Development Process in North-East India

About the Author

Ram Krishna Mandal, the author of 'Developmental Process in North-East India with Special Reference to Arunachal Pradesh' was born in a remote village of West Bengal. Dr. Mandal completed his graduation with honours in Economics from Balurghat College, Balurghat (West Bengal) and did his M.A. in Economics with Distiction, M. Phil. and Ph.D. in Economics, BLIS and B.Ed. from the North Bengal University, Darjeeling (West Bengal). Dr. Mandal has to his credit 55 published research papers in National and International Journals on different issues of national as well as regional importance.

By virtue of his merit and perservance, Dr. Mandal has so far produced eight books : (i) Micro-economic Theory (Atlantic Publishers, New Delhi), (ii) Socio-economic Transformation of Arunachal Pradesh (Omsons Publishers, New Delhi), (iii) Money, Income and Rational Expectations in Indian Economy (Mittal Publications, New Delhi), (iv) Macro-economic Theory (Atlantic Publishers, New Delhi, jointly written), (v) Value Added Tax in North-East India. (Mittal Publications, New Delhi, edited), (vi) Women in North-East India (Mittal Publications, New Delhi, jointly written), (vii) Entrepreneurship and Rural Development in North-East India (DVS Publishers, Guwahati, edited) and (viii) Industry, Trade and Economic Development in North-East India (Mittal Publications, New Delhi, jointly edited). He has three UGC sponsored research projects in his credit. He is also a Post-Doctoral Research Awardee UGC Fellow. Presently, he has been rendering his service as an Associate Professor in Economics in Dera Natung Government College, Itanagar, Arunachal Pradesh.

Development Process in North-East India

with Special Reference to Arunachal Pradesh

RAM KRISHNA MANDAL

CONCEPT PUBLISHING COMPANY PVT. LTD.
New Delhi - 1100059

ISBN-13 : 978-81-8069-956-6

First Published 2014

Published and Printed by

Since 1974

Concept Publishing Company Pvt. Ltd.
A/15-16, Commercial Block, Mohan Garden
New Delhi-110059 (India)
T: 25351460, 25351794, *F*: 091-11-25357109
E: publishing@conceptpub.com, W: www.conceptpub.com
Editorial Office: H-13, Bali Nagar, New Delhi-110 015, India.

Cataloging in Publication Data--*Courtesy:* D.K. Agencies (P) Ltd. <docinfo@dkagencies.com>

Mandal, Ramkrishna, 1966-
Development process in North-East India : with special reference to Arunachal/ Pradesh / Ram Krishna Mandal.
p. cm.
Includes bibliographical references and index.
ISBN 9788180699566

1. Economic development—India—Arunachal Pradesh. 2. Forests and forestry India—Arunachal Pradesh. 3. Women in development—India—Arunachal Pradesh. 4. Women in development—Government policy—India—Arunachal Pradesh. I. Title.

DDC 338.954163 23

Dedicated to

Prof. Chandan Kumar Mukhopadhyay

with Reverence and Affection

Preface

The present study is an attempt at a comprehensive and critical analysis of socio-economic development of North-East India with special reference to Arunachal Pradesh. So far, whatever information was available about the state's economy was fragmented and not subjected to any critical study. In the present study, taking due account of the factors promoting socio-economic transformation, as well as factors retarding development, attempt has been made to devise ways and means for accelerating the rate of economic growth of the State against the background of the existing structure of the state's economy and the trends of its transformation. The State covers an area of 83,743 sq. kms., which is 2.5 per cent of the total area of the country. Out of its total geographical area, 70 per cent of its topography constitutes broad and narrow valleys, 10 per cent foot-hills and flat areas and 20 per cent snow clad peak mountainous areas. The agricultural operations are confined to only 5 per cent of the total geographical area, of which 62 per cent to 65 per cent land are under shifting cultivation (*jhum*). The total population as per 2001 census is 10,97,968 which constitutes 0.11 per cent of the national population. Majority of the people (around 85 per cent) live in 3,863 villages and 42 per cent of its people live Below Poverty Line. The State is the richest state in terms of having the highest per capita availability of natural resources, yet it is one of the most economically backward regions in India. Social capital of the State has not been utilized to its fullest capacity due to structural and functional inefficiency of the delivery institutions. The State formed on February 20, 1987 is situated near the tropic of cancer lying between latitudes 26°28′N and 29°30′N and longitude between 91°30′E and 97°30′E on the North-East extremity of India surrounded by Bhutan on West (157 kms.), China on the North and the North-East (1080 kms.), Myanmar on the East (441 kms.) and Assam and Nagaland on the South. The great Himalayan ranges in the State run from the east of the Bhutan Himalayas to the Tsangpo up to Mishmi hill.

The socio-economic development of the State has not been treated as an isolated phenomenon but as an integral part of the economic development of the country as a whole. The work is based on diverse source materials which consist of official reports, published journals, books and findings of field work. I have weighed my occasional writings in different reputed national journals of the region and found that most of them are either on the social structural aspects or on the social dynamism and rapid regional socio-economic transformation or on the empowerment of women. I have felt the need to put some of them together so as to enable the readers to get an overall idea about the region. Some of them have been updated, revised and edited for the purpose. I hope that the readers will find it relevant for understanding the region in a better way.

I express my deep gratitude to the esteemed editors of the journals and the seminar editors who published my papers on varied topics of national as well as regional importance. I pray to them and take their permission to publish the papers in this volume in the large interest of the academic world. I am also thankful to the individual scholars and the different agencies from whom I have drawn optimum.

I am conscious of the bulk of the work which becomes largely inevitable on account of the intrinsic sweep of the subject. I acknowledge my gratitude to all writers—Indian and foreign, whose books were consulted in the preparation of this volume. I am also thankful to the officers and staff of the Administration in the State without whose sincere cooperation and help, it would not have been possible for me to collect necessary source materials. I am also indebted to the Directorate of Economics and Statistics, Government of Arunachal Pradesh, Librarian of State Central Library, Itanagar, Librarian of Dera Natung Government College Library, Itanagar for permission to use the library facility.

I had a desire to dedicate this volume to the name of my beloved teacher Prof. Chandan Kumar Mukhopadyaya (Department of Economics, NBU) as a token of my regard and respect to him. He gracefully accepted my dedication of this volume to him for which I feel gratified. Before the raw idea of publication took a distinct shape, a number of my colleagues especially Mrs. Mudhuparna Bhattacharjee, Dr. Rishikesh Mishra, Dr. S.D. Jha, Dr. A.I. Singh, Dr. D. Choubin, Mr. B.L. Behara, Dr. Manisha Mohanty and Dr. D.K. Padhi helped me in various ways to clarify the issues through occasional interaction. For that I am obliged to them and 'others' whose names do not appear in the volume.

I also acknowledge the inspiration received from my colleagues Dr. S.K.Sharma and Mrs. Nibedita Sharma, Associate Professors, Dera Natung Government College, Itanagar. I am also thankfut to my students especially the students of B.A.-III Year and B.A.-II Year Honours.

Mrs. Uma Chetry who did the typing all alone of the volume, for which she deserves my special appreciation. I am thankful to Ashok Kumar Mittal, Concept Publishing Company, Pvt. Ltd., New Delhi not only for attractive and quick publication of the book, but also for his various professional advices. Lastly, I am grateful to the members of my family – Mrs. Archana Mandal (Wife) and Miss Anusree Krishna Mandal (Daughter) and Master Avinandan Krishna Mandal (Son) for their untiring support and patience during the work of this volume.

Ram Krishna Mandal

Contents

Preface VII

1. Development Process in North-East India 1
2. Overview of Arunachal Pradesh 56

Section-I
Developmental Activities

3. Constraints of Economic Development with Special Reference to Globalization and Inner Line System 105
4. Information Technology with Special Reference to Post Office and Telecommunication 134
5. Road Network in Arunachal Pradesh Since 1947 163
6. Employment and Rural Industrialization 182
7. Khadi and Village Industries in North-East India with Special Reference to Arunachal Pradesh 202
8. Entrepreneurial Innovation and Economic Development 230
9. Trade Potentialities of North-East India 243
10. Urbanization : Trends and Patterns 275
11. Quality Assurance in Higher Education 307

Section-II
Forest

12. Forest Resources and Its Contribution 351
13. Biodiversity :
A Threat Perfection to Sustainable Development 376
14. Flora and Fauna
Economic Viability and Sustainability 429
15. Floriculture Industry 468

Section-III
Women Empowerment

16. Empowerment of Women Through Education
and Some Selected Opinions 481
17. Tribal Women in the State 495
18. Gender Discrimination : A Holistic Approach
Towards Intervention in Frontier State of
Arunachal Pradesh in India 505
19. Socio-Economic Status of Tribal Women in
Present Economic Environment 536
20. Work Participation of Women in Agriculture
A Case Study in West Siang District 555
21. Panchayati Raj Insitutions PRIs and
Women Empowerment 575
22. Women's Micro Entrepreneurship and
Economic Development in the State : Need of the Day 600

Index 619

1

Development Process in North-East India

Introduction

Previously the North-East Region, i.e., the seven political units was popularly known as the Land of 'seven sisters' consisting of the States of Arunachal Pradesh, Assam, Manipur, Meghalaya, Mizoram, Nagaland and Tripura. In 1971, following the North-Eastern Reorganization Act, 1971, the State of Assam was constitutionally recognized and Meghalaya, Manipur and Tripura became full-fledged States. But Mizoram and the erstwhile NEFA (present Arunachal Pradesh) were made Union Territories. In 1987, these two Union Territories were elevated to the status of States. These States are comparatively small in area and/or population. It was felt necessary to involve inter-state cooperation in sharing of costs of building basic infrastructure for the development of the region. Consequently, in 1971 another important Act was passed to establish in 1972 the North-Eastern Council (NEC) as an advisory body for formulating regional development plans with these seven States as members. Execution of projects under the plans was, however, the responsibility of the State Governments concerned. But Nagaland decided to remain outside the purview of the NEC.

Recently, the State of Sikkim also has come under the umbrella of this region owing to its proximity to the area and somewhat similar type of developmental and other problems. For the purpose of Developmental Activities, Sikkim has also come under the purview of the North Eastern Council, which is a Regional Planning Body, by an Act of Parliament, in December, 2002 as per the NEC Reorganization Act. This Act provided for the inclusion of Sikkim as a member of the NEC. Presently, for development purposes the North-Eastern Region (NER) consists of eight States i.e., Arunachal Pradesh, Assam, Manipur, Meghalaya, Mizoram, Nagaland, Tripura, and Sikkim.

Map 1.1

India has the largest concentration of tribal people anywhere in the world except perhaps in Africa. The tribals are children of nature and their lifestyle is conditioned by the Ecosystem. India, with a variety of ecosystems, presents a varied tribal population throughout its length and breadth. The areas inhabited by the tribal constitute a significant part of the underdeveloped areas of the country. The tribal people live mostly in isolated villages or hamlets. A smaller portion of their population has now settled in permanent villages as well as in towns and cities. On the whole, as per rough estimates, the prominent tribal areas constitute about 15 per cent of the total geographical area of the country. Tribal people over the years have become the most disadvantaged, exploited and the neglected lot in our society. The tribal basically stand averse to the modern lifestyles and hardly willing to change until and unless they encounter a very strong social mobilization.

Map 1.2

According to Ralph Linton, the legendary and respected anthropologist of mid-20th century, a 'tribe is group of bands occupying a contiguous territory or territories having a feeling of unity deriving from numerous similarities in culture, frequent contacts and a certain community of interests'. Indian tribal society can be underlined as a social group with strict territorial affiliation, possessing characteristics of endogamy, with no specialisation of functions ruled by tribal officers hereditary or otherwise, united in language or dialect recognising social distance with other tribes.

An enormous section of Indian tribal societal population depends on agriculture as their sole way for survival. Characteristically too Indian tribal society possess their own set of languages, which are unwritten. Hence, the degree of communication both in time and space is predictably narrow. At the same time, tribal societies demonstrate an outstanding economy of design and have a compactness and self-sufficiency surprisingly lacking in modern city society. There are as many as 573 tribes and sub-tribes in India. They have been broadly classified into different classes, groups depending upon their present state of development and factors namely, mode of living in forest, shifting villages, forest villages, community villages and revenue villages. They have got a heterogeneous cultural pattern with variegated economic condition and activities largely based on ecological settings and ethnic environment.

In this era of globalisation, it has become a common practice in developing countries to formulate their developmental plan programmes within the framework of international development discourse. Obviously, these countries broadly lay their emphasis on participatory, decentralised and sustainable development. In other words, there is a shift in development paradigm from top-down to bottom-up, centralised approach to decentralisation and from 'people around development' to 'development around people', i.e, people centred development. Essentially, the focus lies on the participation of the people in the process of their own development. 'Globalisation' defined in broad terms encompasses every aspect of human life. Whether we like it or dislike it, today, globalisation, liberalization and privatization have become the ***mantra*** for economic development of countries. In recent times, globalization has made its maximum impact on economic integration through free movement of goods, capital, services, information and technology across national boundaries. Economic integration offers vistas of opportunities for individual countries to achieve higher rates of growth, efficient utilization of resources through import of new technology, increased living standards, increased purchasing power, availability of cheap foreign capital, access to larger markets, finances and so on. Toeing to the compulsions of globalisation,

India started its new economic reforms of globalisation in 1991-92, in consultation with the international bank and its policies. Since then India has witnessed rapid and high growth rate of Gross Domestic Product (GDP) which was 5.6 per cent during 1980-90 and 7 per cent during 1993-2001. Over the last four years, the GDP growth rate on average was 8.5 per cent and Government of India is confident of having an average of 10 per cent growth rate during Eleventh Five Year Plan. In addition, India has a very high foreign exchange reserve of $180 billion till 2007. India is also the fourth largest country to have Rs. 1, 81,566 crores of FDI inflow in 2006. Again, India is placed in fourth position in respect to market capitalization with $894 billion. As per Forbes latest list of billionaires in 2007, India has 40 numbers of it having combined wealth of $ 170 billion and total assets of worth Rs. 7.50 lakh crores.

In a country, however, there are heterogeneous constituents along such divides as religions, regions, ethnic groups and many such other factors. In the process of globalisation, all these constituents are required to be integrated to the market forces. Market being competitive in nature, it is but logical to think that all constituents cannot be equal partners given unequal levels of efficiency/skill endowment. There are weaker sections in every developing country. It is evident from the existence of urban-rural divide. Moreover, there are backward communities like tribal people who have their unique way of living. They are undoubtedly weak partners as compared to advanced sections in the country. Many studies are available which substantiate to this point.

Encounter of tribal communities to globalisation through state policies needs to be considered from different angles. The tribal people are tradition bound and their tradition is quite different from that of in the market economy. In a way, it can be stated that their tradition tells on their efficiency/level of skill endowment, which fall short of market requirements. Since independence, the special benefits available to Scheduled Tribes have convinced many groups, that they will enjoy greater advantages if so designated. The Schedule gives tribal people incentives to maintain their identity. A number of traits have customarily been seen as establishing tribal rather than caste identity. These include language, social organization, religious affiliation, economic patterns, geographic location, and self-identification. Recognized tribes typically live in hilly regions, somewhat remotely located from caste settlements; and they generally speak a language recognized as tribal.

There are five major geographical areas or zones in the country where there is concentration of tribal population. The tribal communities living in each of these zones, by and large, have common racial, linguistic, cultural and even economic characteristics. The five zones, which are thus distinguishable, are the North, North-Eastern, the Central, the Western and the Southern.

There are 533 tribes as per notified Schedule under Article 342 of the Constitution of India in different States and Union Territories of the country with the largest number of 62 being in the State of Orissa. Some of the major tribes of North-Eastern India are as follows. They are Nyishi, Adi, Tagin, Apatani, Wangcho, Dafla, Khampti, Singpho, etc. in Arunachal Pradesh, Boro, Kachari, Mikir (Karbi), Lalung, Rabha, Dimasa, Hmar, Hajong etc. in Assam, Garo, Khasi, Jayantia, etc. in Meghalaya, Chakma, Kuki, Lusai, Liang, Santhal etc. in Tripura, Lusai, Kuki, Garo, Khasi, Jayantia, Mikir etc. in Mizoram, Lapcha, Bhutia, Nepali, etc. in Sikkim.

All the States of this region, except Assam are mostly hilly. Assam is also having hilly regions, but it is comparatively less than the plain areas of the state. The states of this region are very much unique in their own ways. There is a wide variation in the altitude ranging from 300 to 5000 metres. The North-Eastern region of India occupies a strategic geo-political situation due to its international boundaries with Bangladesh, Bhutan, China, Myanmar and Nepal. No doubt, these states constitute a homogeneous natural region of the hills, plains, valleys, flora and fauna and other related geographical features. Though the North-Eastern region reflects some ecological and cultural adaptive contrasts between the hills and the plains, there are also significant elements of continuity in the biological, cultural and social factors between these segments. Also, as per available records, we find a lot of independence and interactions between the hills and the plains in this region.

The North-Eastern mosaic is a replica of the Indian mosaic but with the prominence of some other special ingredients. There are nearly 150 ethnic groups and sub-groups. All the known anthropological offshoots, e.g., Negroids, Mongoloids, Austro-Asiatic, Tibeto-Burmans, and the equally important Caucasians are here in the North-Eastern part of India with Assam having more than 20 major ethnic groups.

The total Geographical Area (notional area) of the North-Eastern Region including Sikkim is 2,63,179 sq. kms. accounting for 7.9 per cent of the total land space of the country. These eight States of NER together have a total population of 3,88,57,769 as per 2001 Census and constitute about 3.8 per cent of the total population of the country (NEDFi, quarterly data bank, 2005). The State of Assam, though, is the second largest in area, but it is the homeland of the highest number of persons i.e., 68.60 per cent of the population of this region with an equally highest density of 340 persons per sq. km. The State of Arunachal Pradesh is though the largest, but there is only 2.28 per cent of population of this region with a density of 13 persons per sq. km. which is the lowest in this region. North-east region of India with its absolute pristine virginal territory remains completely unexplored. The valley is beautified with lush green vegetation, grandiose mountains and feral rivers. North-east India is also abode of exceptional range of flora and fauna and the brilliant tribal life. North-East Indian tribes are perhaps some of the most mysterious and yet most studied and observed band in the country, with host of things to offer in a slice of everyday life.

"India lives in villages". Because, 72.18 per cent of its population is living in rural areas and only 27.82 per cent in urban areas. This is also very true for the North-Eastern Region as it is seen that 84.34 per cent of people of this region is living in the rural areas only and 15.66 per cent of people is living in urban areas. One of the bases of Indian economic growth has been the transformation of the hill-forest regions for the use of the mineral resources therein, and the utilization of the hydropower and irrigation potential. These developments have increased power availability, irrigated water to increase agricultural productivity and the development of an industrial base. The benefits of these developments, however, have been largely concentrated among Indians in the plains, including workers who have secured employment. The inhabitants of the hill-forest regions, the indigenous peoples (or Scheduled Tribes as they are legally termed) on the other hand, have had to bear the brunt of involuntary displacement and destruction of their traditional, livelihoods through mines, dams, etc.(Nathan, Dev. 2009). States viz. Arunachal Pradesh, Meghalaya, Mizoram and Nagaland are tribal dominated states. So far North-East region is concerned, it is a new approach. The region has been neglected even by the centre so long and is lagging behind on all fronts, so far any type of modern resources are concerned. And to talk about the tribal population in the North-East region and the Impact of Globalization on Tribal Women of North-East, is completely a new concept.

It is a homeland of a large number of tribes. In India, there are about 212 major Scheduled Tribes and in North East alone we find more than 145 tribes. The development of villages has become the need of the hour, especially the hill villages in North-East India. However, it goes beyond the conventional development models; it focuses also on social, political, and other aspects of development. Majority of the world's poor live in villages. Basic necessities of life of these people are much lower than that of the people living in the town or city. Definitely, a hill village is different from the village in the valley. So, the tribal hill village, particularly in the North-East is quite different from other villages in the country. They have some uniqueness in their structure, socially, culturally, and economically. Social life here is organized along definite ritual and secular principles, such as those of caste, kinship, economy, politics, and religion. The physical character of the village is influenced by its dynamic interaction with these principles and patterns of settlement. A village could be clustered or dispersed in its settlement pattern. Every village has a definite pattern of social relations based on traditional principles of kinship and marriage, such as those of village exogamy. These relations extend the interactive network and social space of a village well beyond its boundaries into neighbouring. The bond of kinship (real or fictive) and marriage govern not only intra-familial interaction but also that between larger kin groups, often across village boundaries. The typical rural family in rural India is the patriarchal (or it is a matrilineal in the case of Meghalaya) joint family the members of which, even when divided into number of households, live together in the village and own property in common (community land especially in the hill villages in NE). More importantly, unlike in other parts of India predominantly ruled by orthodox Hindu caste system or hierarchy in the hill villages of NE region, community land plays a vital role in shaping their economy. The economic system of these communities revolves around their social structure. It is the village law or social norm which binds the people of a village. Traditional norms and beliefs deeply rooted in people's minds are more difficult to change than formal laws so that they are likely to become more fetters on modern economic development. Trust is the social capital, which can reduce social transaction cost. Community institutions and organizations are inflexible and fail to adjust to changing economic needs. Traditional norms and conventions in communities have been formed slowly over many, many years.

The share of population of North-East Region (NER), in comparison to all India, increased from 2.89 per cent in 1951 to 3.78 per cent in 2001. Among various states of NER of India, the geographical area of Arunachal Pradesh is the highest at 83,743 sq. kms. In terms of population, Mizoram is the smallest state among NER of India. The decadal growth rate of population (1991-2001) is the lowest in the state of Tripura 16.03 per cent followed by Assam (18.92%) and highest in the state of Nagaland (64.53%) followed by Sikkim (33.06%). The region's growth rate of population (21.61%) is higher than the national average of 21.35 per cent during 1991-2001. The density of the population varies from 13 in Arunachal Pradesh to 340 in Assam followed by 305 in Tripura. The density of the population of the region is 147.65 which are almost half of the national density (324) in 2001 while it was only 34.29 in 1951. The growth of population is shown below in Table 1.1.

The share of population of NER to the total population of India as low as 1.70 per cent in 1901, since then it has been steadily increasing and reached at nearly 3.8 per cent with a total population of 39.04 million, as per 2001 census. The Region is inhabited by more than 150 ethnic groups and sub-groups, constituting almost 30 per cent of the total population. Assam is the most populous State and accounts for about 70 per cent of the Region's population. According to India's Health Ministry, India's population which was 238 million in 1947 touched 1.012 million in March 2001 and is expected to be 1.263 billion by 2016. The share of population of NER, in comparison to all India, increased from 2.89 per cent in

1951 to 3.78 per cent in 2001.The density of population varies from 13 per sq. km. in Arunachal Pradesh to 340 per sq.km. in Assam.

Table 1.1: Population Trend in North-East Region (in'000).

Year / *State*	*1951*	*1961*	*1971*	*1981*	*1991*	*2001*
ANP	—	337	468	632	865	1091
ASM	8029	10837	14625	18041	22414	26638
MNP	578	780	1073	1421	1837	2389
MGH	606	769	1012	1336	1775	2306
MZM	196	266	332	494	690	891
NGN	213	369	516	775	1210	1989
SKM	138	162	210	316	406	540
TRP	639	1142	1556	2053	2757	3191
NER	10260	14501	19582	24752	31547	38495
IND	361088	439235	548160	683329	846303	1027015

Fig. 1.1 shows that the total number of tribal population is 104.66 lakh in 2001 which is approximately 26.93 per cent of the total population. The percentage of Scheduled Tribes varies from 12.41 per cent (Assam) to 94.46 per cent (Mizoram) which are above the country's figure (8.2%). However, more than 80 per cent of the population belong to Scheduled Tribe in the States of Mizoram (94.46%), Nagaland (89.15%) and Meghalaya (85.94%), while in Tripura (31.1%), Manipur (34.2%) and Assam (12.4%), these are below 50 per cent. It is to be noted that although percentage of total tribal population of NER has increased from 25.71 per cent in 1991 to 26.93 per cent in 2001, proportion of tribal population has decreased in some of the States of NER like Arunachal Pradesh, Assam, Manipur in 2001. But the State of Assam though having only 12.41 per cent of its population as tribal, but this number of 33,08,570 tribal population is greater than the total population of any other state of this region.

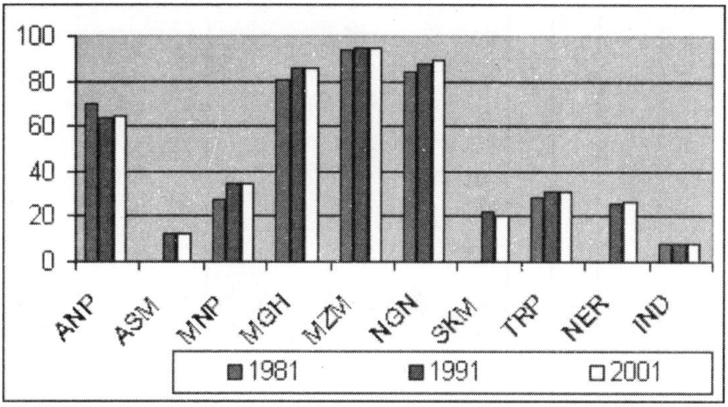

Fig. 1.1: Percentages of ST Population in NER, 1981, 1991 and 2001.

The educational scenario (excluding the children of the age group of 0-6 years) of the North-Eastern Region (NER) is not uniform. It varies from state to state. The people of Mizoram are more educated than the people of any other State of this region and their average percentage of literacy is 88.80 per cent. The percentage of literacy of the rural peoples of Mizoram though a bit low to the level of 81.27 per cent, but it is quite high to the extent of 96.13 per cent for the urban people. In some of the States of North-Eastern Region, though the percentage of literacy is quite high, but the literacy or the level of education alone cannot increase the efficiency of the workforce, quality education, professional courses, proper training facilities, etc. are very much necessary to keep the workforce abreast with the changing Educational and Technological Development. The general demographic profile of NER, 2001 along with educational scenario is shown below in Table 1.2.

Table 1.2: Demographic Profile of NER, 2001.

State	*Area in sq. km.*	*Population*			*Density per sq. km.*	*Literacy*		
		Total	*Male*	*Female*		*Total*	*Male*	*Female*
1	*2*	*3*	*4*	*5*	*7*	*9*	*10*	*11*
Arunachal Pradesh	83743	1091117	573951	517166	13	54.74	64.07	44.24
Assam	78438	26638407	13787799	12850608	340	64.28	71.93	56.03
Manipur	22327	2388634	1207338	1181296	107	68.87	72.87	59.70
Meghalaya	22429	2306069	1167840	1138229	103	63.31	66.14	60.41
Mizoram	21087	891058	459783	431275	42	88.49	90.69	86.13
Nagaland	16579	1988636	1041686	946950	120	67.11	71.77	61.92
Sikkim	7096	540493	288217	252276	76	69.68	76.73	61.46
Tripura	10486	3191168	1636138	1555030	304	73.66	81.47	65.41

Source: (i) Census of India, Series-13, Arunachal Pradesh, Provisional Population Totals, Paper-1 of 2001, p.15;
(ii) NEDFi Data Bank Quarterly, Vol. 1, Issue-1, July, 2002. p. 2.

The population including male and female for north-east states as per 2001 census are shown in Fig. 1.2 as under.

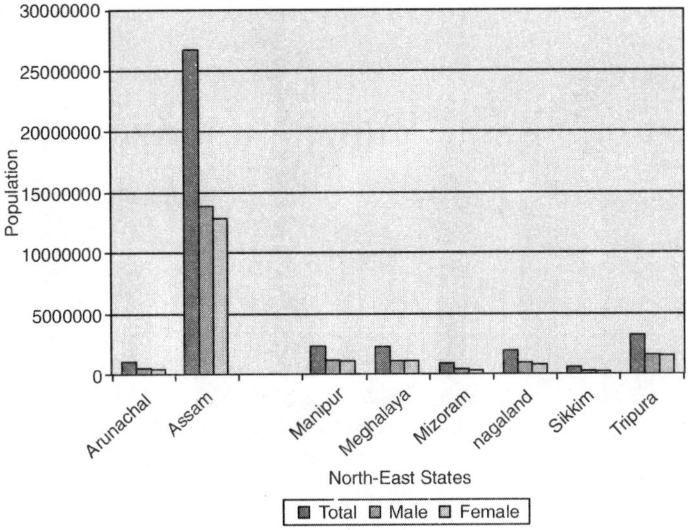

Fig. 1.2: Trend of Growth of Population in North-East States as per 2001 Census.

The area in sq. km. and population per sq. km. i.e., population density in NER as per 2001 census are shown in Fig. 1.3 as under.

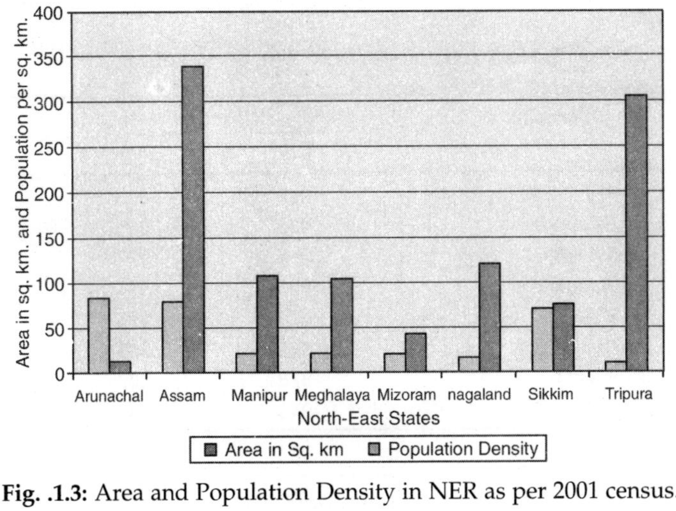

Fig. .1.3: Area and Population Density in NER as per 2001 census.

The literacy in North-East States as per 2001 census is shown in Fig. 1.4.

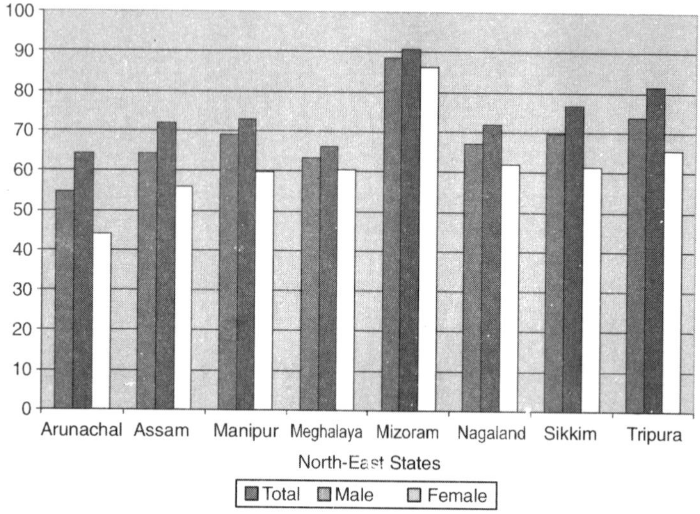

Fig. 1.4: Literacy of Male and Female in NER as per 2001 census.

A Comparative Statement of Sex Ratio in North-East States

A comparative statement of sex ratio in North-Eastern States and India in 1991 and 2001 is shown below in Table 1.3 and in Fig. 1.5.

Table 1.3: Sex Ratio of N-E States and India

States/Country	*Sex Ratio*	
	1991	*2001*
Arunachal Pradesh	859	893
Assam	923	935
Manipur	958	977
Meghalaya	955	971
Mizoram	921	935
Nagaland	886	900
Sikkim	878	800
Tripura	945	948
India	927	933

Source: Population Census 1991 and 2001.

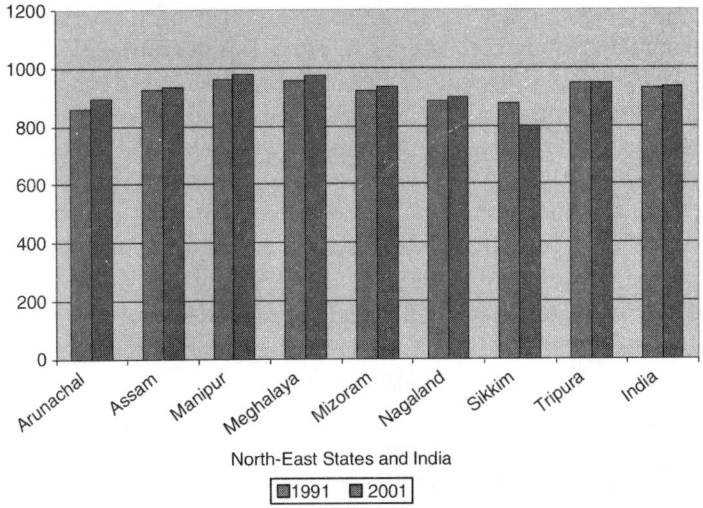

Fig. 1.5: Sex Ratio in North-East States and India.

Sex ratio in Manipur, Meghalaya and Tripura is higher than the All India average in 1991. Sikkim shows the least sex ratio among the North-Eastern States in both the censuses. However, it may be noted that there has been considerable improvement of sex ratio during 1991-2001 in all North-eastern States except Sikkim where sex ratio has declined from 878 to 800.

Sex ratio in Arunachal Pradesh, Nagaland and Sikkim is lower than the All India average in 2001. This may happen due to two reasons: Predominance of male migration and higher female death rate. Moreover, infant mortality among girls may be higher in the hill States. The burden of bearing children at early age, the lesser use of birth control devices, lack of adequate family planning measures, and heavy workload of the female members in the hills may also increase the death rate among the females.

Improvement in sex ratio in Assam, Tripura and Meghalaya over the period is partly due to immigration from other states on account of migration of tea garden labourers and partly due to influx of refugees from neighbouring countries to these states.

Urbanization and Growth of Urban Population

Urbanization, in demographic sense, is an increase in the proportion of the urban population to the total population over a period of time. Rapid urbanization has been a worldwide phenomenon in the 21st century. In developing countries like India, the challenge of urbanization becomes more serious in the context of unplanned urbanization and growing urban poverty, which is largely an extension of rural poverty. Urbanization generally indicates technological, institutional, educational, communicational, industrial and organizational development from time to time and is being brought about by development, modernization, and migration. It is also closely related with economic development and social transformation of a state or a region and stimulates each other with structural changes on a large scale. Economic development in this regard is generally associated and follows in the company of the growth of urbanization. The trend and pattern of urban growth and pattern of state level migration in the context of growing spatial and economic inequality have also been analyzed in the proceeding sections explaining the increasing pace of mobility of population across the State and from rural to urban areas leading to the emergence of a new urban culture. The general reasons for urbanization thus can be attributed to: (1) the natural increase of the urban population over a period of time, (2) The large scale migration of population from the rural areas of the state itself and immigration from other states to its urban areas (the administrative headquarters). Thus, both the push and pull factors have played their role in the migration of population from the rural to urban areas or from other states to this region on a large scale in the post liberalization period due to educational and employment opportunities as well as expansion of service sectors.

Urbanization in this regard may also be defined as a process that is characterized by transition or take off in which a region/ nation can jump out of the transition from total agrarian base to industrial society (Rao *et al.*, 2004). In other words, it is delimitated as a process of massive shifts of labour and capital from predominantly rural to urban areas.

In fact, it is in general, have been very helpful in contributing positively to poverty reduction in the rural areas. Different levels of urbanization, however, reflect different degrees of modernization and development in the economy (Prasad, 1995). It is a multi-dimensional process and largely, it depends upon the incentives for industrial and service sector development. The opinion of Mills Becker (1986), holds that "Urbanization is an inevitable process that is experienced by all nations in their transition form agrarian to industrial and service societies and is a necessary factor behind the economic growth". What is more is that, capital accumulation, technological change and the growth of socio-economic infrastructure seem to be the most important determinants of this shift (Kundu, 2004). They are positively associated with industrial and service sector development in contrast to agriculture.

It is also true that in a growing economy, there is mounting demand of industrial and service sector products. Consequently, there is spontaneous increase in industrial and service sector production and thus, employment generation in the economy. This also follows increase of service facilities for various purposes like the distribution of increased output, financial management through banking and financial institutes as well as civic services for the population experiencing increase in income levels (GoI, 2003). Economic development, therefore, foretells industrialization and that itself promotes the concentration of people in the urban areas, where maximum attempt is made to economize the land inputs (i.e., the land requirement per unit of output being less than the agricultural sector). On the whole, growth of industrialization necessitates urbanization in particular and economic development in general. The growth of urbanization can also enlarge through availability of socio-economic infrastructure in the economy. In the modern world, problem of large urban concentrations not only affects the advanced countries but also all the areas with dense population.

In India, the trend towards concentration of urban population in a small number of large urban centres has been taking shape over a century. While the number of urban centres doubled between 1901 and 1991, urbanization increased eight-fold, resulting in a top heavy urban hierarchy. Future demographic and economic growth is likely to concentrate in and around the large cities in the country having a population of a million people or more. The demographic trends towards urbanization are accompanied by a change in the management and financing of urban development as a result of liberalization. Decentralization of municipal governance has led to a substantial reduction in budgetary allocations for infrastructural development. Greater reliance is now placed on institutional financing and capital markets for resource mobilization and on private companies for service delivery.

Many researchers and governments in the developing countries considered that the rapid growth of urban population and high primacy (concentration of population and activities in the leading cities) have a major impediment in realizing their development goals of equitable development. Several explicit and implicit policies were adopted by governments of many developing countries for slowing down the urban growth particularly the population growth in large cities, by focusing on reducing the migration to these cities from rural areas. The latest data on world urbanization, however, show that at the beginning of the twenty-first century, a number of developing countries do not have even one-third of their population in urban areas. There is also a considerable slowing down in the rate of urbanization as well as the rate of urban population growth in most of the developing countries in the last two decades. In India, the latest census data also confirms the same.

The rural to urban migration is an important component of urbanization in most of the countries and regions. Both urbanization and migration are regarded as one of the most important indicators of economic development and social transformation of a region. Economic growth is accompanied by a gradual reduction in the relative share of agriculture and an increase in the relative share of industry and services in total output and labour force. This indicates a movement of population from agricultural areas to the industrial centres.

As a result, migration from rural areas to urban areas takes place with the growth of industrial and service sectors. So, migration and urbanization is an integral part of economic development. S. Kuznets emphasized that there is a relationship between migration and economic development that takes place in terms of the selectivity of people. He opines that migrants are dynamic, risk-bearing persons who respond favourably to economic stimuli and have high capacity to detach themselves from traditional surroundings and adapt themselves to unfamiliar environments. Thus, the migrant people are most productive from the viewpoint of economic development in the sense that they are risk bearing section of population (Mitra, 1997, p. 1).

For understanding the dynamics of urbanization and development, it would be important to analyze the spatial pattern of urban growth in different size classes of towns. During the first four census decades since independence, urban growth has generally been high in relatively backward and less urbanized States. (Kundu, 1994).This is primarily due to the fast growth of small and medium towns and emergence of new towns.

In the instant case of State like Arunachal Pradesh, a sizeable proportion of these fast growing and new towns are circle or block or district headquarters where implementation of government sponsored development schemes are in full swing including the new central scheme popularly known as JNURM (Jawaharlal Nehru Urban Renewal Mission).

The relationship between urban growth and development, in this case, works out to be negative. This can be attributed to government investment in district headquarters and transfer of funds from centre to state and from state to local bodies through a need based or what is popularly known as "a gap filling" approach. (Kundu, 2006). A large part of rural-urban migration into smaller towns from their rural hinterland in backward states like Arunachal can, however, be explained in terms of push factors, owing to lack of diversification of agrarian economy and pull factors, owing to demand of high skill, semi-skilled, and unskilled workforce required for the all round development of the State.

As observed in Table 1.4 above, the urban population of the state in the year 2001 was 20.34 per cent against 27.78 per cent for all India. In terms of absolute numbers, the urban population of Arunachal Pradesh in 2001 was 2,22688 against 285 million of that of India. Since 1961, the urban population has steadily increased and it has shown a considerable rise from negligible share to 20.34 per cent of the total population in 2001.

However, it is also to be taken in view that while the pace of urbanization is growing at a faster rate, this considerable rise in urban population and their livelihood strategies are at different levels of economic development spread over the three different belts which are territorially different and varies in terms of economic opportunities that the terrain provides. Additionally, the pace of urbanization in the region has never attracted any external investment. The Municipal Act of the state is in the pipeline and this will usher a new era attracting attention of the urban local bodies to provide for the basic amenities that generally follows in other parts of the country.

The pattern and level of urbanization along with the growth of urban population in the entire region of North-Eastern States is shown in Table 1.4 below. The annual exponential growth rate of entire region as compared to all India scenarios is quite misleading. This can be attributed to fast growth of small towns in the region due to influx of internal and international migrants especially in the States of Arunachal, Assam, Mizoram, Meghalaya, Nagaland and Sikkim.

The census-wise increase in percentage of urban population since 1971 is shown below in Fig. 1.6.

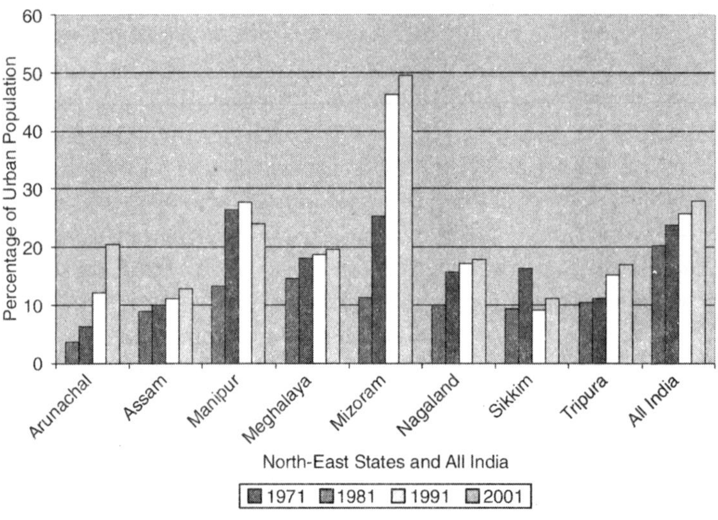

Fig. 1.6: Percentage of Urban Population since 1971 Census.

The rank-wise position of urbanization of North-East States on the basis of percentage of urban population of 2001 Census is depicted in Fig. 1.7 as under.

Table 1.4: Pattern and Level of Urbanization and Growth of Urban Population across N.E. States.

State	*Percentage of Urban Population*					*Annual Exponential Growth Rate*		
Year	*1971*	*1981*	*1991*	*2001*	*RANK*	*1971-81*	*1981-91*	*1991-01*
Arunachal	3.70	6.32	12.21	20.41	3	8.32	9.28	7.00
Assam	8.82	9.88	11.09	12.72	7	3.29	3.29	3.09
Manipur	13.19	26.44	27.69	23.88	2	9.70	2.98	1.21
Meghalaya	14.55	18.03	18.69	19.63	4	4.87	3.10	3.16
Mizoram	11.36	25.17	46.20	49.50	1	11.79	9.57	3.27
Nagaland	9.95	15.54	17.28	17.74	5	8.49	5.58	5.27
Sikkim	9.37	16.23	9.12	11.11	8	9.55	-3.23	4.83
Tripura	10.43	10.98	15.26	17.02	6	3.26	6.19	2.53
All India	20.22	23.73	25.72	27.78		3.79	3.09	2.73

Source: Calculation on the basis of Population Censuses, 1971,1981,1991 and 2001.

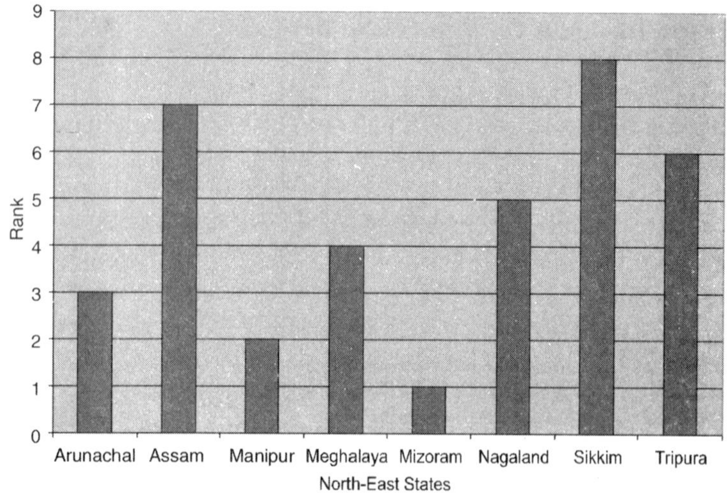

Fig. 1.7: Rank of Urbanisation on the basis of 2001 Census.

The annual exponential growth rates for 1971-81, 1981-91 and 1991-2001 are shown in Fig. 1.8.

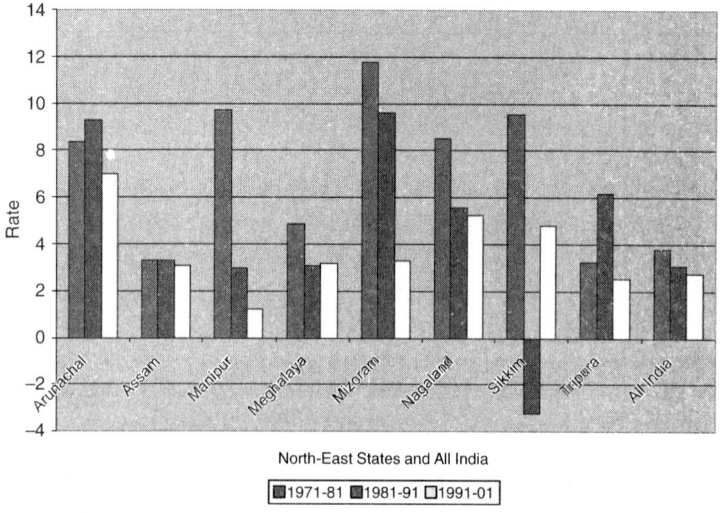

Fig. 1.8: Annual Exponential Growth Rate Population for 1971-81, 1981-91 and 1991-2001.

The impact of globalization on socio-economic life of tribals of North-East cannot be ruled out. If a part of change occurs, evolution and revolution on the totality of life are likely to take place. The impact on traditional lifestyle of tribals is unavoidable, but there is need to prevent loss of indigenous knowledge systems besides ethnicity. When we think of the social problems faced by women, it is true that the women of North-East are deprived of several privileges as enjoyed by their counterparts in advanced states. Education may be one of the major factors for the women of North-East not making much progress in life, especially to fight for the legitimate rights. But much more important is the grip the man exercises over the society through the age old social taboos, forcing the women to play a subdued role in the development process. The women are subjugated to various myths and beliefs and the lack of ignorance about their rights have made their life restricted to doing household duties and raising their family. The workshops is an attempt to focus as the equal participation of women in political, economic, social and cultural life at the national, regional and international awareness among the people which calls for involvement of women in every sphere of social activities. This would encourage the women to have a lager role to play in decision making and making them economically self-reliant. Unless there is a collective wisdom brought about in framing policies suitable for the society in general, the socio-economic status of women will receive a set back.

After the opening of the North-East region some decade past people have been witnessing significant socio-economic and political development and having the influence of new scored high in respect of well-being of women in the region. Socially advanced Meitei dominated Manipur has ranked top followed by tribal dominated Nagaland and Mizoram. Other States except Assam with lack of social and infrastructural development has brought tribal people at the lower standard with existing socio-economic backwardness particularly among the Scheduled Tribes. In-migration has been a major factor of demographic change. This affects the social behaviour, economic condition, employment and even political atmosphere. This migration has affected very badly on the tribal life in North-East region.

The important segment of the tribal society in the North-East region has not been seen quantitatively and qualitatively in proper direction which has resulted in the economic and social backwardness, inspite of many social constitutional guarantees, etc. Of course, with the spread of education and training in States like Assam, Meghalaya, mobility skill and developmental awareness has been seen. So to see the impact of globalization on the tribal women has to be considered keeping in view the area, topography, isolation, communication, infrastructure and introduction of new developmental activities tradition, skill, education, need, etc. Globalization is a new concept so far tribal women are concerned. The tribal women in some of the states and society are so much tradition bound closed, and with difficult natural barriers that they could not think of crossing the village boundary, though they are capable of extending their great help to the society and nation as a whole.

Globalization gives the scope of benefit both ways. It opens the door for restructuring the reformation of the ways for production export, import from outside of the area which has been so long closed, creating isolation and limitation of production export or import of new technology, raw materials, awareness and contact in this region which is a necessity for proper development of the socio-economic life in the tribal society in North-East Region. The dimension of globalization covers the field of social-economic, cultural, technological and environmental. But these days the most emphasis has been given on economic. There are about five processes of globalization so far located on the basis of experience in the last century, (1) creating credit money, (2) growth of importance of knowledge in the system of production, (3) continuing development creating larger share of money from multinational organization, (4) growth of international class and contact with the regional centres or entrepreneurs, and (5) on the whole rise of international, multinational diplomacy and state power.

With this process new type of national and international competition and global production increases and the same is followed on the regional and local level which gives a new approach of thinking. Within globalization some factors like the movement of social and cultural elements, financial flows, eco-system and financial flows, human resources in the globalization process affecting tribal women; labour migration. India's North-East India witness many different complex demographic and socio-economic and cultural pattern but forms the integral part of their society. Mostly they like villages of course some migration to urban area has also been observed, from interior hill for different purposes. When we see the location of the tribal in all eight states, one has to consider the topographical condition, one group lives near the plains and some are urbanized location, 2nd group may be located in the middle part of the state where communication, contacts from the outside area trade with few small item and the 3rd group is the interior areas where no road, and type of trade less impact of even primary education, lack of awareness of any type of social, political, economic, etc. However, to generate the addition of finance, labour socio-economic, cultural and eco-environment with the globalization process, a new structure of international competition may develop from the growth of global market in this region also and the tribal women have to see the new horizon and approach. Whether, the simple tribal women will gain or lose they are not in a position to forecast now. The tribal society in North-East Region is a male dominated society except some tribes in Meghalaya where women get preference. In such a condition it is difficult for the women to have an independent view. But again when the total tribal group is affected with the world family concept for the development, women too will be affected.

Handloom, handicraft, cottage industries, woollen product, brass metal, cane and bamboo, village industries, agriculture base industries is the field where tribal women are engaged at home along with their household work. The products are limited if proper infrastructures are provided they may increase the production, they will be benefited in the competition with globalization. They gain and add to the knowledge of the world community. Not much impact has been on the surface since there is no easy communication and contact from outside. However, globalization during the modern period of history of the world was attempted at the initiative of the member countries of the Non-aligned Movement in 1975 when they initiated a move in the General Assembly of the United Nations Organization. At their initiative the programme was adopted by the U.N. General Assembly which included: (i) opening Northern markets to Southern industrial exports, (ii) improving terms of trade for tropical agricultural products and minerals, (iii) better access to international finance, and (iv) creating more normal condition for technology transfer. Simultaneously, the developed industrial countries made a counter move against this programme by taking advantage of stiff rise in oil price and debt trap to impose current pattern of globalization consisting of five monopolies: (a) technological monopoly, (b) control of worldwide financial markets, (c) monopoly access to planet's natural resources, (d) media and communication monopoly, and (e) monopoly of weapons of mass destruction.

In 1991 the industrialized countries fostered their own model of globalization which has become a new mantra for integration of national economics with the world economy. It is being carried out through removal of barriers on the way of flow of trade, capital, technologies and labour across national frontiers with a view to export led growth. The process of globalization started in Indian Economy in 1991 when India joined the World Trade Organization (WTO). Since then, about a decade and half have passed and appraisal of the impact of globalization must be evaluated now to formulate strategic move for the future course of action. Linkage multiplicity, interconnections between the different states, societies, which opens the door for economic, cultural goods, technology, labour etc. may be termed as globalization. This affects greatly the integration in several manners on the national economy, multinational production corporations' foreign direct investments, consumption production etc.

Coming to the question of globalization in the context of North-East Region, we find that the region is lagging behind on all fronts so far as the technology aided articulations of its resources are concerned. The issue is further complicated by the fact that the study of the tribal women in the North-East region is a new concept arising out of the worldwide emphasis over empowerment of women. The declaration of General Assembly of the UNO on the "elimination of discrimination against women" has still to go a long way for empowerment of women. However, we cannot sit idle since women's full services and talents are needed alongside those of men for the full and complete development of a country, the welfare of the world and the cause of peace. Thinking on this line the Research Centre for the Himalayan and Tribal Regions has ventured under the sponsorship of the North-Eastern Council, Shillong to organize the present national seminar to assess and evaluate the attitudinal, structural and functional impacts of Globalization on Women.

In this context, it is to be noted that social change is possible only by empowering and educating women. Pt. Nehru once said, "to awaken the people, it is women who is meant to be awakened, once she is on the move, the family moves, village moves and the nation moves". Swami Vivekananda also once said, "there is no change for the welfare of the world unless the condition of women is improved. It is not possible for a bird to fly on one wing." Likewise no nation can flourish keeping half of its population in negligence and ignorance, as women constitute half of its human capital. A modern society cannot bring all round development without utilizing the talent of its women.

The full and equal participation of women in political, economic, social and cultural life at the national, regional and international levels and eradication of all forms of discrimination on grounds of sex are priority objectives of the international community. The Vienna Declaration and programme of action, 1993 June and Beijing Resolution, 1995 enunciate the Human Rights of Women, among others to strengthen affirmative action programme in order to increase the number of women serving in decision-making positions at all levels of government. Tribal women have developed their own interesting design of weaving, knitting, carpet making, wood carving, cane and bamboo work, etc., which is locally marketed, and some of them have outside market also, with local materials and skill. The workers are too simple, ignorant of outside developed skills, materials and not capable of competing with developed society. Import of material from outside is cheaper since they have been produced on large scale with ordinary cheap matter, no aesthetic concept which works against the local product. There is every danger of surpassing the local artisan and art materials. But again, if import of new item is done with protection of local indigenous products, capital infrastructure may help on both sides. This implies to tribal women in North-Eastern region. On the other side, globalization may help women with opening of socio-cultural, political and economic awareness in the region. Women share equal responsibility with man in this tradition bound subsistence economy in all the States in North-East Region. Besides, economic loss or gain, socio-cultural indigenous material etc. is an aspect where there is fear of cultural and economic aggression by developed society on the simple and primitive society, particularly the women. All the tribal women of North-East region have not faced such complex system of global change, and they have retained precious culture. Some of the States have faced such contacts, conversion, assimilation and cultural aggression. They have lost the tribal culture, custom, tradition etc. Neither they could fully merge with the westernized culture or economic system nor they are in position to face the real tribal identity, uprooting them out from own moorings resulting in feeling of separation, frustration, loss of ethical and cultural moorings. It is a difficult deal on every aspect of the tribal women to assess the impact of globalization on tribal women. But one thing is clear that loss and gain has been assessed considering most developed group and the primitivism of the tribal women in North-East region. However, tribal women are gaining with the development of the rest part of the world with the flow of modern facilities available in India now and may extend with the globalization process in the air now. With development and change in the world on all front of life like economy, culture, political, trade, industry, education to the women movement have been noticed for the rights and welfare which indicate all round development and awakening. It may be the distance impact of the world family or globalization. To cope up with the global change, tribal women require infrastructural facilities, mobility, new mechanized training, and socio-economic open contact. For that is required, support of the financial institutions, government's full support, NGO's involvement, education, skill training, etc.

The NER is considered as an undifferentiated unit for all practical purposes. For purposes of the policy, the most of the socio-economic characteristics of Assam, including poverty ratios have been assigned to the remaining states in NE India (GoI, 1993). Even in understanding of development problems and potentials, the region is treated as a homogeneous unit while selecting the sample. It is evident from India's Human Development Report, 1999 in which all the seven States have been clubbed together into a NER category and data collected from Assam have been made the basis to draw inference on NER as a whole. In fund allocation, the states are not considered separately. Each Central Department/Ministry (except those exempted) is required to earmark at least 10 per cent of Gross Budget support for the Region. Evidently, there have been no serious efforts to understand the region from its heterogeneous reality. Besides, very little data is available across states making the task of interventions equally difficult. The region is bountifully endowed with biodiversity, hydro-power potential, oil and gas, coal, limestone and forest wealth. It is ideally suited to produce a whole range of plantation crops, spices, fruit and vegetables, flowers and herbs, much of which could be processed and exported to the rest of the country and worldwide. Markets must be developed and problems of transportation, power, infrastructure, finance and services overcome. Its natural beauty, serenity and rich flora and fauna invite trekking and tourism. In terms of potentials the following are the strength of this region:

Tea

Northeast produces more than 50 per cent of tea in the country. Tea being an agricultural plantation crop and a major revenue generator, it plays a vital role in improving the socio-economic condition of the States of North-Eastern Region of India. Assam is the largest producer of tea in India. The recent technical survey carried out by the Tea Board indicate that there is possibility of bringing sizeable areas under tea in the States of Nagaland, Meghalaya, Mizoram, Manipur, Arunachal Pradesh and Tripura. As new clones proven for their quality and yield are being used for plantation in these States, the quality of tea to be produced in these regions are expected to be far superior. There is also good scope for producing organic tea from these regions since tea is being planted in virgin areas. In view of the positive developments, there is good scope for export of good quality tea also from the North-Eastern States in the long run. While good quality tea produce is assured in the years ahead, the focus would be on marketing of the output in a more systematic and value added form in order to reach the peak of the value chain both in traditional and non-traditional markets.

Bamboo

Bamboos play an important role in the rural economy. Bamboos are a sub-family of grasses that include over 1,200 species worldwide.18 genera and 130 species are so far known from India. The region has abundant bamboo resources. The heavy rainfall and temperate climate has assured an abundance of bamboo and cane in the region over the ages. Out of 136 species of bamboos found in India, 63 species in 22 genera are found in Northeast India, spread over an area of 30,500 sq. kms. Distribution patterns of bamboos in the region reveal that the species of Bambùsa, Dendrocalamus, Dinochloa, Cephalostachyum and Neohouzeoua are mostly confined to the lower altitude ranging between sea level and 600 m. above the sea level. Species of Arundinaria, Chimonobambusa, Semiarundinaria, Sinobambusa, Thamnocalamus and Phyllostachys are found in altitudes between 800 and 3500 m. The largest contribution to the growing stock is from Dendrocalamus strictus (45%), followed by Melocanna baccifera (20%), Bambusa bamboos (13%), D.hamiltonii (7%) and B. tulda (5%), with the rest sharing 6 per cent. About 25 species of bamboo are considered rare in North-east India.

Tourism

The North-Eastern Region of India with its large untapped potential for development of Tourism, still remains in the backward of development in so far as the tourism sector is concerned. The natural wealth of the region should have changed its own face with significant social and economic development. Each of the eight constituent states of the region has too enormous a potential for development of tourism industry.The eight States of the North-Eastern Region form part of the East Himalayan region, which extends from Sikkim eastwards and embraces the Shillong Plateau of Meghalaya. The rich natural beauty, serenity and exotic flora and fauna of the area are invaluable resources for the development of eco-tourism. The Region is endowed with diverse tourist attractions and each State has its own distinct features. The attractions are scattered over the entire region and are largely located in remote areas within highly fragile environments. These attractions and the people of the Region constitute the tourism resources at large.

Handloom and Handicraft

In the North-East States, KVIC took initiative to put foothold of its presence and established its field officials in the entire region. KVI occupy a unique position in the rural economy of this region and collaborative approach has been initiated. Spices Board of India and Khadi and Village Industries Commission (KVIC) have jointly extended financial and technical support for setting up of spices making units in Assam and Arunachal Pradesh .The Central Leather Research Institute (CLRI) under its Leather Technology Mission has extended support for setting up leather products manufacturing projects in Manipur and Negaland. From time immemorial handloom industry has been playing a vital role in the economy of the north-east region. The traditional skill of handloom weaving was not only a status symbol for the womenfolk but it was also an indispensable aspect of the socio-economic life of the people in this region. The NER has a rich and fairly ancient tradition of handloom weaving. On a conservative estimate there are about 1.3 ml. handlooms and nearly 1.4 ml weavers in the entire region. The total production of handlooms in the NE region is valued around Rs.1145 million on an annual basis. The commercial production of cotton handloom is oriented heavily towards meeting the requirement of the local market. In Assam, items like Gamucha, Chaddhar, Mekhala, Lungi and Dhoti, etc. which are basically the local dresses, dominate the product mix. The pattern is almost identical in the other states. In Arunachal Pradesh the traditional 'Galley' and 'Galluk' account for bulk of the production. In Meghalaya, items like 'dakmanda' (a traditional dress worn by Garo women) 'dhara' or 'jainsems' (worn by Khasi and Jaintia ladies) and dakhana (tribal dresses) are the most popular articles of manufacture. Shawls and skirts are the major items in respect of Nagaland. Near about 70 per cent of the production of cotton handloom fabrics in Manipur, comprise phanek (Lungis) and scarff shawls, though of late, some diversification in the product mix is being undertaken in the state. In Tripura, over 90 per cent of the production is still being accounted for by janata and plain sarees, gamucha and lungis. The Mizo lungi locally known as a 'puan' has a share of over 80 per cent of the total handloom fabric production in Mizoram. Handloom and Handicraft sector in the Northeast has a strong potential to stand on its own and act as an engine of growth for the entire region. The artisans are endowed with considerable amount of human capital. However, they are constrained by the insignificant size of the market for their product.

Biodiversity

The climatic factors of NER are high humidity (80-90%), frequent and heavy rainfall and moderate to mild temperature without extremes of heat or cold. The average rainfall is heavy but varies from 2,000-12,700 mm. The Brahmaputra flows through to the whole length of Assam valley with alluvial deposits on either side. The NER is an area of rivers, hills and plains, extraordinarily rich in vegetation: a part of the Khasi hills above the pine zone (2,000 m) is considered to be the richest, not only in India, but perhaps in the whole world. The forest of NEI is divided into: (i) tropical wet evergreen forest (5860,000 ha.), (ii) tropical moist forest (5474,000 ha.), (iii) sub-tropical broad leaved forests (300,000 ha.) and (iv) montane wet temperate forest (2628,000 ha.).

Forests are a unique storehouse of plant and animal genetic resources. Their contribution to the country's biological diversity is very significant. Biological diversity acts as an insurance against any possible crisis in food production. Forests meet nearly 40 per cent of the energy needs of the country (above 80 per cent in rural India). They also account for about 25 per cent of our fodder needs. Forest products are crucial to rural and tribal economy of India. While wood is the major forest product, resins, gums, lac and khus are some of the minor forest products. Many of the products provide sustenance to the rural people as a large part of their day-to-day necessities including food and medicines, are met by the forests. The forests are integral to the alleviation of their poverty. For landless families, forest-related activities often constitute the primary source of income.

The northeast India, being at the confluence of three major bio-geographical realm of the world, is extremely rich in floral and faunal biodiversity with several endemic species. North-east India is blessed with a wide range of physiography and eco-climatic conditions. The State of Assam has extensive flood plains, while Khangchendzonga in Sikkim stands 8586 m. tall. Cherrapunjee in the State of Meghalaya holds the record for the highest rainfall in a single month (9,300 mm) as well as the most in a year (26,461 mm) in India, while the nearby Mawsynram has the world's highest average rainfall (11,873 mm). The forests in the region are extremely diverse in structure and composition and combine tropical and temperate forest types, alpine meadows and cold deserts. There are regions, for example, in the State of Sikkim, where the faunal assemblages also change rapidly from tropical to sub-tropical, temperate, alpine and finally to cold desert forms.

Energy

Uninterrupted power supply is one of the crucial prerequisites for the growth of industries in any region/state. The present energy sector, constitute the valuable component of industrial scenario of North-Eastern Region, has the special role to play in the region's economic development. This sector is also deserved as the important component for improving the quality of life of the people. Energy is an economic good and both energy production and energy utilization are the main indicators of a country's progress. The region has an abundant supply of hydro-resources, coal existence, petroleum existence, but of little use of them due to the remoteness from the centre as it is characterized as industrially backward.

In the industrial scenario of Assam, petroleum industry is highly mechanized and highly capital intensive. The petroleum manufacturing sector has long been the most valuable and important source of energy in the economic history of the region. The persistent backward nature of the region stands as a great contrast to its development potential since independence. It is, therefore, due to this reason, special concentration should be drawn on those sectors which has much potentiality to contribute better in the development process. There is the great potentiality of oil sector in Assam to contribute in the national capital formation and in turn may help in achieving the goal of marching towards progress.

Oil Resources

North-east accounts for slightly less than half of the total crude oil production in the country. The North-Eastern Region has been a pioneer in the country in as far as exploration and production of Petroleum is concerned. Asia's first successful mechanically drilled oil well was drilled in Makum (Assam) way back in 1867. The first commercial discovery of crude oil was however, made in the year 1889 at Digboi (Assam) and this also marked the beginning of oil industry in India. In the year 1959, the Oil India Ltd. (OIL) and Oil and Natural Gas Commission (ONGC) were set up and since then, these two state owned companies have been continuously engaged in the exploration and production of hydrocarbons in the North-East.

In addition, the North-east region is the host to a variety of economic minerals. The important minerals are coal, dolomite, limestone, graphite, marble, etc., besides crude oil and natural gas. Most of the mineral deposits are found in forest area which calls for economic exploitation and development with due regard to ecosystem.

Water Resources

Endowed with a sub (extra) tropical type of monsoonal climate, the region shows remarkable variability of weather and climate on a regional scale and forms a distinct climatic zone within the Indian landmass. Comprising mainly of the basins of three of the large river systems of the world viz. the Brahmaputra, the Barak (Meghna) and the Irrawady, the NER possesses the richest treasure-trove of water resources in India. It possesses about 30 per cent of the total water resources potential and about 41 per cent of the total hydropower potential of India. The per capita and per hectare availability of water in this region is the highest in the country. The NE India is one of the wettest as well as most acutely flood prone zones of the world.

Horticulture

Each state has vast possibilities for growing a range of fruit and vegetables, tuber crops, tapioca and spices. This region is home to certain citrus and rice strains and is yet to be completely mapped for the full range of its bio-diversity. Productivity could also be greatly improved in the case of citrus, pineapple, banana and other varieties through tissue culture and the development of breeder seed farms. Likewise, vegetables Ratoon crops like banana can be replaced by more productive and disease free annuals. The hills can exploit niche markets and provide oft-season fruit and vegetables to the plains, including Bangladesh.

The National Horticulture Board (NHB) has urged the North-east states for "crop zoning" of horticultural products so that it could help boost the product's quality to capture the international market. Addressing the newspersons, NHB managing director, J.N.Chamber said that North-East Region has tremendous potential for horticultural farming and if proper care is taken, it will become the horticulture destination of the world. He visited Assam, Meghalaya, Mizoram and Arunachal Pradesh to acquaint himself with various horticultural schemes and different varieties of unique fruits and vegetables. Special focus was given to the north east for its several unique products, which are not available in other parts of the world (*Arunachal Times*, September 13, 2005).

Floriculture

The North-East region is endowed with the rich natural resources, which needs to be transformed into wealth though entrepreneurship development. Floriculture is a labour intensive economic activity generates large employment opportunities. Hence, Floriculture will be one of the avenues for employment and empowerment for women, unemployed educated youth and development of weaker sections of the society and overall poverty alleviation programmes. Diversification of cut flowers with high value flower crops, which have the export demand, is urgent need of the hour for the Floriculture Industry. Anthurium, which is important exotic commercial cut flower, which can be grown in North-Eastern Region of India (Mizoram, Meghalaya, Nagaland, Arunachal Pradesh). Other crops like orchids, gerbera, lilium, bird of paradise, etc. can be cultivated successfully in this region. Government of India has also declared some of the hill states as Special Economic Zones (SEZ) for Floriculture due to certain strategic advantages in Sikkim and Jammu and Kashmir for Floriculture, Uttarakhand for growing Gladiolus flower crop. The potentials of Commercial Floriculture are increasingly recognized and the expectations are that the Floriculture is an important growth engine for sustainable and widespread development, augmenting economic opportunity, income and employment in hilly states of the region *viz.*, Arunachal

Pradesh, Mizoram, Nagaland, Meghalaya and Sikkim. The economy of the north-east people can be strengthened through the Floriculture Village or cluster village model for rural development in areas with good accessibility. This involves the sustainable use of natural resources and introduction of the market driven non-farm enterprises business opportunities through post harvest processing and value addition to primary products through cultivation of commercially important flower crops suitable to the region.

Trade

The North-Eastern region of India has often been visualized as the remote landlocked backward region of a dynamic economy. The difference between the potential and actual economic performance is most startling for the region that has large international borders with several neighbours like Bangladesh, Bhutan, China, Myanmar and Nepal. The North-East region of India comprising of eight states has a unique geographical configuration with 98 per cent of its borders shares with neighbouring Asian countries. This along with the fact, that most of these states distinctly vary in terms of their ethnic composition, political ideologies, socio-economic characteristics and cross border interactions make a major differences in the national and local perspectives of borders. The most critical aspects of the border trading regime is to bring forth the genuine traders who are looking forward to a sustainable exchange of goods and services with the neighbouring countries. The 'Look East Policy' of the Union Government and the emerging trends of sub-regional cooperation among Bangladesh, Bhutan, India, Myanmar, Nepal, Sri Lanka and Thailand Economic Cooperation (BBIMNSTEC) and South Asia Growth Quadrangle (SAGQ) have in them cross border policy intervention with a view to harness the comparative advantages of all the eight North-Eastern States. The 'Look-East Policy' of India is of added importance to this region that all goods from and to India in the trade relation with South-East Asian market have to pass through this region and hence, it will reap an extra advantage of commercial transaction benefits. The then Indian Prime Minister, Atal Bihari Vajpayee's Southeast Asian tour to participate in the Association of Southeast Asia Nations (ASEAN) summit in Bali, Indonesia on 7th and 8th

October, 2003, marks the success of a decade-long shift in Indian foreign policy— known as the "Look East" strategy—initiated by former Prime Minister, Narasimha Rao in the early 1990s. On November 23, 2004, Prime Minister, Manmohan Singh flagged off the first ever India-ASEAN car rally in Guwahati. The non-competitive rally, organised by CII, has emphasized India's new found stress on the 'Look East' policy signifying new trade initiatives with the country's eastern neighbours and ASEAN nations. The Indo-ASEAN car rally has revived the speculation on vast possibilities of reaping benefits from trade that could take place between the north-eastern states and South-East Asian nations. If the concerned governments, particularly that of India, Myanmar and Thailand, and local authorities of these countries are serious about their declared intentions, then these new initiatives would indeed rediscover, renew and rejuvenate the age-old cultural and historical ties between the peoples of South-East Asian nations. In turn, greater interaction would undoubtedly boost trade, commerce and tourism prospects in the entire region.

The 'Look East Policy' when successfully implemented will make NE Region the gateway of India to Asian countries. It is a fact that once trade with Myanmar is in full swing, it could enter the South East Asian market. Since all goods from and to India have to pass through the north-eastern region, the latter will certainly develop commercially through the 'Look East Policy' of the Government. With Myanmar being an ASEAN member, common markets of as many as 500 million consumers are at the doorstep of North-Eastern region for which Myanmar will be the entry point to South-East Asian market. However, to achieve the end, it is not only that the road conditions have to be improved but also that the already experienced frequent disruption of transport due to agitations and militant activities of insurgent groups have to be brought under control. The most urgent need at this moment is to develop Special Economic Zones (SEZ) at appropriate places of the region to start with the trade ventures.

There is no doubt that this vast population could have great advantage for establishing any kind of trade and commerce. But the vary geographical condition basically the rivers and mountains of the country stand as a barrier and create geopolitical tensions which ultimately act as most disadvantages factors in creating a conducive atmosphere in the path of developing trade relation among those countries. But in the recent developments in the field of communication and technology, some visible changes are taking place. Now, the NER have felt the need of the hour regarding the modern facilities of lives. They have realized that in order to develop the economy of the nation, the border trade could be an effective solution. Border trade would help to great extent in the field of economic development and also the route between production points of India to the Northern district of Myanmar via North-East region is economic viable as it is much shorter than sea route.

The term 'development' is used for the process of allowing and encouraging people to meet their own aspirations. It, therefore, must relate to transforming the entire society enmeshing together its economic, social, political and administrative aspects on all round balanced upward change (Basu, A.R., 1985).

Epstein (1972) rightly pointed that the study of development requires the simultaneously analysis of a large number of variables and relationships on both the individual and the social level in the several major institutions of any community. Development process has to be ultimately assessed for impact on quality of life and human well-being.

Vidyarthi (1981) defines development as 'growth' plus 'change'. It involves material and human factors. He is of the view that the economic approach of development is not acceptable for an anthropologists who firmly believes that socio-cultural factors are integral part of the dynamics of growth and that social change is not a simply a non-functional effect of planning. Thus, development is a holistic phenomenon.

Belshaw (1977) described development as an increase in the capacities of the society to organise for its own objectives and to carry out its programmes more effectively. From this point of view, development is an organised activity and a multi-dimensional process to improve the social, cultural, economic and human conditions of the people for balanced growth of the society.

What Happens?

All the States in the NER are Special Category States whose Development Plans are centrally financed on the basis of 90 per cent

Grant and 10 per cent loan. Further, the Special Category States are allowed to use up to 20 per cent of the Central Assistance for Non-plan expenditure. Development of NER has always remains high on the agenda of both the Central Government and the respective States Government. The North-East Council (NEC) which was set-up in 1972 has been playing a major role. As a regional planning body, it has taken up a series of projects for balanced regional development of the region. To provide further focus to the development initiatives of this region, the Government had also set-up Department of North-East Region (DONER) in 2001.

Per capita devolution of Central Assistance to the state plans in NER is among highest in the country; the average per capita Central Assistance for State plans in NER was placed at Rs. 1,546 in 2001-02 as compared to Rs. 356 at the All-India level. The Government of India has also been providing special Central Assistance in respect of some of the States in the region for special programme such as the Hill Area Development Programme (HADP) and Border Area Development Programme (BADP). Other policy initiatives includes announcement of a new industrial policy for NER (December, 1997) which encompassed a comprehensive incentive package to stimulate development, creation of non-lapsable central resource pool (1998-99) to ensure speedy development of infrastructure in NER, the PM special packages. In addition, Projects of inter-State nature in the Region are funded through by the North-Eastern Council (NEC), which has a separate additional budget for the purpose. Thus, this region is not lacking in policy attention and programmes. The flow of funds is also not a problem.

The regional economies are simple, heavily deficit and dependent on the rest of the country for many basic needs. All states in north-eastern region are special category states whose development plans are almost entirely centrally financed on the basis of 90 per cent grant and 10 per cent loan. The development funding pattern for the special category states accords them built-in preferential treatment. There is no agricultural surplus and limited capital formation and entrepreneurial skills. Assam has seen development activities around tea, oil and timber; the region is, however, basically pre-industrial despite a number of saw mills and plywood factories, a few cement plants and other miscellaneous enterprises apart from oil and coal. Handlooms and handicrafts, once the pride of the North-east, are on the decline but have a considerable potential if it is given contemporary functionality through design, marketing and other inputs. After independence, some efforts were made to diversify the economic activities, but industries that came up were mostly remaining concentrated in certain pockets of Assam. The prospects for modern industries are not encouraging, as there is a lack of local or regional markets and distance from the main land of the country. Another important reason for the economic stagnation of the north-eastern region is the socio-economic resistance of the people and the structural rigidity of the society. Development has been a major casualty of insurgency and rampant violence. Hence, the region continues to remain mainly dependent on subsistence agriculture. Further, the agriculture has not undergone any significant transformation and the most primitive farm practices of slash and burn (jhum) is still dominating the sector. It is an irony that despite being an agriculture economy, the northeast remains food deficient.

The hilly States of Northeast are the most densely administered region of the country. Uncontrolled and unproductive employment in government sector resulted in the stagnation of the development process. On the whole, the economy of this region reflects underdeveloped agrarian societies with very weak industrial sector and inflated services (government) sector. Today, the saturation point has reached in most of the North-East States. The region is bountifully endowed with rich mineral deposits, hydropower potentials, forests, bio-diversity, etc. It is ideally suited to produce a whole range of plantation crops, spices, fruit and vegetables, flowers and herbs much of which could be processed and exported to the rest of the country and worldwide (Shukla Commission, 1997). But the region is considered as one of the backward regions of the country. It indicates that a high percentage of households is lying below poverty line. It varies between 55.48 per cent in Meghalaya and 78.39 per cent in Arunachal Pradesh. The unemployment problem in the region is also higher than the national scenario. A study of Srivastav and Dubey (2003) shows that in the age group of 15-23 years in NER in 1993-94, 8.70 per cent of the rural youths and 12.62 per cent of all the urban youths are unemployed as against all

India level of 7.8 per cent and 11.36 per cent respectively. Out of the total unemployed youths in this age group in the region, the urban unemployed youths constituted 66.99 per cent as against all India level of 37.74 per cent. Contrary to unemployment situation, there is demand for labour from outside as the intensity of development activities increases with successive plan periods. In another study, Dutta (2003) has found the per capita Net Domestic Product of the north-eastern states lying below the national level. In 1996-97 the all India per capita NDP at current prices was Rs. 12,237 while that of Arunachal Pradesh was Rs. 10,205, Assam Rs. 6,663, Manipur Rs. 7,510, Meghalaya Rs. 8,474, Mizoram Rs. 9,758, Nagaland Rs. 9,985 and Tripura Rs. 5,083.

Corruption

The local tribal people especially in Arunachal Pradesh do not pay income tax. The National Government is extending liberal financial aid to the state for her socio-economic development. An appreciable amount of this state sponsored for investment finds channelized to a new category of contractor-entrepreneur-politicians. This newly emerged neo-rich class has been to control a good amount of what is known as the 'black money'. A chunk of this is being spent in acquiring luxurious items (Sinha, 1994). All the states of North-eastern region depend on the financial aids of the centre. 90 per cent of their states' budget comes from the centre. In addition to that, funds for different developmental activities of the north-east states are granted by the centre. Hardly, a nominal amount of these funds are utilized for the concerned activities. Most of the funds are channelized by the officers or political leaders from top to bottom. This is the real economic scenario of the north-east states.

Some people within a very short period of time have experienced income and wealth inequalities to a high degree. Very few of them have been found to become very rich overnight and enjoy luxurious life and prefer conspicuous consumption which has been adversely affecting the rest of the society. The income inequalities in the north-east states' society are very much strong. Some are very rich and some are very poor. Some peoples in rural areas are living on self-growing food and common property resource forest product without functioning of money. The presence of high degree of corruption at all levels and existence of underground economy has also gone against in development of market economy. The consumer durables and non-durables are purchased by the easily earned money or easily available credit (consumption loans) from the markets located in big cities of the country or some growing urban centres in the State. This has regrettably led to the emergence of the consumption economy without the economy of production and hence obstructed the growth of market economy.

Development Policy

The term 'economic development' is generally used in many other synonymous terms such as economic growth, economic welfare, secular change, social justice and economic progress. As such, it is not easy to give any precise and clear definition of economic development. But in view of its scientific study and its popularity, a working definition of the term seems to be quite essential.

Economic development, as it is now generally understood, includes the development of agriculture, industry, trade, transport, means of irrigation, power resources, etc. It, thus, indicates a process of development. The sectoral improvement is the part of the process of development which refers to the economic development. Economic development is a long process in which several forces and factors of production work together to bring about an economic change for the betterment. The chief objective of an economic development is to maximize the production of consumer goods and services in the society which will positively increase the economic welfare of masses in general.

'Development' is generally used in connection with the poor or underdeveloped regions. Development differs from economic growth in that it pays attention to the conditions of production; for example, the environments affected by economic activity, and to the social consequences, for example, income distribution and human welfare. Stemming from Enlightenment notions of the use of the modern, scientific mind for improving existence, development entails human emancipation in two senses: liberation from the vicissitudes of nature through advanced technology and self-emancipation, that is, control over social relations, conscious control over the conditions under which human nature is formed. In both senses, development entails economic, social, and cultural progress, including, in the latter sense, finer ethical ideals and higher moral values. Development means improvement in a complex of linked natural, economic, social, cultural, and political conditions. Developmentalism is the belief in the viability and desirability of this kind of economic progress. A resource-rich region can be developed only when it is exploited efficiently in right direction. The NE region especially the hill areas are poor in the midst of abundant resources due to non-exploitation, under-exploitation or non-utilization of resources.

For rural development to succeed in a global environment, three things are essential: human capital, physical infrastructure, and adequate financing. For human capital and infrastructure (public capital) are critical components of sustainable community development. However, they feel that the third element should be social capital. Communities that have thriving social networks and institutions and good human capital will have adequate financing as well. Another component, which is very much talked about today, is social capital. Importance of infrastructure in the development of village economy is accepted by everyone, but the equally important factor which is not noticed by everyone is the social norms.

As for improvement of social capital, T. W. Schultz's research suggests that economic growth is largely the result of investment in the human capital. He further argues that increase in the capital income-ratio is largely due to human capital development, not material capital (i.e., reproducible, non-human capital), which was originally thought to account for all increases in income and subsequent economic growth. Investment in human knowledge and skill is the critical determinant of economic growth and is necessary if regions lacking human capabilities ever expect to attract and fully benefit from infusions of new capital. No matter how powerful the computer hardware or how user-friendly the software, most functions provided by computers still require hands-on human contact to be productive.

Development in north-east India is lopsided with disproportionate growth of the service sector, for the development that has taken place in the region is largely government sponsored. A high percentage (more than 50%) of working population is recorded as cultivators and agricultural labourers. In agriculture related activities, the percentage of female workers is higher than the male workers. Conversely, the percentage of male main workers exceeds the female workers in 'other services' category. A comparative high percentage of female workers in household industry category implies the traditional nature of industrial activities in rural areas. It can also be seen in the table of reference that the percentage of people engaged in 'other services' is much higher in urban areas. In other words, service sector is more developed in urban areas. It can be argued that the service sector has developed around government jobs which are mainly concentrated in urban areas. It can also be noted that in NER most of the urban centres are Administrative centres. There are many such centres which are not recognized as urban centres and, therefore, the service sector in such places is enumerated in rural sector. This implies that except the government jobs in Administrative centres, there are no, or very less of, other activities under otherwise very low intensity of 'other services' category in rural areas. Conclusively, there is a rural-urban difference in the level of development as reflected in differences in percentage of main workers in different activities and the economy in general is not diversified with a high percentage of workers in agricultural related activities and a comparatively low percentage of workers in 'household industry', and 'other services' categories. In the last category, however, a high percentage is attributed to government sector only.

In the industrial field, the region has only 1.8 per cent of the registered factories employing less than 2 per cent of the factory workers of the country (Datta Ray and Baishya, 1998). The spirit of entrepreneurship has not emerged to take up the challenges of industrialization and the constraints to entrepreneurship lies more in socio-cultural domain (*ibid.*) than in economic explanation. Besides socio-cultural constraints, there are also infrastructural bottlenecks. Evidently, the space of industrialization is slow (Shukla Commission, 1997). The indices of investment incentives are also not encouraging. Almost every item of mass consumption and every item of conspicuous consumption is imported from the rest of the country. Arunachal Pradesh, Nagaland, Mizoram,

Meghalaya, Manipur and Tripura still do not produce 'universal intermediaries' like cement, iron and steel, chemicals, machine tools, etc. which Ganguly considered to be one of the important contributing factors to the low rate of growth in terms of industrial employment. The economic policy since 1991 has left the major initiative for economic development to private sector. Even the infrastructural development responsibility is being entrusted to private initiatives. Under this situation, the development issue in north-east India bears scrutiny, for the new development paradigm focuses on enlarging people's choices (UNDP, 1990) through participation in order to ensure equitable and sustainable development.

The issue of development in North-East India draws attention to the 'problems of social, political, economic and cultural engineering of our diverse society' (Haksar, 1984). The region has its own peculiarities and its rich natural resources, but comparatively economic backwardness. The reason of comparatively poor performance lies at the root of financial crisis threatening these States (Bhattacharjee, 2002). There is a great deal of racial, linguistic and ethnic diversity, presenting complex problems to regional and national partnership in development efforts and of regional and national integration. The region is further burdened with problems relating to the assertion of national, sub-national and ethnic identity and to refugee issues. The insurgency problem and the recurring floods/natural calamities annually require a lot of financial resources meant otherwise for development purposes.

The issue of development in the north-eastern region is more of challenges than of opportunities in this era of globalization. There is a shift in development paradigm along with the process of globalization that emphasizes on 'reversals' of the approach, more precisely, 'putting the last first'. Put otherwise, the new development paradigm that has emerged and is taking shape right from early 1990s, precisely with the first Human Development Report of 1990, emphasizes on 'enlarging people's choices'. Bottom-up approach to development gets into practice within the theoretical and empirical frame of good governance, decentralized and micro-level planning, and for a participatory development. Obviously, the context is rural development as policy and practices, and also as process *vis-à-vis* globalization.

But the challenges are tough. In one way or another they relate to the theoretical and practical problems of development in a diverse society. In spite of 'reversals', the core-periphery syndrome is not only in the application of international development discourse to such less development areas and peoples as in the case of NER, but in all such efforts directed from central authority through bureaucracy. In an obvious line of reasoning it can be stated that the involvement of bureaucracy in the development process at various levels and bureaucratic misunderstanding of peripheral issues affects the process itself. Liberalization prescribes state interventions at selected sectors to correct market irregularities that create and widen existing social inequalities. Bureaucracy requires an understanding not only of the functioning of market under liberalization but of peripheral issues of the nation in relation to developed countries and within these countries. A balance has to be sought in perspectives of development at three levels, international development perspectives, national perspectives and perspectives of people at peripheral level. Government has its own agenda, perspectives and priorities, compulsions and constraints and programmes and above all a bureaucracy as functional machinery. Bureaucracy, however, functions within a professional frame, and bureaucrats have their mind set in appreciating people's development perspectives. Obviously, there remains a gap; put simply, a misunderstanding by bureaucracy of development perspectives of the people that differ greatly from national and international perspectives and from their own professional understanding. Because of bureaucracy and their professionalism, ideologies of the core always dominate that of the periphery. The strength of professionalism is specialization. Simplification and assimilation remain dominant 'through training and rewards, conservative and well defined and therefore is stable' (Chambers). This stability makes the new requirements, which are associated with new development paradigms of rural development, instable and weak, and thus render rural development plans and policies ineffective.

According to Schumpeter economic development and growth are two different things. By the former he means qualitative development of the economy and by the latter the quantitative changes as brought about by population growth. The economic development is also meant as increased national income and wealth, which can be possible from increased aggregate production. Production is the function of land, labour, capital, technology, organization and enterprise. The growth of output is relative and responsive to the rate of changes in the productive factors. The structural determinants of economic development are: (1) the rate of capital formation, (2) capital output ratio, (3) rate of growth of population, and (4) socio-economic environment. The rate of economic development and growth depends on the plans for expansion of the various growth agents. Their simultaneous attempts to carry out those plans based on anticipations about economic environment in future and the actual rate of growth that result from these activities, which, in turn, determine the plans and activities of succeeding plan periods need no elaboration.

The investments through Five Year Plans have, no doubt, resulted into physical achievements which are clearly visible in relation to the level of development existing during 1947 in North East. Under the label of development, the changes may be grouped into two: (1) Changes in the growth agents, and (2) Changes in general with a view to attempting objective analysis and arriving at valid conclusions, the resulted change in growth agents during all the previous plan periods are more relevant and important to account for. This is why the changes in growth agents may only be referred to which are defined by Leibenstein as, "the quantum of capacities residing in the members of the population to carry out growth contributing activities. The outcome of such growth contributing activities is to increase the quantum of productive capabilities of the population, their entrepreneurial capabilities, their skills, their stock of knowledge etc."

The central theme of the above definition is to build up productive capabilities in the manpower. Necessarily, the human capital is the foremost capital for any development. Mr. J. Panda and P. K. Sahu note, that the "process of acquiring and increasing the number of persons who have the skill, education and experience which are crucial for economic and political development should be vitalized." Human capital formation is thus associated with investment in man and his development as a creative and productive resource. Simultaneously, the physical means of development are equally important by dint of which the creative capabilities of human factor result into economic growth and so on. In view of this, the changes, on account of above plan investments, which have taken place with regard to infrastructural facilities and resource development in North-East economy may specifically be taken into consideration because only they can sustain changes and help bring desirable changes in future years to accelerate development.

Even today, the economy of Northeast has not been able to fully overcome the gravitational pull of stagnation. Its economy is faced with vicious circle on demand side as well as supply side. There is no denying the fact that its economy is constrained with low income followed by inadequate size of market, low and poor inducement to invest, lagging capital formation and low productivity. Thus, Northeast economy is passing through the preparatory stage of economic development. Now, how to break the deadlock of vicious circle is the main concern.

In order to have better grasp of the economy of Northeast it may be imperative to refer to Rosenstein Rodan, who remarks that the gravitational pull of stagnation in a given economy can be overcome by means of concerted attempt with due regard to complementary investments in different fields. He says, A big push must jerk the economy out of the grip of the forces of stagnation—a large expenditure in social and economic overheads to invest in various industries. He further says that big-push can also help overcome the inadequacy in the size of market created by the low per capita income and constrained consumer's basket. The complementary investment can help a lot in generating external economics which may sustain the development activities and propel the economic growth further. This changed situation may pave way for the economy heading towards market oriented industrialized one. Such transformation in the economy may automatically further lead to desirable changes in the outlook of the people and motivate them towards honorific activities, and more drive them towards risk taking profit earning and monetary gains. Structurally only such changes in the outlook of the masses can precede economic growth in a given economy successfully. In this regard, some achievement has been made, yet much is to be achieved in Northeast economy.

The immediate requirement in Northeast economy is to break the growth barriers on priority. In order to translate the above idea into practice and break the deadlock of vicious circles the 'system approach' may be adopted, in view of which the whole economy may be distributed into tile following five broad sectors: (A) Infrastructure comprising: (i) social and economic overheads—transport, communication, energy and power, (ii) services-education and training, consultancy services, physical services e.g. maintenance and repair of capital equipments, entrepreneurial motivation, institutional facilities, etc. (B) Resources comprising: (i) manpower, (ii) physical resources-forest, mineral, agriculture, livestock, others, and (iii) financial-farm and non-farm; (C) Production comprising: (i) primary-agriculture, animal husbandry and veterinary, fisheries. forestry, and (ii) secondary industries (D) Social Services comprising: (i) mass literacy, (ii) rural water supply, (iii) village approach roads, (iv) village electrification, (v) public health, hygiene and sanitation, (vi) rural housing, etc. (E) Miscellaneous; which may fulfil the requirement of nucleus plan, big-push, complementary investment, generation of external economics, minimum critical effort and bring about sustainable changes.

In the light of the above referred system approach the investment criteria of scarce means which have alternative uses may be projected practically so that maximum possible utility is derived from Leibenstein remarks, "Not everything can be done at once. A certain expenditure stretched over ten years may be more effective than the same expenditure spent all at once or all in one year. This implies that the critical minimum effort viewed as a minimum of all possible efforts that would lead to sustained real income growth involves an optimum time pattern of expenditure or effort." Besides, further in the light of the above deliberations the plan investments may be preferred on the following considerations:

1. Projects/schemes having total linkages, backward linkages, and foreward linkages, relating to promotion of social and economic overheads, production and productivity may be preferred to.

2. Projects / schemes having potential of ensuring faster economic growth with socio-economic justice e.g. dotting up of labour intensive industries etc. may be desirable.
3. Projects/schemes having potential of promoting growth agents viz. hydel projects roads and communication etc. may be preferred to.
4. Projects/schemes envisaged to promoting concentration of activities along with generating external economics instead of diverting activities during the given period in view of proportionate size of the plan in relation to total absorbing capacity of the economy may merit all due consideration and preference.
5. Projects/schemes having regard to existing set of circumstances under which they are to be operated may be preferred to.

The economic thinkers right from the Mercantilists to Karl Marx and Keynes also paid their attention to the problem of economic development, but they dealt merely with the problems which were static in nature and largely related with the Western European countries. The main objective of Keynesian economics was to help advanced countries to get out of depression. In the forties, they were otherwise busy in Second World War, and therefore, had no time to think of the economic development of the backward economies in the world. After the Second World War, the leaders of the Asian and African countries desired to promote rapid economic development in their countries because they felt that poverty anywhere is a threat to prosperity everywhere. Meier and Baldwin rightly remark, "A study of the poverty of nations has even more urgency than a study of the Wealth of Nations."

With the publication of Keynes' General Theory of Employment, Interest and Money in 1936, a revolutionary change in economic thinking has come forward so far. The problems of underdeveloped countries like poverty, hunger, high death rate due to chronic diseases, illiteracy and lack of opportunity for self-employment have attracted economists now to study them deeply and find their solutions. People in these countries in general suffer from the problems of starvation and illiteracy, and they look enviously towards the high and very prosperous societies of the developed countries. It is with this view that their mind has become development-biased. People in the developed countries also realize that their interests coincide with the development of poor countries.

Most important feature of underdeveloped countries is their dependence on vicious circles of poverty which may be considered as the highest bottleneck in the process of their economic development. Poverty is not only distressing but it is also demoralizing. A poor man is one who is regarded as a disgrace to the society and a cause of humiliation to himself, and who is unable to have proper food and a suitable house. Neither he helps himself, nor he is able to serve others. He is burden on society. A poor man always finds himself having been caught in a vicious circle of poverty. Since, he lacks the means to prosper, he remains poor. What is true to an individual is also true to the country as a whole. Since, an underdeveloped economy lacks the proper and modern means of economic development, its economic development becomes an uphill task. Since its rate of investment and growth potential is so little, it has to remain poor.

We find circular relationships, known as the "vicious circles of poverty" which reveal the low level of economic development in Less Developed Countries (LDCs). Prof. Nurkse defines the concept of "Vicious Circles of Poverty" in these words: "It implies a circular constellation of forces tending to act and react upon one another in such a way, as to keep a poor country in a state of poverty. Although it is not easy to break the vicious circle, yet it should be broken from both ends. The supply of savings both from domestic and foreign resources must be raised by the state under a suitable monetary and fiscal policy, so as to increase the level of investment in the country. As we know, the low level of real income, resulting in low productivity is a very important point both on the demand and the supply sides. Of these two ends, the supply side is more difficult to break than the demand side. In other words, it is obviously easy to create demand for capital but it is not easy to increase the level of capital formation and hence to make up the shortage of capital. But the lack of natural resources along with other deficiencies can be ultimately removed, provided the people are educated and the problem of capital formation is solved successfully.

According to Malthus, the process of economic development is not automatic or natural. But it requires consistent efforts on the people's part. He conceives that the economy is likely to have slumped many times before achieving its optimum level of development, and do not point out any phase of the stationary state. For him, the process of development is, thus, not a smooth functioning of various economic activities, but it is merely an activity of ups and downs in the economy. Malthus recognizes progress of wealth as economic development of a country. The wealth of a country is dependent both on the quantity of goods and their valuation. But "the wealth of country does not always increase in proportion to the increase in value, because an increase in value may sometimes take place under an actual diminution of commodities." According to Malthus, the underdeveloped countries have dualistic economies where the agriculture sector retards the development of the industrial sector, because the former operates subject to the Law of Diminishing Returns while the latter works under the Law of Increasing Returns. His division and analysis of an underdeveloped economy is rather realistic. Similarly, his analytical approach to study the causes of poverty in the poor economies is also highly realistic even in the modern times.

According to the most of the economists, the economic development is to be ensured through a more efficient allocation of resources. They are, therefore, chiefly concerned with short-run problems and most of them are interested in the interrelations with the various sectors of the economy at a particular point of time rather than analyzing their behaviour over a long period of time.

Marx believes that the 'mode of production' is the base to change the human behaviour. The mode of production and the relations of production determine the structure of the class in a society. Under capitalism, this structure consists of the 'haves' and 'havenots', i.e., the small rich and dominant class of exploiters and the poor and exploited workers among the masses. The class struggle between the two brings a change in the material forces of production and, thus, the society also undergoes a change.

Labourers are largely exploited for the interest of the capitalist which led to the concentration of capital in the hands of a few people. "Even today, in most of the underdeveloped countries that are politically free, wages are nearly at the subsistence levels; the increasing misery of masses is visible; the chronic and disguised unemployed exists; the problem of under-consumption is universal and the society is sharply divided into two classes—the rich and the poor masses." As we know, in the Marxian model of development, the dualistic economy has been emphasized, which consists of a capitalist sector and a subsistence agriculture and small-scale sector. Marx calls them two departments. The basic strategy of planning in these countries has been to promote these two sectors—industrial and agriculture simultaneously, so as to achieve the rapid economic growth and create larger opportunities of employment within the economy.

The Schumpeterian theory of development lies in the breaking up of the circular flow with an innovation in the form of a new product by an entrepreneur for the purpose of earning profits. The circular flow can be broken up by entrepreneurs raising the level of investment in the economy. The bank credit can help largely in this context. Once the new innovations prove to be more profitable and quite successful, other entrepreneurs also follow them. Again, Leibenstein's thesis is more realistic and has more relevance than Rosenstein-Rodan's "big push" theory. A big push for the rapid economic development is impracticable in underdeveloped countries for capital deficiency, whereas Leibenstein's thesis which emphasizes the critical minimum effort, broken up into a series of smaller efforts to lead the economy on the way to sustained economic development, has rather much relevance in underdeveloped countries. This theory also includes the idea of demographic transition and population control which is the main problem of most of the underdeveloped economies.

No underdeveloped country possesses capital and other resources in such quantities as to invest simultaneously in all sectors. Therefore, investment should be made in a few selected sectors or industries for their rapid development, and the economies accruing from them can be utilized for the development of other sectors. Thus, the economy gradually moves from the path of unbalanced growth to that of balanced growth. Economists like Singer, Kindleberger, Streeten, etc., have expressed their views in favour of the unbalanced growth doctrine which are in fact the criticisms of the theory of balanced growth. It is, however, Hirschman who has propounded the doctrine of balanced growth in a systematic manner. According to Hirschman, investments in strategically selected industries or sectors in the economy will lead to new investment opportunities and so pave the way to further economic development. He maintains that "development has of course, proceeded in this way, with growth being communicated from the leading sectors of the economy to the followers, from one industry to another, from one firm to another." He regards development as a "chain of disequilibria" that must keep alive rather than eliminate the disequilibria, of which profits and losses are symptoms in a competitive economy.

REFERENCES

Ahmed, J.U. (2007): *Industrialisation in North-Eastern Region*, Mittal Publications, New Delhi.

Ali, N. (2007): "Constraints in Growth in Market Institutions in Arunachal Pradesh" in Borbora, S. and Gogoi, J.K.(ed): *"Development Issues in Northeast in the Turn of the Century", NEEA*, Papyrus, Guwahati.

Arunachal Times, Vol. 19, No. 251, February 20, 2008, Itanagar, Arunachal Pradesh.

Arunachal Times, Vol. 17, No. 98, September 13, 2005, Itanagar, Arunachal Pradesh.

Behera, M.C. (2004): *Globalisation and Development Dilemma: Reflections from North-East India*, Mittal Publications, New Delhi.

Behera, M.C., (2000): 'Tribal Development and Environmental issues in Arunachal Pradesh' in Sharma P.D. (Ed): *Environment, Health and Development: An Anthropological Perspective'*, S.C.Roy *Institute of Anthropological Studies*, Ranchi.

Bhattacharjee, P.R. (2002): 'The Problem of Ensuring Financial Efficiency in the North-Eastern States', *Dialogue*, Vol. 4 (1), July-September.

Datta Ray and Baishya, P., (1998): *Sociological Constraints to Industrial Development in North-East India*, Concept, New Delhi.

Ganguly, J.B. (1998): 'Status of and Sociological Constraint on Industrial Development in North-East India', in Datta Ray and Baishya P., (eds): *Sociological Constraints to Industrial Development in North-East India*, Concept Publications Pvt. Ltd., New Delhi.

Government of India: *Census Reports*, 1961, 1981, 1991 and 2001.

Haksar, P.N.(1984): 'Problem of Building a Diverse Society', in North-East Region, Problems and Prospects of Development, Abbi, B.L., (ed), *Centre for Research in Rural and Industrial Development*, Chandigarh.

Kulshrestha, U.C.(2003): *Economic Development and Planning*, Educational Publishers, Agra.

Kundu, A. (2004): *Infrastructure, Financing and Emerging Pattern of Urbanization: Vision 2020*, India Vision 2020, *Planning Commission*, New Delhi.

Kundu,A. (2006): "Social Development Report",Oxford Univ.Press,New Delhi.

Mandal, R.K. (2005), "Trend of Diversification of Arunachal Economy with Special Reference to Agriculture: A Strategy for Sustainable Development" *Resarun: Journal of the Directorate of Research*, Vol. 29, Itanagar.

Mandal, R.K.(2008): "Position of Women in Tribal Society of Arunachal Pradesh with special Reference to Galo Women" in Pandey, B.B.(ed): *Impact of Globalisation on the Himalayan Tribes of India*, Himalayan Publishers, New Delhi, Itanagar.

Mandal,R.K.(2005): "Arunachal Pradesh Emerging as Power House" *Journal of Global Economy*, Vol. 01, No. 4.

Megu, K. (2007): *Development Issues in North-East Region*, Mittal Publications, New Delhi.

Mitra, A. (2002), *"Internal Migration and Economic Development in the hill*, Omsons Pub., Gauhati, New Delhi.

Nathan, Dev (2009): "Social Security, Compensation and Reconstruction of Livelihoods", *EPW*, Vol. XLIV, No. 30, July 25-31, Mumbai.

NEDFi, quarterly data bank, 2005.

Pandey, B.B.(2008): *Impact of Globalisation on the Himalayan Tribes of India*, Himalayan Publishers, New Delhi, Itanagar.

Pandey, G.S.: *Buddhism and Khamtis*, San Park Press Pvt. Ltd., Ashok Vihar I, Delhi.

Prasad, P. (1995): *Urban Slums: Health, Education and Development*, Delta Publications, New Delhi.

Rao, N.A. *et al.* (2004): "Urbanization Trends in Andhra Pradesh: A Region-wise Study", *Asian Economic Review*, 46(1).

Sen, A. (2002): 'Globalisation, Inequality and Global Protest', *Development*, 45, June, pp. 11-16.

Shukla Commission, (1997): 'Transforming North-East, Tackling backlogs in Basic Minimum Services and Infrastructural Needs', High Level Commission Report to the Prime Minister, Planning Commission, New Delhi.

Singha, Komol (2009):Village Development in North-East India, Concept Publishing, Company Pvt. Ltd., New Delhi.

Sinha A.C. (1994): *"North-Eastern Frontier of India: Structural Imperatives and Aspects of Change"*, Indus Publishing Company, New Delhi.

UNDP(1993): Human Development Report.

2

Overview of Arunachal Pradesh

Introduction

Arunachal Pradesh, the land of rising sun situated in the North Eastern part of India formed on February 20, 1987 is the 13th geographically largest State in all the States and UTs of India. It has 83,743 sq. kms. area covering around 2.5 per cent of the total geographical area of India. The State is predominantly mountainous and like a horseshoe in shape. This State is situated near the tropic of cancer, lying between latitudes 26°28′N and 29°30′ N and longitude between 91° 30′ E and 97°30′ E on the North-East extremity of India. It is bestowed by nature with beautiful ranges of snow-clad Himalayan peak which is locally called as "Paradise on the earth". Arunachal Pradesh is one of the largest States in the northeast region with a population of about 11 lakh showing only 0.11 per cent of the population of India. Arunachal Pradesh falls within the Eastern Himalaya, which extends from Bhutan and southern China to the tri-junction of India, China and Mynamar where the Himalaya makes its dramatic U-turn to form the Patkoi Hills. This is the region where the pre-Tertiary Tethys Sea first began to close, opening up a pathway for the Palaeoarctic biota of Tibet and Malayan elements from the south east, which resulted in enormous ecological and floristic diversity. The State has a long international border with Bhutan to the West (160 kms.), China to the North and North–East (1,030 kms.) and Myanmar to the East (440 kms.). The geo-strategic importance of the State becomes evident from the fact that the State has more than 1630 kms. international border. The international border of the State runs from one tri-junction of Tibet (China), Bhutan and India in the north-west to another tri-junction of China, Myanmar and India in the north-east along with high peaks of the Himalayas. The great Himalayan ranges run from the east of the Bhutan Himalayas to the Tsangpo up to Mishmi hills. The border is under dispute particularly with Tibet (China) regarding Mac-Mohan Line until date. This border dispute led to the Chinese aggression of India in 1962, which was a turning point not only in the history of India but also in the development of the region.

Arunachal Pradesh is one of the two globally designated areas of the "Biological Hotspot" region in India. Major portion of the geographical land area in the state is mountainous and hilly terrains, which are inaccessible and underdeveloped. Natural resources, particularly forest and land are the vital components of all socio-economic activities for livelihood sustenance of indigenous tribal communities living in the State. Sustainable utilisation of these resources need proper planning, as the development of the any region is largely dependent on availability of resources, proper planning and local community participation. In this context, the passage of the 73rd Constitutional Amendment Act, 1992 marks a new era in the federal democratic set-up of the country and provides constitutional status to the Panchayati Raj Institutions (PRIs), which help planning from grassroots level and ensure community participation in developmental activities. In the extreme east, the State meets another series of mountain ranges where the Himalayan range turns from East-West direction to South-West direction and hastens on, prominently southwards into the hills of Nagaland. Its great range of elevation form the outer Siwalik type hills rises to a height of 300 metres and further in a series of knife like ridges from the plains of Assam to the inner or Greater Himalaya which encompasses heights from 4,900 metres to 7,000 metres along the border of Tibet (China). Though once forbidden and formidable area; it is, at present developing at fast pace and the people are enjoying a better life in social, economic, political and religious spheres.

A major portion of the habitat that North-East Indian tribes inhabit is hilly and forested. The native people of Arunachal Pradesh are tribes with heart-warming legacy of arts and crafts and engaging folk-songs. The tribal people have their own patois and cultural identities. Each tribe possesses its own lively folk-songs and kaleidoscopic traditional dances, depicting an inimitable outline of unity in diversity. Though the tribes possess their own dialect, but Hindi and Assamese are also extensively spoken and used in communication with non-tribal people.

According to Indian aboriginal traditions, the tribal societies inhabit and remain within a definitive and common topography. Members of a tribe possess an awareness of mutual unity. Tribes follow their own political organisation which preserves eternal harmony. Religion is of supreme importance in an Indian tribal society. Tribal people make up 8.2 per cent of the nation's total population, which adds to over 84 million people, according to the 2001 Indian census.

Elwin (1957), the then Anthropological Advisor to the Government of NEFA, recommended some measures on the basis of which government policy was formulated. He elucidated the social, cultural, economic and psychological goals for the administration in tribal areas with particular reference to NEFA. He advised to dealt with tribal problems under the heading of material needs, social, religious and cultural problems.

As a matter of fact, this border region State, Arunachal Pradesh acquired an identity of its own for the first time in 1914 when some tribal areas were separated from the then Darrang and Lakhimpur districts of Assam to form North-East Frontier Tract (NEFT). The North East tract was further subdivided into the Balipara frontier tract, Lakhimpur frontier tract, Sadiya frontier tract and the Tirap frontier tract during various stages of evolution between 1914 and 1948. These frontier tracts were collectively renamed as North East Frontier Agency (NEFA) in 1954. The North East Frontier Agency was reconstituted into the Kameng frontier division, Subansiri frontier division, Tirap frontier division, Siang frontier division, Lohit frontier division and Tuensang frontier division. The Tuensang Frontier Division was later separated from NEFA in 1957 and merged with newly constituted Naga Hills after creation of a new State of Nagaland. In 1950 under the Constitution of India these areas were rechristened as Tribal Areas.

The NEFA was upgraded to Union Territory and renamed as Arunachal Pradesh on 20th January, 1972 in pursuance of the North-East Frontier Areas Reorganization Act of 1971 by the then Prime

Minister of India, Late Indira Gandhi at Ziro, the headquarter of Subansiri District. Consequently, the Agency Council was replaced by Pradesh Council which in turn was converted to Legislative Assembly in 1975. The first election to 30 members Assembly was held in 1978.

Since 15th August, 1975 this Union Territory was endowed with a Legislative Assembly having Chief Minister with a cabinet of four Ministers to assist the Lt. Governor appointed on the same day as the Administrator of the Union Territory. People's participation in decision-making process in Arunachal started as late as in 1967 with introduction of a Panchayat system. The General Election for the first time were held in 1977 for the Parliament and the first General Election to the 30 member Arunachal Pradesh Legislative Assembly was held in 1978, constituting a landmark in the political history of the territory. The headquarter of this Union Territory was then shifted from Shillong to the newly constructed capital complex at Itanagar under Subansiri District in 1974. Arunachal Pradesh was Union Territory till 19th February, 1987.

On 20th February, 1987 Arunachal Pradesh was upgraded from UT to a full-fledged State by the then Prime Minister of India, Sri Rajiv Gandhi at Itanagar, the State capital in the district of Papum Pare. On the attainment of Statehood, the Lieutenant Governor of the Territory was redesignated as the Governor of the State and the number of seats in the Legislative Assembly was increased to 60. Administrative responsibility for Arunachal Pradesh passed from the Ministry of External Affairs to the Ministry of Home Affairs of the Government of India in 1965 consequent to which the five frontier divisions of the territory became the five original districts. These districts have been further subdivided with the passage of time.

The administration and resources necessary to control and develop an area is directly proportional to its size and population. In regard to this fact, China had a much larger task in Tibet than the Indian Government did in Arunachal Pradesh, and this may have had a degree of impact upon the militaristic strategies that the Chinese employed. As far as development is concerned, Arunachal Pradesh has progressed by leaps and bounds. The region now, to varying degrees, has a modern infrastructure that includes paved roads, electricity, medical services, schools, colleges, and basic facilities. Many of the residents of the areas have access to aspects of the developed world that it previously did not have before outside intervention. To a modest extent, the tribals of Arunachal Pradesh are becoming more and more settled, making more money, and are living lives that are more tied in with the functions of industrial societies.

Until the twentieth century the tribal people of Arunachal Pradesh lived in virtual isolation and autonomy from the nearly all forms of outside influence. The first recorded contact with the British colonial authority was not until 1897, and this was only a brief encounter which lasted two days and had little direct effect.

It has been segregated all the tribes of Arunachal Pradesh into groups quite independent of each other, living their lives on their own terms. All the tribes follow 'endogamy' and strictly observe the rule of 'clan exogamy'. With the societies of the tribes of Arunachal Pradesh, polygamy is highly endorsed and practiced by all. Festivals are an integral part of all the tribes of Arunachal Pradesh thereby mirroring the cultural exuberances and artistry. The Adi tribes by nature are democratic and organized village council called Kebang. Adi women are good weavers. Apatani tribes produce paddy and fish in large numbers. Unlike other tribes of Arunachal Pradesh, the economy of Apatani tribes is stable. Agriculture is one of the main occupations of Bugun or Khowas tribes, just like any other tribes of Arunachal Pradesh. They are also cordial by nature. Aka tribes are mainly traders. The Singpho are mainly farmers. Khamba and Memba do farming activities. Mishmi women are expert weavers. Although agriculture is the main occupation of the people, some of them also carry of with the trade of various items like, wild medicinal plants etc. Amongst various tribes of Arunachal Pradesh, the Sulung or Puroik are considered to be one of the ancient tribes in the area. The society of Wancho is divided into four classes—the Wanghams (chiefs), the Wangpana, the Wangaue and Wangaas . They have a strict sense of the law and the village council protects the law and order of the society.

The main occupation of the local population is agriculture, which is based primarily on swidden cultivation, the slash-and-burn method that is known in North-East India as *jhum*. However, in the foothill and plain areas of the district people are increasingly adopting permanent agricultural practices. Paddy, maize and millets are the main crops. Fruits like apple, pear, plum, peach and almond are grown in the higher reaches of the district whereas pineapple, papaya, litchi, banana etc. are grown in the foothills and plain areas. The climate and soil of the lower parts are suitable for sericulture. People residing in these places grow mulberry and eri silk worms. However, there are distinctly two types of agricultural practices: (i) settled cultivation, and (ii) shifting cultivation. The agricultural operations are confined to only 5 per cent of the total geographical area, out of which 62 per cent to 65 per cent are under shifting cultivation .The shifting cultivation is also called as slush and burn method of cultivation. It is labour-intensive process of farming with extensive use of land. It is also claimed that slash and burn agriculture leads to deterioration of the vegetative cover on the hills: forest lands degenerate into infertile grassland and barren land space. Therefore, it is contended that this system of agriculture is unsustainable and economically impoverishing of the tribal people depended on it.

It is generally agreed that growing monetization of the economy should lead to the spurt in investment. Nevertheless, due to very low level of farm and non-farm production, output has not registered a noticeable growth that evidently adds to constraints to the economic development. Third, social capital of the State has not been utilized to its fullest capacity due to structural and functional inefficiency of the delivery institutions.

It also stretches from snow-capped mountains in the North to the plains of Brahmaputra Valley (Assam) in the South. Out of the total area of 83,743 sq. kms., the State has recorded forest cover of about 51,540 sq. kms. forming 61.5 per cent of her total geographical area. The proportion of arable plain land is very low. This topographical situation has direct influence on the economy of the State. From the economic point of view the whole State may be divided into three lateral belts each having a distinct pattern of economic development. The upper belt bordering international frontiers has very little economic opportunities as well as constrained with negligible or no facilities of modern civilization. The lower belt consisting mainly of the foothills has intimate economic ties with the adjoining plains of Assam. The people of lower belt enjoy almost all facilities of modern life. The middle belt acted as a bridge between the upper and the lower belt. The people inhabiting the three belts are at different stages of economic development. The low levels of population mobility are due to the regional disparity in the levels of economic development in Arunachal Pradesh. Arunachal Pradesh has one of the highest per capita availability of natural resources, yet it is one of the most economically backward regions in India. By the first half of the 19th century, surveyors, botanists and administrators, besides Catholic and Hindu religious missionaries, had made their way up the banks of the Brahmaputra, and into the formidable Mishmi Hills of Lohit. Towards the end of the century, an adventurous British tea planter got as far as the Apatani plateau in Subansiri.

The People of the State have a rich tradition of craftsmanship and are very adept at crafts such as weaving, woodcarving, carpet weaving, cane and bamboo works, smithy works, etc. Khadi and Village Industries (KVI), therefore, offer enormous prospects for increasing the opportunities for income and employment generation in the State. The State bears a testimony to an extravagant history of art and craft. The tribal people exhibit finesse in this field. Weaving is the universal craft in this region as in other parts of northeast India, with beautiful and highly coloured fabrics being made largely by women. The handicrafts of the State include a wide variety in weaving, painting, pottery, basketry and wood carving. The tribal people make exquisite carpets, paintings on wooden vessels and silver articles. The Village and Small-Scale Industries and traditional un-organized industries constitute an important segment of Arunachal's planned economy. This sector has not only continued to play a vital role in fulfilment of socio-economic objectives but also offers an excellent opportunity for industrial self-employment. The aim and objective of the department of Industries in the State is to promote the industrial activities in the State and thereby to provide employment opportunities to the rural and urban and to improve the economic conditions of the people. There are two Industrial Training Institutes and one Rural Industries Development Centre that are functioning in the State who are also helping the local youth to generate self-employment. Small Scale and Cottage Industries in Arunachal Pradesh are the largest and most potential source of economy and also the mainstay of economic progress of the people. Almost all the major tribes in Arunachal Pradesh use to practice, to some extent, weaving, the widespread household industry. Everywhere it is the exclusive business of the women. The women are good weavers and only the family members of the village headman carry out with it. They are proficient in wood carving also. Arunachal Pradesh is proud of her traditional and fantastic indigenous handicrafts and most colourful handloom products. In the past years, the role conceived for the Industries Department in Arunachal Pradesh was one of the revival and revitalization of the traditional handloom and handicrafts. The notable activities have been the establishment of craft centres, production centres in the board areas, extension of sericulture programme and setting up of small scale industrial units.

The south west monsoon makes the State one of the wettest in the country, with the rainfall as high as 4,500 mm a year in the foothills. The higher altitudes are relatively drier with 800 mm a year, giving the State an average annual rainfall of 3,000 mm. The rains extend from the tempestuous pre-monsoon showers in March through the heavy, incessant downpours in June and July, to taper off in September-October. This makes the foothills almost constantly hot and humid, with temperatures touching 38 degrees in the summer. The Middle or Lesser Himalayan area has a temperate climate but even in spring, certain locations can be quite chilling as the wind tears through the deep gorges. The alpine belt has less precipitation of snow than at similar altitudes in the western Himalaya, but the winters can be freezingly cold.

The striking feature of the topography of the region is that the mountainous routes follow the river system excepting in the places where the mountain sides are very steep. The landscape of Arunachal Pradesh is dissected by mighty rivers and their tributaries which drain into the Brahmaputra in the Assam valley. From Tibet the Tsangpo swerves around into Arunachal, where it is called the Dihang or Siang, and when it enters Assam this becomes the great river, Brahmaputra. The river system in the territory is as important as the geography of the land. The five major rivers: Kameng, Subansiri, Siang, Lohit and Tirap with a large number of tributaries have drained the waters of this vast area in the mighty Brahmaputra. These rivers, besides becoming an important source of protein rich fish, have of late begun to provide hydel powers to illuminate the hitherto formidable land.

Growth of Population

During every tenth year, population census is undertaken in India. The growth behaviour of population is accounted for this period, which is known as decennial growth of population. From the standpoint of economic development, to know decennial growth rate of population is one of the most essential requirements. Because, the decennial growth rate and the economic benefit out of economic development at constant rate relate inversely considering that other things remain as constant. That is why, the technique of decennial growth rate is used as barometer to reflect the growth phenomena of population. In the absence of decennial population growth rate, the requirements can neither be identified nor quantified properly. Thus, population is the pivot around which all types of economic activities rotate.

The State of Arunachal Pradesh is sparsely populated by the indigenous population predominantly. During the Census year1961, the tribal people comprised 88.76 per cent of total population. According to 2001 census, the State has a population of 10,97,968 persons consisting of 5,79,941 males and 5,18,027 females as against 1991 census of 8,64,558 comprising 4,65,004 males and 3,99,554 females. The sex ratio of Arunachal Pradesh at 901 females to 1000 males is lower than the national average of 933. The State has 0.11 per cent of the All India Population with a total of 10252.51 lakhs. The decennial growth rate of the population from 1991 to 2001 is about 26.85 per cent against an increase of 21.34 per cent at all India level. The density of population in the State as per 2001 census is 13 persons/sq.km.as compared to10 persons/sq.km. in the 1991 census. What is more is that, the population density of the State is the lowest among the States in India. According to 2001 census, the tribal population of the State at present is 705,158, which is 64.22 per cent of total population in this State in which the highest percentage is in Kurung Kurmey district with (97.89%) while in Lohit district scheduled tribes account for only a third of the population (32.42%). The sparsely inhabited hilly terrain State, Arunachal Pradesh is a predominantly tribal inhabited State. Obviously in the past, the Scheduled Tribe (ST) people purely inhabited it. During 1961, the tribal people formed

88.67 per cent of total population. The percentage of S.T. population was 78.85 per cent in 1971, 69.82 per cent in 1981, 63.66 per cent in 1991 and 64.22 per cent in 2001. Census-wise population growth including males and females and also ST population growth with its percentage to total population of Arunachal Pradesh since 1961 census is depicted as follows in Table 2.1 and in Figs. 2.1, 2.2, 2.3 and 2.4. In Figs. 2.3 and 2.4, it is observed that the percentage of ST population is continuously decreasing since 1961 (first census).

Table 2.1: Population Growth Since 1961.

Year	Persons	Males	Females	ST population	ST population as % of total population
1961	336558	177680	158878	298439	88.67
1971	467511	251231	216280	369408	78.85
1981	628050	335941	292109	441167	69.82
1991	864558	465004	399554	550351	63.66
2001	1097968	579941	518027	705158	64.22

Source: Directorate of Economics and Statistics (Various issues).

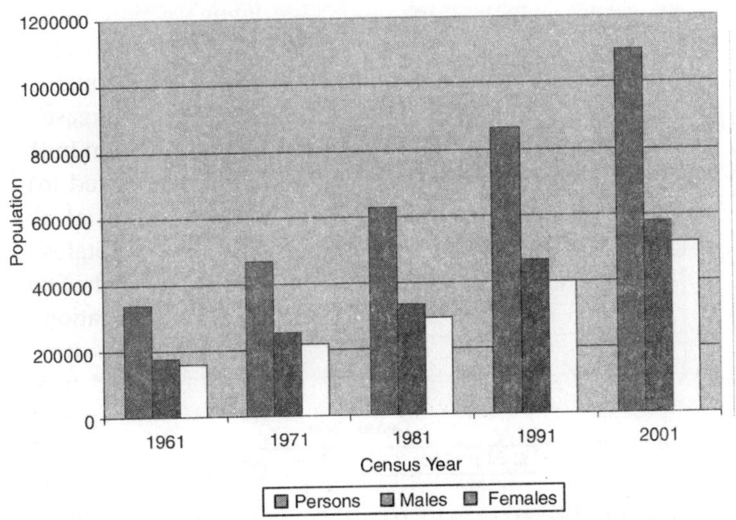

Fig. 2.1: Population Growth in Arunachal Pradesh since 1961.

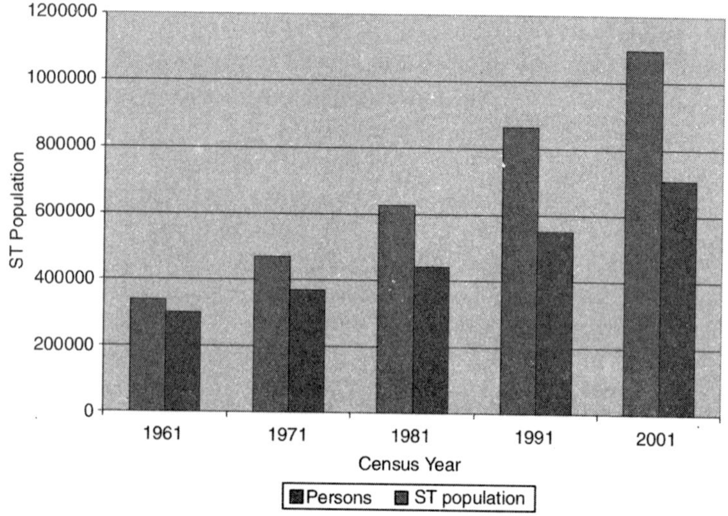

Fig. 2.2: Growth of General and ST Population since 1961.

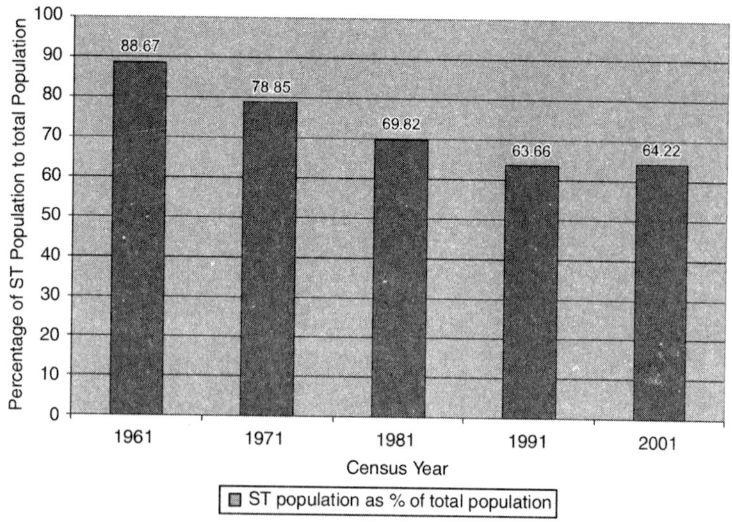

Fig. 2.3: Percentage of ST Population to Total Population.

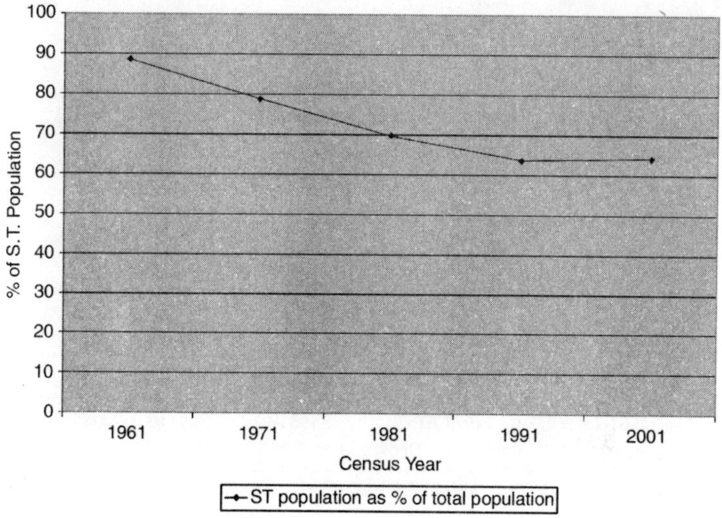

Fig. 2.4: Time Plot of ST Population as % of Total Population.

The decennial growth rate of population of Arunachal Pradesh and India since 1961 is shown in Table 2.2 and in Figs. 2.5 and 2.6.

Table 2.2: Decennial Population Growth Rate Since 1961.

	1961-71	*1971-81*	*1981-91*	*1991-2001*
Arunachal Pradesh	38.91	35.15	36.83	26.21
India	24.80	24.66	23.86	21.34

Source: Census Report, Arunachal Pradesh, 2001.

Note:

(i) Decennial Growth

$$= \frac{\text{(Population of previous census – Population of current census)}}{\text{Population of previous census}} \times 100$$

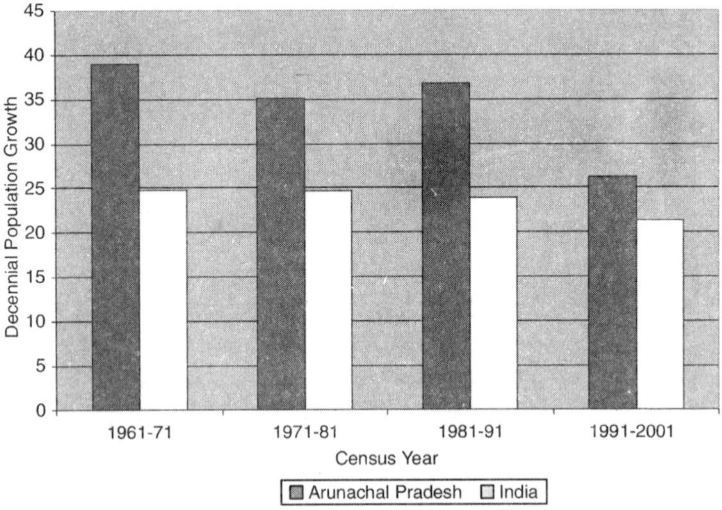

Fig. 2.5: Decennial Growth of Population for India and Arunachal Pradesh since 1961.

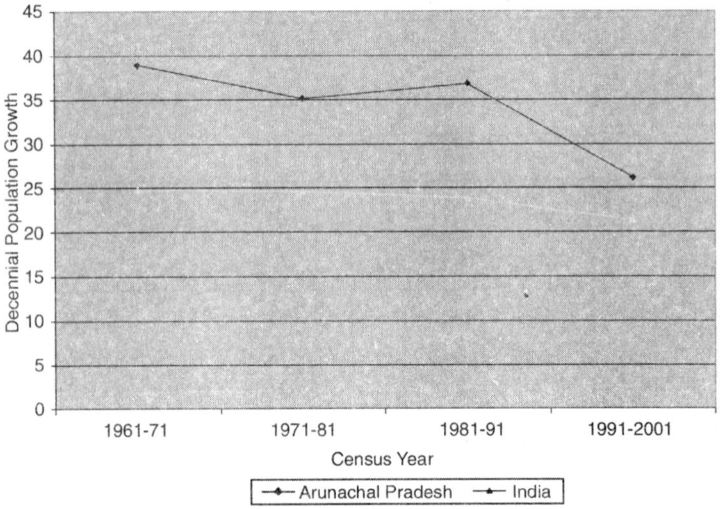

Fig. 2.6: Time Plot of Decennial Population Growth Rates of India and Arunachal Pradesh since 1961.

If we form a line diagram considering decennial population growth of Arunachal Pradesh and India along the 'Y' axis and Census Years along the 'X' axis, we see the line for Arunachal Pradesh standing always higher than that of India. It is observed from Figs. 2.5 and 2.6 that the decennial population growth in Arunachal Pradesh can be divided into three categories: (i) Population growth rate was declining from 1961 to 1981; (ii) It was slightly increasing from 1981 to 1991; (iii) Again, it was declining from 1991 to 2001 very significantly. But, in context of India, it was declining smoothly during the period concerned.

From Table 2.2, for Arunachal Pradesh, census figures earlier to 1961 are not available. During 1961-71, the population grew by 38.91 per cent and during 1971-81, 1981-91 and 1991-2001; it grew 35.15 per cent, 36.83 per cent and 26.21 per cent respectively. But at the national level the growth was 24.80 per cent in 1961-71, 24.66 per cent in 1971-81, 23.86 per cent in 1981-91 and 21.34 per cent in 1991-2001 respectively. It is clear that the decennial growth of population in Arunachal Pradesh is very high as compared to that of the country as a whole. Therefore, the decennial growth rate of population of Arunachal Pradesh decreased in 1971-81 in comparison to 1961-71 and slightly increased in 1981-91 and finally decreased in 1991-2001. But the decennial growth rate of population of India is continuously decreasing and remains always below Arunachal Pradesh for concerned census year.

The reason of sliding down of the population growth rate in Arunachal Pradesh from census 1991 might be due to the reduction of labour force engaged primarily in extraction of forest and forest products after the imposition of ban on these. Because of this ban, almost all the saw mills, veneer mills and felling of logs throughout the State had been stopped functioning. Thereby, the labourers were forced to be employed in other sectors or to leave the State. Again, the consciousness of family planning and the advantages of small family norms are seen not only in literate couple but also in illiterate couple.

Geographical area is fixed, but the population varied at increasing rate. Population increased in 1971 census by 38.91 per cent, in 1981 census by 86.61 per cent, in 1991census by 156.88 per cent and in 2001 census by 226.23 per cent in comparison to the population of 1961 census. Population has increased 3.26 times in comparison to that of 1961 within the span of 40 years. The percentage variation of population from 1961 to subsequent census year is shown in Table 2.3 and Fig. 2.7 as under. If we put the time plot data regarding percentage variation of population from 1961 to subsequent census years as shown in Fig. 2.8, we see that the line goes continuously upward very sharply.

Table 2.3: Percentage Variation of Population from 1961 to Subsequent Census Years

Census Year	*1961 to 1971*	*1961 to 1981*	*1961 to 1991*	*1961 to 2001*
Percentage Variation of Population from 1961	38.91	86.61	156.88	226.23

Note: Construction on the basis of Table 2.1.

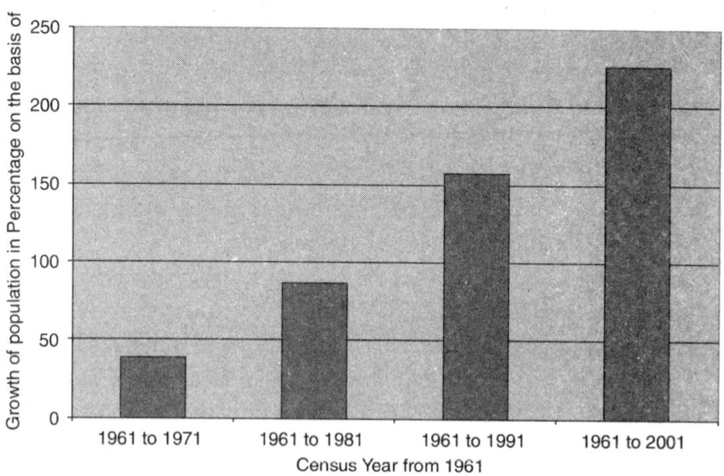

Fig. 2.7: Percentage Variation of Population from 1961 to Subsequent Census Years.

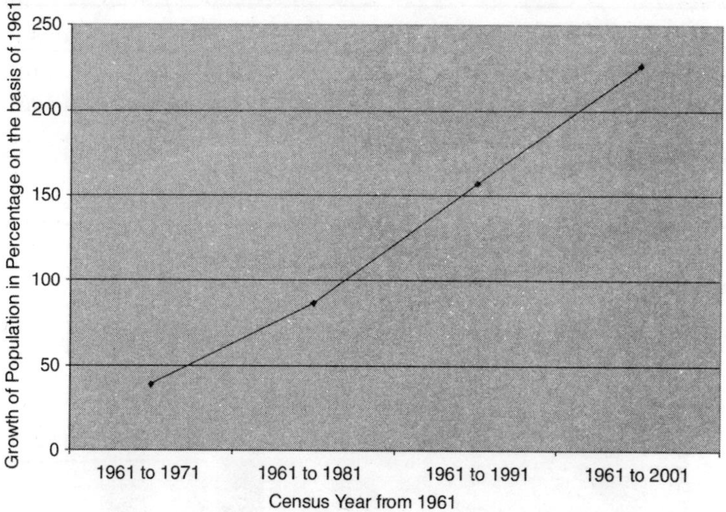

Fig. 2.8: Time Plot of Percentage Variation of Population from 1961 to Subsequent Census Years.

The population density figures as shown in Table 2.4, also shows an important demographic characteristic. Density is calculated on the basis of the population living per sq. km. That is, density of population is obtained by dividing total population by the area where they are living. This is a relationship between the area and the population. In other words, it can be said that density of population is the number of people living in per unit of area of a village, or a district, or a State, or a country. Thus, the density of population means the number of people living per square kilometre of area as per the presently existing census practice in our country. Arunachal Pradesh is a thinly populated hilly State with approximately 83,743 sq. kms. At first, it should be noted from Table 2.4 that the density of population has increased since 1961 census. It was 4 in 1961 census, 6 in 1971 census, 8 in 1981 census, 10 in 1991 census and 13 in 2001 census. It has been constantly increasing. It is also shown in Figs. 2.9 and 2.10.

Table 2.4: Population Density since 1961

Census Year	*Population Density*
1961	4
1971	6
1981	8
1991	10
2001	13

Source: Population Census Reports.

Note: Population Density = Total Population ÷ Area in sq. kms.

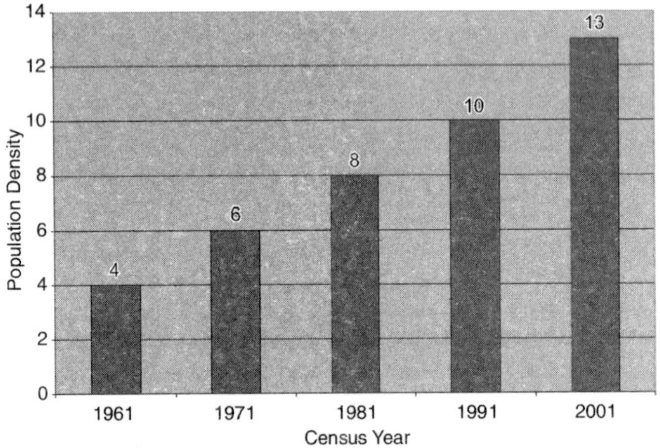

Fig. 2.9: Population Density since 1961

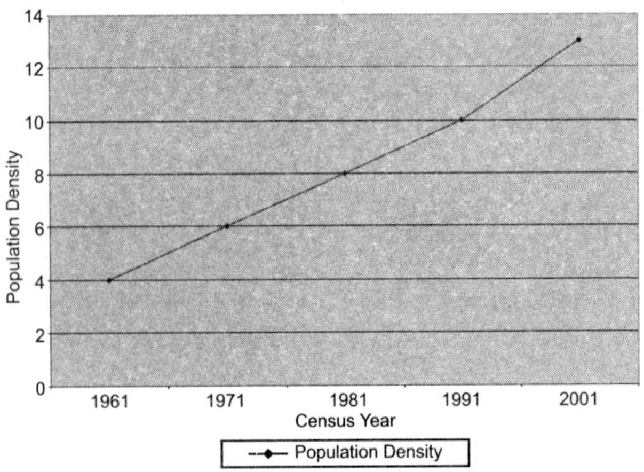

Fig. 2.10: Time Plot of Population Density since 1961

Pattern of Sex Ratio

Table 2.5, Table 2.6 and Fig. 2.11 given below highlight the details about the sex ratio from 1961 to 2001 censuses concerning the population of Arunachal Pradesh and India. This may be significant to mention here that the first population census in Arunachal Pradesh took place in the year 1961.

Table 2.5: Sex Ratio in Arunachal Pradesh: 1961-2001.

Census	*Sex Ratio-General*	*Sex Ratio-ST*
1961	894	1013
1971	861	1007
1981	862	1004
1991	859	998
2001	901	1003

Table 2.6: Sex Ratio in India: 1961-2001

Census	*Sex Ratio General*
1961	941
1971	930
1981	933
1991	927
2001	933

Source: Census Report 1961, 1971, 1981, 1991, 2001.

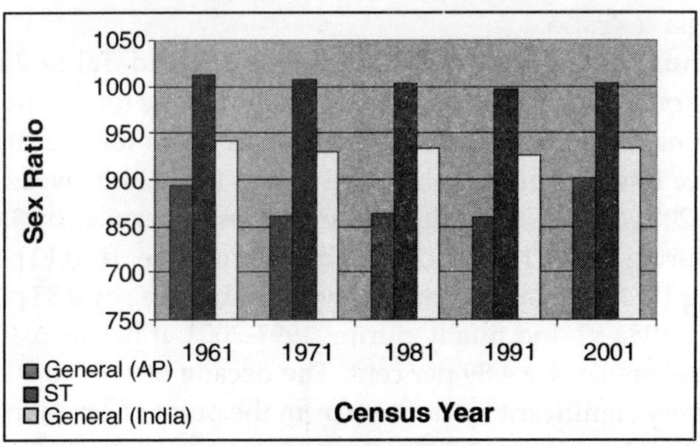

Fig. 2.11 Sex Ratio—Arunachal Pradesh (General and ST) and India : 1961 - 2001

The overall trend of general sex ratio in the State of Arunachal Pradesh as well as for the country as a whole shows a continuous decline, except for a marginal improvement in 1981. In 2001, there is an improvement in the proportion of females to 901 in Arunachal Pradesh and to 933 for India as compared to 1991 census. If we look at the change in sex ratio for India as a whole in the period flanked by 1991-2001, then it is observed that there is an addition of +6 for all India in contrast to the substantial addition in case of Arunachal Pradesh to +42. The comparison of sex ratio in context of General population and Scheduled Tribes population in the State and the country has been represented in Fig. 2.11, with the help of bar diagram. The child sex ratio in the age group of 0-6 years on the other hand, recorded for India as well as Arunachal Pradesh was –18. (Chandna, 2005, p. 291).

A comparative analysis of sex ratio of Arunachal Pradesh and All India in respect of the general total population reflects that the sex ratio of Arunachal Pradesh in general was much lower than All India level. The general sex ratio in Arunachal has been steadily declining over the central periods. In 1961 census, the figures of females were 894 per 1,000 males in Arunachal Pradesh, as compared to 941females for all India i.e. less by 47 numbers. The sex ratio of Arunachal Pradesh shows a paucity of females in general which was always lower than that of all India since 1961. It was lower by 5.26 per cent in 1961, 8.01 per cent in 1971, 8.23 per cent in 1981, 7.92 per cent in 1991 and 3.55 per cent in 2001 than the all India sex ratio.

Thus, as evident from the Table 2.5 and Table 2.6, the comparative analysis of sex ratio in respect of the total population of Arunachal Pradesh in different census years reflects that it is more or less declining continuously since 1961, with an exception in the 2001 census. It has decreased by 33 numbers i.e., by 3.69 per cent during 1961-71, but increased by 1 number i.e., by 0.12 per cent during 1971-81, again decreased by 3 numbers i.e., by 0.35 per cent during 1981-91 and finally during 1991-2001, it has increased by 42 numbers i.e., by 4.89 per cent. The decade of 1991 to 2001 has been very significant in the State from the point of sex ratio as the number of females per 1,000 males has increased remarkably. Thus, it follows from the above discussion that general paucity in the number of females per thousand males in the State of Arunachal Pradesh is no exception as compared to All India sex ratio statistics.

However, considering the fact of geographical isolation and inhospitable terrain, low levels of development in the State, as well as lack of modern facilities and technology in the health services sector, the general paucity of females in the State may be attributed.

The people of Arunachal Pradesh are with a glorious heritage of arts and crafts, enchanting folk songs and are a simple, friendly and hospitable people. Their colourful festivals are a manifestation of their faith and belief, conceived by their ancient forefathers, in the power of nature. Their hospitable nature is known worldwide. The different census reports have given different classification of total number of tribes and sub-tribes. According to 2001census, an approximate number of 110 tribes and sub-tribes inhabited the entire State. The principal inhabitants of the State of Arunachal Pradesh from east to west are the tribes of Wancho, Nocte, Tangsa, Singpho, Khamti, Mishmi, Adi, Galo, Padam, Minyong, Pailibo, Bokar, Bori, Memba, Khamba, Apatani, Nyishi, Hill Miri, Nah, Tagin, Aka, Khowa or Bugun, Miji, Sulung, Sherdukpen and Monpa. They exhibit a distinctive culture, customs and traditions. These tribes are scattered over an area of 83,743 sq. kms. in hilly terrain of Eastern Himalayas. The concentration of tribal population throughout the border region though very high is scattered in small villages with uninhabited habitations in higher altitudes.

Arunachal Pradesh has been peopled by several waves of migration from ancient times to the present. At first, Mongoloid tribes may have ventured into the region as early as 2,000–2,500 years ago into north-west India. Some groups may have spread further through Assam, Bengal and North Bihar. The early migrants perhaps came from Bhutan, Tibet, Burma and Yunan. Recent migrants have come mainly from Burma (Myanmar) and Bangladesh. For centuries the vast mountainous terrain has served to keep the tribal clans virtually isolated from one another. Inter-tribal warfare was intermittent and indecisive. No dominant tribe emerged, and there was not much homogenisation. Instead, there seems to have been a process of diversification with small tribal groups having their own languages, belief systems and lifestyles. As per 1991 census, 15 major tribes out of 25 have populations of over 5,000 each. It is depicted in Table 2.7.

Table 2.7: Major Tribes of Arunachal Pradesh (population > 5000 in 1991).

Sl. No.	*Tribes Name*	*Population*
1.	Adi	1,58,059
2.	Nishing/ Nyishi	1,16,258
3.	Monpa	38,862
4.	Wancho	38,528
5.	Nocte	33,720
6.	Mishmi	31,329
7.	Tagin	28,860
8.	Tangsa	26,016
9.	Apatani	22,526
10.	Hill Miri	11,017
11.	Khamti	8,339
12.	Mishing	5,899
13.	Miji	5,779
14.	Sulung	5,443
15.	Deori	5,200

Source: Census 1991.

From Table 2.7, it is seen that Adi is more populous tribe followed by Nyishi and Deori has lowest populous tribe having only 5,200 populations as per 1991 Census. The comparison among the tribes on the basis of having populations is seen in Fig. 2.12.

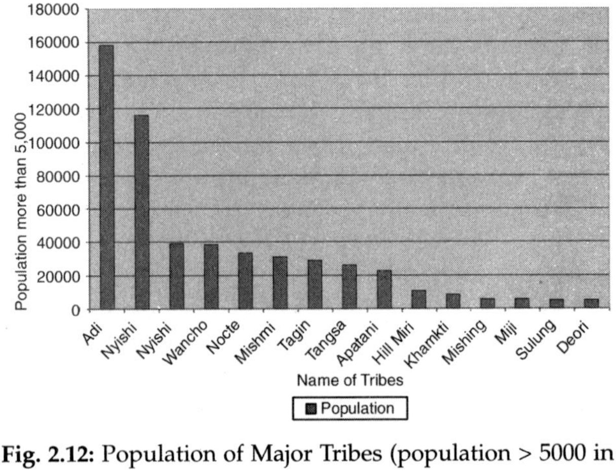

Fig. 2.12: Population of Major Tribes (population > 5000 in 1991).

Again as per 2001 census, we get 26 major tribes. Their populations are shown in Table 2.8 given below and the comparison on the basis of population is depicted in Fig. 2.13 as under.

Table 2.8: Distribution of Tribes-wise Population of Arunachal Pradesh as per 2001 census.

Sl.No.	*Name of Tribe*	*Total Population*	*Male Population*	*Female Population*
1.	Adi (Abor)	120118	60165	59953
2.	Aka (Hrusso)	5140	2528	2612
3.	Apatani	27576	13346	14230
4.	Deori	5693	2921	2772
5.	Galo	75368	37643	37725
6.	Hill Miri	4471	2293	2178
7.	Khamba	346	170	176
8.	Khampti	12925	6614	6311
9.	Khowas (Bugun)	1616	822	794
10.	Lisus (Yobins)	2105	1017	1058
11.	Memba	12655	6168	6487
12.	Meyor	391	198	193
13.	Miji	6721	2920	2801
14.	Mishing/Miri	13591	6976	6615
15.	Mishmi	35085	17523	17562
16.	Monpa	43344	21462	21882
17.	Nocte	36299	18152	18147
18.	Nyishi	163020	80341	82679
19.	Sherdukpen	3260	1628	1632
20.	Singpho	4539	2339	2200
21.	Sulung	3945	2083	1862
22.	Tagin	39129	19390	19739
23.	Tangsa	29538	14791	14747
24.	Wancho	47788	24389	23399
25.	Other Naga Tribes	6978	3698	3280
26.	Generic Tribes	1831	100	823
27.	Other	2686	1402	1284
	Total	**705158**	**352017**	**353141**

Source: Resarun, the Directorate of Research, Itanagar, A.P. (Figures are subject to correction).

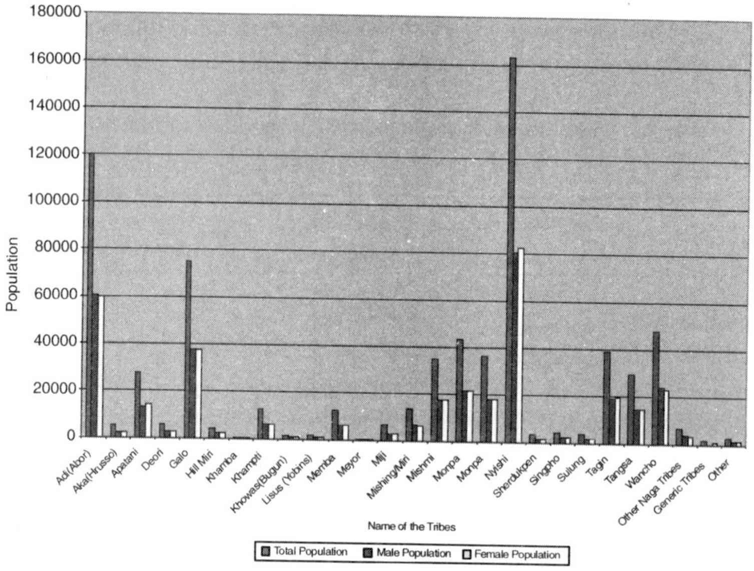

Fig. 2.13: Population as per 2001.

The tapestry of Arunachal Pradesh has so many overlapping hues that any categorisation of the tribes remains somewhat unsatisfactory. Anthropologists have attempted to group them by their geographic location, belief systems, lifestyles and crafts. Conventionally, the tribes have also been grouped by the five original administrative units of the State: Kameng, Subansiri, Siang, Lohit and Tirap, more or less demarcated by the major rivers. The Buddhist tribes include the Monpa and Sherdukpen in Kameng in western Arunachal Pradesh, the Memba and the Khamba of Siang along the northern border, and the Khampti and Singhpo in Lohit at the eastern end of the State. The majority of the tribes in the central Subansiri-Siang region, like the Adis, are Dony-i-polo (sun-moon) worshippers, but there are infinite variations from tribe to tribe. Some tribes are animist. Others have been influenced by Hindu Vaishnavism. For some tribes, like the Nyishi and the Mishmi, the village community has less significance than the individual household does. The Nyishi household is literally a "long house", which is internally partitioned off for an extended family. In the past, the households were scattered, and may have had little to do with one another. The larger tribes are in fact conglomerates of many groups—the Adi group is made up of the Galo and its associated tribes like the Minyong, Padam and various others. The Apatani, a much smaller tribe of seven original villages is confined to a small plateau. The Milang, a sub-tribe of the Adi-Padam, occupy just three villages, but have a distinct language.

Literacy and Educational Level

As per the records, there were 14 schools by the end of 1947. These schools were confined mostly in Siang and Lohit region. Out of these, there were 6 in East Siang, 2 each in West Siang, Lower Dibang Valley and Lohit and 1 each in Upper Siang and West Kameng Districts (Joram, 2008). In the State, till independence, literacy rate was only less than 1 per cent. In the succeeding five year plans, an increasing percentage of expenditure on education has given good results despite of formidable constraints like inaccessibility of territory, people's unawareness of the need of education and traditional dependence on children for domestic and field work. Thus, with increasing emphasis through successive plans the State has achieved commendable progress in the field of education. The literacy rate census-wise from 1961 to 2001 in Arunachal Pradesh is shown in Table 2.9 and Fig. 2.14 given below.

Table 2.9: Literacy Rate in Percentage.

Year	*Person*	*Male*	*Female*
1961	7.13	12.5	1.42
1971	11.29	17.82	3.71
1981	25.55	35.12	14.02
1991	41.59	51.45	29.69
2001	54.74	64.07	44.24

Source: Census Report, Arunachal Pradesh, 1961, 1971, 1981, 1991, and 2001.

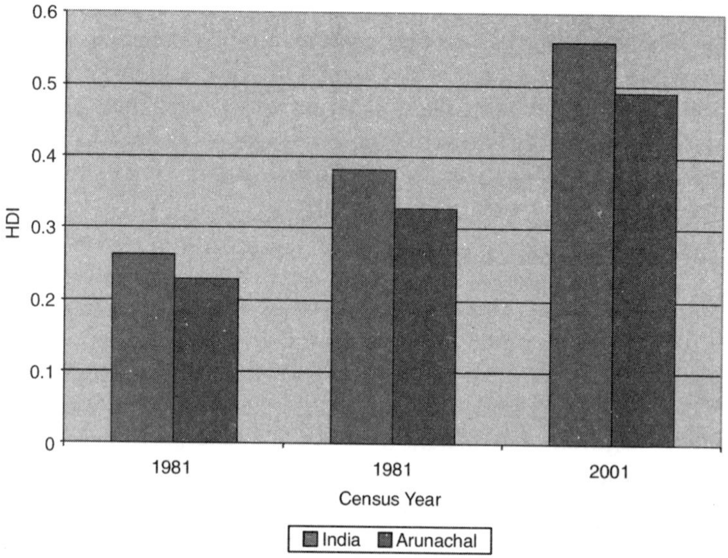

Fig. 2.14: Literacy Rate in Percentage Regarding Person, Male and Female.

From Table 2.9 and Fig. 2.14, it is observed that the good fruit of education in the State is achieved though the females are lagging behind the males. Higher education in Arunachal Pradesh needs a far-reaching structural reconstruction. According to sixth NCERT survey only 45 per cent of total school teachers in the region are trained. The corresponding figure for the national level was about 87 per cent. The situation was particularly bad in Assam and Nagaland where only about 30 per cent teachers at the secondary and higher secondary levels were trained. Even in a State like Mizoram, which has almost 90 per cent literacy, about 76 per cent could not complete high school.

In this State, higher education started first with the set-up of Jawaharlal Nehru College at Pasighat in 1964. Next Dera Natung Government College was set-up in 1979. Gradually, Indira Gandhi Government College was set-up in 1986 at Tezu, Bomdila Government College in 1988 at Bomdila, Donyi-Polo Government College in 1996 at Kamki, Rang Fra Government College in 1996 at Changlang and Wangcha Rajkumar Government College at

Deomali in 1997. Rajiv Gandhi University (Central University) (previously it was named Arunachal University) at Rono-Hills, Doimukh, Itanagar, Papum Pare District was set-up in 1984 and North-Eastern Regional Institute of Science and Technology (Deemed University) at Nirjuli, Itanagar, Papum Pare District was also set-up in 1984.

Thus, there are at present 20 institutions (Private and Government) of Higher and Technical Education functioning throughout the State. Number and Type of Institutions of Higher and Technical Education in the State as on 30th September, 2008 is shown in Table 2.5. Out of these colleges, Jawaharlal Nehru College and Dera Natung Government College are imparting general education like Arts, Science and Commerce while the remaining colleges are imparting only Arts. In addition to Arts, Commerce is also taught in Indira Gandhi Government College and Donyi Polo Government College. Nevertheless, this is, indeed a phenomenal growth of education in the State within a small span of 61 years of its existence. The growth of institutions of higher and technical education in the State is depicted in Table 2.10 and their location and year of establishment are given in Table 2.11.

Table 2.10: Number and Type of Institutions of Higher and Technical Education in the State as on 30th September, 2008.

Sl. No.	*Name of Institutions*	*Number*
1.	University	01
2.	Deemed University	01
3.	Govt. Degree Colleges	08
4.	Private Degree College	04
5.	Professional/Technical College	04
6.	Polytechnic	02
	Total	20

Source: Directorate of Higher and Technical Education, Itanagar.

Table 2.11: Higher and Technical Institutions in the State with Location and Year of Establishment.

Sl. No.	Name of Institutions	Location	Year of Establishment	Status
1.	Rajiv Gandhi University	Rono-Hills, Doimukh, Itanagar, Papum Pare District	1984	Central University
2.	North Eastern Regional Institute of Science and Technology	Nirjuli, Itanagar, Papum Pare District	1984	Deemed University
3.	Jawaharlal Nehru College	Pasighat, East Siang District	1964	Government Degree College
4.	Dera Natung Government College	Itanagar, Papum Pare District	1979	Government Degree College
5.	Indira Gandhi Government College	Tezu, Lohit District	1986	Government Degree College
6.	Bomdila Government College	Bomdila, West Kameng District	1988	Government Degree College
7.	Rang-Frah Government College	Changlang, Changlang District	1996	Government Degree College
8.	Donyi Polo Government College	Kamki, West Siang District	1996	Government Degree College
9.	Wangcha Rajkumar Government College	Deomali, Tirap District	1997	Government Degree College
10.	Government College	Yachuli, Lower Subansiri District	2007	Government Degree College
11.	College of Horticulture and Forestry	Pasighat, East Siang District	2001	Under Central Agriculture University, Imphal
12.	Don Bosco College	Jully, Itanagar, Papum Pare District	2002	Private Degree College
13.	North East Homeopathic Medical College and Hospital	Vivek Vihar, Itanagar, Papum Pare District	2002	Private Professional and Technical College

(Contd...)

(*Table 2.11 Contd...*)

14. Rajiv Gandhi Polytechnic	Itanagar, Papum Pare District	2002	Government Polytechnic Institution
15. St. Claret College	Ziro, Lower Subansiri District	2003	Private Degree College
16. Doying Gumin College	Pasighat East Siang District	2004	Private Degree College
17. Hills College of Teacher Education	Naharlagun, Papum Pare District	2006	Private Professional and Technical College
18. Tomi Polytechnic College	Basar, West Siang District	2006	Private Polytechnic Institution
19. St. Francis De Sales College	Aalo, West Siang District	2007	Private Degree College
20. Arunachal Law Academy	Itanagar, Papum Pare District	2007	Private Law College

Source: Directorate of Higher and Technical Education, Itanagar.

Human Development Index (HDI)

The HDI attempts to rank all countries on a scale of 0 to 1. It consists of three indices, income index, health index and education index. With respect to HDI Arunachal Pradesh is the least developed States among eight north-eastern States in India.

Other than HDI, there are other indices to measure level of development from various angles these are GDI (Gender Development Index), GEM (Gender Empowerment Index), HPI (Human Poverty Index) etc., according to GDI nation's development cannot be possible without the development of female. The main components of these index is

(1) with respect to per capita income how much females are getting compared to male,
(2) with respect to education how girl students are progressing compared to boys, and
(3) the male-female ratio with respect to enrolment in school and average life expectancy of female compared to male etc.

Therefore, according to this index though high HDI implies high level of development, but it does not reflect the status of women of a nation. It is only through GDI which reflects the status of women of a nation and whose development is the true reflection of the development of a nation. HDI is shown in Table 2.12 given below regarding India and Arunachal Pradesh.

Table 2.12: Human Development Index.

Country/States	*HDI*		
	1981	1991	2001
India	0.263	0.381	0.56
Arunachal Pradesh	0.228 (L)	0.328 (L)	0.49 (L)

Source: Human Development Report, Arunachal Pradesh.

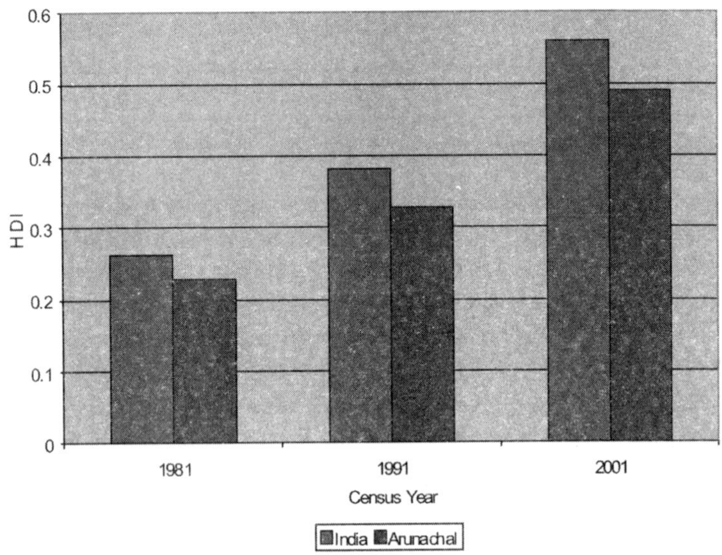

Fig. 2.15: HDI in respect of India and Arunachal Pradesh.

Table 2.12 and Fig. 2.15 show the Human Development Index of India and Arunachal Pradesh. The rank of Arunachal Pradesh is lower than India.

Panchayati Raj in Arunachal Pradesh

Panchayats have been the backbone of the India's village since 'Vedic' Period. Panchayat in Arunachal Pradesh has been in existence from very old days. The people used to manage their daily affairs at village and community levels through the traditional village Institutions. The traditional village councils were in existence, which got the status of Gram Panchayats later on.

The traditional village councils recognized under the North-East Frontier Administration of Justice Regulations, 1945. These village councils were accorded the status of Gram Panchayat under NEFA Panchayati Raj Regulation, 1967. This Regulation was passed an Act by the Government of India in 1967. As per provision in this Act, the Agency Council was formed at apex level, followed by Zilla Parishad at district level, Anchal Samiti at Block level and Gram Panchayat at village level. In the erstwhile North Eastern Frontier Areas, Panchayati Raj was formally inaugurated by the then Governor of Assam on 2nd October, 1968, with the following tiers: (i) Gram Panchayat at village level, (ii) Anchal Samiti at circle level; (iii) Zilla Parishad at district level; (iv) Agency Council at Agency level. The members of the Panchayat were elected by the traditional tribal system, with three years tenure. Elections of the Panchayats were held for 7 times between 1968 and 1992 (through secret ballot system) except the Gram Panchayat Elections. The Gram Panchayat elections were held according to traditional Tribal Custom.

The 73rd Constitutional Amendment Act, 1992 a background had been created to move towards turning Panchayat into an instrument of self-government rather than working as a mere implementing agency of the Government's line of function. Gandhiji's dream from "*Gram Swaraj*" has been transmitted into reality with the introduction of three tier Panchayati Raj System to ensure people's participation in the great task of rural reconstruction.

The enactment of the 73rd Constitutional Amendment Act, the NEFA Panchayati Raj system was dissolved on 14th September, 1997, and the Arunachal Pradesh Panchayati Raj Act, 1997 was passed. This Act mandated provision for establishment of Gram Panchayat/Gram Sabha, Anchal Samiti and Zilla Parishad. The election to the above bodies has been scheduled to be held after every 5 years under the supervision of State Election Commission. The State Election Commission was constituted on 18th June, 2002 and the first Panchayat election in Arunachal Pradesh as per the new system were conducted in April, 2003.

Tribal Empowerment and the Role of Panchayat

In August, 2007, the Arjun Sengupta Committee reported that the 836 million Indians i.e., over 75 per cent of our people, "the poor and the vulnerable" surviving on a daily average expenditure of under Rs.20 a day. The north-eastern region as a whole and the central regions, which have large tribal populations, are lagging behind. So it is the key component of India's "Strategy of inclusive growth" must be inclusive governance as the means of empowering the disadvantaged with the aim of enabling them to overcome their poverty. It is the effective empowerment of the disadvantaged through the effective devolution of functions, finances and functionaries to representative institution of local self-government such as panchayats, and village councils, village development boards and similar such institutions elsewhere, on the principle of subsidiary.

The Arunachal Pradesh Activity Mapping Order, 2007 was released by the Chief Minister, Arunachal Pradesh on 25th October, 2007 and the executive order for devolution of 29 subjects of activity mapping was issued on 21st February, 2008. The executive order was issued for devolution of 29 subjects covering 20 departments. There is overlap of some of the functions devolved to Panchayat. More clarity of three Tiers of Panchayat is required in terms of specifying the functions in terms of policy, planning, implementation, coordination/control devolved to different tiers. So the role of representatives of various tiers of Panchayats is very important.

In Arunachal Pradesh all representatives of three tiers of Panchayats are Sceduled Tribes. Panchayat election of 2003 is the first election of Panchayats under new system, all elected members are tribals. In 2003, Panchayat election was held in 14 Zilla Parishad. The total numbers of elected members of Zilla Parishad are 136. Out of these number 45 are woman members, which is more or less equal to the national level reservation policy.

Total number of Anchal Samitis are 150. Out of these Anchal Samitis, election was held in 136 Anchal Samitis. Total number of elected representatives of Anchal Samiti's are 1639. All of the members of Anchal Samitis are tribals. Out of 1639 members 577 are women. The percentage of women representatives is 35.2, which is higher than the national level reservation policy.

The total number of Gram Panchayat in Arunachal Pradesh is 1744 according to 2003 Panchayat election. Election was held in 1639 constituency in 2003. Total number of elected Gram Panchayat members are 6485. All of the elected Gram Panchayat members are tribals. Out of them 2561 are women members, which is 39.5 per cent. This percentage is also higher than the national level reservation policy. The following Table 2.13 shows the elected representatives of three tiers level.

It is clear from above discussion that the Panchayati Raj Institutions of Arunachal Pradesh has given ample scope to the rural tribal people in decision making process. Panchayati Raj Institutions of Arunachal Pradesh has given them right to realize their voice independently. Panchayati Raj Institutions as a vehicle of rural development has given the tribal people of Arunachal Pradesh more and more power in the process of economic development and social justice. If Panchayati Raj Institution is vehicle; representatives are the driver of this vehicle. Representatives of Panchayat as a driver of rural vehicle (Panchayati Raj Institutions) are playing an important role for the development of their respective areas. So it is right to say that Panchayati Raj Institutions is taking important role for empowering tribal people in Arunachal Pradesh.

After all, the State of Arunachal Pradesh faces some problems in her developmental processes. The main hindrance in development in Arunachal Pradesh is her geographical location. Arunachal ranked as the lowest-infrastructure index of only 0.44 for her geography. Even today, 34 administrative centres and 2741 habitations of villagers, are not connected by all weather roads, more than 50 per cent of villagers do not have electricity and safe drinking water even today. Poor health infrastructure is a drawback due to her geographical location. Lack of sufficient Educational Institutions is another drawback for tribal developments in Arunachal Pradesh. Lack of finance is the main problem of

Table 2.13: Elected Representatives of Three Tiers Level.

Level of Panchayats	Total numbers of constituency	Election held	Total number of elected represe-ntatives	General		SC		ST		ST
				Male	Female	Male	Female	Male	Female	Female%
Zilla Parishad	15	14	136	Nil	Nil	Nil	Nil	91	45	33.1
Anchal Samiti	150	136	1639	Nil	Nil	Nil	Nil	1062	577	35.2
Gram Panchayat	1744	1639	6485	Nil	Nil	Nil	Nil	3924	2561	39.5
Total	1909	1789	8260	Nil	Nil	Nil	Nil	5077	3183	107.8

Source: 2003 Panchayat Election, 2003.

Panchayati Raj Institutions for making this self-institution. The source of finance of Panchayati Raj Institutions is Centre and State Government funds. Own finance source of Panchayati Raj Institutions is very limited. Corruption is another hindrance of development plan and programme of Panchayati Raj Institutions. Lack of proper training within the members of Panchayati Raj Institutions is one of the most important drawbacks of Panchayati Raj Institutions. Lack of people's consciousness about Panchayats activities is another drawback of Panchayati Raj Institutions.

Religion

The total ST population, 47.2 per cent has been returned under the category of "Other Religion Followers". Besides, 26.5 per cent of the STs are Christians, 13.1 per cent Hindus, and 11.7 per cent Buddhists. In Arunachal Pradesh, unlike Nagaland, Mizoram, and Manipur, considerable ST population are still adhering to original tribal faith. Individual ST-wise, Khampti, Monpa, Momba, Sherdukpen, and Singpho are mostly the followers of Buddhism, while quite sizeable population among Adi, Nishi, Nocte, and Wancho are going to be converted to Christianity.

Urbanization

During the colonial period, large parts of the region of the North-Eastern States were "Excluded Areas" or "Partially Excluded Areas". Further, under the Inner Line Regulation Act, Arunachal Pradesh remained secluded and restricted to outsiders. The entries as such were permitted based on administrative necessity otherwise outsiders were strictly prohibited entry in the tribal territorial area beyond the inner line. The British, through such measures, sought to protect the tribal culture from so called exploitation by others (the non-tribal). Tribes were thus left to themselves to pursue their traditional methods of livelihood and manage their affairs in accordance with their traditional/ancestral customs.

Consequently, the pace of urbanization in the region was negligible or very low. But after independence and particularly since the planning era began, along with the thrust of Statehood in 1987, a substantial amount of investments have been made in expanding the basic infrastructure in the region and setting up of a large number of administrative headquarters and circle administrative centres at the different levels. Such development interventions have resulted in the growth of 17 urban centres in the region at a rapid pace.

The process of urbanization and economic development are interrelated in many respects. Urbanization leads to greater access to modern amenities of life, education, health and other civic amenities/services as compared to their rural counterpart. Nevertheless, urbanization may also give rise to host of other problems like over crowding, water and sanitation problems, environmental pollution, social evils like crimes etc. On account of historical and geographical factors, the rates of urban growth and pattern of urbanization as well as nature and extent of urban problems vary from State to State in the North-East region.

The process of urbanization in Arunachal Pradesh may be attributed to the setting up of administrative headquarters at different levels and mainly administrative set-up of district headquarters, and circles. Spatial variation in the level of urbanization in this hilly State gets highly accentuated due to local differences in topography and altitude as well as accessibility and nearest neighbour factors. The pattern is remarkably clear showing higher level of urbanization restricted to the river valleys of varying width. The small river valleys of Lohit, Dibang, Siang and Subansiri river in Arunachal Pradesh are experiencing urban growth at a very fast pace while the neighbouring highland areas continue to be entirely inaccessible and rural.

During 1961 census entire Arunachal Pradesh was treated as rural. But from 1971 onwards urbanization started with the declaration of 3 districts HQ and 1 sub-divisional HQ as Census Town. As per 2001 census, there are 17 towns.These are Tawang, Bomdila, Seppa, Naharlagun, Itanagar, Ziro, Daporijo, Along, Basar, Pasighat, Roing, Tezu, Namsai, Changlang, Jairampur, Khonsa and Deomali. There is no statutory town in the State.

Thus, urbanization and development in Arunachal Pradesh is confined to the low altitude foothill zone. The process of urbanization is yet to take off in areas with a strong concentration of indigenous (tribal) population. In developing countries like India, and the economically backward States like Arunachal the challenges of urbanization becomes more serious in the context of urban poverty, and growing urban hazards due to negligence of topographical characteristics in urban planning. Table 2.14 below shows district-wise status of urbanization in the State of Arunachal Pradesh in 2001.

Table 2.14: District-wise Urbanization Status in the State of Arunachal Pradesh, 2001.

Sl. No.	District	Total Population	Town	Urban Population Total	Urban Population %age	Town Class
1.	Tawang	38924	Tawang	8376	21.52	V
2.	West Kameng	74599	Bomdila	6693	08.97	V
3.	East Kameng	57179	Seppa	15002	26.24	IV
4.	Papum Pare	122003	Itanagar,	35022	28.27	III
			Naharlagun	27020	22.15	III
5.	Lower Subansiri	98244	Ziro	12384	12.61	IV
6.	Upper Subansiri	55346	Daporijo	15756	28.57	IV
7.	West Siang	103918	Aalo,	17033	16.39	IV
			Basar	4079	3.93	VI
8.	Eest Siang	87397	Pasighat	21965	25.13	III
9.	Upper Siang	33363	-	-	-	-
10.	Dibang Valley	57720	Roing	10107	17.57	IV
11.	Lohit	143527	Tezu,	15015	10.46	IV
			Namsai	11747	8.18	IV
12.	Changlang	125422	Changlang,	6469	05.16	V
			Jairampur	5919	04.72	V
13.	Tirap	100326	Khonsa,	9233	09.20	V
			Deomali	6061	06.64	V
14.	Arunachal Pradesh	1096702		227881		

Growth of Urban Population in India, 1961-2001(million) and Arunachal Pradesh 1971-2001

The information about total population as well as urban population in India from 1961 to 2001 is depicted in Table 2.13. India's population was just above 439 million in the year 1961, (17.97%), which increased to about 548 million in 1971 (19.90%), about 686 million in 1981 (23.31%), about 846 million in 1991 (25.71%) and about 1027 million in 2001(27.78%). During the year 2005, the total population of India was about 1099 million. But the percentage share of urban population in Arunachal Pradesh is 3.70 in 1971, 6.32 in 1981, 12.91 in 1991 and 20.41 in 2001. It is estimated that about 17 per cent of the world's population live in India with just 2.4 per cent of the geographical area of the world.

The Gross State Domestic Product of Arunachal Pradesh at market prices estimated by the Ministry of Statistics and Programme Implementation with figures in millions of Indian Rupees is depicted in Table 2.15.

Table 2.15: Gross Domestic Product

Year	*1980*	*1985*	*1990*	*1995*	*2000*
Gross State Domestic Product	1,070	2,690	5,080	11,840	17,830

Arunachal Pradesh's gross state domestic product for 2004 was estimated at $706 million in current prices. Agriculture primarily drives the economy. Recorded forests of Arunachal Pradesh is 61.5 per cent of its geographical area. Hence, forest products are the next most significant sector of the economy. Among the crops grown here are rice, maize, millet, wheat, pulses, sugarcane, ginger, and oilseeds. Arunachal is also ideal for horticulture and fruit orchards.

Flora and Fauna

This area is the habitat of as many as 55 major mammalian species of which 17 are rare or extremely rare. 21 rare species of extremely rare birds are found in this region and there are innumerable species of insects. As such, there are different species of wild lives found in this region. Almost all of them are dared as protected species under the Protection Act of 1972. All the forest resources are disappearing and become rare due to deforestation and illegal felling of trees.

The biogeographically strategic location, the distinct topography and the unique influence of the monsoon together support a diversity of ecosystems, different forest types and wetlands. Some four fifths of the State is covered by forest-evergreen and semi-evergreen forests constitute 69 per cent of the geographic area, and the degraded forests (mainly in the foothills) another 13 per cent. Arunachal Pradesh has a third of the flowering plant diversity and a fifth of the faunal diversity in India. The Eastern Himalaya as a whole also has a high degree of species endemism: 114 endemic species, including 29 genetic resource species. About half of these endemics are believed to be under various categories of threat. The rivers mark the distributional boundaries of certain species. The capped langur is found throughout the State except in the stretch of land between the Siang and the Dibang rivers. This suggests that some capped langur came from the east but could not cross the Dibang, while others came down the Assam valley and up into the western end of Arunachal but could not cross the Siang River.

The landscapes and the flora and fauna in Arunachal Pradesh follow an altitudinal zone from the alpine to the foothills area, and vary from the western end of the State to the east, and also between the areas north and south of the Brahmaputra. All along the northern borders is a thin ribbon of alpine forest and meadows (4,000-5,000 m), with dwarf rhododendrons, small alpine plants like *Saxifraga, Saussurea,* rhubarb (*Rheum*) and a few ground orchids.

Next comes a wide band of temperate forest mainly conifer at 2,800-3,500 m and broad leaved forest at 1,800-2,800 m. The conifer forest has trees like the *Abies* species, which occur in associations with other trees which change according to the gradient—at the higher altitudes *Abies* and *yew* (*Taxus baccata*); a little lower down *Abies* and larch, juniper or spruce, interspersed with shrubs of rhododendron, *Berberis* and *Gaultheria*; and at the lower elevations *Abies* with *Tsuga* species, *Pinus wallichiana* and rhododendrons. Cypress trees occur in pure stands as at Rupa and Shigao in West Kameng. Temperate bamboo form shrubby undergrowth in many places. The temperate broad-leaved forest includes magnolia, oak, rhododendron, poplar and chestnut species; specific tree associations also occur. There is a diversity of orchid species, growing on tree trunks and on the ground, on moss-covered rocks, and on decaying logs.

The local tribes of Arunachal Pradesh still prefer to rely on the traditional methods of health care. These people are very familiar with the herbal medicines that are abundantly available from the surroundings. Vast climate variations in the region have resulted in existence of almost all types of medicinal plants and timber wealth ranging from tropical teak in foothills jungles to coniferous and alpine of high mountains. The State is very rich in fauna and flora. It has 20 per cent of species of country's fauna and about 4500 species of flowering plants, 400 species of pleridophytes, 23 species of coniferous, 35 species of bamboos, 20 species of canes, 25 Rhododendron species. No doubt, Arunachal Pradesh offers an ideal agro-climate with vast potentials for growing varieties of orchids round the year. Out of about 1150 species of orchids known in India, about 550 species occur only in Arunachal Pradesh. These species occur in varying climatic and habitat conditions in varying concentration from the warm foothills to the cool temperate hills in the State. Such a diverse climatic situation has favoured the occurrence of about 550 species of orchids in the State which is a highest number for any State in India thus making it an "Orchid Paradise" of our country. There are over 500 medicinal plants recorded from Arunachal Pradesh of which 250 are used in various Ayurvedic formulations.

In the rain-shadow areas of the temperate and sub-tropical belt there are pockets of pine, which grow in association with different trees in different places. In the western parts, there are three different species of pine. In the central parts of Arunachal, the Indian blue pine *Pinus wallichiana* grows with oak and wild plum. In the Dibang valley, pines occur with Nepalese alder, birch and shrubs of *Lyonia*. The pine forest of West Kameng has a wondrous richness of epiphytic orchids, including *Dendrobiums*, some rare *Cymbidiums* and the celebrated lady's slipper *Paphiopedilum fairieanum*.

Sub-tropical evergreen forest with trees growing at 25-40 m. high, occur between 800 m. and 1,900 m. Here, there is a diversity of species including *oak, chestnut, Schima, Michelia, Acer* and *Ficus* species. Orchids are abundant in these wet evergreen forests. Different species of orchids grow in a range of microhabitats from exposed sites (e.g. *Kingidium taenialis*) to dark humus-rich sites on the forest floor (e.g. *Phaius mishmensis*). Bamboo occurs as a secondary succession in *jhumed* lands and in the evergreen forest up to 2,000 m. This zone is also rich in fern species, which differ in different locations from west to east—Dirang, Bomdila and Sessa in Kameng; Hapoli in Subansiri; Jenggin in East Siang; and Roing in the Dibang Valley.

The tropical evergreen forest in the foothills on the north and south banks of the Brahmaputra are distinct from each other, but both are rich in trees which have been heavily exploited for timber. In the foothills on the north bank from Kameng to Siang, there are discontinuous stretches of diverse species, many of which attain great girths and heights and are buttressed and fluted—including *Altinga, Mesua, Syzygium* (*jamun*) and oak. As elsewhere, here too are ferns, and epiphytic and terrestrial orchids. The south bank in Tirap and Changlang districts is characterised by the distinct *hollong* forest (*Dipterocarpus macrocarpus*) and other timber trees, climbers and epiphytes.

A narrow band of tropical semi-evergreen forest forms the southern boundary of Arunachal in the foothills and along the river banks up to 600 m. The tallest trees are deciduous, with evergreens forming the lower canopy, and a dense undergrowth of shrubs and climbers.

The floodplains where the Mountain Rivers join the Brahmaputra form complex and varied wetland habitats. In East Kameng, the Pakhui wetland lies in the floodplain of the Kameng-Pakke rivers, near Seijosa. In East Siang the river beds of the Siang and Sibia rivers, and the river islands which are seasonally flooded, form a combination of wetland and grassland, home of the wild buffalo and several bird species. (This is now the D. Ering wildlife sanctuary, named in memory of Daying Ering, the architect-Statesman of modern Arunachal Pradesh.) The grasslands have patches of deciduous forest and scattered trees of Chinese mimosa (*Albizia chinensis*), the wild date (*Ziziphus nummularia*), and the silk cotton (*Bombax*). Small ponds (*beels*) are formed by the backwaters. The swamp partridge and the rare Bengal florican are resident birds, and a large number of migratory water birds flock here in the winter.

The Eastern Himalayan has been a virtual *charduar*, with its "gates" open for floristic elements from India, China, Malaya, and Myanmar (Burma). Its species diversity attracted intense botanising in colonial times by Kingdon-Ward and others; later by the Botanical Survey of India and more recently, by the Arunachal State Forest Research Institute (SFRI). Yet, vast tracts remain unexplored. So, field explorations in Arunachal continue to yield reports of new plant species, or new distributional records for plants and animals not sighted here before. For example, a new orchid species *Gastrodia mishmensis* has been reported from Lohit. A rare gymnospermous plant (*Amentotaxus assamica*) was found in a forest patch between Mithumna and Mailang villages also in Lohit nearly a century after its last collection by Kingdon-Ward in 1892 (Haridasan, 1989). Recently, a miniature orchid *Dendrobium monticola* which was earlier known only from the north-west Himalaya and Sikkim, was reported from West Kameng.

Arunachal is especially rich in rhododendrons, magnolias, aroids, balsams and primroses. It has some 500 species of orchids, nearly half of all the orchid species in India. Some 18 species are extinct or nearly so; and 105 are endangered and threatened (Hegde, 1996 and pers. com. 1997). The fern flora has not been comprehensively surveyed but there may be over 400 species.

Not much is known about diversity at the genetic level, except in the case of orchids and bamboos. Both are being conserved *in situ*. Orchid centres at Dirang, Tipi, Sessa, Itanagar, Jengging and Roing under SFRI have a germ plasm collection of 400 species and about 100,000 plants being grown in *ex-situ* conditions.

There are 16 genera and some 63 species of bamboo in the northeast, which is considered the centre of genetic diversity for four major genera *Arudinaria, Bambusa, Cephalostachyum,* and *Dendrocalamus*. The maximum diversity is in Arunachal, Meghalaya and Assam. Arunachal has some 45 species of bamboo, and nowhere else are bamboos found at such a high altitude (Haridasan, pers. com. 1997) Rare species like *Dendrocalamus sahnii* and *Pleioblastus simonii* are confined to Arunachal. Tribals around Namsai are also able to recognise some intra-specific variability, which is yet to be studied by geneticists.

More is known about the genetic diversity of crop plants. Arora and Nayar (1984) recorded over 80 wild relatives of crop plants from the Eastern Himalaya. These include local varieties of both established and lesser known food crops. Arunachal is a significant sub-centre of diversity for fruit crops, with wild cherries, plums, pears and gooseberries. A recent survey (Puri, *et. al.*, 1995) of the small Talle Valley near Ziro in Lower Subanasiri found 21 wild relatives of crop plants.

Information on medicinal plants is still very meagre, although some preliminary listings have been made. All kinds of fauna are also used for various medicinal purposes (Borang, 1996). Often, practices of medical value are not easy to separate from superstitions and ritual sacrifice; in many tribal communities the dispensing of medicine is also still in the hands of traditional medicine men (occasionally women), who do not easily part with their knowledge.

The best known medicinal plant of Arunachal is the root of the *Coptis teeta* (*mishmi teeta*) a local cure for stomach ache and an antidote for poison. It is believed that the shrub is the umblical cord of the sky, Dote-Abu. If the plant is picked, the sky is hurt and his tears fall as rain. The root must be dug out secretly; unseen by people or the sky, and the plant must be left in the soil as if it were untouched. Verrier Elwin (1970) recounts an incident in 1955 when the Palibos and the Ramos attacked the Boris for digging for the plant on the Bayur Hills, which they believed would cause heavy rain. In another incident, when month-long rain prevented the Palibos of Tagur from burning their *jhum* crops, they captured a mithun from another group as compensation for digging for *Coptis teeta* without taking the necessary precautions.

The flora has immense pharmaceutical and commercial potential. The *Aquilaaria agallocha* tree, from which the expensive aromatic *agar* oil is produced, has already been decimated. At higher altitudes, on the forest floor in the Dibang Valley, the Mishmi cultivate *Coptis teeta,* which sells at Rs. 300 per kg. at the Tinsukhia market in Assam. They also grow *Clerodendrum colebrookianum* at lower altitudes. The common yew *Taxus baccata,* whose leaves produce taxol a drug used for treating cancer, occurs in the temperate forests throughout the State. The *pipli (Piper longum)*—one of 20 species of long pepper in Arunachal - is cultivated in parts of Siang, Dibang Valley and Lohit. The local tribes in Kameng collect and sell the vitamin-C rich fruit *amla* (*Emblica officianalis*) to ayurvedic companies. There are also three varieties of ginseng. The Arunachal Pradesh Department of Environment and Forests is setting up a medicinal plant sanctuary in Lohit, and will soon establish a separate Medicinal and Aromatic Plant Corporation (Haridasan, pers. com. 1997).

In conclusion, it is right to say that at first the need of infrastructural development of Arunachal Pradesh is very urgent. To connect all district headquarters by roads. It is very necessary to connect important places of Arunachal Pradesh with other parts of India by rail linking. To increased central funds for rapid development of Arunachal Pradesh – need to proper propaganda as a tourist destination Arunachal Pradesh to the peoples. Need to set-up more and more hydro-power project, which strengthen the State economy. I think it is very necessary to engage all sections of peoples to developmental plan and programme. To hold Gram Sabha in time is very necessary for grass root development. Proper training should be given to the PRI members to increase efficiency and consciousness about developmental plan and programmes. Consciousness also decreased corruption. If grass root peoples are understand that development need for them, they spontaneously engaged themselves in development. So at last, I can say that Panchayati Raj Institutions is a most important vehicle for tribal development not only for Arunachal Pradesh, also elsewhere.

The tribal people should be brought into main stream, if they are to be benefited from the progress on the development front. The Tribal people are facing a number of problems like land alienation, displacement, rehabilitation and degradation of Common Property Resources. They still suffer from poverty, unemployment, and poor access to health and sanitation. 42 per cent people are living below poverty line in the rural areas. The poor are very poor especially in the rural areas and rich are very rich in the urban areas. The good fruit of modern civilization is not reaching among the rural people living along the border frontier region. The tribal way of life is under threat under the impact of globalization. Indebtedness is high among tribal farmers. A serious problem is the small size of the landholding. Other constraints are: poor quality of soil, absence of improved techniques, lack of use of better seeds and chemical fertilizers. These problems must be considered while framing plan and policies.

The basic approach is to promote processes of awareness

generation, legal literacy, social analysis and mobilisation for self-selecting group formation among disadvantaged women and marginalised groups.

The tribal teachers should be given incentives to try to generate motivation among tribal girls and their families about the value of education, especially girls' education. The government must organize mass awareness programmes. The teachers and government must try to encourage gender equitable values and the role of men in household activities may be encouraged and taught as part of the curriculum as well so that the boys and men also share the household activities and the tribal girls get time for studies.

Tribals constitute the largest single group of population that has been subjected to systematic harassment and displacement from their homeland in the name of developmental projects in independent India. This has resulted in an endless saga of inordinate human sufferings in socio-economic as well as cultural and psychological terms. This must be stopped and the inalienable right of the tribal people to live in their homeland cannot be sacrificed at the alter of corporate good.

Various Programmes should be undertaken to develop and should be implemented a replicable model properly which ensures household food security and improves livelihood opportunities and overall quality of life of the tribal population of the State in particular and NER in general based on the sustainable and equitable use of natural resources. To achieve this, the programme: (i) empowers tribal grass roots associations and users' groups, including women and other marginal groups; (ii) promotes activities which generate sustainable increases in production and productivity of land and water resources; and (iii) generates sources of income outside of agriculture, particularly for the landless.

The well-being of tribal community depends very much on the women. Status of tribal women relating to their socio-cultural problems, their economic rights, their participation in management, their access to employment, food, health, etc. have not been properly focused. Nutritional status of tribal is compromised by unequal access to food, by heavy work demands, and by special nutritional needs (such as for iron), females are particularly susceptible to illness, particularly anemia, trapped in a cycle of ill health exacerbated by childbearing and hard physical labour. There are many taboos and myths which are barriers to health practices and growing body of adolescence tribal girls. In the region different tribal communities are at different stages of development; as such the status of women differs from community to community. However, in general the position of women in some of the States is respectable but not very high. The prevalence of polygamy, victim of bride price, sex abuse and child marriage are quite in common. It has no doubt lowered their position in the society. They are generally devoid of equal political and property rights.

There has always been interaction and trade between the hill tribes and the plains people of Assam. But the demographic character of Arunachal Pradesh began to change only in the 1970s. Modern administration has brought large numbers of non-Arunachalees into the region. The Nepali and Bengali are the most numerous, engaged in manual labour, as domestic helper, and in services and trade. Many of the junior functionaries like village school teachers are from the Assam plains. Retired jawans of the Assam Rifles were also resettled in some areas. In Itanagar, the capital, and most district headquarters, stenographers and other clerical assistants are Malayali. In the 1991 census, out of a total population of 864,558, 64 per cent were Scheduled Tribes (ST), 36 per cent were non-tribals. Besides, there is a floating population of migrant workers.

The discrimination from one to another depends on their socio-cultural background. Phenomenon of gender discrimination is not caused by a single factor. It has multiple causes and, therefore, need a multiple strategy to tackle the problem. The problem of gender discrimination may be viewed from the various angles like the roles they assume – who does what, the responsibilities they share – who is responsible for what, the resources they enjoy – who owns what, the constraints they face – who has access to what, the regards they are entitled to – who deserves what, the recognition they need – who gets recognized for what, the remuneration that is due – who gets how much for the work, the representation they make – who represents where, the regulations they make – who decides what, the restrictions imposed on them – who submits to whom or what; Man or Woman! This is very much prevailing in tribal society in particular and in Indian society especially in rural communities in general. This gender discrimination leads to inequality, injustice, dissatisfaction and disputes. When gender discrimination is eliminated, many problems would be solved and peace would be established. The positive way to eliminate gender discrimination is to generate awareness level of the people about the causes and consequences of the phenomenon. Without development of tribal people at beforehand in the State it is difficult to bring any type of development of the State. The tribal youth enjoys reservation facility in respect of both education and jobs. That is not enough. In tribal education; the emphasis should be on agriculture, poultry, forestry and carpentry etc.

It is necessary to evaluate the total configuration of the performance of different agencies and the government and to identify the problems of the people and also to know who are the beneficiaries of the facilities and incentives provided by the different agencies and the government for the development of the region.

REFERENCES

Alam, K. (ed.) (1985): *Planning in North-East*, Omsons Publications, New Delhi.

Alam, K., (ed.) (1985): *Planning in North-East*, Omsons Publications, New Delhi.

Arora, R.K. and K.R. Nayar (1984): *Wild Relatives of Crop Plants in India*, NBPGR, New Delhi : Indian Council of Agricultural Research.

Aggarwal, A.K. (1985: "Changing Pattern of Demography in Arunachal: An Analysis" in Ray Datta, B.(ed), *"The Pattern and Problems of Population in North-East India*, Uppal Publishing House, New Delhi, p. 348.

Basu, A.R. (1985): *"Tribal Development Programmes and Administration in India"*, National Book Organisation, New Delhi.

Borang, A. (1995): Ecological status of capped langur (*Presbytis pileatus Blyth*, 1843) in Arunachal Pradesh, *Arunachal Forest News*, Vol. 13, 1 and 2.

Borang, A. (1996): Studies on certain ethnozoological aspects of Adi tribes of Siang, *Arunachal Forest News*, Vol. 14, 1.

Chandna, R.C. (2005): *Geography of Population Concepts, Determinants and Patterns*, Kalyani Publishers, New Delhi, pp. 272-293.

Chowdhury, J.N. (1976): *Evidence of some caste-like features in some Arunachal*

Tribes, Resarun, Directorate of Research, Government of Arunachal Pradesh, Itanagar.

Chowdhury, J.N. (1979): Arunachal Panorama Itanagar: Directorate of Research, Deptt. of Information and Public Relations.

DoEF. (1993): Arunachal Forests Itanagar: Department of Environment and Forests, Government of Arunachal Pradesh.

Dutta, P. (1976): *Women in Arunachal and their Status in the Socio-Cultural Life*, Resarun 1975, Itanagar: Research Deptt: Government of Arunachal Pradesh.

Elwin, V. (1959): *A Philosophy for NEFA*, Shillong: North-East Frontier Agency. (2nd edition).

Elwin, V. (1970) (reprinted 1991): *A New Book of Tribal Fiction, Itanagar*: Director of Research, Arunachal Pradesh.

Haridasan, K. and A.N. Rao. (1995): "Dendrobium monticola—A miniature orchid new to N.E. India from Arunachal Pradesh", *Arunachal Forest News*, 13, 1&2.

Joram, Begi (2008): "Education Scenario in Arunachal Pradesh", *Arunachal Review*, Directorate of Information, Public Relations and Printing, Government of Arunachal Pradesh, Vol. X, No.2, June –August, Naharlagun, Government of Arunachal Pradesh.

Mandal, R.K. (2008): "Dependence of Arunachal Economy on Central Grants-in-Aid", *Journal of North-East Indian Council for Social Science Research*, Vol. 32, No. 1, April, North-Eas India Council for Social Science Research, Shillong, Meghalaya.

Pandey, G.S.: *Buddhism and Khamtis*, SanPark Press Pvt. Ltd. Ashok Vihar, Phase I, Delhi.

Puri, S.K., M. Ahmedullah, A.R.K. Sastry, and Amenita Ivan. (1995): *Bio-diversity of Arunachal Pradesh*, New Delhi: Worldwide Fund for Nature-India (booklet).

SECTION I
DEVELOPMENTAL ACTIVITIES

3

Constraints of Economic Development with Special Reference to Globalization and Inner Line System

Introduction

The British penetrated fully into the North-East Region (Arunachal Pradesh) in 1826 when the Burmese authority was badly defeated by the British in the first Anglo-Burmese war in 1824-1826. The war was terminated by the treaty of Yandabo in February, 1826. The outcome of the treaty was that the king of Burma (Myanmar) renounced all claims upon Assam and agreed to abstain from all future interferences with Assam and its dependencies. Since then, the British had to take over the charges of the administration in Assam.

This event forced the British Government to deal with the hill tribes of Arunachal Pradesh as the tribesmen had age old prescriptive claims over the plains of Assam bordering hill as their own land and were accustomed to collect posa (payment in kind) and taxes annually from the Assamese inhabitants since the Ahom times. To secure the British interests, it was necessary to expel the hill tribes of Arunachal Pradesh from the foothill areas bordering Assam. The British policy of appeasement failed in due course of time as the tribesmen carried on feudatory incursions into the plains of Assam with a view to punish the refractory subjects who moved away from the detriment of the hill masters and who refused to pay posa or taxes defying the age old tradition.

The economy of Assam had become promising and trade and industry had made a good start. Tea, petroleum, coal, rubber and wood became flourishing industries and elephant-catching and ivory were engaging growing attention. Besides, the revenue of the Assam valley increased as good surplus and huge fallow lands could yield more if tenants were invited to cultivate. But the economy depended upon the Administration's capacity to maintain law and order in the province. All the districts of the Assam valley were bordered on some hills inhabited by the tribes. The unrestricted intercourse between the people who had come for commerce and who knew very little about the tribes led to many disputes and sometimes these took violent dimensions. Moreover, the tribes driven into the hills sometimes had to fall upon the plains with a view to punish the refractory subjects who moved away from the detriment of the hill masters and who refused to pay taxes defying the age old tradition. The problem of regulation of the intercourse between the tribes and the businessmen of the Assam plains therefore, drew the attention of the Administration. To solve the hill tribes' problem the British had to create a barrier between the hills and the plains which reduced contact and consequently friction between the civilized valley-dwellers and the primitive hill tribes. Thus, to check the movement of the hill people into the valleys i.e., to separate the hill people by a line, an Inner Line System was introduced under the Bengal Eastern Frontier Regulation Act in 1873, which came into force in 1875. It is commonly known as the Inner Line Regulation of 1873. However, the term 'Inner Line' originated from the suggestion of Arthur Hobhouse who observed in his draft for the Regulation of 1873 that the line to be prescribed under the Regulation might be called 'Inner Line'. The Local Government was empowered to prohibit all British Subject or any person residing in or passing through such districts, from going beyond such Line without a pass under the hand and seal of the executive officer or such officer as might be authorized to grant such pass. The Local Government was also given the power to suspend or vary this prohibition from time to time. Any person who went beyond the Inner Line was fixed according to the above process. Without a pass he was liable to conviction before a Magistrate of first or second class and to a fine not exceeding Rs.100 for the first offence; for each subsequent offence there could be a fine not exceeding Rs.500 or simple or rigorous imprisonment for a term not exceeding three months or both.

The Objective of the Inner Line before Independence

The object of the Inner Line Regulation was to keep outside the boundary all tracts in which semi-savage tribes lived and to complicate their free intercourse with the people of the plains. It was clearly mentioned that the Government of India would not be responsible for life and property of the people beyond such Line and if necessary, people might not be allowed to go beyond the Line. The Government of India had suggested the Government of Bengal that while prescribing such Line, they should see that the line corresponding to the natural features of the country, and if there was no such feature, it was to coincide with obligatory points like crossing of a road. The place where a road crossed the Line was to be clearly shown in map. If any tea garden was there on the frontier, that should be brought within the Line, if possible, for avoiding possible complications.

Commerce beyond the Inner Line could be carried on pass basis. The people who wanted to catch elephants, to cut wood, to collect forest products like rubber etc. could carry on their trade in the tribal area on the basis of pass which was issued from the government. But they were subject to payment of tolls to the tribes inhabiting in the region where such trade was to be carried on. Miju Mishmis even collected tolls from the Hindu pilgrims visiting the Parasuram Kund as it was regarded lying outside the administered area.

The Objective of the Inner Line after Independence

After independence, the Government of India decided to continue to follow the restriction of the Inner Line. But the purpose for which the Inner Line had been designed in 1873 was changed. The main purpose of the Inner Line is to restrict the free movement of Non-Arunachalees is NEFA now Arunachal Pradesh, i.e., the free flow of entrance of Non-Arunachalee is prohibited in the State. A Non-Arunachalee who wants to cross beyond such Line has to get first an Inner Line Pass (ILP) issued by Arunachal Pradesh Government authorized Gazetted Officer for a limited period of time after fulfilling some formalities.

Again, it is thought that the territory is located at strategic point from the standpoint of defence. Besides, the Government of India feels it necessary to protect the land and forest of the innocent tribal people of the State from the Non-Arunachalees' hunger of grabbing. It is well thought that the protected Arunachalees can make economically a smooth progress. They will not be disturbed from their socio-cultural and economic dimension.

To pursue the avenues of development, Pandit Jawaharlal Nehru prescribed five fundamental principles in his speech delivered at the opening session of the Scheduled Tribes and Scheduled Areas Conference held at New Delhi in 1952. The five principles are:

1. People should develop along the lines of their own genius and we should avoid imposing anything on them. We should try to encourage in everyway, their own traditional arts and culture.
2. Tribal rights in land and forests should be respected.
3. We should try to train and build up a team of their own people to do the work of administration and development. Some technical personnel from outside will no doubt, he needed, especially in the beginning. But we should avoid introducing too many outsiders into tribal territory.
4. We should not over-administer these areas or overwhelm them with the multiplicity of schemes. We should rather work through and not rival to our own social and cultural institutions.
5. We should judge results not by statistics or the amount of money spent, but by the quality of human character that is evolved.

Pandit Jawaharlal Nehru had rightly cautioned the Administration: "what I am anxious about particularly, is to avoid large number of outsiders being sent to the tribal areas in some capacity or other. If that happens, whatever well we may train them, the mere numbers, will produce what I could call a revolutionary situation in the tribal areas. We will lose grip of the situation then, and will have to content ourselves with drifting and accepting many things that we do not like".

Globalization and its Meaning

Today no country in the world, including India, can afford to isolate itself from the ongoing rapid process of globalization. Economic liberalization in India is almost a decade old phenomenon. A number of multinational companies have come into the country. Corporationization of huge public sector undertakings has already taken place. Indian Airlines Limited, Indian Oil Corporation Limited, Oil and Natural Gas Corporation Limited, Gas Authority of India Limited, and so on are good examples of this process. Disinvestment from many public sector undertakings is on the card. In course of time, the university system is likely to be privatized. People have begun to realize that resistance is of no use. Utter disillusionment with the fifty years of Indian Independence seems to be working behind many of the privatizing initiatives.

As the advocates of globalization have pointed out, it is essentially a means of meaningful growth and development. India can catch the markets of other countries as others will have their markets in India. Now goods and services of international standards can be made available to the common people. Most of the unhealthy monopolized trade practices can be checked. The non-productive and non-viable economic sectors will be compelled to arise from their long slumber. The people of all sectors now realize that they have to work to earn their bread and not treat the customers nonchalantly.

There are also disadvantages of this globalization, especially to the poorer sections of the society whose earning and buying capacity is next to nothing. The Small Scale Industries will have to face the challenges from the multinationals. India, having the second largest population in the world, will have to look after the food, shelter, clothing, health, education, and employment of the illiterate and unskilled people. In Professor Amartya Sen's words, Indian economy has to be people-oriented as against the multinational economy, which is commodity-based. As the well-known industrialist from Tamil Nadu Dr. N. Mahalingam (1998: 5-6) has emphasized, Gandhian economic principles cannot be sacrificed, if the whole of India has to survive.

Whatever, the consequences, India is very much in the thick of globalization. Even some of the sensitive sectors like telecommunications and defence have partially been liberalized. Gradually more such sectors are being thrown open to foreign direct investments.

India initiated the process of globalization and liberalization since 1991. Over the past decade globalization and liberalization in India has been discussed mainly in terms of foreign investment, industrial development, information technology and the tremendous growth of service sector, etc. and there has been substantial media coverage of all these aspects of the Indian economy.

Globalization is considered as an important element in the reform package. But what constitutes globalization? The term globalization has four parameters: (i) reduction of trade barriers so as to permit free flow of goods across national frontiers; (ii) creation of an environment in which free flow of capital can take place among nation-states; (iii) creation of environment, permitting free flow of technology; and (iv) last, but not the least, from the point of view of the developing countries, creation of an environment in which free movement of labour can take place in different countries of the world. The advocates of globalization, more especially from developed countries, limit the definition of globalization to only three components, viz., unhindered trade flows, capital flows and technology flows. They insist on the developing countries to accept their definition of globalization and conduct the debate on globalization within the parameters set by them. However, several economists in the developing world believe that this definition is incomplete and in case the globaliser's ultimate aim is to look upon the world as a 'global' village, then the fourth component, unrestricted movement of labour cannot be left out. But the entire issue whether debate at the World Trade Organization (WTO) or at other forums blacks out the 'labour flows' as an essential component of globalization. The effect of globalization, 1991 in favour of annual average growth rate is shown in Table 3.1 where 1990 is pre-globalization period while 1999 is post-globalization period.

However, globalization refers to a process of increasing economic integration and growing economic interdependence between countries in the world economy. It is associated not only with an increasing cross-border movement of goods, services, capital, technology information and people, but also with an organization of economic activities which crosses national boundaries.

Table 3.1: Merchandise Exports of Selected Countries of the World.

Country	Export US$ million		As % of World Exports		Percentage increase in 1999 over 1990	Annual Average growth rate (1990-99)
	1990	1999	1990	1999		
India	17,975	36,560	0.54	0.67	103.4	8.2
Chila	62,091	195,150	1.86	3.59	214.3	13.6
South Korea	65,016	144,745	1.95	2.66	122.6	9.3
Mexico	40,711	136,703	1.22	2.51	235.8	14.4
World Exports	3,328,357	5,442,226	100.0	100.0	63.5	5.6

Source: Compiled and Computed from the data provided in World Bank, World Development Indicators (2001).

The restrictive import policy along with thrust on export promotion continued till 1975-76 to alleviate adverse Balance Of Payments (BOP) problems (the rupee was devalued in June, 1966). Then a stage came when the government adopted a policy of import liberalization with a view to encourage export promotion. However, our experience with this policy was also not good and India faced a serious BOP crisis in the middle of 1991. The foreign exchange reserves had fallen to a level barely adequate to meet essential imports for a few weeks. Thus, India seemed to be entering into a situation of imminent default on foreign payments. To cope with the imminent problem India adopted the policy of economic reforms. The external sector was at the centre stage of reform package that included exchange rate devaluation in 1991, introduction of the market-based exchange rate system in a phased manner, dismantling of tariff and non-tariff barriers and encouragement of Foreign Direct Investment (FDI). The FDI plays an important role for the industrial development of developing countries because of the fact that it brings in not only capital but also technology, skills and sometimes even market access. In India, the policy toward FDI has also evolved through different phases along with the trade policy. It was sought on mutually advantageous terms and local ownership was preferred.

The WTO has already completed more than ten years of its existence with 148 members in February, 2005 and 95 per cent of the global trade is governed by the rules and regulations of the WTO. On the whole, India did well during the period. It has entered the ranks of the ten largest economies of the world in dollar terms between 2003 and 2004. The restructuring of the economy has been going on steadily with the tertiary sector and the secondary sector improving their share in the GDP at the cost of the primary sector. It is interesting to note that during 1990-91 to 2002-03, the share of the primary sector in the real GDP has declined from 35 per cent to 24 per cent and the share of the service sector increased from 41 per cent to 51 per cent. The overall growth of the economy during the 1990s has been impressive compared to the same during the earlier decades. The rate of growth of real GDP was 3.1 per cent per annum during 1970-71 to 1980-81, which increased to 5.6 per cent during 1980-81 to 1990-91 and continued to grow at that rate during 1990-91 to 2000-01. Further, it grew at the rate of 6.4 per cent during 2000-01 to 2004-05 with the service sector growing at the highest rate during the later periods. So far as the behaviour of the external sector was concerned, the values of export and import as percentage of GDP were increased especially after the trade liberalization such that the relative share of the former has more than offset that of the latter (Chattopadhyay and Ghosal, 2006).

The advent of globalization brings with it a marked change in our outlook as far as management of national economy is concerned. Under economic globalization, country after country has opened up their economies to free flow of finance capital, technology and goods. The three pillars of globalization: the death of distance (as globalization is often referred to), the services revolution and the mobility of capital present tremendous opportunities for India. However, the transition from a close lethargic economy to a vibrant, globally integrated economy cannot be painless. It has led to the reduction in the role of the State and a shift from welfare to a market-friendly system of governance. In urban sector it has meant handling over the responsibility of providing certain basic amenities to the private sector or bringing the public utilities under commercial framework. While this has been the case in all urban areas, it can be seen more clearly in large cities, specially the metropolitan centres.

Foreign Capital plays a crucial role in the economic development of all the Nations. The Foreign Capital flows in a country in two ways one is Foreign Direct Investment and Foreign Portfolio Investment. For any country's development foreign capital is vital. The developing nations require much doses of foreign investment. Where foreign investment is more that country is said to be prosperous and economically sound. So far India is concerned; it faced severe external imbalances in the 1990's. To overcome the problems, India welcomed the New Economic Policy advocated by IMF. After the implementation of the NEP (New Economic Policy), India saw tremendous novelties in the economic development. The trend pattern of Foreign Capital flows in India after Globalization has increased drastically. The states in India are competing to invite Foreign Direct Investment to achieve their economic goals. The progress of FDI is partially depends on the States response. The Political instability in such states hinders the flow of FDI, which in turn block the unique development of India where there are wide regional imbalances. This paper examines the hidden facts that hamper the flow of FDI.

FDI is seen as a means to supplement domestic investment for achieving a higher level of economic growth and development. FOI benefits domestic industry as well as the Indian consumers by providing opportunities for technological upgradations, access to global managerial skills and practices optimal utilization of human resources making Indian industry internationally competitive, opening up export markets, providing backward and forward linkages and access to internationally quality goods and services. Most importantly, FDI is central for India's integration into global production chain, which involves production by Multinational Corporation spread across all over the world.

India is the world's largest democratic, the second-most populous country and the' 7th largest in terms of land area. As one of the oldest civilization of world, India represents a nation rich in diversity in terms of its culture, people, language, geographic and climatic conditions and natural resources. To fully realize the country's immense economic potential, the Government launched the Economic Reform Programme in July 1991. Since, then, successive Governments have progressively liberalized and deregulated the economy. Today the Government policies are simple, transparent and promote domestic and foreign investment. This has brought a radical change in the course of the economy.

Foreign Direct Investment (FDI) has played an important role in the economic development of Southeast Asia and India. The Asian Development Bank (ADB) points out that FDI has led a transfer of production of labour intensive products and exports from high wage source nations to lower wage host nations. Transfer of technology from developed countries was substantial. FDI benefits developing countries by:

- Providing additional sources of capital and expanding countries production. Transferring crucial technology to the host country.
- Promoting trade and exports, especially in more open host nations.
- Generating employment opportunities and training skilled workers and
- Improving the international allocation of capital, particularly if the return on capital is higher in the host country than in the source country.

India's share in world FDI is minor, notably when considering its size. The entire world is watching the miraculours growth of India and China. China opened up to FDI a decade before India did. Indeed, the opening of the India is relatively new and the history of its FDI on a large scale is very short. Officially, at the end of 2004, India's stocks of inward FDI amounted to $ 38.7 bn i.e. only 0.4 per cent of world stock, and investment received by developing countries. These stocks represented 5.9 per cent of GDP in 2004, a very small ratio compared with developing country's average (26.4%). We notice however, that Indian stocks were 23 times greater in 2004 than in 1990. In 2004, India held the 15th slot in terms of inward FDI stock among developing economies (WIR, 2005).

Opening of FDI have really created new opportunities for India's development and boosted the performances of local firms as well as the globalization of some of them. Such a trend has undeniably raised Indian's stature among developing countries.

The strategy of economic development of any nation that envisages measures for alleviating poverty of the masses by providing large scale employment, education and training, capital formation, effective mobilization of resources, dispersal of industry, balanced regional development, expansion of trade and equitable distribution of national income with the effective involvement and participation of all the citizens in accomplishment of the goal, cannot relegate production to the background.

Broadly speaking, the term 'globalization' means integration of economies and societies through cross country flows of information, ideas, technologies, goods, services, capital, finance and people.

But the author is sorry to say that the non-Arunachalee has no right to enter the State without prior Government Permission. It means that we have limited right to move within the region of our own country. Globalization says cross country flows among countries. To get the good effect of globalization in the State it needs first cross state flows among the States in India. Due to lack of free flows of goods (existence of check gate), cost of living is very high. The prices of perishable goods, in the state are almost two or three times more than those of nearly Assam plains. As per example, the prices of green vegetables are at least Rs. 20 per kg. at Itanagar but the prices of same thing are only Rs. 8 or less in Assam plains only at a distance of 30 or 35 kms. away from Itanagar.

This paper seeks to examine an in-depth study to identify the relevant constraints of economic development of Arunachal Pradesh, which are discussed below.

Market and Market Institutions

The term 'institution' has been defined by different people in various ways. In present context, it is necessary to define the concept that would be more appropriate for examining the objective of the institution. According to Wolf, Jr. (1955) institutions refer to organizations of government and private as well. They are considered as the "rulers of society or organization that felicitate coordination among people by helping them from expectation which each person can reasonably hold in dealing with others" (Ruttan and Hayami, 1984). Alternatively, as institution can be viewed as "a complex norms and behaviour that persists over time by serving some socially valued objectives (Uphoff, 1991)". By market institutions we mean the necessary conditions and rules that should exist for perfectly competitive form of production and transactions of goods and services among different engaged economic agents. Unfortunately the impact in transforming the primitive tribal economy into a market economy has been negligible conceivably because supply driven by government efforts is mismatched with the ground realities in regard to the existing institutional structure associated with the tribal mode of production prevailing in the State. Therefore, for the sake of economic progress it is extremely important to know the factors that have been impeding the emergence and development of market institutions which are deemed crucial for transformation of a primitive economy to a modern one. This new economic policy of the State Government, which is considered as a paradigm shift in the country's economic policy, is based on the capitalist mode of production where it is assumed that if markets are allowed to function freely it can efficiently achieve a marked improvement in economic life of the people in a country. Governments in the State have emphasized in building economic institutions through introduction of policies and programmes such as establishing different bank branches from zero in 1971 to 1999 at present for promotion of market-led development like in other parts of the country.

Resources, technology and institutions may be considered as the three essential factors of development. Economic growth and development of a country or region may be realized through the optimum utilization of available resources and the state of technology, which in turn depends on the quality of institutional arrangement or structure that is being the force in production and distribution. Because there is a close connection between the institutions and technology employed and the efficiency of a market economy is directly shaped by the institutional framework. In the whole process of the economic progress, various types of institutions are to function and they work at various levels interdependently. It is evident that institutions are as important as technology for economic development, and they evolve together interactively during the development process. The role of institutions in economic activity is that defining the parameters and processes through which agents use technology, natural and human resources are to increase the level of production and income. However, it should be noted that all the time all the institutions would not be equally effective. While favourable institutional arrangement promotes economic progress, unfavourable arrangement may act as a factor impeding economic development. Under such circumstances, the study of issues such as institutional forms, institutional arrangements, institutional design, institutional constraints and how institutions change has drawn great attention. The modernity of the economy is characterized by the development of markets based on the capitalist mode of production. In capitalist system it is assumed that with the progress of science and improvement in technologies, large scale capital formation will create jobs and specialization in production through division of labour will further expand markets for produced goods and services. The development of market depends on the institutional reforms where government can play a positive role in developing institutional arrangements for private investment which may be private domestic investment or Foreign Direct Investment (FDI). For example, because of the beautiful landscape and natural scenic beauty of the territory, *tourism industry* has very prosperous future subject to the removal of *Inner-Line Pass* and provision of infrastructural facilities. The single industry could be capable in transforming the State economy significantly. It is also important to improve the law and order problem by providing security of life and property.

Agriculture

The process of globalization and economic liberalization opened up several opportunities in agricultural sector, especially in the Indian seed sector. The opportunities were in the form of increase in the distribution of quality seeds, improvement in seed replacement rate and reduction in the requirement— supply gap for quality seeds. Liberalization also enabled augmentation of foreign investment and partnership programmes in seed sector promoting private participation. Due to liberalization, the information on contractual commitments was available for wider acceptance and alliances with domestic firms. Multinational seed firms are participating as active competitors in the seed markets in India. Currently, there are more than 150 companies operating in India with 1/3rd have collaborative linkage with global partners. This study addresses the impact of liberalization on the economic role of the domestic seed sector and their implications for the use of bio-technology and for achieving food security. Seed sector in India witnessed rapid changes since liberalization. In 2001, estimated total value of commercial Indian seed market was Rs. 4,050 crores accounting for 4 per cent of the world seed market. Of this, 98 per cent for domestic and 2 per cent international sales.

Therefore, agriculture plays an important role in the economic development of the developing countries like India and the development of agriculture through increased production and productivity is one phase and the other phase being the crucial role played by its marketing. "A Marketing system which protects the interests of both producers and consumers is the key to agricultural development." "The vital role played by efficient marketing system in the planned economy needs no emphasis. The success of any agricultural development programme rests ultimately on the efficiency of the marketing system."

Agriculture boosts the economy through backward and forward linkages. Sharad Joshi, founder of Shetkari Sanghathan and also a Rajya Sabha member has said "Agriculture is the basic source of wealth and also the prime mover of the demand function. India being a developing country, the role of agriculture sector is even more important. It provides livelihood to over 60 per cent of the population. And in India it also provides a cushion for the ratio between the urban and rural income." Being such an important sector of the economy it cannot be ignored or neglected. Agriculture occupies an important place in the economy of Arunachal Pradesh and forms a major occupation of the people of the State. According to 2001 census about 79.66 per cent of the State's population is living in rural areas and 58.44 per cent of the total workers are cultivators. The share of this sector in State Domestic Product (SDP) or Arunachal Pradesh at current price was 32.07 per cent in 2000-2001.

Most of the landed property is jointly owned by the clans and community. Perhaps the abundance of land resources with the lowest man-land ratio and absence of private property rights, the market for lands could not develop (however, in urban areas many fortunate tribal elites grabbed prime lands and recorded in their names and these lands have now very good markets). Most of the families cultivate their operational holdings and does not allow the tenancy system of cultivation which constitutes a specific institutional form in agricultural relation. The operation holdings of the farmers are very small, because, this is a labour intensive method of cultivation. As a result, large scale agricultural production do not take place. Because of subsistence nature of the crop production, the market for agricultural labour cannot build up. All the operations in agriculture are performed by the family labour including femalefolk and community labour are found to work on mutual and cooperative basis without payment of wage for labour. In all probability, this is the only State in the country where nobody can be considered as landless and the class of agricultural labour in tribal society does not exist. Rural people in simple living with the support of nature are self-sufficient where role of money is not significant at least in production sector, and they are used to exchange goods and services for goods and services among themselves to satisfy their limited but varied wants.

In regard to other modern agriculture inputs such as seeds, fertilizer, pesticides, irrigation, and agriculture implements, the role of market is negligible because of the nature of production (*jhum* cultivation) and production relation prevailing in State. Tribal farmers use their traditional variety of seeds and home made implements are applied in shifting type of cultivation. The modern production inputs are costly and the poor capital deficient farmers may find it difficult to buy them from the market since they have little opportunity to get institutional credit as there is lack of private assets that banks demand as collateral security before sanctioning loans. As a result investment—private or government in the State's agricultural sector could not appear as a reality. However, to some extent modern agricultural technologies in the form of HYV seeds, pesticides and chemical fertilizers are supplied to the farmers by the government to increase the productivity and to modernize agriculture sector and rightly to discourage shifting cultivation which is detrimental to the environment and ecology of this area. But very little impact of this exertion is noticed because of the conflict between the traditional mode of production and the character and nature of the means of production supplied by the government.

Due to existing Inner Line system, the entrance of National and Multinational seed firms are almost *nil* in the State and hence, free flow of information and its utilization regarding modernized agriculture is very limited and thereby agricultural market is not growing.

Production

The production of marketable surplus for some crops like ginger in the State is noteworthy but marketing in Arunachal Pradesh remains backward and underdeveloped due to ignorance of farmers, lack of market information, poor infrastructure, and lack of grading and storage facilities. For example, fruits processing industries are extremely important as some fruits such as orange, pineapple and apple grow plenty but due to lack of marketing and storage facilities farmers do not get attractive prices. So far the institution in production is concerned, for many products such as medicinal and herbal products and processed foods; marketing channel is almost missing in the State. But it is well known fact that more production and unrestricted exchange of goods and services will improve the well being of the community as a whole and an equitable distribution of income and assets may accelerate the tempo of development because all these activities are performed under such as institutional arrangement where economic agents find incentives to maximize benefits.

Industry, Investment and License Issuing System

According to World Development Reports 1999, "Globalization not only ensures efficiency and growth but also equity and development" (Sengupta, 2004). Goals of globalization should be appropriately viewed as the fulfilment of the rights of the people. At its 96th plenary meeting of December 20, 1995, the General Assembly of the United Nations proclaimed the period of 1997 to 2006 as the "First United Nations Decade for the Eradication of Poverty" (Borocz, 2005). But inequality still persists. For example, people living below BPL in Arunachal Pradesh is 40.04 per cent during 1999-2000 in rural areas (NEC, 2002). One of the basic characteristics of globalization is perhaps inviting Foreign Direct Investment (FDI). In this part of globe especially Arunachal Pradesh, the impact of FDI is a far cry. There is restriction between countries in this region due to lack of border trade and restrictions within trade. There is restriction within states in this part of world due to imposition of *Inner Line Permit.*

Industrialization is recognized as a real tool of economic development as it indicates a higher standard of living of the majority of population. Once Nehru told that real progress might ultimately be depend on industrialization. During the last 57 years after independence, our country has been bringing a noticeable growth in industrial production. But the North-Eastern Region of our country has, till now, been lying neglected. Though the region is well endowed with mineral, forest and hydel resource they have been left out of the process of industrialization. It has remained so due to isolation of the region from the main centres of trade and industry, inadequate economic and physical infrastructure, small size of the regional market, low accessibility of the markets outside the region, lack of entrepreneurs, difficult terrain condition, serious law and order problem, etc.

Arunachal Pradesh among the North Eastern States abounds in a variety of natural resources including agricultural, forest and mineral wealth. This State would be benefited with a high degree of industrialization. Unfortunately, the position is just the reverse. The interface with infrastructure will be examined in detail by examining the impact of the major components of infrastructure such as road, power and communication. We shall also examine the industrial policies of these states. The basic objective of industrialization is to be gainful utilization of her resources: material and human. At present there are 15 medium scale industries which are mostly saw mill, plywood and 11 veneer mill functioning in the state. In spite of many obstacles in the way of development of large and medium scale industries, significant numbers of small-scale industrial units have come up in the state over the year due to active support and positive policy of the government. There were 471 registered small scale industrial units functioning at the end of March 2003 mostly engaged in activities like blacksmithy, tin smithy, carpet-making, carpentry, wool-knitting handloom and weaving, cane and bamboo works, printing press, etc.

There is no major industries and hence no large scale industrial production. Neither the government nor private initiated manufacturing enterprises have grown in this region. Like agriculture, there is no industrial labour class in this state among the tribal. This is clear from the figures with respect to the contribution of manufacturing sector to the Net State Domestic Product which has remained almost unchanged at only about 22 per cent from 1970-71 to 2001-02, of which government sponsored construction works occupies the highest share where neither the local labour are found to work nor the construction materials are locally available.

The investment level in this State is low and the firms are of small scale using low capital-intensive technology that is often inefficient. Realizing this fact, the Government of India has been inviting foreign capital by changing the institutional designs that are guiding the economic development before introduction of privatization and structural adjustments. In this connection, it is worthy to note that while local tribal people lacking investment capacity, investors from other States and Foreign Direct Investment (FDI) should be invited. But the system of *Inner Line Permit* does not allow the non-tribal to enter the territory without obtaining permission from the government and also without fulfilling some formalities. So far the trade, commerce and business are concerned; the number of local people engaged in these economic activities is very small. The people from outside this State come for these activities for which they are to obtain *license in the name of some tribal people* who get the rent from the businessmen for their licenses. These trading people earn money and mostly siphon off in their respective home because they do not get the right to buy the property for independent business and trade. This situation hugely restricts the private investors in coming and opening up big manufacturing units within this territory. Banking credit for establishing business and industries are available to the local people but they lack entrepreneurial skills and show little interest in industrial production activities. Therefore, *Inner-Line Permits system and government policy in issuing licenses* only to local people most likely has worked against the opening up of market institution in this part of the country.

Financial Co-operation and Co-ordination

Nature of financial problem in this state is quite different from that prevailing elsewhere. Inadequate banking system, excessive dependence on agricultural economy, less inflow and more outflow of funds, low capital formation rate, lack of expert in knowledge in financial management, lack of co-ordination between financial institutions and the development agencies, lack of appropriate measures of expenditures, excessive procedural formalities, no-repaying tendency of borrowers are the obstacles for the financing of industrial sector.

Small-Scale Industrial Units

The definition of small-scale industry at present is related to investment ceiling on the original value of the installed plants and machinery. A small-scale industry is defined as "an industrial undertaking in which the investment in fixed assets in plant and machinery whether held in ownership terms or on lease or by hire purchase does not exceed Rs. 100 lakhs."

The most common problem regarding to small-scale industrial units in Arunachal Pradesh is not built properly from the point of economic view. Again, most of them fall in the category of tiny units. Such types of tiny units are not capable to achieve cost efficiency. Innovation cannot take place. Product design cannot be improved. The product cannot be competitive. The entrepreneur cannot render his service effectively. The small-scale sector is a very crucial sector both from the economic point of view and in the social context, as it is capable of generating direct employment for a substantial number of local people. The scope for development of this sector is wide. Greater attention should be given first so as to develop this sector. This sector can play an important role for the economic development of this state. Its role has been emphasized in the successive Industrial Policy Resolutions and Five Year Plans.

The Cottage Industries Department was established during 1953-54 in Arunachal Pradesh. Its main objective was to revitalize the traditional handicrafts, handlooms and sericulture industries with introduction of efficient tools and modern techniques.

It is observed that industrial sickness becomes a perennial trouble in the small-scale industries in this region. The main cause of industrial sickness is inadequate supply of raw materials, finance and other inputs, management inefficiency, scarcity of skilled manpower and high transport cost. If this is reduced, the present position of industrial sickness can be wiped out from this region.

Public sector should play a major role in establishing large or small-scale industries in North Eastern Region where the role of private sector is very negligible. Various social infrastructures should be developed in a coordinated way so that all the sectors of economy will be benefited by fuller exploitation of resources.

The state being a developing in position, can ill afford to ignore this most significant labour intensive and capital-sparing sector. Small industries play a key role in the industrialization of our country since they provide immediate large scale employment and have a comparatively higher labour/capital ratio; need shorter gestation period and relatively smaller markets to be economic; need lower investments; offer a method ensuring a more equitable distribution of the state income and facilitate an effective mobilization of resources of capital and skill which might otherwise remain unutilized. They stimulate the growth of industrial entrepreneurship and promote a more diffused pattern of ownership and location.

Entrepreneurial Lack

Economic development of any region is an outcome of purposeful human activity. Both the developed and the underdeveloped world look at the industrialization process as an important key to economic development. Most of the social scientists agree that man stands at the centre of economic activity and he assumes various roles in the development process, namely, as an organizer of human and material resources, worker, consumer and exchange agent. Out of these multiple roles, his role as the organizer of human and material resources is the most important and basic one.

It is widely accepted that the availability of entrepreneurship is the most important determinant in the process of industrialization. The government in its efforts to create entrepreneurship in the underdeveloped regions provides for various monetary and non-monetary incentives like the development of an infrastructure, assistance in marketing and procuring raw materials, providing finance or granting subsidies on investment. With this thrust in view, the State Governments have created various institutions to cater to the different needs of entrepreneurs.

It can be argued that lack of entrepreneurial skill of the local people and their deficient interest to invest and innovate has contributed in preventing the evolution of modern economic system in the State. One example of their lacking interest in manufacturing activities is that those tribal boys and girls who go for crafts training do not want to have their own business but like to join as craft teachers in government organizations (Krishna, 2000). The mindset of the tribal is not to establish their own enterprise or business but to venture either in politics, contract business, or government services to earn "easy money". This mindset can be termed as *psychological barrier* which has emerged very strongly in the context of present socio-political context of the State.

Corruption

The tribal of this region do not pay income tax. The national government is extending liberal financial aid to the state for her socio-economic development. An appreciable amount of this state sponsored for investment finds channelized to a new category of contractor-entrepreneur-politicians. This newly emerged neo-rich class has been to control a good amount of what is known as the 'black money'. A chunk of this is being spent in acquiring luxurious items (Sinha, 1994).

Some tribal people within a very short period of time have experienced income and wealth inequalities to a high degree. Very few of them have been found to become very rich overnight and enjoy luxurious life and prefer conspicuous consumption which has been adversely affecting the rest of the society. The income inequalities in the tribal society are very much strong. Some are very rich and some are very poor. Some peoples in rural areas are living on self-growing food and common property resource forest product without functioning of money. The presence of high degree of corruption at all levels and existence of underground economy has also gone against in development of market economy. The consumer durables and non-durables are purchased by the easily earned money or easily available credit (consumption loans) from the markets located in big cities of the country or some growing urban centres in the State. This has regrettably led to the emergence of the consumption economy without the economy of production and hence obstructed the growth of market economy.

Power Supply and Communication

Underdeveloped economic infrastructure like power supply and communication can also be held responsible for insignificant development of market institutions in Arunachal Pradesh. Perhaps, because of this, not a single case of foreign direct investment has reportedly been established in Arunachal Pradesh during the reforms period when other major States have been trying to attract foreign investment in their respective territories by reforming institutions and offering many soaps to the investors.

The modern economic development involves large-scale use of power. Regarding the set-up of an industry the state needs first some infrastructural facilities of which power is one. Due to its geographical location and its hilly terrain, Arunachal Pradesh has an immense hydel potential to use the power of water to produce electricity in comparison to the other states of the country. The State is of turbulent perennial rivers and major streams, which possess enormous hydro-electric generation potential. In addition to water resource, the stare has oil, natural gas and coal resources that can be used in the production of electricity.

Presently, there is a vast gap between the availability and the requirement of power. As per 2001 census, out of 2,12,615 households, only 116,275 households (54.7%) are having electricity facility and out of 3649 number of villages (as per 1991 census), only 2339 numbers have been electrified accounting 64 per cent of total villages till the end of March 2003. Arunachal Pradesh, having untapped estimated hydro power potential of 49,000 MW, may emerge as Power House of India when this potential is fully harnessed (*Source:* Department of Power, Government of Arunachal Pradesh), this is shown in Table 3.2. Even if a part of the available hydro potential is harnessed, the state will not only be self-sufficient in meeting its own power requirement but at the same time it can earn revenue by supplying power to the other neighbouring states of the country. During 2002-03, 35 numbers of micro/mini hydel projects with an installed capacity of 32.48 MW and diesel sets with an installed capacity of 27.12 MW are the main sources of power supply in the state though the actual power requirement is 95 MW. So the state is highly deficient in power generation.

Table 3.2: Major river basins and their potentials.

Name of the River/Basin	*Probable Hydro Potentials (MW)*			*Name of Districts*
	ROR	*Storage*	*Total*	
Kameng	3799	847	4646	W&E/Kameng
Subansiri	10141	5050	15191	U&L/Subansiri/Kurung Kumey
Siang	3557	11700	15257	W&E/Siang U/Siang
Dibang	5946	1282	7228	U & L/Dibang Valley
Lohit	3594	3075	6669	Lohit
Total Potentials	27037	21954	48991	

Source: Department of Power, Government of Arunachal Pradesh, Itanagar.

Transportation and Communication

The service of Transport and Communication is a precondition of economic development. Revolution in transport and communication would take place first before the advent of industrial revolution. It is well known fact that the prosperity of a country depends on the development of agriculture, mining, industry, services, Banking etc. But without prior development of transport and communication, any type of development is not possible of a region.

The road density i.e., road length per 100 sq. kms. is an index of economic prosperity and the standard of living of a state. Table 3.3 and Table 3.4 as shown below measures the transportation service in the state. The total length of roadways per 100 sq. kms. is adopted to mean the relative development of different areas. In terms of road length per 100 sq. kms., the position of Arunachal Pradesh is very low than any other states in the north-eastern region and again it is low in comparison to the all India average of 40.78 kms., 62.8 kms. and 74.9 kms. per 100 sq. kms. in 1980, 1992 and 1997 respectively. Table 3.3 also shows that between 1980, 1992 and 1997, the road density has increased to a great extent in all the hilly states of North-East India. It signifies that there is a massive investment in building transport system. But the road length per 100 sq. kms. is much more below the requirement. It cannot act as a boost either to modernization of agriculture or to industrialization of the state. Category-wise of roads length in terms of surfaced, un-surfaced, road length per 100 sq. kms., road length per 1000 population and percentage of surface road to total road are shown in Table 3.3 for all states in north east India.

Table 3.3: The Road Length per 100 sq. kms. among the States of North Eastern Region of India, 1980, 1990 and 1997.

State/India	Road length per 100 sq. kms in 1980	Road length per 100 sq. kms in 1992	Road length per 100 sq. kms in 1997
Arunachal Pradesh	5.97	11.9	16.8
Assam	46.62	87.8	87.2
Manipur	28.54	30.3	49.0
Meghalaya	16.16	34.9	37.8
Mizoram	13.89	17.6	22.9
Nagaland	33.76	53.1	110.7
Tripura	51.40	124.1	140.5
All India	40.98	62.8	74.9

Source: (i) Basic Statistics of North-Eastern Region, 1980.
(ii) Basic Statistics of North-Eastern Region, 1994.
(iii) Basic Statistics of North-Eastern Region, 2002.

Table 3.4: Road Length (As on 31.03.1997).

State	Total	Surfaced	Un-surfaced	Road length per 100 sq. kms.	Road per 1000 population	Percentage of surface road to total road length
1	2	3	4	5	6	7
Arunachal Pradesh	14092	3991	10101	16.8	12.81	28.32
Assam	68418	11590	56828	87.2	2.70	16.94
Manipur	10941	3598	7343	49.0	4.75	32.88

(Contd...)

(Table 3.4 Contd...)

Meghalaya	8480	3923	4557	37.8	3.86	46.26
Mizoram	4829	1983	2846	22.9	5.36	41.10
Nagaland	18356	5241	13115	110.7	12.241	28.55
Tripura	14729	4577	10152	140.5	4.33	31.10
Total	139845	34903	104942	54.8	3.81	24.96
All India	2465877	1394081	1071796	74.9	2.58	58.68

Source: Basic Road Statistics of India 1996-97, Ministry of Surface Transport.

Table 3.3 shows the density of road is lowest in Arunachal Pradesh as on 31.03.1997. That is, the state is much behind the rest of the North Eastern states in this regard. As such in the development plans, the government has been attaching high priority to the construction of roads and as a result the total length of roads constructed in the state stood at about 15021.80 kms. including 399.80 kms. under National Highway giving the road density of 17.9 kms. per 100 sq. kms. of area at the end of March, 2004 as against the all India average of 74.9 kms. per 100 sq. kms. during 1997. Category-wise length of road for the last five years with road density is shown in Table 3.5.

Table 3.5: Category-wise Length of Roads and its Density During 9th Plan.

(In. km)

Year	*Black topped*	*Surfaced*	*Un-surfaced*	*Total length of roads*	*Density of roads*
1	*2*	*3*	*4*	*5*	*6*
31.03.2000	4853.93	2182.615	6945.655	13982.20	16.70
31.03.2001	4853.93	2182.615	6945.655	13982.20	16.70
31.03.2002	4853.93	2182.615	6945.655	13982.20	16.70
31.03.2003	5805.416	2496.648	6148.406	14450.47	17.26
31.03.2004	5679.87	3761.13	5127.85	15021.791	17.94

Source: Directorate of Economics and Statistics, Government of Arunachal Pradesh, Itanagar.

Note: Density of Road = Total length of roads ÷ total area.

The above Table 3.5 indicates that out of total length of roads, 15021.791 kms. in 2003-04, only 38.98 per cent are black topped, 25.81 per cent are surfaced and rest 35.19 per cent are un-surfaced.

The progress of development of transport is not up to the expectation. Although the length of roads in the state has increased from 168 kms. in 1947 to 15021.791 kms. in March 31, 2004, a large part of the state particularly the higher belt in the northern part are either inaccessible or ill served by the existing transport facilities. For example, Anini, the district headquarters of Dibang Valley district does not have an all-weather road with the plans even till today. Again, a peculiarity of surface transport of the state is that most of the district headquarters are not interconnected, i.e., one cannot move from one district headquarter to other specially the old district headquarters in Arunachal Pradesh without going down to Assam. The state does not have lateral roads connecting district headquarters and sub-divisional headquarters of the districts. In other places, roads run vertically connecting places of Assam with the places of district headquarters in the State. As a result, the transport cost is not only high but also the state is affected by disturbances and insurgency activities in Assam.

Arunachal Pradesh being predominantly hilly terrain, there is a lot of constraints in the development of railways. In fact, the state was brought under the railway map of India for the first time with the opening of Balipara (near Tezpur, Assam) to Bhalukpong in West Kameng District of Arunachal Pradesh in 1989 with only 1.26 kms. (metre gauze).

Conclusion

The various institutional rigidities such as non-existence of private property, poor infrastructural facilities, restriction in free entry by imposing *Inner-line Permit* system, insurgency problem, traditional and psychological barriers, lack of entrepreneurial skill and incentive, no plan of the government to establish free trade zone or growth centre are to be addressed by reforming the existing institutions for market institutions. The primitive mode of production can't be broken unless suitable institutional arrangement for creation of attractive incentive is done. Main reforms of government institutions related to *withdrawal of inner line permit and license policy* are very urgent to ensure easy entry of investment and skill labour force into the territory for industrialization. In this way, employment of local people will increase and thereby insurgency problem will automatically disappear.

In fact, the history of human society shows that civilization everywhere has been built by the contact and intercourse of peoples, which has been the chief motivating power behind progress. There are innumerable instances of the borrowing of cultural traits by peoples of different countries, such as articles of food, use of metals, domesticated animals, method of agriculture and spread of literacy. So long as the borrowing has been natural and in harmony with cultural setting and the psychological make-up of the people, it has been intensely beneficial and even added to the richness of their culture. (T. Mibang, 1994). This remarks favour less restriction of entrance of Non-Arunachalees in the State.

To strengthen the economy of the State, the Government should provide larger scope to the private sector. At the same time, a number of changes in policy should be introduced with regard to industrial licensing to the non-tribal, removal of Inner Line, technology upgradation, fiscal policy, removal of controls and restrictions, rationalizing and simplifying the system of fiscal and administrative regulation and improving law and order problems so as to encourage for free flow of goods, capital, technology and labour from other States to this State. All these changes will be directed towards creating on uninhabited climate for private sector so that private sector investment can get a big boost to modernize the economy approaching towards global economy.

REFERENCES

Chattopadhyay, A.K. and Ghoshal, R.K.(2006): "WTO and India's External Sector:Trends and Prospects" Artha Beekshan, *Journal of Bangiya Arthaniti Parishad* (Bengal Economic Association) Vol. 15, No. 3, p. 20-22.

Desai, N.R. (1960): "Agricultural Marketing in M.P", *Agricultural Marketing*, Vol. III, No. 1, p. 43.

Elwin, Verrier (1957): *"A Philosophy for NEFA": Forwarded by the then Prime Minister, Shri Jawaharlal Nehru,*—Shillong, Sachin Roy on behalf of the North-East Frontier Agency, p. 59.

Ibid., p. 53.

Ghumare, S.A. and Nagori V.R. (2007): "FDI and Globalization in India" *Southern Economist*, Vol. 46, No. 3, pp. 39-42.

Krishna, Sumi (2000): "Arunachal Pradesh", in M.S. Swaminathan (ed.) *Gender Dimensions in Bio-Diversity Management*.

Mandal, R.K. (2005): "Arunachal Economy: Socio-Economic Transformation", Champion Publications, Itanagar, pp. 2-4.

Mandal, R.K. (2006): "Constraints of Economic Development in Arunachal Pradesh with Special Reference to Globalisation and Inner Line System" Artha Beekshan, *Journal of Bangiya Arthaniti Parishad* (Bengal Economic Association) Vol. 15, No. 3, p. 78.

Mandal, R.K. (2007): "Inner line System and Growth of Arunachal Economy-Some controversial Issues", *Journal of North-East India Council for Social Science Research*, Vol. 31, No.1, April, North-East India Council for Social Science Research, Shillong-3, Meghalaya.

Mandal, R.K. (2008): "Inclusive Development in Arunachal Pradesh: Opportunities and Challenges in the Present Economic Environment", *Arunachal Review*, Vol. X, No. 2., June-August, Directorate of Information, Public Relations and Printing, Government of Arunachal Pradesh, Naharlagun. Arunachal Pradesh.

Mandal, R.K. (2008): Inner Line System in Arunachal Pradesh (Is it necessary in the 21st Century?), *Arunachal Review*, Vol. IX, No. 24, Dec., 2007-Feb., 2008, Directorate of Information, Public Relations and Printing, Government of Arunachal Pradesh, Naharlagun. Arunachal Pradesh.

Memoria, C.B. and Tripathi, B.B., (1989): *"Agricultural Problems of Indians"*, Kitab Mahal Agencies, p. 600.

Mibang, T. (1988): *"Social Change in Arunachal Pradesh"*, Omsons Publication, Rajouri Garden, New Delhi, p. 74.

Osik, N.N. (1999): *"Modern History of Arunachal Pradesh"*, Himalayan Publishers, Itanagar, New Delhi, p. 1-2.

Raghurama, A., (Feb. 1, 2005): "Globalisation and Challenges for Small-Scale Sector in India", *Southern Economist*, Bangalore, Vol. 43, No. 19, p. 13.

Ruddar, D. and Sundharam, K.P.M. (2004): *"Indian Economy"*, S. Chand and Company Ltd., Ram Nagar, New Delhi, p. 247.

Ibid., p. 810

Ruttan, V.W. and Jujiro Hayami (1984): "Towards a Theory of Induced Institutional Innovation", *Journal of Development Studies*, Vol. 20, pp. 203-223.

Uphoff, Norman (1991): *"Managing Irrigation: Analyzing and Improving the Performance of Bureaucracies"*, Sage Publication India Pvt. Ltd., New Delhi.

World Investment Report (WIR), 2004 and 2005.

Wolf, Jr. Charles (1955): "Institutions and Economic Development, *American Economic Review*", December, pp. 867-883.

Borocz, Jozsef (2005): "Globalization and the management of Indian cities", *EPW*, Vol. XXXVIII, No. 25, p. 2535.

Sengupta, Arjun (2000): "Managing Globalization", *EPW*, Vol. XXXIX, No. 6, 2004, p. 549-51.

Sinha, A.C. (1994): "*North-Eastern Frontier of India: Structural Imperatives and Aspects of Change*", Indus Publishing Company, New Delhi, p. 211.

Sreenivasulu, A. (2007): "Issues in FDI—A Bird's Eye View" *Southern Economist*, Vol. 46, No. 6, Bangalore, pp. 17-19.

Khanna, D. and Verma, R. (2006): "Agriculture: Where does the problem lie?", *Journal of Global Economy*, April-June, Vol. 2, No. 2, p. 77.

4

Information Technology with Special Reference to Post Office and Telecommunication

Introduction

No important field of human endeavour remains immune to its influence and no comer of life is left undisturbed. The social application of the advances has resulted in network systems, electronic shopping and banking, business data and government information systems. It gives rise to hopes of an information-rich society. The plain old telephone service is transformed to an image/fax/data/voice network with global connectivity and a gateway to the information superhighway. These innovations have led to the development of new interactive media like e-mail (electronic-mail), online information, video conferencing, etc. They have become great facilitators for faster information flow and quicker decision-making. To say that these developments have been instrumental in eroding the barriers between nations and reduced the entire globe into a village, it is not an exaggeration. Coupled with this is the Indian reality of opening up its economy. Indian economy is getting integrated into world economy. Globalization has become the catch phrase. In this process one needs to interact with people around the world in order to exchange and share views and negotiate terms. As all this is conveniently done in English, English has acquired a great significance for global communication. English is also used as the international language of Information Technology (IT) in general. In fact, the relation between English and IT may be described as symbiotic, each benefiting from the other.

Information Technology (IT) exerts universal appeal in the world of today. It is identified in many countries as perhaps the single most important means to the attainment of economic, social and political ends. Information is that which adds to our awareness or understanding of some topic, problem or event. It is variously perceived as facts, intelligence, data, news and knowledge. It can be printed on paper or can come in the form of computer software, electronic mail, videotex and video, compact audio or optical digital disk, etc. Information is the lifeblood of education. It is the essential ingredient in new ideas, in course content and curriculum development, and in the creation of materials and methods for teaching and learning. The new technologies enhance one's ability in the production and dissemination of this educational information, and its management and control.

The term 'Information Technology' (IT) today is a shifting complex of meanings and interpretations. A simple definition put forward in an exhibition by the Department of Trade and Industry, Great Britain, encompasses information use and content as well as technology itself: "Information Technology is the acquisition, processing, storage, dissemination and use of vocal, pictorial, textual and numerical information by a micro-electronics based combination of computing and telecommunications." Information technology revolution is essentially the product of advances in the three key areas of computing, telecommunications and micro-electronics.

Globalization is an inevitable and irreversible process of economic technological, social and political integration of the world and an economy should capitalize on its positive aspect. In globalization, the domestic economy is opened to the world economy. Major characteristics of globalization include information technology, integration, the Worldwide Web, homogenization and speed-speed of travel, commerce, communication and innovation. The process of globalization is being fuelled by revolution. With IT we have entered a structural transition of global dimension which can be termed as Fourth Logistical Revolution (Anderson, 1886).The earlier revolutions were the Agricultural Revolution, Industrial Revolution (management of large production and distribution systems, vertical integration and introduction of railways) and mass production of automobiles for transport and telephones for order. The fourth revolution is the information and Commerce Revolution. The global IT industry offers India and Indian centric companies unique opportunities in four areas: e-business, value added IT services, software products and IT enabled services (Tikendrajit and Ningombam, 2007).

Globalization and Information technology are two sides of the same coin. If globalization is the end, information technology is the means to achieve that end. Today the whole world can be in one's palm in the form of a palmtop. As a result, the impact of information technology can be felt everywhere—offices, factories, homes, educational institutions, hospitals, railway stations, airports, bus stations, restaurants, giftcorners, grocery shops, and so on. Information Technology seems to be the master technology at present. Previously science used to provide the base for technology. Now the role seems to have been reversed, for no science can advance without the necessary technological base. Even fine arts cannot flourish without technological props. A.R. Rahman's heart-throbbing songs speak volumes for the influence of technology on the common man. "The impact of the microprocessor on society may be as great as that of the automobile or electric light" says the President of the Indian Library Association, Mr. P.N. Kaula (1996: 8).

The main constraint to economic development of our country which is well felt for a long time is infrastructural bottlenecks. Transport, communication, power and other infrastructural facilities are very vital for economic development. Poor quality of infrastructural facility implies higher economic cost, which adversely affects the economic growth and economic development (Parikh, 2007)

Telecommunication infrastructure and economic development are tightly linked. The adequate level of telecommunication infrastructure in a country is necessary both from a policy and a business point of view. Rapid expansion of IT enabled services especially e-commerce and e-governance in the past few years has made the government forced to provide adequate telecommunication infrastructure (Chrishna *et al.*, 1999). Therefore, making the development of an adequate telecommunication infrastructure has become one of the major goals of policy makers. Telecommunication infrastructure consists of many components.It is a combination of civil works, towers, antennae and cables, coupled with hardware and software comprising access, switches and transmission systems all combine to constitute the telecommunication infrastructure. Optical fibre cables, terrestrial wireless, satellite system and internet are all key components of the modern infrastructure (Singh, 2007).

The Telecommunication services were introduced in India soon after the invention of telegraphy and telephone. The first Telegraph line between Kolkata and Dimond Harbour was opened for traffic in 1851. By March 1884, Telegraph messages could be sent from Agra to Kolkata. As in the case of telegraph, telephone service was also introduced in Kolkata in 1881-82, barely six years after the invention of telephone. By 1900, telegraph and telephone started serving Indian Railways. The first automatic exchange was commissioned at Shimla in 1913-14 with a capacity of 700 lines. During the last decade or so, the Indian telecom sector has seen continued liberalization. Telecom services, which were the sole monopoly of the government till1994, were opened to the private sector. The National Telecom Policy announced in 1994 separated the functions of the government from those of providing services, and allowed the private sector to provide telephone services. In 1998, New Internate policy went to effect: ISP business opened up to the operators other than DOT (Department of Telecommunications) and VSNL (Videsh Sanchar Nigam Limited). The policy was further liberalized in 1999 (Rastogi, 2003). The Department of Telecommunications (DOT) was corporatized in the year 2000 with the creation of BSNL (Bharat Sanchar Nigam Limited). The National Long Distance Services on the domestic routes, that were the sole monopoly of the government, were also opened to the private sector in the year 2001 (Kulkarni, 2003). In the same year, International Long Distance (ILD) sector opened to competition by ending VSNL monopoly and in April government allowed restricted IP Telephony. And very recently in 2004, government announced a new broadband policy as'New Broadband Policy, 2004'. In 2005, FDI ceiling in telecom services increased from 49 per cent to 75 per cent. Entry fee for National and International Long Distance licenses reduced to $50 million from $22 million and $5.5 million respectively (Singh, 2007)

No important field of human endeavour remains immune to its influence and no corner of life is left undisturbed. The social application of these advances resulted in network systems, electronic shopping and banking, business data and government information systems. It gave rise to hopes of an information-rich society. The plain old telephone service is transformed to an image/ fax/data/voice network with global connectivity and a gateway to the information superhighway. These innovations led to the development of new interactive media like e-mail (electronic-mail), online information, video conferencing, etc. They have become great facilitators for faster information flow and quicker decision-making. To say that these developments have been instrumental in eroding the barriers between nations and reduced the entire globe into a village is not an exaggeration. Coupled with this is the Indian reality of opening up its economy. Indian economy is getting integrated into world economy. Globalization has become the catch phrase. In this process one needs to interact with people around the world, exchange and share views and negotiate terms. As all this is conveniently done in English, English has acquired a great significance for global communication. English is also used as the international language of IT in general. In fact, the relation between English and IT may be described as symbiotic, each benefiting from the other.

Globalization in India

Today no country in the world, including India, can afford to isolate itself from the ongoing rapid process of globalization. Economic liberalization in India is almost a decade old phenomenon. A number of multinational companies have come into the country. Corporatization of huge public sector undertakings has already taken place. Indian Airlines Limited, Indian Oil Corporation Limited, Oil and Natural Gas Corporation Limited, Gas Authority of India Limited, and so on are good examples of this process. Disinvestment from many public sector undertakings is on the card. In course of time the university system is likely to be privatized. People have begun to realize that resistance is of no use. Utter disillusionment with the 60 years of Indian Independence seems to be working behind many of the privatizing initiatives.

As the advocates of globalization have pointed out, it is essentially a means of meaningful growth and development. India can catch the markets of other countries as others will have their markets ın India. Now goods and services of international standards can be made available to the common people. Most of the unhealthy monopolized trade practices can be checked. The non-productive and non-viable economic sectors will be compelled to arise from their long slumber. The people of all sectors now realize that they have to work to earn their bread and not treat the customer's non-chalantly.

There are also disadvantages of this globalization, especially to the poorer sections of the society whose earning and buying capacity is next to nothing. The small scale industries will have to face the challenges from the multinationals. India, having the second largest population in the world, will have to look after the food, shelter, clothing, health, education, and employment of the illiterate and unskilled people. In Professor Amartya Sen's words, Indian economy has to be people-oriented as against the multinational economy, which is commodity-based. As the well-known industrialist from Tamil Nadu Dr. N. Mahalingam has emphasized, Gandhian economic principles cannot be sacrificed, if the whole of India has to survive.

Whatever, the consequences, India is very much in the thick of globalization. Even some of the sensitive sectors like telecommunications and defence have partially been liberalized. Gradually more such sectors are being thrown open to foreign direct investments.

Impact of Information Technology

Globalization and Information Technology are two sides of the same coin. If globalization is the end, information technology is the means to achieve that end. Today the whole world can be in one's palm in the form of a palmtop. As a result, the impact of information technology can be felt everywhere - offices, factories, homes, educational institutions, hospitals, railway stations, airports, bus stations, restaurants, giftcorners, grocery shops, and so on. Information Technology seems to be the master technology at present. Previously science was used to provide the base for technology. Now the role seems to have been reversed, for no science can advance without the necessary technological base. Even fine arts cannot flourish without technological props. A.R. Rahman's heart-throbbing songs speak volumes for the influence of technology on the common man. "The impact of the micro-processor on society may be as great as that of the automobile or electric light" says the President of the Indian Library Association, Mr. P.N. Kaula.

North-east is geographically isolated, infrastructural backward and predominantly a tribal region. It is located on the international border and this is one of the two meso-regions in the country, which is land-locked. These states are not only ethnically distinct, but also the homes of small ethnic groups, which are not only isolated on the undulating topography, but technologically backward. It is presumed that with the opening of the new telecasting stations, the remote areas will be linked to the national mainstream. The Post and Telegraph Department was created by the British administration as an adjunct to effective administrative control over Indian people. The department was run on the cost-benefit consideration. However, it was also established 'to serve the people' (those who could afford to). The department was rather slow in adopting new technological innovations. But it did increase its network to the length and breadth of the country and with the dawn of independence, the department was geared to the cause of the national priorities and programmes. As a government department, it slowly turned out to be one of the biggest employers of unskilled and semi-skilled persons. With the massive emphasis on rural development and overall demand for social transformation, the department did try to modernize itself technologically to meet the ever increasing demands on it. As a whole, this modernization phase in the department is largely based on technological transfer. No serious efforts are being made to ask whether the technological transfer fits in the national policy of self-reliance. In fact, its adoption is based on the principle of trickling down benefits from the top and what is known as technological diffusion. So far North Eastern region in general and Arunachal Pradesh in particular is concerned, it is not only inaccessible from transport, communication and telecommunication point of view, but it is also economically at subsistence level. By tradition, the vital resources - land, water, forest and even minerals are controlled by the community, in which technological investment is minimal.

Revolution in information and communication technology has drastically changed the very concept of connectivity. It has reduced distances and made possible to disperse business operations by taking advantage of differentials in wage, natural and other resource endowments and thus to bring down dramatically the production cost. The Indian postal network is one of the largest networks in the world in terms of area covered and population served, and constitutes an important mechanism of achieving transportation and communication. The Indian Postal System currently provides 38 services which can broadly be divided into four categories: Communication services (Letters, Post Cards etc.), Transportation services (Parcel), Financial services (Saving Bank, Money Order, Postal Life Insurance) and Premium Value Added Services (Like Speed Post, Business Post). The Post Office Savings Bank is the largest bank in India in terms of network, accounts and annual deposits. As on March 31, 2004, there were 1, 55,669 post offices or outlets, of which roughly 89 per cent were outside cities in the country (*Economic Survey* 2004-05, p. 203).

In the changed industrial system of recent technological progress, innovation and application of sophisticated knowledge to production process have become inevitably common. They are indispensable too. The technological progress encourages interdependence between the enterprises and the environment. The application of sophisticated technical process to an enterprise takes two forms: (a) first is product innovation, that is to say, the innovation in goods and services produced and the programmes of work involved therein which is known as programme change and (b) second is technological innovation that is to say, the innovation in terms of technique applied to production. The use of the term technology is restricted to the visible items of capital equipment used in the work-flows of an enterprise and the relationship of the operations to which the same is applied.

Technological progress is normally associated with environmental change and complexity with the growth of more sophisticated information technology which is increasingly relevant to various functions of an enterprise. The technological progress simultaneously pressures towards growing scale. Obviously, technological progress is associated with closer relations between enterprises and governmental agencies, which bear the tendency to wean away enterprise autonomous power with corresponding magnitude. Besides, product differentiation on account of technological progress, growing scale of production, actions of trade unions, consumer organization and government policies also erode the power of business enterprise (Bose, 230-31). All types of technological development depends more or less on the development of information technology.

Objectives

This paper intends to highlight some economic issues pertaining to discuss the development of IT in the North-East in general and in Arunachal Pradesh in particular.

Methodology

This study is based on both primary and secondary data. While secondary data have been collected from different reports and journals, primary data have been collected through personal investigation from the VSNL personnels. Simple numerical calculations, graphical representations have been used to analyze data.

Case Study of Arunachal Pradesh: Development of Post Offices

No regular attempt had been made to rise in the scale of civilization or to provide any system of direct administration in the north-east region of India, though the Frontier Tracts were divided into three charges in 1914; and in 1919 the names of the Eastern and Western Sections of the Frontier Tracts were changed into Sadiya Frontier Tract and Balipara Frontier Tract, respectively. Roads, postal communication, schools, hospitals and so on, did not exist. Practically, the tribes were living in a paradise of their own almost ignorant of the outside world.

The crude agency created by the British to administer the tribal territories began to develop after independence. At the time of independence there were altogether three Political Officers for the Frontier territories and a few sub-staff to cater to the needs of their offices. Immediately after the independence, the administration of the Frontier Tracts was placed at the disposal of the Government of Assam by Indian Independence Act, 1947, and in 1948 Sadiya Frontier Tract was bifurcated into two charges of Abor Hills and Mishmi Hills. The Constituent Assembly of India viewed the problem of Tribal development carefully and appointed a Committee to investigate and report for a rational administration of the tribals of Assam.

There were 6 post offices in 1953 and the number increased to 70 in 1970. Three post offices in 1956 and 16 in 1972 had telegraph facilities. The development of communication was thus poor (Bhattacharjee, p. 175). As on 31.3.1993, there were 266 number of post offices, 18 post offices had telegraph facilities. During the period, population served per post offices was 3,250. But according to CMIE, there were 269 post offices in the State during 1992-93 with population per post office as 2974 and area served by a post office (sq. km.) as 311.15 which is highest in the country. The vastness of the area served by a post office is unavoidable because of low density and dispersed nature of human habitation. A comparative picture of post offices in North- East India is shown in Table 4.1 given below.

Table 4.1: Post Offices in Arunachal Pradesh—a Comparative Study, (1992-93).

Sl. No.	*States*	*No. of post offices*			*Population per post office*	*Area served by a post office (sq. km)*
		Total	*Urban*	*Rural*		
1	2	3	4	5	6	7
1.	Arunachal Pradesh	269	13	256	2974	311.15
2.	Assam	3780	300	3480	6772	22.31
3.	Manipur	660	35	625	2727	33.33
4.	Meghalaya	470	31	439	3830	44.65
5.	Mizoram	362	39	323	1934	58.00
6.	Nagaland	294	19	275	4082	56.11
7.	Tripura	689	49	640	3774	15.08
8.	All India	152037	16283	135754	5607	21.60

Source: Directorate of Economics and Statistics, Government of Arunachal Pradesh, "Statistical Abstract, 1992", Itanagar.

From Table 4.1, we find that population per post office was 2974 in Arunachal Pradesh – the third lowest in the North-Eastern States after Mizoram and Manipur and fifth lowest after Himachal Pradesh and Sikkim in all India. The area served by a Post Office is extremely high in the State (Bhattacharjee, p. 95-96).

In 1973, there were 73 post offices of which 16 had telegraph facilities. This increased to 283 in 1995 of which 17 had telegraph offices (Bhattacharjee, p. 211).

In respect of communications, total number of post offices with telegraphic facilities is noted 28 and without telegraphic facilities 166 during 1979-80. Now telecommunication facility is available, but its effect cannot be experienced on account of inadequate infrastructure. Telephone connections are confined to few pockets only, and therefore, their effects are localized so far (Jha, p.196). In the state the growth of post offices since 1960 onwards is shown in Table 4.2, percentage of villages with postal and telegraph facilities on the basis of distance covered (1991) in Table 4.3, percentage of rural population with access to post and telegraph facilities on the basis of distance covered (1991) in Table 4.4 and number of postal institutions with telegraph facilities as on 31.3. 2001 in Table 4.5 given below.

Table 4.2: Growth of Postal Facilities in Arunachal Pradesh (1961-2001).

Year	*No. of Post Office*	*Population per Post Office*	*Area served by Post Office (sq.km.)*
1960-61	23	14,632	3,641
1970-71	70	6,678	1,196.33
1980-81	200	3,159	418.72
1990-91	249	3,447	363.32
2000-01	303	3,388	276.38

Source: Statistical Abstracts of Arunachal Pradesh.

Table 4.3: Percentage of Villages with Postal and Telegraph Facilities on the Basis of Distance Covered (1991).

Districts	*0 km*	*0-5 km*	*5-10 km*	*Above 10 km*
Tawang	5.52	33.13	28.83	32.52
West Kameng	4.78	8.82	11.77	74.63
East Kameng	4.36	11.27	8.00	76.37
Papum Pare	2.66	14.45	13.31	69.58
Lower Subansiri	2.19	11.76	12.77	73.28
Upper Subansiri	2.50	8.15	9.60	79.75
West Siang	4.90	25.49	16.18	53.43
East Siang	13.24	22.55	12.25	51.96
Dibang Valley	10.08	14.29	10.50	65.13
Lohit	6.78	21.97	15.81	55.44
Changlang	8.42	28.42	15.09	48.07
Tirap	15.38	10.90	17.31	56.41
Arunachal Pradesh	5.76	17.04	13.70	63.50

Source: Census of India, 1991, District Census Handbook of different districts of Arunachal Pradesh.

Note: Postal facilities are calculated on the basis that there is at least one extra-departmental branch post office in the villages, i.e., at least, basic facilities are available where postcards, stamps, etc., are sold, and a letter box is maintained.

Table 4.4: Percentage of Rural Population with Access to Post and Telegraph Facilities on the Basis of Distance Covered (1991).

Districts	*0 km*	*0-5 km*	*5-10 km*	*Above 10 km*
Tawang	23.56	36.59	18.69	21.16
West Kameng	35.88	10.49	10.31	43.32
East Kameng	26.22	9.59	10.64	53.55
Papum Pare	22.97	13.30	17.44	46.29
Lower Subansiri	18.10	13.95	11.82	56.13
Upper Subansiri	32.94	7.72	7.43	51.91
West Siang	23.20	18.82	15.32	42.66
East Siang	30.58	23.94	8.84	36.64
Dibang Valley	51.38	20.92	4.34	23.36
Lohit	29.10	30.79	13.15	26.96

(Contd...)

(*Table 4.4 Contd...*)

Changlang	27.08	33.13	9.05	30.74
Tirap	25.26	15.83	8.27	50.64
Arunachal Pradesh	27.94	20.29	10.99	40.78

Source: Census of India, 1991, District Census Handbook of different districts of Arunachal Pradesh.

Table 4.5: Number of Postal Institutions and Telegraph Facilities in Arunachal Pradesh as on 31-3-2001.

Districts	*No. of Post Offices*	*No. of Telegraph Facilities*
Tawang	13	1
West Kameng	22	3
East Kameng	14	1
Papum Pare	25	3
Lower Subansiri	23	1
Upper Subansiri	13	1
West Siang	28	2
East Siang	30	2
Upper Siang	10	3
Dibang Valley	22	2
Lohit	45	5
Changlang	28	5
Tirap	30	2
Arunachal Pradesh	303	31

Source: Statistical Abstract of Arunachal Pradesh, 2001.

The postal and telecommunication services in the State are growing steadily in the recent years. There were one Head Post Office, 48 Sub-Post Offices and 256 EDBPO's functioning in the state at the end of 2003-04. Thus, during 2003-04 the average area and population served by each post office were 207.77 sq. kms. and 3675 persons respectively. The growth of post offices is shown in Table 4.6 given below.

Table 4.6: Growth of Post Offices in Arunachal Pradesh Since 2000.

Sl.No.	*Indicator*	*Unit*	*Post Offices as on 31st March*				
			2000	*2001*	*2002*	*2003*	*2004*
1.	Post offices	No.	301	303	304	305	305
	(a) Head post office	No.	1	1	1	1	1
	(b) Sub-post office	No.	46	46	47	47	48
	(c) E.D.B.P.O.	No.	254	256	256	257	256
2.	Telegraph office	No.	21	21	31	31	-
3.	Population served per post office	Person	3005	3601	3675	3675	3675
4.	Area served by one post office	Sq. Km	278	276	207	207	207

Source: Director of Postal Services, Itanagar.

Development of Telecommunication

After the announcement of New Telecom Policy 1999, progress in telecom in India has been extremely rapid. The structure and composition of telecom growth has undergone a substantial change in terms of mobile *versus* fixed phones and public *versus* private participation. Mobile phones were once considered a luxury. In recent years, it has become clear that the capital costs of mobile telephony are lower, which makes mobile telephony the technology of choice for low-price telephony. Few areas of India's economy have enjoyed as sharp a pace of structural change as that in the telecom sector. The rapid pace was the outcome of vigorous competition among firms and technologies. This drastic pace of structural change highlights the possibilities in other segments of infrastructure for eliciting massive investment by the private sector and for benefiting the consumers through competition between old and new technologies. The total number of telephones (basic and mobile) rose from 22.8 million in 1999 to 88.62 million at the end of October, 2004 in India. Although India's 88.62 million (2004-05) strong telephone network, including mobile phones, is one of the largest in the world, with the low telephone penetration rate of about 8.20 phones per hundred population, the country offers vast scope for growth of its present projections which suggests that by the end of 2007, the total number of phones will reach 250 million in India. While tele-density (number of telephones per 100 people) has risen sharply, India continues to lag far behind countries like Brazil and China, where the tele-density is more than 40 as shown in Table 4.7.

Table 4.7: International Comparison of Tele-density, December, 2003.

Countries	*Tele-density*
Australia	126.18
Bangladesh	1.56
Brazil	42.38
China	42.32
India	6.60
Indonesia	9.17
Nepal	1.70
Pakistan	4.42
Sri Lanka	9.57
U.K.	143.13
U.S.A.	116.43

Source: ITU.

Some important policies are taken to develop the telecom sector. In order to 'catch up', there is a need to maintain vigorous pre-competitive efforts in terms of public policy, rapidly shift to new technologies, encourage entry of new players, and drive prices down through competition. The policy initiatives taken in the telecom sector recently address some of these issues.

Evolution of Telecommunication in Arunachal Pradesh

1. Establishment Year: First telephone exchange was installed at Bomdila in 1968.
2. In 25th May, 1974, SDOT in Arunachal Pradesh was created under DE(T), Guwahati. The SDOT (Tezpur) and AE Phones (Military), Tezpur looked the charges of SDOT of Arunachal Pradesh. Mr. K.C.Mukherjee was the first SDOT of Arunachal Pradesh.
3. On May 1976, the Office of SDOT of Arunachal Pradesh was shifted from Tezpur to North Lakhimpur.

4. On 31st December, 1979, the same office was shifted from North Lakhimpur to Itanagar, capital of Arunachal Pradesh. At that time, there were 15 working exchanges.
5. In December,1985, it was converted to DET Office under the control of Area Manager, Dibrugarh, Mr. Motilal, who joined as DET. At that time the entire North-East was under the administrative control of North-East Circle, Shillong.
6. In 1987, the post of DET was upgraded to TDM. Mr. M. Ukeel was the first TDM.
7. In the year 1988, the North-East Circle was bifurcated into two Telecom Circles: one circle with headquarters at Guwahati and another circle with headquarters at Shillong as North-East Circle. The DET, Arunachal Pradesh was under the control of CGM, North-East Circle, Shillong.
8. On 27th May, 1999, the post of TDM was upgraded to GMTD. Mr. A.S. Egaya was the first GMTD of Arunachal Pradesh.
9. In the year 2000, North-East Circle, Shillong was further bifurcated into NE-I Circle covering the area of Meghalaya, Mizoram, Tripura with HQ at Shillong and NE-II Circle covering the area of Arunachal Pradesh, Manipur, Nagaland with HQ at Dimapur. At the beginning there were approximately 500 connections.

Over the past years the State has been making slow and steady progress in creating telecommunication network. The state is at present divided into eight Telecom-Sub-Divisions, viz; Itanagar, Naharlagun, Bomdila, Tezu, Pasighat, Anini, Khonsa and Changlang. The number of telephone exchanges in the state at the end of 31-3-2004 was 105 as against 95 at the end of 31-3-2002. The total equipped capacity has increased from 82868 during 2002-03 to 83,000 during 2003-04. The total number of working telephone connections which was 53,862 at the end of March, 2003 has increased to 57,700 at the end of March, 2004 registering a rise of about 7.25 per cent over the year. The achievement made during 2001 to 2004 in Arunachal Pradesh is highlighted in the Table 4.8 given below.

Table 4.8: Growth of Telecommunication Facilities for the Public for Last Four Years (up to March 2004).

Sl. No.	*Indicator*	*Unit*	*As on March*			
			2001	*2002*	*2003*	*2004*
1	2	3	4	5	6	7
1.	Telephone Exchange	No.	94	95	105	105
2.	Total Capacity	No.	62816	73208	82868	83000
3.	Working telephone connection	No.	39269	44388	53862	57700
4.	No. of Mobile connections	No.	NA	NA	NA	3750
5.	Internet Connection	No.	53	NA	NA	1107

Source: General Manager, BSNL, Itanagar.

The USOF has been entrusted with the responsibility for setting up infrastructure for providing Mobile Services in rural and remote areas, which have not been covered with wireless signal (August, 2007). The three service providers will share each of the towers. In Arunachal Pradesh, Bharat Sanchar Nigam Limited (BSNL) is the infrastructure provider and Reliance Telecom Limited, Dishnet Wireless Limited and BSNL are Universal Service Providers sharing the tower.

The entire state has been divided into seven clusters and 62 numbers of sites have been selected all over the state for setting up of the towers. The state government has to provide the land and power connection up to the tower sites and share the responsibility of removal of problems that may arise during the execution of the scheme. The state government will also nominate a coordinating officer for liaison with the Department of Telecommunication (DOT) (*Arunachal Review*, Vol. VIII, No. 22, June-August, 2007, p. 31).

The Role of Telecom in the Process of Development

The role that telecom plays in development has remained obscure because of difficulty in measuring its impact. Such difficulties arise because of its point-to-point benefits i.e., telecom generates immense indirect benefits to the users and local economy, which is difficult to be measured statistically. In addition to the direct benefits to the users, its social benefits are likely to contribute to improve the quality of life in rural areas. These emphases reflect current concern with equity, decentralization and self-reliance. To achieve these goals, developing nations such as ours must pay greater attention to rural human development (Hudson, H.E.: 1984). As it is considered to be a socio-economic need of the bulk of the population residing in rural areas, it has to be provided on a subsidized basis. It is imperative to expect certain level of infrastructural, economic and administrative activities to reach for expecting an appreciable rate of even indirect benefits. "Although telecommunications can be used on occasion as a substitute for transport, their effectiveness in coordinating the movement of goods in reducing inventories, in finding the best markets for produce and so on depends on the adequacy of the transport system. The same is true of the role of telecommunications played in emergencies. The telecommunications link between patient and doctor will not fulfil its purpose unless transport is available to move the patient to hospital or to deliver drugs and other supplies" (ITU: 1984: 10). And only the telecom infrastructure plus other complementary infrastructures can together lead to more economic growth and more effective social service delivery. The need is not only to increase the telephone density, but also give a thrust on the accessibility of communication for rural masses. We realize that the modernization process has to relate to the larger sections of the community. As a whole, the telecommunication (i) provides information; (ii) plays a vital role in emergencies and health services; (iii) increases efficiency of public administration, commerce and other economic activities; (iv) assist in national integration, self-reliance and political stability; (v) reduces regional disparity within the country; (vi) helps shrink distance; (vii) can reduce need to travel, and (viii) facilitates better use of exiting transport facilities. However, full utility of rural telecom can be realized only when most of the villages are telephonically linked and other associated infrastructural amenities are extended to the area. Though its indirect and imperceptible impacts take time to be felt, the measurable economic impact for the use of telecom channel in an area like Arunachal Pradesh will depend on two factors: (i) the increase in information flows achieved by telecom in comparison to other communication networks, and (ii) the extent to which new messages change economic agents' opinion of the probability of events (i.e. the social receptiveness of the rural folk to new information). The existing telecom infrastructure suffers from serious problem of accessibility, reliability and credibility of the service. Thirdly, because of its strategic location, a reliable telecom will have an impressive demand in future that all the villages in the sub-division, district, state or region will have to be linked telecommunicationally; supporting secondary information sectors such as education, health care, industries etc. move in to take advantage of telecom; and laws of land are liberalized to encourage interaction at social, economic and industrial levels. And lastly, access to telecom amenities may affect the social equilibrium widening the gulf between the elite and the masses (Sinha-pp. 210-27).

WEBSITES

The World of online communications explodes daily with new multi-media content involving animation, video and sound. Web is a network of programmes and stored files designed to be accessed by using software known as 'search engines' or 'browsers'. By opening a Website we have access to publication lists, research projects, disaster research centres and relevant disaster organizations Government/NGO. These organizations provide online assistance as well as preparedness and mitigation, response and recovery information. An array of mitigation information is accessible including but not limited to information on how to prepare one's home for a cyclone, flood or earthquake.

E-MAIL

Electronic Mail is a means by which individuals can communicate with one another by electronically mailing text through cyberspace. Through using e-mail software one individual can correspond with another anywhere on the net. Their personal communication stored in the host computer. In the process, one can communicate with the disaster faculty members and research and clarify some of the points connected to disaster management and mitigation process.

Connectivity for e-mail or website browsing is currently cost often achieved through desktop/laptop computers, modems and telephones access to one of the services available for such e.g., AOL within the academy faculty are often connected directly to the host computer through their computers and a modem or hardwired directly through fibre optic cable.

At present, distance learning is most often characterized as that which occurs through satellite linkage rather than connectively though cyberspace. The instructor or trainer is viewed by trainees at divers' geographical locations throughout a nation or around the world via televised often closed circuit broadcaster. With the advance of new technologies we will incur more learning training and conferencing through these means in the area of planning management and mitigation of disasters. And it is increasingly used form of face-to-face interaction for conferencing and training of participants who are in geographically diverse locations.

Distance learning is primarily that which occurs through either tell conferencing or satellite connectivity. While current practice is likely to increase in the future distance learning will encompass so much more. For example, linkage of websites, use of e-mail and chat rooms and increased incorporation of digetivicy cameras between individual desktop (laptop) users will greatly increase distance learning options for educational training and response purpose in the area of preparedness, mitigation and management of disaster situations.

INTERNET

In the present era of electronic communication, the INTERNET provides a useful platform for disaster mitigation communications. Launching of a well defined Website is a very cost-effective means of making an intro-national and international presence felt. It provides a new and potentially revolutionary option for the rapid, automatic and global dissemination of disaster information.

A number of individuals and groups and several meteorological services are experimenting with the Internet for real time dissemination of weather observation, forecasts, satellite and other data. It may be observed that in the most crucial phase of disasters, electronic communication have provided the most effective and the only means of communication with the outside world.

Furthermore, the Internet technology offers great opportunities to build and share resources. Development of research (risk communication and policy) together with scientific assessments of risk and vulnerability provide a basis for effective programme and implementation. The emergence of the Internet, as global channels of communication empowered organizations to collaborate across disciplines, jurisdictions and geographical regions. In the field of disaster information collection, integration and delivery, most significant is the advance being made in the way disaster information can be integrated and delivered to users of global disaster information specification. The present status of NE II Circle is shown in Table 4.9 given below.

Table 4.9: Status of Telecom Services in NE II Circle

Sl. No.		*NE II Circle as on 31st Dec., 2006 (Arunachal, Manipur and Nagaland)*	*Arunachal Pradesh as on 31st April, 2007*
1.	Area (in sq.km.)	122500	83,743 sq. kms.
2.	Population (in lakh)	53.89	1,09,67,968
3.	No. of Telecom connections		
	(a) Land line	150777	55,832
	(b) WLL	21558	7,094
	(c) Mobile	212382	103837 as on 31.07.2007
4.	Equipped Capacity		
	(a) Land line	210448	86,452
	(b) WLL	36250	24,000
	(c) Mobile	225454	94,259
5.	Internet Connections	15895	4,213
6.	Broad Band	696	223 (Capital complex only)
7.	Dias	186	49
8.	PCOs	7240	1,823
9.	Total no. of villages	7340	968 out of 3,863
10.	Total no. of DHQs	36	16 DHQ with Mobile service
11.	Total no. SDHQs	115	39
12.	Total no. of SDCCs	56	31

(Contd...)

(*Table 4.9 Contd...*)

13.	Total no. of Block HQs	145	58
14.	Total no. of WLL BTSs	64	24
15.	Total no. of GSM BTSs	192	59
16.	Total no. of Telephone Exchanges	219	104
17.	OFC Route Kilometres	2748.2	1,196.6
18.	Microwave Kilometres	1745.4	1,083.54 kms

Source: General Manager, BSNL, Itanagar.

The USOF has been entrusted with the responsibility for setting up infrastructure for providing Mobile Services in rural and remote areas, which have not been covered with wireless signal (August, 2007). The three service providers will share each of the towers. In Arunachal Pradesh, Bharat Sanchar Nigam Limited (BSNL) is the infrastructure provider and Reliance Telecom Limited, Dishnet Wireless Limited and BSNL are Universal Service Providers sharing the tower.

The entire state has been divided into seven clusters and 62 numbers of sites have been selected all over the state for setting up of the towers. The state government has to provide the land and power connection up to the tower sites and share the responsibility of removal of problems that may arise during the execution of the scheme. The state government will also nominate a coordinating officer for liaison with the Department of Telecommunication (DOT). (*Arunachal Review*, Vol. VIII, No. 22, June-August, 2007, p. 31)

Present Position

At present, the tele-density is 15.21 in the state as on 31.07.2007. Since January, 2007, there is prevailing competition among BSNL and private companies in the cell phone market. Airtel, Aircell, Reliance and BSNL try to enlarge their own market through cut-throat competition. Day to day the number of cell phone customer is increasing. It is not possible to get the exact figure of cell phone connections. But this facility is limited within the urban areas in the state.

To

The AGM(OP)

O/o the CGMT, NE-II, Circle, Dimapur.

Sub: Tele-Density SDCA-wise in ARP SSA

Enclosed herewith the Data of SDCA-wise Tele-Density of ARP SSA for the month of August, 2007

Sl. No.	SDCA	SSA	No of Exge	Fixed Capacity	DEL's as on 31-8-07	WLL connec-tion as on 31-8-07	GSM connec-tion as on 31-8-07	Total (DEL+ WLL+ GSM)	Waiting list	Population as per 2001 census.	Telly-Density %
1.	Along	APSSA	4	3292	2848	157	5913	8918	0	67472	13.22
2.	Anini	APSSA	1	320	311	0	45	356	0	5957	5.98
3.	Arda	APSSA	1	152	53	0	0	53	0	1489	3.56
4.	Bameng	APSSA	1	152	5	0	0	5	0	24571	0.02
5.	Basar	APSSA	5	3268	1576	40	3995	5611	0	39147	14.33
6.	Bomdila	APSSA	7	5736	2584	1067	7312	10963	0	35393	30.98
7.	Changlang	APSSA	2	1552	1285	0	3225	4510	0	43564	10.35
8.	Chowkham	APSSA	4	3476	1756	1184	3252	6192	0	58834	10.52
9.	Daporijo	APSSA	3	2748	1645	138	2808	4591	0	49622	9.25
10.	Dirang	APSSA	2	1152	607	0	895	1502	0	19750	7.60
11.	Hayuliang	APSSA	1	488	268	0	545	813	0	25316	3.21
12.	Itanagar	APSSA	12	24976	13979	2008	43810	59797	0	107043	55.86
13.	Jairampur	APSSA	3	1800	995	214	1087	2296	0	25162	9.12
14.	Khonsa	APSSA	6	3528	1835	149	4283	6267	0	99370	6.31

(Contd)

(Contd...)

15.	Koloriang	APSSA	7	4040	2418	739	5084	8241	12	98772	8.34
16.	Mariso	APSSA	1	152	27	0	0	27	0	5389	0.50
17.	Mariyang	APSSA	2	336	265	0	0	265	2	14576	1.82
18.	Mechuka	APSSA	1	336	168	0	0	168	0	10752	1.56
19.	Miao	APSSA	4	3072	1717	278	794	2789	0	53398	5.22
20.	Nafra	APSSA	1	152	0	0	0	0	0	15731	0.00
21.	Pakkeshang	APSSA	1	488	120	0	0	120	0	9680	1.24
22.	Panging	APSSA	2	1304	496	2	50	548	4	16722	3.28
23.	Pasighat	APSSA	8	5988	3706	821	9887	14414	25	62961	22.89
24.	Roing	APSSA	3	2792	1889	565	4136	6590	0	32004	20.59
25.	Sagalee	APSSA	5	3480	1025	0	1192	2217	0	17264	12.84
26.	Seppa	APSSA	2	2152	1376	0	2119	3495	7	25480	13.72
27.	Tali	APSSA	1	304	148	0	119	267	0	10247	2.61
28.	Taliha	APSSA	0	0	0	0	0	0	0	6714	0.00
29.	Tawang	APSSA	6	4140	2139	326	2044	4509	0	37545	12.01
30.	Tezu	APSSA	5	3404	2634	305	3810	6749	0	49834	13.54
31.	Tuting	APSSA	1	336	226	0	0	226	7	7195	3.14
32.	Yingkiong	APSSA	2	1368	976	0	2346	3322	0	14121	23.53
33.	Huri	APSSA	0	0	0	0	0	0	0	45	0.00
			104	**86484**	**49077**	**7993**	**108751**	**165821**	**57**	**1091117**	**15.20**

SDE(OP)
O/o the GMT, BSNL, Itanagar.

Bharat Sanchar Nigam Limited
(A Government of India Enterprise)
Office of the General Manager Telecom
Arunachal Pradesh -791111
No.OP- 65/2006-07/33

Dated at Itanagar, the 6th September, 2007

The Next Frontier: Broadband

Indian telecom is set for high growth rates embracing the wider population, when it comes to ordinary voice telephony. While India's tele-density lags behind the world, present trends suggest that catching up is presently underway. India also lags behind the world to a considerable extent in the field of broadband telecom. At end-December, 2003, penetration of Broadband, Internet and Personal Computer (PC) in the country was 0.02 per cent, 0.4 per cent and 0.8 per cent respectively. As per the Broadband Policy announced on October 14, 2004, broadband has been defined as an "always-on" data connection supporting interactive services including Internet access with minimum download speed of 256 Kbps per subscriber. The broadband policy aimed to target three million broadband subscribers and six million Internet subscribers with a timeframe of December, 2005. Further, it is targeted that, by 2007, the broadband subscribers would be 9 million. By the end of the year 2010, the policy aims to target of 40 million Internet subscribers. The rapid growth of Internet has created huge new demand for the broadband access.

The prime consideration guiding the policy includes affordability and reliability of broadband services, incentives for creation of additional infrastructure, employment opportunities, induction of latest technologies, national security and bringing in a competitive environment to reduce regulatory interventions. The new policy encourages creation and growth of infrastructure through various access technologies which can mutually coexist like optical fibre technologies, digital subscriber lines on copper loop, cable TV network, satellite, and terrestrial wireless technologies. The choice is left to the service provider.

Ability to emulate the success of many other Asian countries in the broadband area will have major implications for smoothing intra-India commerce and industry, knowledge flows into India, e-governance, greater integration into the world economy through international voice and video conferencing traffic and lower prices for NLD and ILD traffic, and services exports such as software and "business process outsourcing". Broadband services have already been launched by BSNL on January 14, 2005. They proposed to cover 198 cities in India in addition to Delhi and Mumbai by April 2005 (*Economic Survey* 2004-05, p. 201).

In Arunachal Pradesh the **Broadband** facility for internet is, at present, only at Itanagar, the capital city of the state. Manager, Telecom, Itanagar is very much optimist. He expects that he will be able to give facility of Broadband in almost all district towns in Arunachal Pradesh within two years.

Problems Faced by the Telecommunication Department

1. To Take Fibre Cable Underground

To take fibre cable underground is not only a time taking matter but also a very problematic issue because of peculiar shape of hilly terrain and stone like soil. Very often it is taken along the side of road. Generally, one side of road is river and another side is drain. As a result, it is not an easy task to get the cable underground. Again the road leads not in a straightway but in a semi- circular way because of lying so many streams. Sometimes it is not possible to get the cable underground because of high peak and solid stone. Therefore, it is a very time taking and expensive matter. One cannot say how much costlier it is than that of plain areas.

2. Road Sliding

In the hilly terrain of the state like Arunachal Pradesh, road sliding is very common matter especially during rainy season. The quantum of rainwater in the North-East Region is much high especially in Arunachal Pradesh. Fibre cable is torn with land sliding.

3. Flood

Due to heavy rainwater in the state, flood is also another problem. During rainy season there occurs flood frequently and again rainy season exits for a long time in comparison to the other areas in the country.

4. Lighting

Lighting is also another problem in the state. As there is frequent raining for a lengthy period of time, lighting disturbs not only the function of the telecommunication but also damage the machines.

5. Voltage Fluctuation

For better functioning of the machines in the telecom department, the stabilization of electric power is necessary. If it goes on frequently up and down, it takes sometimes to stabilize the voltage. Again sometimes machines are damaged by sudden high voltage of power. Therefore, for smooth functioning of the telecom department voltage fluctuation must be minimized.

6. Local Pressure

The local people create pressure to the authority of the telecom department to be engaged as contingency staff to participate in the field work. They have no expertise regarding field work and again are not willing to do such type of hard work, but simply want to earn easy money after having been appointed. It creates delay and disturb to the authority.

7. Population

The state is very much thinly populated in our country. As per 2001 Census, the population density per sq. km. is 13 only which are lowest in the country. To provide telephonic facility through optical fibre underground in the remote villages is not economically viable.

8. Establishment of Sub-exchange

Due to existence of so many high peaks of hill it is necessary to establish frequent sub-exchange which is practically not possible. Again to connect sub-exchange with main exchange through satellite is not possible due to non-economic viability.

9. Scarcity of Power

Though the state is emerging as power house as Arunachal Pradesh is the home of unexploited hydro-power potential, there is much below of supply of electricity generated by diesel and hydro set in comparison to demand. As a result, the exchange cannot do function properly due to non-availability of power. Another problem is that to run exchange with the help of generator, fuel is not at hand. For better efficiency of the machine of telecom department, air conditioning is highly required. Due to power shortage air conditioning is not possible in many telecom offices.

10. Poor Road Network

The state is much behind the rest of the North-Eastern states regarding road network.. As such in the development plans, the government has been attaching high priority to the construction of roads and as a result the total length of roads constructed in the state stood at about 15021.80 kms. including 399.80 kms. under National Highway giving the road density of 17.9 kms. per 100 sq. kms. of area at the end of March, 2004 as against the all India average of 74.9 kms. per 100 sq.kms. during 1997. Due to lack of transportation it is very much difficult to set up sub-exchange in remote villages.

Education can involve the use of television and radio for the delivery of software and access to courseware written for specific subject areas. It can make use of micro-computers for access to view data and videotext, as well as to on-line databases. It can involve the use of a wide variety of interactive multi-media packages.

The computer has enormous potential as an educational aid providing new language learning opportunities. Used properly it can be very effective enabling the individual to carry out tasks inconceivable by other means. By virtue of its multi-media capacity and its capabilities as a data storage and retrieval system, it may be used very effectively in the learning process. Multi-media technology exemplified today by the CD-ROM allows a variety of media (text, graphics, sound, animation, and video) to be accessed on a single machine.

Acknowledgement

The author is grateful to the G.M., Mr. Ranjan Datta who has supplied the necessary information of Tele-Com. Department.

REFERENCES

Arunachal Review, Vol. VIII, No. 22, June-August, 2007, p. 31.

Balachandrudu,K.(2007), "Information Technology: Disaster Mitigation and Management", *Southern Economist,* June 15, Vol. 46, No. 4, pp. 13-14.

Bhattacharjee, R.P. (2000): *Economic Development of Arunachal Pradesh,* Himalayan Publishers, Delhi, Itanagar, p. 175, 95, 211

Bose, M.L. (1997): *History of Arunachal Pradesh,* Concept Publishing Company, New Delhi, p. 230-31.

Government of Arunachal Pradesh (2005): *Economic Review,* Directorate of Economics and Statistics, Itanagar, p. 41.

Government of India, Ministry of Finance, Economic Division (2004-05): *Economic Survey,* pp. 201-03.

Jha, S.D. (1988): *Socio-economic and Demographic Dimensions of Arunachal Pradesh,* New Delhi, p. 196.

Mandal, R.K. (2005): "Arunachal Pradesh Emerging as Power House" *Journal of Global Economy,* Vol. 1., No. 4, Research Centre for Social Sciences, Mumbai.

Mandal, R.K. (2007): "Development of Information Technology in North-East India with Special Reference to Arunachal Pradesh (Regarding Post Office and Telecommunication)", *Journal of Global Economy,* Vol. 3, Nos. 5 & 6, Research Centre for Social Sciences, Mumbai.

Parikh Kirit S. (2007): "Making the Growth Process Inclusive: India's Next Economic Challenge" in Borbora, S. and Gogoi J.K. (eds.): *Development Issues in the Northeast in the Turn of the Century,* NEEA, Papyrus, Guwahati.

Sinha, A.C. (1994): *North-Eastern Frontier of India,* Indus Publishing Company, New Delhi, pp. 210-27.

Singh, S. (2007): "Telecommunication Infrastructure in India: An Uphill Journey", *Journal of Global Economy,* Vol. 3, Nos. 5 & 6, October-December, Research Centre for Social Sciences, Mumbai.

Shailaja, P. (2001): Introduction, in Damodar, G. *et al.* (eds.): IT Revolution, *Globalisation and the Teaching of English,* Atlantic Publishers and Distributors, New Delhi, pp. 1-2.

Tikendrajit Paonam and Ningombam Jayanti (2007): "Globalisation, IT and E-Commerce in India : Issues and Challenges", *Journal of Global Economy,* Vol. 3, Nos. 5 & 6, October-December, Research Centre for Social Sciences, Mumbai.

5

Road Network in Arunachal Pradesh Since 1947

Introduction

The economic development of a region or a state largely depends upon the development of a sound infrastructural base. The infrastructural facilities of Arunachal Pradesh are inadequate, despite concerned efforts by the State Government to improve the situation. For example, road is a basic necessity to the infrastructure thereby isolation can be broken only through roads. The service of Transport and Communication is a precondition of economic development. Revolution in transport and communication would take place first before the advent of industrial revolution. It is well known fact that the prosperity of a country depends on the development of agriculture, mining, industry, services, Banking, etc. But without prior development of transport and communication, any type of development is not possible of a region.

Transport is a means or system of carrying passengers or goods from one place to another using vehicle. It is an indispensable part of today's modern civilization. It is a lifeline of economic, social, commercial and cultural progress. If agriculture and industry are seemed to be the body and bones of the economy, transport and communications will be its nerves which circulate men and materials. Today's economy is the market economy of branded commodities which are manufactured in different places based on economies of scale and circulated in different other places for sale. The movement of raw materials, fuel, machinery etc., to the places of production is essential. The more extensive and continuous the production in any branch of activity, the greater will be the need for transport facilities. Transport development helps to open up remote regions and resources for production and thereby to broaden the market for goods. Regions may have abundant supplies of agricultural, forest and mineral resources. But they cannot be developed if they are lying to continue to be remote and inaccessible. Transport is only the means to link the backward regions with relatively more advanced regions and thereby to utilize the idle resources in a place where industries are growing. Transport makes possible large scale production. Thus, transport and communication stand at the root of development of a region, or of a state or of a country. It is transport and communication system that enable a given region to get rid of both unwarranted and natural separation from the rest of the world. An improvement in transport and communication system in a given region, undoubtedly, facilitates development of trade and commerce and consequently, promotes human satisfaction and augments considerably the wealth of the community as well as it helps to break up caste restrictions, false customs, traditions, superstitions and other barriers to rapid economic development and economic growth. Dealing with the role of transport and communication in England's economic growth, Marshall said, "Probably more than three-fourths of the whole benefit she has derived from the progress of manufactures during the nineteenth century has been through its indirect influence in lowering the cost of transport of men and goods, of water and light, of electricity and news for the dominant economic fact of our own age is the development not of the manufacturing, but of the transport industries."

The impact of road transport is wide ranging which includes agriculture, industry, trade and commerce which cumulatively affect overall development of a region. The present investigation is an attempt to assess and examine existing transport network of this state and to suggest possible and meaningful strategy for efficient transport network in order to accelerate development process in the state. The road network pattern and the size of towns in the hills are found to be too poor to help mobilize resources to diffuse innovations for modernization and to ensure sustainable development. The accessibility pattern in the state would have been different. Accessibility greatly influences the size and spacing of towns. The prevailing differences in the pattern of road accessibility and in the number and size of towns in different physical units of the state indicate the regional disparity in the socio-economic attainments among them. The state needs special attention in this respect. Its calls for an integrated transport planning to eradicate the existing imbalances and to pave the way for a more effective and economic transport system in the State. Transportation network is an important factor for the adoption of modern farm technology. The adoption of an improved agricultural practice by a farmer is directly effected by the road/rail distance from agricultural markets and urban centres to the villages. With the help of transportation network, the farmer can acquire and absorb knowledge about new techniques of agriculture and can convert the acquired knowledge to practise in this field. That is why, the villages which are located on or near the transportation network get advantage to avail this opportunity, whereas the villages located away from this network may be deprived of such facilities. Therefore, the transportation network gives birth to the adoption of modern farm technology and improves agricultural practices in the villages of India.

Transport is not merely an amenity but a key factor in economic development. It provides an enduring basis for a developing economy and is thus, a basic requirement of its infrastructure. Since times immemorial, means of transport have also been changing according to particular requirements. Amongst the different means of transport, the most ancient is the road transport. Later on, came the sea route and still later the rail route. Air routes have come last. In this industrial and commercial age, mechanical transport is of paramount importance. W.A. Lewis observed, "A cheap and extensive network of communications is the greatest blessing which any country can have from the economic point of view". Further, the degree of transport development is an indicator of the economic prosperity of a country.

The association between infrastructure and economic development is now widely accepted by economists considering it as a necessary pre-condition of development within this framework, transport has a multi-dimensional role of play. As Youngson remarks, "the more closely one examines the impact of transport improvement, the more closely one realizes how pervasive this impact is, in what a multiple of ways the transport system helps to determine the scope and direction of economic development and how important are transport improvements in creating new opportunities and new incentives".

Road networks are the lifeline of mountain area. They are one of the pre-requisites for any development activity and integrate the production, marketing and consumption of various commodities and social-economic function of the community. In hills, the role of roads is more vital as other means of transport cannot operate in this undulating and rugged terrain.

Transport and Regional Development

Transport being a seminal factor for any kind of economic activity plays a crucial role in the process of development, particularly in terms of spatial economic integration, a key element of regional development and planning. In general, there has been observed a reciprocal relationship between transportation and regional development, the former providing infrastructural base for the latter and the latter acting as stimulant to evolution and expansion of the former.

The positive role of transportation in regional development has been better acknowledged. In this regard, Wheeler (1973) stressed the need for study of transportation in societal perspective underlining its contribution to the process of industrialization, economic specialization and socio-economic underdevelopment. Hoyle bearing the similar idea observed that the interaction between the level and pattern of transport facilities and the average level of living of the population of an area is a critical factor affecting economic and social progress and it needs to be taken into account at all stages of national and regional development planning. As a matter of fact, the formation of regional hierarchies is initially related with the levels and patterns of development of network of transportation and communication. In many cases, in order to avoid bottlenecks in execution of the plan it becomes imperative to provide for a well coordinated transport network with requisite capacity in advance. Belousov observes that no regional planning scheme can be considered complete or can be properly evaluated if it does not provide for transport links and does not envisage transport network necessary to achieve the planned development.

Economic and social development of Arunachal Pradesh depends mostly on efficient system of roads and communication. Roads are the mainstay of the people of the state as there are practically no other means of transport. Realizing importance of construction of roads for connecting production areas with market centres and for providing much needed employment to rural population so that marginal farmers with cash income from employment would sustain themselves as well as invest a little bit in development of their agro-based economy till the time it can be remunerative.

Arunachal Pradesh is situated on the north-east extremity of India and has a long international border with Bhutan to the West by 160 kms., China to the North and North-east by 1030 kms and Myanmar to the South-East by 440 kms. The state is bounded on the south by Assam and Nagaland in our country. It is predominantly a hilly terrain state. Its topography is rugged and typical. The whole topography is occupied and characterized by lofty hill ridges and deep valleys. Its terrain does not allow even a smooth motorable transport. Landslide is a common phenomenon during the rainy season. It is the home of more than twenty major tribes and one hundred and ten sub-tribes and it is acknowledged to be one of the most splendid and multilingual tribal areas of the world.Possibly, this is the only state in India which is having an international border with three countries and the length of international border is around 1,630 kilometres.

The state has vast area of 83,743 sq. kms., out of which 51,540 sq. kms. are forest forming 62 per cent of her total geographical area. Arunachal Pradesh, having untapped estimated hydro power potential of 49,000 MW, may emerge as Power House of India when this potential is fully harnessed. Again, this region is endowed with mineral resources including a vast oil reserve. As per 2001 census, its total population is 10,97,968 out of which 79.66 per cent are living in rural areas and 58.44 per cent of the total workers are cultivators. Agriculture based on traditional system occupies an important place in its economy constituting 30.30 per cent its SDP in 2001-02. Considering the economic potentialities including forest and a long international border, Arunachal Pradesh is very much important on economic point of view as well as very much sensitive on political point of view in our country. The state needs first immediate development of transport and communication. This paper seeks an in-depth study about the need for an effective approach on transport and communication in Arunachal Pradesh. The paper is divided into three sections. The first section concentrates on the development of transport since 1947. The second section devotes to the challenges for development of transport in the state. The third section deals with the suggestions regarding the speedy qualitative development of transport and finally the conclusion follows.

SECTION - I

Development of Transport Since 1947

An analysis of the role of transport in regional development is considerable theoretical interest as well as of great practical value especially with reference to Arunachal Pradesh. Road construction in Arunachal Pradesh is a very hard task because of the nature of terrain. The hills are high and steep and rivers are turbulent and difficult to negotiate. Thus, due to non-availability of resources, severe weather and typical topography, transport facilities were not in existence in the region under study till the country's political independence. This conspicuous absence led the people to remain in complete isolation from another and consequently stood as a great stumbling block in the way of trade and commerce in the region. The infrequent movement of goods used to take place either through porters or their head loads or animals, mostly ponies.The porters were regular government employees, designated as Auxiliary Labour Corps (ALC) and the casual porters were engaged occasionally in the villages for the purpose of transportation. Each circle, sub-division and district headquarters maintained certain number of ALC to meet the transport needs. The reason was that vehicles could not go to the places not connected by roads. To supplement the porters' business, the Administration kept bridle also and so bridle path was constructed. Mule path was also considered necessary as the locals used the mule transport system. It may be mentioned that the Monpas in the region used the mule, cow-mithun cross animal and yak transport very frequently.

Till 1947, there were only three jeepable roads between Pasighat and Kobo by 35 kilometres, Sadiya-Tezu-Denzing by 77 kilometres and still well road 56 kilometres (*Source:* N.C.A.E.R – Techno-Economic Survey of NEFA, 1967, p. 91). So, the total length of roads was only 168, till 1947. Before independence the colonial government did not take any effort to initiate the development process and the British indifference towards the area was mainly due to the fact that the area did not possess any readily exploitable resources. After the independence of the country, the Government of India undertook the development of transport and communication with a view to open up this remote state of India and therefore to facilitate the rapid development of the State. Observing the conditions of Arunachal in 1964, the North-Eastern Frontier Association Administration requested the National Council of Applied Economic Research to conduct a techno-economic survey of the territory. The council in its report published in 1967 recommended action on three areas on priority basis: (a) Transport access both to and within the region, (b) Development of natural resources, and (c) Improvement in human resources.

Regarding transport, the council advocated the construction of road links between district headquarters and administration centres and inter-village road construction. However, since 1950-51, special emphasis was being given in various Five Year Plans of the State government to improve the transportation infrastructure. Table 5.1 and Table 5.2 indicate the outlays in Transport and Communication sector as a percentage of total outlays in the various Five Year Plans and One Year Plans in Arunachal Pradesh.

Table 5.1: Percentage Outlay on Transport and Communication Sector in Arunachal Pradesh since the First Five Year Plans

Plan Period	*Outlay on Transport and Communication out of Total Outlay in percentage form*
First Plan (1951 – 56)	35.06
Second Plan (1956 – 61)	41.33
Third Plan (1961 – 66)	26.98
Fourth Plan (1969 – 74)	28.75
Fifth Plan (1974 – 79)	33.02
Sixth Plan (1980 – 85)	31.60
Seventh Plan (1985 – 90)	31.78

Source: (i) Basic Statistics of North-Eastern Region, 1980.
(ii) Basic Statistics of North-Eastern Region, 1994.

Table 5.2: Plan Outlays on Transport and Communication since 1990-91 in Arunachal Pradesh.

Period	*Outlays (Rs. in crore)*	*Outlay on Transport and Communication out of Total Outlay in percentage form*
1990 – 91	54.33	29.68
1991 – 92	69.27	29.47
1992 – 93	73.02	29.80
1993 – 94	85.18	29.37
1994 – 95	91.80	27.40
1995 – 96	102.67	23.37
1997 – 2002	929.51 (Transport only)	26.03

Source: Basic Statistics of NER, 2002.
Note: 1. Outlay under 9th Plan is at 1996-97 prices.

Table 5.1 and Table 5.2 show that a substantial part of the plan funds are being deployed for the development of transport and communication in this state. Even the sectoral outlays for North-Eastern Council (NEC) constituted in August 1, 1972 also show a similar pattern with a greater emphasis on transport and communication sector. Table 5.3 reflects this issue and show the outlays prescribed on Transport and Communication over the period 1974-90.

Table 5.3: NEC Outlays on Transport and Communication during 1974-90 in percentage form in Arunachal Pradesh.

Years	*NEC Outlays on Transport and Communication in percentage form*
1974 – 78	32.66
1978 – 79	27.90
1979 – 80	31.91
1980 – 85	43.98
1985 – 90	44.07

Source: (i) North-Eastern Council Secretariat, Shillong.
(ii) North-Eastern Council Sixth Five Year Plan, 1980–90.
(iii) North-Eastern Council Seventh Five Year Plan, 1985–90.

It is evident that place of road construction in the region has been accelerated since latter part of the sixties. That is, road construction works took place with a sense of urgency only after the Chinese invasion in 1962. While bridle path and mule path received attention during the early fifties, porter tracks had been given increasing attention thereafter. Table 5.4 depicts district-wise length and type of roads in the State as on 31-03-1973.

Table 5.4: District-wise Length and Type of Roads as on 31.03.1973 (In km.).

District/ state	*National highway*	*Cement concrete*	*Painted*	*Metalled*	*Gravelled*	*Fair weather and up tracks*	*Total*
1	*2*	*3*	*4*	*5*	*6*	*7*	*8*
Kameng	—	—	—	33.80	96.00	219.86	349.66
Subansiri	—	—	—	10.00	—	176.36	186.36
Siang	—	—	61.25	67.75	—	462.80	591.80
Lohit	—	—	38.13	41.85	50.40	147.85	278.23
Tirap	—	—	137.10	92.40	159.80	200.50	589.80
Arunachal Pradesh	—	—	236.48 (11.8)	245.80 (12.3)	306.20 (15.1)	1207.37 (60.8)	1995.85 (100)

Source: Statistical Hand Book, Arunachal Pradesh, 1972-73 (Provisional, p. 14).

As shown above in Table 5.4, more than 60 per cent of existing land communication is that of fair-weather tracks. While gravelled roads' share comes to a little more than 15 per cent, metalled and painted roads' shares workout almost equally that is 12 per cent each. In this time, out of 82 administrative centres, only 39 were connected by roads; and only 25 per cent of the people had the advantage of roads running by the side of their villages. For reasonable development of the economy the present total length of 1995.85 kilometres of general road plus 931 kilometres of forest road (*Source:* Chief Conservator of Forest, Arunachal Pradesh) fell much short of requirements of Arunachal Pradesh.

The present position of roads as compared with the other states of North Eastern Regional is depicted in Table 5.5.

Table 5.5: The Road Length per 100 sq. kms. among the States of North-Eastern Region of India, 1980, 1990 and 1997 (In km.)

State/India	*Road length per 100 sq. kms. in 1980*	*Road length per 100 sq. kms. in 1992*	*Road length per 100 sq. kms. in 1997*
Arunachal Pradesh	5.97	11.9	16.8
Assam	46.62	87.8	87.2
Manipur	28.54	30.3	49.0
Meghalaya	16.16	34.9	37.8
Mizoram	13.89	17.6	22.9
Nagaland	33.76	53.1	110.7
Tripura	51.40	124.1	140.5
All India	40.98	62.8	74.9

Source: (i) Basic Statistics of North-Eastern Region, 1980.
(ii) Basic Statistics of North-Eastern Region, 1994.
(iii) Basic Statistics of North-Eastern Region, 2002.

The road density i.e., road length per 100 sq. kms. is an index of economic prosperity and the standard of living of a state. Table 5.5 and the Table 5.6 as shown below measures the transportation service in the state. The total length of roadways per 100 sq. kms. is adopted to mean the relative development of different areas. In term of road length per 100 sq. kms., the position of Arunachal Pradesh is very low than any other states in the north-eastern region and again it is low in comparison to the all India average of 40.78 kms., 62.8 kms. and 74.9 kms. per 100 sq. kms in 1980, 1992 and 1997 respectively. Table 5.5 also shows that between 1980, 1992 and 1997, the road density has increased to a great extent in all the hilly states of North-East India. It signifies that there is a massive investment in building transport system. But the road length per 100 sq. kms. is much more below the requirement. It cannot act as a boost either to modernization of agriculture or to industrialization of the state. Category-wise of roads length in terms of surfaced, un-surfaced, road length per 100 sq. kms, road length per 1000 population and percentage of surface road to total road are shown in Table 5.6 for all states in north-east India.

Table 5.6: Road Length as on 31.03.1997 (In km.).

State	*Total*	*Surfaced*	*Un-surfaced*	*Road length per 100 sq. kms*	*Road per 1000 popu-lation*	*Percentage of surface road to total road length*
1	*2*	*3*	*4*	*5*	*6*	*7*
Arunachal Pradesh	14092	3991	10101	16.8	12.81	28.32
Assam	68418	11590	56828	87.2	2.70	16.94
Manipur	10941	3598	7343	49.0	4.75	32.88
Meghalaya	8480	3923	4557	37.8	3.86	46.26
Mizoram	4829	1983	2846	22.9	5.36	41.10
Nagaland	18356	5241	13115	110.7	12.24	28.55
Tripura	14729	4577	10152	140.5	4.33	31.10
Total	139845	34903	104942	54.8	3.81	24.96
All India	2465877	1394081	1071796	74.9	2.58	58.68

Source: Basic Road Statistics of India 1996-97, Ministry of Surface Transport.

Table 5.6 shows the density of road is lowest in Arunachal Pradesh as on 31.03.1997. That is, the state is much behind the rest of the North-Eastern states in this regard. As such in the development plans, the government has been attaching high priority to the construction of roads and as a result the total length of roads constructed in the state stood at about 15021.80 kms. including 399.80 kms. under National Highway giving the road density of 17.9 kms. per 100 sq. kms. of area at the end of March, 2004 as against the all India average of 74.9 kms. per 100 sq. kms. during 1997. Category-wise length of road for the last five years with road density is shown in Table 5.7.

Table 5.7: Category-wise Length of Roads and its Density during 9th and 10th Plan

(In. km)

Year	*Black topped*	*Surfaced*	*Un-surfaced*	*Total length of roads*	*Density of roads*
1	*2*	*3*	*4*	*5*	*6*
31.03.2000	4853.93	2182.615	6945.655	13982.20	16.70
31.03.2001	4853.93	2182.615	6945.655	13982.20	16.70
31.03.2002	4853.93	2182.615	6945.655	13982.20	16.70
31.03.2003	5805.416	2496.648	6148.406	14450.47	17.26
31.03.2004	5679.87	3761.13	5127.85	15021.791	17.94

Source: Directorate of Economics and Statistics, Government of Arunachal Pradesh, Itanagar.

Note: Density of Road = Total length of roads ÷ total area.

Table 5.7 indicates that out of total length of roads, 15021.791 kms. in 2003-04, only 38.98 per cent are black topped, 25.81 per cent are surfaced and rest 35.19 per cent are un-surfaced. The progress of development of transport is not up to the expectation. Although, the length of roads in the state has increased from 168 kms. in 1947 to 15021.791 kms. in March 31, 2004, a large part of the state particularly the higher belt in the northern part is either inaccessible or ill served by the existing transport facilities. For example, Anini, the district headquarters of Dibang Valley district does not have an all-weather road with the plans even till today. Again, a peculiarity of surface transport of the state is that most of the district headquarters are not inter connected, i.e., one cannot move from one district headquarters to other specially the old district headquarters in Arunachal Pradesh without going down to Assam. The State does not have lateral roads connecting district headquarters and sub-divisional headquarters of the districts. In other places, roads run vertically connecting places of Assam with the places of district headquarters in the state. As a result, the transport cost is not only high but also the state is affected by disturbances and insurgency activities in Assam.

In order to cope with the rising demand, the Government of Arunachal Pradesh introduces State Transport for departmental operations to ensure coordinated regular bus service at reasonable rates. Arunachal Pradesh State Transport Services (APST) came into existence in 1975 with only two buses. The department is now operating a fleet strength of 236 buses (as on 31.03.2004) on 148 routes within and outside the state. The average daily passengers carried by the buses were 6275 Nos. Apart from APST bus services, a large volume of traffic is operated by private operators.

In the interior parts and especially border area of this State, the communication is still hazardous, journey to many places from headquarters involve one week or more than one week on foot march through hazardous foot track where even mules cannot travel. These tracks are maintained and communicable by negotiating rivers and streams through indigenous cane bridges and bamboo ladders. During the rainy season most of the big rivers are unaffordable.

Arunachal Pradesh being predominantly hilly terrain, there is a lot of constraints in the development of railways. In fact, the State was brought under the railway map of India for the first time with the opening of Balipara (near Tezpur, Assam) to Bhalukpong in West Kameng District of Arunachal Pradesh in 1989 with only 1.26 kms. (metre gauge). Regarding railway lines, Table 5.8 reflects the position of each state in North-East India.

Table 5.8: Railway Network in NER (As on 31.03.2002).

(in kms.)

State	*Broad Gauge (BG)*	*Metre Gauge (MG)*	*Narrow Gauge (NG)*	*Total Gauge*
1	*2*	*3*	*4*	*5*
Arunachal Pradesh	NIL	1.26	NIL	1.26
Assam	1227.71	1288.55	NIL	2516.26
Manipur	NIL	1.35	NIL	1.35
Meghalya	—	—	NIL	—
Mizoram	NIL	1.50	NIL	1.50
Nagaland	11.13	1.72	NIL	12.85
Tripura	NIL	44.72	NIL	44.72
Total	1238.84	1339.10	NIL	2577.94

Source: General Manager (Works) N.E. Railway, Maligaon, Guwahati.

Inland-Water Transport

Although there are many rivers in the state, navigation is almost impossible due to typical terrain as well as strong cross current of the rivers of the region. Again, almost all the rivers remain turbulent during monsoon while during winter, water level in the rivers is so low that it is not possible for water transport. In a few places in the foothills particularly people in Pasighat take their agricultural products to Dhola market near to Dibrugarh through the Siang river for commercial purposes. This implies that navigation is practised in Arunachal Pradesh on a very nominal basis.

Air Transport

Arunachal Pradesh is the only state in the North-Eastern Region which is outside the Indian Airlines air map till 1995. In view of remoteness and long distance between the capital and district headquarters and due to absence of a good surface communication there was a long felt need for air communication for movement of passengers and for supply of ration items to the remote parts of the State. As a first step towards the effort the State government introduced a single helicopter service basically for passengers through Pawan Hans Helicopter Limited (A Government of India Enterprise) with effect from December, 1995. The Government has acquired another aircraft in 2003 making the total strength to two. The passenger service was initially started on two routes viz., Naharlagun-Guwahati and Naharlagun-Mohanbari and subsequently extended to few other places of the state.

The helicopter service is also extended to other locations on emergency situations like lifting of stranded passengers due to disruption of road communication, lifting of VIP's etc. At present, there are 85 helipads and 11 ALGs for transportation of men and materials by Pawan Hans Helicopter Services [*Economic Review* of Arunachal Pradesh, 2004].

SECTION - II

Challenges for Development of Transport

This section consults the challenges for construction of roads in the State as follows:

1. In hills, the construction as well as the reconstruction of roads involves rock cutting, soiling in soft patches, construction of retaining walls, etc. which requires a lot of human labour throughout the year. The whole of topography was dissected into isolation by numerous rivers and streams, many of which being big and at the same time full of rocks as well as subjected to very strong cross currents rendering navigation impossible to a considerable extent. As per State Forest Report, 1999 published by the Forest Survey of India, forest cover of Arunachal Pradesh is 6895 sq. kms. accounting for 82.21 per cent of its total geographical area. Again out of its area, 70 per cent constitutes broad and narrow valleys, 10 per cent foothills and flat areas and 20 per cent constitutes snow clad peak areas. Such type of characteristics of this area signifies how much difficulties to construct roads in this area the agencies face.
2. Arunachal Pradesh is isolated in its location with respect to the rest of the country. As the region is a cul-de-sac, surrounded by three foreign countries, and as it is far away from the industrial areas of the country, the lines of transport and communication have not been developed to the desirable extent.
3. As the region has very heavy rainfall, the roads suffer from surface and gully erosion. The situation is further deteriorated by the loose soil-base derived largely from alluvium in the plains and such sedimentary rocks as sandstone, mudstone, shale etc. in the hills. The roads have, therefore, to be constantly repaired and maintained in serviceable condition, needing a huge expenditure.
4. The north-east region of the State, especially its plains in Lohit district and Lower Dibang Valley district having a number of turbulent rivers, annually experiences devastating floods which often damage roads and bridge. On the other hand, heavy deluges cause landslide and soil creep in the area damaging the roads. These again necessitate repairs and renovation of the roads requiring huge expenditure. That is why, till today, it is not possible to interconnect all the district headquarters by roads in the State.

5. The region has numerous turbulent rivers and hill-streams which flow with fury during the rainy season. Besides, many of them change their course very often. Some of them, again, are very wide. In this connection, it can be mentioned that Arunachal Pradesh is a land of five big rivers. They are Kameng, Subansiri, Siang, Lohit and Tirap. They are not only wide but also subject to very cross current. The roads need to be frequently bridged and many culverts, retention walls, spurs etc. have to be constructed requiring huge labour and expenditures.
6. The state government is not financially well off to afford sufficient expenditure to construct and maintain a well-knit transport system. The government has to depend very much on central grant-in-aid. Hence, construction of new roads is rare and maintenance of existing roads is poor.

SECTION - III

Suggestions for Construction of Roads

This section relates suggestions for construction of roads in this state and conclusion as follows:

1. Formulation of transport network model may be on the basis of a composite view of all the relevant spatial, structural and functional variables. It should necessitate balanced emphasis on both the morphological and functional properties while identifying gaps and bottlenecks in the transport system. The planners, in this regard, should aware with the multi-dimensional nature of the problems associated with economic, social, political and spatial aspects of transportation.
2. In order to develop rural transport to increase overall accessibility in view of rural development it should be desired to link the farms to the villages, village to the market, market to the town and soon so that industrial and agricultural development can take place in rural areas to strengthen the agricultural economy of the state. Regarding this the construction of the new roads should be immediately started to interconnect all the district headquarters and also the all towns declared by 2001 census.

3. A comprehensive repair and renovation of the existing roads should be taken up on the basis of the nature of problems and demands in various parts of the state.
4. An effort should be made to determine the type of barriers in the development of the transport network of this hilly state and appropriate engineering structures should be adopted on the basis of cost-benefit analysis.
5. The existing *Kaccha* road particularly in mineral and forest based region must be immediately transformed into *Pucca* roads for increasing mobility of people and raw materials.
6. Due to the inadequate coverage of roads, a large area of the rich forest is still inaccessible and as such potentialities of cash crops, hydro-power, animal husbandry and tourism remain unexploited. Similarly, many of the other schemes for Arunachal Pradesh have become prohibitive due to inadequate progress of road transport. Such areas should be stressed first for the construction of road.
7. Although special emphasis is given for the development of transport and communication during Five Year Plans, but still a large part particularly the higher belt in the northern part (border area) is either inaccessible or ill-served by the existing transport facilities. In fact, where road is the only communications link it should have top priority over other sectors. East-west connecting roads in the state approved under Eighth Five Year Plan connecting Tezu, the headquarters of Lohit District to Ruksin in East Siang District is now under construction without touching Assam. This type of road construction in a phased manner is very much urgent for rapid economic development of Arunachal Pradesh. Road communication without touching Assam should be given top priority as to exempt the people of the state to face bandh or insurgency in Assam during their journey period.

Conclusion

Needless to mention that in the light of regional development being a joint venture of experts from various associated disciplines, the geographers equipped with their unique integrative synthesizing technique embodying theories and methodologies based on spatial variable and economic models and generalization can contribute significantly in this field.

The proposals for the transportation planning suggested above, if properly implemented, will not only solve the problems of transport but will also enhance the efficiency of the network mobility of goods and people and pace of rural development and growth.

In view of the alarming situation arising due to environmental deterioration, roads in hill areas are required to be built on the principle of minimum necessity and net maximum possible gain both in socio-economic as well as in ecological perspectives. Inter-departmental collaboration and co-ordination, particularly, among road, forest and soil conservation departments will be inevitable if roads are to be planned, constructed and maintained in such a way as to channelize the process of socio-economic development in the region, to desire destinations with ensuring minimum possible environmental and ecological implications.

REFERENCES

Belousov, I.I. (1964): "Transportation and the Formation of Economic Regions", *Soviet Geog., Rev. and Trans.*, Vol. 5, p. 19.

Bhattacharjee, R.P. (2000): "*Economic Development of Arunachal Pradesh*", Himalayan Publishers, Delhi, Itanagar, p. 91.

Datt, R. and Sundharam, K.P.M. (2004): "*Indian Economy*, S. Chand and Company Ltd., Ram Nagar, New Delhi, pp. 128-129.

Government of Arunachal Pradesh (2004): "Economic Review of Arunachal Pradesh," *Directorate of Economics and Statistics*, Itanagar, p. 38.

Holye, B.S. (ed.) (1973): "*Transport and Development*, Macmillan Press, London, p. 9.

Jha, S.D. (1986): "*Arunachal Pradesh: Rich Land and Poor People*", Omsons Publications, New Delhi, Guwahati, p. 195.

Mandal, R.K. (2007): Expansion of Road Network in Arunachal Pradesh (since 1947), *Arunachal Review*, Vol. VIII, No. 18, June-August, Directorate of Information, Public Relations and Printing, Government of Arunachal Pradesh, Naharlagun, Arunachal Pradesh.

Mandal, R.K. (2003): "Trend of Diversification of Arunachal Economy with special reference to Agriculture: A Strategy for Sustainable

Development", Resurun: *Journal of the Directorate of Research,* Government of Arunachal Pradesh, Itanagar, pp. 108-109.

Mitra, A. and Mitra, D. (1998): "Role of Transport and Communication in the Economic Development of Arunachal Pradesh" in Vaidya, B.C. (ed.): *Readings in Transport Geography: A Regional Perspective,* Devika Publications, Delhi, pp. 286-289.

Singh, D.N. (1998): "Perspectives on the Role of Transportation in Regional Development in Vaidya, B.D. (ed.): *Readings in Transport Geography: A Regional Perspective,* Devika Publications, Delhi, pp. 7-8.

Taher, M. and Ahme, P. (2002): "*Geography of North-East India,* Mani Manik Prakash, Panbazar, Guwahati, p. 216.

Wheeler, James. O. (1973): "Transportation Geography: Societal and Policy Perspective", *Economic Geography,* Vol. 59, p. 11.

6

Employment and Rural Industrialization

Introduction

Economic, political and social processes are interwoven inextricably in the course of development. Developmental economics is sterile without an understanding of the accompanying developmental politics, which involves the interaction of the State with the major actors. At the core of this politico-economic process is the role assigned to industrialization. Thus, the current debate about industrialization is essentially a debate about how the economic and political factors would drive, in an interlocked manner, the transformation of our economy, polity and society, and it should not be trivialized into statistics about growth rates.

India lives in its villages where rural development is one of the topmost priorities of Indian's development strategies. Rural development is considered as one of the important tools to eradicate the chronic problems like poverty and unemployment. The term rural development is rightly defined by the World Bank that "Rural development is a strategy to improve the economic and social life of a specific group of people, the rural poor, including small and marginal farmers, tenants and the landless".

Similarly *Desai*, underlined that the objectives of rural development encompasses improved productivities, increased employment, higher incomes for target groups as well as a minimum acceptable levels of food, clothing, shelter, education and health. Whereas, Prof. V.K.R.V. Rao, entrusted that the rural development is a process of optimum utilization of the natural and human resources of a given rural area for the enrichment of the quality of life of people.

While going through the available definitions it is clear that the rural development is synonymous of upliftment of people with regard to physical, intellectual economic and social welfare in society. It is well known that the rural industrialization plays a pivotal role in rural development by providing employment, income, and infrastructural facilities etc.

Importance of Rural Industries

The development of the Indian rural industries in rural areas has been one of the most important elements of industrial policy and programmes for rural development, though the scale of priority on it has differed from period to period during the last few decades. In over populated countries like India, agriculture alone cannot absorb the entire surplus workforce. It is obvious that new opportunities for employment in the rural areas are found largely in the non-agricultural sector. As rural industries are labour intensive in nature, therefore, they provide additional employment opportunities in the rural areas. The distinguishing characteristic of the rural industries is that it also provides a major proportion of employment opportunities to the women.

Another major feature of rural industries is its decentralized production through a network of well-knit rural industries which obviates the necessity of complicated managerial and competitive marketing techniques, thus, reducing the costs on account of overheads and paving avenues for managerial development in rural areas. These challenges and issues will lead to the establishment of village republics and human resources development centres at industrial establishments in the rural areas.

It will also provide ample scope for the promotion of artistic achievement and creativity that has been suppressed in rural areas for a long period of time. It is also well observed that in agrarian countries like India the rural industrialization has been promoting agricultural development and *vice versa*. The rational behind rural industrialization in the Indian context today consists in the immediate need for reducing the rural-urban economic imbalance, avoiding explosive social costs of over urbanization or urban agglomeration and providing of remunerative employment to the surplus labour in rural areas.

In addition, it utilizes the optimum level of local manpower, skill and available resources. Only rapid rural industrialization can help developing countries substantially, therefore, when opportunities increase for employment in the non-agricultural sector which will in turn increase the production of inputs needed to increase agricultural output and thereby the number of plants available for processing farm commodities will increase.

One of the major myths regarding setting up of big industries is that it eradicates many economic problems, this is found to be still a myth in many areas, for instance, the Rourkela Steel Plant was set-up in a tribal region in Orissa, but the plant did not help tribal people to improve their financial condition and their day to day living. Similarly, there are many other examples that can be quoted as far as India is concerned setting-up of big units is not going to help the local rural people, hence the setting up of rural industries alone would help towards the development of rural areas specifically in India.

It is recognized that development planning in India has to concentrate on generation of more employment as it is the only effective way of poverty alleviation, reduction of inequity and meaningful growth. Rural industrialization is important not as a means of generating employment opportunities in the rural areas with low capital cost and raising the real income of the people, but because it contributes to the development of agriculture and urban industries. Without rural industries, it would be considerably more difficult to solve the problem of agricultural unemployment. Rural industrialization promotes rural industry. The problem of mass unemployment and underemployment and poverty is likely to persist unless some supplementary avenues of generation of employment for the masses are devised for the rural areas. Employment due to industrialization is the surest way to enable the vast numbers living below the poverty level to rise above it. Rural industries are capable of offering employment opportunities at the place of residence to a large section of population. Rural industries have the capacity to correct regional imbalances by initiating industrial activities on dispersed basis in the most neglected, backward inaccessible areas where perhaps large scale sector is unable to penetrate. Rural industrialization is a key to rural development and rural prosperity. It helps not only in the growth of the economy but also paves the way for urbanization. So, urban expansion is linked up with economic development arising out of Industrial development and this is inevitable. It is a wide ranging process. It implies not merely development of certain industries, also changes in the structure, technology and organization of economic activity. Industrialization is recognized as a real tool of economic development as it indicates a higher standard of living of the majority of population. Once Nehru told that real progress might ultimately be depend on industrialization. During the last 62 years after independence, our country has been bringing a noticeable growth in industrial production. But the North-Eastern Region of our country has, till now, been lying neglected. Though the region is well endowed with mineral, forest and hydel resources they have been left out of the process of industrialization. It has remained so due to isolation of the region from the main centres of trade and industry, inadequate economic and physical infrastructure, small size of the regional market, low accessibility of the markets outside the region, lack of entrepreneurs, difficult terrain condition, serious law and order problem, etc.

Developing industries in the rural areas is essential because

1. Rural industries are labour intensive.
2. By providing employment, these industries have also high potential for income generation in the rural areas.
3. These industries encourage dispersal of economic activities in the rural and thus, promote balanced regional development.
4. Rural industries also help protect and promote art and creativity i.e., the age-old rich heritage of the country.
5. Rural industries being environment-friendly lead to development without destruction.

Rural Employment Programme

The Government through Khadi and Village Industries Commission is implementing this programme for the promotion and development of Agro and rural industries. The revised target for the Tenth plan under the REGP is to generate 25 lakhs additional employment opportunity and Rs. 369.95 crores has been provided for the rural employment generation programme in 2005-06 Budget.

Under this scheme, the KVIC provides margin money assistance at the rate of 25 per cent of the project cost up to Rs. 10 lakhs and for projects above Rs. 10 lakhs and up to Rs. 25 lakhs rate of margin money is 25 per cent of Rs.10 lakhs plus 10 per cent on remaining cost of the project. In the case of SC/ST/OBC/women/ physically handicapped and other special category, the margin money grant is 30 per cent of the project cost up to Rs. 10 lakhs and for projects above Rs. 10 lakhs and upto 25 lakhs, it is 30 per cent of Rs. 10 lakhs plus 10 per cent of the remaining cost of the project. Under this scheme the beneficiary's contribution is 10 per cent of the project cost. In the case of SC/ST and other weaker sections, beneficiary's contribution is 5 per cent of the project cost.

Arunachal Pradesh among the North-Eastern States abounds in a variety of natural resources including agricultural, forest and mineral wealth. This State would be benefited with a high degree of industrialization. Unfortunately, the position is just the reverse. The interface with infrastructure will be examined in detail by examining the impact of the major components of infrastructure such as road, power and communication. We shall also examine the industrial policies of this State. The basic objective of industrialization is to be gainful utilization of her resources: material and human.

Unemployment Position in Arunachal Pradesh

The data of unemployment position can be obtained from the employment exchange of the State. The data given below include all categories of degree holders. But it does not give the correct picture of the unemployment situation, as many candidates do not register their names in the Employment Exchanges. It is important to note that no micro-level survey is done to find out the actual position of unemployment position in Arunachal Pradesh.

The number of job seekers as per live register of District Employment Exchanges is shown in Table 6.1.

Lack of technical education and faculty manpower planning is responsible for the existence of educated unemployment. Again, in the absence of vocational education and professional guidance, these educated unemployed youths cannot become self-employed. There are only three technical institutions in this state. They are

Table 6.1: Number of Job Seekers as On 31-03-2003.

Items	*2000-2001*	*2001-2002*	*2002-2003*
Candidates registered during the year	6903	6098	4018
Candidates sponsored	1764	614	790
Placement of candidates in employment during the year	20	41	26
Candidates in live register	22031	23160	23952

Source: Directorate of Economics and Statistics, Government of Arunachal Pradesh, Itanagar.

NERIST at Nirjuli (Itanagar), Polytechnic College at Itanagar and Horticulture and Forestry College at Pasighat. A good number of students of the state are sent every year to other states for higher studies in technical courses like Engineering, Medicine, Vetrinary, Agriculture, etc., to colleges located outside the State. On completion of courses, these students use to fill up the vacuum of technical manpower need of the state and almost all the technical graduates are absorbed by the Government Department. The outturn of engineering graduates to employment market in the state is surplus. Employment avenues in private and corporate sectors need to be developed to stop wastage of skilled engineers.

Of late, it has been well established fact that in our country although GDP growth has accelerated, it has not been accompanied by a commensurate increase in employment leading to a worsening in the employment situation. These considerations have led to a demand for greater attention to the employment objective in the Eleventh Plan document. There is also a concern on youth and educated unemployment as increase in it will lead to waste of human resources and social tensions. If these factors are not properly understood and solved in time, it could jeopardize all the developmental activities and can nullify the gains achieved so far. Particularly, the employment generation strategy cannot be distinguished from the broader policy thrust for growth and structural changes in the economy as a whole [GoI (2001), "*Report of Task Force on Employment Opportunities*", *Planning Commission*, Government of India].

Present Position of Industry

At present there are 15 medium scale industries which are mostly saw mill, plywood and 11 veneer mill functioning in the State. In spite of many obstacles in the way of development of large and medium scale industries, significant numbers of small-scale industrial units have come up in the State over the year due to active support and positive policy of the government. There were 471 registered small scale industrial units functioning at the end of March 2003 mostly engaged in activities like blacksmithy, tin smithy, carpet making, carpentry, wool knitting handloom and weaving, cane and bamboo works, printing press, etc. The rural industry in the State has scope for tremendous growth, but it has been facing lot of problems for a long time.

This chapter seeks to examine an in-depth study to identify the scope for industrialization specially in rural areas in Arunachal Pradesh and relevant issues and challenges for its growth.

Scope for Industrialization

New Industrial Policy of Arunachal Pradesh 2001

This policy resolution is the second of its kind and will be known as "New Industrial Policy of Arunachal Pradesh 2001".

Policy Resolution

(a) The State Government will encourage the establishment of industrial undertaking in the private and cooperative sectors for the sustainable development of the State.

(b) Employment opportunities and gainful self-employment in industrial and allied sectors for the local population of Arunachal Pradesh will be given priority.

(c) Investors from outside the State will be encouraged to invest in the state. Hundred per cent equity ownership of an industrial unit by entrepreneurs will be allowed for a maximum period of 30 (thirty) years by the end of which period such equity holding will be reduced to 49 per cent, the remaining 51 per cent will be held by a local Arunachal Tribal entrepreneur or a group of local tribal entrepreneurs or the state government, if it considers necessary to do so.

(d) Outside entrepreneurs may be allowed to hold land on lease for a period of 30 years, after which the lease may be renewed for a further period of 30 years. The consideration for the lease may be in the form of annual or lump sum payments or as equity. (The lease may be used as security for loans from financial institutions).

(e) Development of all industries will be encouraged. To being with, the following industries will have priority :

  (i) Industries based on agricultural, horticultural and plantation produce.
  (ii) Industries based on locally available raw materials.
  (iii) Textiles (handlooms and powerlooms) and handicrafts.
  (iv) Electronics and knowledge based industries.
  (v) Industries based on non-timer forest produce.
  (vi) Infrastructure, such as power and communications.

Forest Based Industries

There is vast scope for forest based industries in the State. We concentrate only on medicinal plants and tender bamboo shoots.

Medicinal Plants

As per the State Forest Report-1999, published by the *Forest Survey of India*, forest cover of Arunachal Pradesh is 68,951 sq. kms. accounting for 82.21 per cent of its total geographical area. The recorded forest area of the state is 51540 sq.kms., which is about 61.5 per cent of its total geographical area. Thus, the state is fortunate to have such high percentage of its area under valuable forests cover against the national percentage of 23.28 per cent. The important types of forests found in the State are Tropical Ever Green, Semi-Green, Wet Ever Green, Wet Temperate, Deciduous Mixed Coniferous, Alpine, Bamboo brakes, etc. It is well known fact that more than 80 per cent of the world's medicinal flora is found in the Himalayan ranges of India. Since, the State has remained a generally inaccessible area with scarce means of communication and transport, very little written record is available about medicinal flora. Mostly, the knowledge and informations were passed from generation to generation by word of mouth and through folklores.

Out of about 1150 species of orchids known in India, about 550 species occur only in Arunachal Pradesh which is a highest number for any State in India thus, making it an "Orchid Paradise" of our country. These species occur in varying climatic and habitat conditions in varying concentration from the warm foothills to the cool temperate hills in the State. There are over 500 medicinal plants recorded from Arunachal Pradesh of which 250 are used in various Ayurvedic formulations [Directorate of Economics and Statistics, Itanagar and Regional Research Institute (Ayurveda), Itanagar]. It may also open up a new avenue in commercial cultivation for large production, processing and packaging, marketing and industrial application.

Good agricultural and collection practices of medicinal plants and its processing can also be potential source of economic development and ecologically safer too to the state

Bamboo and Bamboo Based Industry

Bamboos play an important role in the rural economy.Bamboos are a sub-family of grasses that include over 1,200 species worldwide. 18 genera and 130 species are so far known from India. 26 species belonging to 9 genera occur in Arunachal Pradesh, such as Bambusa (4 species), Chimono Calamus (2 species), Dendro-calamus (6 species), Dinochloa (1 species), Drepano-stachyum (1 species), Gigantochola (1 species), Neomicro Calamus (1 species), Phyllostachys (3 species) and Schizostachyum (7 species) (*Source:* BSI, Itanagar).

They are widely distributed and occur abundantly in most regions of India except in the Rajasthan desert or upper reaches of Kashmir.In addition to the bamboo based industry, we can use tender bamboo as food as bamboo shoots. In addition to the domestic demand there is large scale demand in the international market.

The National Mission for Bamboo Applications (NMBA) is an initiative of the Department of Science and Technology (DST), Government of India, and is being implemented by the Technology

Information, Forecasting and Assessment Council (TIFAC), an autonomous organisation under DST.

TIFAC brings to this endeavour a decade and more of experience in key areas of economy covering various societal initiatives. TIFAC brings to the bamboo sector its unique mission-mode modality, a tested and successful mechanism to bridge the laboratory-user-market gap, one that helps implement industrial technologies speedily. Focusing on applications and markets, sourcing knowledge and technology from diverse resources and working intensively with its partners, TIFAC has developed innovative models of technology absorption, development and dissemination.

- The Mission takes a multi-disciplinary and multi-dimensional approach to:
- Develop and promote environment friendly, value-added bamboo based products, practices, technology and processes.
- Improve industry-lab-user linkages.
- Develop and disseminate technologies for value added products.
- Develop small and medium enterprises.
- Empower people and communities by focusing on areas and regions with natural competitive and comparative advantages.

NMBA endeavours to achieve its goals by focusing on the industrial growth of the bamboo sector by functioning as:

- A funder of industrial initiatives
- A catalyst and demonstrator of technologies and processes.
- A platform for exchange of ideas and a repository of sectoral knowledge.
- A facilitator and promoter, and
- In pivotal and limited areas as an implementer.

Market Scenario

A market potential study has elaborated upon the potential of shoots and relevant findings are given below:

- A 4 per cent penetration in the very rich class households, consuming one kg of bamboo shoot per year and a 2.5 per cent penetration among the climbing class consuming the same amount at a price of Rs. 50 per kg. results in a domestic market of Rs. 105 crore which can be targeted.

- The total international export market for bamboo shoot has been estimated at US$ 720 million. This is equivalent to Rs. 3,600 crore. A 5 per cent penetration in the export market would yield a market size of Rs. 200 crore for the Indian bamboo shoot processing units to start with. The international market has been increasing rapidly at almost 25 per cent per year on higher acceptance of bamboo shoot as a delicacy.
- Domestic market volumes as they stand today are hardly indicative of the potential of bamboo shoots. The consumption of 132 tonnes per annum also reflects lack of availability and promotion in the market leading to poor depth of supply.
- Increase in usage at hotels, restaurants, and clubs will lead to an increase in demand of home cooking, which will help drive volumes in the long term.
- The market for shoots exists as a three-tiered structure:
  - The local market is at the first tier and at the low end of the value chain with the shoots being sold fresh as a vegetable for consumption by local communities.
  - The second tier comprises metro and urban markets within the country procuring the shoots through an established distribution chain in a packaged form primarily for oriental cooking needs.
  - The third tier is the export market that will yield best value for the produce but will have stringent requirements of quality and taste.
- Entrepreneurs looking to enter the bamboo shoot sector should target marketing efforts towards the second tier, that of the national domestic market, and then move up to the third tier, the larger export market once they are confident about addressing aspects of consistent quality and quantity supply. Smaller manufacturers could target local markets which in consumptive regions can offer reasonably high volumes.

International Trade Potential

The international trade for bamboo shoots is shown in Table 6.3:

Table 6.2: International Trade for Bamboo Shoots.

Country	*Import (tonnes)*	*Export (tonnes)*
Japan	134,000	—
USA	44,000	—
Australia	12,000	
Korea	12,000	—
Others	93,000	42,000
Thailand	—	68,000
Taiwan	5,000	40,000
China	—	150,000
Total	300,000	300,000

Source: Department of Forest, Itanagar, Government of Arunachal Pradesh.

The Department of Agriculture and Co-operation, Ministry of Agriculture, Government of India has recently launched a centrally sponsored scheme "National Bamboo Mission" (NBM) for addressing the issues relating to the development of bamboo in the country. The cost of the Mission is estimated at Rs. 5.68 billion with 100 per cent assistance of the Central Government. The Scheme will be implemented by the division of Horticulture under the Department of Agriculture and Co-operation in the Ministry of Agriculture, New Delhi, informed B.J. Lhungdim, Coordinator, Cane and Bamboo Technology Centre, Guwahati.

State Bamboo Mission

Ministry of Agriculture, Government of India launched National Bamboo Mission in 2006 for development of bamboo as resource for economic development. Following this, the Government of Arunachal Pradesh has also started State Bamboo Mission and made institutional arrangements for the development of bamboo as a resource. State Bamboo Steering Committee, Bamboo Development Agency and District Level Agency on Bamboo have already been constituted. The State Bamboo Steering Committee is headed by PCCF and Principal Secretary (Environment and Forests) while, Director of State Forest Research Institute (SFRI) acts as its Member-Secretary. Bamboo Development Agency and District Level Agency on Bamboo are headed by Director of Horticulture and District

Horticulture Officer. State Bamboo Technical Support Group headed by Director, SFRI has also been constituted with officers, scientists belonging to the Departments of Environment and Forests, Horticulture and Panchayati Raj.

National Bamboo Mission Scheme has been included in the Eleventh Five Year Plans of the Government of India. Action Plan under National Bamboo Mission is prepared under the supervision of State Bamboo Steering Committee (SBSC). The action plan is implemented in the state in forest areas by the Department of Environment and Forests in various forest divisions through Forest Development Agency (FDA). FDA has to function through Village Forest Management Committees (VFMCs). Scheme of National Bamboo Mission is implemented in forest areas in Joint Forest Management mode. The Departments of Horticulture and Panchayati Raj have implemented the National Bamboo Mission Scheme in non-forest areas through individual Entrepreneurs, Non-governmental Organizations and SHGs.

For development of bamboo as enterprise, the State Government has constituted Arunachal Pradesh Bamboo Development Agency (APBDA). This Agency is presently headed by Shri Tame Phassang with Director, SFRI as its Member-Secretary. It also includes senior officials and prominent industrialists as members. APBDA is planning to revive closed wood-based industries by converting them into bamboo based industrial units. It is being supported by State Government, National Mission on Bamboo Application (NMBA), Cane and Bamboo Technology Centre (CBTC) and State Forest Research Institute (SFRI) (*SFRI Information Bulletin* No. 27).

Under the NBM, an area of 1,76,000 hectares will be brought under bamboo cultivation during Tenth and Eleventh Five Year Plans in both forest and non-forest areas of land. Under this mission it is proposed to generate employment of 9.7 lakh mandays through nursery and plantation activity.

The main objectives of National Bamboo Mission are:

- To promote the growth of the bamboo sector through as an area based regionally differentiated strategy;
- To increase the coverage of area under bamboo in potential areas, with improved varieties to enhance yields;

- To promote marketing of bamboo and bamboo based handicrafts;
- To promote, develop and disseminate technologies through a seamless blend of traditional wisdom and modern scientific knowledge; and
- To generate employment opportunities for skilled and unskilled persons, especially unemployed youths.

According to the Coordinator, state activities relating to National Bamboo Mission will be implemented through the respective Bamboo Development Agencies / Forest Development Agencies or any other agencies approved by the respective State Governments. The fund earmarked for the year 2006-07, as approved by the National Level Steering Committee have been released to the respective states and altogether an amount of Rs. 6570.98 lakhs has been released to eight North-Eastern States under NBM. The details about the National Bamboo Development Agencies may be obtained from respective State Bamboo Mission Director or Bamboo Development Agencies/Forest Development Agencies.

Bamboo can be used as charcoal and even some countries are trying to extract fuel from bamboo. A Bangalore based firm has come up with a model that can generate electricity from Bamboo. The model called Bamboo Based Biomass Gasification System was displayed at the first-ever Enterprise show organized by the Confederation of Indian Industries at the Assam Engineering College Ground, Chandmari, Guwahati. The model developed by the Indian Institute of Science, Bangalore and demonstrated by the Department of Energy, Tezpur University (*Times of India*). Government of India is planning to confer more rights to the tribal in their own land especially in hills in the next session of Parliament by the Department of Tribal Affairs. This should include scientific utilization of forest resources for Economic Development of all states in general and Arunachal Pradesh in particular (*Arunachal Review*, Vol. VIII, No. 22, June-August, 2007, p. 31). Thus, bamboo plays a vital role in livelihood security in terms of poverty alleviation, ecology, security through conservation, and providing food and shelter.

The backwardness may be due to its inhospitable hilly terrain, accidental topography, its late start in the development process, cost intensive nature of construction of road in the hills of Arunachal Pradesh. A more detailed analysis of the available infrastructure in Arunachal Pradesh is carried out in the following sub-section.

Power

Uninterrupted power supply is one of the crucial prerequisites for the growth of industries in any region/state. In spite of the state's estimated hydel potential of 26,505 MW (which is the highest among the states of North East India), it generates only 66.86 MW, which is the lowest among the states of North-East India. The state has a very low base of installed and generating capacity and nearly 52 per cent of power requirement of the state are met from diesel generating set. At the same time, power consumption in Arunachal Pradesh is mainly domestic with only 14 per cent being used in the industrial sector. The absence of consumption by the agricultural sector underlines the prevalence of labour intensive, primitive agricultural practice i.e. shifting cultivation. In spite of small population, the State shows a low per capita consumption which signifies the lack of domestic or industrial facilities to utilize power. In 1998, 58.43 per cent of villages in the State were electrified which is far below the national average of 84 per cent and it is only better than Meghalaya (49%) amongst the North-Eastern States. The slow electrification act as a major obstacle to the growth of entrepreneurship and small scale industries. However, the commissioning of the Ranganadi Hydel Project in Lower Subansiri district increases the state's power resources significantly.

Transport and Communication

Road transport is predominant in Arunachal Pradesh since it is barely connected by Railways (i.e. only 3.5 kms.). At the same time, the road development in the state has been slow on account of difficult mountainous terrain, lack of road alignment, etc. The present road density in Arunachal Pradesh is only 15.45 kms. per 100 per sq. km., which is the lowest in the country. Of the available road, only 49 per cent is motorable and 30 per cent is surfaced. At the same time, the state does not have lateral road connecting the district headquarters and sub-divisional headquarters of the district.

However, the road density may not throw proper light of the lack of proper road communication in Arunachal Pradesh since the villages in Arunachal Pradesh are scattered and many of the interior villages are yet to be connected. Therefore, this indicator has been supplemented by another relevant indicator i.e. the percentage of total villages having connectivity status of roads in a district. The villages within the radius of one kilometre in hilly area terrain from constructed road are deemed to have been connected. The data has been collected from the status of village connectivity in Arunachal Pradesh compiled by the Chief Engineering, Eastern Zone, Public Works Department, Itanagar. On that basis, Lower Subansiri district has the lowest road connectivity (16.30%) and East Siang district has the highest road connectivity (73.68%).

Banking infrastructure

The banking network in Arunachal Pradesh is not very developed. There are around 69 bank offices with an average of 9.07 offices per lakh population in 2001. There are very few nationalized banks which have their branches in the state. The State Bank of India has around 42 branches accounting for nearly 60.86 per cent of the total number of branches in the year 2001. Itanagar and Naharlagun town (capital of the State) of Papum Pare district can only avail of the banking facilities offered by other commercial banks like Vijay Bank, Central Bank of India and UCO Bank. At the same time, the credit-deposit ratio of Arunachal Pradesh is the lowest among the States of North-East India, which is only 20.89 per cent. The low credit-deposit ratio signifies that the bank have not been able to support sufficient investment opportunities in the State. The recovery rate in industrial sector is only 30 per cent which is a matter of grave concern. It shows that the loans forwarded by the banks is either consumed or invested in unviable capital stock. The reason behind this poor recovery rate is the predominance of central scheme loans over other commercial loans.

Social Infrastructure

The development of settlements around centres of economic and commercial activities is necessary not only as a source of supply of manpower but also for development of markets. The availability of social infrastructure determines the quality of life of the population and contributes to human capital formation. The social infrastructures as provided by the Government and appropriate policy measures are required to guarantee a minimum quality of life to the people. The medical facilities are one of the important components of social infrastructure. In Arunachal Pradesh there has been a perceptible improvement in the public health facilities. For example, the number of hospitals are 18 in the state and there are around 221 beds per lakh population, which is better than most States of North-East India. As a result, in Arunachal Pradesh, health condition has improved significantly in the course of last five decades. In 1971 the country's crude death rate was 16.9 per cent as against the Arunachal Pradesh's crude death rate, which stood at 20.9 per cent (during 1971-73) which is big difference. Over the years, the difference between the country's crude death rate and that of Arunachal's declined as health condition in the latter improved at a faster rate than the national average.

Education is also an important social infrastructure which helps in human capital formation and thereby industrial development. So, it is necessary to strengthen the educational infrastructures. Arunachal Pradesh has a fair number of primary, middle and secondary schools. As a result, in literacy, the state has made a significant progress. With only a 7.12 per cent literacy rate in 1961, the state covered a long route in four decades in achieving a 54.74 per cent literacy rate by 2001.

Conclusion

The creation of basic infrastructures is highly essential for industrial development of a region or a state. In fact, it is the infrastructure which can help the industries to grow. In other words, lack of proper infrastructural facilities (both physical and financial) can act as a major obstacle for industrial development as it happens in the case of Arunachal Pradesh. However, the industrialization of any area does not depend exclusively on the infrastructural development. It is now increasingly maintained that local entrepreneurship plays a pivotal role in any process of industrialization and the availability of local industrial entrepreneurs is one of a region or a state. However, it shows that in Arunachal Pradesh there is dearth of industrial entrepreneurs and the entrepreneurial skill among the local people. In this study, attempt is made to identify the factors which has prevented the growth of local industrial entrepreneurs in the State. It is found that relatively high risk and transaction cost are the important factors for the slow growth of local entrepreneurship. Hence, it is necessary to develop the market fully so as to make possible the better trading of risk and to evolve the institution in a way which would reduce the cost of transaction. At the same time, the local entrepreneurship development programme are to be conducted by various institutes from time to time to guide and motivate the prospective industrial entrepreneurs.

The various institutional rigidities such as non-existence of private property, poor infrastructural facilities, poor market facilities, restriction in free entry by imposing "Inner-Line Permit" system, insurgency problem, traditional and psychological barriers, lack of entrepreneurial skill and incentive, no plan of the government to establish free trade zone or growth centre are to be addressed for the growth of industry in the State. The primitive mode of production cannot be broken unless suitable institutional arrangement for creation of attractive incentive is done. Main reforms of government institutions related to "withdrawal of inner line permit and license policy" are very urgent to ensure easy entry of investment and skill labour force into the territory for industrialization. In this way, employment of local people will increase and thereby insurgency problem will automatically disappear.

In fact, the history of human society shows that civilization everywhere has been built by the contact and intercourse of peoples, which has been the chief motivating power behind progress. There are innumerable instances of the borrowing of cultural traits by peoples of different countries, such as articles of food, use of metals, domesticated animals, and method of agriculture and spread of literacy. So long as the borrowing has been natural and in harmony with cultural setting and the psychological make-up of the people, it has been intensely beneficial and even added to the richness of their culture. (T.Mibang, 1994). This remarks favour less restriction of entrance of Non-Arunachalees in the State.

To strengthen the economy of the State, the Government should provide larger scope to the private sector. At the same time, a number of changes in policy should be introduced with regard to industrial licensing to the non-tribal, removal of Inner Line, technology upgradation, fiscal policy, removal of controls and restrictions, rationalizing and simplifying the system of fiscal and administrative regulation and improving law and order problems so as to encourage for free flow of goods, capital, technology and labour from other States to this State. All these changes will be directed towards creating on uninhabited climate for private sector so that private sector investment can get a big boost to modernize the economy approaching towards "global economy". When the Government takes these steps and creates private investment, the State will grow automatically with industrialization.

REFERENCES

1. *Arunachal Review*, Vol. VIII, No. 22, June-August, 2007, p. 31.
2. Bhaduri Amit and Patkar Medha (2009): "Industrialisation for the People, by the People, of the people", *EPW*, Vol. XLIV, No. 1, January 3-9.
3. Desai, N.R. (1960): "Agricultural Marketing in M.P", *Agricultural Marketing*, Vol. III, No. 1, p. 43.
4. Elwin, Verrier (1957): "*A Philosophy for NEFA*": Forwarded by the then Prime Minister, Shri Jawaharlal Nehru, - Shillong, Sachin Roy on behalf of the North-East Frontier Agency, p. 59.
5. *Ibid.*, p. 53.
6. Krishna, Sumi (2000): "Arunachal Pradesh", in M.S. Swaminathan (ed.) *Gender Dimensions in Bio-Diversity Management*.
7. Mandal, R.K. (2005): "Arunachal Pradesh Emerging as Power House" *Journal of Global Economy*, Vol. 01, No. 4.
8. Mandal, R.K.(2006): "How to Develop Arunachal Pradesh", *Arunachal Review*, Vol. VIII, No. 18, June-August, Directorate of Information, Public Relations and Printing, Government of Arunachal Pradesh, Naharlagun, Arunachal Pradesh.
9. Memoria, C.B. and Tripathi, B.B., (1989): "*Agricultural Problems of Indians*", Kitab Mahal Agencies, p. 600.
10. Mibang, T. (1988): *Social Change in Arunachal Pradesh*, Omsons Publication, Rajouri Garden, New Delhi, p. 74.
11. Osik, N.N. (1999): *Modern History of Arunachal Pradesh*, Himalayan Publishers, Itanagar, New Delhi, pp. 1-2.

12. Raghurama, A., (Feb. 1, 2005): "Globalisation and challenges for small-scale sector in India", *Southern Economist*, Bangalore, Vol. 43, No. 19, p. 13.
13. Ruddar, D. and Sundharam, K.P.M. (2004): *Indian Economy*, S. Chand and Company Ltd., Ram Nagar, New Delhi, p. 247.
14. *Ibid.*, p. 810.
15. Reddy A.V. (2007): "National Rural Employment Guarantee Scheme: An Approach to Inclusive Growth", *Southern Economist*, Vol. 46, No. 3, p. 21.
16. Ruttan, V.W. and Jujiro Hayami (1984): "Towards a Theory of Induced Institutional Innovation", *Journal of Development Studies*, Vol. 20, pp. 203-223.
17. Uphoff, Norman (1991): *Managing Irrigation: Analyzing and Improving the Performance of Bureaucracies*, Sage Publication India Pvt. Ltd., New Delhi.
18. Wolf, Jr. Charles (1955): "Institutions and Economic Development, *American Economic Review*", December, pp. 867-883.

7

Khadi and Village Industries in North-East India with Special Reference to Arunachal Pradesh

Introduction

The main principle of Gandhian approach is to set up a system of village self-sufficiency. In this regard, the hypothesis of M.K. Gandhi was establishment of 'gram swaraj' in the countryside which means the complete independence of the Indian villages. The ultimate goal of Gandhian planning was to make Indian villages fully independent. Mahatma Gandhi often used to say that the real India was to be found in the villages, not in the cities and towns. This sector has not only continued to play a vital role in fulfilment of socio-economic objectives but also offers an excellent opportunity for industrial self-employment.

It was Mahatma Gandhi, who pioneered the revival of the age-old self-sufficiency (*Gram Swavalamban*) and leased a new life and extinct glory to the concept of Swadeshi. According to Gandhi, the law of *Swadeshi* was the *Swadharma* of the *Gita* interpreted in terms of one's physical environment. Gandhi advocated Khadi as the necessary and most important corollary of the principle of *Swadeshi* in its application to society, he warned that "it is the greatest delusion to suppose that the duty of *Swadeshi* begins and ends with merely spinning some yarn and wearing Khadi made from it. In Swadeshi there is no for illwill. It is a doctrine of selfless service and has its roots in the purest *ahimsa*, love".

Gandhiji had realized the dent made in the rural society and its economy by the machine economy, when he advocated Khadi and

Village Industries and self-sufficiency of the village. He worked for the removal of the stigma of unsociability and low status of the artisan so that the artisan could get his due place and share in the rural society, its economy and their development. These and other ideas culminated in the "*Sarvodayas*" concepts had facilitated the development of rural economy.

Rural industrialization is important not as a means of generating employment opportunities in the rural areas with low capital cost and raising the real income of the people, but because it contributes to the development of agriculture and urban industries. Without rural industrialization, it would be considerably more difficult to solve the problem of agricultural unemployment and widespread underemployment. Rural industrialization promotes rural industry.

According to Khadi and Village Industries Commission (KVIC), "rural industry or village industry is the one which is located in the rural area and produces any good or renders any service with or without use of power and in which the fixed capital investment per head of an artisan or a worker does not exceed rupees 50000." The definition of village industry has been recently modified by the government so as to enlarge its scope. Accordingly, any industry located in rural areas, village or town with a population of 20000 and below and an investment of Rs. 10 million in plant and machinery, is classified as a village industry.

Rural industry embraces different kinds of village and small industries. All the village industries have been grouped into seven major categories as follows:

(i) Mineral based industry
(ii) Forest based industry
(iii) Agro-based industry
(iv) Polymer and Chemical based industry
(v) Engineering and non-Conventional industry
(vi) Textile industry (excluding khadi) and
(vii) Service industry.

Village Self-sufficiency

The main principle of Gandhian approach is to set-up a system of village self-sufficiency. In this regard, the hypothesis of M.K. Gandhi was establishment of '*Gram swaraj*' in the countryside which means the complete independence of the Indian villages. The ultimate goal of Gandhian planning was to make Indian villages fully independent. Mahatma Gandhi often used to say that the real India was to be found in the villages, not in the cities and towns.

India lives in its villages; right from the historical phase, rural development is one of the topmost priorities of Indian's development strategies. Rural development is considered as one of the important tools to eradicate the chronic problems like poverty and unemployment. The term rural development is rightly defined by the World Bank that "Rural development is a strategy to improve the economic and social life of a specific group of people, the rural poor, including small and marginal farmers, tenants and the landless".

Similarly, Desai, underlined that the objectives of rural development encompasses improved productivities, increased employment, higher incomes for target groups as well as a minimum acceptable levels of food, clothing, shelter, education and health. Whereas, Prof. V.K.R.V. Rao, entrusted that the rural development is a process of optimum utilization of the natural and human resources of a given rural area for the enrichment of the quality of life of the people.

While going through the available definitions it is clear that the rural development is synonymous of upliftment of people with regard to physical, intellectual economic and social welfare in society. It is well known that the rural industrialization plays a pivotal role in rural development by providing employment, income, and infrastructural facilities etc.

Importance of Rural Industrialization

Developing industries in the rural areas is essential because:

1. Rural industries are labour intensive.
2. By providing employment, these industries have also high potential for income generation in the rural areas.
3. These industries encourage dispersal of economic activities in the rural areas and thus, promote balanced regional development.
4. Rural industries also help protect and promote art and creativity i.e., the age-old rich heritage of the country. Rural

industries being environment-friendly lead to development without destruction.

The Government has taken a number of policy initiatives through various Central Ministries for overall promotion of village and small scale industries.

The development of the Indian rural industries in rural areas has been one of the most important elements of industrial policy and programmes for rural development, though the scale of priority on it has differed from period to period during the last few decades. In overpopulated countries like India, agriculture alone cannot absorb the entire surplus workforce. It is axiomatic that new opportunities for employment i.e., in the rural areas are found largely in the non-agricultural sector. As rural industries are labour intensive in nature, therefore, they provide additional employment opportunities in the rural areas. The distinguishing characteristic of the rural industries is that it also provides a major proportion of employment opportunities to the women.

Another major feature of rural industries is its decentralized production through a network of well-knit rural industries which obviates the necessity of complicated managerial and competitive marketing techniques, thus, reducing the costs on account of overheads and paving avenues for managerial development in rural areas. These challenges and issues will lead to the establishment of village republics and human resources development centres at industrial establishments in the rural areas.

It will also provide ample scope for the promotion of artistic achievement and creativity that has been suppressed in rural areas for a long period of time. It is also well observed that in agrarian countries like India the rural industrialization has been promoting, agricultural development and *vice versa*. The rational behind rural industrialization in the Indian context today consists in the immediate need for reducing the rural urban economic imbalance, avoiding explosive social costs of over urbanization or urban agglomeration and providing of remunerative employment to the surplus labour in rural areas.

In addition, it utilizes the optimum level of local manpower, skill and available resources. Only rapid the rural industrialization can help to developing countries substantially, therefore, when opportunities increase for employment in the non-agricultural sector which will in turn increase the production of inputs needed to increase agricultural output and thereby the number of plants available for processing farm commodities will increase.

One of the major myths regarding setting up of big industries is that it eradicates many economic problems this is found to be still a myth in many areas for instance, the Rourkela Steel Plant was set-up in a tribal region in Orissa, but the plant did not help tribal people to improve their financial condition and their day to day living. Similarly, there are many other examples, that can be quoted as far as India is concerned settingup of big units is not going to help the local rural people, hence the setting up of rural industries alone would help towards the development of rural areas specifically in India.

In his hypothesis of '*Gram Swaraj*' M.K. Gandhi explained that every village should produce all needed crops, food and non-food items. Each village should possibly produce its own goods such as cloth, shoes and leather products and similarly a village should have essential amenities, such as schools, hospitals, entertainment facilities and playground. Gandhiji's assumption was that India lives in villages and majority of its population depends on agriculture and its allied occupations. In case of '*Gram Swaraj*' is established, India would get naturally an economic freedom and would stand as a prosperous and independent country in the world.

We have to generate mass employment at the same time; the produced goods should have sustained market. The investment part should also be affordable. Cloth may be one such commodity which can be bought by all the people irrespective of their economical standard so it has market both sustainable and permanent. Take for example, khadi, though it has great potential to generate employment facilities in the rural areas.

Evolution of Khadi and Village Industries (KVI)

Originally, Gandhi conceived khadi as the best instrument for giving concrete expression to the '*Swadeshi*' spirit and for making effective the boycott of foreign goods in general and foreign cloths in particular. Khadi was also expected to provide an opportunity to India for cultivating self-discipline and self-sacrifice as a part of non-cooperation movement. For coordinated development of Khadi throughout the country, Gandhiji set-up, the All-India Khadi Board (AIKB) with branches in all provinces in December, 1923. This organization was an integral part of the Indian National Congress and worked under its control. Initially the first phase of khadi movement in India started in 1918 and ended in 1924.

The second phase started in 1925 with the formation of an autonomous body called All India Spinners Association (AISA) of Akhil Bharat Charkha Sangh. It was organizationally independent of Indian National Congress. However, Gandhiji continued to distinguish and play important role in the affairs of the Sangh. In 1930 Gandhiji's attention was to form other village industries; as a result the All India Village Industries Association. (AIVIA) was established on the basis of a resolution passed by the Indian National Congress in 1934. The association under the Chairmanship of Gandhiji did distinguish service for the development of village industries. He wrote; "Khadi is the central sun around which the other village industries revolve like so many planets. They have no independent existence nor Khadi can exist without other village industries, they are absolutely interdependent". Among those that conceded a role for KVI, some stressed the need for adopting better technology and a flexible attitude to the use of machine. It was an answer to these doubt and hesitancies, Gandhiji wrote in the *Harijan* dated June 20, 1946 as follows: "Khadi (including Village Industries) is the only true economic proposition in terms of the millions of villagers until such time, if ever, when a better system of supplying work and adequate wages for every able bodied person above the age of sixteen, male or female, is found for his field, cottage or even factory in everyone of villages or displace the villages so as to give the villages the necessary comforts and amenities that well regulated life demands and is entitled to". "What I object to is the craze for machinery, not machinery as such. The craze is for what they call 'labour saving machinery'. Men go on 'saving labour' till thousands are without work and thrown on the open street to die of starvation. I want to save time and labour, not for a fraction of mankind, but for all".

Perhaps, the first move to make Khadi, a Governmental programme was made in 1946 by the Government of Madras, which deputed a senior officer to obtain advice from Gandhiji and set-up a department of khadi soon thereafter. This was followed by the Central Government's recognition of the importance of rural cottage industries in the Industrial Policy Resolutions of 1948. The Constituent Assembly also included development of cottage industries in rural areas among the Directive Principles of the Constitution in Article 43. These ideas were elaborated in the First Five Year Plans, which began in 1951-52.According to the First Five Year Plans, Village industries have a central place in the rural development programme and their development should be matter of State's concern. The Government of India has set-up the All India Khadi and Village Industries Board (AIKVIB) in January 1953. The main function of the Board was to prepare and organize programmes for the development of KVI, including training of personnel, manufacture and supply of equipment, supply of raw materials, marketing and research and study of the economic problems of different village industries. Again Khadi and Village Industries Commission (KVIC), a statutory body was created by an Act of Parliament (No.61 of 1956).Accordingly KVIC was established in April 1957 look after the work of the former AIKVIB.

The aim and objective of the Khadi and Village Industries (KVI) in the state is to promote the industrial activities in the state and thereby to provide employment opportunities to the rural and urban and to improve the economic conditions of the people. About 94 per cent population of Arunachal Pradesh lives in the rural belt making agriculture the main occupation. The world is moving towards natural and Eco-friendly Products. More and more people are becoming conscious of responsibility towards the environment and ecology and products like plastic, etc. are highly looked down upon and greater demand is being generated for bio-degradable and Eco-friendly products. The KVI Sector produces a wide range of exclusive products which are having distinct characteristics. Most of the projects of KVIC are local resource based and eco-friendly and which is very much suitable for a place like Arunachal Pradesh.

Khadi Industries have played a pioneering role in restoring the lost glory of the time tested for self-employment model, the model of just distribution of wealth, the model that generates maximum number of employment, the model that employs local resources and local talent to produce for masses. As we know, the advent of the British in India saw an emergence of a new politico-economic policy, which aimed at annihilating the traditional industry and handicrafts to find an outlet for its own products in the Indian market. The shear discrimination and oppressive policy totally led to destruction of the Indian handicrafts *vis-a-vis* the village self-sufficiency. It was Mahatma Gandhi, who pioneered the revival of the age-old self-sufficiency (*Gram Swavalamban*) and leased a new life and extinct glory to the concept of *Swadeshi*. Initially, Khadi and Village Industry was entirely a non-governmental effort under the inspired guidance of Gandhi. In 1923, he founded the All India Khadi Board, an integral part of the Indian National Congress. In 1925 he formed an autonomous organization called All India Spinner Association (AISA). In 1935 for promotion of other village industries he set-up All-India Khadi and Village Industries Association (AIVIA). To Gandhi, Khadi and Village Industries are absolutely inter-dependent and so later the AISA and AIVIA were merged into a single entity under the banner of Akhil Bharat Sarva Seva Sangh. After Independence, the Government of India set-up the All India Khadi and Village Industries Board in 1953. This Board, aimed to function in close cooperation with the State Governments and the Akhil Bharat Sarva Seva Sangh plagued with procedural handicaps. It was then decided in 1955 to replace this Board by a statutory body. Accordingly, the Khadi and Village Industries Commission (KVIC) came into being in 1957. The broad objectives of the KVIC are: (i) The social objective of providing employment, (ii) The economic objective of producing saleable articles, and (iii) The wider objective of creating self-reliance amongst the people and building up a strong community spirit.

The State Khadi and Village Industries Boards have come into existence in response to advice of the All India Khadi and Village Industries Board which was required by the Government Resolution of January 14, 1953 to work "in close cooperation with the State Government". Today there are 33 States and Union Territories Khadi and Village Industries Boards in the country.

The Arunachal Pradesh Khadi and Village Industries Board (APKVIB) was created by a State Act. The Board was initially under the administrative control of Department of Industries lately on bifurcation of this department and on creation of Department of Textile and Handicrafts it was placed under latter's administrative control. This Board like any other State Boards was positioned to promote the KVI sector and to act as a replica of KVIC at the State level. The Board is a promotional body with no income of its own as it does not undertake any commercial operation but generally channelizes and monitors utilization of central sector developmental funds provided by KVIC. The broad objectives are similar to that of the KVIC within the jurisdiction of the State of Arunachal Pradesh. However, the state government has to bear its establishment and administrative expenses. The APKVIB act was amended in 1998 and also framed its Rules and Regulations in this year. The Board got its first developmental fund from the KVIC in the year 1991-92.

The tribal communities were extremely self-reliant; they constructed their own inter-village path, build their own cane bridge, devised their own indigenous equipments to husk or grind rice and millets, weaving their own cloths, ornaments and jewels, hats, cooking vessels, weapons. This shows the exceptional similarities of Gandhian concept of self-reliance in the tribal Communities of the state. However, there was hardly any development. The economy and the society at the dawn of independence were primitive. But, now the days are fast moving far from culture of self-sufficiency in this tribal soil. Thus, in the context of changing scenario, the study aims at making a study that the KVI sector is relevant in the tribal soil of Arunachal Pradesh.

Thus, in the context of changing scenario, the study aims at making a study that the KVI sector is relevant in the tribal soil of Arunachal Pradesh. In view of this, the chapter attempts to address the objectives:

1. To ascertain the present scenario of KVI in North-East States.
2. To investigate the growth and development of Khadi and Village Industries and Employment Scenario.
3. To find out the major problems faced by Khadi and Village Industries, and
4. To find the probable solutions of the problems in the state.

Present Scenario of KVI in North-East States

In order to have better implementation and monitoring of KVI programme in the North-East States, KVIC took initiative to put foothold of its presence and established its field officials in the entire region. KVI occupy a unique position in the rural economy of this region and collaborative approach has been initiated. Spices Board of India and Khadi and Village Industries Commission have jointly extended financial and technical support for setting up of spices making units in Assam and Arunachal Pradesh. The Central Leather Research Institute (CLRI) under its Leather Technology Mission has extended support for setting-up leather products manufacturing projects in Manipur and Nagaland.

Table 7.1: Summary of Performance of KVI in NE States and India (2002-03).

(Rs. In lakhs, employment in lakh person)

India/NE State	*Production*	*Sales*	*Employment*	*Earning*
India	856936.82	1019333.80	66.45	330507.44
North East	26079.27	28619.14	2.91	12300.77
Arunachal Pradesh	317.88	446.85	0.01	150.86
Assam	6074.74	5721.56	1.22	2416.18
Manipur	5997.52	5656.74	0.62	2632.11
Meghalaya	3100.46	3842.30	0.25	1949.88
Mizoram	3769.44	5063.82	0.23	1492.67
Nagaland	4583.94	5508.02	0.30	3011.71
Tripura	2235.29	2379.85	0.28	647.3

Source: Annual Report of KVIC (Ministry of Agro and Rural Industries, Government of India 2003).

The North Eastern has a great diversity in respect of culture, tradition and ethnicity. They have a tradition of artistic craftsmanship wide variety of crafts such as weaving, painting, pottery, smithywork, basketry, wood carving, etc. Therefore, development of KIV activities in NE region is considered as priority area under KVI programme. In addition to this, attention is focused on to provide better infrastructure facilities and liberalized assistance to motive rural population of the region to take up KVI programme in a large way. Accordingly, various policy decisions were taken from time to time for the benefits in this region. A major policy decision was taken for allocating 10 per cent of KVIC's budget in the NE region. During the year 2002-03 the Government of India also earmarked separate budget allocating under KVI programme exclusively for the region. Under Rural Employment Generation Programme (REGP), concession facilities are extended to the weaker section. Accordingly, 30 per cent Margin Money is provided to the entrepreneurs of north-east region. Whereas, margin money for other than north- east is 25 per cent .In spite of many concession facilities extended to the region, Table 7.1 shows that contribution of KVI sector is not satisfactory, though KVI has a bright future in this region.

Growth and Development of Khadi and Village Industries and Employment Scenario

Prior to independence, the present State Arunachal Pradesh had nothing in respect of industrial sector with exception of home-crafts. In view of the craft practices in the territory, the Department of Cottage Industries came into function in the year 1952-53. The Arunachal Pradesh Khadi and Village Industries Board (APKVIB), a statutory body of the Government of Arunachal Pradesh was lately created by an Act of Legislative Assembly viz. the APKVIB Act 1989.The board started its function in 1991-92 under the administrative control of the Department of Textile and Handicrafts, Government of Arunachal Pradesh. The Act was further amended during the year 1998 as per Government of India's direction which has ensured that State Government exclusively control over administrative affairs of the board. The APKVIB has a Chairman, who is non-official head of the board. The Secretary, Industry to the Government of Arunachal Pradesh is the *ex-officio*, Member-Secretary of the Board. The Director, Textile and Handicrafts is the *ex-officio*, Chief Executive Officer of the Board. The Board has a full time Executive Officer.

The nodal agency for implementation of KVI programmes in the state is APKVIB. The Arunachal Pradesh Seva Sangh runs HRD Programme in the MDTC including Khadi Spinning and Weaving. The KVIC's state office headed by Assistant Director with 9 other supporting staff has been implementing Rural Employment

Generation Programme (REGP) and other Programme. The APKVIB is in a shocking position. It devoids the attention of the authority. The Chairman is appointed casually. There is no regular or full time CEO. The post of vice-chairman is non-functional and creates unnecessary strains on hard earn resources. State Government's funding is abysmally meagre with no long term plan on anvil. Indifference of the state authorities coupled with lack of institutional in-built capacity has resulted *inter alia* a low treatment by KVIC in sharing developmental funds. The Board has ended up by distributing KVIC funds without further follow up/monitoring. The KAVIRC observes, 'although these Boards were supposed to be replicas of the KVIC at the state level, but in reality they have not gone beyond the disbursement of KVIC funds. The Boards have even not efficiently and properly performed their primary functions' (Report of KAVIRC, 1987). 'Organizational weakness, lack of trained manpower and technical expertise, inadequate support from the state governments are some of the reasons for inability of the Board in making any significant impact' (Majumdar, 2000). The number of units of KVI established in different years is shown in Table 7.2.

Table 7.2: Number of Units of KVI Established in Different Years.

Year	*No. of units*
1999 – 00	9
2000 – 01	60
2001 – 02	23
2002 – 03	16
2003 – 04	14
2004 – 05	20
2005 – 06	19
2006 – 07	30
Total	**191**

Source: The Arunachal Pradesh Khadi and Village Industries Board.

The year-wise employment generation, total investment and per capita investment are shown in Table 7.3.

Table 7.3: Year-wise Employment generation.

(Rs. in Lakh and employment in No.)

Year	Employment	Total investment	PCI
1991 - 92	107	26.70	0.250
1992 - 93	98	24.62	0.251
1993 - 95	222	55.48	0.250
1995 - 97	160	132.79	0.830
1999 - 00	100	41.52	0.415
2000 - 01	378	187.21	0.495
2001 - 02	168	95.79	0.570
2002 - 03	190	103.83	0.546
2003 - 04	78	67.78	0.869
2004 - 05	137	99.64	0.727

Source: The Arunachal Pradesh Khadi and Village Industries Board.

Per Capita Investment (PCI) low and almost fixed then sudden high in 1995-97. The PCI has been near stabilized from 1999-00 to 2002-03. Then sudden jump and again in 2004-05 fall considerably. Again the year-wise employment generations in different industries are shown in Table 7.4.

Table 7.4: Industry-wise Employment generation.

Year	Khadi	Mineral based	Agro-based	Chemical based	Engineering and NCE	Textile	Forest based	Service industry	Total
1991-92	10	—	2	—	33	42	20	—	107
1992-93	10	—	23	—	24	36	2	3	98
1993-95	2	16	52	8	37	18	89	—	222
1995-96	—	—	19	38	46	18	39	—	160
1997-99	—	—	—	—	—	—	—	—	Nil
1999-00	—	22	16	—	34	—	22	6	100
2000-01	—	—	79	—	98	66	57	78	378
2001-02	—	24	48	—	46	—	32	18	168
2002-03	—	36	14	—	78	18	20	24	190
2003-04	—	—	—	—	38	26	14	—	78
Total	22	98	253	46	434	224	295	129	1,501

Source: The Arunachal Pradesh Khadi and Village Industries Board.

With the impact of globalization and development of education the number of job-seeker is increasing drastically. The Khadi and Village Industries in the state are playing a significant role in employment generation.

In spite of having abundant natural resources and tradition of artistic craftsman KVI programme is not visible in ground level. In cursory observation, KVI programme is suitable for the State like Arunachal Pradesh and should keep priority for growth of KVI to solve the unemployment problem. APKVIB being catalyst agent of KVI sector in the State, a number of KVI units have come up. Table 7.5 shows that, as on 31.03.2003 there were 326 units with investment of Rs.698.78 lakhs and 1478 persons engaged in this sector.

Table 7.5: District-wise Distribution of KVI unit in A.P. as on 31-03-2003.

(Rs. In lakhs, unit and employment in No.)

District	*Unit*	*Investment*	*Employment*
Papum Pare	138	282.21	582
Lower Subansiri	67	140.72	309
Upper Subansiri	7	9.91	22
East Siang	46	121.39	256
West Siang	28	78.11	163
Changlang	23	14.09	39
Dibang Valley	1	9.77	20
Tawang	1	0.54	1
West Kameng	3	10.82	20
East Kameng	4	28.65	58
Tirap	4	0.80	4
Lohit	4	1.20	4

Source: Directorate of Textile and Handicraft, Itanagar.

Revival and revitalization of the traditional handlooms, handicrafts and best utilization of local raw materials available in the State should be the basic aims of the KVI programme because fundamentals of the KVI establishment is to relief of poverty by finding employment to the villagers and make equitable distribution of goods produced. Further to Mahatma Gandhi who opined that KVI was symbolized economic freedom and equality. Therefore,

Arunachal Pradesh, a land of beautiful handicrafts, traditional craftsman and natural khadi and village industries' potentiality in every district should use KVI as tools for rural development. For this, APKVIB should identify and uplift the economic condition of those who fall below the poverty line and encourage them to enter into KVI activity. Table 7.5 reveals that there is a wide difference in the growth and development of KVI programme in different districts. Some districts of the State have yet to open account of the KVI activity. There is also dispersion in terms of establishment in all districts of the State. Therefore, APKVIB should sincerely implement the programme in view of equal distribution.

Industrial Policy Resolution of 1948, while appreciating the role of heavy and basic industries, and cottage and village industries as having very special role in the national economy, because it is most conducive for employment generation, decentralization of economic and industrial concentrate, and for a more equitable distribution of national wealth. Less population, industrially backward but growing State like Arunachal Pradesh should take advantage of KVI programme, because KVI sector is useful for mobilizing resources of small and middle class for investment in industrial ventures and it facilitates a more even distribution of incomes originating from village industries sector through a large number of retails outlets. Further, it is suitable for better utilization of local resources and for the achievement of local self-sufficiency in respect of certain types of essential consumer goods like food, cloth and agriculture equipment, etc.

Table 7.6: Bank Term Loans to KVI sector in A.P. as on 31-03-2003.

	Bank	*KVI unit (In number)*	*Amount (Rs. in lakh)*
1.	Centralized Bank		
	(a+b+c)	46	151.41
	(a) SBI Bank	24	48.90
	(b) UCO Bank	19	87.25
	(c) Vijay Bank	3	15.26

(*Contd...*)

(*Table 7.6 Contd...*)

2.	Arunachal Pradesh Bank (d+e)	68	166.90
	(d) A.P Rural Bank	67	160.54
	(e) A.P Co-op. Apex Bank	1	6.36
	Total (I+II)	114	318.31

Source: Directorate of Textile and Handicraft, Itanagar.

Finance is rightly regarded as the lifeblood of any commercial enterprises irrespective of its size and nature. Inadequacy of finance prevents the process of raising industrial growth. As such banks and financing institutions are a vital importance in the process of industrialization. Many times the committee is constituted to look into various aspects relating to the flow of institutional credit to KVI sector. They have submitted their report after study and observations regarding institutional credit flows and recommended different pattern and sources of finance to KVI sector. However, recommendations could not support both positive and pro-active to the KVI Programme in one way or the other.

Presently KVIC introduced a Margin Money Scheme with the adoption of project approach. In respect of KVI in rural areas, credit can be made available by nationalized banks to the enterprises directly, up to Rs. 10 lakh for individual units and up to Rs. 25 lakh for institution, for which 25 per cent of project outlay would be the margin money granted by the KVIC/State KVIB. Margin money eligibility in respect of weaker sections including women and special area like NE States, 30 per cent of the project cost up to Rs. 10 lakh. Hence, bank finances 95 per cent of the project cost in the form of term loan to the Arunachal Pradesh Scheduled Tribes beneficiary/ institution and 5 per cent in the form of beneficiary contribution, in the process of KVIC/ APKVIB grant 30 per cent of the project cost as a subsidy.

Table 7.6 shows the term loans granted by bank to KVI sector in the State and disbursed Rs. 318.31 lakh of which centralized banks disbursed Rs. 151.41 lakh and Arunachal Pradesh banks Rs. 166.90 lakh. Thus, nationalized bank have got prospect of credit for the KVI sector in the State. In spite of having many inhabiting factors in the development of agriculture sector; the State is exclusively reliance on it. Understanding, the increasing population and limited employment absorption capacity in agriculture and Government job, it is desirable to go for alternative source of income generation, employment expansion. One desirable alternate may be the rural industrialization through KVI programme. Because this sector has distinct advantages over large and medium scale industries. KVI provides immediate large employment, ensuring more equal distribution of wealth. This sector is labour intensive, less capital, less skill and has short gestation period and advantage of decentralization. KVI programme is good for accelerating the tempo of rural industrialization in the State. But the success of KVI programme is largely dependent on the dedication of KVIC and APKVIB officials, degree of co-operation from various concerned agencies and the involvement of people, their honest and fair participation which can make KVI programme success and living reality. Thus, the industry receives considerable help from the state government in the form of finance, improved looms, accessories and raw materials at reasonable rates. To promote production of handloom and handicraft products and generate self-employment, the Directorate of Textiles and Handicrafts is running 88 numbers of weaving and craft centres and 6 numbers of Handloom Development and Quality dyeing units in the State.

With a view to popularize handloom and handicraft products being manufactured by the industrial units in the State, the department has been participating in various fairs, festivals and exhibitions. Besides running 18 numbers of Emporia and 5 numbers of Show Rooms cum Sales Counters in the State, there are 2 numbers of Emporia functioning in Delhi and Kolkata. The department has also acquired a plot of land in New Mumbai for establishment of a Guest House and an Emporia to exhibit the State's traditional craft with a view to develop rich heritage of handloom and handicraft products of Arunachal Pradesh, the Department has taken up number of schemes viz. participation and organizing of Exhibition to create awareness amongst the local entrepreneurs and artisans of the State. The achievement of Craft/Weaving Centres during 2003-04 is shown in Table 7.7.

Table 7.7: Physical Achievement of Craft/Weaving Centres in Arunachal Pradesh during 2003-04.

Sl.No.	*Particulars*	*Unit*	*2001-2002*	*2002-2003*	*2003-2004*
1	*2*	*3*	*4*	*5*	*6*
1.	Craft/ Weaving Centres	No.	88	88	88
2.	Trainees in Craft/ Weaving Centres	No.	247	302	303
3.	Handloom Development Centre and Quality Dyeing Units	No.	6	6	6
4.	Value of Production of Cloth/ Craft	Rs. in lakh	NA	NA	28.59
5.	Emporium	No.	15	15	18
6.	Show Room-cum Sale Counter	No.	3	3	5
7.	Annual sale proceed of Emporium and Show Room cum Sales Counter	Rs. in lakh	39.80	40.09	
	Cash				6.72
	Credit				38.26

Source : Directorate of Textile and Handicraft, Itanagar.

Major Problems Faced by Khadi and Village Industries

The KVI are not commercially viable due to—(i) lack of interest of weavers, (ii) lack of raw materials, (iii) lack of working capital, (iv) lack of marketing facilities, (v) lack of capacity-utilization, (vi) lack of technical know-how, (vii) shortage of organizational strength, (viii) competition from power loom and other modern products, (ix) lack of entrepreneurial knowledge, (x) lack of power, (xi) lack of transportation,etc. Some of these problems are discussed below in brief.

Market

Market is not necessarily confined to any particular geographical location in which buyer and seller are brought into contact with one another. The buyer may be in Delhi and seller in Mumbai or even in London. What is essential for a market is that the buyers and the sellers are able to get in touch with one another that the exchange of goods and services for money takes place between them. The contact for the exchange of goods can be performed with the help of e-mail, internet, telephone, telegraph, ordinary post, etc. It is undisputedly accepted that the success of an industry depends on the market of its products. It has no well organized market outside this State and even inside the State. It has no worldwide website and no regular advertisement through T.V. and Radio and not even in daily newspaper inside or outside the State. Again there is no organized agent to whom its products are sold. Only the local entrepreneurs are encouraged to participate in different Fares and Expo inside and outside the State like N.E. Trade Expo, Indian International Trade Fare, New Delhi and Regional Level Exhibitions where the products of KVI are exhibited and sold.

Inner Line System

After Independence, the Government of India decided to continue to follow the restriction of the Inner Line System. But the purpose for which the Inner Line had been designed in 1873 was changed. The main purpose of the Inner Line is to restrict the free movement of Non-Arunachalees in NEFA now Arunachal Pradesh, i.e., the free flow of entrance of Non-Arunachalee is prohibited in the State. A Non-Arunachalee who wants to cross beyond such Line has to get first an Inner Line Pass (ILP) issued by Arunachal Pradesh Government authorized Gazetted Officer for a limited period of time after fulfilling some formalities.

Again, it is thought that the territory is located at strategic point from the standpoint of defence. Besides, the Government of India feels it necessary to protect the land and forest of the innocent tribal people of the State from the Non-Arunachalees' hunger of grabbing. It is well thought that the protected Arunachalees can make economically a smooth progress. They will not be disturbed from their socio-cultural and economic dimension.

Globalization refers to a process of increasing economic integration and growing economic interdependence between countries in the world economy. It is associated not only with an increasing cross-border movement of goods, services, capital, technology information and people, but also with an organization of economic activities which crosses national boundaries. Broadly speaking, the term 'globalization' means integration of economies and societies through cross-country flows of information, ideas, technologies, goods, services, capital, finance and people. Globalization says cross-country flows among countries. To get the good effect of globalization in the State it needs first cross-state flows among the States in India.

Industrialization is recognized as a real tool of economic development as it indicates a higher standard of living of the majority of population. Once Nehru told that real progress might ultimately be depend on industrialization. During the last 58 years after independence, our country has been bringing a noticeable growth in industrial production. But the North-Eastern Region of our country has, till now, been lying neglected. Therefore, Inner Line System stands as a main hindrance for the growth and development of KVI as well as globalization.

License Issuing System

The people from outside of this State comes for the activities for which they are to obtain license in the name of some tribal people who get the rent from the businessmen for their licenses. These trading people earn money and mostly siphon-off in their respective home because they do not get the right to buy the property for independent business and trade. This situation hugely restricts the private investors in coming and opening up manufacturing units within this territory. Banking credit for establishing business and industries are available to the local people but they lack entrepreneurial skills and show little interest in industrial production activities. Therefore, "Inner Line Permits system and government policy in issuing licenses" only to local people most likely has worked against the opening up of KVI in this part of the country.

Entrepreneurial Lack

Economic development of any region is an outcome of purposeful human activity. Both the developed and the underdeveloped countries look at the industrialization process as an important key to economic development. Most of the social scientists agree that man stands at the centre of economic activity and he assumes various roles in the development process, namely, as an organizer of human and material resources, worker, consumer and exchange agent. Out of these multiple role, his role as the organizer of human and material resources is the most important and basic one.

It is widely accepted that the availability of entrepreneurship is the most important determinant in the process of industrialization. The government in its efforts to create entrepreneurship in the underdeveloped regions provides for various monetary and non-monetary incentives like the development of an infrastructure, assistance in marketing and procuring raw materials, providing finance or granting subsidies on investment. With this thrust in view, the State Governments have created various institutions to cater to the different needs of entrepreneurs.

It can be argued that lack of entrepreneurial skill of the local people and their deficient interest to invest and innovate has contributed in preventing the evolution of modern economic system in the State. One example, of their lacking interest in manufacturing activities is that those tribal boys and girls who go for crafts training do not want to have their own business but like to join as craft teachers in government organizations (Krishna, 2000). The mindset of the tribal is not to establish their own enterprise or business but to venture either in politics, contract business, or government services to earn "easy money". This mindset can be termed as "psychological barrier" which has emerged very strongly in the context of present socio-political context of the State. Some tribal people within a very short period of time have experienced income and wealth inequalities to a high degree. Very few of them have been found to become very rich over night and enjoy luxurious life and prefer conspicuous consumption which has been adversely affecting the rest of the society. The income inequalities in the tribal society are very much strong. Some are very rich and some are very poor. Some peoples in rural areas are living on self-growing food and common property resource forest product without functioning of money. The presence of high degree of corruption at all levels and existence of underground economy has also gone against in development of market economy.

Power

The modern economic development involves large-scale use of power. Regarding the set-up of an industry, the State needs first some infrastructural facilities of which power is one. Due to its geographical location and its hilly terrain, Arunachal Pradesh has an immense hydel potential to use the power of water to produce electricity in comparison to the other states of the country. The state is of turbulent perennial rivers and major streams, which possess enormous hydro-electric generation potential. In addition to water resources, the state has oil, natural gas and coal resources that can be used in the production of electricity. Presently, there is a vast gap between the availability and the requirement of power. As per 2001 Census, out of 2,12,615 households, only 116,275 households (54.7%) are having electricity facility and out of 3649 numbers of villages (as per 1991 Census), only 2339 numbers have been electrified accounting 64 per cent of the total villages till the end of March 2003. Arunachal Pradesh, having untapped estimated hydro-power potential of 49,000 MW, may emerge as Power House of India when this potential is fully harnessed (*Source:* Department of Power, Government of Arunachal Pradesh).

Transportation

The service of Transportation is a precondition of economic development. Revolution in transport and communication would take place first before the advent of industrial revolution. It is well known fact that the prosperity of a country depends on the development of agriculture, mining, industry, services, banking etc. But without prior development of transport, any type of development is not possible of a region.

As such, in the development plans, the government has been attaching high priority to the construction of roads and as a result the total length of roads constructed in the State stood at about 15021.80 kms. including 399.80 kms. under National Highway giving the road density of 17.9 kms. per 100 sq. kms. of the area at the end of March, 2004 as against the all India average of 74.9 kms. per 100 sq. kms. during 1997.Thus, in comparison to the All India Road density , the State has a very low road density in the country, which is the basic barrier to the development of industry. Again, a peculiarity of surface transport of the State is that most of the district headquarters are not interconnected, i.e., one cannot move from one district headquarters to other specially the old district headquarters in Arunachal Pradesh without going down to Assam. The State does not have lateral roads connecting district headquarters and sub-divisional headquarters of the districts. In other places, roads run vertically connecting places of Assam with the places of district headquarters in the State. As a result, the transport cost is not only high but also the state is affected by disturbances and insurgency activities in Assam.

Arunachal Pradesh being predominantly hilly terrain, there is a lot of constraints in the development of railways. In fact, the State was brought under the railway map of India for the first time with the opening of Balipara (near Tezpur, Assam) to Bhalukpong in West Kameng District of Arunachal Pradesh in 1989 with only 1.26 kms. (metre gauge).

Solutions

New objectives, strategy, organizational change required for Handlooms: The handloom sector is beset with manufacture problems such as obsolete technology, unorganized problem, low productivity, inadequate working capital, conventionally protected range, weak marketing strategies; competition from powerloom sector and the like. However, with an effective State intervention through development and welfare schemes implemented mainly through co-operatives, the sector has been able to tide over some of these disadvantages.

Efforts of politicians, government and regulatory agencies like RBI and NABARD, the staff and members of the co-operatives are required for this. What is required is a political will to make the cooperatives competent and concerted efforts should be made to make them competent. This requires technological and design intervention with institutional support, apart from effectively implementation of the present and proposed development and welfare scheme intended for the handloom weavers.

The following suggestions may be considered with a view to strengthen the KVI in Arunachal Pradesh.

1. First, this industry needs well organized advertisement for its product through T.V., Radio, even through daily newspaper outside and inside the State. It must have been own website.

2. The State Government should give priority to develop border trade with Bhutan, China and Myanmar. If border trade comes into effect with undivided sincerity, I hope, it will give fillip not only generating a new avenue of employment but also it will make a self-generating and self-sustaining economy of Arunachal Pradesh. In this way the market for Arunachal products including KVI will be automatically developed.
3. A comprehensive techno-economic survey of entire region of Arunachal Pradesh by a competent agency should be performed to find out the potentiality of such type of small scale industries.
4. Establishment of various technical and managerial institutions should be set-up for imparting training to the existing and potential entrepreneurs.
5. Complete financial support and its use in proper way in any probable selected unit should be shouldered by the government agent.
6. The flow of relevant information relating to these small scale industries should be circulated in a regular way so that the entrepreneurs can get up-to-date information about technology, manpower planning, etc.
7. The bank has to play more vital role in addition to lending credit assistance to such type of small scale industries. Bank may offer a special scheme to the entrepreneurs so that they can take short-term interest free loan. The bank can detect the sickness of industrial units and draw up a nursing plan for their rehabilitation. It can set-up a special cell for close monitoring during the rehabilitation period until the unit becomes self-sufficient again.
8. Tourism industry must be developed on the priority basis as this State has a great potentiality regarding this so as to attract large number of tourists to come in Arunachal Pradesh. The development of tourism industry will bring the development of KVI in the State.
9. Last of all, we can say that to bring small scale industrial development, the State should be self-sufficient in raw materials, technical knowledge, machine and tools, skilled labourers, technicians and overall marketing facilities.

10. In the context of to-day's global liberalization, the existence of inner line between Arunachal and the rest of the economy of India may be deemed irrelevant as because, the observance of inner line is obstructing the inflow of capital, other inputs and technology. In such a situation, how can Arunachal Pradesh expect to avail of the benefit of liberalization so as to boost up the state market economy? Here, precisely. It may be within reasonable limit while recommending that the inner line should go.
11. The weavers must be in a position to change the pattern and method of weaving i.e., they must adapt to change market situations. They should not stick to the same items.
12. The focus could be turned towards readymade items to attract the young customers who are fond of modern dresses. The Government may extend rebate to readymade items also.
13. There must be a handloom complex for marketing of handlooms in addition to the Co-opted, Loom world and so on. Places may be provided for individual primaries to have stalls in main parts of every town and city.
14. The Co-opted must settle the dues in time. This will ensure uninterrupted production.
15. The Government could strictly implement the Reservation Policy at all levels.
16. The Government authorities may also clear the wrong conception of the rebate i.e., 'the rebate is bogus.

Therefore, the KVI needs:

- Sustaining the existing weaving population on hand weaving by stopping their exit through developmental and welfare schemes.
- Making weaving a remunerative and economic avocation for the new generation.
- Ensuring long-term sustainability of the sector by providing higher income level to the weavers through the Self-Help Groups.
- Utilizing the 'Handloom Mark' throughout the country effectively.
- Involvement of Non-Governmental Organizations (NGOs) such as SHGs and the others in implementation of schemes.

- Regularizing supply of quality yarn through State and Centre Institutions at a reasonable price.
- Regularizing multi-level training scheme for the existing as well as new generation weavers by creating new centres apart from strengthening the existing infrastructure for training.
- Organizing the women weavers into exclusive SHG in all the villages. These groups can be encouraged to undertake weaving activity with modern designs (CAD).
- Encouraging the production of unique products in handlooms, this cannot be easily copied or mass-produced by powerloom and mill sectors.
- Encouraging manufacture of value added items.
- Securing market for certain handloom items through meeting clothing requirements of Government Departments and Public Sector Undertakings.
- Organizing buyer seller meets and overseas exhibitions to enhance market awareness and to enable the weavers understand the emerging consumer tastes and preferences.
- Motivating the Public to patronise handloom cloth and motivating the weavers to produce the product as per the taste of the modern market.
- Explaining to the weavers the benefits of social security and welfare schemes like Mahatma Gandhi Bunkar Bima Yojana Scheme.
- Making the concept of 'social audit' mandatory in respect of all the handloom exporters.
- Conducting market survey to create fashion market on design intervention, the infrastructure and other facilities, for which National Institute of Fashion Technology and National Institution of Designs and others may be utilized.

Conclusion

In an age in which mechanical inventions are the prime factor in economic progress, it is difficult to realize that in certain lines, hand-made goods are unsurpassed in excellence by the products of modern machinery. The efforts taken by both Central and State Governments must be made to reach the beneficiaries. The implementing agencies and machineries must take it as a venture with all commitment and positive attitude. The feedback as well as follow-up is *very* much needed to revive and sustain this sector in the global context.

In the process of industrial development the importance of cottage industries should not be ignored. To set-up heavy industry is not so much possible in different places of this State as its major portions are not easily accessible. But to set-up small scale industries in the State is not so much difficult. That is why; top priority must be given to those small scale industries like Khadi and Village Industries which need light machine tools and other equipments in order to produce qualitative products because today, a State's progress is measured by the quality of goods it produces.

To strengthen the economy of the State, the Government should provide larger scope to the private sector. At the same time, a number of changes in policy should be introduced with regard to industrial licensing to the non-tribal, removal of Inner Line, technology upgradation, fiscal policy, removal of controls and restrictions, rationalizing and simplifying the system of fiscal and administrative regulation and improving law and order problems so as to encourage for free flow of goods, capital, technology and labour from other States to this State. All these changes will be directed towards creating on uninhabited climate for private sector so that private sector investment can get a big boost to modernize the economy approaching towards global economy.

Employment is the surest way to enable the vast numbers of people living below the poverty level to raise them above it. KVI is capable of offering employment opportunities at the place of residence to a large section of population. This has the capacity to correct regional imbalances by initiating industrial activities on dispersed basis in the most neglected, backward inaccessible areas like most of the areas of North-East States where perhaps large scale sector is unable to penetrate. KVI is a key to rural development and rural prosperity.

REFERENCES

Borgohain, H. (2004): "Development of Industries and Handicrafts in Siang Region" in Pandey, B.B. (ed), "*Patterns of Change and Potential for Development in Arunachal Pradesh,"* Himalayan Publishers, Itanagar, New Delhi, pp. 133-139.

Das, G.D (1995): *"Tribes of Arunachal Pradesh in Transition"*, Vikas Publishing House Pvt. Ltd., Jangpura, New Delhi, pp. 30-33.

Das, N.C. (1998): "Handloom Development Programme under five year plans in Assam" in Bhorali, D. (ed), *"Economic Development of the North-Eastern Region"*, Spectrum Publication, Guwahati, Delhi, pp. 177-185.

Government of Arunachal Pradesh (2000, 2001, 2002, 2003 and 2004): *"Economic Review of Arunachal Pradesh"*, Directorate of Economics and Statistics, Itanagar.

Jeyakodi, K. (2007): "Strategy for Handloom Sector: An Evaluation", *Southern Economist*, June 15, Vol. 46, No. 4, p. 15-16.

Jha, S.D. (1985): *"The Wealth of Arunachal Pradesh"* Mittal Publications, Delhi, p. 375.

Joram, A. (2006): "Khadi and Village Industries Movement in Arunachal Pradesh", *Arunachal Review*, Vol. VII. No. 19, Sept.-Nov., pp. 1-4.

Krishna, Sumi (2000): "Arunachal Pradesh", in M.S. Swaminathan (ed.) *Gender Dimensions in Bio-Diversity Management*.

Mandal, R.K. (2006): "Arunachal Pradesh as Emerging Power House", *Journal of Global Economy*, Vol. 1, No. 4, Oct.-Dec., p. 223.

Mandal, R.K.(2005): "Emergence of Marketing of Handloom and Handicraft Products of Arunachal Pradesh" a paper presented in the 7th Annual Conference of North-Eastern Economic Association (NEEA) held at Rajiv Gandhi University, w.e.f. 21st to 22nd October.

Mandal, R.K. (2007): "Khadi and Village Industries in North-East India with Special Reference to Arunachal Pradesh: Retrospect and Prospect", *Journal of Global Economy*, Vol. 3, No. 2, Research Centre for Social Science, 403, Kalina, Mumbai-400098.

Mandal, R.K. (2009): *"Khadi and Village Industries: Problems and Prospects in Socio-Economic Development of Arunachal Pradesh"*, UGC Sponsored Major Research Project.

Mandal, R.K. (2007): "Constraints of Economic Development in Arunachal Pradesh with Special Reference to Globalization and Inner Line System", *Artha Beekshan*, Vol. 15, No. 3, December, IIDS, 221A, APC Road, Kolkata-700 004.

Patri, Neelakant (2007): "Operation 123—Will it Take Off?" *Southern Economist*, Vol. 46, No. 8, Bangalore, pp. 6-7.

Sankaran, A. and Kumar, Jagdish (2007): "Performance of Khadi and Village Industries in India", *Southern Economist*, Vol. 46, No. 1, Mangalore, p. 34.

8

Entrepreneurial Innovation and Economic Development

Introduction

Rural industrialization is important not as a means of generating employment opportunities in the rural areas with low capital cost and raising the real income of the people, but because it contributes to the development of agriculture and urban industries. Without rural industrialization, it would be considerably more difficult to solve the problem of agricultural unemployment and widespread underemployment. Rural industrialization promotes rural industry. According to Khadi and Village Industries Commission (KVIC), "rural industry or village industry is the one which is located in the rural area and produces any good or renders any service with or without the use of power and in which the fixed capital investment per head of an artisan or a worker does not exceed Rs. 50,000." (N.K. Trikha, 2005). The definition of village industry has been recently modified by the government so as to enlarge its scope. Accordingly, any industry located in rural areas, village or town with a population of 20000 and below and an investment of Rs. 10 million in plant and machinery, is classified as a village industry.

Rural industry embraces different kinds of village and small industries. All the village industries have been grouped into seven major categories as follows.

(i) Mineral based industry
(ii) Forest based industry
(iii) Agro-based industry

(iv) Polymer and Chemical based industry
(v) Engineering and non-Conventional industry
(vi) Textile industry (excluding khadi), and
(vii) Service industry.

Need for Rural Industrialization

Developing industries in the rural areas is essential because:

1. Rural industries are labour intensive.
2. By providing employment, these industries have also high potential for income generation in the rural areas.
3. These industries encourage dispersal of economic activities in the rural areas and thus, promote balanced regional development.
4. Rural industries also help protect and promote art and creativity i.e., the age-old rich heritage of the country. Rural industries being environment-friendly lead to development without destruction.

The economic development of India largely depends upon the success of industrial and agricultural sectors. The agricultural sector has not been able to contribute adequately to the national economic development. Therefore, the industrial sector has assumed greater importance in economic development. Realizing this fact, our planners have aimed of speedy industrial development through utilizing the natural and physical resources that the country processed plenty. They also realized that the people and their potential ability have supreme role to play for economic development. The growing needs of the public on the one hand, and the inability of the government machinery to fullfil the ever-growing needs of people efficiently and effectively on the other hand, has accelerated the process of marketisation. This trend could be clearly seen in the field of industry and the business where the potential entrepreneur comes forward to take up industrial ventures. It is worthwhile considering what role the women entrepreneurs can play in the context.

Entrepreneurial drive among youth is considered an important factor for the socio-economic development of community and country. Entrepreneurial initiative is a key factor for the development of any community. Communities where entrepreneurial ingenuity is high enough to optimally and effectively use the scarce resources at the disposal of the community, the economic development is more and correspondingly the quality of life of the members is better. In India, especially since the Eighth Five Year Plan period, it is realized that self-employment and small business initiatives have a very important role in generating employment and developing the economy.

Entrepreneurship is a vital input to industrial development as entrepreneurial talents and efficiency made the fortune of an enterprise.

Entrepreneurs are those who initiate organize, manage, control the affairs of business or industrial unit and confine the factors of production with supply of goods and services. They are dynamic force in the economic life of a society and have organized its productive resources.

Cantillon's (1755) remarked on uncertainty has been widely interpreted as, the first introduction of the term entrepreneurship into economic theory. According to him, entrepreneur as one "who assumes the risk of buying goods, or parts of goods, at once price and attempts to sell them for profit, either in their original states or as new products. Knight (1921) viewed the entrepreneur as an "economic pioneer who initiates change or innovation by managing uncertainty and risk. According to him, an entrepreneur is the person who willingly carries on those responsible activities which are neither insured nor salaried.

Schumpeter (1934) described the leadership role of the entrepreneur in an economy in his belief that entrepreneurs are continually reorganizing the economic system. Schumpeter also distinguishes his entrepreneur from the 'inventor' by claiming that 'as long as they are not carried into practice, inventions are economically irrelevant. Thus, entrepreneurial talents make themselves felt by introducing new ideas, new combinations, with the consequence that established firms are challenged and the pre-existing ways of economic life the disrupted.

Human resources are one of the most strategic and critical determinants of growth. Inspite of abundant physical resources, a country cannot make rapid economic and social advancement unless it has enterprising people with necessary knowledge, skills and attitudes. In any developing country, human resource development is the key to development in all sectors of the economy, more particularly rural sector where a majority of the people are *very* poor, illiterate and lack the necessary knowledge, skills but also *creativity*, interpersonal relations, team building, leadership, *motivation*, training, education, health, nutrition, employment, empowerment and rights of the people.

Concept of Entrepreneur

An entrepreneur is basically an *innovator* who introduces something new into the economy. He is a person who is capable of taking investment decisions, calculated risks under conditions of uncertainty, can plan and *innovate*, take prompt and wise decisions in selection of a product or product mix, technology mix and marketing. Therefore, an entrepreneur is a dynamic agent of change, or catalyst who transforms the physical, natural and human resources into corresponding production possibilities. He is the key person who envisages new opportunity, new techniques, new lines of production, new products and co-ordinates all other activities. Basically an entrepreneur is a person who is responsible for setting up a business or an enterprise, and *strives* to maximize profits by adopting innovations.

Concept of Entrepreneurship

Entrepreneurship is the *creative* and *innovative* response to the environment, which can take place in *variety* of fields of social endeavour—business, industry, agriculture, education, social work and the like and it is the potent limiting factor in economic development. It is an act of assuming risk of business ownership. In fact, it is the mental urge to take risk in the face of uncertainties and an initiation and capacity of seeing things in a way afterwards, proves to be true. And it is an individual set-up of managing things in a proper manner. It is multidimensional encompassing financial, managerial and functional aspect.

Entrepreneurship Development

Economic development is a process, the ultimate aim of which is to raise the standard of living of the people. Effective utilization of the resource endowments in the country hastens this process. Many countries have achieved this. This calls for certain higher qualities in human talent described as entrepreneurship. This existence and its level of competence set the limit to the degree of development and the speed with which the same is achieved. The absence of such qualities is held to be the causative factor for the tardy development of many of the developing economies. Promotion of these qualities have been recognized as necessary today and accorded critical importance in national efforts.

Role of Entrepreneur

The functions and the role of an entrepreneur *reveal* the uniqueness of the qualities in entrepreneurship. The functions are classified into internal and external. The internal functions include assembling of factors of production, organization of the enterprise and take up the responsibilities of engineering and the like; the external functions include purchasing of raw materials, entering into contacts, determination of quality and quantity of output and pricing and marketing of goods. The performances of these functions require foresight, shrewd judgment, business acumen, and a capacity to work and extract work.

The entrepreneur need not do all the functions himself; they can be delegated. But this can be only decision-making and risk-taking in anticipation of the success of the venture. This responsibility solely rests on the entrepreneur. In tune with his actions, the enterprise either capacity to successfully initiate, co-ordinate, *motivate* and lead the enterprise. This is easily said than found. The motivated needs to have a mental set-up which is highly *motivated* with a strong will and bold determination to pursue one's path irrespective of the uncertainties and the risk involved. This spirit is hard to be found in preference to a peaceful and steady life.

The entrepreneurial activity may manifest itself in two ways. It can emerge as a result of individual efforts or collective and co-operative efforts including the state. The first category is known as individual entrepreneurship where type is based on techno-structure, which is a systematic outcome of mechanization, division of labour, large scale production and production in anticipation of demand. This type of leadership is shifted from one individual to an organized group.

In many of the developing economies, this techno-structure though have helped to strengthen the economic development base and the process have failed to have spread effects and intimates the process of industrialization in real terms. They have been able to create largely social overheads and townships only. These points to the necessity of fostering the individual and local entrepreneurial talents are to make the process of economic growth meaningful and sustained. Fundamentally, this involves an effort at raising the general level of human talent in the country as it forms the source of supply of such entrepreneurship.

The problem in many of the developing countries is that the entrepreneurial supply and its competence are at a very low level. This leads to economic inequalities and exploitation. The social systems, cultural values, lack of infrastructural facilities and the technological backwardness are held as the inhabiting factors in developing entrepreneurial attitudes in the people.

The Government of India has taken many steps through institutional props, fiscal policies and public sector enterprises in accordance with the national objectives to create the climate for the promotion of the entrepreneurial talent in the country. Formation of industrial estates, establishment of financial institutions and institutes for motivation, training and service are given stressed on priority basis but there is a few to cite. However, these have proved to be insufficient and have been largely available only to the urban areas. India is said to live in villages and the rural people remain still ignorant and unable to reach to these facilities and use them. A vast change can be witnessed in the mental frame of the people, if only they are activated.

As an innovator who commercially applies the Invention, he developed new product, modifying the existing products and services. He promotes capital formation by mobilizing the idle savings of the household sector. The profit, which he earns ultimately, goes to capital formation. Every productive venture involves risk. Entrepreneur takes risk and gets a reward of profit. The quantity of profits depends upon the quantity of moderate risk taken.

Institutional Support for Entrepreneurs

In India various institutions were set-up to promote Entrepreneurial development. During the last two decades many banks either solely or with the help of other Agencies have taken up the task of advising the prospective entrepreneur about the preparation planning, evolution and execution of projects called as merchant banking, Entrepreneurial banking, new entrepreneur scheme. Government also offers a range of incentive measures to Entrepreneur for providing an impetus to industrialization.

Developing countries aims at the decentralization of industrial structure to remove the regional imbalances and they prepare to export more so that the entrepreneurs start the Industry in backward areas so as to remove the imbalances and fulfil the export promotion. Entrepreneur create wealth, generate employment and income and they increase the standard of living etc.

District Industries Centre (DIC)

District Industrial centre was introduced on 1st May, 1978 with the intention that under a single roof a entrepreneur should be able to get necessary benefits and guidance about all related matter of Industries. Each District has a DIC at its headquarters. The main responsibility of DIC is to act as the chief co-ordinator or multifunctional agencies for various Government Departments and other Agencies.

Function of DIC

The functions of DIC can be summarized as Identification of project, Selection of projects, Provisional registration under SSI, Acquiring of land and building, Purchase of plant and machinery Power connection, Clearance from various departments, SSI registration, Raw material allotment, Import of machinery and raw materials, Assistance to Village artisans, Interest free sale tax loan, Power subsidy and various Training Programmes, Self-employment for unemployed youth etc.

Small Industries Development Organisation (SIDO)

SIDO is a policy making coordinating and monetary agency for the development of small entrepreneur. It maintains a close link with the government and other financial organization which are involved in the promotion and development of small scale industries. It provides a good consultancy services, technical, managerial, economic and marketing assistance to SSI units.

Technical Consultancy Organizations (TCO)

All Indian Financial Institutions and the state governments have set-up a net work of technical consultancy organization in the country. The activities of the TCO include conducting survey on industrial potential, preparation of project, profiles and feasibility studies, undertaking techno economic appraisal of projects, carry out market research, providing technical and managerial assistance to entrepreneur, assistance in modernization of technology upgradation, rehabilitation programme and organizing information cell and Databank regarding industrial environment potential.

Women Entrepreneurs

The girl today needs to be exposed to the new values system that will enable her to emerge as 'new women'. Women have a predominant role to play in our country and there is a need to bring them into mainstream of economic development in general and industrial development in particular. But they have not responded favourably. As traditionally, women are confined to the four walls of their homes. But, now times have been changing they should be motivated and encouraged to force themselves to enlarge their field of activities. In view of their proverbial capacity for hard work, dedications, commitment and sense of duty and responsibility, they have been properly motivated and in their note talents and canalized into newer and fruitful activities and entrepreneurship. In the interest of the nation's all round development is necessary, that Indian women both urban and rural be drawn into them without delay. There can be no doubt that they can make substantial contribution to the nation's development, and in industrial field also the small scale sector provides many opportunities for their entrepreneurship.

The importance of the economic development of women takes on an added dimension in India when considered in the context of the prevailing social, legal and economic norms. The government has, therefore, taken several steps to promote women entrepreneurship.

In view of the initiative shown by women in various economic activities, promotional organizations have been organizing special programmes for them. This trend indicates a shift towards a gender-specific approach to such programmes in order to enhance the competence of women in the establishment and management of SSIs. The 1991 Industrial Policy has envisaged special training programmes to support women entrepreneurs. Accordingly, women entrepreneur are receiving training through Entrepreneurship Development Programmes (EDPs) conducted by various institutions and organisations both at the Central and State levels.

The SIDO, with its field officers all over the country, has been carrying out development programmes for women entrepreneurs and is providing technical schemes for the setting up of SSI units. In view of changing outlook of the promotion of women enterprises, the SSI Board in 1991 revised the definition of women enterprises by omitting the condition of employing 50 per cent of women workers. This provided a boost to women entrepreneurs to take up businesses and avail of facilities as are applicable to all SSIs.

The SIDBI has instituted various developmental initiatives towards promoting women enterprises. The Bank has designed programmes, with a focus on women, viz. Mahila Vikas Nidhi, Mahila Udyamik Nidhi, Micro Credit Scheme, Women Entrepreneurship Development Programmes, etc. These programmes have been formulated with the twin objectives of: (i) providing training and extension services support to women entrepreneurs through a comprehensive package suited to their skills and socio-economic status; and (ii) extending financial assistance on liberal, to enable them to set-up industrial units in the small scale sector. Andhra Pradesh has set-up an exclusive Industrial Estate for Women Entrepreneurs. The other states can take lesson from Andhra Pradesh.

State Industrial Policies

Incentives are needed to remove regional disparities in the development of any region or area, to promote entrepreneurship and strengthen the entrepreneurial base in the economy, to provide competitive strength, survival and growth of entrepreneurs, to generate more employment and remove underemployment and unemployment and to provide self-sustainability to educated youth.

The State/UT Governments pursue the Central Government Industrial Policies and assistance is obtained under different centrally sponsored schemes/incentives for disbursement among eligible SSIs. This Central policy framework serves as a guiding principle for States, which evolve respective Governments also to design suitable incentives to encourage existing units to expand, diversity products and support entrepreneurs to establish new units. In this context, Government provides technical and other support service to SSIs through the Directorate of Industries and DICs. The main areas of support and facilities are listed below:

1. To develop and manage industrial areas by respective Industrial Development and Investment Corporation.
2. Financial support service by State Financial Corporations (SFCs).
3. Technical guidance by Technical Consultancy Organizations (TCOs).
4. Human resources development by a host training institution.
5. Infrastructure development by Infrastructural Development Corporations.
6. Export promotion by Small Industry Export Corporations.
7. Single Window Assistance by District Industries Centres.

Present Industrial Scenario of Arunachal Pradesh

Arunachal Pradesh, though endowed with abundant natural resources is still lagging behind in industrial development as compared to other states of the country. Lack of transport and communication, dearth of skilled/ technical personnel, poor literacy among local people, low capital formation and the atmospheres being non-conducive for setting-up industries in this hilly region are some of the major factors for industrial backwardness.

At present, the main thrust of the Industry Department is to promote traditional village and small scale industries and thereby provide employment opportunities and improve the economic conditions of the people of the state. At present, there are 14 district industries centres in the state. Three DICs provide all possible help and guidance to the prospective entrepreneurs for taking up industrial ventures and provide services for identification of suitable schemes, preparation of project reports, supply and management of raw materials and marketing of finished products, etc. The DICs also organize trainings at district level to create awareness amongst the entrepreneurs. They also assist entrepreneurs to avail incentive packages and facilities given by both Central and State Governments.

There are two industrial training institutes and one rural industrial development centre functioning in the state which impart vocational education to the local youths in the trades like Electrician, Motor Mechanic, Wireman, Fitter, Plumber, Surveyor, Mechanic (TV and Radio), Draughtsman (Civil), Carpenter, Welder, Shorthand and Secretarial Practice. A total number of 106 trainees passed out from different ITI's and RIDC of the state in different trade during 2005-06.

The Government of India, Ministry of Labour has approved for establishment of two new ITI's at Yupia (for woman) and Miao (General) and upgradation of Rural Industrial Development Centre, Dirang into ITI for which an amount of Rs. 468.41 lakhs has been sanctioned.

Under Centrally Sponsored Scheme (CSS), Government of India has approved for establishment of one Growth Centre at Niglok-Ngorlong within an estimated cost of Rs. 10.71 crores. The Government of India has also approved for establishment of 4 Industrial Infrastructure Development Centres (IIDC) at Bame, Dirang, Bhalukpong and Miao under CSS for which project report amounting to Rs. 5 crores has been submitted to SIDBI for onward submission to the Government of India for approval. Table 8.1 given below shows up-to-date position of industries and schemes implemented under CSS.

Table 8.1: Districtwise Village and Small Scale Industries as on 31.03.2006.

Sl.No.	*Particulars*	*Number*
1	*2*	*3*
1.	Medium Scale Industries	15
2.	No. of Village and Small Scale Industries registered permanently(functioning)	525042
3.	No. of Industrial Estates	1413

Source: Director of Industries, Itanagar.

Conclusion

In conclusion, we can say that "entrepreneurship" has proven to be an exceptionally fertile concept within economic theory. But how to motivate the youth and direct them into entrepreneurial field is still a big puzzle in the state like Arunachal Pradesh. Indeed, this term has played such a valuable role within economics that each era has adapted it to meet the innovations and spirit of the times. Though consensus on a precise definition of entrepreneurship may be impossible, what cannot be denied is the economic power of entrepreneurship and its way of inspiring creative individuals to pursue opportunities and take risks? Now it is necessary to extend the facilities created to the rural areas to promote agro-based and locally available raw material based industries in the rural areas and ensure markets for their products. Therefore, the authority should conduct research surveys to guide the prospective entrepreneurs. The small-scale industries hold much prospect and afford good opportunities for the rural individual entrepreneurship to flourish in the State like Arunachal Pradesh. Because, the State is hilly terrain where it is difficult to set-up large scale industry but on the contrary, there is much opportunity to set-up small scale type industries.

Preventive measures should be taken to provide a check on the mall practices of small units. Banks and financial institutions may follow liberal procedures in regard to surity and reduce the delay in sanction and disbursement of loan amounts to small scale units. Different lending institutions may introduce uniform lending norms to increase the efficiency of the lending system.

Employment is the surest way to enable the vast numbers of people living below the poverty level to raise them above it in the state. Rural industrialization through the development of Entrepreneurial Innovation is capable of offering employment opportunities at the place of residence to a large section of population. This has the capacity to correct regional imbalances by initiating industrial activities on dispersed basis in the most neglected, backward inaccessible areas of the state and thereby to bring rural economic development and rural prosperity.

This is a pity. The people of the state have tremendous potential, but like the Indian cricket team in recent years, the potential is not used fully. It seems that the root cause of our comparatively poor performance is total lack of self-reliance, spirit of innovation and capacity for hard and concentrated work. The dependence on foreign technology and money that is evident in recent years, as part of economic liberalization so-called, is shocking. For everything we want funds from the centre for roads, schools, hospitals, bridges, canals, etc.

REFERENCES

Alroaia,Y.V. (2008): Entrepreneurial Innovation : Theories and Policies in Some Countries", *Southern Economist*, Vol. 47, No. 10, Semtember, 15, Jamia Masjid Complex, Palace Guttahalli, Bangalore.

Anbalagan (2008): "Role of Entrepreneur and Institutions in Economic Development", *Southern Economist*, Vol. 47, No. 6, July 15, Jamia Masjid Complex, Palace Guttahalli, Bangalore.

Government of Arunachal Pradesh (2006): *Economic Review of Arunachal Pradesh*, Directorate of Economics and Statistics, Itanagar, Arunachal Pradesh.

Kamalakannan, K. (2008): "Rural Industrialistion and Poverty Alleviation", *Kurukshetra, A Journal of Rural Development*, Ministry of Rural Development, May, Vol. 54, No. 52, New Delhi.

Mandal, R. K. (2008): "Entrepreneurial Innovation and Economic Development in Arunachal Pradesh", a paper submitted in the ICSSR Sponsored National Seminar organized by Dera Natung Government College, August 9, Itanagar, Arunachal Pradesh.

Reddy, C. Srinivas (2008): "Introducing Technology to the Market", *Southern Economist*, Vol. 47, No. 9, September 1, Jamia Masjid Complex, Palace Guttahalli, Bangalore.

Subramanian, K., Bose, D. and Sundaram, K. (2007): "Entrepreneurship Development and Economic Development", *Southern Economist*, Vol. 46, No. 12, Oct. 15, Bangalore.

9

Trade Potentialities of North-East India

Introduction

The North-East Region (NER) of India which comprises of eight states, namely Arunachal Pradesh, Assam, Manipur, Meghalaya, Mizoram, Nagaland, Sikkim and Tripura shares most of its boundary with China, Bangladesh, Bhutan and Myanmar. The NER accounts for about eight per cent of the country's geographical area and about four per cent of population. Tribals account for more than 30 per cent of the total population of NER. Inadequate and poor infrastructure, inhospitable terrain and a comparatively late start in the development process are some of the reasons for economic backwardness of the region. However, the NER has certain strengths in different angles to achieve economic development in easy way. From the geopolitical angle, the NER is located in a strategic location as it is bounded by these several foreign countries. Naturally, it has got both advantages and disadvantages due to its location. So far advantages are concerned, it is connected with the South-East Asian countries mainly China, Myanmar, Bhutan, Bangladesh, Malaysia, Thailand, Philippines, Cambodia and Indonesia etc. where almost half of the world's population live. There is no doubt that this vast population could have great advantage for establishing any kind of trade and commerce. But the vary geographical condition basically the rivers and mountains of the country stand as a barrier and create geopolitical tensions which ultimately act as most disadvantages factors in creating a conducive atmosphere in the path of developing trade relations among those countries. But in the recent developments in the field of communication and technology, some visible changes are taking place. Now, the NER have felt the need of the hour, regarding the modern facilities of lives. They have realized that in order to develop the economy of the nation, the border trade could be an effective solution. Border trade would help to great extent in the field of economic development and also the route between production points of India to the Northern district of Myanmar via North-East region is economic viable as it is much shorter than sea route.

Border trade has special significance for the economies of the North-Eastern States, which have a large segment of international border on their boundaries. Of the border trade conducted through the international border of these states, it has been mentioned in the report of the Inter-Ministerial Task Force that the trade with Bangladesh and Myanmar is especially important for a variety of reasons. Apart from the fact that these two nations account for the major portion of the border trade with the North-Eastern States, India has to forge special trade relationship with both Myanmar and Bangladesh in view of the Inter-country trade issues. It is also important in view of the need to promote trade in locally produced goods in which the region has strength. The report suggests that a focus or promotion of export through the border trade will promote greater value addition in the North-East and help in shifting the export initiatives from the trading centres located outside the region to those located within the region. So a special importance needs to be given to the measures connected with simplification and facilitation of border trade.

In the context of globalization and liberalization and of the emerging 'Look East Policy' of the Government of India, the issues of border trade across the North-Eastern States of India has attracted the attention of the governments, planners, development agencies and the academics in India. Considering the geographical proximity and huge potentialities, the existing value and volume of bilateral trade between the neighbouring countries like Bhutan, China, Myanmar and Bangladesh on the one hand, and India on the other, appear to be too small. It is because, trading between these countries is quite difficult due to transport bottlenecks and the protectionist policy followed in the pre-globalization period. Lack of wider markets had impeded the economic development and the process of exploitation of potentialities of all these countries. With the initiation of liberalization policy, border trade is now viewed as one of the important instrument for the development of the bordering regions. Border trade lessens the insecurity and hardships of life in border areas particularly if it is far away from national market places. It may observe that besides economic implications, unlike sea or air borne trade, border trade unifies the interest of the people across the border and it tends to strengthen the links among the people living in the bordering areas which in turn help in a greater way to make better border management possible. Recent developments widen the scope of India's trade with countries bordering North-East India like academic initiatives, a regional cooperation among these countries; proposed development in transport and communication, prospects of border trade of the regions by exploring new frontiers with its rich bio-diversity like beautiful orchids horticultural crops, major and minor forest products, economic mineral resources, tourism products, plantation sector including tea, coffee, rubber, bio-diesel products (viz. jatropha) etc.

The objectives of this paper are three-fold to analyze the emerging scenario of trade potentialities of North-East India in view of its challenges and opportunities. (i) It examines the trends in export from North-East India, (ii) It seeks to find out the current dynamics of India's proactive attitudes and multilateral initiatives in this direction, (iii) It is designed to examine the potentialities of border trade pertaining to India's North-East region, and (iv) It tries to investigate the underlying challenges for the development of North-East border trade and its opportunities in the event of emergence of a strong regional cooperation among Bangladesh, China, India, Myanmar and Bhutan and finally conclusion follows.

Trends in Export from North-East India

The export from North-East Region (NER) takes place both directly and indirectly. Direct trade flows through Land Custom Stations (LCSs)/custom check post along the international border. The items of trade, quantity and value are recorded at LCSs. However, in case of indirect trade, it is hard to estimate the contributions of NER as the items produced in the region are exported from outside its geographic boundaries after a value addition in the process of production.

Table 9.1 depicts the NER's export over the last 10 years. NER's export to neighbouring countries viz., Bangladesh, Bhutan and Myanmar consists of diversified products and varies from primary commodities to manufacturing items. NER also exports to countries like UAE, UK, Sri Lanka, Germany, USA, Ireland, Pakistan, Egypt, Indonesia, Japan and Netherlands. It mainly exports tea to these countries. The export from NER has exhibited a fluctuating trend in past ten years. Meghalaya dominates the total export from NER to Bangladesh followed by Assam. NER Export to Myanmar through Moreh (Manipur) LCS initially gained momentum and reached its peak but started declining from 1997-98. It could not sustain initial thrust due to various factors. Apart from exporting tea to various countries, NER exports perfumery compound and aquilaria agallocha. NER export to Bhutan through Hatisar (Assam) LCS is also negligible. Having discussed about the trend in the export from NER, an attempt has been made to study the composition of export from this region.

Composition of Exports from North-East India

The composition of exports from NER in terms of value and its percentage in total value of export from NER during the period 1996-97 to 2005-06 are presented in Table 9.1. The bulk of items exported from NER are grouped under mineral, agricultural and allied products, and other products. Minerals are mainly consisting of coal and limestone. Other minerals are boulder stone, crushed stone, sand stone, crude marble etc. and are exported without any value addition. Agricultural and allied products mainly consists of tea, fruits and some horticultural products like ginger, oranges, citrus, fruits, garlic, pears etc. Other products include synthetic and woollen fabrics, construction items like brick, cement, tiles, plywood, door, frames and low-value manufacturing products. The main exports from NER consist of mineral, agricultural and allied products as portrayed in the Table 9.2. Table 9.2 also reveals a very high fluctuating trend of export from NER in case of mineral and agricultural and allied products. It ranges from 25.74 to 48.35 per

Table 9.1: Total Exports from NER.

(Value in Rupees Crores)

Year	*NER Export to Bangladesh*				*NER Export to Mayanmar*	*NER Export to other countries*		*NER Export to Bhutan*	*Total Export from NER*
	Meghalaya	*Assam*	*Tripura*	*Total Export*	*Manipur*	*I.C.D. Amingaon*	*L.G.B.I. Airport*	*Assam*	
1996-97	86.08	17.42	0.16	103.67	30.86	182.90	—	—	317.43
1997-98	80.77	43.71	0.97	125.45	23.84	251.75	—	—	401.04
1998-99	85.24	51.26	2.24	138.75	5.03	244.95	—	—	388.72
1999-2000	129.99	37.51	2.31	169.81	3.31	222.77	—	—	395.89
2000-01	129.83	20.64	0.75	151.23	5.53	247.01	0.30	—	404.07
2001-02	166.93	17.69	1.28	185.89	1.23	190.60	1.43	—	379.15
2002-03	171.99	28.97	1.59	202.55	5.00	201.16	1.26	0.15	410.12
2003-04	188.51	48.29	1.38	238.18	9.41	184.90	0.71	1.82	435.02
2004-05	163.79	25.14	1.49	190.42	6.49	188.73	0.90	5.49	392.03
2005-06	179.51	35.68	0.74	215.93	3.87	199.82	0.65	17.55	437.82

Source: Office of the Commissioner of Customs, Shillong, Meghalaya.

cent in case of mineral and 45.31 to 74.01 per cent in case of agricultural and allied products. It cannot be denied that the major driving force behind the NER growth in export is tea, particularly that of Assam which produces around 53 per cent of the total production. Other products including textiles, building materials and other constitute a very negligible part of total export from NER ranging from 0.12 to 4.12 per cent.

The exports from NER to Bangladesh mainly comprise of mineral and agricultural and allied products. There are two types of minerals—(i) coal, and (ii) limestone. Both are mined in southern belt of Meghalaya and directly exported to Bangladesh. They are also found in Sutarkandi and Karimganj (Assam) and are exported without any value addition. The bulk of other items exported from NER include boulders, fruits, agricultural products and low-value manufacturing products. Horticultural products like ginger, oranges, citrus fruits, garlic, pears etc. have a contribution in the total NER's export volume. These are cultivated mainly in Meghalaya and N.C. Hills of Assam. The complementarities between the resource base of hills of NER and the plains of Bangladesh provide a firm basis of trade between them. The people residing on both sides would certainly find their lives much easier with border trade and commerce since marketability is least costly as compared to respective main land alternatives in their own countries. The distance to nearest port of NER is Kolkata which is about 1100 kms. to 1700 kms. from different capitals of North Eastern States.

Meghalaya has become important amongst eight sister States with regard to volume of trade with Bangladesh. The cement plant at Chattak in Bangladesh, the only major public sector cement manufacturer, depends solely on the limestone brought from Shella and Nongtrai areas of Meghalaya. Lafarge, the international cement giant, has reiterated its commitment to implement its $25 million investment for mining limestone in the State. The French company has established a joint venture to feed its mammoth cement plant at Chattak in Bangladesh. Chairman of Japan Development Institute (JDI), Mr. Shoichi Kobayashi during his recent visit to North-East observed that Bangladesh is deficient in cement production and requires not less than "8 million metric tonnes of cement" annually for its domestic consumption. Bangladesh is currently importing

Table 9.2: Composition of Exports from NER.

Items	*1996-97*	*1997-98*	*1998-99*	*1999-2000*	*2000-01*	*2001-02*	*2002-03*	*2003-04*	*2004-05*	*2005-06*
Mineral	102.34	106.62	100.04	165.29	148.00	182.50	197.39	235.58	185.05	211.69
	(32.24)	(26.59)	(25.74)	(41.75)	(36.63)	(48.14)	(48.13)	(54.15)	(47.20)	(48.35)
Agricultural and	215.08	294.42	287.70	230.11	254.81	195.04	210.38	197.10	200.03	208.07
Allied Products	(67.76)	(73.41)	(74.01)	(58.12)	(63.06)	(51.45)	(51.30)	(45.31)	(51.02)	(47.53)
Others	0.00	0.00	0.98	0.49	1.26	1.57	2.35	2.33	6.96	18.05
			(0.25)	(0.12)	(0.31)	(0.41)	(0.57)	(0.54)	(1.77)	(4.12)
Total	317.42	401.04	388.72	395.89	404.07	379.11	410.12	435.02	392.03	437.81

Source: Self-Compilation from Official Data.

limestone from South-East Asian nations. "Meghalaya which has abundant limestone can set-up a cement plant and export it to Bangladesh, " Kobayashi said. (Sikidar, Bora and Adhikari, 2010).

Current Dynamics of India's Proactive Attitudes and Multilateral Initiatives in this Direction

Bilateral trade exchanges with some of the countries in the region have not only grown exponentially, but there has also been a rapid increase in bilateral, sub-regional and regional linkages and institutional interactions aimed at enhancing and consolidating all round cooperation. In order to demonstrate the current dynamics of India's proactive attitudes and multilateral initiatives in this direction, we may cite just a few examples:

1. India and ASEAN Countries

India maintains continuous dialogue with ASEAN and Southeast Asian countries. Ministerial meetings and official level discussions are held in order to fulfil the 'Look East Policy' agenda. India is now one of the four summits levels partners of ASEAN, the other three being China, Japan and Korea. During December 2005, India participated in the ASEAN Summit interactions and East Asia Summit interactions held in Kaula Lumpur. Ministerial level meetings had also been held with a number of ASEAN and East Asian dignitaries. These had provided the frameworks and directions for the various issues involved in enhancement of trade and investment relations (Ministry of Commerce and Industry. Annual Report: 2005-06). India has also suggested the formation of Asian Economic Community including ASEAN, China, Japan, Korea and India.

During 2003-04, South-East Asia, East Asia and ASEAN countries taken together accounted for 21.3 per cent of the total volume of India's international trade. India's trade relation with North-East Asians countries like China, Japan, Republic of Korea and Hong Kong has also increased tremendously over the years. China has now emerged as India's third highest trading partner after the US and UAE, overtaking countries like UK and Belgium in 2003. To provide physical connectivity, India has already signed Trans-Asian Highway projects, initiated by Union Nations

Economic and Social Commission for Asia Pacific (UNESCAP). On the political fronts, India has made efforts to improve relationships with neighbouring countries especially with China, Myanmar and Bangladesh.

2. BCIM Forum for Regional Co-operation

If a regional co-operation among the countries of BCIM (Bangladesh, China, India and Myanmar) is established through extensive trade through various bilateral and multilateral trade agreements, all the participating partners will be benefited immensely. A modem transport and communication network between India, Myanmar and China can only break the existing impediments. The improvement of the transportation network between India, Myanmar and China includes construction of railway, road and air routes. For example, the construction of a Trans Asian Railway route, which will connect Lekhapani railway head in Assam, India with Kunming in South China through Myitkyina in Myanmar may be considered, as proposed by the Economic and Social Commission for Asia and Pacific (ESCAP). The construction work of the 1360 kms. India-Myanmar-Thailand connecting Highway is to be started very soon at the cost of $700 million dollars will go a long way in improving trade relationship between India and ASEAN countries.

The BCIM countries have also taken a few steps in this regard at diplomatic level. They have signed several diplomatic and bilateral trade agreements. For example, India and China have already launched a determined bid in 2003 to chart out a roadmap to forge an enduring and string partnership based on the principles of co-operation and mutual sensitivity to each other's concerns and equality. The roadmap in the form of a joint declaration, the first-ever between India and China, was signed during the then Prime Minister, Atal Behari Vajpayee's historic visit in Beijing in June, 2003, leading to a flurry of high-level exchanges, including the launch of a new political initiative for the early resolution of boundary issue that bedeviled bilateral relations. The year 2003 also saw the continued expansion and intensification of Indo-China economic co-operation. During Vajpayee's visit, it was decided with his Chinese counterpart Wen Jiabao, to form a joint study group to examine the potential complementarities and also draw up a programme for development of India-China Trade and Economic Cooperation for the next five years. This economic cooperation between India and China, the two giant nations, having nearly 38 per cent of world population, in collaboration with the ASEAN, can transform the entire Asian Continent into the biggest trading zone in the world. The existing intervening obstacles both natural and political between these countries will disappear when strong economic forces through active and vibrant trading activities are generated in the region.

BCIM Forum for Regional Co-operation also popularly known as Kunming Initiative—a second track diplomacy was an exercise to promote and explore regional co-operation between Bangladesh, China, India and Myanmar focusing on their contiguous region. The exercise began in August 1999 in Kunming, capital of Yunan, one of south-western provinces of China convened jointly by institutions from the four countries. These included the Yunan Academy of Social Sciences from China, the Institute of Chinese Studies and the Centre for Policy Research from India, the Centre for Policy Dialogue from China and Co-operating institutions from Myanmar. Scholars and academicians, representatives of governments, industry and business, as well as media persons from all four countries attended it. The Forum represented the combined effort by the four countries to increase connectivity, culture, trade and tourism ties and people-to-people contact among them, in border areas in particular. The BCIM project also hoped to encounter issues of trans-border crimes, such as drug-trafficking, gunrunning, illegal migration etc. through increased inter-country co-operation and greater harmonization of border policies. The Forum had already held its conference in New Delhi (2000), Dhaka (2002), Yongon (2003), Kunming (2004). The Sixth Forum was held in New Delhi on March 2006. It addressed issues like conceptual framework for regional and multilateral cooperation, livelihood issues of the peoples of the border areas in the context of national economic co-operation, social and human development and culture as well as strategies for the economic development of the region including co-operation in the health sector, especially in the field of HIV / AIDS.

India and China Trade Relations: The rapid economic growth of China in recent years has opened the possibilities of expanding trade relationship further with India. China's huge population and growing per capita income and rapid infrastructural development have created opportunities for exporting several new products from India. India with its current economic reforms and growing GDP can emerge as a good market for Chinese goods. The recent bilateral trade agreements between India and China can act as a catalyst in this emerging scenario of trade potentialities between the two countries.

As a first step, India and China signed a memorandum on expanding border trade through Nathula Pass on the Indo-China boundary. This was followed by a move by the Chinese Foreign Ministry which stopped showing Sikkim as an independent country in Asia on its official website and India also recognized that Tibet is part of the territory of the People's Republic of China. Another area where India and China have made solid progress in 2003 is in the defense sector, where mutual suspicion had prevented the two largest armed forces in Asia from engaging and interacting with each other. The two sides were also decided to step up bilateral military exchanges at different levels to boost mutual trust and understanding. For example, on November 14, 2003, the Indian and Chinese Naval Ships successfully conducted the search and rescued exercise off the coast of Shanghai in the East China Sea.

Trade Routes: Considering topography and geographical nature of the BCIM zone, rail and road transport seem to be more realistic and economical viable for all BCIM countries. In addition to the existing roads, the Kunming initiatives have identified the following land routes for multilateral and bilateral transport connectivity between the BCIM countries.

1. The Kunming – Baoshan – Myitkyina – Ledo Road (popularly known as Stilwell/Ledo Road);
2. The Kunming – Mandalay – Yangon Road (with outlet to the sea);
3. The Kunming – Kyauphyu Road (with outlet to the sea);
4. The Kunming – Mandalay – Monywa – Moreh Road;
5. The Chittagong – Yangon Road.

The Stilwell was built during the Second World War connecting Kunming Boashan (China)—Myitkyina (Myanmar)-Ledo (India).

The total length of the road between Kunming and Ledo is about 1700 kms. of which 800 kms. is in Yunnan Province of China, 727 kms. in Myanmar and 173 kms. in India. But between Myitkyina in Myanmar and Ledo in India, a stretch of about 160 kms. to 200 kms., this route needs rebuilding because beyond Myitkyina up to Kunming the road is already well developed. From Myitkyina the road takes a southern turn towards Lashio via Bhamo; from Lahio it takes north-eastern turn towards Kunming. Since Kunming is already connected with Hong Kong by an express highway, the North-East India, for that matter India as a whole, could establish direct road link with Hong Kong if the Stilwell Road is well developed. Moreover, since Lashio is well connected by rail and road with provinces of south and central Myanmar, bordering Laos, Thailand, Malaysia and Singapore, the Stilwell Road can connect North-East India with the entire South-East Asian countries. If the Stilwell Road is reconstructed as a Trans-Asian Express Highway and along with it, if a Trans-Asian Railway line is built-up, then in near future not only the North-East India but the entire nation would be connected by both road and railway with Myanmar, South Chinese trading centres and the entire South-East Asian region.

Another land route recently opened (2001) is the 160 kms. Tamu-Kalewakalemy road. If this road is extended by another 250-300 kms. across Myanmar, it can meet the Stilwell Road at Bhamo from where Kunming is already well connected. The Governments of India and Bangladesh have recently proposed to extend this road by a distance of about 300 kms. across Manipur and Southern Assam to Bangladesh border so that it can be the shortest land route between Bangladesh and Myanmar through North-East India. In this case the distance to Chitagong seaports from Agartala, Imphal, Shillong, Guwahati etc. will be shorter than that to Kolkata.

In recent years the possibilities of foraging regional cooperation including formation of a trading block among the BCIM countries have been highlighted in various academic as well as diplomatic forums. The first such academic initiative was taken by the Institute of Chinese Studies, New Delhi in collaboration with the Indira Gandhi National Centre for Arts, New Delhi in a conference on Regional Development in India and China held on 19-20th November, 1998 in New Delhi. The second major step involving all the BCIM countries in this regard was the famous 'Kunming Initiatives' held for the first time at Kunming in Yunnan Province of China in 1999. The second, third and fourth meeting of the Kunming Initiatives were held in New Delhi in 2000, in Dhaka in 2002 and in Yangon in 2003 respectively. The five noble principles of the Kunming Initiatives are equality and mutual benefit, sustainable development, comparative advantage, the adoption of international standards and infrastructure development. However, the Kunming Initiatives are yet to be implemented for the mutual benefit of the zone.

3. Indo-Myanmar Co-operation

Myanmar constitutes one of the critical components for the success of India's Look East Policy. It has not only a common land border of 1,643 kms. with India's North-East states like Mizoram, Manipur and Nagaland and Arunachal Pradesh but also share a long maritime boundary. Besides border trade between India and Myanmar, India has involved in oil and gas sector and infrastructure development of Myanmar. India and Myanmar formally signed Border Trade agreement on January 1994 to exchange goods produced locally by people living along both sides of the border as well as to create mechanism to deal with foreign trade transaction. Both governments agreed to open border trade through the following points: (i) Moreh (Manipur) in India and Tamu in Myanmar, (ii) Champhai/Zokhawthar (Mizoram) in India and Rhi in Myanmar. Effort is also underway to open border trade between Bangladesh and Mizoram. The states of Assam, Meghalaya and Tripura had already operated border trade relations with Bangladesh. Sino-Indo Border trade is expected to grow up in a big way in the North-East following the reopening of the historic Nathula Pass in Sikkim. India has already constructed the 160 kms. long Tamu-Kaewa-Kalemyo road at a cost of Rs. 90 crores and also offered to upgrade Rhi-Tiddim and Rhi-Falam roads.

India is actively participating in the currently proposed Indo-Myanmar-Thailand Superhighway Project, 1400 kms. long to connect Moreh in Manipur to Maesot in Thailand, running through the ancient city of Bagan in Central Myanmar. Another project called Kaladan Multimodal Transport Project (approximately 411 kms.) providing connectivity between India and Myanmar along the

Kaladan River in southern Mizoram up to the Sittwe port (Myanmar) in the Bay of Bengal has also been approved by the Government of India. The total estimated cost is US$ 105 million. India is to provide US$ 95 and Myanmar US $ 10 million. The Government of India has further agreed to provide the amount in the form of a Line of Credit to Myanmar Government. India has also been taking interest in Myanmar's large gas reserves that would help to address its energy security concerns. A trilateral deal between India, Myanmar and Bangladesh has already been negotiated to export Myanmar's natural gas from Shwe natural gas field in the Bay of Bengal to India through Bangladesh. The Shwe pipeline consortium comprised of 4 entities: Daewoo International 60 per cent, Korean Gas Corporation 10 per cent, India's ONGC and Videsh Ltd. 20 per cent and Gas Authority of India 10 per cent. (The Shew Gas Pipeline Campaign Committee (India).

Considering the geographical proximity between India and Myanmar, the overland trade and transit trade seem to be more suitable, effective and profitable between the two countries. Myanmar's entry into ASEAN block, its signing of an MoU with India in 1994 recognizing two border trading points between Myanmar and India, viz., Tamu (Myanmar) - Moreh (India) and Rhi (Myanmar) - Champhai (India), the opening of 160 kms. Tamu-Kalewakalemy Road in February, 2001, the opening of the Myanmar-India Friendship Centre at Yagoon and signing of a bilateral trade agreement between India and Myanmar in October, 2003, the bilateral trade agreements between India and China and ASEAN block in October, 2003, are likely to play a major role in improving the regional economic co-operation between the three countries.

The signing of an MoU between Senior General Than Shwe, the Chairman of the ruling State Peace and Development Council (SPDC) of Myanmar and Mr. Kamal Nath, Minister of Commerce and Industry, Government of India, on 25th October, 2004, at New Delhi, for cooperation on economic and security issues, is a landmark in the process of bilateral cooperation between Myanmar and India. In addition to the issues like terrorism, drug trafficking, smuggling, money laundering, international economic crimes, cyber crimes, the MoU covers several economic issues as well. India has agreed to upgrade the Yangon-Mandalay rail link, to help in laying fibre optic network in Myanmar and to conduct a feasible study of deep-water port and cooperate in energy sector. Both the Governments have agreed to upgrade Mizoram-Chin State road and Kaladan multi-model transportation system.

There are a number of cooperation agreements at bilateral level too. For instance, an Indo-Myanmar bilateral agreement of far-reaching significance to Northeast is the Multi-Modal Inland Waterway-cum-highway project on the Kalodyne River, estimated to cost $104 million. Under this project, Sittwe Harbour in Rakhyne, Myanmar and navigation on Kalodyne as also Highway from south Mizoram will be developed so that Northeast is directly linked to a seaport. All the attendant protocols to the agreement have been signed and the project is ready to take off.

4. Indo-Bangladesh Border Trade

Bangladesh has long border of 4100 kms. with the north eastern Bangladesh and North-East India because of their geographical proximity. But no lasting foundation of cooperation has yet been laid between Dhaka and New Delhi for a beneficial trade relation. Several thorny socio-political and border issues, some real and some imaginary, have stood in the way of regional economic cooperation between these two countries. The Indo-Bangla Joint Economic Commission (JEC) has so far failed to settle any of the above issues, delaying economic cooperation between the two countries. The proposed Indo-Bangla Free Trade Agreement (FTA) can go a long way in establishing regional cooperation between these two countries. Prof. Nurul Islam and Prof. Rehman Sobhan, who were associated with the Bangladesh Planning Commission, has suggested joint venture manufacturing units like cement, fertilizer and sponge-iron to accelerate further trade between the two next-door neighbour. Prof. Nurul Islam further stated that the administrative and professional skill supported by elaborate study on formal and informal trade between Bangladesh and India were essential before establishing a free trade area between the two countries. The implementation of the proposed FTA between Bangladesh and India was possible only when Bangladesh got itself rid of the suspicion against the big neighbouring country like India.

The first Trade Agreement signed between India and Bangladesh on 28th March, 1972, incorporated a specific provision for border trade "in order to meet the day to day requirements of the people living within a 16 kms. belt of the border between West Bengal, Assam, Meghalaya, Tripura and Mizoram on the one side, and Bangladesh on the other". Before the provision could be implemented and the necessary instructions for issue of permits, finalization of routes, check posts, travel and custom documents and inspection facilities could be finalized, the Government of Bangladesh reported large scale smuggling across the border and asked in October 1972 for the border trade to be scrapped. It was conveyed that its meaningful implementation was not possible unless adequate checks and controls were established along the entire length of the border. In absence of any formal agreement with the long and open border between the two countries, the situation had led to a thriving informal trade smuggling across the border. In a trade talks between India and Bangladesh the Indian Delegation led by the Commerce Secretary insisted on giving transhipment facilities i.e., carrying Indian goods from one Indian state to another (Northeast) through Bangladesh land routes. But the Bangladeshi Delegation led by its Commerce Secretary, Suhel Ahmed, pointed out that the Indian demand of transhipment did not meet now because of its politically sensitive nature.

5. South Asia Free Trade Agreements (SAFTA)

The leaders of the South Asian Association for Regional Cooperation (SAARC) during the Twelfth SAARC Summit held in Islamabad, Pakistan on 4-6th January, 2004 have finalized the formation of South Asian Free Trade Area (SAFTA) which would accelerate the trade among the SAARC countries and the Agreement on SAFTA was signed and would be effective from January 2006. Under SAFTA, a phased Trade Liberalization Programme (TLP) is envisaged under which, Non-Least Developed Contracting States (NLDCSs) (India, Pakistan and Sri Lanka) would reduce their existing tariffs to 0-5 per cent for other NLDCSs within a time-frame of seven years from the coming into force of the Agreement. NLDCSs shall be the same for Least Developed Contracting States for LDCSs (Bangladesh, Bhutan, Maldives and Nepal). The LDCSs would reduce their existing tariff to 0-5 per cent within a time-frame often years from the date of coming into force of the Agreement.

6. Trans-Asian Highway

The Trans-Asian Highways comprising the Asian Highway (AH), the Trans-Asian Railway (TAR) and facilitations of land projects were initiated in 1959 to promote regional cooperation, international trade and tourism to provide access to the landlocked countries and territories across Asia. Thirty-two Asian countries already endorse the Asian highway project and it will cover a network of 141,000 kms. of standardized roadway crossing these countries with linkages to Europe. When completed, it will be the largest road network in the world. India is also a party to this project. Asian Highway (AH-l) will pass through four states of North-East India. It will enter Meghalaya after crossing Bangladesh, then enter Assam and pass through two more states, Nagaland and Manipur before entering Myanmar. The project is expected to promote trade, commerce, tourism etc. in the region. It will provide a critical linkage between North-East India and South East Asian countries.

7. BIMST-Economic Cooperation

Bangladesh-India-Myanmar-Sri Lanka-Thailand Economic Cooperation was an important element in India's "Look East" strategy and added a new dimension to India's economic co-operation with South-East Asian countries. This multilateral initiative involved 3 members of SAARC (India, Bangladesh and Sri Lanka) and 2 members of ASEAN (Thailand and Myanmar). This group was expected to provide a vital link between ASEAN and SAARC countries. Initiated by Thailand in 1994, BIMST-EC tried to explore economic co-operation on a sub-regional basis involving contiguous countries of South East and South Asia grouped around the Bay of Bengal. Nepal and Bhutan also had already joined this grouping. The aim, principle and purpose of this group were contained in Bangkok Declaration of 6th June, 1997. The first Ministerial meeting held in 1998 agreed that free trade agreement would be the main objective and decided to focus on activities that facilitated trade, increased investment and promoted technical co-operation among member countries. Six areas were identified for co-operation, namely, trade and investment, technology, transportation and communication, energy, tourism and fisheries. Bhutan, India, Myanmar, Nepal, Sri Lanka and Thailand signed the Framework Agreement on BIMST-EC Free Trade Agreement on 8th February, 2004 in Phuket, Thailand. The Framework Agreement included provisions for negotiations on FTA in goods, services and investment.

8. Mekong-Ganga Cooperation (MGC)

MGC is an effort to link the countries situated on the shores of the Indo-Chinese Rivers. The main agenda has been to consolidate cultural and tourist exchange between these countries. The first meeting was held in Vientene, the Laotian capital, on November 10, 2002. These countries included China, India, Cambodia, Laos, Vietnam and Thailand.

9. South Asia Growth Quadrangle (SAGQ)

Since Bangladesh, Bhutan, Nepal and North-East India, all located in the eastern fringe of South Asian, have several critical and strategic advantages in jointly initiating the development process of the region; the idea of having a South Asia Growth Quadrangle has emerged recently. The Foreign Ministers of these countries, in their meeting in Delhi, on April 8, 1997, formally launched a sub-regional economic co-operation initiative among the four countries. The entire initiative would be outside SAARC and that development projects to be undertaken would be from six sectors viz., multi-modal transport and communications, energy, trade and investment facilitation and promotion, tourism, optimum utilization of national resources endowment and environment. However, like any other regional initiative in South Asia, the SAGQ has not really taken off mainly because of the poor political commitment of the member countries and the non-inclusion of the real stakeholders in the decision making process, i.e., the states of the Northeastern region (Lama, 2003).

10. Free Trade Area (FTA) Agreements

India has already signed Free Trade Agreements (FTA) with Thailand and Singapore. The Framework Agreement for establishing Free

Trade Area between Thailand and India was signed on 9th October, 2003 in Bangkok. The agreement covered FTA in Goods and Services, and Areas of Economic Co-operation. The modalities for the first phase of the FTA between India and Thailand involving the reduction of tariff on 82 agreed items in three years had already been finalized. To be implemented in a phased manner, the two countries will have a fully free trade regime by 2010. There are also plans to implement FTA with other ASEAN countries like Indonesia, Malaysia and Brunei by 2011 and also with the Philippines, Cambodia, Laos, Myanmar and Vietnam by 2016.

Potentialities of Border Trade Pertaining to India's North-East Region

The potentialities of growth in India's trade with the neighbouring countries are immense. The North-Eastern region can also be a partner of this emerging trade scenario. The major impediment towards the growth of Border trade with India's Eastern neighbours is found to be the absence due to lack of strong and efficient transport and communication networks between India and the countries of BCIM because of their geographical proximity to each other. To achieve such benefits from Border trade, the physical linkages among the trading partners in the form of Trans-National Highways, Railways, Waterways and Airways, wherever possible, are essential. A huge amount of capital expenditure would be necessary to build such infrastructural facilities. It is possible only through financial assistance from international financial institutions and the participation of Multi-National Corporation (MNCs).

The prosperous East and South-East Asian countries are attractive destinations for Indian exports. ASEAN markets provide big opportunities for India. Most of the ASEAN populations have similar cultural background as in India. Affinity in cultural background will make Indian products acceptable and saleable in ASEAN markets. By the end of the year 2000 Indian exports to Indonesia, Malaysia and Singapore increased impressively (87 per cent increase to Indonesia; 47 per cent to Malaysia and 39 per cent to Singapore.). Export figures to other countries of the region have also shown market increase. Seeing such export figures India realized that East and South-East Asian region offered attractive destination for exports. Accordingly, India decided to diversify its export direction towards the East. This is another aspect of India's Look East Policy. It is hoped that spectacular success would be achieved in this endeavour. The NER has the following resources:

1. Forest and Horticulture Products

North-East India is famous for its exotic flora and fauna. The North East is one of the few bio-diversity zones in the world. It has immense flora and fauna. The world's annual trade on medicinal and aromatic oil/plants is of amount, over $60 billion. North East only supplies the raw materials for many of the industries inside and outside the country. Out of the 925 varieties of orchids available in India, as many as over 650 can be grown in the region due to the favourable climatic conditions. In fact, approximately 200 varieties are unique to this region and 60 per cent of these are ornamental in nature with high demand at the international markets. It is also ideally situated to produce spices, fruits and vegetables, flowers and herbs. Therefore, the North-East India can emerge as an exporter of orchids, flowers, apple, orange, pineapples, spices, herbs, etc. Some of the best and rare quality fruits and vegetables are produced in North-East region for example, pineapples produced in North-East are considered to be of the highest quality. Moreover, the forests of North-East offer a vast array of aromatic plants which can be used in the aromatic industry for the manufacture of perfumes, incenses, etc. In fact, there is an increasing international trend towards natural perfumes and room freshners, shifting the focus from chemical ones. With proper planning there exists scope for establishing aromatic industry in the region. The climate of North-East is also suitable for wide range of agro-horticultural as well as exotic floricultural products. With support services like training, tissue culture labs, production, finance, marketing tie-ups and farm to market roads, the region can produce both for domestic market and international market.

2. Tourism

The North-East India is well known for its bio-diversities and heritage sites. Tawang in Arunachal Pradesh, Majuli, Kaziranga, Manas, Pabitara etc. in Assam can be developed further as tourist spots attracting more tourists from Europe and America. The multi-ethnic culture coupled with snow capped mountains and mighty Brahmaputra provides ideal setting for development of tourism. The name Tawang was given by Mera Lama in the 17th century. Tawang Monastery popularly known as the 'Tawang Gompa' is the second oldest Monastery in Asia more than 460 years old and the largest Monastery in the Himalayan region constructed by Lama Lodre Gyatso in 1681 AD. Tawang is the birth place of the sixth Dalai Lama, the only Indian so far who rose to the highest position in Gelupa Sect of Buddhism. If modern transport and communication system between the ASEAN countries and India along with the requisite infrastructural facilities are developed, then tourists visiting the ASEAN countries are likely to extend their tour programmes to the North-East India, a few hundred miles away, for visiting its exotic bio-diversity and heritage sites. In 1996, an internationally reputed consultancy firm, Coopers and Lybrand submitted a report to the Government of Assam, which state that if the vast tourism potentials of the North-East India are fully tapped and developed, within 20 years the region will receive more tourists than Singapore or Bangkok. Because almost all the Western and Japanese tourists visiting South-East Asian region would fly or drive a few hundred kilometres more to enjoy the scenic and cultural beauties of the North-Eastern Region. This alone can boost the economy of the entire North-East. But for this, road and airways between the South-East Asian region and India have to be developed. All this is possible only when the region can attract foreign direct investment complemented with domestic investment.

Recently, the Madrid-based World Tourism Organization has evinced interest in promoting tourism in North-East India and already identified Nagaland and Sikkim as its priorities. These United Nations-affiliated organizations will assist initially Nagaland in preparing a suitable tourism development programme with emphasis on employment, especially for women and other disadvantaged groups. The World Tourism Organization has advised the Union Tourism Ministry to constitute a panel of consultants for framing suitable tourism development programmes in Nagaland and Sikkim in the areas of rural tourism, eco-tourism, social-tourism, architecture-tourism and historical tourism.

3. Medical Tourism

Now-a-days, India is in a position to give world class medical treatment at a low cost in comparison to the developed countries. India has advantage due to low cost of treatment, large number and high quality of Indian health care professionals, world class corporate hospitals (Apollo, Escorts), presence in niche areas. It attracts the patients throughout the world especially the African and Middle East countries. Presently, patients from developing and developed countries are coming to receive treatment in Indian hospitals. Health tourists from Middle East, CIS countries, neighbouring countries, Non-Resident Indians in developed countries, foreigners from some developed countries are coming everyday. It is observed that 130000 international patients came to India (2003) from South Asia, Africa, Gulf mainly for treatment in India. Again, many foreign patients seek treatment in traditional and alternative medicine (unani, ayurvedic, herbal treatment). The north-eastern region is the home of ayurvedic and herbal medicine. 90 per cent herbal medicine of India is seen in this Himalayas belt. The State like Arunachal Pradesh where almost all of herbals are available has a bright scope to attract health tourists to give treatment at a low cost.

The Central Council for Research in Ayurveda and Siddha, Department of Ayush, Ministry of Health and Family Welfare, Government of India has initiated research programmes in this state from the early seventies. Accordingly, it has taken up a special survey tour programme to study the traditions, culture, customs, folk medical practices and the extent of availability and the quality of the medicinal plants in the State. Consequently, the council has also initiated other important research programmes, such as clinical research programme in the State and established Regional Research Centre at Itanagar in May, 1979. The status of the centre has been upgraded to Regional Research Institute with effect from 9th September, 1999.

4. Hydroelectricity

Due to its geographical location and its hilly terrain, the North-East Region has an immense hydel potential to use the power of water to produce electricity. The region is of turbulent perennial several rivers, big and small having high gradients which possess enormous hydroelectric generation potential. Arunachal Pradesh, which possessing a huge hydro-power potential, may alone fulfil 60 per cent of the existing demand of the country if the potential is fully harnessed. The National Hydroelectric Power Corporation (NHPC) has already undertaken to construct several mega multipurpose hydro-power projects in upper reaches of the Brahmaputra River in Arunachal Pradesh, estimated to generate 25,000 MW of power. The projects included Subansiri upper, lower and middle; Dihang, Dibang and Siang hydro projects. In near future Arunachal Pradesh is expected to be made a Power Surplus State so much that after fulfilling the home demand it would earn much revenue by exporting power to rest of the country. The hydro-power potentialities of the major five rivers in Arunachal Pradesh are shown in Table 9.3.

Table 9.3: Major river basins and their potentials.

Name of the River/Basin	*Probable Hydro Potentials (MW)*			*Name of Districts*
	ROR	*Storage*	*Total*	
Kameng	3799	847	4646	W&E/Kameng
Subansiri	10141	5050	15191	U&L/Subansiri/Kurung Kumey
Siang	3557	11700	15257	W&E/Siang U/Siang
Dibang	5946	1282	7228	U & L/Dibang Valley
Lohit	3594	3075	6669	Lohit
Total Potentials	27037	21954	48991	

Source: Department of Power, Government of Arunachal Pradesh, Itanagar.

Therefore, Arunachal Pradesh, having untapped estimated hydro-power potential of 49,000 MW, may alone emerge as Power House of India when this potential is fully harnessed. The power sector will herald a golden era for the region once its hydel potential is harnessed to make it the power house of the country. A major part of this power can be exported to neighbouring countries. But the development of these power projects requires huge investment and technological support, which is possible only through foreign direct investment. The WTO regime has given an opportunity to develop these power potentialities of the region.

5. Oil and Gas

Assam alone has an estimated 1,300 million tonnes of oil and 156 billion cubic metres of natural gas. Not even 40 per cent area has been explored. Assam, Mizoram, Tripura, Nagaland, Arunachal and even Brahmaputra have a number of oil bearing strata, still to be explored. Other mineral resources like Thorium, Limestone etc. are available in huge quantities.

6. Plantation

(i) Tea: Assam alone produces about 50 per cent of country's tea and tea industry in India needs new international markets. However, to capture such market, tea industry needs attention on the fronts that the tea industry has to overcome the two major problems of low productivity and high cost of production faced by the tea industry of the country. However, Indian tea will have to compete with other tea producing countries of the world in terms of quality also and tea industry of Assam, *vis-à-vis* North-East should also take up the challenge in the coming years.

(ii) Coffee: Although coffee regions in India are in the three southern states of Karnataka (53%), Kerala (28%) and Tamil Nadu (11%), a small quantity (approx. 8%) is grown in the non-traditional belts of Andhra Pradesh and the North-Eastern States such as Assam, Nagaland and Arunachal Pradesh. However, the non-traditional coffee areas of North-East is certainly preserving not only the natural forests in these areas by preventing shifting cultivation and providing employment to the tribal force (90% of whom are women and uplifting their socio-economic status) but also enabling the preparation of some fine distinct coffees from the areas. Therefore, such qualitative coffee plantation in North-East India has great prospects for exports.

(iii) Rubber: The world natural rubber production was 6.8 million tonnes in 2002. There is a high demand for natural rubber in the world market. At present, India is producing about 613000 tonnes and India's production is projected at 720,000 tonnes by 2010. The Government of India selected North-East as a major production centre of natural rubber during the Tenth Five Year Plan (2002-07). The rubber planters have been guaranteed a grant of Rs. 20,000 per

hectare for holdings up to 5 hectares and Rs. 16,000 per hectare for holdings about 5 hectares to 20 hectares. The target of plantation and re-plantation of rubber for the entire North-East has been fixed at 7050 hectares by the end of the Tenth Plan against 1410 hectares at the end of the Ninth Plan. The highest target of 3500 hectares has been fixed for Tripura followed by Assam at 2000 hectares. Considering the potentialities of the region and the growing global demand for natural rubber the target in the Tenth Plan appears to be too conservative. Therefore, during Eleventh Plan Period (2007-12), rubber plantation in this region should get top priority so that plantation coverage can be expanded by at least ten-fold increase.

(iv) Bio-Diesel Plantation/Jatropha: Another emerging potentiality of the North-East is the plantation of jatropha plants from which bio-diesel can be produced. This plant is grown wildly in the entire North-East. If its scientific captive cultivation can be undertaken in a large scale, the region can save lot of foreign exchange in terms of reduced import of crude oil, the price of which is increasing sharply. The plant produces seeds with oil content 37 per cent and the oil can be combusted as fuel without being refined. It burns with clear smoke-free flame and is fit for diesel engine. The byproduct is pressed-cake which can be used as fertilizer. The plant grows relatively quickly, producing seed within 4-5 years and survives for about 40-50 years. The Government of India has emphasized for the plantation of Jatropha plants throughout the country. The Ministry of Petroleum and Natural Gas, Government of India has announced bio-diesel Purchase Policy 2005, declaring the procurement price of bio-diesel at Rs. 24 per litre. For such economic viability, several NGOs, Government and Private companies, etc. have shown interest for Jatropha plantation in the North-East Region. If large scale cultivation of these plantation crops is undertaken in the region, it will protect region's environment. This can be an important source of income of rural people and thereby diverting the jhumia from their shifting cultivation. But it is not economically viable and very much labour intensive cultivation. But from the ecological point of view only barren land can be used for the purpose.

Challenges for the Development of North-East Border Trade and its Opportunities

Challenges

To develop border trade there are so many barriers that should be overcome first. Some of these are given below.

1. *Insurgency-Related Issues:* Insurgencies in the region have already caused serious damage to the regional economy and taken away a number of valuable human lives. A consensus is emerging among scholars that contrary to popular belief, civil wars and ethnic conflicts in several parts of the world are not due, primarily to ethnic and religious diversity, but rather to high levels of poverty, failed political institutions and economic natural resources. Deep political and economic development failures, not tribalism, ethnic hatred and linguistic fragmentation, are the root causes of the problem. The implication of these findings is significant. Something can be done to reduce the prevalence of violent conflicts in the affected countries and prevent their recurrence. Democratic reforms, improved political governance and institutions for economic management are needed in the societies to manage effectively the challenges to maintain political stability and also to diversify their economies. Based on the observations, Central Government and State Governments in the regions need to restructure the styles and systems of governance to address the root cause of conflicts in the regions.

2. *Transport and Communication and other Facilities:* Trade between BCIM countries can flourish only when people, goods and vehicles can move with minimal technical and procedural obstacles across the borders. Development of an efficient transport and communication system greatly contributes to rapid progress of the merchandize trade. Transport cost being a significant determinant of competitiveness, cheaper mode of transportation is essential for the development of trade and services between the BCIM countries. In hills, the construction as well as the reconstruction of roads in the north-east region involves rock cutting, soiling in soft patches, construction of retaining walls, etc. which requires a lot of human labour throughout the year. The whole of topography was dissected into isolation by numerous rivers and streams, many of which being

big and at the same time full of rocks as well as subjected to very strong cross current rendering navigation impossible to a considerable extent. Such type of characteristics of this area signifies how many difficulties to construct roads in this area the agencies face. As the region has very heavy rainfall, the roads suffer from surface and gully erosion. The situation is further deteriorated by the loose soil-base derived largely from alluvium in the plains and such sedimentary rocks as sandstone, mudstone, shale etc. in the hills. The roads have, therefore, to be constantly repaired and maintained in serviceable condition, needing a huge expenditure. It is completely disrupted during every monsoon season. Railway services are yet to reach the nooks and corners of the region while the road network is not free and smooth. The Telex-communication facilities are available only in and around the urban centres and the postal services cannot be said to be satisfactory.

The region has numerous turbulent rivers and hill-streams which flow with fury during the rainy season. Besides, many of them change their course very often. Some of them, again, are very wide. They are not only wide but also subject to very cross current. The roads need to be frequently bridged and many culverts, retention walls, spurs etc. have to be constructed requiring huge labour and expenditures. But it must be noted that unless exportable surpluses are produced within it, regarding roads, airports, power, railways, telecommunication, banking and finance the North-Eastern Region could not be able to derive the full benefits of all developments simply by acting as a corridor of exports of other countries.

3. *Institutional and Structural Corruption:* There is no dearth of funds to hasten the development of the NER since 1996 when the former Prime Minister, H.D. Deva Gowda first declared a package of Rs. 6,100 crores for the infrastructural development in the region. But one does not know how much of these huge funds actually flowed down the development pipeline. The leakages of development funds in the region have been at a higher level than it is in the rest of the country. All financial allocations for development and the wealth generated thereof have flowed out of the region or into the hands of the corrupt politicians, bureaucrats and contractors. The region has remained still cut off both physically and emotionally from the national mainstream primarily due to the absence of a coherent perspective on development.

4. *Lack of Transit Facility:* The North-East States are very far from the main land of India. So far trade is concerned; distance is also a vital factor in view of transport cost. This distance will be reduced if Bangladesh gives transit facility to India. If it is occurred, both the countries will be benefited. It will help to stimulate not only the bilateral trade between North-East States and Bangladesh, but also the international trade between India and ASEAN through Bangladesh and Bangladesh and ASEAN through North-East States. The transit facilities through Bangladesh would help bypass the difficult chicken neck corridor that connects the landlocked North-East States with the rest of India. If Dhaka provides transit facilities to India and allows the use of Chittagong international port and other ports in Bangladesh, commodities and machinery can be transported to the North-East Region from various parts of India and abroad, saving huge time and money. Agartala, the capital of Tripura is 1,650 kms. from Kolkata and 2,637 kms. from New Delhi via Guwahati, whereas the distance between Agartala and Kolkata via Bangladesh is 350 kms. only (*Arunachal Front*, March 07, 2009)

Opportunities

There are a vast economic opportunities and benefits to link North-East Region with dynamic Asia including the deepening social and cultural ties between the people of northeast and its neighbouring countries.

1. There are a variety of benefits that India can extract through North-East India from FTA with ASEAN:
   (a) Free Trade Agreement (FTA) has the potential to speed up the reforms process in North-East India. There will be a greater urgency to align India's economic policies with those of ASEAN. Clearly, economic liberalization under the provisions of FTA would happen even in areas that are considered sensitive. It creates incentives for countries to liberalize in the context of these agreements, which, in turn, favours deeper liberalization in the context of multilateral negotiations. Proponents of this view argue that 'competitive regionalism' can catalyze global trade liberalization (Hilaire *et al.*, 2004).

(b) There would be significant gains for North-East India's economy and industry in terms of free flow of trade, services and investment. Besides, being a part of an important regional block will also enhance India's bargaining capacity at the WTO.

(c) If a zero duty imports are allowed in certain sectors then cost-benefit analysis of a number of Indian companies may alter. It will be an opportunity to establish new units and create new capacities to cater the local market in the northeast region and ASEAN markets. Indian companies can also set-up plants in ASEAN and export to the entire ASEAN region through this region. By setting up plants abroad Indian companies can leverage some of the cost efficiencies that may come from better infrastructure and lower tariff and non-tariff barriers in this region.

(d) It will put immense pressure on Indian policy makers to align their own tax policies with those of other ASEAN so as to make investments equally attractive in North-East India.

2. Regional cooperation through trade and investment among the BCIM countries is the only way for rapid economic development in the zone. The following areas and measures that need immediate attention of the BCIM governments in this regard are discussed below.

   The border disputes among some of the BCIM countries are to settle for good immediately;

   (a) To sign joint trade agreements;
   (b) To actively promote plural and diversified trade;
   (c) To develop and expand overland transit through cross-border infrastructural development;
   (d) To establish BCIM trade centres, research and training institutions for promotion of trade and human resource development;
   (e) To establish BCIM free trade zone in due course of time.

3. Border Haat:

   (a) The Border Haat may be established to cover a well-defined geographical area of about 1 km radius on both sides of the border at specified locations so as to enhance the living standard and to facilitate the good fruits of modern age in the border areas. The border crossing should be at specified entry points and proper record of entry/exit should be kept.

(b) The Traders may be allowed to carry goods by head load, rickshaw and other non-merchandised means of transport only. Merchandised Transport should not be permitted.

(c) Identity cards may be issued to the traders by the respective Governments for which a common procedure/system may be worked out.

(d) In the specified zone of the Border Haat, the traders should be allowed to do transaction in the local currency of the respective countries. The transaction should be duty-free and there should be no requirement for customs documentation, licensing etc.

(e) Border Haat may be held 2-3 days per week.

4. The economic liberalization will have a bearing upon the present volume of trade and commerce between India and its neighbouring countries. If the Government of India takes positives steps for the development of routes between India and its neighbouring countries and improve the relations, whole economic scenario of the North-East India would be changed which would ultimately solve many of our existing problems specially unemployment and over dependence on agricultural sector.
5. There is a very strong case both on economic and political grounds for India regarding its northeast region to extend unilateral duty-free and quota-free access to its market for products from the least developed countries of the region.

Conclusion

It is true that along with bringing in lot of benefits, the outward looking development strategy of the region may also import a few vices such as erosion in social bond in tribal society, emergence of economic inequality at the initial stage, spread of HIV, drug addiction, women trafficking etc. These are the costs of development. What is necessary is to find out a trade-off. The economic benefits of the market- oriented, trade-led, outward looking economic strategy would definitely outweigh the costs in the form of importation of vices, imaginary or real. Thus, the globalization and India's 'Look East Policy' can accelerate trade/border trade between India and the South-East Asian countries, which can bring in progress and prosperity for the entire country including North-East India.

With the developments discussed above, the North-East India with its geo-strategic location advantage could emerge as a business transit centre for the BCIM, SAARC and ASEAN groups of nations.

REFERENCES

Arunachal Front, Vol. 17, No. 1888, March 7, 2009.

Das, Gurudas (2000): "Trade between the North-Eastern Region and Neighbouring Countries: Structures and Implications for Development" in Das, Gurudas and Purkayastha, R.K. (eds) "*Border Trade: North-East India and Neighbouring Countries*" Akansha, New Delhi.

Dubey, Muchkund (2007): "SAARC and South Asian Economic Integration", *EPW*, Vol. XII, No. 14 April 7-13, Mumbai.

Goswami, H. and J.K. Gogoi, (2003): "Regional Cooperation between China, Myanmar, Bangladesh and India through bilateral Trade: Impact on North East India", *Assam Economic Journal*, Vol. XVI, Dibrugarh.

Government of India, Ministry of Commerce and Industry (Department of Commerce) Annual Reports (various years).

Hilaire, Alvin *et al.* (2004): "Regional and Bilateral Free Trade Schemes should be pursued with caution" *IMF Survey*, June 14.

Lama S.P. Mahendra (2003): "N-E Region and South Asia Growth Quadrangles: Opportunities and Growth Prospects", in *Gangtok Times*, September 11. (Accessed from www.gangtoktimes .com)

Mandal, R.K. (2007): "Expansion of Road Net Work in Arunachal Pradesh (since 1947)", *Arunachal Review*, Vol. VIII, No. 22, June-August, Itanagar.

Mandal, R.K. (2005): "Arunachal Pradesh as an Emerging Power House", *Journal of Global Economy*, Vol. 1, No. 4, October-December, Mumbai.

Majumder, Chandrika Basu (2007): "Border Trade and Border Inhabitants with Special Reference to Tripura", *Journal of North-East India Council for Social Science Research*, Vol. 31:1, April, Shillong.

Passah, P.M. (2007): "North-Eastern Region of India and the Look East Policy", *Proceedings of the 8th Annual Conference of NEEA*, Mizoram University, Aizawl.

Sarma, Atul (2005): "Northeast as a Gateway to Southeast Asia-Big Dream and Home Truths", *Presidential Address, 7th Annual Conference of NEEA*, Rajiv Gandhi University, October 21.

Sikidar, S., Bora, B. and Adhikary, A. (2010): "Export from North-Eastern Region of India: Opportunities and Challenges" in Ahmed, J.U. (ed): *Development Vision of North-East India*, Concept Publishing Company, (P) Ltd. New Delhi, pp. 25-30.

Srivastava, R.K. (2007): "Indo-Asian FTA: Constraints and Opportunities", *Southern Economist*, October 15, Bangalore.

The Statesman, 30th July, 2004, Kolkata.

The Assam Tribune, 26th October, 2004.

10

Urbanization
Trends and Patterns

Introduction

Urbanization is a socio-economic phenomenon. It plays a significant and dynamic role in changing the ways of life of the people. It transforms, civilizes as well as modernizes the human societies. It serves as a significant agent in patterning and organizing the social processes in space. Urbanization is an essential component of development, a necessary transformation which society will and must go through if it is to move from one stage of development to another. Urbanization, in the vocabulary of development economics, is a necessary structural adjustment if the development process is to go forward. This does not mean that one must like urbanization, as one need not approve of many social transformations, which come with economic growth. It does mean, however, that one cannot turn a blind eye to urbanization. To do so means running the risk of letting urbanization evolve in directions, which can impose high costs on society and on future generations? The consequences of such negligence can be truly momentous.

Urbanization, as a social transformation, is very sensitive to public policy. The transformation is indeed inevitable, but the form it takes can vary greatly from one situation to another. The manner in which a society chooses to organize its cities, be it in terms of governance structures, social legislation, or physical planning, will greatly determine the environment in which future generations live. Some urban forms are more conducive to harmonious and sustainable development than others. For instance, within the industrialized world, cities have evolved in different ways, some clearly offering a superior quality of life to their citizens than others. For developing nations, the message is clear: learn from both the successes and the failures of the industrialized world (Rao, 2006).

An overview of the process of urbanization in the State of Arunachal Pradesh during the last two decades brings out the inadequacy of the existing institutional structure in managing urban centres in the "borderless" world of today (Ohmae, 1991, in Kundu, 1994). These institutions are noted to have least capacity to deal with the demands and pressures that are being generated as a result of the present focus of globalization. Managing these processes was considered to be an exclusive responsibility of the government and state owned and state led institutions, just a few decades back.

Now, under a decentralized system of planning, it is viewed as a joint responsibility of stakeholders like industrial and business enterprises, public and private organizations and resident associations, etc. These tasks include providing the infrastructural services and other civic amenities, etc. for the urban dwellers. Cities and towns are a product of complex forces that include market dynamics, over which town and city managers have only a limited control. Consequently, the extent to which an individual city or town can accelerate or retard its economic, social, or for that matter, demographic growth, depend largely on internal dynamics and external circumstances.

The new perspective, thus, urges the government at different levels in the hierarchy to function in collaboration with the other stakeholders, if they want to make an impact on the pace, pattern and trend of urbanization.

Urbanization, in demographic sense, is an increase in the proportion of the urban population to the total population over a period of time. As long as, urban population to the total population increases, there is urbanization. Rapid urbanization has been a worldwide phenomenon in the 20th century. In developing countries like India, the challenge of urbanization becomes more serious in the context of urban poverty, which is largely an extension of rural poverty.

Urbanization indicates technological, institutional, educational, communicational, industrial and organizational development from time to time and is being brought about by development, modernization, and migration. It is also closely related with economic development and social transformation of a state or a region. Urbanization and economic development stimulates each other with structural changes on a large scale. Economic development is generally associated with the growth of urbanization. The census definition of urban area takes into account these criteria: (i) all places with a municipality corporation, cantonment board or notified town area committee, (ii) all other places which satisfy these minimum criteria: (a) a minimum population of 5,000, (b) at least 75 per cent of male working population engaged in non-agricultural pursuits, and (c) a density of population of at least 400 persons per sq. km.

This research paper attempts to assess the nature of urbanization, urbanism and migration in Arunachal Pradesh in the context of the recent globalization. The trend and pattern of urban growth and pattern of state level migration in the context of growing spatial and economic inequality have also been analyzed in the proceeding sections explaining the increasing pace of mobility of population across the State and from rural to urban areas leading to the emergence of a new urban culture. The article is organized as follows. Section-I focuses on Regional Characteristics and Physical Setting of Arunachal Pradesh. Section-II reviews Generalities and Conception Urbanization. Section-III shows the Genesis of Urbanism and Urbanization in Arunachal Pradesh. Section-IV analyses Pattern and Level of Urbanization in Arunachal Pradesh. Section-V discusses the Trend and Features of Urbanization in Arunachal Pradesh. Section-VI examines the Population Mobility i.e., migration in Arunachal Pradesh. Section-VII searches the Problems for Urbanization in Arunachal Pradesh. Section-VIII detects the Consequences of Urbanization in Arunachal Pradesh. The final Section-IX summarizes the basic findings and puts forward a perspective for future growth and Section-X concludes.

SECTION - I

Regional Characteristics and Physical Setting of Arunachal Pradesh

Arunachal Pradesh, the land of rising sun situated in the North-Eastern part of India has 83,743 sq. kms. area and has a long international border with Bhutan to the West (160 kms.), China to the North and North–East (1,030 kms.) and Myanmar to the East (440 kms.). It also stretches from snow-capped mountains in the North to the plains of Brahmaputra Valley (Assam) in the South. Out of the total area of 83,743 sq. kms., the State has forest cover of about 51,540 sq. kms. forming 62 per cent of her total geographical area.

The proportion of arable plain land is very low. This topographical situation has direct influence on the economy of the State. From the economic point of view the whole State may be divided into three lateral belts each having a distinct pattern of economic opportunities and choice of economic development. The upper belt bordering international frontiers has very little economic opportunities as well as constrained with negligible or no facilities of modern civilization. The lower belt consisting mainly of the foothills has intimate economic ties with the adjoining plains of Assam. The people of lower belt enjoy almost all facilities of modern life. The middle belt acted as a bridge between the upper and the lower belt.

The people inhabiting the three belts are at different stages of economic development. The level of population mobility are also distinct and varies between and within the belts due to the regional and territorial disparity in terms of amenities and facilities available based on the levels of economic development in the State of Arunachal Pradesh. The State has one of the highest per capita availability of natural resources, yet it is one of the most economically backward regions in India.

SECTION - II

Generalities and Conception Urbanization

The process of urbanization and economic development in many respects are interlinked with each other. It is generally accepted that the average urban dweller have greater access to modern amenities of life as compared to the rural counterpart. This, therefore, provides a contrasting picture with regard to overall opportunities and choices available to the people at large for rural and urban dwellers and therefore a contrasting level of quality of life.

The variation in terms of quality of life may be attributed on account of historical and geographical factors that led to differential rate of growth and pattern with regard to urbanization over space and time. Thus, the pattern and process of urbanization as well as the nature and extent of urban problems vary from place to place. The challenges of proper management of civic amenities in the urban centres are also not uniform.

Pattern of urbanization in the North-East region presents a paradoxical situation; while the hilly areas, with their quasi-subsistent tribal economies have been experiencing a phase of urban explosion in recent years, the valley areas having surplus producing peasant economy are experiencing stagnation in terms of the growth of urban areas (Mitra, 1997).The following section highlights the several important aspects and dynamism of urbanization as a phenomenon over the space and time.

Urbanization as we all know is a socio-economic phenomenon. It plays a significant and dynamic role in changing the overall quality of life. It transforms or enhances as well as modernizes the human societies, and serves as a significant agent in the patterning and organizing the social process in *spatio-temporal* context. Urbanization is an essential component of development which every society at one point of time must go through if it is to move from one stage of development to another. Urbanization is also considered as a necessary structural adjustment in the process of forward mobility of human society as a whole. This does not mean that one has to or one must like many of the social transformation which follows. It does mean, however, one cannot turn a blind eye to urbanization. The consequences of such negligence can be truly momentous.

Urbanization *vis-à-vis* social transformation is also very sensitive to public policy. The transformation is indeed inevitable but the form varies to a great degree from one situation to another. Some urban forms are more conducive to harmonious and sustainable development than other.

The general reasons for urbanization thus can be attributed to: (1) the natural increase of the urban population over a period of time, (2) The large scale migration of population from the rural areas of the state itself and immigration from other states to its urban areas being the administrative headquarters. Thus, both the push and pull factors have played their role in the migration of population from the rural to urban areas or from other states to this region on a large scale in the post-liberalization period due to educational and employment opportunities as well as expansion of service sector like transportation and communication.

Urbanization in this regard may also be defined as a process that is characterized by transition or take off in which a region/ nation can jump out of the transition from total agrarian base to industrial society (Rao *et al.*, 2004). In other words, it is delimitated as a process of massive shifts of labour and capital from predominantly rural to urban areas. Urbanization in this sense can be considered as an index of modernization and largely associated with economic growth and development (Prakash, 2005).

In fact, it is very helpful in contributing positively to poverty reduction in the rural areas. Different levels of urbanization, however, reflect different degrees of modernization and development in the economy (Prasad, 1995). It is a multi-dimensional process and largely, it depends upon the incentives for industrial and service sector development.

According to Mills Becker (1986), "Urbanization is an inevitable process that is experienced by all nations in their transition form agrarian to industrial and service societies and is a necessary factor behind the economic growth". Capital accumulation, technological change and the growth of socio-economic infrastructure seem to be the most important determinants of this shift (Kundu, 2004). They are positively associated with industrial and service sector development in contrast to agriculture. In fact, the latter depends upon climatic conditions along with soil and other geographical factors of the economy.

It is true that in a growing economy, there is mounting demand of industrial and service sector products. Consequently, there is spontaneous increase in industrial and service sector production and thus, employment generation in the economy. This also follows increase of service facilities for various purposes like the distribution of increased output, financial management through banking and financial institutes as well as civic services for the population experiencing increase in income levels (GoI, 2003). Economic development, therefore, foretells industrialization and that itself promotes the concentration of people in the urban areas, where maximum attempt is made to economize the land inputs (i.e., the land requirement per unit of output being less than the agricultural sector). On the whole, growth of industrialization necessitates urbanization in particular and economic development in general.

The growth of urbanization can also enlarge through availability of socio-economic infrastructure in the economy. In the modern world, problem of large urban concentrations affects not only in the advanced countries but also all the areas with dense population and consequently, in large cities. In a mature system of cities, standardized manufacturing production trends to be de-concentrated into smaller and medium size metropolitan areas. However, the production in large metropolitan areas focuses on services, R & D and non-standardized manufacturing. The problem in today's developing countries is that they appear to be strong bias toward excessive concentration (Henderson, 2002 in Pradhan, 2006).

In India, the trend towards concentration of urban population in a small number of large urban centres has been taking shape over a century. While the number of urban centres doubled between 1901 and 1991, urbanization increased eight-fold, resulting in a top heavy urban hierarchy. Future demographic and economic growth is likely to concentrate in and around 60-70 large cities in the country having a population of a million people or more. The demographic trends towards urbanization are accompanied by a change in the management and financing of urban development as a result of liberalization. Decentralization of municipal governance has led to a substantial reduction in budgetary allocations for infrastructural development. Greater reliance is now placed on institutional financing and capital markets for resource mobilization and on private companies for service delivery.

Many researchers and governments in the developing countries considered that the rapid growth of urban population and high primacy (concentration of population and activities in the leading cities) have a major impediment in realizing their development goals of equitable development. Several explicit and implicit policies were adopted by governments of many developing countries for slowing down the urban growth particularly the population growth in large cities, by focusing on reducing the migration to these cities from rural areas. The latest data on world urbanization, however, show that at the beginning of the twenty-first century, a number of developing countries do not have even one-third of their population in urban areas. There is also a considerable slowing down in the rate of urbanization as well as the rate of urban population growth in most of the developing countries in the last two decades. In India, the latest census data also confirms the same.

The rural to urban migration is an important component of urbanization in most of the countries and regions. Both urbanization and migration are regarded as one of the most important indicators of economic development and social transformation of a region. Economic growth is accompanied by a gradual reduction in the relative share of agriculture and an increase in the relative share of industry and services in total output and labour force. This indicates a movement of population from agricultural areas to the industrial centres.

As a result, migration from rural areas to urban areas takes place with the growth of industrial and service sectors. So, migration and urbanization is an integral part of economic development. S. Kuznets emphasized that there is a relationship between migration and economic development that takes place in terms of the selectivity of people. He opines that migrants are dynamic, risk-bearing persons who respond favourably to economic stimuli and have high capacity to detach themselves from traditional surroundings and adapt themselves to unfamiliar environments. Thus, the migrant people are most productive from the viewpoint of economic development in the sense that they are risk bearing section of population (Mitra, 1997).

SECTION - III

Genesis of Urbanism and Urbanization in Arunachal Pradesh

Any study on urbanization is constrained by definitional and conceptual problems across the countries in the world. In the Indian context, the definition of "Urban" remained same for the period up to 1957. Nevertheless in 1961 census, several modifications were made and definition of town was adopted. Subsequently, 1991 census (series I, Vol. II, p.34) reviewed and adopted a definition for urban place. According to this definition urban place is defined on the basis of administrative and population criteria as:

1. All statutory towns, i.e., all places with a municipality, corporation, cantonment board or notified town area committee etc. (Administrative criterion).
2. All other places which satisfy the following criterion.
   (a) A minimum population of 5000.
   (b) At least 75 per cent of male population engaged in non-agricultural activities.
   (c) A density of population of at least 400 persons/sq. km.
   (d) Important tourist centres, and
   (e) Outgrowth of urban centres.

According to the above-mentioned criteria, Indian census has classified the Indian towns into six categories, such as:

Class I	Towns having more than 1,00,000 population
Class II	Towns having 50,000 – 99,999 population
Class III	Towns having 20,000 – 49,999 population
Class IV	Towns having 10,000 – 19,999 population
Class V	Towns having 5,000 – 9,999
Class VI	Towns having less than 5,000 population.

Similarly, different classification of towns have been suggested by different scholars from time to time which include categorization based on density (Wilcox in Sharma, 2008), occupation (Dickinson 1964, in Sharma, 2008),technological characteristics (Mumford,1966 in Sharma, 2008), and migration characteristics (Ray Chaudhury, 1993 in Sharma, 2008).

As far as Arunachal Pradesh is concerned all the urban centres are declared urban due to two different criteria viz: (1) based on the transformation of the urban centres from 'EOPOLIS' to 'POLIS' stage growing out of the existing villages having a market outlet or a link with a market outlet beyond the state boundary, (ii) criterion is based on population characteristics along with prospective and important tourist centres. The following paragraphs outline the genesis of urbanism and urbanization in the state and the region.

Urbanism and Urbanization: A Distinct case

During the colonial period, large parts of the region of the North-Eastern States were "Excluded Areas" or "Partially Excluded Areas". Further, under the Inner Line Regulation Act, the tribal state like Arunachal remained secluded and restricted to outsiders. The entries as such were permitted based on administrative necessity otherwise outsiders were strictly prohibited from entering the tribal territorial area beyond the inner line. The British, through such measures, sought to protect the tribal culture from so called exploitation by others (the non-tribal). Tribes were thus, left to themselves to pursue their traditional methods of livelihood and manage their affairs in accordance with their traditional/ancestral customs.

Consequently, the pace of urbanization in the region was negligible or very low. But after independence and particularly since the planning era began, along with the thrust of statehood in 1987, a substantial amount of investments have been made in expanding the basic infrastructure in the region and setting up of a large number of administrative headquarters and circle administrative units/centres at the different levels. Such development interventions have resulted in the growth of 17 urban centres in the region at a rapid pace.

The process of urbanization and economic development are interrelated in many respects. Urbanization leads to greater access to modern amenities of life, education, health and other civic amenities/services as compared to their rural counterpart. Nevertheless, urbanization may also give rise to host of other problems like over crowding, water and sanitation problems, environmental pollution, social evils like crimes, etc. On account of historical and geographical factors, the rates of urban growth and pattern of urbanization as well as nature and extent of urban problems vary from state to state in the North-East region.

The process of urbanization in Arunachal Pradesh may be attributed to the setting up of administrative headquarters at different levels and mainly administrative set-up of district headquarters, and circles. Spatial variation in the level of urbanization in this hilly state gets highly accentuated due to local differences in topography and altitude as well as accessibility and nearest neighbour factors. The pattern is remarkably clear showing higher level of urbanization restricted to the river valleys of varying width. The small river valleys of Lohit, Dibang, Siang and Subansiri river in Arunachal Pradesh are experiencing urban growth at a very fast pace while the neighbouring highland areas continue to be entirely inaccessible and rural.

Thus, urbanization and development in Arunachal Pradesh is confined to the low altitude foothill zone. The process of urbanization is yet to take off in areas with a strong concentration of indigenous (tribal) population. Urbanization, in demographic sense, is an increase in the proportion of the urban population to the total population over a period of time. Rapid urbanization has been a worldwide phenomenon in the 20th century. In developing countries like India, the challenge of urbanization becomes more serious in the context of urban poverty, which is largely considered as an extension of rural poverty.

In an idealistic sense, urbanization generally indicates technological, institutional, educational, communicational, industrial and organizational development from time to time and is being brought about by development, modernization, and migration. It is also closely related with economic development and social transformation of a state or a region. Urbanization and economic development stimulates each other with structural changes on a large scale. As we all understand that economic development is generally associated with the growth of urbanization.

The census definition of urban area takes into account these criteria: (i) all places with a municipality corporation, cantonment board or notified town area committee, (ii) all other places which satisfy these minimum criteria: (a) a minimum population of 5,000, (b) at least 75 per cent of male working population engaged in non-agricultural pursuits, and (c) a density of population of at least 400 persons per sq. km. Table 10.1 below shows district-wise status of urbanization in the State of Arunachal Pradesh in 2001.

Table 10.1: District-wise Urbanization Status in the State of Arunachal Pradesh, 2001.

Sl.No.	*District*	*Total Population*	*Town*	*Urban Population*		*Town Class*
				Total	*% age*	
1.	Tawang	38924	Tawang	8376	21.52	V
2.	West Kameng	74599	Bomdila	6693	08.97	V
3.	East Kameng	57179	Seppa	15002	26.24	IV
4.	Papum Pare	122003	Itanagar,	35022	28.27	III
			Naharlagun	27020	22.15	III
5.	Lower Subansiri	98244	Ziro	12384	12.61	IV
6.	Upper Subansiri	55346	Daporijo	15756	28.57	IV
7.	West Siang	103918	Aalo,	17033	16.39	IV
			Basar	4079	3.93	VI
8.	Eest Siang	87397	Pasighat	21965	25.13	III
9.	Upper Siang	33363	—	—	—	—
10.	Dibang Valley	57720	Roing	10107	17.57	IV
11.	Lohit	143527	Tezu,	15015	10.46	IV
			Namsai	11747	8.18	IV
12.	Changlang	125422	Changlang,	6469	05.16	V
			Jairampur	5919	04.72	V
13.	Tirap	100326	Khonsa,	9233	09.20	V
			Deomali	6061	06.64	V
14.	Arunachal Pradesh	1096702		227881		

SECTION - IV

Pattern and Level of Urbanization in Arunachal Pradesh

The information about total population as well as urban population in India from 1961 to 2001 is depicted in Table 10.2. India's population was just above 439 million in the year 1961, which increased to about 548 million in 1971, about 686 million in 1981, about 846 million in 1991 and about 1027 million in 2001. During the year 2005, the total population of India was about 1099 million. It is estimated that about 17 per cent of the world's population live in India although we have just 2.4 per cent of the geographical area of the world.

During the last four decades, there has been fast urbanization in our country. The urban population was about 18 per cent of the total population in the year 1961 that increased to about 20 per cent in 1971, about 23 per cent in 1981, about 26 per cent in 1991 and about 28 per cent in 2001.

Table 10.2: Growth of urban population in India, 1961-2001 (Million) and Arunachal Pradesh 1971-2001.

*India **				*Arunachal Pradesh***
Year	*Total Population*	*Urban Population*	*%age share of Urban population*	*%age share of Urban population*
1961	439.23	78.94	17.97	NA
1971	548.16	109.11	19.90	3.70
1981	686.18	159.73	23.31	6.32
1991	846.30	217.61	25.71	12.91
2001	1027.02	285.35	27.78	20.41

Source: *Population Census, Paper II, 1981, 1991,2001.
** Statistical abstract of Arunachal Pradesh, various issues.

Table 10.3 shows the pattern and level of urbanization along with the growth of urban population in the entire region of North-Eastern States. The annual exponential growth rate of entire region as compared to all India scenarios is quite misleading. This can be attributed to fast growth of small towns in the region due to influx of internal and international migrants especially in the states of Arunachal, Assam, Mizoram, Meghalaya, Nagaland and Sikkim.

Table 10.3: Pattern and Level of Urbanization and Growth of Urban Population across N.E. States.

State	*% of Urban Population*					*Annual Exponential Growth Rate*		
Year	*1971*	*1981*	*1991*	*2001*	*RANK*	*71-81*	*81-91*	*91-01*
Arunachal	3.70	6.32	12.21	20.41	3	8.32	9.28	7.00
Assam	8.82	9.88	11.09	12.72	7	3.29	3.29	3.09
Manipur	13.19	26.44	27.69	23.88	2	9.70	2.98	1.21
Meghalaya	14.55	18.03	18.69	19.63	4	4.87	3.10	3.16
Mizoram	11.36	25.17	46.20	49.50	1	11.79	9.57	3.27
Nagaland	9.95	15.54	17.28	17.74	5	8.49	5.58	5.27
Sikkim	9.37	16.23	9.12	11.11	8	9.55	-3.23	4.83
Tripura	10.43	10.98	15.26	17.02	6	3.26	6.19	2.53
All India	20.22	23.73	25.72	27.78		3.79	3.09	2.73

Source: Population Census, Paper 2, 1971, 1981, 1991, 2001.

For understanding the dynamics of development, it would be important to analyze the spatial pattern of urban growth in different size classes of towns. During the first four census decades since independence, urban growth has generally been high in relatively backward and less urbanized states. (Kundu, 1994).This is primarily due to the fast growth of small and medium towns and emergence of new towns.

In the instant case of State like Arunachal Pradesh, a sizeable proportion of these fast growing and new towns are circle or block or district headquarters where implementation of government sponsored development schemes are in full swing including the new central scheme popularly known as JNURM Mission (Jawaharlal Nehru Urban Renewal Mission).

The relationship between urban growth and development, in this case, works out to be negative. This can be attributed to government investment in district headquarters and transfer of funds from centre to state to local bodies through a need based or what is popularly known as "a gap filling" approach.(Kundu,1994) A large part of rural to urban migration into smaller towns from their rural hinterland in backward states like Arunachal can, however, be explained in terms of push factors, owing to lack of diversification of agrarian economy and pull factors, owing to demand of high skill, semi-skilled, and unskilled workforce required for the all round development of the state which is in the infant state of development in terms of all round development.

Table 10.4: Trend, Natures and Extent of Urbanization in the State 1961-2001.

Year	*Total No. of Towns*	*Total Population*	*Total Urban Population*	*% of Urban Population*	*Decennial Growth (%)*	*Annual Exponential Growth*
1961	—	336558	—	—	—	—
1971	4	467511	17288	3.70	—	—
1981	6	631839	41428	6.56	139.63	8.74
1991	10	864558	110628	12.80	167.04	9.82
2001	17	1096702	222688	20.34	101.64	7.01

Source: Calculation based on Census Data, 1961-2001.

As observed in Table 10.4 above, the urban population of the state in the year 2001 was 20.34 per cent against 27.78 per cent for all India. In terms of absolute numbers, the urban population of Arunachal Pradesh in 2001 was 2,22688 against 285 million of that of India. Since 1961, the urban population has steadily increased and it has shown a considerable rise from negligible share to 20.34 per cent of the total population in 2001. However, it is also to be taken in view that while the pace of urbanization is growing at faster rate, this considerable rise in urban population and their livelihood strategies are at different levels of economic development spread over the three different belts which are territorially different and varies in terms of economic opportunities that the terrain provides. Additionally, the pace of urbanization in the region has never attracted any external investment and attention of the urban local bodies to provide for the basic amenities that generally follows in other parts of the country. The following Table 10.5 gives the details of classification of urban towns based on its demographic characteristics and Table 10.6 depicts the GINI coefficient ratio for the year 2001.

Table 10.5: Classification of Urban Centres in Arunachal Pradesh 2001.

Size of Urban Place	*Class*	*No. of Units*	*Name of Towns*	*Class-wise Urban Total Population*
100000	I	—	—	—
50,000-99,999	II	—	—	—
20,000-49,999	III	3	Itanagar, Naharlagun, Pasighat	83855
10,000-19,999	IV	7	Seppa, Ziro, Roing, Daporijo,Aalo,Tezu, Namsai	96257
5,000-9,999	V	5	Bomdila, Changlang, Jairampur, Khonsa, Deomali	34286
<5,000	VI	2	Tawang, Basar	8290
Total		17		222688

Source: Calculation based on 2001 Census.

From Table 10.5 above, the computed value of GINI concentration ratio for urban population living in various size categories of urban centres in the State of Arunachal Pradesh is 0.30647. It is a very low coefficient of urban concentration, implying that only three urban centres (as shown in Table 10.5) have a disproportionately somewhat large share of state's total urban population that ranges between 20,000-49,999, categorized as III Class towns. The remaining 14 small urban centres account for only an insignificant proportion of state's total urban population.

Growth of urban centres

Till 1961 census the State of Arunachal Pradesh was entirely rural having no urban centre. Census-wise trend in urbanization is shown in the following Table 10.7.

Table 10.6: Computation of GINI Concentration Ratio, 2001.

Size of Urban Place	No. of Units	Population	Proportion of Unit	Cumulative Proportion of			$X_i Y_{i+1}$	$Y_i X_{i+1}$
				Population	Units X_i	Popu. Y_i		
100000	—	—	—	—	—	—	—	—
50,000-99,999	—	—	—	—	—	—	—	—
20,000-49,999	3	83855	0.1765	0.3766	0.1765	0.3766	—	—
10,000-19,999	7	96257	0.4118	0.4322	0.5883	0.8088	0.14275	0.22155
5,000-9,999	5	34286	0.2941	0.1540	0.8824	0.9628	0.56641	0.71368
<5,000	2	8290	0.1176	0.0372	1.0000	1.0000	0.8824	0.9628
Total	17	222688	1.0000	1.0000			1.59156	1.89803

GINI Concentration Ratio (GCR) =1.89803-1.59156=0.30647.

Table 10.7: Census-wise List of Urban Centres since 1961.

Census	*No. of Census Town*	*Name of Census Town*
1961	Nil	None
1971	4	Along, Bomdila, Pasighat and Tezu.
1981	6	Along, Bomdila, Pasighat ,Tezu, Naharlagun and Itanagar.
1991	10	Along, Bomdila, Pasighat, Tezu, Naharlagun, Itanagar, Ziro, Roing, Namsai and Khonsa.
2001	17	Along, Bomdila, Pasighat, Tezu, Naharlagun, Itanagar. Ziro, Roing, Namsai, Khonsa, Tawang, Seppa, Daporijo, Basar, Changlang, Jairampur and Deomali.

Source: Census Report of various years.

All these towns are administrative centres. In most cases before the establishment of administrative centres; these places were full of forest.

Table 10.8: Growth of Urban Population in Arunachal Pradesh.

Year	*Decennial Growth Rate of Urban Population*
1971-1981	139.63
1981-1991	167.04
1991-2001	101.64

Source: Calculation based on Census Data 1971-2001.

According to 1991 census 12.80 per cent people live in ten urban areas while as per 2001 census 20.41 per cent people live in seventeen urban areas. The decennial urban growth rate in the State has been recorded as 139.63 in 1971-81, 167.04 in 1981-91 and 101.24 in 1991-2001.

SECTION - V

Trend and Features of Urbanization in Arunachal Pradesh

To find out the trend and features of urbanization in Arunachal Pradesh we need to observe what are the (a) degree of urbanization, (b) rate of urbanization, (c) growth of urban centres and (d) estimation of internal migrants to urban areas?

Degree of Urbanization: The degree of urbanization of Arunachal Pradesh in 1971, 1981 and 1991 was 3.70 per cent, 6.65 per cent and 12.21 per cent respectively as against all India average 23.3 per cent in 1981 and 25.72 per cent in 1991. It was declared that Arunachal Pradesh was poorly urbanized state of India (calculated from population census).

Rate of Urbanization: Again, the rate of urbanization in 1971-81 and 1981-91 and 79.73 per cent and 83.6 per cent respectively (calculated from population census).

Where Degree of Urbanization

= (Urban Population ÷ Total Population) × 100

and Rate of urbanization

= {(Degree of urbanization in second census – Degree of urbanization in first census) ÷ Degree of urbanization in second census} × 100

Regarding urbanization, it should be mentioned that there was no urban centre in 1961 census.

Table 10.9: Degree and Rate of Urbanization of Towns in Arunachal Pradesh.

Towns	*Degree of Urbanization/Classification*				*Rate of Urbanization*		
	1971	*1981*	*1991*	*2001*	*1981*	*1991*	*2001*
Bomdila	0.6785(VI)	0.6109 (VI)	0.6540 (V)	0.6095 (V)	–9.96	7.05	–6.80
Along	1.0305 (VI)	1.2778 (V)	1.5313 (IV)	1.5349 (IV)	23.99	19.83	0.23
Pasighat	1.0943 (V)	1.4464 (V)	1.6932 (IV)	2.0035 (III)	32.17	17.06	18.32
Tezu	0.8945 (VI)	0.9874 (V)	1.4673 (IV)	1.3690 (IV)	10.38	48.60	–6.69
Itanagar	—	1.0138 (V)	1.9136 (IV)	3.1886 (III)	—	88.75	66.62
Naharlagun	—	1.2202 (V)	1.6620 (IV)	2.4539 (III)	—	36.19	47.64
Ziro			1.0250 (V)	1.1205 (IV)			9.31
Roing			0.8069 (V)	0.9215 (IV)			14.20
Namsai			0.9224 (V)	1.0560 (IV)			14.48
Khonsa			0.8209 (V)	0.8415 (V)			2.51
Tawang				0.4063 (VI)			
Seppa				1.3645 (IV)			
Daporijo				1.4382 (IV)			
Changlang				0.5830 (V)			
Deomali				0.5525 (V)			
Basar				0.3495 (VI)			
Jairampur				0.5396 (V)			

Thus, to understand the dynamics of urban growth there is fundamental and pertinent question about migration which holds a place of prominence in a geographical analysis of population change in an area. Migration is most fundamental to the understanding of continuously changing space content and space relationship of an area. The trends in migration have also been considered as a sensitive index of changing pattern of economic opportunities in an area. The section below highlights the population mobility, reasons and causes of migration for the state of Arunachal Pradesh.

Section - VI

Population Mobility in Arunachal Pradesh

The patterns of urbanization of Arunachal Pradesh in particular have been accelerated by migration and natural increase to a remarkable extent. Naturally, the impacts of migration have been heavier on urban areas as these are more accessible and attractive to migrants. Thus, our main concern is to estimate and analyze the internal migration in the urban centres of the districts of Arunachal Pradesh classified by direction of movement and distance covered on the basis of 'place of birth.'

The average annual growth rate of population of north-eastern state is much higher than the all India average during 1961-71 and 1971-81 period. This is due to only in-migration in north-eastern states.

Internal migration is a very important component in the population structure of Arunachal Pradesh. The share of mobile population to total population is the highest among the states of North-Eastern India. According to 1971 census, the percentage of internal migrant population was 31.83 per cent of the total population of the State and it has increased to 35.58 per cent of the total population of the State in 1981 census. This can perhaps be attributed to the following reasons:

(i) The policy of NEFA administration which was formulated to develop the territory with the politico-administrative 'main stream' without disturbing the tribal ethos and sentiments and bringing all types of workers from outside of the State.

(ii) Large number of military personnel in the border districts of the State after Indo-China War in 1962 is deputed.

(iii) The fast development of the state and the implementation of various development projects are considered after emerging as a Union Territory in 1972.

(iv) Accommodation is given to the people from other states serving in this State.

In Arunachal Pradesh, the share of total internal migrants varies between 26.41 per cent in Tirap District to 47.87 per cent in Dibang valley district while the share of male migrants to total migrants varies between 33.50 per cent in Upper Subansiri to 58.95 per cent in East Siang District.

Observing the share of migrants to total population, Dibang Valley, Lower Subansiri and Lohit District stand top in the list with the highest share followed by East Kameng, West Siang, Upper Subansiri and East Siang in the high category and West Kameng and Tirap in low category.

Again, on the basis of male migrants to total migrant population, East Siang has a very high category followed by Tirap and Dibang Valley Districts in high category. In the Foothill districts like East Siang and Tirap enjoying more fertile foothills plain land and other infrastructure facilities have high share of male migrants while Upper Subansiri and East Kameng which are lacking in fertile land and other infrastructural facilities, have failed to attract male migrants.

Reasons for urbanization

1. The first reason is being the natural growth of the urban population over a period of time.
2. The large scale migration of population from the rural areas of the state itself and outside of the states to its urban areas. Both the push and pull factors had played their role in the migration of population from the rural to urban areas or from other states to the states on a large scale in the past liberalization period due to employment opportunities.

Reasons and Causes of Migrations

There are some factors which force the people to move from their birth place to another place. These factors are: (i) Political issues, (ii) Better transport facilities, (iii) Growth of industries, (iv) Development of cities, (v) The expansion of irrigation system, (vi) Search of employment, (vii) Better lifestyle, (viii) Education facilities, (ix) Medical facilities and (x) Education facilities etc.

There may be more than one or several reasons for increasing urban population in a country or a state. Natural growth rate of urban population is of course, one reason. Reclassification of previously rural population centres as urban and net migration from rural to urban areas is the other major reasons. In some contexts, a net gain of migrants from other countries could also be important. Apart from the continuous migration of people from rural to urban areas, a major reason for this shift is the rapid growth in the hundreds of towns reclassified as cities in recent years.

Williamson (1988) has noted that rates of migration in developing countries as a group have been quite comparable to that in developed countries at a similar level of development in the 19th century. Over time the share of immigration in urban areas has begun to decline in developing countries as it did in the developed countries. Even in Africa, there are now signs of declining rates of rural-urban migration. A major trend in rural to urban migration in recent years has been the increasing participation of women. In comparison with other developing regions, Latin America and the Philippines have always had the most feminized net urban in migration. In Latin America, for every three rural-urban male migrants there were four female migrants. However, recent data indicate that this pattern is now appearing elsewhere too. This is especially the case in the cities of South-East Asia. Even India, where women usually do not migrate independently of men, there has been an increase in the share of women in the rural-to-urban migration flow. All of these would appear to suggest a historical transition from a preponderance of men to a preponderance of women in net rural-urban migration (Bhattacharya, 2002).

There is a consensus among researchers concerning the determinants of migration. Migrants tend to move from areas of lower economic opportunity to those of higher economic opportunity. Migrants tend to find jobs quickly after moving. Yap (1977) and others have shown conclusively that migrants improve their income over their rural options immediately upon finding an urban job. Urbanization and a great deal of rural-urban migration are inevitable consequences of economic development (Bhattacharya, 2002).

In the instant case for Arunachal Pradesh urban centres are economically dynamic places not only because of the agglomeration effects commonly considered, but also because they are places where ideas spread and people learn about new goods or new ways of doing things. Majority of the urban centres in the State are functionally administrative and military in nature as the State has a strategic location bounded by International border. International experience also demonstrates the futility of attempts to regulate the size of mega-cities through direct controls on growth or movement of people.

Internal Migration

Redistribution of population through movement is defined as Migration. Migration is reticent for those changes of residence that involve a complete change of the community affiliations of the individual. Thus, migration is a form of geographic or spatial modality involving a change of usual residence between clearly defined geographic units. Migration is divided into two categories: (i) internal migration, and (ii) international migration.

A migrant who crosses a migration defining boundary in the process of changing residence and enters a given community from some other parts of the same nation is an internal migrant and is termed as 'in-migrant'. But on the other hand, the term 'immigrant' refers to an international migrant who comes from a sovereign country to live permanently in a country that is not their own. On the other hand, 'emigrant' refers also to an international migrant who leaves his own country to live in another.

The term 'gross-in-migration' denotes the sum of the arrivals and departures of migrants and it is a measure of total volume of population turnover that a community is experiencing including both internal and international migration. Any particular area may simultaneously be receiving migrants from some areas and countries and losing migrants to other areas and countries. The net balance between arrivals and departures is termed as 'net migrants'. Net migrants may be positive or negative depending upon the number of arrivals and departures.

The area from which a migrant departs is termed as the area of 'origin' and the area to which he arrives are termed as area of 'destination'. When a large number of migrants depart from a common area of origin and arrive at a common area of destination during a particular period of time, it is known as a 'migration stream'. A particular period of time is taken to observe migration and it is known as 'migration interval'. Time interval of one year, two years, etc. is used in migration analysis. The development indicators which are likely to exert influence on the total migration in Arunachal Pradesh can be grouped into four categories as given below:

(i) Economic Indicators,
(ii) Socio-Demographic Indicators,
(iii) Indicators of Infrastructural Development, and
(iv) Changing nature of religious composition of population.

Migration is now recognized as an important factor in determining plans for social and economic development, especially in an underdeveloped state like Arunachal. The economists and demographers alike are interested in the relation of migration to regional economic growth, business cycle, the supply of skilled and unskilled labour, the growth of industry, outflow and inflow of money income, wage difference between the place of origin and the place of destination of migrants etc. Similarly, the socialist is interested in the social and cultural amalgamation of the migrants as well as the general population in the place of destination.

Economic Consequences of Migration

Migration may influence the growth of the economy and the level of living both in the place of origin and the place of destination. The different effects of migration are shown below:

1. *Effects of Migration on Employment and Unemployment:* Migration has important economic implications on employment and

unemployment for both the emigrating and the immigrating increase unemployment while emigration tends to reduce it. Many governments have imposed limitations on immigration and the employment of immigrants while some other governments have tried to alleviate unemployment by promoting emigration.

2. *Effects of Migration on Regional Development:* Migration plays an important role on regional development. The freedom of migration ensures the maximum efficiency and productivity of the factors of production, leading to maximum output and optimum use of resource endowments so as to bring a country is proper development.
3. *Effects of Migration on Wage Levels:* When immigrant workers are employed for native works which may be performed by the native workers, the wage level is naturally changed.
4. *Effects of Migration on the Balance of Payments and the Multiplier:* Migration affects the balance of payments through the funds which the migrants carry with them or the remittances which are sent by thereto the home market.
5. *Effects of Migration on Demographic Consequences:* Migration influences the demographic structure both at place of origin and place of destination in two ways: (a) through sex-age structure as very often migrant streams have high proportions of males in the young working age group and (b) through differences in labour force participation rates between migrants and non-migrants in the same age group.

Migration in Arunachal Pradesh

The patterns of urbanization of Arunachal Pradesh in particular have been accelerated by migration to a remarkable extent. Naturally, the impacts of migration have been heavier on urban areas as these are more accessible and attractive to migrants. Thus, our main concern is to estimate and analyze of the internal migrants in the urban centres of the districts of Arunachal Pradesh classified by direction of movement and distance covered on the basis of 'place of birth.'

The average annual growth rate of population of north-eastern state is much higher than the all India average during 1961-71 and 1971-81 period. This is due to only in-migration in north-eastern states.

Internal migration is a very important component in the population structure of Arunachal Pradesh. The share of mobile population to total population is the highest among the states of North-Eastern India. According to 1971 census, the percentage of internal migrant population was 31.83 per cent of the total population of the state and it has increased to 35.58 per cent of the total population of the state in 1981 census. We can consider some reasons behind this.

(i) The policy of NEFA administration which was formulated to develop the territory with the politico-administrative 'mainstream' without disturbing the tribal ethos and sentiments and bringing all types of workers from outside of the state.

(ii) Large number of military personnel in the border districts of the state after Indo-China war in 1962 is deputed.

(iii) The fast development of the State and the implementation of various development projects are considered after emerging as a union territory in 1972.

(iv) Accommodation is given to the people from other states serving in this state.

SECTION - VII

Problems for Urbanization in Arunachal Pradesh

"Urbanization is still at a nascent stage in the Eastern Himalayan region of Bhutan, Arunachal Pradesh, Sikkim and the hills of Darjeeling in West Bengal. In the Indian portion of the Eastern Himalayas the history of the growth of towns does not go back beyond the late 19th century—while urban centres emerged in Bhutan only in the 1960s. Most of the hill urban centres that have subsequently emerged are small with population even less than a 1000 in some cases.

The problem of urban development is a complicated process in the Himalayas as the entire human habitation is largely controlled by the natural environment. The unstable nature of terrain, heavy rain, soil erosion and mass wasting create many problems in the physical distribution of the towns and sometimes further complicates the situation in the long run.

Problems are accentuated by the uneven distribution, unbalanced growth and disparity in the size of these small towns. Unplanned developmental activities, particularly concrete modern construction are increasing day by day without consideration of the risks and vulnerabilities due to earthquakes. Population pressure is forcing people to construct their houses on hill tops and slopes, and thus disturbing the natural slope and making them prone to landslide hazards. The point of concern is not only of the increasing population, but also of the urban character in the delicate eco-system which is prone to natural hazards.

In fact, everyone have a desire to settle down in urban towns which have developed and mushroomed over the years. However, the land resources for urban settlement are limited and, thus, almost all the capital, urban and business towns in these regions have reached the critical level of their load bearing capacity. Due to paucity of land in the plain areas and valleys the local inhabitants have started encroachment of land on hill tops and slopes for construction of residential and commercial complexes. In this process of unregulated constructions, people have even started occupying natural drain areas for construction of buildings, misusing the modern construction technology by creating tunnel passage to the natural drain without due consideration to the volume of rainfall water in the catchment's area. Slope cutting and blocking of the natural drains in an unscientific manner are causing serious threat to the hill slopes and settlements.

SECTION - VIII

Consequences of Urbanization in Arunachal Pradesh

1. Rapid mushrooming of squatter settlements on land pockets may be observed as usual fallout of urbanization. The factors identified for the formation and growth of squatter settlements are poverty, absence and inadequacy of urban planning, migration, economic development of urban centres, shortfall in existing housing stock, political reasons, refugee influx especially Bangladeshees and other miscellaneous spatio-demographic reasons.

2. As the demographic trends unfold, the contours of urban life in almost all urban centres in the State must be in a flux. The world is in the midst of an epochal change characterized by an ongoing fundamental economic restructuring towards ever escalating pace of urbanization, driven by globalization and the revolution in information and communication technology which in turn, impinge upon practically all spheres of human life. The trend of the increase in urban population since 1971 (census year) will be more in the next decades, which will lie crux of the problems seen in different cities in India.
3. As urban centres grow and evolve, certain other paramount challenges come up like ensuring adequate urban infrastructure, its improvisation and upgradation, infrastructure investment, management. Appropriate macro-economic policies which are in tune with the rising urban demands must alone remain relevant and useful. In view of the huge challenges facing urbanizing the State, its urban demand appropriate shifts in the national macro-economic policies to ensure raising of infrastructure investment as well as facilitating fresh approach to modern planning and professional management of urban centres including development of effective mechanisms for disaster management.
4. Rapid rate of urbanization brings in its wake the increasing number of environmental, economic and social problems that adversely affect health and well-being of urban dwellers. These are already seen in the urban centres due to rapid unscientific deforestation. Urbanization up to a certain level seems to have associated with good health. But most densely developed artificial urban environment seems to be associated with negative health outcomes. Unplanned urban growth is often associated with poverty, environmental degradation and population demands that outstrip service capacity. These conditions place human health at risk (Judd, 2002). Patterns of immigration, migration, change in the global economy and sharpening the income inequalities are identified as having a direct bearing upon urban health.

SECTION - IX

Findings

It is in these terms of the spatial character due to special emphasis on the investment on infrastructure and economic development, guided by the national and international capital markets resulting in the emergence of 17 administrative urban centres of Arunachal Pradesh by the year 2001.

Arunachal Pradesh is one of the poorest States in Indian economy. It is not only poor in economic development but also in human development. In fact, its performance in human development is worst among the major non-special category states in India. In terms of urbanization, Arunachal Pradesh is one of the least urbanized States in India. In spite of substantial growth of urban population in the State, the proportion of urban population to total population is about 20.41 per cent only as per 2001 census. This is comparatively very low in contrast to most of the states of the country. In addition, the level of urbanization in the State also varies substantially from district to district. Briefly, urbanization in Arunachal Pradesh reveals one important feature: First, the low level of urbanization and its inter-districts variations. It is expected that slowing down of urbanization not only puts pressure on already crowded agriculture but also widen disparities in the rural development across the districts of Arunachal Pradesh as well as rural-urban disparities within the less urbanized districts. This is a matter of serious concern and requires attention from national policy makers and planners. This also provides the planners and administrators an opportunity to take corrective actions in order to make the towns more conducive for economic and social development and improve upon the quality of life with respect to physical and social environment. Since, there is migration of unskilled labour from villages to urban centres for their livelihood and that is leading to poverty alleviation in the rural areas, it is creating disturbance and high pressure of population in the towns which need more investment in social amenities. The government has to create some facilities in the form of vocational training and extension centres to upgrade the skills and technical competency of rural labour so that they can be easily absorbed in the industrial and service sector. There is also need to improve the urban infrastructure, as it is very supportive to employment generation and making the towns as an engine of economic growth.

Urbanization in Arunachal Pradesh is mainly due to administrative expansion and not due to industrialization as it is seen in developed countries rather than the growth centres. These urban centres can be termed as 'induced' urban centres as opposed to the 'sequent occupance' of urbanization process of plain areas. It can also be safely said that the growth of urban settlements in Arunachal Pradesh is not an outcome of social process; rather, it is the result of conscious politico-administrative efforts (Mitra, p.159). Again migration has played an important role in the urbanization process of Arunachal Pradesh.

Therefore, sustainable development in urban areas in Arunachal Pradesh may not be expected as the resources of government are shrinking. Moreover, there are no statutory bodies in urban areas that can look after the development of towns. The urbanization in Arunachal Pradesh is going on in the way of unplanned growth of buildings, residential houses and complexes, commercial buildings. Thus, the impact of urbanization is destructing the scope of social forestry and leading to ribbon development in all urban areas of the State especially in the capital complex. The unplanned construction is leading towards land slides, soil erosion, waterlogging especially during rainy season and loss of fertility of nearby land. Again, it is creating sewage problems and traffic congestation.

SECTION-X

Conclusion

The level of disparity in the rate of urbanization can be minimized by giving importance to socio-economic development between rural and urban areas. There is need of broad based policy to urbanize the poor State like Arunachal Pradesh in the interest of overall economic development of the country. However, the present study raises a number of vital questions which can be answered more satisfactorily with the help of further research, preferably at more micro level, into this less explored but economically and socially important field of inquiry. Hence, it is expected that the present study will form the basis for future research work on the original topic relating to the entire North-Eastern Region.

REFERENCES

Asif, M. and Wali, T. (2006): "Asian Urbanization: Certain Public Health Consequences of Urban Social Stress" in Jugale, V. B. and Jugale, Y.V. (eds.): *The State of Indian Economy*, Serials Publications, New Delhi.

Bhattacharya, Prabir C. (2002): "Urbanization in Developing Countries", *EPW*, Vol. XXXVII, No. 41.

Chandna, R.C. (2005): *Geography of Population: Concepts, Determinants and Patterns*, Kalyani Publications, New Delhi.

Census Reports, 1961, 1981, 1991 and 2001.

Datt, R, and Sundharam, K.P.M. (2004), *"Indian Economy"*, S. Chand and Company Ltd., Ram Nagar, New Delhi.

Jha, S.D. (1989), *"Policy Imprecation of Rural Delhi migration in India"*. Vani Pub. New Delhi.

Judd, F.K. *et al.* (2002) : 'High Prevalence Disorders in Urban and Rural Communities,' *Australian NZ Journal of Psychiatry*, 36(1).

Kundu, A. (2004): Infrastructure, Financing and Emerging Pattern of Urbanization: Vision 2020, *India Vision 2020*, Planning Commission, New Delhi.

Mandal, R.K. (2005), "Trend of Diversification of Arunachal Economy with Special Reference to Agriculture: A Strategy for Sustainable Development" Resarun: *Journal of the Directorate of Research*, Vol. 29, Itanagar.

Mandal, R.K. and Bhattacharjee, M. (2009): "Globalization and Emerging Patterns of Urbanization in Arunachal Pradesh: Trend and Features" submitted to *EPW* for publication.

Mazumdar, D.N. (1990), "An assessment of Shifting Cultivation in North-East India" in Majumdar D.N. (ed.): *"Shifting Cultivation in North-East India"*, Omsons Pub., New Delhi.

Mitra, A. (2002): *"Internal Migration and Economic Development in the hill"*, Omsons Pub., Guwahati, New Delhi.

Osik, N.N. (1996): *"A brief history of Arunachal Pradesh"*, Omsons Publications, Guwahati.

Pradhan, R.P. (2006): "Urbanization in Orissa: An Inter-State and Inter-District Analysis", in Jugale, V.B. and Jugale, Y.V.(eds): *The State of Indian Economy*, Serials Publications, New Delhi.

Prakash, H. (2005): "Urban Infrastructure—A Glimpse", *Southern Economist*, Vol. 44, No. 9, Bangalore.

Prasad, P. (1995): *Urban Slums: Health, Education and Development*, Delta Publications, New Delhi.

Rao, N.A. and *et al.* (2004): "Urbanization Trends in Andhra Pradesh: A Region-wise Study", *Asian Economic Review*, 46(1).

Rao, J.N. (2006): "Population Growth and Economic Development in India", *Southern Economist*, Vol. 45, No. 1, Bangalore.

Sharma, Manish (2008): *Economy of Arunachal Pradesh: Problems, Performances, Prospects*, DVS Publishers, Guwahati.

Sidhu, M.S., Toor, M.S. and Dhadli, T.K. (2006): "Urban Proverty in India: Some Issues", *Southern Economist*, March 1, Vol. 44, No. 20, Bangalore.

Yap, L. (1977): "The Attraction of Cities: A Review of the Migration Literature", *Journal of Development Economics*, Vol. 4, No. 3.

11

Quality Assurance in Higher Education

Introduction

Societies will increasingly become knowledge-based and promote knowledge-based industries. India has a distinct advantage with a population profile concentrated in the younger age group, where many new opportunities can be fully optimized, for which equipping our human resources with required skills and knowledge becomes an essential condition. Education is the process whereby society passes on the accumulated knowledge and experience of past generation to its youth in a systematic and abridged form, so that it can begin where past generations have ended and move on from there. Being at the apex of this educational pyramid, higher education has a key role to play in the system as it provides people an opportunity to reflect on the critical social, economic, cultural and spiritual issues of the country. Traditionally, higher education has provided the wisdom and expertise, which equips young people for their future role as social leaders. This remains valid since higher education must uphold education and values, which moulds socially responsible citizens. Higher education is now regarded as a constitution not only for developing knowledge and training young minds, but also for disseminating and applying such knowledge. Today performance evaluation, accountability and higher standards have become watchwords in any discussion on revamping higher education. Hence, it is very much essential to ensure quality of higher education at a nationally comparable and internationally expectable standard.

It is the education that it would accelerate economic growth, that it would improve the levels of living and knowledge of the people and that it would encourage modern attitudes. Education is also recognized as a basic input for empowerment to individual and overall development of the society. Almost all third world nations believe that it is the rapid expansion of educational opportunities that holds the basic key for national development. Despite its importance, education continues to be a neglected area at the policy level. After many years of planning and promises total literacy in India remains to be a distant dream.

The literacy rate for the country as a whole in 2001 worked out to 65.38 per cent for the population aged seven years and above. The corresponding figures for males and females are 75.85 and 54.16 per cent respectively. Kerala with a literacy rate of 90.92 per cent holds the first rank while Bihar with a literacy rate of 47.53 per cent ranks last in the country.

Education is a vital channel to prepare people for the kind of effective role mentioned above, to achieve a sound democratic system, with full knowledge of the citizens' duties and rights. The benefits of education are many. Investment in education is the best investment that a country could make of lasting benefit.

The General Agreement on Trade Services (GATS) is an agreement between countries who are signatories to World Trade Organization (WTO). Education is one of the services covered under GATS as, marketing "education" is now-a-days a more profitable proposition with very great potentials and possibilities. It is included in 12 classified sectors covering 161 services. Free unfettered trade in education seems to be imminent. The educational systems of all the countries of the world are to be opened up as per GATS mandate. Therefore, education must possess inbuilt quality and saleable skills while competing with other best trades of the world. In a globally competitive world, India will be a loser in the international educational trade market, if quality and relevance of education are not inbuilt.

Globalization is the emerging reality of the 21st century and the advent of the 21st Century accompanied by tremendous development in science, technology, information and communication technology is witnessing unforeseen changes and is posing new challenges in the realm of higher education. We have become a world-wide community living in a global village. World-wide economic, scientific, cultural, political and knowledge interdependence (knowledge is power) dictated by opening up under the pressure of free trade theories of Word Trade Organization (WTO) and General Agreement on Trade in Services (GATS) of economic and financial frontiers and finding an instrument in new information technologies is becoming even more securely established. Globalization means integration of economics and societies through cross country flow of information, ideas, technology, goods, services, capital, finance and the people. In another sense it refers to removal of barriers to free trade and the close integration of national economy-"a world in one nest". WTO classification list has divided educational services in to five parts—*viz.*, (a) Primary Education Services, (b) Secondary Education Services, (c) Adult Education, (d) Other Education Services (Professional Technical etc.) India being one of the founding members of WTO cannot close its door to globalizations of education. There is an apprehension that GATS would jeoparadize the academic autonomy of a country as India "Educational health" is not satisfactory as a whole (except a few) and majority of the institutions are substandard in comparison with the institutions of the developed and developing countries of the world.

In a globally competitive world, India will be loser in the international educational trade market, if quality and relevance are not inbuilt, empowerment and status of the teachers are not enhanced, suitable infrastructure is not available, obsolete curriculum and courses are not properly substituted and revamped, research specially mass action researches are not strengthened and evaluation and monitoring are not inbuilt. Without a world-class education, the out-flow of students will comparatively become more than the inflow along with more brain drain to brain gain. Thus, in a globally competitive world, it is quality of education that can sustain a nation. Quality education will produce knowledgeable persons and in the modern world "knowledge is power."

Concept of Quality in Higher Education

Quality may mean different things to different people who, therefore, demand different quality outcomes and methods of assessing quality. Harvey and Green (1993) describe quality as a 'relative concept'. Quality is relative to the user of the term and the circumstances in which it is involved. It means different things to different people. This also raises the issue of whose quality? There are a variety of stakeholders in higher education, including student, employers, teaching and non-teaching employees, government and its funding agencies, accreditors, validators, auditors, and assessors (including professional bodies). Each of these stakeholders has a different view about quality, influenced by ones own interest in higher education. To the government a high quality system is one that produces trained scientists, engineers, architects, doctors and so on in numbers judged to be required by society. To an industrialist a high quality education institution may be one that turns out graduates with wide-ranging, flexible minds ready to acquire skills, and adapt to new methods and needs. This idea is resonant with what Barnett (1994) conceives as a threefold connection between different conceptions of higher education, different approaches to quality, and the identification of different outcome behind the various notions of what constitutes quality, there lies, whether explicitly formed or held tacitly, a view as to the ends that higher education should serve. In turn, these prior conceptions will generate different methodologies for evaluating quality in particular and call for alternative sets of outcome in general.

The Quality Assurance in Higher Education is gaining wider acceptance amongst the stakeholders across the globe. Even though the quality assurance mechanisms in different countries are at different levels of maturity and capacity, there is a broad agreement on need and effectiveness of quality assurance. Of the three factors involved in production: land, labour, and capital, it is labour and more particularly the quality of labour that is the key determinant for a country's competitiveness. It is, therefore, not surprising that there is a strong positive correlation between endowment of skilled labour and the gross domestic product per worker across countries. The quality of higher education enhances a country's capacity for participation in an increasingly knowledge-based world economy and has the potential to enhance economic growth and reduce poverty.

Education is an important index of human development alongwith economic growth and empowerment; it forms the core of every social and human development doctrine. Jawaharlal Nehru accepted education as the most important means to bring about social change. His belief was that "It is only through right education that a better order of society can be built up. Education is the most important requisite to open up the individual". Among various levels of education, higher education has pervasive and influential impact on development, since it empowers the individual with necessary skills and competence for achieving important personal and social goals and thereby contributing to the social development. It is widely believed that the state of higher education in a country is an index of its future well-being. Higher education is needed as a vital tool for intellectual, cultural and aesthetic development and means for achieving wider social aspirations. It also has an increasingly crucial role to play in producing change agents for moving the country along the development continuum. The phenomena of liberalization, globalization, and privatization of the Indian economy coupled with revolution in information technology have brought new challenges to higher education.

The relationship between education and human beings is very close. Man has achieved success in almost every field and made his life comfortable. But this development or achievement has been gained at the cost of his knowledge and skills which has been acquired through education, as it is regarded as the most powerful instrument for emancipation and empowerment of human beings. Indeed, education is a process of human enlightenment and empowerment for the betterment and quality of life. It not only enhances man's knowledge, skills competencies, potential, values and attitudes but also transforms his belief and thoughts. At the same time, it is assumed as the training of the human soul in the pursuit of truth and the practice of virtue, (Dongaonkar-2004).

The Human Development Report published in 1990 opened with the words, "the real wealth of nation is its people". It is seen that more physical and capital resources alone are not sufficient input to make a country developed (Sudha Rao-2002). A nation dreaming to be developed should use its human resource judiciously and convert it into national asset. In this context, Prof. Galbraith rightly observed, "we now get the large part of the industrial growth not from more capital investment, but from investment in men and improvements brought about by improved men". No physical capital can be utilized productively without skilled and technically trained personnel. Similarly, Marshall regarded education as a national investment and the most valuable of all capital is that invested in human beings. Human capital means acquired abilities to play a more important role for economic growth and economic development. The study of human resource is vital from the point of view of economic welfare. It is particularly important because human beings are not only instruments of production but also ends in them. Human resource development is the process of increasing knowledge, skill, capacity for sustained work, aptitudes and all other human qualities conducive to higher output and accelerated economic growth.

The dream of India to become a knowledge super power by 2020 will be a mirage unless there is massification of higher education and technological empowerment of the working class. In the introduction to his work "Buffalo Nationalism" (2004) Kancha Iliah has forcefully presented a case for imparting higher education to the working classes. According to him, the prime cause of India's underdevelopment is the disassociation of intellectual labour from physical labour.

The strategy for bridging the democratic deficit in our way of life through education was outlined by the UNESCO Conference in Geneva on "Quality Education for all Young People". The conference declared: "Promoting quality education and training for all young people between the ages of 12 and 20 is essential to securing a better future and constitutes an essential mechanism for combating social exclusion at the local, national and global levels. As both a basic right and a public good, this education must respond to the needs and interests of all young people with a view to ensuring the realization of their full potential, their successful integration in the world of work, as well as their capacity to participate in active life and as responsible citizens".

The National Policy on Education, 1986 and its Programme of Action, as reviewed in 1992, envisaged improvement and expansion of education in all sectors, a stress in improvement in quality and relevance of education at all levels, alongwith technical and professional education. The strength of a country either in economy or even in defence depends not in having its material resources but only in having its qualitative people. The quality of people is achieved through only the quality of education. The greatest and the most precious asset of a country is its people as it is they who exploit all natural resources and potentials of a region. Thus, the people form the wealth of a nation. The Task Force on Higher Education and Society appointed by the World Bank and UNESCO in year 2000 suggested that without more and better education, developing countries would find it difficult to benefit from the global-knowledge-based economy.

The present millennium is witnessing phenomenal global changes and no nation can isolate itself from the process. In the process of global changes and development, India has achieved success in various fields i.e., agriculture, industrialization, modernization, urbanization, trade and commerce, transport, communication, science and technology, production and so on. With the result of these phenomenal changes, educations are expanding at every corner in India, as it is assumed as the Human Resource Development (HRD) in the country. However, after Independence, the country has become more conscious to educate her people. Therefore, it has introduced various educational schemes and programmes to attain higher level of education and also to achieve socio-economic as well as overall development. But this educational expansion or change has not taken place for everyone and all sections of society. The Scheduled Castes (SCs), Scheduled Tribes (STs) and underprivileged people are still lagging behind in all stages of education. Despite constant efforts both by Central and State governments to spread the education of S.Cs., S.Ts and other weaker section, the level of education among them is very low in comparison to general castes and other community and this level of education exhibit high degrees of dispersion and disparities. Majority of them are still away from educational accessibility. The reasons behind this low education are due to:

(i) Poverty and backwardness,
(ii) Social discrimination and exploitation,
(iii) Lack of aspiration and awareness,

(iv) Marginalization in the society,
(v) Lack of political will,
(vi) Faulty in the education system,
(vii) Absence of a balanced, sensible and realistic approach,
(viii) Negative approach in handling educational programmes, and
(ix) Non-implementation of education policies for the progress of SC and ST education level.

Higher Education in India has successfully resisted all attempts for reform that was contemplated in two National Policies (1968 and 1986); recommended by the Higher Education Commission 1948 headed by Dr. S. Radhakrishnan; and numerous committees and commissions thereafter. If it is to remain competent, meet emerging challenges and serve the needs of the nation, it has necessarily to undergo a major revolution.

Higher Education in India

The modern higher education system is only 150 years old, when the first three universities were set up in 1857 under the British rule. The role of these universities was defined by the policy guidelines of Macaulay and Wood's Dispatch. The period between 1857 and 1947 saw a slow growth of institutions of higher education with focus mainly on liberal arts education. India with its huge population in the working age group and a large system of higher education has attracted world attention in recent times. There is a sense of euphoria about the Indian success in the IT services and now IT-enabled services. At a recent international exposition on trade in services, the Prime Minister talked about India becoming a knowledge supplier to the world. Industry leaders, on the other hand, express concerns about the severe shortages of qualified people and unacceptable attrition rates. Most countries are faced with similar problems.

At present there are around 247 Universities and 95 Deemed to be Universities, more than 16 thousand colleges, 97 lakh students and 4.5 lakh teachers in India. When India became Independent, there were just 18 Universities, 500 colleges, 2.28 lakh students and about 25 thousand teachers. These figures shown in Table 11.1 give impression that the massive expansion of higher education has taken place after 1947. However, it is not completely true.

Table 11.1: Some Basic Information on Higher Education in India

Sl.No.		1947	2003-04
1	Universities	18	343
2	Colleges	500	16000
3	Students	228804	9463821
4	Teachers	<0.24 lakh	4.36 lakh
5	Budget	55 crores	> 78000 crores

Source: University News, Aug. 14-20, 2006, Vol. 44, No. 33, p. 3.

Although, enrollment of 95 lakh students appears to be huge but it accounts only far less than 1 per cent of total population of India. The large population of the country either has no access or does not afford to go for higher education. Therefore, the efforts are need to be made to provide the access to higher education to as many people as possible. It is required in the interest of our country. Access to education is first and essential step to empowerment of people.

In statistical terms, the number of institutions engaged in providing higher education has increased manifolds. The numbers of beneficiaries of this educational set up have grown more than ten times since Independence. The number of higher education institution is shown in Table 11.2.

Table 11.2: Number of Higher Education Institutions in the Country

Year	Central Universities	State Universities	Deemed to be Universities	Institutions of National Importance*	Private Universities	Total
1950-51	3	24	—	—	—	27
1960-61	4	41	2	2	—	49
1970-71	5	79	9	9	—	102
1980-81	7	105	11	9	—	132
1990-91	10	137	29	9	—	185
2005	19	204	95	18	7	343

Source: UGC Annual Report and Government of India, Department of Education.

* Includes five institutions established through State Legislative Acts.

Table 11.3 shows the number of Universities in some of the leading/important countries alongwith their population.

Table 11.3: Number of Universities in some leading countries

Sl.No.	*Countries*	*Population (crores)*	*Universities*	
1	Japan	12.7	684	
2	USA	27.6	2364	
3	UK	5.98	104	(231 autonomous institutes)
4	Germany	8.2	330	
5	India	100	247	+ 98 deemed to be Universities

Source: University News, Aug. 14-20, 2006, Vol. 44, No. 33, p. 2.

The young Indians between the age group of 17-26 years are also large in number. This age group of students is expected to be enrolled in higher education. It is a matter of great concern that most of them (approximately 93%) are out of higher education system and have no access to higher education. Mere six-seven per cent of the said age group is enrolled for higher education. In countries like Canada, USA and Australia the students' enrollment of the same corresponding age group is between 80 per cent - 88 per cent. We are even behind Thailand, Brazil and Indonesia where enrolment in higher education is 19 per cent, 12 per cent and 11 per cent respectively (Table 11.4). The main objective of the Tenth Plan of UGC is to raise enrollment in higher education from present 6 per cent to 10 per cent by the end of the Plan Period. It will be great achievement, if we succeed in enhancing the enrollment by three to four per cent by the year 2008 (Kale, 2006).

Table 11.4: Student Enrollment in Higher Education in some Selected Countries

Sl. No.	*Country*	*% Enrollment*
1	Canada	88
2	Australia	79.8
3	USA	80.9

(Contd...)

(*Table 11.4 Contd...*)

4	UK	52
5	Thailand	19
6	Brazil	12
7	Indonesia	11
8	India	6

Source: University News, Aug. 14-20, 2006, Vol. 44, No. 33, p. 2.

As many as 80,000 students in the year 2005 went to USA, UK, Australia, New Zealand and Germany for higher education. The trend is increasing. It is because education in India, of the quality in foreign, is simply not available. Each student has to spend around Rs. 15 lakh per year. Yet they are going. We need to make introspection to build our institutions qualitative and competitive by world standards. This is essential to save our money as well as to avoid brain drain and to achieve the dream of becoming a developed nation by 2020. India can fulfil the aspirations of younger generation, if and only if, it leads in quality in research, innovation, patenting and hi-tech start ups etc.(Naik, 2006).

Massification of education, including higher education, is the key to massification of human welfare. It is generally accepted that an enrolment rate of atleast 20 per cent of the relevant age group (between 17 and 23) is an essential condition for development today. Whereas the developed countries have crossed the 50 per cent mark, India still lags behind at around nine per cent of its total population. Again if we say about Arunachal Pradesh it will around 7.10 per cent of its total population

Several recent studies in India have revealed that the overall state of Indian higher education is dismal. This poses a severe constraint on the supply of qualified manpower. While problems have been identified and solutions found, the studies have failed to map the contradictions that exist. Unfortunately, there are far more contradictions in the Indian higher education system than most countries of the world. Based on a recent comprehensive review of the Indian higher education, this chapter seeks to map the contradictions in Indian higher education with special reference to Arunachal Pradesh.

Education Scenario in Arunachal Pradesh

The Christian Missionaries, who followed the British Administration, established their centres at the adjacent places like Sadiya, North Lakhimpur etc. They operated their religious preaching to the present Arunachal Pradesh through education in the schools established at these centres. They also penetrated to some places in the foot hill areas of the State. The first of such attempt was made in 1839 by establishing a school at Namsang near present Deomali in Tirap District. This was done by Mr. Bronson of American Baptist Mission of Joypur centre, Assam. Similar schools were recorded to have established at Balek near Pasighat around 1915, Ningroo in 1934, Bolung in 1940, Dambuk in 1945 etc.

The Anglo-Abar war of 1911-1912 compelled the British Government to establish a regular administrative centre with the posting of an Assistant Political Officer at Pasighat. This necessitated the establishment of a Govt. Lower Primary School at Pasighat in 1918 and another at Riga (an Army base camp) in 1941. From the old records, it has been found that some venture schools were also established by the initiative of some individuals like Late Tamik Dabi at Tene village near Koyu, East Siang District in 1946 and Yomcha in West Siang District in January 1947. Teachers of Assam were said to have engaged to teach in these schools and their honorarium paid by the villagers in kind or cash. In this context it is to be pointed out that many of the official records it has been stated there were only two primary schools with enrollment of 35 students existed at the time of Independence of the country in 1947. Perhaps, this indicates the govvernment schools at Pasighat and Riga and it did not include the schools at other places mostly run by the Christian Missionaries. However, these schools were taken over by government after Independence in 1947.

In real sense, the formal education in Arunachal Pradesh began only after the Independence of the country in 1947 with the appointment of Mrs. Indira Miri as the Education Officer. She started the office as an Education Office at Sadiya most probably in the month of October and functioned as the Head of the Department of Education. She also established a Teachers Training Centre at Sadiya at the end of the same year and trained 10 teachers in the first batch of the training centre. Their training completed in the month of August in 1948 and they were sent out to establish new schools in different places of the State like Dening in Lohit, Nijam Ghat in Lower Dibang Valley, Taki-Lalung in East Siang Districts etc. Also existing schools at Pasighat, Bolung, Dambuk etc. were strengthened by posting some of these teachers.

In the initial period imparting education to the tribal children was so difficult task that Indira Miri in her book "Moi Aru Nefa" stated Hoi Polayan Nahai Akramon" which means students will either run away from school or become violent when they were prevented from doing so. Due to poor response from both students and parents many schools had to be closed down.

As per the records, there were 14 schools by the end of 1947. These schools were confined mostly in Siang and Lohit region. Out of these, there were 6 in East Siang, 2 each in West Siang, Lower Dibang Valley and Lohit and 1 each in Upper Siang and West Kameng Districts (Joram, 2008).

In this State, higher education started first with the set up of Jawaharlal Nehru College at Pasighat in 1964. Next Dera Natung Government College was set up in 1979. Gradually, Indira Gandhi Government College was set-up in 1986 at Tezu, Bomdila Government College in 1988 at Bomdila, Donyi-Polo Government College in 1996 at Kamki, Rang Fra Government College in 1996 at Changlang and Wangcha Rajkumar Government College at Deomali in 1997. Rajiv Gandhi University (Central Univetsity) (previously it was named Arunachal University) at Rono-Hills, Doimukh, Itanagar, Papum Pare District was set-up in 1984 and North Eastern Regional Institute of Science and Technology (Deemed University) at Nirjuli, Itanagar, Papum Pare District was also set-up in 1984.

Thus, there are at present 31 institutions (Private and Government) of Higher and Technical Education functioning throughout the State. Number and Type of Institutions of Higher and Technical Education in the State as on 31st March, 2012 is shown in Table 11.5. Out of these colleges, Jawaharlal Nehru College and Dera Natung Government College are imparting general education like Arts, Science and Commerce while the remaining colleges are imparting only Arts. In addition to Arts, Commerce is also taught in Indira Gandhi Govt. College and Donyi Polo Government College. Nevertheless, this is, indeed a phenomenal growth of education in the State within a small span of 61 years of its existence. The growth of institutions of higher and technical education in the State is depicted in Table 11.5 and their location and year of establishment are given in Table 11.6.

Table 11.5: Number and Type of Institutions of Higher and Technical Education in the State as on 31st March, 2012

Sl. No.	*Name of Institution*	*Number*
1.	University	01
2.	National Institute of Technology	01
3.	Deemed Uhiversity	01
4.	Degree Colleges	16
5.	Professional/Technical Colleges	10
6.	Polytechnic College	02
	Total	31

Source: Directorate of Higher and Technical Education, Itanagar, 2011-12.

Table 11.6: Higher and Technical Institutions in the State with Location and Year of Establishment

Sl. No	*Name of Institution*	*Location and Year of Establishment*	*Status and NAAC* Accreditation	*Status*
1	Rajiv Gandhi University	Rono-Hills, Doimukh, Itanagar, Papum Pare District, 1984	-	Central University
2	National Institute of Technology	Yupia, Itanagar, Papum Pare District, 2010	-	Central Institution
3	North Eastern Regional Institute of Science and Technology	Nirjuli, Itanagar, Papum Pare District, 1984	-	Deemed University
		GOVERNMENT COLLEGES		
4	Jawaharlal Nehru College	Pasighat, East Siang District, 1964	B++	Government Degree College
5	Dera Natung Government College	Itanagar, Papum Pare District, 1979	B+ (Reaccreditated in Dec.,2011)	Government Degree College

(*contd...*)

(Table 11.6 contd...)

6	Indira Gandhi Government College	Tezu, Lohit District, 1986	B+	Government Degree College
7	Bomdila Government College	Bomdila, West Kameng District, 1988	B	Government Degree College
8	Rang-Frah Government College	Changlang, Changlang District, 1996	C	Government Degree College
9	Donyi Polo Government College	Kamki, West Siang District, 1996	B+	Government Degree College
10	Wangcha Rajkumar Government College	Deomali, Tirap District, 1997		Government Degree College
11	Government College	Yachuli, Lower Subansiri District, 2007		Government Degree College
12	Government College	Seppa, East Kameng District, 2009		Government Degree College
13	Government College	Nyapin, Kurung Kumey District 2009		Government Degree College
		PRIVATE COLLEGES		
14	Don Bosco College	Jully, Itanagar, Papum Pare District, 2002		Private Degree College
15	St. Claret College	Ziro, Lower Subansiri District, 2003		Private Degree College

(contd...)

(Table 11.6 contd...)

16	Doying Gumin College	Pasighat East Siang District, 2004	Private Degree College
17	Central Institute of Himalayan Culture Studies	Dahung, Mon-Bomdila, West Kameng District, 2007	Private Degree College
18	St. Francis De Sales College	Aalo, West Siang, 2007	Private Degree College
19	Arunachal Community College	Vivek Vihar, Itanagar, Papum Pare District, 2009	Private Degree College
	TECHNICAL AND PROFESSIONAL COLLEGES		
20	College of Horticulture and Forestry	Pasighat, East Siang District, 2001	Under Central Agriculture University, Imphal
21	North East Homoeopathic Medical College and Hospital	Vivek Vihar, Itanagar, Papum Pare District, 2002	Private Homoeopathic Medical College
22	Hills College of Teacher Education	Naharlagun, Papum Pare District, 2006	Private B. Ed. College
23	Arunachal Law Academy	Itanagar, Papum Pare District , 2007	Private Law College
24	Ranjeev College of Fine Arts	Itanagar, Papum Pare District , 2009	
25	M.T.M. B. Ed. College	Ziro, Lower Subansiri District, 2010	

(contd...)

(Table 11.6 contd...)

26	D. Ering College of Teacher Education	Pasighat, East Siang District, 2010		
27	Puri Symbiosis College	Naharlagun, Papum Pare District, 2010		
28	Siang Royal Academy	Pasighat, East Siang District, 2011		
29	Marjum Memorial B. Ed. College	Aalo, West Siang District, 2011		
		POLYTECHNICS		
30	Rajiv Gandhi Government Polytechnic	Itanagar, Papum Pare District , 2002	Government Polytechnic	AICTE Approved & Recognized (ISO 90001: 2008 Certified)
31	Tomi Polytechnic College	Basar, West Siang District, 2006	Private Polytechnic Institution	AICTE Approved & Recognized

Source: Directorate of Higher and Technical Education, Itanagar, 2011-12

In Arunachal Pradesh, till Independence literacy rate was only less than 1 per cent. In the succeeding five years plans, an increasing percentage of expenditure on education has given good results despite of formidable constraints like inaccessibility of territory, people's unawareness of the need of education and traditional dependence on children for domestic and field work. Thus, with increasing emphasis through successive plans the State has achieved commendable progress in the field of education. The literacy rate census-wise from 1961 to 2011 in Arunachal Pradesh is shown in Table 11.7. Census started first in the state from 1961.

Table 11.7: Literacy Rate in Percentage

Year	*Person*	*Male*	*Female*
1961	7.13	12.5	1.42
1971	11.29	17.82	3.71
1981	25.55	35.12	14.02
1991	41.59	51.45	29.69
2001	54.34	**63.83**	**43.53**
2011	**66.95**	**73.69**	**59.57**

Source: Census Report, Arunachal Pradesh, 1961, 1971, 1981, 1991, and 2001.

From Table 11.7, it is observed that the good fruit of education in the State is achieved though the females are lagging behind the males. Higher education in Arunachal Pradesh needs a far-reaching structural reconstruction. The enrolment of students in the colleges in the State during academic session 2008-09 is shown in Table 11.8. Year-wise their enrolment in all institutions of higher and technical education and also sex-wise enrolment of teaching staff in all institutions of higher education during this academic session are shown in Tables 11.9 and Table 11.10 respectively in the State.

Table 11.8: Enrolment of Students in the Institutions of Higher Education in State during Academic Session, 2008 – 09

					APST			NON-APST		
Sl.No	Name of Institution	Boys	Girls	Total	Boys	Girls	Total	Boys	Girls	Total
1	Rajiv Gandhi University Rono Hills, Doimukh	484	485	969	393	408	801	91	77	168
2	J.N. College, Pasighat	1263	958	2221	1111	846	1957	152	112	264
3	D.N.Govt. College, Itanagar	1598	1237	2835	1457	1117	2574	144	117	261
4	I.G. Govt. College, Tezu	696	639	1335	449	440	889	247	199	446
5	Govt. College, Bomdila	310	325	635	263	270	533	47	55	102
6	D.P. Govt. College, Kamki	568	393	961	538	406	944	13	4	17
7	R.F. Govt. College, Chalanglan	116	124	240	110	117	227	6	7	13
8	W. R. Govt. College, Deomal	203	190	393	197	147	344	24	25	49
9	Govt. College, Yachuli	58	29	87	57	28	85	1	1	2
10	Don Bosco College, Jully, Itanagar	234	252	486	228	239	467	6	13	19
11	St. Claret College, Ziro	132	150	282	124	136	260	8	14	22
12	Doying Gumin College, Pasighat	223	145	368	200	129	329	23	16	39
13	St. Francis De Sales College, Aalo	44	41	85	37	33	70	6	9	15

(contd...)

(*Table 11.8 contd...*)

14	Arunachal Law Academy, Itanagar	84	11	95	84	10	94	0	1	1
15	North Eastern Regional Institute of Science and Technology, Nirjuli	898	297	1195	121	38	159	777	259	1036
16	Rajiv Gandhi Govt. Polytechnic, Itanagar	223	156	379	129	109	238	94	47	141
17	College of Horticulture and Forestry, Pasighat	77	56	133	13	12	25	64	44	108
18	North East Homoeopathic Medical College and Hospital, Itanagar	46	98	144	16	39	55	30	59	89
19	Tomi Polytechnic, Basar	263	58	321	253	54	307	10	4	14
20	Hills College of Teacher Education, Naharlagun	43	57	100	26	31	57	17	26	43
	Grand Total	**7563**	**6701**	**13264**	**5806**	**4609**	**10415**	**1760**	**1089**	**2849**
				(42.98)		**(44.25)**			**(38.22)**	

Source: Directorate of Higher and Technical Education, Itanagar

N.B. Figures in parenthesis show percentage

Table 11.9: Year-wise Enrolment of Students in Institutions of Higher Education in the State

Sl. No	Session	Boys	Girls	Total	APST Boys	APST Girls	APST Total	NON-APST Boys	NON-APST Girls	NON-APST Total
1	2004 - 2005	5016	2785 (35.70)	7801	3469	2095 (37.65)	5564	1547	690 (30.84)	2237
2	2005 - 2006	5446	3289 (37.65)	8735	3920	2555 (39.46)	6475	1526	734 (32.48)	2260
3	2006 - 2007	6050	3896 (39.17)	9946	4471	3110 (41.02)	7581	1549	816 (34.50)	2365
4	2007 - 2008	6667	4828 (42.00)	11495	5017	3901 (43.74)	8918	1650	927 (35.97)	2577
5	2008 - 2009	7563	5701 (42.98)	13264	5806	4609 (44.25)	10415	1760	1089 (38.22)	2849

Source: Directorate of Higher and Technical Education, Itanagar

N.B. Figures in parenthesis show percentage.

Table 11.10: Number of Teaching Staff during Session 2008-09 (Sex-wise)

Sl.No	*Name of Institution*	*Male*	*Female*	*Total*	*APST*		*NON-APST*	
					Male	*Female*	*Male*	*Female*
1	Rajiv Gandhi University Rono Hills, Doimukh	66	19	85	17	10	51	07
2	North Eastern Regional Institute of Science and Technology, Nirjuli	122	18	140	06	01	116	17
3	College of Hortiulture and Forestry, Pasighat	31	03	34	01	01	30	02
4	J.N. College, Pasighat	53	09	62	17	04	36	05
5	D.N. Govt. College, Itanagar	44	18	62	17	10	27	08
6	I.G. Govt. College, Tezu	23	01	24	06	01	17	00
7	Govt. College, Bomdila	16	04	20	05	04	11	00
8	D.P. Govt. College, Kamki	19	03	22	14	02	05	01
9	R.F. Govt. College, Chalanglan	11	03	14	07	03	04	00
10	W.R. Govt. College, Deomal	08	05	13	03	03	05	02
11	Govt. College, Yachuli	07	02	09	06	02	01	00
12	Rajiv Gandhi Govt. Polytechnic, Itanagar	13	06	19	02	05	11	01
13	St. Claret College, Ziro	10	08	18	03	05	06	04
14	Don Bosco College, Jully, Itanagar	11	12	23	07	08	04	04
15	Doying Gumin College, Pasighat	09	06	15	06	02	03	04
16	St. Francis De Sales College, Aalo	10	01	11	02	00	08	01
17	Arunachal Law Academy, Itanagar	07	02	09	05	01	02	01
18	North East Homoeopathic Medical College and Hospital, Itanagar	20	04	24	05	02	15	02

19	Tomi Polytechnic, Basar	25	02	27	01	01	24	01
20	Hills College of Teacher Education, Naharlagun	07	04	11	02	00	05	04
	Grand Total	**512**	**130**	**642**	**132**	**65**	**381**	**64**
			(20.25)			(10.12)		(9.97)

Source: Directorate of Higher and Technical Education, Itanagar
N.B. Figures in parenthesis show percentage

From Table 11.8, enrolment of girls in all the institutions of Higher and Technical Education in the State during the academic session, 2008 – 09 is 42.98 per cent in regard to total students including tribal and non-tribal. Enrolment of tribal girls is 44.25 per cent among tribal students and also enrolment of non-tribal girls is 38.22 per cent among the non-tribal students during the same academic session. But the percentage of enrolment of girls increases with the increase in enrolment of students. If we see from the academic session, 2004 – 2005 to 2008 – 2009, the percentage of girls including all increases from 35.70 in 2004 – 2005 to 42.98 in 2008 – 2009. If we want to see separately in case of tribal and non-tribal girls, we get same trend shown in Table 11.9. Again in teaching staff during session 2008-09, the percentages of female staff is 20.25 in overall, 10.12 in tribal and 9.97 in non-tribal only in respect of total teaching staff shown in Table 11.10. It is clear that girls are lagging behind their male counterpart, though the proportion of female population is more than the male population as per 2001 census, if we consider only tribal population. As per 2001 census, the tribal sex ratio is 1003.

In respect of Technical and Professional education, there are only seven institutions. One is North Eastern Regional Institute of Science and Technology (NERIST) set up at Nirjuli, Itanagar in 1984 with limited seats for the State. In order to fulfil technical manpower requirement of this State, Rajiv Gandhi Polytechnic has been set up at Itanagar in 2002 under the World Bank Assisted Project. The institute offers technical level diploma courses in Information Technology, Travel Tourism and Hotel Management, Costume Design and Garment Technology, Herbal Remedies and Cosmetology, Automobile Engineering and Electrical and Electronic

Engineering. There is only one private Homoeopathic college set up at Itanagar in 2002. A Horticulture and Forestry College has been set up in 2001 at Pasighat under the sponsorship of Central Agricultural University, Imphal, Manipur. As there is practically no college for studying in medicine, veterinary, agriculture, fishery etc. under government as well as private sector, students are sent to study there disciplines of Higher & Technical education in the institutions of other States of the country.

A number of students are sponsored by the State Government through seat quota allotted to this State by different institutions. The following Table 11.11 shows the total number of students sent for medical, veterinary, agriculture, horticulture, engineering, pisciculture, etc. outside of this State since 1994 onwards.

Table 11.11: Students Sent for Education outside of this State since 1994–2003

Year	*Medicine*			*Agriculture*	*Veterinary*	*Horticulture*	*Engineering*		*Pisciculture*	*Handloom Technology*
	MBBS	*BDS*	*BHMS*	*B.Sc. (Agri)*	*B.V. Sc.*	*Degree Course*	*Degree*	*Diploma*	*Degree*	*Degree*
1994	31	6	4	44	14	1	70	104	-	2
1995	32	5	3	45	14	-	130	108	3	1
1996	31	5	3	25	9	1	131	123	1	5
1997	36	5	2	-	11	-	131	126	-	4
1998	39	5	3	25	7	-	142	132	1	3
1999	41	6	4	10	6	1	150	161	-	4
2000	34	5	5	13	10	4	154	158	-	3
2001	34	5	4	10	8	4	150	162	-	-
2002	34	5	6	8	11	9	116	111	-	-
2003	34	5	6	10	8	4	150	102	-	-

Source: Directorate of Economics and Statistics, Itanagar, Govt. of Arunachal Pradesh (Various Issues)

Challenges

Arunachal Pradesh cannot side track itself from world-wide trends taking place throughout the globe for adopting strategies regarding higher education for its youth. There are various factors responsible for the present day changes in Higher Education. They are enumerated us under:

(i) Liberalization, Globalization of trade.
(ii) Technological advancement particularly in the field of communication network and systems.
(iii) Governments increasing emphasis on Market Economy.
(iv) Increased international labour mobility.
(v) Growing importance of life-learning.

Quality assurance is one of the Central issues in higher education today. The serious issues and challenges including teaching, admission and infrastructure are discussed below. Many countries are moving toward instituting more careful quality assurance and regulation of degree offerings. International efforts are under way in the field of quality assurance, although national mechanisms are necessarily at the heart of a system of ensuring higher education quality and relevance. Quality assurance in higher education is Central issues of the current period.

1. Present Environment: There are many changes and new challenges in terms of how present environment is affecting internalization and how the growing international dimension of higher education is an agent of change itself. Globalization has been regarded as a powerful and pervasive factor for changing the overall environment. Higher education will have to find out ways of dealing with, responding and ideally, benefiting from these trends. The national and international dimensions of higher education are therefore becoming increasingly important and at the same time more complex. It is the national analytical judgement on the part of Central/State Governments to frame and follow higher educational policies for its and other nationalists.

2. Education Delivery Methods: Fast changing information and communication technologies system demand new education delivery methods to be installed to compete with those using especially on line and satellite based methods. How is it possible for the students of Arunachal who are accustomed to follow the traditional method of classroom lecture using only blackboard to compete with the students of outside of the State, who are the follower of modern methods of teaching? Apart from classroom lecturers, more attention has to be given to the accreditation of these programmes and recognition of qualifications for domestic and cross border education.

3. Skill based/vocational and professional educational institutions: It is the need of the hour for the development of Arunachal Pradesh. This policy would assist unemployed educated youth to find the relevant jobs in their related field of specialization. At the same time this will also provide opportunities for self-employment.

4. Industry Based Education: Arunachal Pradesh is endowed with natural resources. The State is presently looking for industries to be established so as to generate income and provide employment. Technology intensive knowledge should be imparted by the professional institutions so as to establish different types of industries in the State where the educated persons get job as per their eligibility. Education without utility is meaningless not only that it will also be harmful to the society.

5. Higher Education in Arunachal Pradesh suffers from many problems:

(i) There are insufficient teaching and non-teaching staff in every college.

(ii) Poor library facility, coupled with no cataloging system, untrained staff and non-computerized, is seen in every college.

(iii) Explosion of student population in D.N.Govt. College whereas very few students are enrolled in other colleges. The class-rooms in D.N. Govt. College are unable to accommodate the strength of existing students.

(iv) No transfer policy of teaching and non-teaching staff exists.

(v) Classroom teaching persists with conventional method. There is no use of computer with internet, video conferencing, overhead projector, etc.

6. Quality is systems improvement: It is an unending journey. It requires a deliberate and persistent attempt in a systematic way. Quality does not come by chance or by accident. The quality in system is every one's job, from top to bottom. Institutions where systems are good, people tend to work efficiently. It stands on the following aspects.

- Quality is a continuous improvement i.e., slowly and steadily.
- Quality comes when the teachers are passionate.
- Quality comes through the strategy of better Human Resource Development.
- Quality comes when every teacher succeeds in igniting the minds of students.
- Quality is empowering teachers.
- Quality is fear reduction in the minds of employers.
- Quality comes through better teamwork with better co-operation from top to bottom.
- Quality comes when every one works in systematic proper way.

7. Julius Nyerere writes, "Higher Education is an unjustified luxury (in developing countries) unless it directly sub-serves the developmental needs of the nation". Higher Education does not merely comprise of dissemination of specialized knowledge and skills, but needs to focus also on lacking of crucial moral dilemmas and existential traumas, through proper training of human resources. The Rammurti Committee Report (May 17, 1990) of the Government of India accorded highest priority to education both as a human right and as the means for bringing about a transformation towards a more humane and enlightened society.

In Arunachal Pradesh, the Government are sponsoring the candidates outside of this State to take higher education spending a lot of money. They are coming back with higher education but job as per education is not easy to get. Again some are not willing to perform the job. The mindset of the local student is not to establish their own enterprise or business but to venture either in politics, contract business or government services to earn "easy money". This mindset can be termed as psychological barrier which emerged very strongly in the context of present socio-political context of the State.

8. Ethical values: Today what we see not only in this state but throughout the country. The youth of a nation where truth has been the keyword, a part of the national motto *Satyameva Jayate* is brimming with falsehood, fraud and dishonesty. If students are even partially conscious and desirous of awakening and improved function, there is a way out of the darkness of unknowing into the light of understanding. This will come with the apprehension of our need to awaken and grow; commitment to learning and growing and practical application of ethics and values which may lead to a transformative experience. But it is must that the soil prepared at the level of school education can be richly cultivated in the higher education. Higher education is steadily worsening ethical values in students and the dire need to deliberate jointly is to seek solutions. Values may be social, religious, ecological or ethical. Ethical values include one's capacity to be one's own self, to harmonies the contradictions within and to be of service to other. Higher education can enhance qualitatively by giving depth to each curriculum and emphasizing those values of life which are beyond the phenomenal subject and add eternity to education, "Education is not limited to the imparting of information or the training in skills. It has to give the educated a proper sense of values", wrote Radhakrishnan. Students in higher education prepare to take place in administration, industry, commerce and other vital areas of civil life. In the absence of some kind of ethical enlightenment, the specialized knowledge may be used to cause harm to the self or to the society. Therefore, in order to overcome physical, mental, social, moral, national and international crises, higher education must give preponderant place to inculcation of ethical values, even if these constitute a hidden aspect of the curriculum. We, the Indians expect that Higher Education should intend to inculcate in the young students the quality of self-reliance, self potential and self-confidence through awareness of the social, intellectual and moral environment, problems of the Indian Society. But it is disliked true that common people are badly treated sometimes by the literate people. That is why; today it is high time and essential to insert certain topics in almost all disciplines of higher education to build moral character so as to bring all-round development of Arunachal Pradesh. This is a new challenge of higher education particularly in Arunachal Pradesh. Today, students of higher education are self-centered, grasp at fleeting promise of pleasure, psychologically conflicted and therefore dysfunctional. All kinds of ethical value whether related to self-like, self-esteem, self-respect, self-actualization, or interpersonal like-tolerance, forgiveness, concern, or social like patriotism, equality and co-operation are conspicuously lacking even in the so-called highly educated young generation. The fire of competition has defeated co-operation just as material gains have replaced misanthropy, as insensitivity stamps minds instead of compassion. To get rid of these problems, ethical values can be cultivated fortuitously by examples from lives of religious and spiritual leaders alongwith extracts from scriptures of the world that are of a universalistic nature. The detached atmosphere of an academic institution can be used to study the deepest ideologies with an open mind.

In 1946, a committee headed by Rev G.D. Barne proposed that spiritual and moral teachings common to all religions should be an integral part of the curriculum and provision of facilities for instruction therein should be a responsibility of the State. Indian culture and heritage offer a rich spectrum of ethical and spiritual renderings which can give students an edge over their contemporaries from other parts of the world, winning them a scoring point in the stiff competition that higher education of developed countries is facing presently. A return to the seeds of all knowledge in Vedic Sciences and the practice of meditation can become a positive step in resolving inner turmoil. It is a proven fact that meditation and contemplative prayers aid the concentration of mind and channelize thoughts on ethical lines. This can result in progressive and accelerated knowledge of higher reality and enhanced intellectual powers.

Ethical values need to be emphasized in higher education because they lead to actualization of innate capacities and elimination of all non-essentials from life. The enlivening influence of high ethical values can promote a flow of creative ideas and all thoughts, emotional states and actions can channelise into a constructive direction. Vivekananda believed that the means of work are as important as the end—if the means are ethical, the end is bound to be productive.

The importance of ethical life in every sphere of activity has been recognized and it is now a question of both study and discussion of the nuances of ethical life and, more important for the application without a break of ethical principles. Without this, there seems to be no hope for humanity which is now immersed in the dangerous ocean of selfishness, greed, violence, uncertainty, growing fears, break down of law and order, collapse of government machinery and anarchy, eventually. These evil forces should be checked. This calls for extraordinary and patient effort. It is also clear that something of the best aspects of religion have also to be brought into achieving the rise of *Dharma* everywhere through proper value-based education.

9. Recruitment Policy: The World-Wide Web, looming as the cornerstone of the information age has revolutionized methods of learning. Knowledge comes almost knocking at our doors with just a click of the mouse. However, the role of the teacher has become even more crucial in making that available to students which is beyond texts. Our humble entry into the world-wide orbit decidedly expands the scope of our firm commitment to the creation and sustenance of a climate congenial not only to cognitive knowledge but also knowledge which is founded on ethical values and moral standards of import in every walk of life. Students are subliminally influenced by the character and conduct of their teachers. As transformative intellectuals, teachers must address themselves to individual students when they need direction, recognizing the heterogeneity of the class. For example, if he/ she spots an over ambitions pupil who wishes to rise at the cost of beheading his/ her peers, the teacher should train the student to keep ambition within ethical bounds.

Moral character of students, which will lead him throughout his lives, depends upon the moral character of the teachers. That is why; recruitment of teachers especially in higher education must be done very carefully. The candidates applied for lectureship must be judged psychologically by a psychologist before recruitment. When entire life of student and the well-being of the country depend on the teacher, why is special strategy for recruitment of lecturer not taken? There is proverb that last is good, all are good. Therefore, teachers of higher education must be unique. Teacher will be like 'Parash Pathar' which will turn the lives of the students into perfect noble persons through teaching. Teachers, in fact, play a more vital role in the society than the administrator at the highest level. Administrators keep on changing and their actions do not have any direct bearing on common men. Teachers on the other hand are role-models for the new generation. Their actions not only affect everyone but have a bearing on future. It is, therefore, imperative that something should be done to improve the method of recruitment (Jafri 2006).

10. Promotion Policy: Improving teaching by upgrading teacher qualifications, training and performance are imperative. Teacher must be nurtured to perform their job. There must be measured by a rigorous assessment of prospective teachers' competency in the content areas. Teaching should get as much importance as research. Good teaching can be ensured only by giving career incentives. Job security, service incentives and promotion of teacher depending on only academic performance including teaching must be confirmed. This will attract not only brilliant candidates in teaching profession but also reduce the intention of teacher to leave this job.

11. Caste-based Quotas in Higher Education: Reservation in public sector education is a particularly Indian practice enshrined in the Constitution, a legal form of affirmative action designed to provide greater opportunities to communities and social groups that have been traditionally deprived and excluded. While the quotas in public sector education that are allocated for Scheduled Castes (S.Cs) and Scheduled Tribes (S.Ts) are now taken for granted in most discussions, the current debate is around the recent decision of the Ministry of Human Resource Development to provide quotas for backward castes in all institutions of higher learning funded by the Central Government.

Those who oppose the policy of reservation operate primarily with the following arguments:

I. It does not address the basic problem of inadequate expansion and poor quality of public education at elementary and secondary levels.

II. It militates against "merit" and allows degrees and qualifications to be awarded with less than deserving aptitude and performance.

III. It is "inefficient" compared with openly competitive and therefore implicitly "market-based" systems.

IV. It creates perceptions of "victimhood" and democratically undesirable identity politics.

V. Inequalities within the specified communities allow a "creamy layer" to take advantage of the reservations and benefit unduly while depriving the rest of the community.

VI. The rigid and inflexible nature of the instrument of reservation does not allow for more creative modes of affirmative action.

VII. It privileges caste-based discrimination and therefore ignores other and possibly more undesirable forms of exclusion.

VIII. It compresses the notion of social justice into only reservation, instead of encompassing broader socio-economic policies such as land reform and other asset redistribution, strategies of income generation, etc.

There is certainly some relevance to each of these points. Certainly one would deny that the system that has operated in India thus far has been inadequate not only in addressing these issues, but even in achieving the goals set in terms of filling the allocated quotas for SCs and STs in public education and employment. It is also true that caste-based quotas are relatively crude and blunt instruments to address a very complex socio-economic reality (Jayati Ghosh, 2006).

The author thinks that as entire development of a nation depends on the quality of education, education should be kept outside of reservation. Admission and recruitment of teacher in educational institution should strictly be considered only on the basis of merit. Only "merit-based selection" can ensure to maintain quality of higher education. To bring the backward classes including SCs and STs into the mainstream of the nation, government can bear entire economical burden of the SC/ST students so that they cannot feel any want during their study in educational institutions. Again government can give allowance to the poor family from where the student has come to take education. In the State, the 40 per cent of the total population live under BPL. They are mostly living in rural areas. Their son/daughter engaged in jhum-based cultivation are their livelihood. Jhum is a labour intensive and low productivity-based cultivation. That is why, they cannot afford to send their son/daughter for higher education. Those who afford their son/daughter for education should be given allowances.The most common argument against reservations is that they will affect quality and undermine "merit". But the supposed contradiction between reservations on the one hand, and merit and efficiency, on the other, is a false one.

We are all agreed that there is huge excess demand for higher education in the country, and that good quality in higher education is extremely under-provided. Therefore, there is severe rationing for places, especially in the best institutions. The question is, therefore, not whether we should have rationing or not, but which form of rationing is the best in the prevailing social circumstances. If we accept that intelligence and talent are not the monopoly of any particular social group but are normally distributed across society, then this means that the current system is inefficient since it is effectively picking up candidates from only a small section of society instead of the whole population. It is elementary logic that this would give sub-optimal results for society. This is an argument on social efficiency grounds, which is quite separate from other arguments about creating a more democratic and inclusive educational process in general. Caste-based reservations are often critiqued on more sophisticated grounds as well. One criticism is that they promote unhealthy forms of identity politics that distract from more substantive and critical social issues.

In context of the current system of reservation, the author opines in this way that the basic issue, of course, is that the roots of discrimination go so deep that social and economic disparities are deeply intertwined, although in increasingly complex ways. In this imperfect world, none of the proposed solutions is perfect either: The choice is between imperfect instruments with different degrees of effectiveness. That is why we still need reservations for different groups in higher education – not because it is the perfect instruments to rectify longstanding discrimination, but because it is still the most workable method to move in this direction. And most of all, because the nature of Indian society ensures that without such measures social discrimination and exclusion will only persist and be strengthened.

12. Quality of Teachers: The National Policy document suggested a better deal for teachers (Art: 7.2). It also stated that

"The status of the teacher reflects the socio-cultural ethos of a society; it is said that no people can rise above the level of its teachers. The government and the community should endeavour to create conditions which will help motivate and inspire teachers on constructive and creative lines. Teachers should have the freedom to innovate to devise appropriate methods of communication and activities relevant to the needs and capabilities of end the concerns of the community" (Art. 9.1).

"The methods of recruiting teachers will be reorganized to ensure merit, objectivity and conformity with spatial and functional requirements. The pay and service conditions of teachers have to be commensurate with their social and professional responsibilities and with the need to attract talent to the profession. Efforts will be made to reach the desirable objective of uniform emoluments, service conditions and grievance-removal mechanisms for teachers throughout the country. Guidelines will be formulated to ensure objectivity in the postings and transfers of teachers. Teachers will continue to play a crucial role in the formulation and implementation of educational programmes" (Art. 9.2). A number of developed countries have introduced the system of peer feedback for improving quality of teaching. Bell (2002) has reported about peer feedback of teaching as an established procedure for improving teaching skills of higher education teachers. Should such a system be introduced in the State? The NPE 1986 stated that Teachers' performance will be systematically assessed. All posts will be filled on the basis of merit" (Art. 5.31). It also stated that "A system of teacher's evaluation – open, participative and data-based – will be created and reasonable opportunities of promotion to higher grades provided. Norms of accountability will be laid down with incentives for good performance and disincentives for non-performance. Teachers will continue to play a crucial role in the formulation and implementation of ê national programmes" (Art. 9.2) (Mohanty, 2006).

Our sages defined the teacher thus: "A teacher should have the ability to build up the students under this charge. He must never be proud of his knowledge. He should be a glorious as fire and possess qualities of leadership. He must be specialist of his branch of knowledge. Just as a cow collects milk in her udders after grazing grass, a teacher should collect knowledge through reflection and self-study. He should make teaching an enjoyable experience even as food items are made tasty and palatable before they are served. He should be popular among his students and be their benefactor. Sitting in the midst of his students he must look distinguished because of his knowledge"— (Rig-Veda 1/69/2).

13. Examination system: In our university examination pattern, there is a frequent possibility of errors arising from erratic marking on answer books. It has been practically observed that:

(i) The standard of marking varies from teacher to teacher.

(ii) Again, the standard of marking varies from same teacher in two different points of time.

(iii) Some teachers are more liberal than others in evaluating answer books.

(iv) Some of teachers are interested to evaluate as many answer books as possible within a minimum time to get maximum remuneration. This practice is always a disadvantage to the brilliant students.

(v) Sometimes, some numbers of answer books are evaluated by university teacher and some of same papers are evaluated by collegiate teacher. There must be a possibility of differentiating in marking.

In such a manner, examination papers are quite failure to test the ability of the students to catch the facts, interpretation and application of knowledge.

How to overcome these problems

The following steps may be suggested.

(a) Every answer book may be evaluated by two teachers without writing the marks on answer book. If the two marks differ beyond 15, then the answer book will go to third examiner and two nearest marks will be considered and taken average.

(b) If possible, single paper may be evaluated by single examiner.

(c) Re-evaluation will be considered on student's demand.

The author thinks that

(i) In most states, the teaching skill and level of knowledge of a teacher is not taken into consideration in assessing performance of a teacher. Generally, the qualifications, programmes attended and papers presented and publications are taken into consideration. Unfortunately, skill in teaching has been overlooked at the time of selection of teachers of different categories in higher education or at the time of promotion to a higher post.

(ii) There is a need of major shift of attention to make education as a priority sector in respect to higher education as well as primary education. Education development urgently requires a shift in focus to bring out intensive educational programmes to achieve higher level of education.

(iii) There is a need of quick implementation of strong and effective education policies in the State. For this, a monitoring body should be constituted under the supervision of high cabinet level and action should be taken to the persons and officers who show any negligence.

The policy-maker has to develop the higher education by equalizing the syllabi as national standard so that our students can compete with the outside students in the job market in order to be employed in the outside of the State. Again, the State Government has to create more and more jobs in the State so as to engage the higher educated persons as because, unemployment problem can give birth of another problem.

(iv) The authority should innovate such type of higher education which will help the educated persons to be self-employment. In all the institutions of higher education, job-oriented vocational courses should be imparted. For competitive examinations at State and national level, the student should be prepared by providing special coaching at all the centres of higher education.

(v) Higher proportion of the State's budget needs to be spent towards the development of higher education.

(vi) As education among scheduled tribe suffers due to acute poverty, unemployment and lack of awareness, however, providing full financial supports and scholarships, counseling and guidance to parents.

(vii) It is also essential to create a congenial atmosphere in the State. For this, government and people's participation is equally required.

(viii) Quality of teaching can be improved only when teachers get feedback regarding their teaching. This can be ascertained only through inspection of classes. Inspections may be carried out by Director, Principal or other officers.

(ix) Provision will be made to give minimum facilities to the students to get healthy environment in the college campus and admission will be regulated according to the capacity of the college.

Many years ago, Gurudev Rabindranath Tagore had suggested teaching skill test for selection of higher education teachers. The NET conducted by UGC needs to reconsider its strategies for recognizing good scholar. But the good scholar may not be good communicator i.e., may be a bad teacher. For selection of teacher, class teaching should be given more weightage. The methods of recruiting teachers will be reorganized to ensure merit, objectivity and conformity with spatial and functional requirements. The pay and service conditions of teacher should be commensurated to attract talent to this profession.

The whole study demonstrates a very complex scenario and suggests that there is a need of change of people's mind and attitude and put collective efforts to improve educational level of scheduled tribe in the State. The realization of dream can come true if the government takes strong and effective steps in the implementation of State's education policies with this assumption that education is the essence of human beings and the best contraceptive to socio-economic development.

Last but not the least, the author thinks that today's people of the State requires that type of education which must be equipped with the skills needed to face the challenges of 21st century and overall to get prestigious jobs in the State in particular and in the country in general. This requires that the education providers or the higher authority of education has to study the changing needs of the students from time-to-time. The challenges ahead are for the policy-makers of higher education as to what interests of the student communities are not being served?

The author strongly believes that the effective and dedicated teachers have profound impact on the success and lives of their students. Personally, teaching has always given me pace, variety, challenge and the opportunity to keep on learning because it is always inquiring ,questing , debating and sometimes controversial but always alive ,and this continues to be the source of endless satisfaction for me. As I teach young people grow and change in front of my eyes. There appears nothing more exciting for me than to witness human minds blossom and determined to accomplish their career goals and eventually go out and empower the communities they live in. The student-teacher relationships and mutual trust established during students formative years are seldom forgotten and often alumni themselves become educational philanthropists.

The quality of academic standards is inextricably linked with the quality of inputs received by the students and the quality of education of any country depends on many factors and one of the crucial factors is teacher competence. The teacher competence in turn depends mostly on their own capacity as well as quality of training and other support provided to them.

Without educating girls, the State never brings all-round development as women constitute a half of its total population. The State should enforce women's empowerment through higher education giving different favourable facilities such as bearing total educational expenses coupled with healthy environment in colleges like separate rest room for leisure period in co-education colleges and separate girls' college, etc. Female literacy, particularly in rural areas, in our country is extremely low, the drop-out rate among girls is very high. Girls are normally burdened with household chores. They are deprived of education and exposure to the outside world and therefore, they remain ignorant and superstitious. There is a need to convince the illiterate parents for girls' education *vis-à-vis* motivating these parents for adult education programmes. Female students can interact with such girls and persuade their mothers for their enrolment in colleges / schools. Cognitive empowerment of women carries her to self-confidence and self-reliance i.e., psychological empowerment which can lead to further social action or economic activity that stimulates political and economic empowerment. Different academic strategies and other plans are drawn out for this purpose. Training and education for empowerment of women in the State result in individual empowerment and social transformation whereby, women have more control over their lives and more of an effect in the changing society to eliminate of reduce gender bias and discrimination.

President **A.P.J. Abdul Kalam** said "empowering of women was a prerequisite for creating a good nation, "when women are empowered, society with stability is assured. Empowerment of women is essential as their thoughts and their value systems lead the development of a good family, good society and ultimately a good nation".

The first and foremost task of Higher Education is to re-examine its role and responsibilities in the context of a fast changing socio-economic milieu. It is expected to ensure quality and relevance of education to meet emerging needs of the society. As it plays an important role not only in the progress of education but also in the overall development of the society. Its growth and status indicate the level of development as it is an important indicator of socio- economic development and a prominent component of population studies. Equally, it is considered as an essential trait of civilization and overall development of human beings. Emancipation and empowerment of people can be achieved only through the quality of education. Indeed, the country's advancement and development largely depends upon the level and quality of education as it provides enlightenment, power, privilege, protection and prestige to the people.

REFERENCES

Agarwal, Pawan (2006): "Higher Education Policy", *EPW*, Nov. 11-17, Vol. XLI, No. 45, p. 4645.

Dongaonkar, D. (2004): "Higher Education in India: The Varies Dimension", *University News*, 42(21).

Ghosh, Jayanti (2006): "Case for Caste-based Quotas in Higher Education", *EPW*, Vol. XVI, No. 24, p. 2428-2432.

Jajri, H.A.S (2006): "Higher Education: Maladies and Remedies", *University News*, Oct 23–29, Vol. 44, No. 43, p. 2.

Joram, Begi (2008): "Education Scenario in Arunachal Pradesh", *Arunachal Review*, Directorate of Information, Public Relation and Printing, Government of Arunachal Pradesh, Vol. X, No. 2, June-August, Naharlagun, Government of Arunachal Pradesh.

Joseph, Thomas (2006): "Higher Education in the changing Global Scenario", *University News*, April, 03–09, p. 2.

Kale, R.K. (2006): "Higher Education and Development of the Nation", *University News*, Aug 14–20, Vol. 44, No. 33, p. 2-3.

Mandal, R.K. (2006): "How to Develop Arunachal Pradesh", *Arunachal Review*, June-August, Vol. VIII, No. 18, p. 8.

Mandal, R.K. (2006): "Development of Education in Arunachal Pradesh (Since 1947)", *Arunachal Review*, December, 05, February, 06, p. 11-12.

Mandal, R.K. (2005): "How to Develop Education in Arunachal Pradesh", *Alokarun (Research Journal)* Vol. XXVI, D.N. Government College, Itanagar, p. 23.

Mandal, R.K. (2005): "Literacy in Arunachal Pradesh: Trend, Features and Growth, *Rajiv Gandhi University Research Journal*, Vol. 8(2), December, Rajiv Gandi University, Itanagar.

Mandal, R.K. (2008): "Quality Assurance in Higher Education in Arunachal Pradesh: Issues and Challenges", in Joram Begi (ed): Dynamics of Higher Education: Local, National and Global Perspectives, Commonwealth Publication, New Delhi.

Mandal, R.K. (2007): "Human Resource Development in North-East Region with special Reference to Arunachal Pradesh, Kangki, M.(ed.): Development Issues in North-East Region, Mittal Publications, New Delhi.

Mishra, P.N., Singh, A.K. and Tripathi, B.K. (2006): "Human Resource Management: An Emerging Area of Research in Institutions of Higher Learning", University News, Vol. 44, No. 35, August 28 – Sept. 2003, p. 1 – 6.

Mahapatra,P.C. (2006): "Opportunities and Challenges to Higher Education" University News, Vol. 45, No. 01, January 01-07, p. 1.

Motiram (2006): "Scheduled Castes' Education in India: Issues and Challenges" University News, March 27-April' 02, pp. 1-5.

Mohanty, Sunil Behari (2006): "Does the Nation Need a New National Policy on Education for High Quality Higher Education?", University News, Vol. 44, No. 38, Sept. 18-24, pp. 6-7.

Naik, B. M. (2006): "Quality Assurance system in Higher and Technical Education: Can we afford to ignore it?" University News, July 24-30, Vol. 44, p. 10.

Pathak, N. (2006): "Good Means for Good Ends: Towards Value-Centered Higher Education", University News, August 21-27, pp. 10-12.

Ramappa, P. (2007): "Primary Education in Andhra Pradesh" Southern Economist, June 15, Vol. 46, No. 4, p. 23.

Ravichandran, A. (2006): "Human Resource Climate in Self- Financing Institution", University News, February 20-26, Vol. 44, No. 08, p. 17.

Rawat, M.S. (2006): "Strategy for Higher Education Development in Uttranchal", University News, Vol. 44, No. 40, Oct 02 – 08, p. 18.

Simha, S.L.N. (2006): "Economic Impact of Bad Politics", Southern Economist, Vol. 44, No. 19, Bangalore, p. 5-6.

Sharrma, J.P. and Jain, T. (2006):"Academic Staff College:An assessment",University News, July 24-30, Vol. 44, No. 30.

Singh, S.P. (2005): "Role of Philanthropy in Education: An American Experience", University News , December 12-18,Vol.43,No.50, pp. 11-12.

Vashistha, K.C. & Malik, S. (2002): *"Some Strategic Efforts towards the Empowerment of Women"*, University News, February 4-10, Vol. 40, No. 5, p. 16.

SECTION II
FOREST

12

Forest Resources and Its Contribution

Introduction

Forests contribute significantly to the economic, social and environmental well-being of a country. In a developing country like India, their role is even more pronounced because such a country is predominantly agriculture-based. Adequate forests and trees lead to a stable environment which in-turn is conducive to sustained agricultural production. Forests protect and enrich the soil mantle by reducing soil erosion and nutrient loss, and by facilitating nutrient recycling and microbial activities. They protect the hydrological systems and regulate stream flow, thus augmenting the availability of water—a critical requirement for agriculture. Forest is an important natural resource of India. It helps to control flood and thereby protects the soil against erosion. It supplies timber, fuel wood, fodder and a wood range of non-wood products. It is the natural habitat for bio-diversity and repository of genetic wealth. Forest, thus, plays an important role in environmental and economic sustainability. Despite its potentiality to reduce poverty and contribution to economic growth and its significant contribution to local and global environment, forest resources are not given their due importance. Forests are recognized as a renewable natural resource. Forests play a very significant role in the national economy and directly influence the rural life of a large number of people living in or near forests. Forests are important for maintaining environmental and ecological balance. Therefore, development of forestry is vital to the socio- economic advancement of the country for of a particular region. The North-Eastern Region, rich in forest resources has good potentialities for the development and expansion of forest-based industries like paper mills, match factories etc. but there is no significant growth of these industries in this region due to a number of factors such as (a) peculiar physical geographical features, (b) infrastructural bottlenecks, and (c) institutional and other shortcomings. But the most tragic part is that the forests remain unutilized and unexploited. The State Forest Department should resort to institutional finance for developing their forests.

The diversity of topographical and climatic conditions has favoured the growth of luxuriant forests which are home to myriad plant and animal forms, adding beauty to the landscape. Living in this incredible cradle of nature are the colourful and vibrant tribes of Arunachal Pradesh for whom the forests and the wildlife are of special significance.

Storehouse of Natural Resources

Forests are a unique storehouse of plant and animal genetic resources. Their contribution to the country's biological diversity is very significant. Biological diversity acts as an insurance against any possible crisis in food production. Forests meet nearly 40 per cent of the energy needs of the country (above 80 per cent in rural India). They also account for about 25 per cent of our fodder needs. Forest products are crucial to rural and tribal economy of India. While wood is the major forest product, resins, gums, lac and *khus* are some of the minor forest products. Many of the products provide sustenance to the rural people as a large part of their day-to-day necessities including food and medicines, are met by the forests. The forests are integral to the alleviation of their poverty. For landless families, forest-related activities often constitute the primary source of income.

Area under Forest in India: Under land utilization pattern, the Government of India estimated the total area under forests as 68 million hectares or 22 per cent of the total geographical area shown in Table 12.1.Using remote sensing technology, the Forest Survey of India assesses the forest cover of the country biennially since 1987.

Table 12.1: Forest Cover Estimates from 1987 in India.

Assessment Year	*Forest (million hectares)*	*Percentage of Geographical Area*
1987	64.1	19.5
1991	63.9	19.4
1995	63.9	19.4
2001	67.6	20.5

Source : 1. Tenth Five Plan (2002-07), Vol. II, p. 1056.
2. Statistical Abstract, India 2002, p. 43.

The assessments since 1987 show clearly that the forest cover in India had stabilized around 19.4 per cent of the total geographical area (i.e. around 64 million hectares). However , the 2001 assessment shows that only about 38 million hectares are dense forests (i.e., 12 per cent) and the rest are open forests on degraded forests (about 8 per cent); the rest are mangroves. In our country, forest has generally been undervalued in economic and social terms. The contribution of the forest sector to GDP was put as 1 per cent in 1996-97 (measured at 1980-81 prices). A recent estimate puts the gross value of goods services provided by the forest sector at 2.4 per cent of GDP. These estimates, however, do not take into account the huge economic value of the ecosystem services of the forests (which obviously cannot be quantified).These values are indeed important and should be given weight in all policy decisions affecting forestry. Forest also supplies fire-wood; it is on account of the shortage of fire-wood, cow dung is used as fuel. For both these purposes, area under forest should be extended.

Forest Covers in North-East States: A Comparison

The climatic factors of NER are high humidity (80-90%), frequent and heavy rainfall and moderate to mild temperature without extremes of heat or cold. The average rainfall is heavy but varies from 2,000-12,700 mm. The Brahmaputra flows through to the whole length of Assam valley with alluvial deposits on either side. The NER is an area of rivers, hills and plains, extraordinarily rich in vegetation: a part of the Khasi hills above the pine zone (2,000 m) is considered to be the richest, not only in India, but perhaps in the whole world. The forest of NEI is divided into: (i) tropical wet evergreen forest (5860,000 ha.), (ii) tropical moist forest (5474,000 ha.), (iii) sub-tropical broad leaved forests (300,000 ha.) and (iv) montane wet temperate forest (2628,000 ha.).

Forest has acquired increasing interest during few years for their role not only in meeting the material requirements but also for their ecological and environmental functions. Forests have been playing a pivotal role in socio-economic development of our country in general and North East Region in particular. Forests are important source of subsistence, employment, revenue and raw materials for industry. In Arunachal Pradesh forest plays an important role in its economy and also in the ecology of North Eastern Region. The repeated occurrence of floods in North Eastern Region is claimed to be due resources including forest resources in the region. The forest resources of the region are under tremendous pressure due to increasing demand for human and livestock. Too much of extraction has led to forest degradation and disaster in ecological balance in recent time in this region. The forests cover of Arunachal Pradesh in comparison to North Eastern States is shown in Table 12.2 given below.

Table 12.2: Forest Covers of Arunachal Pradesh: A Comparison

(in sq. km.)

States	*1987*	*1989*	*1991*	*1993*	*1995*	*1997*	*1999*
Arunachal Pradesh	64132	69002	68757	68661	68621	68602	68847
Assam	25160	24832	24751	24508	24061	23824	23688
Manipur	17475	17685	17685	17621	17558	17418	17384
Meghalaya	16466	15645	15875	15769	15714	15657	15633
Mizoram	10984	18170	18853	18697	18576	18775	18338
Nagaland	14394	14399	14321	14348	14291	14221	14164
Tripura	5953	5535	5535	5538	5538	5546	5745
NER	162664	165268	165777	164842	164359	164043	163799
%Change of NER		+ 1.6	+ 0.3	– 0.56	– 0.3	– 0.2	– 0.15

Source: State Forest Report, 1987-1999

In above Table 12.2 we find that the forest cover in Arunachal Pradesh was 76.6 per cent during 1987 compared to geographical area and this has increased to 82.21 per cent during 1999. There has been gain of forest cover in the State during the period under review. The North Eastern Region, the forest cover during 1987 was 162,664 sq. km. which is 163,799 sq. km. during 1999. Thus during 1980s and 1990s, there was no enormous decrease of forest cover in North Eastern Region. Rather depletion of forest was more in outside of North Eastern Region (NER), which is more concerned for our country. During 1999, the North Eastern States had dense forest of 95,285 sq. km. and out of that Arunachal Pradesh had 57,756 sq. km. This shows that 60.6 per cent of dense forest in NER belongs to Arunachal Pradesh. This is an indication of huge untapped forest resources in the State.

Forest Cover in Arunachal Pradesh

Forest cover (recorded and reserved), district-wise forest cover, land use classification, legal forest status of the forest, forest type and species diversity of plant and animal, forest type and species diversity of plant and animal, plant groups, families, genera and species and dominant families of angiosperms of Arunachal Pradesh, India and world are shown in Tables 12.3 to 12.8 and 12.9.

Table 12.3: The State is ranked second among States and UTs in terms of area under forest cover

Forest Cover	
Very Dense Forest	13,907 km^2
Open Forest	14,508 km^2
Moderately Dense Forest	39,604 km^2
Total	**68,045 km^2**
Of State's Geographic Area	81.22 per cent
Of Country's Forest Cover	10.03 per cent
Recorded Forest Area	
Reserved Forest (RF)	10,178 km^2
Protected Forest (PF)	9.536 km^2
Unclassed Forest (UF)	31,826 km^2
Total	**51,540 km^2**

(contd...)

(Table 12.3 contd...)

Of State's Geographic Area	61.55%
Of Country's Forest Area	6.65%

Source: Statistical Abstract of Arunachal Pradesh, 1998

Table 12.4: District-wise Forest Cover in Arunachal Pradesh (Area in Sq.Km)

District	*Geographical*	*Forest cover*				*Per cent*	*Change*
		Very	*Moderately*	*Open*	*Total*		
	Area	*Dense*	*Dense*	*Forest*	*Forest*		
Changlang[TH]	4,662	1,879	1,539	888	4,306	92.36	-46
Dibang Valley[TH]	13,029	851	5,836	2,736	9,423	72.32	12
Kameng East[TH]	11,556	2,583	5,548	2,107	10,238	88.59	4
Kameng West[TH]							
Lohit[TH]	11,402	1,955	4,224	1,615	7,794	68.36	34
Papumpare[TH]	3,462	754	1,699	834	3,287	94.95	7
Siang East[TH]	3,655	448	1,944	480	2,872	78.58	9
Siang Upper[TH]	7,050	736	3,676	1,198	5,610	79.57	11
Siang West[TH]	7,813	997	4,884	946	6,827	87.38	-69
Subansiri Lower[TH]	9,548	2,286	4,745	1,704	8,735	91.49	-53
Subansiri Upper[TH]	7,032	849	3,803	1,155	5,807	82.58	67
Tawang[TH]	2,172	110	664	453	1,227	56.49	12
Tirap[TH]	2,362	459	1,042	392	1,893	80.14	-14
Total	**83,743**	**13,907**	**39,604**	**14,508**	**68,019**	**81.22**	**-26**

Source: Statistical Abstract of Arunachal Pradesh, 1998

Table 12.5: Land use classification in Arunachal Pradesh

Sl. No.	*Land Use*	*Area (in Km²)*	*% of Geographical Area*
1.	Total Geographical Area	83743	
2.	Forest Area	51540	61.54
3.	Fallow Land	646.3	0.771
4.	Land under misc. tree crops	444.55	0.53
5.	Cultivable wasteland	330.94	0.395
6.	Cropped Area	1931.93	2.307
7.	Area not available for cultivation	427.89	0.5109

Source: Statistical Abstract of Arunachal Pradesh, 1998

Table 12.6: Legal Forest Status of the Forest in Arunachal Pradesh

Sl. No.	*Legal Classification*	*Area (Km²)*	*% of Recorded Forest*	*% of Geographical Area*
1.	Reserve Forests	9722.69	18.86	11.61
2.	Protected Forests	694.3	1.35	0.82
3.	Anchal Reserve Forest	329.38	0.64	0.39
4.	Village Reserve Forest	300.24	0.58	0.36
5.	National Parks	2468.24	4.79	2.94
6.	Wild Life Sanctuary	7059.75	13.70	8.43
7.	Unclassified State Forest	30965.39	60.08	36.90
	Total:	**51540**	**100**	**61.55**

Source: 'Forest Statistics (Up to Year 2000-2001) Arunachal Pradesh'.

Table 12.7: Forest type and Species Diversity of Plant and Animal in Arunachal Pradesh

Sl. No.	Zone	Forest Type	Plant spp.	Animal
1	Tropical (Plains)	Tropical evergreen 4A/b1/1 tropical semi-evergreen 2/B/C1/1a Reverie Semi evergreen	Altingia excelsa, Diptorocarpus gracils, D.retusus,	Asian Elephant, Tiger, Leopard, Snow Leopard, Clouded leopard, Takin, Chinese Pangolin,
2	Sub Tropical (upto 900-1800 mtr).	Sub-Tropical broad leaved $3C_3/B_b$, $3c/Is_2$	Castonopsis, Quercus, Populus, Tsuga, Acer, Abies, Cupressus, Pine.	Himalayan Black Bear, Hoolock gibbon, Capped langur, Slow loris,
3	Sub Tropical (upto 900-1800 mtr.)	Sub-Tropical pine forest (1200-1800 mtrs) 11/9/DS/1	Pinus roxburghii, Pinus Wallichiana, Pinus mesksii	Assamese macaque, Stump tailed macaque, Pig tailed macaque,
4	Temperate (1800-2750 mtrs.)	Temperate broad leaved forests $IV/II/IIB/C_1$ $IV/II/IIB/C_2$ sub-ayrine and Alpine	Quercus lamsllosa, Castonopsis India Acer hookeri	Rhesus macaque, Black mutjac, Leaf deer, Musk deer etc.
5	Alpine	V/C_2, VI/ISC_3, $VI/16/C_1$, E_1		

Source: Department of Forests & Environment, Government of Arunachal Pradesh

Table 12.8: Plant groups, families, genera and species in Arunachal Pradesh

Sl. No.	*Plant groups*	*No. of families*	*No. of genera*	*No. of species*
1	Angiosperm	192	1295	4117
2	Dicotyledons	165	970	2986
3	Monocotyledons	27	325	1131
4	Gymnosperm	8	18	29
5	Pteridophytes	43	133	452

Source: Department of Forests & Environment, Government of Arunachal Pradesh

Table 12.9: Dominant families of Angiosperms of Arunachal Pradesh, India and World

Sl. No.	*Name of the family*	*Arunachal Pradesh*		*India*		*World*	
		Genera	*Species*	*Genera*	*Species*	*Gen.*	*Species*
	Orchidaceae	122	545	184	1229	735	15000
	Leguminoceae	67	196	191	1152	690	17600
	Asteraceae	68	186	167	950	900	1300
	Rubiaceae	52	159	115	659	500	6000
	Ericaceae	9	158	15	199	50	1350
	Poaceae	76	153	260	1200	620	10000
	Urticaceae+Moraceae	25	129	25	114	45	550
	Rosaceae	18	111	44	492	100	2000
	Cyperaceae	22	96	38	545	90	4000
	Euphorbiaceae	39	94	84	528	300	5000

Source: Department of Forests & Environment, Government of Arunachal Pradesh.

Arunachal Pradesh contains only 0.11 per cent of population of the country while its geographical area constitutes 2.5 per cent of total area of the country. The State, which is the extension of Eastern Himalayas, is very rich in forest-wealth mainly due to non-interference of the forest by mankind. Due to botanical richness, it has attracted many plant explorers in the past. From 1956, the Botanical Survey of India has been actively exploring different parts of the State. As per the State Forest Report-1999, published by the Forest Survey of India, forest cover of Arunachal Pradesh is 68951 sq. km. accounting for 82.21 per cent of its total geographical area. The recorded forest area of the State is 51540 sq. kms., which is about 61.5 per cent of its total geographical area and the largest among the States of North-East India and second highest among the States of India only next to Madhya Pradesh (Forest Statistics, 2000- 2001). Thus, the State is fortunate to have such high percentage of its area under valuable forests cover against the national percentage of 20.5 as per 2001 assessment.

Forests have acquired increasing interest during last few years for their role not only in meeting the material requirements but also for their ecological and environmental functions. Forests have been playing a pivotal role in Socio-Economic development and also in containing the ecology of our country in general and North East Region in particular. Forests not only provide the tribal people with food, construction materials, fuel, fodder and employment opportunities in various forests–based occupations but they also satisfy their deep-rooted sentiments. Their folklore, songs and dances revolve around forests and in times of natural calamities, forests are their last succour. According to legal status, there are seven-fold classifications of forests in Arunachal Pradesh.

In the absence of cadastral survey of land and other resources, there is a dispute (Community *vs.* State) regarding the ownership of the forest resources. However, in general, village forest and unclassified State forests are claimed to be the community (common) forest in the State of Arunachal Pradesh. Thus, forests are important source of subsistence, employment, revenue and raw materials for industry. In Arunachal Pradesh forest plays an important role in its economy. The repeated occurrence of floods in North Eastern Region is claimed to be due to unplanned exploitation of natural resources including forest resources in the region. This chapter seeks to an in-depth study to identify the contributions of forest and how to make it more beneficial to the people of the State.

Contribution of the Forest

Flora and Fauna: It is well known fact that more than 80 per cent of the world's medicinal flora is found in the Himalayan ranges of India. Arunachal Pradesh is lying within the Himalayan belt has almost of all medicinal plants. Since the State has remained a generally inaccessible area with scarce means of communication and transport, very little written record is available about medicinal flora. Mostly the knowledge and information were passed from generation to generation by word of mouth and through folklores. However, under Monasteries of Monpa (Buddhist), there were monks who had expertise and who trained some selected persons in the area of identification, collection and processing, and use of various active parts of the herbs. It is a common knowledge that only certain plants and certain parts of plants like flower, leaf, bark, root are of medicinal use.

Arunachal Pradesh offers an ideal agro-climate with vast potentials for growing varieties of orchids round the year. Out of about 1150 species of orchids known in India, about 550 species occur only in Arunachal Pradesh. These species occur in varying climatic and habitat conditions in varying concentration from the warm foot-hills to the cool temperate hills in Arunachal Pradesh. Such a diverse climatic situation has favoured the occurrence of about 550 species of orchids in the State which is a highest number for any State in India thus making it an "Orchid Paradise" of our country. There are over 500 Herbs recorded from Arunachal Pradesh of which 250 are used in various Ayurvedic formulations.

Vast climatic variations in Arunachal Pradesh have resulted in existence of almost all types of Herbs and timber wealth ranging from tropical teak in foothills jungles to coniferous and alpine of high mountains. The State is very rich in flora. It has about 4500 species of flowering plants, 400 species of pleridophytes, 23 species of coniferous, 35 species of bamboos, 20 species of canes, 25 Rhododendron species. Overall, Arunachal Pradesh is, as if, a natural garden of more than 20,000 identified species of medicinal plants and so many still remain unidentified. About 300 plant species out of native flora in North-Eastern India are used for edible purpose. Of these, over 25 provide tubers/rhizomes etc., which are eaten raw or boiled. Over 50 are consumed as green with their leaves/tender shoots cooked as vegetable; about 170 ripe fruits, which are pulpy and sweet/sub-sweet are eaten raw and many of these are used for pickles/vegetables when unripe; about 15 have edible seeds which are eaten raw or roasted.

Like flora, the deeply wooded terrains of Arunachal Pradesh are also rich in fauna. There are believed to be more than 100 species of mammals in its forests. These include four major cats (tiger, leopard, snow leopard and clouded leopard), three antelopes (serow, goral and takin) and the highly endangered hispid hare. The State is home to 8 out of 16 species of primates found in India. Bison or Gaur and Mithun are two important mammals found in the state. Additionally, at least six species of squirrels, mongoose, civet cat are some of the smaller mammals found in the wild. There are four types of deer: Sambar, hog deer, barking deer, and musk deer. Red panda, binturong, black bear, sun bear, sloth bear, wolf, wild boar, wild goat and wild pig, monkey, elephant are the other animal species found in the State. There are about 650 species of birds, including three species of hornbills and the endangered white winged duck and rare pheasants. In addition, there are 105 species of fishes, 42 species of amphibians, besides a large numbers of reptiles, butterflies and other terrestrial mammals.

Natural Environment and Ecological Balance: There is a great need today to create a comprehensive awareness of the need to have adequate safeguards against the destruction of the natural environment. The concern for preservation of environment is multi-dimensional and it relates itself to many disciplines and facets of the administration. The protection of environment and ecological balance are the concern of the people all over the globe. The Northeastern region of the country, which forms major part of the Indian portion of the Eastern Himalayas, is not only rich in forest and related natural resources, but also very much rich in bio-diversity. It has myriads of complex problems with distinct constitutional and legal features.

It is clear that there is a need for conservation of forest in the region. As there are many people maintaining their livelihood from forest, we should chalk out proper aforestation programme which will ultimately satisfy the growing demand for products. But at the time of aforestation we should use multiple species for plantation. Environmentalists have been warning about the damage of planting a single species over a large area. This is because any insect or disease outbreak can wipeout the entire tree plantation, leading to ecological and financial crisis. Monoculture may deplete the nutrients at a particular profile of the soil and cause nutritional deficiency in the long run. The principle behind bio-diversity is to encourage the conservation of a wide range of flora and fauna in a given area to ensure an ideal nutrient cycle, as well as, food chain which are important aspects of ecological balance. Preservation of plants and animals are necessary, because our present knowledge about them is confined to a small number of species and the benefits of the remaining millions of plants and animal species are not known to us today. Nevertheless they play an important role in maintaining the ecological balance.

Ecotourism: Arunachal Pradesh is the largest in area among North- Eastern states and is the second largest forest covered state next to Madhya Pradesh in the country. The State is already in the tourist map of India because of its unique, diverse culture, beautiful river valleys, snowcapped mountains, archaeology and mythology of ancient culture and religion.

Ecotourism is a visible means for communities and individual to earn their livelihoods because of:

- Increasing the awareness and value of natural wildlife on both local and international levels.
- Contributing to the socio-economic incentives to preserve the natural wildlife population and habitats. This may contribute to the influx of foreign currency much needed for capital investment.
- Creating socio-political pressure on the local and international level in order to preserve the biological resources for current and future generations.

Ecotourism is a form of tourism that is inspired primarily by the natural history and the environment of an area. Profits that may originate from this programme are used for sustainable economic development and to fund local conservation projects for the preservation of the environment. Tourism is one of the faster growing industries in the world today. It creates employment especially for guides, restaurants, hoteliers, local shopkeepers, merchants etc. and brings in foreign currency to economically marginal areas. And also it plays an important role in the social culture and economic development of the nations, and has the potential to preserve the heritages.

Hydro Power Potential: Arunachal Pradesh, having untapped estimated hydro power potential of 49,000 MW, may emerge as power house of India when this potential is fully harnessed (*Source:* Deptt. of Power, Govt. of Arunachal Pradesh), this is shown in Table 12.10. Even if a part of the available hydro potential is harnessed, the State will not only be self-sufficient in meeting its own power requirement but at the same time it can earn revenue by supplying power to the other neighbouring states of the country. During 2002-03, 35 numbers of micro/mini hydel projects with an installed capacity of 32.48 M.W. and diesel sets with an installed capacity of 27.12 M.W are the main sources of power supply in the state though the actual power requirement is 95 M.W. So the State is highly deficient in power generation.

Table 12.10: Major river basins & their potentials

Name of the River/Basin	*Probable Hydro Potentials (MW)*			*Name of Districts*
	ROR	*Storage*	*Total*	
Kameng	3799	847	4646	W&E/Kameng
Subansiri	10141	5050	15191	U&L/Subansiri/Kurung Kumey
Siang	3557	11700	15257	W&E/Siang U/Siang
Dibang	5946	1282	7228	U & L/Dibang Valley
Lohit	3594	3075	6669	Lohit
Total Potentials	27037	21954	48991	

Source: Deptt. of Power, Govt. of Arunachal Pradesh, Itanagar.

Forest Revenue: Forest has several uses and functions. Forest is scarce and is becoming increasingly scarce due to pressure on it. It can be attributed to increase in population and demand for forest resource. The forest resources of Arunachal Pradesh are under tremendous pressure due to increasing demand for human and livestock. Too much of extraction has led to forest degradation and disaster in ecological balance in recent time in this region and this led to famous Supreme Court verdict on 12/12/96 banning exploitation of forest resources specially industrial wood in Arunachal Pradesh and other State. If we refer to Table 12.3 shown above we find that the forest of Arunachal Pradesh was at higher side except during 1989 when the forest cover was 69,002 sq. km. only 0.22 per cent of forest cover reduction during 1999 compared to 1989. If we accept state first report, then there was not much depletion of forest cover in the State. Forest revenue plays an important role in Forest economy of any State. Table 12.11 below shows the forest revenue of Arunachal Pradesh during last few years.

Table 12.11: Forest Revenue in Arunachal Pradesh

Year	*Rs. in Crores (Approx)*
1992-1993	28.48
1993-1994	39.65
1994-1995	34.89
1995-1996	49.04
1996-1997	25.24
1997-1998	07.53
1998-1999	12.43
1999-2000	15.44
2000-2001	13.00
2001-2002	25.24
2002-2003	15.61
2003-2004	9.63

Source: Directorate of Economics and Statistics and Different Publication.

It may be seen from above Table 12.4 that the forest revenue of Arunachal Pradesh has decreased substantially specially after the Supreme Court verdict during 1996-97. The forest revenue during 1992-93 was Rs. 28.48 crores approximately while during 1993-94, it was Rs. 39.65 crores and Rs. 34.89 crores during 1994-95. It was Rs. 49.04 crores during 1995-96 and fell down to Rs. 25.24 crores during 1996-97 and further to Rs. 7.53 crores during 1997 -98. There is some improvement in recent years while it was Rs. 15.61 crores during 2002-03 and Rs. 9.63 crores during 2003-04.

The State economy of any state consists of 13 sectors and these are agriculture; forestry and logging; fishing; mining and quarrying; manufacturing; construction; electricity, gas and water supply;

transport, storage and communication; trade, hotel and restaurant; banking and insurance; real estate, ownership of dwellings and business services, public administration and other services.

Forestry and logging sector played an important role in State Economy or Net State Domestic Product (NSDP) of Arunachal Pradesh. This is shown in Table 12.12 given below.

Table 12.12: Contribution of forestry in State Economy of Arunachal Pradesh

(at current prices)

Year	*NSDP (Rs.crores)*	*Contribution of Forestry (Rs.crores)*	*Contribution in %*
1970-1971	21.34 #	4.42	20.7
1980-1981	97.70@	9.99	10.2
1990-1991	231.11@	22.12	9.6
1991-1992	264.24@	22.39	8.5
1992-1993	271.07@	30.73	11.3
1993-1994	812.13*	93.24	11.5
1994-1995	872.68*	119.82	13.7
1995-1996	1071.45*	116.55	10.9
1996-1997	1082.71*	116.87	10.8
1997-1998	1192.18*	53.68	4.5
1998-1999	1353.82*	70.97	5.2
1999-2000	1457.08*	72.99	5.0
2000-2001	1594.86*	71.28	4.5
2001-2002	1730.21*	77.13	4.5
2002-2003	1744.36*	75.92	4.4
2003-2004	1970.66*	76.75	3.9

#At 1970-71 series, @ at 1980-81 series, *at 1993-94 series.

Source: SDP Publication of Department of Economics and Statistics, Government of Arunachal Pradesh, Itanagar

From Table 12.12 we find that the contribution of forestry in State Economy was 20.7 per cent during 1970-71,which decreased to 10.2 per cent during 1980-81 and further to 9.6 per cent during 1990-91.During 1990s the contribution in NSDP of the State was 8.5 per cent during 1991-92, 11.3 per cent during 1992-93, 11.5 per cent during

1993-94, 13.7 per cent during 1994-95, 10.9 per cent during 1995-96, and 10.8 per cent during 1996-97, and fell down to 4.5 per cent during 1997-98. This is an effect of Supreme Court verdict on exploitation of forest resources in the State. The contribution of the forest economy further declined to 3.90 per cent during 2003-04 estimates of NSDP at current prices. Beside the above, the forest-based industries were closed down after the famous judgment and as a consequent 14 forest-based industries out of 17 medium scale industries went to oblivion and as a consequence the contribution of manufacturing sector had little impact in State Economy since 1997-98. The contribution of manufacturing was Rs. 36.17 corers during 1997-98 compared to Rs. 49.31 corers during 1996-97. It was Rs. 40.34 crores during 2003-04. Even the new industrial policy resolution of 2001 had very little impact in the manufacturing sector of the State.

Some Suggestions to Make the Forests More Beneficial

In order to maximize the monetary gains and maintenance of ecological balance, there is an urgent need for quick growing species to supply wood for fuel. Again, systematic plantation of suitable types on waste and semi-waste land would be the right answer. Reserved forests are maintained by the State not only for ecological reasons, but also for economic benefit.

1. The first step in planting trees is the selection of species that will thrive on a given site. This has to be done on the basis of local observation, experience and ecological understanding. The purpose of planting should be to establish a protective cover that would help to conserve and increase soil fertility to achieve rapid progress. The government must directly take step with its full authority, acquire all forests and waste lands, plant them with selected species of quick-growing trees and protect, control and manage them in the initial stages. All this can be done by the State forestry department which needs to be suitably strengthened for the purpose. After reaching the harvesting stage, the actual operation can be contracted out to qualified tribal people.

For planned forest management, quick-growing species should be planted. Wastelands should be brought under the scheme of *Haryali* through forestation and so on. There may be scheme for bamboo used in industry and also plant different species of bamboo compared to the neighbouring countries like China,

Myanmar etc. In fact 61 species out of 127 species of bamboo are available in India and most of them are indigenous to the NER. If a proper planning is made, all of them would be very useful in the industries of the State.

2. The Poor tribal people need to be rehabilitated in their own natural setting by enabling them to develop their skill and potential for production of forestry. What is required for this? It is sympathetic understanding of their needs and facilitating fuller use of their man-power by making them active partner in social forestry. Actually the team spirit to do challenging tasks which the tribal have can be institutionalized through multipurpose service co-operatives. In this way the intermediaries will also get wiped out.

3. Forest-based industries such as paper pulp, paper mills, match, wood factory, fibre board factory, plywood and hard-wood manufacturing, timber treatment and seasoning, resin, turpentine manufacturing industry should be economically feasible. The finished goods can be marketed through co-operatives and Forest Corporation. The government can help by providing all infra-structural facilities to the local entrepreneurs to set up a network of wood-based small scale industries. The tribal people will then no longer remain mere collecting agents of minor forest produce but the skill, experience and capability generated in them would open out their entrepreneurial abilities. This will enhance their capacity to take up new jobs and help them to learn new skills so as to enable them to earn.

4. The unemployed youth can find employment in the rubber plantations as well as in the rubber-based industries. Rubber-based industries can also lead to the economic development of the State. Apart from the economic aspects, rubber plantations can play a vital role in the ecological and climatic conditions prevailing in the region. Rubber plantations have an important role to play in soil conservation. The vast stretches of fallow land of the region can be made productive and being man-made forests. As a whole, the cultivation of rubber and the growth of rubber-based industries will improve the status of the economy of the eight states of the north-eastern region and will contribute much to the prosperity of the region as well as of our country. On the other hand, rubber plantations will help to control the climate of the region to a great extent.

Forest planning and policy should be framed in such a way so as to provide maximum employment and income to the tribal people. In this case, the cultivation of rubber can hold out a big promise due to its shorter gestation period and also its foreign exchange saving role if it is made stronger in view of the sufficient availability of tilla lands in the state. Again, the future strategy of industrial development in the state hinges upon the development of small scale and cottage industries rather than upon large industries, it has a direct linkage with the development of forest resources in the State.

5. Forest Corporations will also help to market the various forest products including medicinal plants collected by the local people so that the exploitation by middlemen and contractors can be eliminated. So the development of forestry in the State means the upliftment and economic development of the tribal population in this region. In the development of village forests in the North Eastern Region, the main problem is one of eliminating shifting cultivation (known as *Jhum* cultivation in this region) which has been going on from generations to generations. The local people of this region have been practicing shifting cultivation for the past several centuries. If the positive rate of growth is to be achieved, the practice of shifting cultivation has to be controlled and regulated. It is also to be noted that not only are the *Jhumias* facing serious economic problem but society as a whole is also having to pay price for deforestation in the region in the form of soil erosion, flood and drought.

For conserving and managing natural vegetation the *jhum* cultivation and illegal felling of trees, which are the root cause of deforestation, must be stopped immediately but not without rehabilitation of the *jhumias*. If the government is successful to protect the natural vegetation, the State will be the richest in having the Herbs which can be sold in national and international markets. Hence, it is necessary first to develop the market for herbs within the State where the local cultivators will be benefited economically. It will give an incentive to the local people to protect the valuable herbs from extinction. Shifting cultivation and illegal failing of trees are the main cause of disappearance of flora and fauna in Arunachal Pradesh. The Central Government as well as the State Government should give top priority to protect the herbs of economic value in the State which are endowed more than 50 per cent of herbs of the country. Days are not far when the Governments can generate employment as well as earn foreign currency from the export of the State's herbs if they try to take keen interest to protect the existing herbs from disappearance.

6. Forest Management: Though the North Eastern Region is no doubt one of the forests richest regions of India but still a large portion of forest area remains unutilized and unexploited due to its difficult terrain, heavy rainfall and transport bottleneck. The Government is no doubt trying to develop the forest resources in the North Eastern Region. But the finance and outlay for the forestry sector during the Five Year Plans are not sufficient. Forest management should be so oriented as to serve the best interests of the region.

Preservation of forest is a heavy task to the State. The interests of people depending on the forests products for their livelihood would have to be protected by providing training and employment opportunities in alternative occupations. The population increased and modernization are realities of the day when we plan for the future, new ideological statements are not enough, but one should have proper action plan. It is necessary that systematic forestation and plantation programmes are to be undertaken to increase the forest cover. All barren lands to be brought under forest cover by private sector.

7. Convention on International Trade in Endangered Species of Fauna and Flora (CITES): In the present Export Policy all wild animals and products are prohibited to export. All items of plants of the Convention on International Trade in Endangered Species of Wild Flora and Fauna (CITES) and Wild Orchids are banned as per the current Export/Import Policy. This policy further includes 29 species of plants obtained from wild and their portions derivatives and extracts which are not allowed for export. The remaining items other than these are permitted for export subject to no-objection from the Regional Deputy Director (Wildlife Preservation) of Government of India and legal procurement certificate/cultivation origin certificate from Divisional Forest Officer of the State Government. For CITES species, specific permits are issued by the

Regional Deputy Directors (Wildlife Preservation) designated as Assistant Management Authorities under the CITES depending on the placement of the items. Import restrictions are equally rigid. Import of Ivory and species found in India and its products is prohibited. Other species are allowed against an Import license and recommendation of Chief Wildlife Warden of the state. All export and imports of wildlife and its products are examined by officials of Regional Deputy Director (Wildlife Resurrection) before granting customs clearance.

India became a signatory to CITES in 1976. In nutshell CITES is a system of permits and certificates to regulate International wildlife trade. The specie are divided into three appendices depending upon their status in wildlife and volume of trade. In case any species is smuggled out of a country, the importing country co-operates by insisting on CITES documents. Presently, the Convention is signed by 144 countries. CITES has become an instrument to control the activities of elements, who tried to meet the demand of wildlife products by illegal means. Wildlife products from North-East States enter the illegal wildlife trade in live, raw or semi-finished forms only. A very large and diverse group of species are involved in such trade. The endangered species of plants and animals are greatly threatened owing to illegal trade in this region. CITES should be strictly followed in India in general and also in North-East States in particular.

8. Plantation of Reserved Forest: The measure involves the policy of restocking the degraded reserved forest areas with high quality species of trees. The strategy is to plant the trees at close spacing commensurate with the silvicultural need and bearing capacity. The restocking measure is expected to restore the quality and quantity of flora in the reserved forest. The schemes adopted under this measure are: (a) Teakwood Plantation Scheme; (b) Plywood Plantation Scheme; (c) Matchwood Plantation Scheme; (d) Regeneration of Degraded Forest Scheme; (e) Quick Growing Industrial Species Plantation Scheme; and (f) Minor Forest Product and Medicinal Plantation Scheme.

Social Forestry: Social forestry refers to the plantation outside the area of reserved forest. It broadly means taking forestry to the people. It was first started by the Central Government during the

Sixth Five Year Plan. Assam also along with other states launched this project during the same plan period. The social forestry scheme was originally designed to plant up all the vacant and community land and also to afforest the land where encroachment had already begun. To this end, extensive plantation programmes had been taken up on government waste lands, roadside lands, railways track side lands, canal embankments, village grazing reserves and institutional lands. In course of time, the social forestry scheme has been diversified to include planting in fallow private lands and block planting or single planting on homesteads, bunds and boundaries of the fields by persuading people to agree to this type of plantation for their own benefit and for the benefit of healthy environment. For this purpose, the necessary seedling raised in departmental nurseries is supplied to the people free of cost. Later on, plantation of avenues in the towns and cities, ancient tanks and other historical places, along with the creation of recreational parks have also been taken up under the extended scheme of social forestry to improve the bio-aesthetic impact. The implementation of the social forestry scheme, although vigorously pursued by the government has achieved only partial success because of several constraints afflicting the project.

Farm Forestry: Farm forestry is another important measure to increase the forest cover of the state. Farm-based forestry under non-governmental organization in the form of private or public limited company or corporation with investment from members of the public is being practiced with good amount of success in many states. Farm forestry is generally devoted towards developing Argo-forestry, social forestry and also plantation of commercially valuable trees. Farm forestry can go a long way in accelerating the growth of forest including production of food crops, fuel-wood, fruits, fodder etc. for the benefit of the society along with generation of income for the investors of the farm forestry projects.

Forest protection and regeneration programme, particularly social forestry schemes to be a success, involvement of people should be ensured. Participation of people can be expected only when they are made partners not only in formulating and implementing the various schemes of plantation-based on local needs, potentials and availability of inputs, but also in sharing the benefits of these programmes to meet the basic needs of the people in respect of fuel wood, fodder, minor forest produce and small timber.

Everybody should realize that forest represent the proverbial goose that lays golden eggs. If man decides to kill the goose to grab all the forest wealth at one time, the future would be bleak.

Conclusion

We find that the forest economy had a great impact on the State Economy especially during last decade. Again, we are satisfied with the intervention of the Supreme Court on preserving ecology and environment in North-East States in general and Arunachal Pradesh in particular. But this had a great impact on the economy of the state. The forestry-logging sector and manufacturing sector were affected very badly and as a result the revenue of the State decreased sharply. The socio-economic effect is badly affected more specially in the eastern part of the state where forest-based industries were largely concentrated. Now the need is for alternative ways and means to compensate the state revenue. The State should try for enhancing the entrepreneurship among the indigenous people based on other alternative resources like mining, bamboo, etc. For the State, alternative resource has to be mobilized for higher matching of state share to Central aids and grants. There must be ways and means to reduce dependency on Central Government and Central fund for self-sufficiency of the State. Given such multi-facet dimension of complexity, conservation and management of forest resources, including eco-development of the region continue to remain a special challenge. For the betterment of lives, urbanization, transportation, industrialization are necessary but we can try to minimize the deforestation.

The recent debates and developments with regard to the draft of National Environment Policy (NEP), 2004 and the Scheduled Tribes (Recognition of Forest Rights) Bill (STB), 2005 are illustrative in different ways of the manner in which social concerns are dealt with environmental policy and legislation in India. Yet, while the pros and cons of specific policies and legislations have been central to the academic debates on the environment, very little attempt has been made to trace the changes in environmental policy-making and the way of social concerns have been still problematized.

REFERENCES

Agarawal, A.K. (1986): "Planning for the Development of Arunachal's Forest—An Approach",in Das Gupta and *et. al* (ed): *Forestry Development in North-East India*, Omsons Publications, New Delhi.

Bhattacharjee, R.P. (2000): *Economic Development of Arunachal Pradesh*, Himalayan Publishers, Delhi, Itanagar, pp. 17-18 and pp. 45-49.

Bhattacharjee, R.P. (2006): "Forest Economies in Arunachal Pradesh and its Impact on State Economy", *Arunachal Review*, Directorate of Information, Public Relation and Printing, Govt. of Arunachal Pradesh, Vol.VIII,No.18, June–August, Naharlagun, Govt. of Arunachal Pradesh.

Datt, Rudder and Sundharam, K.P.M. (2004): *Indian Economy*, S. Chand & Company Ltd., New Delhi p. 92.

Diksit,V.K. (2002): "International Trade and its Impact on Wildlife Resources of North East" in Roy B.Datta and Alam K. (ed): *Forest Resources in North East India*, Omsons Publication, New Delhi.

Dutta, Nani Ranjan (1986): "Assessment of Forestry Planning in Tripura During the Five Year Plans" in Das Gupta and *et. al.* (ed): *Forestry Development in North-East India*, Omsons Publications, New Delhi..

Ghosh, A.K. (1990): "Impact of shifting cultivation in Living Natural Resources", in Majumdar, D.N. (ed): Shifting cultivation in North-East India, Omsons, Publications, Guwahati and New Delhi, pp. 178-197.

Govt. of Arunachal Pradesh (2006): *Economic Review*, Directorate of Economic and Statistics, Itanagar.

Govt. of Arunachal Pradesh (2006): Arunachal Pradesh: Human Development Report 2005, Rajiv Gandhi University, p. 171-72.

Hegde, S.N. (1988): "Coptis Teeta Wall (Mishmi Teeta): A Rare Medicinal Plant from Arunachal Pradesh", Arun for News 6(I), pp. 27-29.

Josh, M.C. (1997): Role of Herbs and Drugs in Economic Development in Pandey B.B. (ed): Patterns of Change and Potential for Development in Arunachal Pradesh, Himalayan Publishers, Itanagar, New Delhi, pp. 174 -184.

Kanjilal, U.N. Kanjilal, P.C. and Das, A. (1934): Flora of Assam, Vol. I, Govt. of Assam, Shillong.

Mandal, R.K. (2006): "Sustainability of Medicinal Plants and its Economic Viability in Arunachal Pradesh", Resarun (Journal of the Directorate of Research), Govt. of Arunachal Pradesh, Itanagar, Vol. 31, pp. 1-10.

Mandal, R.K. (2007): "Flora and Fauna in Arunachal Pradesh: Economic Viability and Sustainability" Arunachal Review,Vol. VIII, No. 23, Sept.-Nov., Naharlagun, Govt. of Arunachal Pradesh.

Mandal, R.K. (2005): ".Arunachal Pradesh Emerging as Power House"

Journal of Global Economy, Vol. 1, No. 4, , Research Centre for Social Sciences, Mumbai.

Mandal, R.K. (2008): "Forest and its Sustainability in Arunachal Pradesh" in Joseph, T.M.(ed): New Governance Paradigm: Issues in Development, Kalpaz Publications, New Delhi.

Mandal, R.K. (2007): "Herbs in Arunachal Pradesh: Economic Viability and Sustainability, Resarun: Journal of the Directorate of Research, Vol. 33, Directorate of Research, Govt. of Arunachal Pradesh, Itanagar.

Mandal, R.K. (2007): "Common Property Resources and Sustainable Development with Special Reference to Forest in Arunachal Pradesh", Ali, N. (ed.): Natural Resource Management and Sustainable Development in North-East India, Mittal Publications,New Delhi.

Mandal, R.K. (2007): "State Income in Arunachal Pradesh: Trend and Growth", *Southern Economist*, Vol. 46, No. 1, May 1, Bangalore.

Menon, Ajit (2006): "Environmental Policy Legislation and Construction of Social Nature", *EPW*, January 21-27, Vol. XLI, No. 3, pp. 188.

Mitra, Amitava (1986): "An Assessment of Forestry Planning During Five Years Plans in the North-East India" in Das Gupta and *et. al* (ed): Forestry Development in North-East India, Omsons Publications, New Delhi.

Pandey, H.C. (1988): "Some Healing Herbs of the Monk's Amongst the Minor Forest Produce", *Arun for News* 6(I), pp. 1-10.

Rao, V.M. (2003): Tribal Women of Arunachal Pradesh, Mittal Publications, New Delhi, pp. 21.

Forest and Forestry in Arunachal Pradesh, SFRI *Information Bulletin* No. 27, Director, State Forest Research Institute & Mission Director, State Bamboo Mission, Itanagar.

Website: www.sfri.org

❑❑❑

13

Biodiversity
A Threat Perfection to Sustainable Development

Introduction

In a world plagued by the proliferation of weapons of mass destruction, menace of global terrorism, global warming and climate change, owing to environmental destruction and ecological imbalances, global epidemics like HIV/AIDS, and growing incidence of poverty related death as fallout of Liberalization, Privatization, and Globalization (LPG), Gandhi as well as his philosophy appears relevant forever. Nature had evolved a wonderful pattern in forest environment. Forest is not merely a collection of trees, herbs and shrubs, but it is a complicated structure which is the result of combined influence of climate, soil, biotic interference, topography and time. The components of the natural resources exist in a delicate balance in the ecosystem. A slight change in any of the factors may alter and damage the structure of the ecosystem permanently.

When the whole world is crying for the mercy to get rid of current state of environmental degradation in the form of depletion of ozone layer, global warming and climate change, Gandhiji's very notion of development appears as a savior to the world community. Sustainability is the core to his developmental process which appears to be a best viable alternative model of development in the recent years. Long before the "World Commission on Environment and Development", coined and defined the concept sustainable development, Gandhi talked about the philosophy of the concept but in a different terms. Today, from United Nations to Government of India, everybody is talking about a form of development which will balance the fulfilment of human needs with the protection of the natural environment so that these needs can be met not only in the present, but in the indefinite future. Now the concept of sustainable development becomes indispensable to the development of the human civilization because of the limited nature of the world's resources. Knowing this inherent limitation of mother earth Gandhi warned the human society not to exploit beyond of its capacity to withstand the exploitation of natural resources for our development. Rather Gandhi advocated for the "optimal utilization" of our natural resources. For him using anything extra is a stealing. Depicting this Gandhian thought very brilliantly Satish Kumar in his article "Five Elements of Ecology" writes "the crisis of environment comes out of a utilitarian, materialistic, non-sacred, non-spiritual world-view—the Earth is there for us to use, for our comfort, for our convenience." As a consequence we have taken from nature without knowing its limits. When we have a sense of reverence, we shall take from nature only what meets our vital needs. And when we take something, we thank, we show gratitude like we take milk from the mother's breast; the mother is very happy to give her milk in the same way as the Earth is happy to give its fruits as long as we take only what we need. When the baby is full, he or she stops sucking and does not go on sucking. Well, unfortunately we humans go on sucking the Earth.

The environment assumed a central role in India, to a large extent, as a result of the first major international conference on the environment, namely, the United Nations Conference on the Human Environment (UNCHE) held in Stockholm in 1972. In preparation for this meeting, each member country was asked to prepare a report on the state of the environment. India set-up a committee on the human environment under the chairmanship of Pitambar Pant, a Planning Commission member. The outcome was three reports, one on the state of the environment, one on the problems of human settlement and one on the possible strategies to manage resources. Environmental goals were subsequently incorporated in the Fifth Five Year Plan onwards. Legislations such as Wildlife Protection Act, 1972 and the Water (Prevention and Control of Pollution) Act, 1974 were passed soon after as well (Menon, 2006).

What is Biodiversity?

Nature has varied forms of creation (plants and vegetation, fauna, insects, birds and microorganism etc.) if all these survive, living would be smooth for all the species on the earth. Thus, biodiversity would mean that there is need for diverse biological varieties to co-exist without the threat of extinction. Thus, biodiversity would simply mean "varieties of species right to existence" it also would mean that no one has the right to threaten a species right to existence. Man being the homosapien should restrain from actions that would erode species but do everything to protect them from extinction. This will not only protect the environment but also enable smooth human survival as well. Thus, all species are equally important for the sustenance for all human and sub-human species. Hence, there is an urgent need to strengthen the food-chain of all living creatures with sustainable and judicious use. Thus, the *mantra* of the century should naturally be "protect species from perish". This would call for truly holistic concerns. In the nature's scheme of things, all species play complementary and supplementary role for the survival of all living entities. One life supports the other, which is an unalterable law of nature, thus, all species have dual role — (a) every species depends on other species, and (b) every species adds to the food basket of other species as well. In this sense, all species on this planet could be deduced as food basket. Planet earth is unique in many ways, which is the only one shelter of innumerable species to coexist, though at the same time, each of them is feeding or nourishing one another. Without these diverse varieties putting up together, a few sacrificing in favour of several others, living would have come to a naught. It is for man's smooth existence that he should strive for the maintenance for biodiversity order. The unlimited greed of man is threatening the healthy and diverse biological order that needs immediate correction. He is exploiting both biological and other precious natural resource beyond the replacement levels, besides polluting them badly thereby posing greater danger to the future generation's smooth survival. In an effort to save erosion of natural resources, several threatened regions are declared as biodiversity hotspots' which includes the Western Ghats and the Eastern Himalayan that are treasure houses for several flora and fauna. It is time to make man realise the negative impact of nature on 'biodiversity' and make him act as a 'trustee' or 'conservator' of nature in true sense. Otherwise, a day may not be far off when our future generation would be compelled to face several risks including shortage of food and other requirements. The time is most appropriate to realise importance for biodiversity conservation for the good of all species. It also calls for a well planned strategy to adequately compensate people involved in biodiversity conservation by foregoing benefits of opportunity costs accruing from commercial crops or exploitation of natural resources.

Forest is the most important resource in Arunachal Pradesh. This can also be called 'primary source' in the words of Norman Myers, the famous ecologist. This resource is the mother of unique culture and traditions of local tribes and is also at the root of abundance of water, biodiversity and soil formation. Forestry is a multi-faceted business and the Department of Environment and Forest is committed to managing forestry resources in a balanced way so that a full range of benefits (economic, social and environmental) are delivered not only today but for generations to come.

Environment conservation and sustainable development are closely interlinked such that one cannot be achieved at the expense of the other. The preservation of natural resources is one of the important components of environmental conservation in the hilly areas. Forests are the most important natural resources in the hilly state and they play an important role in the economic life of the indigenous people in the State. At the same time forest represent a complex economic resource. In addition to their timber value, they are a valuable source of biodiversity, as a carbon store and in reducing the severity of floods.

The broad aim of this paper is to analyze and discuss the factors and issues that are associated with effective operations in degradation of forest and searching the ways for its conservation with the changes of traditional institutions and customary laws that may exist in managing natural resources in a self-governed tribal society of Arunachal Pradesh. However, the specific objectives are:

- To examine the real causes of deforestation and its impact in the State including institutional failures.
- To search the possible ways to conserve the forest in the State for sustainable development.

Therefore, this paper is divided into two sections. The first section seeks to an in-depth study to identify the causes of degradation and its impact of biodiversity while the second tries to find out the possible ways to conservation of biodiversity under sustainable development and conclusion flows.

SECTION - I

Causes of Deforestation and Its Impact

In Arunachal Pradesh we are destroying a good percentage of forest area every year. Now, the question arises what factors are responsible for deforestation. Among the factors we may mention is poverty, inequality in the distribution of land, low agricultural productivity, lack of infrastructural facilities, low level of economic development, industrialization, urbanization and rapid growth of population. Major causes of forest degradation are legal and illegal land-use changes; use pressure from villages inside and outside the reserve in the form of fuel wood collection and grazing of livestock; and institutions that fail to manage the forests. The grabbing of common land by the individual has been observed to a significant extent. In consequence, average distance to be covered by a household to collect CPR products has increased significantly. The size of human and livestock population, scarcity of resources (emergence of new-rich class with commercial interests), distance of the reserve area from the residential area and the quality of the management etc. are some of the important factors that determine the extent of degradation. Market close to the villages cause more severe degradation of forest resources i.e. market plays the promotional role of forest degradation. Scarcity of commons in relation to population leads to its degradation. Though the imposition of a ban on the extraction of forest and forest products by the Supreme Court in 1996 has formally checked the illegal felling of trees, the emerging neo-merchant class are taking the advantages of local power to exploit the forest resources, and in consequence, the state ownership and management have failed to prevent the conservation and degradation of many forests.

A brief analysis of the causes of natural resource degradation and depletion in the region shows that various factors, from a long time, have resulted to the worsening of the situation causing various socio-economic hazards. By this we mean the distribution of total land area among different uses. The pattern of land use, which is a complex phenomenon, in general is the result of the action and interaction of factors like physical characteristics of land, supply of resources like labour and capital, the framework of socio-economic institutions, etc. There is virtually no planning in the field of land utilization. The existing pattern of land utilization has evolved over the past few centuries under the pressure of increasing population. So far land use is concerned the North-Eastern Region, like other parts of the country, seems to have no planning virtually in this field and a good portion of land is lying as cultivable waste. In the North-East India even though agriculture is the only source of livelihood to the majority of the people, the rational land utilization was not possible because of difficult terrain. Being agricultural backward economy, the productive forces have been arrested by retrogressive agrarian land relations. As a result, more and more area has been brought under cultivation by clearing forests, which meant damage to the ecological balance. In the first place, those who caused this damage were not aware of the repercussions of their actions. There are some major factors which are responsible for destruction of forest and thereby flora and fauna in the state discussed below.

Presently, some of the major issues facing the resource managers, researchers, policy-makers, international institutions, and some NGOs are: (i) loss of biodiversity with its yet unknown potential consequences, (ii) increased rate of deforestation and fragmentation, (iii) inadequate knowledge of ecological functioning and complex relationships between and within biotic and abiotic components of the forest biome, (iv) adverse impact on indigenous communities and forest dwellers, (v) inadequate public awareness and lack of transparency (vi) resources exploitation, and (vii) adverse changes in soil, water and climate due to deforestation.

Shifting Cultivation

However, the problem of natural resources degradation particularly forests in Northeast India appeared to be very serious even during the regime of New Forest Policy explained which envisages that this strategy might have not been implemented with its true spirit. One of the assumptions of the new forest policy was that the forest dependent poor tribal communities are responsible for depletion of these resources as they not only over exploit but also practice shifting cultivation which needs clearing of forests and hence leads to deforestation. Shifting cultivation directly reduces available forest resources and indirectly enhances soil erosion, increases silting of rivers, streams and dams, and causes an imbalance in environmental factors. More specifically, it is argued that the practice of jhum cultivation is the principal factor of deforestation/ degradation although a generalized caused and effect relationship between loss of forest and shifting cultivation is misleading because deforestation is a complex socio-economic, cultural and political phenomenon. Moreover, the degradation caused to forests as a result of shifting cultivation depends on the habits and beliefs of the people, the area available, development index, land-man ratio, the population density and the proximity to the market. The forest resources of a specified area may be degraded due to a variety of reasons including government policy of issuing timber permits, market penetration, economic development, and practice of subsistence agriculture and so on. So far management of natural assets is concerned; the question of property rights plays an important role. Most of these resources are treated as open access due to absence or undefined property rights. But unlike other tribal regions, in Northeast India communities and private individuals in most cases enjoy the rights of ownership of forest lands. As a result, it seems that the new Bill on Forest Rights will have little impact on forest condition. Hence, the real problem with respect to the management has to be analyzed in the context of socio-economic, cultural, and political set-up of the tribal communities in this remote and isolated part of the country. It is argued that the traditional institutional arrangements of tribal communities were effective in sustainable management of local resources for a long time and most likely their breakdown in recent times with the introduction of market economy and development has been behind the present situation of rapid degradation of forest and other natural resources.

The practice of shifting cultivation, cropping of forest areas for a year or two, then clearing another area leaving the first one fallow to revert to scrub forests is widely practiced by tribal communities in the hilly mountainous forest regions. The fallow periods have been gradually shortened with increase in population. If the pressure on land increases, the soil has no chance to regenerate and wider and wider tracts of otherwise productive forests get destroyed. It is noticed that the land under shifting cultivation is still increasing in the north-eastern region causing several imbalances in the ecology of the region.

Agriculture occupies an important a major occupation of the people of the state. According to 2001 census, about 79.66 per cent of the State's population is living in rural areas and 58.44 per cent of the total workers are cultivators. Due to scarcity of plain land in the State, the rural people have to practice shifting cultivation, i.e., *Jhum* cultivation in order to fulfil their minimum requirement for food. The shifting cultivation is called slush and burn method of cultivation. It is labour-intensive process of farming with extensive use of land. The technology being primitive, the level of production and income is very low. It occupies a distinct place in the socio-economic fabric of tribal economy of this State. The man who practices *jhum* cultivation i.e., shifting cultivation is called *jhumia.* The jhumia selects the field on the slope of the hill on rotation basis. Due to deterioration in fertility of soil the *jhumia* is compelled to shift his cultivation on another plot. He keeps the land fallow for a number of years for regeneration of forests. Again, he uses the same land after a number of years. That is why, this process is also called 'shifting cultivation'. This practice is not only done in Arunachal Pradesh but also in all north-eastern states due to lack of sufficient plain land. The area under shifting cultivation and number of families are engaged are shown in Table 13.1 in context of North-East States.

Table 13.1: Shifting cultivation in the North-East Region.

State	*Annual Area under Shifting cultivation (sq. kms.)*	*Fallow Period (in years)*	*Minimum Area under Shifting cultivation one time or other (sq. kms.)*	*No. of families practicing shifting-cultivation*
Arunachal Pradesh	700	3 – 10	2,100	54,000
Assam	696	2 – 10	1,392	58,000
Manipur	900	4 – 7	3,600	70,000
Meghalaya	530	5 – 7	2,650	52,290
Mizoram	630	3 – 4	1,890	50,000
Nagaland	190	5 – 8	1,913	1,16,046
Tripura	223	5 – 9	1,115	43,000
Total	3869		14,660	4,43,336

Source: The Task Force Report on Shifting Cultivation, Ministry of Agriculture, 1983.

Not also are the *jhumias* facing serious economic problem because the forests in their traditional economic role are unable to sustain them, but society as a whole, also has to pay a price for the extensive deforestation in the State in the form of soil erosion, floods and droughts. Therefore, any well-designed forest policy will have to divert the *jhumias* from jhuming by providing them with alternative occupations in the long run while in the short run, it will have to ensure that the jhumias can derive a higher income from their forest based occupations. Both the long and the short-term measures have two-fold aim to protect the forests and to improve the economic condition of the jhumias. The two aims are complementary because forests cannot be saved without improving the standard of living of the forest-dwellers and *vice versa*. Any policy to be successfully implemented has to be acceptable to the people for whom it is designed. So an exercise is to be carried out in the course of the study on shifting cultivation in Arunachal Pradesh to find out the opinion of the jhumias themselves regarding their preferred occupation. It is found that although the jhumias are aware of the problems of jhum cultivation and the low economic returns derived from this occupation, the majority of them are not willing to give it up at least in the short run. The other forest-based occupations like plantations of coffee and rubber can prove to be very attractive as a source of earning a living for the jhumias. Social forestry and other reforestation schemes will reduce the dependence of the *jhumias* on the traditional use of forest. These measures, if successfully carried out, will regenerate the economic life of the *jhumias* as well as the forests of the state.

Deforestation, due to practice of shifting cultivation, is considered world's most pressing land use problem. The effects of deforestation on ecology are too well known. The role of forest in maintaining ground-water level, preventing soil erosion and land slide, controlling flood in plains, reducing air pollution have been discussed at length in several publications. The extent of deforestation of tropical forest has caused worldwide alarm as tropical forests provide more than 50 per cent of modern medicine. Tropical forests are living museums and laboratories that have yielded only a tiny fraction of their treasures to scientific study.In course of shifting cultivation remarkable varieties of flora and fauna are disappearing, which need immediate attention for extensive and intensive studies.

The type of vegetations destroyed depends upon the length of jhum cycle. A dense forest of long cycle has more tree species than grasses, whereas a forest of short cycle has more number of grasses. All the forest resources are disappearing and become rare due to deforestation and illegal felling of trees. The ecological balance favouring the complete hydrological cycle has been seriously upset over vast areas due to ignorance or lack of appreciation of methods of conserving and managing natural vegetation (whether a forest, grass land or mixed type) and of clearing the vegetation for cultivation. This misuse and destruction of plants cover combined with great increase in human and livestock population has created intense competition for natural resources. In the continued absence of conservation and correctly integrated land use system, overall habitat deterioration has become very widespread.

Forest Grazing

The practice of indiscriminate livestock grazing leads to forest degradation. The excessive and uncontrolled grazing brings about a physical damage to the vegetation and cause erosion of soil, spread of disease, pests and weeds. The unlimited and continuous grazing in the forest interferes with the productive and protective functions of the forest.

Forest Fires for Shifting Cultivation

Forest fires bring widespread damage to the productive capacity and the protective value of forest, destroy wildlife and damage the recreational and the scenic value. The causes may be natural, accidental or intentional, etc. The preservation of forest ecosystem demands the elimination of the frequency and severity of the fires. In the months of March and April, the *jhumia* generally uses fires the forest for *jhum* cultivation. It is generally seen everywhere in the State even in the surrounding areas of capital city, Itanagar. The Government machinery becomes fails to stop it. After much *hullabaloo* over the burning of forest in the Capital Complex that led to the formation of an action plan and appeals from Governor Gen. (Retd.) J.J. Singh and Chief Minister Dorjee Khandu, forest burning continues, mocking at the 'action plan' (*Arunachal Front*, March 21, 2009).

Impact of Current Development on Forest

Urbanization

The North-Eastern States in general and Arunachal Pradesh in particular are proceeding towards the path of development though the progress is slow and uneven. Because of rapidly growing job facilities, business activities, there is a change of interest from agricultural activities to modern enterprises, government jobs, etc. which leads to the speeding up of cities and towns. Those who migrate to cities or towns are in reality pushed out of villages due to economic and social pressures. Generally, the immediate outcome of urbanization is that the urban areas become over crowded which leads to congestion. For dwelling of large number of people, for opening and widening of business establishment, forests are destroyed/cleared. Finally, overall pollution (air, water, soil, noise) takes place, which are not only responsible for degradation of natural resources but also of environment. Till 1961 census the State of Arunachal Pradesh was entirely rural. There was no urban centre in the State. Census-wise trend in urbanization is shown in the following Table 13.2.

Table 13.2: Census-wise Urban Centres.

Census	*No. of Census Towns*	*Name of the Census Towns*
1961	NIL	-
1971	4	Bomdila, Along, Pasighat and Tezu
1981	6	Bomdila, Along, Pasighat and Tezu, Nharlagun and Itanagar.
1991	10	Bomdila, Along, Pasighat and Tezu, Nharlagun and Itanagar, Ziro, Roing, Namsai and Khonsa.
2001	17	Bomdila, Along, Pasighat and Tezu, Narlagun and Itanagar, Ziro, Roing, Namsai and Khonsa, Tawang, Seppa, Daporijo, Basar, Changlang, Jairampur and Deomali.

Source: Various Census Report.

All these towns are administrative centres in most cases. Before the establishment of administrative centres, *these places were full of forest.* According to 1991 census 12.80 per cent people live in ten urban areas while as per 2001 census 20.41 people live in seventeen urban areas. The decennial urban growth rate in the State has been recorded as 139.63 in 1971-81, 167.04 in 1981-91 and 101.24 in 1991-2001.

Rapid Population Growth

Rapidly increasing population in Arunachal Pradesh caused not only by large scale influx of people from Bangladesh and Nepal, but also by natural growth has put immense pressure on the supply of land for various purposes like housing, industrial and other development projects and also for agricultural production and grazing of animals, etc. As the available land in the state is insufficient for these myriad purposes, additional land had to be procured by illegal encroachment upon the forest lands, first in the unclassified forest, then in the reserved forest also.

Rapid population growth is one of the major factors of the depletion of natural resources in north-east states in general and in

Arunachal Pradesh in particular. Though it is true that population growth is welcome as it initiates and helps in the growth process of any region or country, but it is up to a certain limit beyond which it works adversely. The north-east region is witnessing excessive pressure of population, which acts as one of the causes of natural degradation. Growing population creates extra demand in terms of basic physical requirement of shelter, fuelwood, food; etc. that makes it necessary to exploit forest and other resources directly accelerating the deforestation. The direct impact of the increasing pressure of population has been in terms of absolute decline in the area under forest as forest land that has been converted to agricultural land to meet the growing demand of growing population.

Increasing population coupled with widespread poverty has generated pressure on our natural resources and led to a degradation of agricultural land and forest. The forest resources are threatened due to overgrazing, commercial household needs, encroachment, unsustainable practices like unscientific cultivation (shifting cultivation, burn cultivation, etc.) and development activities. Excessive fuelwood removal, indiscriminate felling of trees for timber needs, inadequate natural regeneration have also threatened to the rich biological diversity of 1,67,486 sq. kms. forest cover of North-East India with widest variety of biomass.

The human population census was conducted for the first time in Arunachal Pradesh in 1961. Population increases in 2001 by 326.23 per cent in comparison to the population of 1961. The growth of population and density of population census-wise are shown below in Table 13.3.

Table 13.3: Population Growth and Population Density Since 1961.

Census	*Persons*	*Population Density*
1961	336558	4
1971	467511	6 (5.58)
1981	628050	8 (7.50)
1991	864558	10 (10.32)
2001	1097968	13 (13.03)

Source: Census Report, Arunachal Pradesh, 1971, 1981, 1991 and 2001.

Notes: (i) Figures in the parentheses show actual values.

(ii) Population Density = Total Population ÷ Area in sq. km.

The decennial population growth rate since 1961 in the State has been recorded as 38.91 per cent in 1961-71, 35.15 per cent in 1971-81, 36.83 per cent in 1981-91 and 26.21 per cent in 1991-2001. It is more than all-India average.

We have observed a high trend of growth of population in Arunachal Pradesh. To see the trend of population in the State in future, we can fit a mathematical equation by the method of least square. Let us now construct the necessary table and make necessary computation where we take Y as population and X as year. We take 1981 census year as origin shown in Table 13.4.

Table 13.4: Calculations for Population Projection through Least Squire Method.

Census Year	*Y (Population)*	*X (Year)*	*X^2*	*XY*
1961	336558	– 2	4	– 673116
1971	467511	– 1	1	– 467511
1981	628050	0	0	0
1991	864558	+ 1	1	+ 864558
2001	1097968	+ 2	4	+ 2195936
Total	ΣY=3394645	ΣX=0	ΣX^2=10	ΣXY=1919867

Now, $Y = a + bX$ ...(1) or, $\Sigma Y = na + b\Sigma X$ ...(2)

and $\Sigma XY = a\Sigma X + b\Sigma X^2$ ...(3)

We substitute the values shown above in the equations (2) and (3), solving them, we get

$$a = 678929 \text{ and } b = 191986.7$$

We put the values in equation (1), we have

$$Y = 678929 + 191986.7\ X$$

After getting this equation, we can find the population strength of any census year.

Suppose for census year 2011, the population,

$$Y = 678929 + 191986.7 \times 3 = 1254889.1$$

For census year 2021, the population,

$$Y = 678929 + 191986.7 \times 4 = 1446875.8$$

And for census year 2051, the population,

$$Y = 678929 + 191986.7 \times 7 = 2022835.9$$

If we compare the population of 1961, the population of 2051 will be six times more. All people especially the rural people have to response to the family programme for their own benefit in particular and for the state in general.

Hypothetically, it is shown with the help of equation. It gives us only idea. With the development of medical science, the population growth can be checked.

Growth of Non-Tribal Population

The tribal communities in North-east India who constitute a very high percentage of the total population being economically week and socially backward are usually dependent on natural resources for their existence. This is so because the tribal people are basically forest dwellers and from pre-historic age, they have been found to live as a close component of natural resources particularly to forest ecosystem. Forest and tribal people have a symbiotic relationship and the existence of both is mutually beneficial. The life of these primitive people is woven around forest ecology and forest resources. Forest satisfy a great range of human needs which vary from tangible raw materials (economic goods) like fuel and fodder, food and shelter, to intangible environmental benefits. The intangible vary from aesthetic enjoyment to protection against soil erosion and regulation of water supply. The primitive tribal communities collect their livelihood needs through hunting, gathering, and fishing, food production mostly at subsistence level. The forests not only provide them food, material to build house, fuelwood, fodder for the cattle, but also satisfy the deep rooted tribal sentiments. It is also necessary to note that woman and children of these communities are found to be engaged in most of the subsistence activities within the forests. Hence, the management of the forests must be for the satisfaction of the day-to-day needs of the tribals and the forest dwellers in respect of firewood, leaf fodder, small timber, edible fruit, leaves, gums, medicinal plants, resins, etc.

The indigenous people have a unique understanding of tropical forest ecology and resources because their culture has been evolved with the forests. They have learned over the centuries how to utilize the bio-resources in sustainable manner. No other person understands and loves forests as the tribal. Their lifestyle totally depends upon the forests. They are integral part of the forest ecosystem. Their biodiversity management and conservation system has proved to be an ideal system. If we see the census data since 1961, we get the following percentage of tribal people in the State shown in Table 13.5. If the trend keeps its same motion, we can calculate the future trend with the help of Least Squire Method taking 1981 as origin shown in Table 13.5.

Table 13.5: Tribal Population (in %)

Census Year	*% of Tribal People*
1961	88.76
1971	79.02
1981	69.82
1991	63.65
2001	64.22

Source: Different Census Issues.

Transportation

Till 1947, there were only three jeepable roads between Pasighat and Kobo by 35 kilometres, Sadiya-Tezu-Denzing by 77 kilometres and still well road 56 kilometres (*Source:* N.C.A.E.R – Techno-Economic Survey of NEFA, 1967, p. 91). So, the total length of roads was only 168 kms., till 1947. Before independence the colonial government did not take any effort to initiate the development process and the British indifference towards the area was mainly due to the fact that the area did not possess any readily exploitable resources. After the independence of the country, the Government of India undertook the development of transport and communication with a view to open up this remote state of India and, therefore, to facilitate the rapid development of the state. In the development plans, the government has been attaching high priority to the construction of roads and as a result the total length of roads constructed in the state stood at about 15021.80 kms. including 399.80 kms. under National Highway giving the road density of 17.9 kms. per 100 sq. kms. of area at the end of March, 2004. The development of roads and its density (Road length per 100 sq. kms.) are shown in Tabie 13.6.

Table 13.6: Category-wise Length of Roads and Its Density during Ninth and Tenth Plan.

(In. km.)

Year	*Total length of roads*	*Density of roads*
1	*5*	*6*
31.03.2000	13982.20	16.70
31.03.2001	13982.20	16.70
31.03.2002	13982.20	16.70
31.03.2003	14450.47	17.26
31.03.2004	15021.791	17.94

Source: Directorate of Economics and Statistics, Government of Arunachal Pradesh, Itanagar.
Note: Density of Road = Total length of roads ÷ total area.

The impact of road transport is wide ranging which includes agriculture, industry, trade and commerce which cumulatively affect overall development of a region. But at the same time the State has to face deforestation and thereby to destroy the herbs.

Industrialization

At present there are 14 district industries centres in the State. Three DICs provide all possible help and guidance to the prospective entrepreneurs for taking up industrial ventures and provide services for identification of suitable schemes, preparation of project reports, supply and management of raw materials and marketing of finished product, etc. The DICs also organizes trainings at district level to create awareness amongst the entrepreneurs. They also assist entrepreneurs to avail incentive packages and facilities given by both Central and State government. In Arunachal Pradesh at the time of independence, there was almost absence of industry excepting cottage industries in the village. But at present there are 15 medium scale industries which are mostly saw mill, plywood and 11 veneer mills functioning in the State. In spite of many obstacles in the way of development of large and medium scale industries, significant numbers of small-scale industrial units have come up in the State over the year due to active support and positive policy of the government. There were 471 registered small scale industrial units functioning at the end of March 2003 mostly engaged in activities like blacksmithy, tin smithy, carpet making, carpentry, wool knitting handloom and weaving, cane and bamboo works, printing press, etc.

Mining and Querrying Activities

In North-East Region the unsystematic extraction of minerals is creating environmental problems thereby ruining the region's land, water, forests and air. Mining practices in large scale has made agricultural and forest land into stockyards, townships, roads etc. and also removed vegetation and topsoil. Further, constant air pollution occurs due to disposal of mining waste and mineral dust from mines and also reduces agricultural productivity. Moreover, water resources get polluted, as rain water that passes through mineral wastes, are flowing into rivers and streams. Furthermore, large-scale deforestation, soil erosion result due to mining operation, which is again responsible for various health hazards to the people.

Impact of Deforestation

Environmental Problems

Deforestation and burning of fossil fuels contribute to global warning, which has now become a local issue for every citizen for action. Therefore, restrictive exploitation of forests now in Arunachal Pradesh leads to reduction in Green House Gas emissions which are the main causes of global warming. Reduction in Greenhouse Gas emissions in Arunachal Pradesh will benefit all mankind on planet earth. This State is, therefore, now contributing its bit in fighting global warming.

Deforestation does not take long, while a forest takes a very long time to develop, often hundreds of years, through a series of successive species, before it becomes a self-contained, viable ecosystem. The strength of a forest system lies in its variety and the inter-dependence of its various elements. A forest maintains the humidity of the soil, its dry leaves, bird droppings and the remaining of the living organisms to add to its fertility, and the various species to support one another. The animals and insects living in the forest maintain a food chain and a balance in the production of the various species. Without forests, agriculture would die. Forest acts as a pumping station as reservoir, hoards an enormous amount of water in the leaves, stems, and roots of trees during the rainy season, and releases it slowly over the year. Without forests, the agriculture would be without water for most of the year, and there would be nothing to resist soil erosion during the months of heavy rains. Forests are necessary for maintaining the balance in the agriculture system. No less important is the need for a sound statistical base on forests, so that the policy makers are aware of what is going on, and are able to implement a system of forest management which augment the total 'stock' of forests while at the same time producing enough of the annual 'flow' to take care of the needs of the country's economy for forest products. Selection of trees is an equally important matter, and again their impact on other species, animal husbandry, and agriculture would have to be examined, in addition to the revenue generating capacity of those trees. While a commercial approach cannot be avoided, this alone should not be the criterion, regardless of its impact on both the physical and the social environment.

The rich and varied altitudinal and climatic conditions in the territory have given rises to a wide spectrum of vegetation in which several of the important forests occur. These are tropical rain forests, the sub-tropical forests, the temperate forests, the sub-alpine forests. The tribal people depend mainly on forests for their survival, livelihood, occupation and employment. The way they exploit forests has pervasive effect on all other aspects of culture, and the socio-culture milieu emerges as an interlocking system in which case and effect are intertwined in a manner that when one element is significantly altered, it has direct and indirect repercussions on the other parts of the system. The tribal people living near the forest areas depend solely on forests and its produce. A house in a tribal village is almost made of forest produce — the roofing leaves, the posts and the walls made of bamboo and small timber, the tying canes, etc. Strips of canes are used as fasteners for the rafters while building houses. The household utensils, the bamboo plates, pipes for carrying water, spoons and ladles, and the drinking cups are all shaped out of the forest produce. The people of the interior areas use beaten barks of forests trees as clothing material for specific uses. They collect many types of tuber, fruits and seeds which help these people to survive during the period of food deficit. The berries, nuts, honey, fruits and roots of all kinds abound and in the process of socializations, the tribal learns to grow which roots, berries and fruits are edible, where these are available , when and for how long etc. Hundreds of such edible items and the time of their availability are commonly known. He learns how to distinguish between poisonous and non-poisonous edible mushrooms which grow abundantly in the rainy season. Certain organic substances, leaves, flowers, roots are known to have intoxication, catalytic and decomposition and medicinal properties. Some of these are used for intoxicating fish while doing river fishing, for fermenting rice and millet beer called Apung, for making dyes and extracting vegetable fibre. For medicines, the tribal discerningly distinguish between various kinds of plants, weeds and herbs which have therapeutic value both curative and preventive. Some of the folk medicines of the main tribes of Arunachal Pradesh namely Nyishi and the Apa Tanis are very important. Various types of timber, bamboo, cane, leaves and fruits of medicinal value and the bark of the trees are the common items which are collected by the tribal from the forests and are sold to the people of the plains. The forests provide a good amount of animal protein to the tribal people who are now supplemented to a considerable extent by domesticated and semi-domesticated animals and poultry. A bulk of the tribal population is still depended directly or indirectly on forest and forest produce. It will remain so, unless there is drastic change in the way of life. They use herb and medicinal plants to cure their diseases. They have evolved their own system of soil and forest conservation because they are vitally concerned with preservation and continuance of forests and exemplify the age-old pattern of co-existence between man and nature.

The forest provides a good amount of revenue to the state exchequer. Other factors responsible include lack of research and market exploration, incentives to develop logging, lumbering and forest-based industries apart from paper, personnel trained in commercial management of forests and modern equipment. With the growing pressure on natural resources various forms of environmental degradation are evident in different parts of the country especially in the north-eastern states. Wildlife resources are highly sensitive to such degradations as habitat destruction which leads to extinction of species in the majority of cases.

The status of wildlife in any area, therefore, may act as a good bio-indicator to measure environmental quality in the natural ecosystem. The important natural resources are land comprising soil, water and associated plant and animal life involving the total ecosystem. Our future depends on the preservation and improvement of the natural resources. Today, on the one side, we are concerned about the nature and its preservation and on the other side, degradation is taking place in land, water, air etc. Soil, water and forest are land-based resources. They exist in a dynamic equilibrium with interaction among all living and non-living components of the ecosystem. Man is the only component of the ecosystem which in spite of being a part of the dynamic milieu, tends to place himself 'apart' from it, and by doing so causes great damage. In reality, the effect of humanity on the ecosystem since the dawn of the modern era has so increased that it has now become a bio-geochemical factor itself.

According to Gandhi "there is enough on earth for everybody's need, but not enough for anybody's greed". So need and greed have to be differentiated and, we must not over use or over-exploit the natural resources in the guise of development. Gandhi advises us to contain our greed and to allow our future generation to taste the fruit of real development. Spirituality helps in keeping our greed for materials and resources in check and sustainable development can take place when we use the resources for our needs and not for our greed. His advices are antidote not only to our consumerist culture but also can save the mother earth from most dangerous phenomena called "Global Warming and Climate Change".

Undoubtedly, because of deforestation the area, quality, quantity, and diversity of forest are fast decreasing. This is mainly due to the rate of deforestation, which is alarmingly faster than the natural regeneration. If a vast area is deforested rapidly, re-growth of forest over that area may take a long time depending upon the rate of regeneration in that climatic zone. Moreover, it may or may not reach to climax regeneration in foreseeable time. Due to cutting of trees not only in forest area there occur innumerable changes in the ecosystem, especially related with depletion of plant and animal species. In fact, the clearance of forest has already caused extinction of a number of species and many are either threatened or at verge of extinction. The World Commission of Forests and Sustainable Development (WCFSD) in their report (1999) has mentioned that survival of about 12.5 per cent of the world's 270,000 species of plant and 75 per cent of the world's mammals is threatened by the decline of the forest cover. The decline in the forest cover would also affect 350 million people of the world who depend entirely on forest for their subsistence (Hussain, 2002).

Loss of biodiversity and disturbance of the ecosystem continue to be a major global threat to future development, says the fourth Report of the Global Environment Outlook (GEO) brought out by the United Nations. Disbalance in the distribution of land, fresh water and marine biodiversity is more rapid than at any time in human history. Ecosystem such as forests, wet lands and dry lands are being transformed, in some cases, irreversibly degraded. The rate of species extinction is increasing, and a great majority of them, including the commercially important fish stocks, is declining in distribution or abundance or both. Biodiversity plays multiple roles in the daily lives of people through the supply of ecosystem services. In agriculture, biodiversity contributes in regulating and supporting services through soil formation, nutrient cycling, and pollination. The Report says that poor people in rural and remote areas tend to be most directly affected by the deterioration or loss of ecosystem services. In view of this, many governments have established and adopted the 2010 biodiversity target to reduce the rate of loss of biodiversity at global, regional and national scales. Though there have been local success stories of sustainable use of biodiversity, at a global level, and in most regions of the world, biodiversity continues to be lost because current policies and economic systems do not incorporate the values of biodiversity effectively in either the political or the market systems, and many policies that are already in place, are yet to be fully implemented, says the report (*The Arunachal Times*, 2007). North-East India is a home of many endemic fauna and flora and many valuable wildlife products which originates from this region. These resources are degrading rapidly due to demand from international trade. Despite strict legislative provisions certain elements resort to illegal and unauthorized wildlife trade. The insurgency and disturbed conditions have made the law enforcement difficult and complicated the matter. Further, ninety eight per cent to the North-East India Border is with neighbouring countries. This border is very porous and constant source of smuggling activities. The region is a store house of biodiversity with its species richness of flora and fauna. The North-East Region (NER) represents a wide range of physiographic and eco-climatic conditions and is endowed with vast and luxuriant vegetation ranging from tropical to alpine with rich gene pool of both wild and cultivated plant species. The flora of the region basically exhibits an Indo-Malayan affinity. However, the flora elements of other parts of India and far off countries have also contributed to its richness and diversity. India is recognized as one of the 12 mega-diversity centres of the world because of its rich diversity of biological resources. The richness of biological diversity of the NER could be established because of its 650 species of orchids, more than 450 species of grasses, 61 species of bamboo, 65 texa of rhododendrons, 42 species of Impatient, 34 species of Hedychin besides a large number of canes, timber trees, ferns, lichens and wildlife of 15,000 flowering plants (6% of world's total) of India 33 per cent are estimated to be endemic to North-East India. Nearly 500 plant species are threatened. Since, North-East India is an area of rich endemism, a large number of endemic plant species of the region are threatened. Mamal fauna comprise of 372 species of which 63 per cent are found in Assam alone and a good number of fauna are threatened due to loss of forest covers (B.K. Sarma, 2002).

The most important natural resources are land comprising soil, water and associated plant and animal lives involving the total ecosystem. Our future depends on the preservation and improvement of the natural resources. Today, on one side we are concerned about the nature and its preservation and on the other side degradation takes place in land, water, air, etc. The forest is now under threat. As a result, Loss of biodiversity and disturbance of the ecosystem continue to be a major global threat to future development, says the Fourth Report of the Global Environment Outlook (GBO) brought out by the United Nations. Disbalance in the distribution of land, freshwater and marine biodiversity is more rapid than at any time in human history. Ecosystems such as forest, wet lands and dry lands are being transformed, in some cases, irreversibly degraded. The rate of species extinction was increasing, and a great majority of them, including the commercially important fish stocks, are declining in distribution or abundance or both. Biodiversity plays multiple roles in the daily lives of people through the supply of ecosystem services. In agriculture, biodiversity contributes in regulating and supporting services through soil formation, nutrient cycling and pollination. Though there have been local success stories of sustainable use of biodiversity in the State, it continues to be lost because current policies and economic systems do not incorporate the values of biodiversity effectively in either the political or the market system and many policies that are already in place, are yet to be fully implemented.

It is pertinent to mention that Eastern Himalayas including Arunachal Pradesh has been identified as one of the world's to 18 biodiversity hotspots. And after Rio Convention (1992), the global concern for preserving the biological diversity has increased tremendously. Forest has been playing an important role in socio-economic development of this region-specially hill tribal inhabited region, as a source of subsistence, employment, and raw-materials for industry. The indigenous people's role in ecological balance, environmental stability and sustainable development has been recognized in National Forest Policy, 1988. The forest resources of the region are under tremendous pressure due to increasing demand for human and livestock. Too much of extraction has led to forest degradation and disaster in ecological balance in recent time in this region. It is clear that North-Eastern India has been fast losing its pride of place in the matter of environment and ecology. There has been exodus of population to the hills causing damage to the forest resources. All these have created severe problems to the whole region in the form of land sliding in the hill and siltage in the rivers. This tells upon not only on the atmospheric condition of the area but also on the livelihood of the people dependent either on forest or on agriculture or on both. Forest dwellers, belonging to different communities, tribes and religion, enjoying for long the traditional and usufractory rights over forest and other natural resources are felling threatened by the forest policies pursued now. There has been a sense of insecurity for the great majority of the rural people who are not only threatened about their present livelihood but also very apprehensive about the future generations. The government, the NGOs and other statutory bodies concerned with improvement of environment should take appropriate and adequate initiatives. All such initiatives should aim at ensuring participation of the broad masses of tribal population. This can only be done by guaranteeing their rights on the forests and lands of the region.

Natural Environment and Ecological Balance

There is a great need today to create a comprehensive awareness of the need to have adequate safeguards against the destruction of the natural environment. The concern for preservation of environment is multi-dimensional and it relates itself to many disciplines and facets of the administration. The protection of environment and ecological balance are the concern of the people all over the globe. The Northeastern region of the country, which forms major part of the Indian portion of the Eastern Himalayas, is not only rich in forest and related natural resources, but also very much rich in biodiversity. It has myriads of complex problems with distinct constitutional and legal features.

Wildlife in the natural situation constitutes the most important component of the ecosystem, which participates affectively in the energy flow and bio-geo-chemical cycling. Animal-plant, plant—plant and animal-animal interactions are the basic milestone of the success of an ecosystem and its productivity. As such, the richness of the ecosystem means the capacity of hold high species diversity but deforestation has threatened the very fabric of the survival of wildlife and the ecosystem in the region. Forests are scarce and are becoming increasingly scarce due to pressure on it. It can be attributed to increase in population and demand for forest resources. The forest resources of Arunachal Pradesh are under tremendous pressure due to increasing demand for human and livestock. Too much of extraction has led to forest degradation and disaster in ecological balance in recent times in this region and this led to famous Supreme Court verdict on 12-12-1996 banning exploitation of forest resources specially industrial wood in Arunachal Pradesh and other States. Timber extraction in the State was taken up on a large scale till 1995-96. Hence, a large number of woods based industries cropped up. A timber trade in the State had also increased through the operation of tree permits. There was halt on this trade after a Supreme Court Judgment on 12th December, 1996 on a writ petition (civil) No. 202 filed by Shri T.N. Godavarman Thirumulkpad. In recent years, the State's rich biodiversity has increasingly come under threat. The hastening paces of developmental activities in the last three decades, and the improvement in the communication network, have meant increased access. Road building has established communication but the blasting process involved has meant the loss of valuable habitat. The rapid monetization of the barter economies has meant increased trade in timber. A number of hydropower projects have been commissioned, and these projects are at various stages of progress. The urbanization process has meant the destruction of the forest cover adjacent to the new townships that have come up. Another significant threat to the fragile ecosystem and biodiversity of the State is due to the shifting cultivation and the shortening of the jhum cycle and introduction of commercial plantation.

Loss of forest on our live can be interpreted in another way which has a long run implication. Destruction of forest disturbs ecological balance also. The forests regulate the earth's temperature regime, water cycle, control floods and droughts and help to balance the CO_2 and Oxygen in the atmosphere. Another cost of deforestation is the loss of biodiversity in the nature. The biodiversity treaty calls for the conservation of ecosystem (Rio-summit, 1992). Because of reckless destruction of forest for domestic fuel and for commercial gains about 17,000 living species are destroyed annually.

In addition, there is the illegal trade of forest projects such as timber, medicinal plants, orchids, animal hide, musk gland and birds, which are smuggled out of the State by poachers. Bio-piracy is a new challenge manifested in a number of ways. Sometimes, the operators enter the State, develop contracts, and smuggle out valuable species, mainly of flora, without the knowledge of the government. Given their highly sophisticated methods of operation, this type of bio-piracy is very difficult to detect. The creation of public consciousness, apart from the enhanced vigilance of the government, can help to control this problem. We know that each of the flora and fauna has its special genetic qualities. Different tree species has specific root system and feeding habits. The Botanical

Survey of India has identified 47,688 of plant out of which 10,400 are known for their rich medicinal properties. In the North-East India, as a result of deforestation, about 650 species of plant and 70 species of animal have been listed as endangered. The region has about 50 per cent montane plants species in India of which many are endemic in nature.

Environmental problems in the State may be attributed to two major reasons: (i) due to negative effects of the process of economic growth and development and (ii) due to conditions of poverty and under-development. As per the Forest Report of 1997 based on visual and digital interpretation of satellite data pertaining to 1995-96, the total forest cover in India is 6,33,397 sq.km which is 19 per cent of the total geographical area of the country. During the period (1989-1995), forest cover in North-East India (NEI) was reduced by 2,037 sq. kms. while in the rest of the country it was increased by 933 sq. kms. This reduction of forest cover in the NEI is quite alarming.

Medicinal Plants under Threat in the State

Due to the shifting cultivation, growth of urbanization, growth of population, growth of transportation, growth of industrialization and overall development programmes, the hitherto virgin vegetation has become a victim of sudden large-scale changes upsetting the balance of nature. At conference in Guwahati, experts from the State Forest Research Institute, Itanagar, Botanical Survey of India and the G. B. Pant Institute of Himalayan Environment and Development, Itanagar made an assessment of 47 plant species lying under threat. Out of the 47, five are threatened at the global level and are red listed by the International Union for Conservation of Nature (IUCN). This endemic species include *Amentotaxus asamica, Coptis teeta, Gymnocladus assamicus, Piper Pedicellatum, P. Peepuloides, Aquilaria malaecensis, Dienia muscifera, Rauvolifia serpentina* and *smilax glabra* are reported to be critically endangered.

Medical Tourism Exports by India

Now-a-days, India is in a position to give world class medical treatment at a low cost in comparison to the developed countries. India has advantage due to low cost of treatment, large number and high quality of Indian health care professionals, world class corporate hospitals (Apollo, Escorts), presence in niche areas. Presently, Patients from developing and developed countries are coming to receive treatment in Indian hospitals. Health tourists from Middle East, CIS countries, neighbouring countries, Non-resident Indians in developed countries, foreigners from some developed countries are coming very day. It is ovserved that130,000 international patients came to India (2003) from South Asia, Africa, Gulf mainly for treatment in India. Again, many foreign patients seek treatment in traditional and alternative medicine (unani, ayurvedic, herbal treatment). The north-eastern region is the home of ayurvedic and herbal medicine. 90 per cent herbal medicine of India is seen in this Himalayas belt. The State like Arunachal Pradesh where almost all of herbals are available has a bright scope to attract health tourists to give treatment at a low cost.

The Central Council for Research in Ayurveda and Siddha, Department of Ayush, Ministry of Health and Family Welfare, Government of India has initiated research programmes in this state from the early seventies. Accordingly, it has taken up a special survey tour programme to study the traditions, culture, customs, folk medical practices and the extent of availability and the quality of the medicinal plants in the State. Consequently, the council has also initiated other important research programmes, such as clinical research programme in the State and established Regional Research Centre at Itanagar in May, 1979. The status of the centre has been upgraded to Regional Research Institute with effect from 09.09.1999 with the following aims and objectives.

Aims and Objectives of the Regional Research Centre

- Intensive Clinical evaluation of selected therapies in assigned diseases.
- Specialized ayurvedic treatment is at OPD and IPD level.
- Morbidity, Survey of population, Health Education, Herbal medication and Medical aids in tribal village.
- Medico-botanical exploration of Arunachal Pradesh.
- Collection and compilation of information on local healing practices from rural tribal areas.
- Development and maintenance of Medicinal Plants Garden and supply of genuine drug materials to the research organization working under the Council.

- Advantage due to low cost of treatment, large number and high quality of Indian health care professionals, world class corporate hospitals (Apollo, Escorts), presence in niche areas.

Hydro Power Potential

Arunachal Pradesh, having untapped estimated hydro power potential of 49,000 MW, may emerge as power house of India when this potential is fully harnessed (*Source:* Department of Power, Government of Arunachal Pradesh), this is shown in Table 13.1. Even if a part of the available hydro potential is harnessed, the State will not only be self-sufficient in meeting its own power requirement but at the same time it can earn revenue by supplying power to the other neighbouring states of the country. During 2002-03, 35 numbers of micro/mini hydel projects with an installed capacity of 32.48 MW and diesel sets with an installed capacity of 27.12 MW are the main sources of power supply in the state though the actual power requirement is 95 MW. So the state is highly deficient in power generation.

SECTION - II

Conservation of Biodiversity under Sustainable Development

Sustainable Development

It appears that the term Sustainable Development (SD) was first used in the context of environmental degradation across generations (Raskin, 1996). However, its scope has since widened to incorporate the new realities of changing times in almost all areas of human concern. Before elaborating on the various dimensions of SD we first explore its meanings.

The notion of SD is derived from two words – sustainable and development. SUSTAIN means 'to maintain' or 'to uphold' something (e.g., a life, a system, etc.) by providing a minimum necessary support and/or a conducive environment. SUSTAINABLE implies 'capable of maintaining' or 'capable of upholding' and has the objective and subjective dimensions of *viability* and *desirability* respectively. Finally, SUSTAINABILITY refers to the capacity or capability of systems for achieving the viable and desirable results from an activity under consideration.

Sustainable Development means 'development that needs the needs of the present without compromising the ability and future generations to meet their own needs'. That is, sustainability implies meeting of current human needs while preserving the environment and natural resources needed by future generations. World Bank Report speaks the sustainable development "a process of managing portfolio of assets to preserve and enhance the opportunities people face". Sustainable Development includes economic, environmental, social sustainability which can be achieved by rationally managing physical, natural and human capital. This term being used by economists and politicians all over the world and the term is constantly being refined. 'Intergenerational' equity would be impossible to achieve unless the groups stops exploitation of other groups or community living in other parts of the world.

Historical example reveals that greater economic development was achieved at the cost of inequality, unemployment, weak democracy, loss of cultural identity, over exploitation of natural resources leading to ecological and economical imbalances resulting in a dire threat for both flora and fauna. To be sustainable, we must rely on certain amount of natural resources available in nature to absorb pollution and regeneration of resources.

In Rio de Janeiro in June 1992, United Nations conference on Environment and Development, 1992, Para 2.1, it is declared, "Human beings are at the centre of concern for sustainable development. They are entitled to a healthy and productive life in harmony with nature". Sustainable development assumes high substitutability among different, components of national wealth. Depletion of natural resources can be compensated with high investment on education i.e., human development and physical capital development which make ways for replacement of old technology to new technology to have effective usage of non-renewable resources at lesser level.

Economic development comes through the judicious and efficient application of three forms of capital – human capital, physical capital and natural capital. The first two types of capital are known as produced capital whereas natural resources are defined as assets gifted by the nature. Non-renewable natural resources such as mineral resources and some other, though renewable like forests and fish resources, may be exhausted if the rate of exploitation exceeds regeneration rate in the process of economic exploitation. As a result, the scope of future development stands limited because of the irreversibility and non-substitutability character of most of the natural resources. To achieving 'sustainable development 'i.e., uninterrupted long-term development, we have to keep ourselves very alert on our exploitation of our natural resources. Sustainable development does not forbid the use of natural resources but restricts their use in such a way that enough, or as much as possible, is left for the future generation; not only for future but even for day-to-day use. When poor people have little access to the capital available in the 'organized' or market economy, they meet their most basic needs as best they can through subsistence activities. The poor live within a biomass-based subsistence economy; all their fundamental needs (food, fodder, fuel-firewood, cow dung, crop-wastes, fertilizer-dung manure leaf-litter, building materials-timber, thatch, and herbal medicines) are collected (often freely) from the immediate environment.

The traditional knowledge of the biological materials of these tribes is very vast which is often kept secret and passed to next generation through verbal tradition as well as through the individuals gifted with a state of spiritual embodiment possessing quality of rare eloquence and power of observation. The system has tremendous potential to evolve planning strategies for conservation and management of biodiversity and improving indigenous economy as well as environmental security of tribal habitat and thus sustainable development of the state.

Major causes of forest degradation are legal and illegal land-use changes; use pressure from villages inside and outside the reserve in the form of fuelwood collection and grazing of livestock; and institutions that fail to manage the forests. The grabbing of common land by the individual has been observed to a significant extent. In consequence, average distance to be covered by a household to collect CPR products has increased significantly. The size of human and livestock population, scarcity of resources (emergence of new-rich class with commercial interests), distance of the reserve area from the residential area and the quality of the management, etc. are some of the important factors that determine the extent of degradation. Market close to the villages cause more severe degradation of forest resources i.e. market plays the promotional role of forest degradation. Scarcity of commons in relation to population leads to its degradation. Though the imposition of a ban on the extraction of forest and forest products by the Supreme Court in 1996 has formally checked the illegal felling of trees, the emerging neo-merchant class are taking the advantages of local power to exploit the forest resources, and in consequence, the state ownership and management have failed to prevent the conservation and degradation of many forests.

1. A periodic exploitation of natural forest should be done on scientific basis. This will help in removing the diseased and unwanted trees to maintain a health density of forest. This, however, should not affect the bio-diversity of the region.
2. People living in and around the forest and largely depending upon the forest resources should be allowed to collect forest products for their subsistence and survival. Even the government is planning to suggest to the Supreme Court to reconsider its decision on the total ban on felling of trees in such areas. In fact, a local need based forest policy can be framed and implemented for forest management, which will keep in mind the interests of the forest and its dwellers. A family depending entirely on forest may even be permitted to collect forest products and sell them to earn enough for their livelihood, of course not for any big commercial purpose. There is a clear-cut distinction between the minimum needs of the family and the commercial exploitation of the forest.
3. Ecosystem based forest management has to be adopted to maintain ecological balance. For example, cutting of forest of tropical belt is much more dangerous than that of the temperate belt. It is because, the nutrients are looked up in the biomass in the former, and in the soil in the later, i.e., organic cycle and physical cycle, respectively. Hence, cutting of the tropical forest leads to breakdown of the ecosystem itself, giving rise to number of environmental problems. Therefore, forest or trees should be grown in the tropical belt, because here nutrient cycle is 'biological'. In the deforested areas of the temperate zone, crops should be grown, as nutrient cycle is 'physical'

here, means all the nutrients are in soil, not in the forest cover. This will give optimum results.

4. Each village, town, industry, and those who need forest products should own tree fields to meet their respective demands.
5. All virgin forest should be declared 'sacred groves' to preserve them for posterity.

Plantation of Jatropha: An Alternative way for Income of Rural People and Fuel for Future

Jatropha curcus is a drought resistant perennial plant growing well in marginal and poor qualitative soil. It is easy to establish, grows relatively quickly and produces seeds for 50 years. The plant produces seeds with an oil content of upto 37 per cent in it. The oil can be combusted as fuel without being refined. It burns with clear smoke-free flame, tested successfully as fuel for simple diesel engine. The by-product is press cake a good organic fertilizer. Its oil contains also insecticide. It is now cultivated in many parts of the country and easily survive with minimum inputs in wastelands. It has also many medicinal values for diseases like cancer, piles, snake-bite, paralysis, etc. A good crop can be obtained with little effort. Oil can be extracted from the seeds after 2 to 5 years after plantation. This can be an important source of income of rural people and thereby diverting the jhumia from their shifting cultivation. But it is not economically viable and very much labour intensive cultivation. But from the ecological point of view only barren land can be used for the purpose.

Incentive and Encouragement to the Poor People

Financial credit, technical assistance and organizational support can help to relieve constraints related to rural poor household's awareness, technology, capacity to invest and local institutional capacity. Co-investment with local communities may be used to mobilize longer term investments through group or micro-credit with labour mobilization or provision of key inputs. Well-organized local participation in project design and management is essential.

Tribal should be encouraged to take up horticulture, floriculture, agro-forestry, growing of medicinal and aromatic plants on hill slope which will not damage the fragile hill ecology. These can play a crucial role in relieving constraints related to a lack of technologies suitable for poor household. Such technologies and resource management systems must raise overall productivity, both increasing household income (to reduce poverty) and protecting or improving the natural resource. Poor rural households have few economic incentives to manage their natural resource more carefully.

Natural Resource Based Entrepreneurship in North-East

In North-East there is tremendous scope for agro-based industries, agro-forestry, horticulture, mushroom farming, herbal, medicinal and aromatic plants, bio-technology, fruit and vegetable processing, handlooms and handicrafts, bee keeping, meat and poultry products, cereal based products, consumer industry, milk and milk based products, food processing, paper products, jute and mestas products, cattle rearing, fishery, edible oil, processing of oils and fragrances, gas based intermediary products, floriculture spices production and processing wood based products, etc.

Explore of Natural Resources in Planned way

People should be made aware of the consequences of the degradation of natural resources due to explore of natural resources and the need to minimize them. Efforts must be made for ensuring optimum utilization and conservation of natural resources which will not only increase national output but also will improve living condition of the people. The schemes of afforestation and tree planting should be extensively done specially by the NGOs and government agencies and proper steps should be taken for continuous maintenance of those areas at least in the initial stages. It may be mentioned that though this type of schemes were undertaken earlier but could not give desired result due to lack of proper maintenance. People should also realize the potent dangers of deforestation and take active interest for successful implementation of the afforestation schemes. In this regard Environment Awareness Schemes seem to be fruitful if the message can reach the remotest corner of the region. Efforts should be made to ensure optimum utilization and conservation of natural resources, which will increase both the national output and improve the living standard of the people of the region.

Forestry development in the region can take place through harnessing the community institutions for the purpose of food-fodder, fuel and timber extraction requirement of the people. Further it is also essential to ensure greater coordination between the government machinery, people and voluntary organizations in regard to enhancement of productivity of forest and forest land under protective care and supervision. Private sector investment should be also encouraged upto some extent. Aforestation of identified areas (wastelands, catchment areas of hydroelectric projects and watershed management projects) and regeneration of forest in abandoned jhum land will be helpful in improving the environment sustainability. The centrally sponsored programmes related to agro-forestry, social-forestry, wasteland development and other employment generation programmes should be given more emphasis on this region.

Land Use Pattern

Basically, the land use pattern of a particular region is by and large determined by the nature and general layout of the physical as well as cultural elements. Primarily, the physical factor like climate, topography set the broad limits upon the capabilities of the land; subsequently, the human factors like length of occupation of the area, density of population, social and economic factors especially, system of land tenure and the technological levels of the people, determine to an appreciable degree the extent to which the physical capacities of land are utilized. Efforts should be made for more intensive people's participation in forest management. It is the people's involvement that will be able to create mass awareness more effectively for preserving the forestry of the region.

Innovations are needed to facilitate poor people's access to natural resources through its more sustainable use whether it is owned or controlled by or shared with others. Land reforms process if taken up in the near future, must ensure secure access by the poor households for both productive and consumptive uses, yet make provision for environmental uses of village commons. Formal arrangements are needed for access to critical resources by the increasing numbers of temporary migrants (e.g., from natural disasters), to limit over exploitation and conflict. Groups of poor people can be involved in land use planning efforts to ensure that their existing use patterns and future needs can be met without increasing poverty or resource degradation. Finally, poor households need insurance systems – cash payments, in-kind provisions or public works employment - to provide subsistence needs after crop failures so natural resources are not over-exploited as emergency reserves. Governments, Non-Governmental Organizations (NGOs) and the private sector should to co-invest in the rehabilitation or improvement of productive on-farm natural resources that are assets of the poor households.

Government Policy

In order to offset the loss of revenue from forests, the Government of India has given direct fiscal assistance to the State on the recommendations of the Twelfth Finance Commission and is promoting development of non-timber forest products particularly bamboo through a fully funded centrally sponsored scheme. Development of bamboo, cane and medicinal plants are thought to have great potentials for employment generation and economic development. The State should particularly evolve a forest sector development policy, bamboo policy and land use policy before any further delay. These measures would go a long way in improving the environmental governance in the State.

Government's Steps

1. The state has to move away from fossil-fuel based, sustainable development processes and adopt alternative sustainable process that provide basic livelihood and social security to all people; this could be done by adopting a clear set of indicators of sustainability (for example, non-conventional energy sources).
2. All leasing of the state's remaining forest areas to mines, industries and other large-scale commercial or development project must halt immediately.
3. Role of NGOs: Government agencies and NGOs need to urgently facilitate communities to derive sustainable forest based livelihoods and provide other sources of employment and livelihood including through the National Rural

Employment Guarantee Act (NREGA). Simultaneously, the government has to identify and arrange alternative health, education and other such amenities that do not end up destroying the forest; this can best be done by building on existing traditional knowledge and process of learning rather than completely replacing them.

One of the important components of effective forestry planning is involving the people in the protection and regeneration of forest because forest can never be protected unless the people are made to feel about the necessity of the forest.

In this respect, the NGOs can also play an important role in forest conservation and preservation among the people of Arunachal Pradesh. The tribes of Arunachal Pradesh had their own system of forest conservation and management but due to modernization and introduction of monetary economy, much of it has been lost. Hence, it is the NGOs who can make the local people more aware about the age-old tradition of the preservation of forest resources and help them to conserve the forest resources of the State. It should be noted that unless social consciousness about forest promotion and conservation do not grow or revive among the people, the government's efforts will be of no use. It is the NGOs, who can motivate people at the grass roots level.

4. The State and Central Governments would do well to take care of the increasing signs of unrest and hostility in the regions where unsustainable development is being imposed.
5. *Forest Management:* With the advent of scientific forestry in 1946, the effort of the State Forest Department (now Environment and Forest Department) has been to conserve the forests and wildlife, to maintain the ecological balance, and to promote sustained socio-economic development of the local people. A humble beginning was made with an area of 534 sq. kms. of reserved forests handed over by the Government of Assam. Over the years rapid strides have been taken in bringing large areas under scientific management besides associating the people in protection, development and management of the forests. The predominantly tribal population of the State lives in close association with and

depends largely on the forest resources. Therefore, forest management efforts seek to elicit the involvement and cooperation of the people while safeguarding their customary rights over the land.

Hitherto, forestry has been confined to reserved forests. But now with the growing emphasis on peoples' participation, forestry is gradually catching up as a land use practice even in the traditionally owned community lands under the schemes of social forestry, wasteland development, national afforestation programme and national bamboo mission. These activities are being taken up in joint forest management mode. For this purpose, forest development agencies and village forest management committees have been constituted in various forest divisions (*SFRI Information Bulletin No. 27*, 2008).

Arunachal Pradesh State Pollution Control Board

Arunachal Pradesh State Pollution Control Board (APSPCB) has been constituted under provisions of the Central Rules - Water (Prevention and Control of Pollution) Act, 1974 by the Government of Arunachal Pradesh on 6th July, 1993 in order to regulate the new rules in the State. Due to increasing concerns for environmental issues and realization about the need for protecting the environment from various polluting ingredients, several acts have been enacted and brought under the purview of Environment Protection Act, 1986. The Board is headed by a full time chairman and a senior IFS officer as Member-Secretary. The Board is required to be further strengthened. The SPCBs/ PCCs, all over the country have been entrusted with the responsibility of monitoring and ensuring the implementation of these acts by various agencies (*SFRI Information Bulletin No. 27*, 2008).

Arunachal Pradesh Biodiversity Board

The Government of Arunachal Pradesh has constituted Arunachal Pradesh Biodiversity Board in March 2005 with Chief Secretary as Chairman and Director, State Forest Research Institute as Member-Secretary and Chief Executive Officer. The Board has other senior officials and scientists as members.

Functions of the Arunachal Pradesh Biodiversity Board are as follows:

(i) Advise the State Government subject to any guidelines issued by the Central Government on matters relating to the conservation of biodiversity, sustainable use of its components and equitable sharing of the benefits arising out of the utilization of biological resources.
(ii) Regulate requests for granting of approvals or otherwise for commercial utilization or bio-survey and bio-utilization of any biological resource by Indians.
(iii) Perform such other functions as may be necessary to implement the provisions of Biological Diversity Act, 2002, or as may be prescribed by the State Government.

The National Biodiversity Authority provides some financial assistance for setting up infrastructure facilities and towards running expenses of the board. Arunachal Pradesh State Biodiversity Strategy and Action Plan prepared by the State Forest Research Institute have been approved by the Central and State Government (*SFRI Information Bulletin No. 27*, 2008).

Compensatory Afforestation/NPV Scheme

In Arunachal Pradesh many developmental projects are implemented after formal diversion/de-reservation of forest land under Forest (Conservation) Act, 1980 by the Government of India. The user agencies remit funds for undertaking compensatory afforestation as per the provisions of Forest (Conservation) Act, 1980. The Hon'ble Supreme Court of India *vide* their order dated 30th October, 2002 and 1st August, 2003 in IA No. 566 in WP (Civil) No. 202 of 1995 ordered realization of Net Present Value (NPV) against the diverted forest land. The user agencies now remit NPV also along with funds for Compensatory Afforestation. The Central Government has constituted a body called the Compensatory Afforestation Fund Management and Planning Authority (CAMPA). The funds received from the user agencies are sent to CAMPA which in turn is released to the State for implementing the Action Plan for NPV fund and Compensatory Afforestation Scheme. Conservator of Forests (Conservation) in the office of PCCF and Principal Secretary (Environment and Forests) is the nodal agency for dealing with the F.C.A cases including implementing the NPV and Compensatory Afforestation Schemes by utilizing the funds received from CAMPA (*SFRI Information Bulletin No.27*, 2008).

All the government rules, regulations and schemes should be strictly carried out. The new Scheduled Tribes and Other Forest Dwellers (Recognition of Forest Rights) Act 2006 is reframed in such a way that community should be given more chance to shoulder more responsibility to manage all the forest regulation Acts.

The debates and developments with regard to the draft of National Environment Policy (NEP), 2004 and the Scheduled Tribes (Recognition of Forest Rights) Bill (STB), 2005 were illustrative in different ways of the manner in which social concerns were dealt with in environmental policy and legislation in India. Yet, while the pros and cons of specific policies and legislations had been Central to the academic debates on the environment, very little attempt had been made to trace the changes in environmental policy making and the way of social concerns still remains problematized.

The government schemes that should have helped communities with securing livelihoods have sometimes done the reverse. For instance, Joint Forest Management (JFM) was meant to create spaces for vulnerable sections of the community to benefit from regenerated forest resources. Certainly in several sites this has helped. However, very often the participation of local people has remained on paper; in any case, the governance framework of JEM is not conducive to power-sharing between the forest department and the communities. In addition to this, JEM has in many cases been superimposed on Community Forest Management (CFM), undermining existing institutions that communities have created.

Community Rights

Our specific focus with regard to social concerns is community rights to resources – a concern that is central to many of the debates on natural resource management. Three arguments are put forth: (i) that while the environment has at one level assumed a non-negotiable presence in policy, social concerns are only highlighted to the extent that they are deemed not to be environmentally destructive, (ii) that the discursive terrain through which social concerns are deemed harmful is overly simplistic and in need of re-examination, and (iii) that the changing nature of environmental discourse can only be understood within the wider shifts in development policy. Although there are many who would claim that the environment itself receives an inadequate attention in development policy, a contention that is at least partly true, we are concerned herewith how emerging policies and legislations tackle social concerns given the socially constructed nature of the environment.

While the discursive thrust of much of environmental policy-making in the late 1970s and early 1980s was on incorporating environmental principles in sectoral planning, something that was matched with legislative intervention, the latter part of the 1980s saw the focus shift towards sustainable development. The importance of this shift was that the link between social and environmental concerns was more forcefully articulated.

The 1988 National Forest Policy (NFP) was the first "environmental" policy document in India that explicitly recognized the linkages between environmental and social concerns in terms of community rights to natural resources. Unlike the previous forest acts that privileged revenue and commercial interests, the NFP was strikingly different. Section 4.6 of the policy highlighted the symbiotic relationship between tribals and forests and the need to involve tribal communities in the management of forests. It also emphasized that domestic requirements of firewood, fodder and minor forest produce should be the first priority of forest management, not commercial or industrial needs.

The 1990 government order on Joint Forest Management (JFM), while giving communities adjacent to reserved forests usufruct rights, was also aimed at improving the protection of forests. As Kolavalli (1995) has argued, citing a number of state-level government orders, JFM was the forest department's way to involve communities in the management of forests as it was incapable of doing it on its own.

But JFM has remained a policy and has not been incorporated into the Forest Act. Thus, while the NFP recognized the symbiocity of forest dependent (tribal) communities with forest, right afforded to these communities have been limited and often no more (sometimes less) than existing settlement rights.

In 2000, the Ministry of Environment and Forest (MoEF) actually gave an NGO Kalpavriksh, the coordinating role in preparing a National Biodiversity Strategy and Action Plan (NBSAP) in consort with 15 members Technical and Policy Core Group. In terms of strategies, the report specified that "empowered local community institutions" should be the implementers of the plan. It would have appeared, therefore, that a good opportunity for decentralized natural resource management where communities were given rights to resources was on the anvil [Kothari, 2004]. However, before the NBSAP was completed in 2003, the National Biodiversity Act, 2002 was passed, although one of the explicit objectives of the act was the recognition of local rights to biodiversity. The National Biodiversity Act, 2002 does recognize the need for local biodiversity committees; the actual powers given to these committees again are mostly managerial in nature. Under Section 41, these committees are constituted for "promoting conservation, sustainable use and documentation of biological diversity including preservation of habitats, conservation of land races, folk varieties and cultivars, domesticated stocks and breeds of animals and micro-organisms and chronicling of knowledge relating to biological diversity" [*NBA 2004:20*].

These three cases have a number of things in common. First, different policies, programmes and laws within particular sectors are often not in consonance with each other in terms of their normative position *vis-a-vis* community rights. For example, while the National Environment Policy (NEP) has made some headway by recognizing tribal rights to forest produce, JFM as a programme has actually given limited usufruct rights to only those who are part of FPCs. Moreover, the Forest Act has remained un-amended with no room for community-based forest management except in the context of village forests (Menon, 2006).

Conservation of biodiversity

The Convention, which was signed by majority of the Nations during the UNCED Earth Summit held in Rio de Janerio in June 1992, is now an International Law. The World Conservation Strategy takes into consideration the human impacts and the perils that may threaten the future of the world's life supporting systems. It clearly defines three global objectives of living resources conservation:

- to maintain essential ecological process and life support systems
- to preserve genetic diversity
- to ensure the sustainable utilization of species and ecosystems.

Conservation of biodiversity is the management of human use of the biosphere so that it may yield the greatest sustainable benefit to present generation, while maintaining its potential to meet the needs and aspirations of future generations. Conservation includes element of b. In this respect, the NGOs can also play an important role in forest conservation and preservation among the people of Arunachal Pradesh. The tribes of Arunachal Pradesh had their own system of forest conservation and management but due to modernization and introduction of monetary economy, much of it has been lost. Hence, it is the NGOs who can make the local people more aware about the age-old tradition of the preservation of forest resources and help them to conserve the forest resources of the state. It should be noted that unless social consciousness about forest promotion and conservation do not grow or revive among the people, the government's efforts will be of no use. It is the NGOs, who can motivate people at the grassroots level.

Systematic Study

It is very important to do a systematic study of these forests products to evaluate their nutritional and medicinal values. On the basis of such study the forest planner may consider the viability of growing such plants commercially for use by a wider array of people.

Other Preservation and Sustainable Use, Restoration and Enhancement

- *In situ* and *ex situ* < >conservation of forest genetic resources through establishment of biosphere reserves, national parks and sanctuaries.
- Protection of exceptional and rare trees in preservation plots.
- Creation of Public awareness of rational utilization of valuable forest resources.
- Promotion of Public involvement in the management of protected areas.

- To increase areas under preservation plots to include all forest types and scientifically monitor of the plots.
- Promotion of eco-restoration of degraded forest areas.
- Regeneration of rare and threatened species and introduction of such plants in suitable habitats.
- Establishment of ethno botanical forest parks.
- Vigorous community participation to medicinal and rare plant conservation.
- Creation of State Information and Data Base (SIDB) centres of forest species, medicinal and aromatic species. Wild relatives of cultivated species, wildlife species along with establishment of bio-resource centres.
- Identification of traditional knowledge base and species exploration to conserve diversity in agro-ecosystems and for promoting sustainability in farming systems.
- High raised areas should be developed in National Parks and sanctuaries for protection of wildlife during flood and other natural calamities, so to prevent from migrating wild animals during flood and drought.
- Reduction and replacement of areas under shifting cultivation system by alternative farming systems.
- Environmental educational awareness building and motivation should form strategy in conservation issues.
- Implementation of clear cut forest policy implementation.

Human interference has greatly threatened the natural ecosystem of the region. The forest of the region have dwindled to a great extent due to indiscriminate human intervention resulting into a large number of plant and animal species are endangered or faced extinction.

We have to grow trees for timber, fuelwood, fodder medicine and other uses on land not meant for agriculture. Trees, especially the timber trees, have to be cultivated on non-agricultural land or 'tree fields'. The grown up trees can be cut to meet the demands. The tree cultivation has to be started in subsequent years in different tree fields, so that annual requirement can be fulfilled from the matured trees in different years. This will enable the tree cultivator to reap the harvest every year or whenever the trees are cut for use. This time-based cultivation of trees would ensure sustainable availability of timber and other forest based products. It is worth mentioning that such practice has already started in various parts of the North-East India.

Local Industries

The absence of local industries to process the forest resources inside the state is another problem. Since no such industries existed or established, the resources have to be exported outside only. If there is local consumption through industries, finished products only will be exported outside and the resources will be able to be utilized in a planned way that will not deplete the natural stock. The Government should try as much as possible to establish local industries based on local resources.

Other Forest Management: This task of managing forest resource cannot be done by foresters alone. Local communities have to realize this and have to come forward to join hands with foresters for protecting and conserving this primary source. Arunachal Pradesh has been declared as one of the hotspots of mega biodiversity in the world.

Forest management practices are implemented in the reserved forest and protected forest only and under the control of the state government, that is, through the approved working plans. So far, the remaining forest of the State under the control of the Autonomous District Councils and private ownership are without working plans which are very essential for sustain harvest and management.

Land Tenure System: The State has a peculiar land tenure system where large extent of the land belonged to the community, villages, clans and private individuals. Enforcement of rules and regulation becomes a difficult task. No doubt the system is very good but proper scientific and systematic management is very difficult especially on the part of exploitation and utilization of forest resources.

Lack of Awareness: In general, the awareness on the environmental aspect is far from expectation. The rural population is supposed to be the main group which lived and depend on forest resources, but they are unaware of the importance of conservation and utilization. Due to their ignorance they are being exploited to the extent that may be detrimental to their existence.

Publicity: Increase appreciation and awareness of environmental values and importance of conservation have to be promoted in order to get a satisfactory result. Through mass communication, awareness programmes, trainings and interactions, seminar, symposium the people are to be made aware of the things around them. Related institutions both Governmental and Non-Governmental will have to be involved to make the population understanding of the importance of environment.

Forest Protection Force: A handsome amount of fund is required to fully equip the forest protection force with sophisticated arms and ammunition against the fully armed timber smugglers and also to carry out regular eviction operations to drive out the encroachers from lands.

Suggestions

No doubt Management of forest is one of the most important and complicated subject and is guided by the variety of factors. The important factors may be forest resources condition, forest policy, local requirements, industrial commitments, economic and ecological considerations etc. Once the decision about the objectives of management of the forest is taken, the detailed procedure of felling trees, regeneration management systems, control of yield and other operations can be easily worked out.

In the physiographical and socio-economic condition of the region, where tribal communities have to depend heavily on traditional practices of forest exploitation, the right approach to forestry is to plan forest development in such a manner that there would be a net addition to a perpetuating stock even after meeting the essential food, fodder, fuel and timber requirement of the people, as well as, the growing requirement of commercial exploitation. It is also necessary to focus other important aspect namely, the conservation of forest resources and control of harmful exploitation. It is worthwhile to introduce the basic elements of community forest management strategy with the community as the unit management. This will help forestry to play a significant role in rural development, maintenance of stream flow and preventation of floods in the plains. Strategies will have to be developed for tackling various problems in connection with forest management in the region.

In India, 1972 Wildlife (Protection) Act was introduced with specific provision to control trade and commerce of wildlife and its products. The Act has been amended thrice i.e., in 1982, 1986 and 1991. Gradually, this trade was discouraged. Initially the Act has divided Animals in five schedules. By Wildlife Amendment Act, 1991 a new Schedule VI was added with imported legislative protection to six species of plants becoming rare and facing extinction. The Act as amended till date prohibits trade in all species of animals included in Schedule - I and Schedule - II (Part II) and increased penalty for violators. No fresh hunting can be done for commercial purpose (Diksit, 2002). But it is a matter of sorry to say that meat of wild animals are sold in open markets of every district headquarters even in capital market, Itanagar till this year, 2009.

If villagers are made partners in the use of potential and over the benefits of, they are more likely to take interest in its protection. A food for work programme may be an example for a successful management. Sharing the responsibilities with local communities and NGO's to interact with all user agencies through forest collaboration, can go a long way for sustainable management of forest and development of society. It is realized that poverty, environmental degradation and population growth are inextricably related and that none of these fundamental problems can be successfully addressed in isolation. However a commonly acceptable sustainable development still remains a challenge for all engaged in development process.

One of the important components of effective forestry planning is involving the people in the protection and regeneration of forest because forest can never be protected unless the people are made to feel about the necessity of the forest.

In the pretext of change in forest policy in 1988, the idea of Joint Forestry Management (JFM) came and it was adopted by various states of the country. However, the JFM model will require suitable modifications to be workable in the hill state like Arunachal Pradesh where 62.17 per cent of the total forest areas are mainly under the traditional ownership of local village committees. At the same time, there is enough scope to shift focus from government forests by bringing more virgin USF to JFM network. The concept of *Apna Van* has received enthusiastic and wide acceptance among some of the local tribes in Arunachal Pradesh.

One of the important components of effective forestry planning is involving the people in the protection and regeneration of forest because forest can never be protected unless the people are made to feel about the necessity of the forest. In the pretext of change in forest policy in 1988, the idea of Joint Forestry Management (JFM) came and it was adopted by various states of the country. However, the JFM model will require suitable modifications to be workable in the hill state like Arunachal Pradesh where 62.17 per cent of the total forest areas are mainly under the traditional ownership of local village committees. At the same time, there is enough scope to shift focus from government forests by bringing more virgin USF to JFM network. The concept of *Apna Van* has received enthusiastic and wide acceptance among some of the local tribes in Arunachal Pradesh.

Conclusion

In the exploitative development model, the forests were looked upon by man as a resource pool of only timber and other industrial raw materials. This idea has since been changed. Forest now managed also for wildlife, medicinal and other beneficial plants, eco-tourism, and soil and water conservation as well as for meeting the local and industrial needs. However, research efforts are necessary to explore new avenues for development and at the same time for restoration and maintenance of ecosystem. Moreover, large patches of the forest of the world still exist as virgin forests which provide a niche to a large number of species of great biodiversity. These offer an excellent situation for study of ecosystem without human influence. Assessing the economic impact of ecological degradation requires an understanding of the value of ecosystem. Particular attention is required to be given to environmental value of the forest because the ecosystems still continue to contribute to the well being of the people.

Given such multi-facet dimension of complexity, conservation and management of forest resources, including eco-development of the region continue to remain a special challenge.

The interests of people depending on the forests products for their livelihood would have to be protected by providing training and employment opportunities in alternative occupations. The population increased and modernization are realities of the day when we plan for the future, new ideological statements are not enough, but one should have proper action plan. It is necessary that a systematic forestation and plantation programmes to be undertaken to increase the forest cover. It is worthwhile to consider allowing barren land to be brought under forest cover by private sector.

For conserving and managing natural vegetation the jhum cultivation and illegal felling of trees, which are the root cause of deforestation, must be stopped immediately but not without rehabilitation of the jhumias. If the government is successful to protect the natural vegetation, the state will be the richest in having the herbs which can be sold in national and international markets. Hence, it is necessary first to develop the market for herbs within the state where the local cultivators will be benefited economically. It will give an incentive to the local people to protect the valuable herbs from extinction.

For the betterment of lives, urbanization, transportation, industrialization are necessary but we can try to minimize the deforestation due to shifting cultivation and illegal felling of trees which are the main cause of disappearance of flora and fauna in Arunachal Pradesh. The Central Government as well as the State Government should give top priority to protect the herbs of economic value in the State which are endowed more than 50 per cent of herbs of the country. Days are not far when the Governments can generate employment as well as earn foreign currency from the export of the State's herbs if they try to take keen interest to protect the existing herbs from disappearance due to impact of the factors mentioned above.

The foresters, wildlifers, conservationists, ecologists, geographers, pedologists and agronomists collectively need to have a good deal of co-ordination with sociologists, and anthropologists for understanding the bad effect of degradation of natural resources and work in the same view for its conservation. A synthesis of traditional knowledge and modern scientific outlook is necessary to evolve a method for improving tribal tradition economy confirming to security.

It is clear that there is a need for conservation of forest in the region. As there are many people maintaining their livelihood from forest, we should chalk out proper aforestation programme which will ultimately satisfy the growing demand for products. But at the time of aforestation we should use multiple species for plantation. Environmentalists have been warning about the damage of planting a single species over a large area. This is because any insect or disease outbreak can wipeout the entire tree plantation, leading to ecological and financial crisis. Monoculture may deplete the nutrients at a particular profile of the soil and cause nutritional deficiency in the long run. The principle behind biodiversity is to encourage the conservation of a wide range of flora and fauna in a given area to ensure an ideal nutrient cycle, as well as, food chain which are important aspects of ecological balance. Preservation of plants and animals are necessary, because our present knowledge about them is confined to a small number of species and the benefits of the remaining millions of plants and animal species are not known to us today. Nevertheless they play an important role in maintaining the ecological balance (Hegde, 1994.)

Total comprehension of the problems is essential and this can only emerge if there are attitudinal changes in both the government and the people. Education on environment from lower classes and training at different levels will go a long way to solve some of these problems.

Development of overall environment will be a nursery bed of cooperation and harmony as opposed to mindless competition and conflicts. We must dare act and go beyond and behind nature to seek the main purpose of existence. Saving the tree is only a first step for saving overselves. Only then sons of the earth will repossess the earth and an enjoyable period of time will be ushered in.

It is found that accessible natural forests particularly in the foothills of Arunachal Pradesh are under great pressure to a large scale due to extraction of timber and illegal felling of trees. Although the demand for wood for local consumption is relatively low due to low population of the state but in view of the increasing demand for industrial timber within the state and other parts of the country, the forest in the state are under great pressure. As per the official estimate, the State contributes to nearly 50 per cent of the timber supply made from the North-Eastern Region of India. At the same time, it is observed that there is large scale illegal felling of trees, which is many times more than the official permits issued for felling of trees. The tree permit system in Unclassified State Forest (USF) which was introduced to enable the local people to earn their livelihood in logging and extraction of timber with a view to generate income has led to the emergence of a 'neo-rich' class in the traditional tribal society to make easy and quick money in collaboration with private forest contractors. There is a growing social and political pressure to over exploit the forest and the protection of forest are becoming increasingly difficult.

China and South East Asian countries have already demonstrated their capability in bio-resource management. China in particular has made great strives in transforming its rural economy through bamboo. Chinese people have replaced wood by bamboo in almost all their industrial, construction and domestic applications. This has considerably reduced pressure on their natural forests. Forest cover in China has increased while India's has remained stagnant. There is, therefore, need for this State to learn about bamboo sector from China particularly in the areas of policy, legal and institutional arrangements which were behind their success story on bamboo (*SFRI Information Bulletin No. 27*, 2008).

REFERENCES

Azad, N.A. (2004): "Poverty and Sustainable Development", S. Bhatt (ed.), *Poverty and Food Security in India*, Aakar Books, Delhi, pp. 106-110.

Bhattacharjee, R.P. (2000): *Economic Development of Arunachal Pradesh*, Himalayan Publishers, Delhi, Itanagar, pp.17-18 and pp. 45-49.

Bhattacharjee, R.P. (2006): "Forest Economics in Arunachal Pradesh and its Impact on State Economy", *Arunachal Review*, Vol. VIII, No. 18, June-August, Naharlagun, Government of Arunachal Pradesh.

B.K. Sarma and *et al.* (2002): "Dwinding Forest Biodiversity of North-East India" in Roy B. Datta and Alam K: *Forest Resources in North East India*, Omsons Publication, New Delhi.

Diksit, V.K. (2002): "International Wildlife Trade and Its Impact on Wildlife Resources" in Roy B. Datta and Alam K: *Forest Resources in North-East India*, Omsons Publications, New Delhi.

Ghosh, A.K. (1990): "Impact of shifting cultivation in Living Natural Resources", in Majumdar, D.N. (ed): *Shifting cultivation in North-East India*, Omsons, Publications, Guwahati and New Delhi, pp.178-197.

Government of Arunachal Pradesh (2006): *Economic Review*, Directorate of Economic and Statistics, Itanagar.

Government of Arunachal Pradesh (2006): Arunachal Pradesh: Human Development Report 2005, Rajiv Gandhi University, pp. 171-72.

Hegde, N.G. (1994): Biodiversity and Ground Realities, *Yojana*, February.

Hegde, S.N. (1988): "Coptis Teeta Wall (Mishmi Teeta): A Rare Medicinal Plant from Arunachal Pradesh", *Arun for News* 6(I), pp. 27-29.

Hussain Zahid (2002): "Tree Cultivation: A Need of the Hour in Forest Management" in Roy B. Datta and Alam K: *Forest Resources in North-East India*, Omsons Publications, New Delhi.

Josh, M.C. (1997): Role of Herbs and Drugs in Economic Development in Pandey B.B. (ed): *Patterns of Change and Potential for Development in Arunachal Pradesh*, Himalayan Publishers, Itanagar, New Delhi, pp. 174-184.

Kanjilal, U.N. Kanjilal, P.C. and Das, A. (1934): *Flora of Assam*, Vol. I, Government of Assam, Shillong.

Mandal, R.K. (2006): "Sustainability of Medicinal Plants and its Economic Viability in Arunachal Pradesh", Resarun (*Journal of the Directorate of Research*), Government of Arunachal Pradesh, Itanagar, Vol. 31, pp. 1-10.

Mandal, R.K. (2005): *Arunachal Economy: Socio-Economic Transformation*, Champion Publishing, Itanagar, p. 116-117.

Mandal, R.K. (2007): "Flora and Fauna in Arunachal Pradesh: Economic Viability and Sustainability" *Arunachal Review*, Vol. VIII, No. 23, Sept.-Nov., Naharlagun, Government of Arunachal Pradesh.

Mandal, R.K. (2005): "Arunachal Pradesh Emerging as Power House" *Journal of Global Economy*, Vol. 1., No. 4, Research Centre for Social Sciences, Mumbai.

Menon, Ajit (2006): "Environmental Policy Legislation and Construction of Social Nature", *EPW*, January 21-27, Vol. XLI, No. 3, p. 188.

Narayana. K.S. (2006): "Biodiversity Conservation Should Be The Mantra of The Century". *Kurukshetra* December, Vol. 55, No. 2, pp. 3-4.

Pandey, H.C. (1988): "Some Healing Herbs of the Monk's Amongst the Minor Forest Produce", *Arun for News* 6(I), pp. 1-10.

Rao,. V.M. (2003): *Tribal Women of Arunachal Pradesh*, Mittal Publications, New Delhi, p. 21.

Sharma, T.C. (1976): "The Prehistoric Background of Shifting Cultivation" in Pakem, B, *et al.*: *Shifting Cultivation in North-East India*, NECSSR, Shillong.

Wani,Milind and Kothari Ashish (2008): "Globalisation Vs. India's Forest", *EPW*, September 13-19, Vol. XLIII, No. 37.

The Arunachal Times, Vol. 19, No. 154, November 11, 2007.

Forest and Forestry in Arunachal Pradesh, *SFRI Information Bulletin*, No. 27, Director, State Forest Research Institute and Mission Director, State Bamboo Mission, Itanagar.

Website: *www.sfri.org*

Arunachal Front, March 21, 2009, Vol. 17, No. 201.

Sinha, G.N. (2008): Forest and Forestry in Arunachal Pradesh, *SFRI Information Bulletin*, No. 27, Issued by Director, State Forest Research Institute and Mission Director, State Bamboo Mission, Itanagar, Arunachal Pradesh.

14

Flora and Fauna
Economic Viability and Sustainability

Introduction

The use of herbs and drugs for treatment of ailments and injuries in the country dates back as early as 4500 B.C., mention of which is found in scriptures (*Rigveda*). More than 2000 items are reportedly used for medicine out of which 200 are of minerals origin and the remaining is of vegetative nature. Forest wealth is one of the important natural aids to mankind which should be utilized judiciously. The forests in Arunachal Pradesh are primarily by large and there is vast wealth of plants, grasses, herbs, orchids and others of immense economic, commercial and medicinal values which may not be available in other parts of the country.

In recent years there has been great demand for plant-derived products in developed countries. These products are increasingly being sought out as medicinal products, nutraceuticals and cosmetics. The WHO estimated that about three quarters of the world's population currently use herbs and other forms of traditional medicines to treat their diseases. The European market for phyto-pharmaceuticals in 1995 was reported to be US $ 1,098 million and to US $ 1,375 million in the year 2001 (Fahishi, 1996). The market for botanical health-care remedies in the USA was reportedly US $ 3.24 billion in 1996 with some 60 million people using herbs to treat minor ailments such as allergies, burns, colds, depression, headache, insomnia, premenstrual syndrome and rashes (Johnston, 1997). Surveys carried out in the USA (Eisenberg *et al.*, 1993) and Australia (Maclennan *et. al.*, 1997) indicates that substantial numbers of people are using complementary health treatments including herbs and herbal products. However, inspite of the popularity of the herbal drugs, several questions have been raised in the recent years regarding their efficacy and safety. There is only limited information available in the literature concerning the interaction of herbal and conventional medicines (Anderson *et. al.*, 1985; D' Arcy, 1993). Herbal drugs have been found to report toxic effects as well as show interactions with food and other drugs. The first report of herb-drugs interaction published in 1970s stated that consumption of cruciferous vegetables resulted in lower plasma level of analgesic drug phenacetin. It was suggested that indoles, which are present in such vegetables enormously, could be responsible for interaction (Pantuck, 1996). In this study herb-drug interactions have been reviewed. The rationale for such interactions is often difficult to explain if knowledge regarding the phytochemical constituents of the herbal products understood. It is well established that patients taking herbal drugs along with prescription medicines can experience drug interactions, which may be detrimental to their health (Mehta, 1998).

Arunachal Pradesh is very rich in medicinal flora. In the absence of any sophisticated system of medicine, the indigenous village elders have been claiming the presence of numerous life saving herbs. Simultaneously, there are numerous known herbs with deadly poisons which when processed become very potent curing medicines. Good agricultural and collection practices of herbs can also be potential source of economic development and ecologically safer too to the State. It may also open up a new avenue in commercial cultivation for large production, processing and packaging, marketing and industrial application. The important types of forests found in the State are Tropical Ever Green, Semi-Green, Wet Ever Green, Wet Temperate, Deciduous Mixed Coniferous, Alpine, Bamboo brakes, etc. The flora of this remote hill state has medicinal values which are utilized by indigenous people to cure their ailment without any side effects like modern medicines have.

Nature has been exceedingly kind and has endowed this beautiful State of Arunachal Pradesh with diverse forests and magnificent wildlife. The richness of life forms i.e. the flora and fauna that occur in these forests presents a panorama of biological diversity with over 5000 plants, about 85 terrestrial mammals, over 500 birds and a large number of butterflies, insects and reptiles. Such an unparalleled occurrence of life forms can be attributed to the peculiar location of the State which is at the junction of the Paleoarctic, Indo-Chinese, and Indo-Malayan bio-geographic regions. Biotic elements from these regions occur in this State making it very rich in floral and faunal resources. The State offers an ideal agro-climate with vast potentials for growing varieties of orchids round the year. Out of about 1150 species of orchids known in India, about 500 species occur only in Arunachal Pradesh. These species occur in varying climatic and habitat conditions in varying concentration from the warm foothills to the cool temperate hills in Arunachal Pradesh. Such a diverse climatic situation has favoured the occurrence of the orchids in the State which is a highest number for any State in India thus, making it an "Orchid Paradise" of our country. There are over 500 herbs recorded from Arunachal Pradesh of which 250 are used in various Ayurvedic formulations. Vast climate variations in Arunachal Pradesh have resulted in existence of almost all types of herbs and timber wealth ranging from tropical teak in foothills jungles to coniferous and alpine of high mountains. The state is very rich flora. It has about 4500 species of flowering plants, 400 species of pleridophytes, 23 species of coniferous, 35 species of bamboos, 20 species of canes, 25 Rhododendron species. Overall, Arunachal Pradesh is, as if, a natural garden of more than 20,000 identified species of medicinal plants and so many still remain unidentified. About 300 plant species out of native flora in North-Eastern India are used for edible purpose. Of these, over 25 provide tubers/rhizomes, etc., which are eaten raw or boiled. Over 50 are consumed as green with their leaves/tender shoots cooked as vegetable; about 170 ripe fruits, which are pulpy and sweet/sub-sweet are eaten raw and many of these are used for pickles/vegetables when unripe; about 15 have edible seeds which are eaten raw or roasted.

Like flora, the deeply wooded terrains of Arunachal Pradesh are also rich in fauna. There are believed to be more than 100 species of mammals in its forests. These include four major cats (tiger, leopard, snow leopard and clouded leopard), three antelopes (serow, goral and takin) and the highly endangered hispid hare. The State is home to 8 out of 16 species of primates found in India. Bison or Gaur and Mithun are two important mammals found in the State. Additionally, at least six species of squirrels, mongoose, civet cat are some of the smaller mammals found in the wild. There are four types of deer: Sambar, hog deer, barking deer, and musk deer. Red panda, binturong, black bear, sun bear, sloth bear, wolf, wild boar, wild goat and wild pig, monkey, elephant are the other animal species found in the State. There are about 650 species of birds, including three species of hornbills and the endangered white winged duck and rare pheasants. In addition, there are 105 species of fishes, 42 species of amphibians, besides a large number of reptiles, butterflies and other terrestrial mammals.

The land and topography of the State is hilly beginning from foothills to snow-clad zones of alpine region. The elevation of the hills ranges from 150 metres to over 7,300 metres. Out of its 83,743 sq. kms., topographically the plains and foothills cover about 10-15 per cent, broad valleys and plateaus about 35 per cent, steep slopes 35 per cent, snow clad peaks and pastoral land 18-20 per cent. The State represents beautiful scenery with irregular mountainous topography. Besides streams, rivers, mountains and peaks, its endless variations in scenic beauty are the first to great sunrise in the country. Rainfall varies from 1000mm. in higher reaches to 5750mm. in the foothill areas, spread over 8-9 months excepting the drier days in winter.

As per the State Forest Report-1999, published by the Forest Survey of India, forest cover of Arunachal Pradesh is 68951 sq. kms. accounting for 82.21 per cent of its total geographical area. The recorded forest area of the State is 51540 sq. kms., which is about 61.5 per cent of its total geographical area. Thus, the State is fortunate to have such high percentage of its area under valuable forests cover against the national percentage of 20.50 in 2001.

Let us take a comparative picture of dense forest area of the State in Table 14.1. We find that in Arunachal Pradesh more area is covered by dense forest as compared to other States.

Table 14.1: Forest Classification: A Comparative Study of Arunachal Pradesh.

Sl.No.	State and Category	1991-assessment	1993-assessment
1	**Arunachal Pradesh**	**100.0**	**100.0**
1.1	Dense forest	79.3	79.4
1.2	Open forest	20.7	20.6
2	**North-Eastern States**	**100.0**	**100.0**
2.1	Dense forest	53.5	53.7
2.2	Open forest	46.5	46.3
3	**Rest of India**	**100.0**	**100.0**
3.1	Dense forest	62.6	62.5
3.2	Open forest*	37.4	37.5
4	**All India**	**100.0**	**100.0**
4.1	Dense forest	60.2	60.2
4.2	Open forest*	39.8	39.8

* = including mangrove.

Source: Government of India, "The State of Forest Report, 1993", Table 1.2, Table 1.4, and Table 1.5, pp. 9-11.

We find that in Arunachal Pradesh, more area is covered by dense forest compared to other States. The State, which is the extension of Eastern Himalayas, is very rich in forest-wealth mainly due to non-interference of the forest by mankind. Due to botanical richness, it has attracted many plant explorers in the past. From 1956, the Botanical Survey of India has been actively exploring different parts of the State.

The vegetation has an altitudinal distribution, following the varied nature of the hills and mountains forming the great Himalayan range. However, the stratification is not clearly discernible as the topography is irregular and disturbed by valleys and plateaus of various extents. Broadly, the following main vegetational types can be indicated as follows:

(i) Tropical Semi-evergreen forests in the foothill regions and adjacent to the Brahmaputra valley up to about 900 m (3000 feet).

(ii) Sub-tropical forests from 900 m to 1900 m (3000-6000 feet).

(iii) Humid sub-temperate forests from 1900 m-3000 m (6000-9000 feet)

(iv) Temperate forests from 3000 m to 4000 m (9000-12,500 feet) and higher up alpine meadows merging to vegetation-less snow-clad peakes.

There is considerable overlap and mixing up of various species of the different broad zones mentioned below.

Perhaps due to this, Forest Department of Arunachal Pradesh relays more on for set-type mapping using Satellite Remote Sensing Technique and identified the forest. These are as follows:

(i) Hollong Forest,
(ii) Nahar Forest,
(iii) Semi-Evergreen Type I,
(iv) Semi-Evergreen Type II,
(v) Sub-Tropical Broad Leaved Forest,
(vi) Sub-Tropical Pine Forest,
(vii) Temperate Forest Type I,
(viii) Temperate Forest Type II,
(ix) Coniferous Forest,
(x) Alpine Shrubs/Grasslands, and
(xi) Bamboo.

The Diptero carpus macrocarpus (Hollong) is in pure form in the state specially in the districts of Tirap and Changlang up to altitude of 610 m. Mesua Ferrea (Nahar) is in pure form found in the eastern parts of the State adjacent to upper Assam. The Hollong Forest and Nahar Forest and upper Assam Valley Tropical Evergreen Forest respectively. Other species found in these forests are shorea assamica (Mekai), Altingia excelsa (Jutuli), Artocarpus chaplasha (cham), Amoora Wallichii (Amari), Kayea assamica (Sia-Nahar), Terminalia Chebula (Hilika, Hartaki), etc.

The Semi-Evergreen Type I conforms with Assam Alluvial plains Semi-Evergreen Forests where the important species grown are Amoora Wallichii (Amari), Pterospermum acerifolium (Hatipolia), Altingia excelsa (Jutuli), Bischofia Javanica (Urium), Gmelina arborea (Gomari), Toona ciliate (Jatipoma, Poma), Sterculia villosa (Udal), Terminolia chebula (Hilika, Hartaki), Artocerpus Chaplasha (Cham), Chukrasia tabularis (Bogipoma), Cinnamomum Cecicodaphme (Gon Sorai) etc.

The Semi-Evergreen Type II forests conform to Sub-Himalayan

light Alluvial Semi-Evergreen forest and East Himalayan Moist-Mixed Deciduous Forest. The main species found in this type of forest are phoebe goal parensis (Bonsum), Terminalia myrocarpa (Hallock), Amoora Wallichii (Amari), Artocarpus Chaplasha (Cham), Tetrameles mudiflora (Bhelu, Tula), Bomba ceiba (Dum bolu/simul), Ailan thus grandis (Borpat), etc. This form is stretched from Bhairab kunda to Sonairupai river in East Kameng District.

The Sub-tropical Board leaved forests conform to East Himalaya Sub-Tropical wet Hill forest. This occurs in lower slope from about 1000m to 2000m. A few species of this forest are calophyllum polyanthum (Kurta), Castenopsis Indica (Hingori), Kydia calycina (Pichola) etc.

The sub-tropical pine forest occurs in between 1000m to 1800m and the species are Pinus roxburghii, Pinus wallichiana and Pinus armandi.

The temperate Forest type conforms to East Himalaya Wet Temperate Forest and East Himalaya Moist Temperate Forest occurs between 1750 to 2750m. The species grown in this forest are *Quercus lamellosa*, *Quercus* sp., *Castonopsis indica* (Hingor), *Acerhookari*, *Acer pectina trum*, *sympolcus spicata* and *Magnolia chambellii*.

The temperate Forest type II conform with Naga Hills wet temperate Forest occurs along Myanmar border from 1800m upward. The species grown here are *Magnalia species* (sopa), *Quercus* sp., *Michulia* sp., *Prunus* sp., *Betula alnoides* (Birch), *Quercus* sp., *Michulia* sp., *Prunus* sp., *Betula alnoides* (Birch), *Acer* sp., *Bucklandia populnae* and *Alunus nepalensis*.

Coniferous forest resembles with East Himalayan Moist Temperate Forest occurs at an altitudinal zone of about 2300 m to 3000 m and the species grown are *Abies* sp., and *Tsuga brunoniana*.

Alpine shrubs/grasslands includes shrubs/grassland of sub-Alpine and Alpine areas occurs for about 4000 m to 5500 m altitude. Here only shrub species like *Rhododendron* sp., *Primula* sp., *Savssura* sp. and *Saxifraga* sp., occur.

And lastly the Bamboo species include *Bambusa palida*, *Bambusa* sp., *Bambusa Tulda*, *Dendroncalemus hamilitonni* (Kakua), *Dendrocalamus hookeri* etc.

Forest wealth is one of the important natural aids to mankind which should be utilized judiciously. The forests in Arunachal

Pradesh are primary by large and there is vast wealth of plants, grasses, herbs, orchids and others of immense economic, commercial and medical values which may not be available in other parts of the country (Bhattacharjee, 2000).

A great diversity is associated with tropical and subtropical vegetation types. All the useful plant species ranging from medicinal herbs to timber plants are closely linked with the economic life of the people. Arunachal is endowed with about a third (5,000 seed plants) of the 15,000 seed plants found in India, thousands of non-flowering plants, and about 500 exotic orchids. The State is rich in faunal wealth, although it is difficult to get exact figures of animal diversity.

This paper basically attempts an in-depth study about the existence of flora and fauna in Arunachal Pradesh. This paper is divided into four sections. The first section concentrates itself about the investigation and survey done by certain botanists, naturalists, foresters and agricultural scientists in regard of existence of flora and fauna. The second section examines the economic viability of flora and fauna in the national and international market. The third section tries to investigate about the sustainability of flora and fauna due to environmental degradation caused by shifting cultivation, growth of urbanization, growth of population, growth of transportation and growth of industrialization in the State and the fourth section deals with suggestions and then conclusion follows.

SECTION - I

This section seeks to identify the existence of flora and fauna in Arunachal Pradesh. It is well-known fact that more than 80 per cent of the world's medicinal flora is found in the Himalayan ranges of India. Arunachal Pradesh is such type of State which is lying within the Himalayan belt. Since, the State has remained a generally inaccessible area with scarce means of communication and transport, very little written record is available about medicinal flora. Mostly the knowledge and information were passed from generation to generation by word of mouth and through folklores. However, under Monasteries of Monpa (Buddhist), there were monks who had expertise and who trained some selected persons in the area of identification, collection and processing, and use of various active parts of the herbs. It is a common knowledge that only certain plants and certain parts of plants like flower, leaf, bark, root are of medicinal use.

The Department of Agriculture of Arunachal Pradesh during seventies made a positive effort to collect and circulate information on plants of medicinal and economic importance. In pursuance of this, an integrated scheme was also submitted to North-Eastern Council for gainful utilization of the medicinal herbs and drugs. Dr. Rajendra Gupta, All India Co-ordinator of Medicinal and Aromatic Plants, Pusa, New Delhi, showed active interest and made some valuable suggestions. Dr. A. S. Rao, Deputy Director, Botanical Survey of India, Shillong, had also undertaken studies of certain plants and orchids of medicinal importance.

In 1976 the upper reaches of Lohit district were explored and the herbs were listed. The main interest in Dibang Valley came on account of this area being the natural habitat of the prised roots of *mishmi teeta* (coptis) which is a rich source of berberin. Dr. Bordoloi of Regional Research Laboratory (RRL), Jorhat toured different districts of Arunachal Pradesh extensively. During 1976, a team headed by Dr. Jamuwal from RRL Srinagar visited West Kameng District in an expedition to explore the herbs around Tawang. A valuable inventory of medicinal herbs and drugs was prepared by them in collaboration with the RRL, Jorhat and the Department of Agriculture of Arunachal Pradesh. During the course of their visit the expedition came across patches of lemon grass, growing naturally in hill slopes between Pamaghar and Lumla, beyond West Siang District. The grass has high lemon oil content and rich in vitamin 'A' which the knowledgeable Monpas claim to be a cure for malignant skin diseases including leprosy. Lemon grass oil is of considerable economic significance besides medicinal value.

RRL subsequently surveyed Wangchu area of Tirap district and conducted trials for cultivation of *mentha piperantha* and also undertook multiplication trail for the *solanum khasyanum* (yellow berries) Manthan yellow berries are the source of solicigin-steroid used as oral contraceptive. This berry was successfully grown in Seneua Farm. There were further trails for diascoreas particularly D. Floribunda, D. Deltoiti etc. which also is a source for steroids.

The Department of Agriculture screened large number of orchids, herbs and other plants of economic significance. Ethno botanical study is an important part of modern plant science, which will get a unique dimension in India in the exploration process of the ethno botanical wealth of different regions among various ethnic groups. The local tribes of Arunachal Pradesh still prefer to rely on the traditional methods of health care. These people are very familiar with the herbal medicines that are abundantly available from the surroundings. Vast climate variations in the region have resulted in existence of almost all types of herbs and timber wealth ranging from tropical teak in foothills jungles to coniferous and alpine of high mountains. The state is very rich flora. It has about 4500 species of flowering plants, 400 species of pleridophytes, 23 species of coniferous, 35 species of bamboos, 20 species of canes, 25 Rhododendron species. Overall, Arunachal Pradesh is, as if, a natural garden of more than 20,000 identified species of medicinal plants and so many still remain unidentified. About 300 plant species out of native flora in North-Eastern India are used for edible purpose. Of these, over 25 provide tubers/rhizomes etc., which are eaten raw or boiled. Over 50 are consumed as green with their leaves/tender shoots cooked as vegetable; about 170 ripe fruits, which are pulpy and sweet/sub-sweet are eaten raw and many of these are used for pickles/vegetables when unripe; about 15 have edible seeds which are eaten raw or roasted.

No doubt, Arunachal Pradesh offers an ideal agro-climate with vast potentials for growing varieties of orchids round the year. Out of about 1150 species of orchids known in India, about 500 species occur only in Arunachal Pradesh. These species occur in varying climatic and habitat conditions in varying concentration from the warm foothills to the cool temperate hills in Arunachal Pradesh. Such a diverse climatic situation has favoured the occurrence of these species of orchids in the State which is a highest number for any State in India thus making it an "Orchid Paradise" of our country. There are also over 500 herbs recorded from Arunachal Pradesh of which 250 are used in various Ayurvedic formulations.

Aromatic Oil Yielding Plants

Java-Citronella: This grass grows luxuriantly all along the foothill area of the territory. It is cultivated by planting two to three slips in a hole three feet apart. The oil is extracted through a distillation plant by direct distillation method. The recovery of oil is between 0.8 to 1.0 per cent from fresh leaves of citronella. The prices are not much less than the other aromatic oil.

Lemon grass: Lemon grass grows in deep clumps in high hills. Natural patches of these have been found in West Kameng in exploitable quantities. Effort is now being made to grow this grass under cultivated conditions for extraction of lemon oil. Lemon oil, besides being a base for perfumery, has been found to be very effective cure for persistent skin diseases and leprosy. Vitamin 'A' contained in lemon grass is said to have strong healing effects on skin and wounds.

Mentha Piperanta: Mentha oil is of medicinal importance and M/s. Glaxo Laboratories have been organizing certain farms and extraction in certain States. For medicinal use menthol has considerable importance.

Musk Dana: There is a plant similar to Bhindi (Okra) plant of malvacceae family which produces musk scented seed known as musk dana. The oils of musk dana is used in high grade perfumery.

Oleoresin Yielding Plants: Ginger, turmeric and Chillies grow widely under varying conditions of soil and agro-climate within the territory. Because of communication and transport limitation these bulky crops hardly attract any significant status. Once oleoresin is extracted from any of these three crops it becomes a low volume high value product and is of great demand in pharmacological industry and for cosmetics. *Oleoresin plants* will serve as an incentive for extensive cultivation of these crops for economic betterment of the rural communities. Basar, Along, Mebo, Roing, Chowkham, Miao and Bordumsa are potential areas for initiating such extraction plants.

Berberin Yielding Plants

Coptis Teeta: (locally known as Mishmi Teeta): This is a widely known herb growing just below the snow line as small herb, at altitude between 9,999 to 12,000 ft. altitude MSL. The cultivation of Mishmi Teeta in Dang Valley around Anini was successfully demonstrated during 1975-76. Presently it is being cultivated by a number of enthusiastic cultivators in Dibang Valley. Seeing the successful cultivation of Mishmi Teeta the Adis-Miniyong in Boleng circle of East Siang district have undertaken successful cultivation of *Coptis teeta* locally known as 'Rinko' by the Adis. In Tuting Singa and Gelling Hills, *coptis teeta* grows naturally in the wild and is being utilized locally for medicinal purposes. It has considerable potential for providing a definite impact on the economy of the people of high hills and also to support a sizeable industry for extraction of berberin for medicinal purpose. *Coptis teeta* is considered as a vital drug by the village medicine men not only as debility tonic, cure for all kinds of stomach disorder, but also as an eye salve (*surma*). The use of *coptis teeta* (memeera) for eye salve is mainly known in J&K Hills of the Western Himalayas.

Tupistra Aurantiasa: Dipo Tale (Rinte) scientifically known as *Tupistra Aurantiasa* is another medicinal herb which grows in similar surroundings as coptis teeta but is more hardy with wider adaptations from elevations between 8000 ft. to 12500 ft. altitude MSL. Its leaves are long, fleshy, smooth and provide luxuriant foliage to the plant with characteristic creeping rhizomes. The creeping rhyzome is long fleshy with long internodes, having active bitter berberine content. The village medicine men use small pieces of the rhyzome also as debility tonic and for curing various kinds of stomach disorders and ailments.

Apatani Ricoh: In the higher hills of Apatani plateau there is a climber, the stem of which is widely used as a cure against all stomach ailments and as debility tonic. The plant is known as Ricoh by the Apatanies. The dry stem is equally bitter as the *Mishmi Teeta* and has medicinal use. Among the Nishyis, the same plant is identified and named as Rik who also use it for medicine.

Aconites: Aconites are some of the oldest well-known items of trade between the hill men of frontier tracts and the Ahom rulers of Brahmaputra valley. *Aconites* provide deadly arrow poison for defense by the local people. *Aconites* are strong base of Ayurvedic medicine for preparing vital life saving drugs. Presently *aconites* are widely used under Ayurvedic preparations.

The Department of Agriculture screened large number of orchids, medicinal plants and other plants of economic significance. Ethnobotanical study is an important part of modern plant science, which will get an unique dimension in India in the exploration process of the ethnobotanical wealth of different regions among various ethnic groups. The local tribes of Arunachal Pradesh still prefer to rely on the traditional methods of health care. These people are very familiar with the herbal medicines that are abundantly available from the surroundings. Vast climate variations in the region have resulted in existence of almost all types of medicinal plants and timber wealth ranging from tropical teak in foothills jungles to coniferous and alpine of high mountains. The State is very rich in fauna and flora. It has 20 per cent of species of country's fauna and about 4500 species of flowering plants, 400 species of pleridophytes, 23 species of coniferous, 35 species of bamboos, 20 species of canes, 25 Rhododendron species. No doubt, Arunachal Pradesh offers an ideal agro-climate with vast potentials for growing varieties of orchids round the year. Out of about 1150 species of orchids known in India, about 500 species occur only in Arunachal Pradesh. These species occur in varying climatic and habitat conditions in varying concentration from the warm foothills to the cool temperate hills in Arunachal Pradesh. Such a diverse climatic situation has favoured the occurrence of about 550 species of orchids in the state which is a highest number for any State in India thus making it an "Orchid Paradise" of our country. There are over 500 medicinal plants recorded from Arunachal Pradesh of which 250 are used in various Ayurvedic formulations. Some important medicinal plants with their application are listed in Table 14.4.

The vegetation of Arunachal Pradesh varies greatly along with the altitude of each separate region. It ranges from a wide belt of swampy rain forests at the foothills and low lying areas, particularly in the eastern section to the tropical and sub-tropical up to an height of approximately 2,134 metres. The trees of the different species and sizes, cane and bamboo of different varieties, wild banana tree etc. are commonly found in the foothill belt. Orchids of numerous varieties are also found abundantly for which an Orchid Research and Development Centre at Tipi in West Kameng district has been set-up by the forest department. The lower elevation area is remarkable for deciduous forest with patches of evergreen tropical vegetables. The Subtropical evergreen tropical vegetations are found at higher elevation too. In the dense forest the common trees are Holloch, Bola, Semalu, Khoman and Makahi, etc. A substantial amount of revenue is earned from these forest products. Wide varieties of medicinal plants are also available. The local inhabitants are well aware of these plants. Between 2134 and 2743 metres, we have the area of deciduous and mixed deciduous forests composed mainly of walnut, oak, chestnut, pine, spruce and rhododendrons. Further up and continuing up to an altitude of 3,658 metre the wide stretch of area is generally claimed by conifers. Beyond 4,877 m and right up to the snowline, one enters the region of alpine meadow. Table 14.2 lists the major plants found in the State.

Table 14.2: Floral Diversity of Arunachal Pradesh.

Sl. No.	*Plant species*	*Number of species (approx.)*
1.	Rhododendrons	52
2.	Hedychium species	18
3.	Oaks	16
4.	Gymnosperms	29
5.	Bamboo	35
6.	Canes	20
7.	Orchids	500
8.	Medicinal plants	500
9.	Pteridophytes	452
10.	Bryophytes	60
11.	Lichens	80

Source: (i) Arunachal Pradesh State Biodiversity Strategy and Action Plan, State Forest Research Institute, 2002.
(ii) Statistical Report: 1999 – 2000, Department of Environment and Forest, Arunachal Pradesh.

Orchids form a dominant group of plants with their attractive and unique blooms. About 500 species of orchids occur in Arunachal Pradesh. These include about 140 species of terrestrial orchids with 15 *saprophytes* and about 340 *epiphytes* found in the different forest types. The prominent species are: *Cymbidium ensifolium, C. grandiflorum, Coelogyne corymbosa, Dendrobium aphyllum, D. fimbriatum var occulata, D. densiflorum, Calanthe masuca, Phaius flavus, Paphiopedilum fairieanum, P. venustum, P. wardii etc.* (*Information Bulletin* No. 27, 2008).

Fauna: Like flora, the deeply wooded terrains of Arunachal Pradesh are also rich in fauna. Zoo-geographically, the fauna of Arunachal Pradesh can be categorized under Palaeartic Indo-Chinese and Indo-Malayan elements. With varying agro-climatic and altitudinal condition from tropical to alpine forests and well distributed precipitation with high humidity rising up to 90 per cent, the area is conducive to the luxuriant growth of vegetation, which in turn determines the faunal communities. The richness in faunal diversity would be evident from the following facts:

The State is the home of more than 210 species of mammals out of which as many as 37 species are categorized under Schedule-I of the Indian Wildlife (Protection) Act, 1972.

- The large herbivores in the foothills and adjoining plans are the Elephant (Elephas maximus), Gaur (Bos gaurus), and Asiatic wild buffalo (Bubalus arnee).
- It is the only state which has tree goat antelopes, namely, *Goral* (Naemorhedus goral), *Serow* (Naemorhedus sumatraensis) and *Takin* (Budorcas taxicolor).
- Perhaps it is the only state that harbours four major cats namely, Tigers (Panthera tigris), Leopard (Panthera pardus), Clouded Leopard (Neofelis nebulosa) and Snow Leopard (Uncia uncoa) and many lesser cats namely *Golden Cat* (Catopuma temmincki), *Fishing Cat* (Prionailurus viverrinus), *Leopard Cat* (Prionailurus bengalensis), *Marbled Cat* (Pardofelis marmarata) and *Jungle Cat* (Felis chaus).
- Seven primates namely Slow Loris (Nycticebus caucang), Hoolock Gibbon (Bunopithecus hoolock), Rhesus macaque (Macaca mulatta), Assamese Macaque (Macaca assamensis), Pig-taile macaque (Macaca nemestrina), Stump-tailed macaque (Macaca arctoides), and Capped Langur (Trachypithecus pileatus) have been reported from the state. In addition, Arunachal Macaque (Macaca munjala), a species new to science, has been added to the checklist from the state.

- The State has more than 2000 elephants having common corridors with Assam, Bhutan and possibly Myanmar.
- Six species of deer namely Sambar (Cervus unicolor), Indian Muntjac (Muntiacus muntjak), Hog deer (Axis porcinus), Musk deer (Moschus chrysogaster), Black muntjac (Muntiacus crinifrons) and Leaf deer (Muntiacus putaoensis).
- The highly endangered Hispid Hare has also been reported from grassy areas like D. Ering Memorial WLS.
- Among the smaller mammals, as many as 12 species of Moles and Shrews, 71 species of Chiropterans, 53 species of rodents, 13 species of Mustelids, 7 species of Civets etc. have been recorded from the State. Of this, the interesting species are Biswamoyopterus biswasi (Namdapha flying squirrel, a new to science from the state), Petaurista nobilis, Marmota bobac, Ratufa bicolor, Myotis longipes, Rhinolophus subbadius, Eonycteris spelaea, Nectogale elegens, Talpa leucura, etc.

The State has amazingly rich avifauna with over 760 bird species. Most of the species are resident and undergo altitudinal migration seasonally, though some winter migrants from the Palearctic region like waterfowls, waders, wagtails, etc. are common in wetland areas. The State has the distinction of having rare and endangered species of birds reported no where else in India, such as Ward's trogon (Harpactes wardi), Spotted Longtailed Wren Babbler (Spelaeornis troglodytoides), Austen's babbler (Stachyris oglei) and Mishmi wren (Spelaeornis badeigularis) which occurs nowhere else in the world. It is the richest state of Pheasants with 10 species. Rare pheasants like Mishmi Blood Pheasant (lthagnis cruentus kuseris), Elwe's earred Pheasant (Crossoptilon crossoptilon harmani), Sclater's or Mishmi Monal Pheasant (Laphophorus sclateri), Temmick's Tragopan (Tragopan temmicki) and Tibetan Graybellied Tragopan (Trogopan blythii molesworthi) etc. are found. Many endangered species of birds like White Winged Wood Duck (Cairina scutulata), Black Necked Crane (Grus nigricollis), Bengal Florican (Haubaropsiss bengalensis), Swamp Partridge (Francollinus gullaris) etc. have been reported. Timilinae babblers (*Pellorneum* sp.), laughing thrushes (*Garrulax* sp.), Fulvetta, Yuhinas, etc. are the family represented by largest number of bird species.

Other vertebrate and non-vertebrate faunal elements also occur in great numbers and forms. The State abounds 49 species of amphibian, 113 species of reptilian and 158 species of pisces and innumerable species of butterflies, moths, beetles and other insects. Some interesting species are Tabanus namdaphaicus, Tabanus shyamarupi, Tabanus tenuifrons (all are new to science from the state), Catapicephala splendens (new to India from the state), Bhagadatta austenia, Lamproptera curius, Delias aealis, Troides aeacus, Troides helena, Appias Iyncida hippoides, Salmostoma boopis, Danio horai, Barilius jayarami, Crossocheilus tirapensis, Aborichthys tikaderi, Noemcheilus arunachalensis, Rhacophorus namdaphaensis, Philautus namdaphaensis, Trimeresurus medoensis, Trimeresurus erythrurus, Calotes mystaceus, Japalura tricarinata, Scinella sikimmensis, Ophisops jerdoni, etc. (*Information Bulletin No. 27*, 2008).

SECTION - II

This section tries to find out the economic viability of flora and fauna in the State. There is a fundamental and strong bond between the people and the environment; for centuries, the forests and the land have given them all that they need. Plants species, which are used as house building and household materials, are abundant in the tropical and subtropical zones. The cane species grow profusely in the phyto-geographical regions. The over exploitation of certain cane species has meant their disappearance in recent years. Thatch grasses and wild bananas which grow abundantly are often used for roofing.

A remarkable feature of the plant diversity in the State is the occurrence of innumerable wild orchid species. Floriculture is now being promoted in the state and individual entrepreneurs have been quite successful in generating income from floriculture.

Wildlife in the natural situation constitutes the most important component of the ecosystem, which participates affectively in the energy flow and bio-geo-chemical cycling. Animal – plant, plant – plant and animal – animal interactions are the basic milestone of the success of an ecosystem and its productivity. As such, the richness of the ecosystem means the capacity to hold high species diversity, but deforestation has threatened the fabric of the survival of wildlife and the ecosystem in the region.

The Mithun (Bos frontalis), the dearest animal of the people of Arunachal Pradesh, is reared in semi-wild condition. It is a rare bovine species. The highest population of Mithuns in Arunachal is 124,730 in 1998. The animal is an integral part of the socio-economic and cultural life of the people. The wealth of a person is often gauged by the number of Mithuns he possesses. The Mithun is regarded as a symbol of prestige and was traditionally used as a medium of exchange, a means to settle disputes and as the bride price. Mithuns determine social status and are essential part of community feasts. The owners leave the Mithuns in the jungles to graze on natural fodder and they are occasionally given a dose of common salt. The Mithuns browse over a considerable range in search of fodder and over two dozen species of trees, shrubs, tall grasses, and bamboos form their diet. To maintain these Mithuns, the protection of the pristine forest is required, a task that is becoming increasingly difficult.

Majority of the rural poor of Arunachal Pradesh depend on the forest resources for at least four purposes such as food, livestock rearing (grazing and fodder), fuelwood and irrigation of crops. The floral and faunal diversities of the State and the dependence of Arunachal people on natural bio-resources for sustenance have resulted in a rich Indigenous Knowledge System (IKS). These systems have played a pivotal role in the conservation of the unique biodiversity over the centuries. It is imperative that the ethno-medicinal knowledge base of the ethnic groups in Arunachal is documented. Scientific exploitation of some of this rich biodiversity may hold the key to the development of the State. Both the State's biodiversity and its rich IKS are under threat due to the ineffective system of deforestation.

The economic viability of flora and fauna is to protect and preserve the rich wildlife through the creation of awareness among the people on the point of view of tourism. Different varieties of birds migrate from other regions during winter, which enrich the bird sanctuaries. The great Indian Hornbill has attained the status of State symbol. Its feather and beak form an important item of decoration of the traditional headgear of the tribes of the State. To preserve these wild birds and animals a number of sanctuaries and parks have been set up by the State Government. The scheme is implemented in two parts: (i) Protected area network management which includes management of National Parks and Sanctuaries, and (ii) Management of Zoological Parks.

There are two National Parks and ten Wildlife Sanctuaries spread over 9528 sq. kms. of its geographical area. The list of National Parks and Wildlife Sanctuaries are given in the Table 14.3.

Table 14.3: National Parks and Wildlife Sanctuaries.

Sl. No.	*Name of National Parks*	*Area in sq. km.*	*Important Fauna*	*Year of Notification*
1	*2*	*3*	*4*	*5*
A. NATIONAL PARKS and TIGER PROJECTS				
1.	Namdapha National Park (Tiger Project)		Tiger, Hooloek Gibbon Musk Deer	May 1983
2.	Mouling National Parks		Serow, Black Bear, Takin	Dec 1986
B. WILDLIFE SANCTUARIES				
1.	Pakui W/L Sanctuary	861.95	Elephant, Tiger, Bear, Sambhar Hornbill and Bison	March 1997
2.	Itanagar W/L Sanctuary	140.30	Elephant, Tiger, Bear	June 1978
3.	D. Ering W/L Sanctuary	190.00	Hog, Deer, Hare	Dec. 1980
4.	Mahao W/L Sanctuary	281.50	Red Panda, H.Gibbon, Takin	Dec. 1980
5.	Kamlang W/L Sanctuary	783.00	Capped, Langur, Bear, Deer	Oct. 1989
6.	Eagle Ness W/L Sanctuary	217.00	Elephant, Tiger, Red Panda	Oct. 1989
7.	Tele W/L Sanctuary	337.00	Clouded Leopard, Deer, Hornbill	July 1995
8.	Kame W/L Sanctuary	55.00	Elephant, Small Cats, Tiger	Sept. 1991
9.	Dibang W/L Sanctuary	4149.00	Trago pan, Kalis, Takin, Pheasan, Mask Deer	Nov. 1991
10.	Ydi-Rebe-Supse W/L Sanctuary	496.15	Capped, Langur, Clouded Leopard, Hornbill, Lesser cats	Feb. 1998

Source: PPCF, Itanagar.

At present, the important attractions of tourists in the State are the above parks and wildlife sanctuaries. On economic point of view, the State has to develop the nature based tourism industry as much as it wants to attract the national and international tourists.

The only one university, Rajiv Gandhi University in the State should establish a Herbal Science Department with following major areas of research as part of teaching and extension programmes.

(a) Development of natural products as drugs from living resources.
(b) Standardization of herbal drugs that are already developed.
(c) Validation of commercially available herbal drugs and formulation.
(d) Development of Agrotechnics for herbal plants.
(e) Development of human resources by commencing job oriented short-term teaching and training programmes on herbal sciences.

The existing Research Institute (Ayurvedic), Itanagar should be well equipped with enthusiastic field experts who have considerable expertise in dealing with herbal research so as to be awarded national and international patents on herbal products.

Traditional Use

India has one of the richest and most diverse cultural heritages associated with the use of medicinal plants. It represents a striking example of intimate link between biological diversity and cultural diversity. India is one of the 17-mega diversity countries and is home to 7 per cent of the world biodiversity. There are 16-agro climatic zones, 45,000 different plants species of which about 7000 to 8000 species are used in various traditional and folk systems of medicine. The richness of Indian civilization with its glorious past has given the humanity vast knowledge about the usage of plants for food and health care. The strong tradition of health care practised and documented for more than 3000 years in the form of Ayurveda, Unani, Siddha and Yoga and Naturopathy systems of medicine have evolved through centuries of usage and have stood the test of times in providing holistic healthcare to the people and are based on a very intimate and well researched understanding that biotic and non-biotic components of the environment play in promoting holistic health care.

Ayurveda is an ancient philosophy based on a deep understanding of eternal truths about the human body, mind and spirit. It is the science of living, developed meticulously by the devout '*Rishis*' of ancient India. This is the study based on the fundamental principles of '*Panchabhootha*' (Earth, Water, Air, Fire, and Space) existing in nature and inside man. Ayurveda teaches that the body and the mind are one entity with gross and subtle manifestations. The term '*Ayurveda*' is composed of two Sanskrit terms. '*Ayu*' means life and '*Veda*' means knowledge. Thus, Ayurveda is the knowledge of life or science of life. It is defined as the science, through which one can obtain knowledge about the useful and harmful ways of life, conditions that lead to the above types of life, as well as, the very nature of life.

There is growing interest in the world about the use of these systems and increasingly the developed world is prepared to adopt Indian systems. Today, *Yoga* has become popular the world over. It is now globally recognized that traditional, alternative complementary systems of medicine provide health care to almost 80 per cent of the population in developing and less developed countries. Even in the developed world, there is a growing realization that the modern system of medicine alone is not able to address all the health problems, particularly related to the lifestyle diseases like diabetes, hypertension, AIDS, cancer, etc. It is in this context that scientific wisdom contained in the traditional health care system can be used to find solutions to the present day problems. India is fortunate to have inherited rich biodiversity, both in plants and animals and the ethno-botanical knowledge which need to be explored and researched to find solutions to the health problems. It is this philosophy that the Government of India is very actively promoting for development and promotion of the traditional systems of medicines like Ayurveda, Unani and Siddha. One of the important initiatives in this direction has been to mainstream AYUSH systems of medicine in the health care under the National Rural Health Mission (NRHM).

Standardization

A major challenge facing the traditional systems of medicine world over today, however, is the question of standardization, quality and safety. Although traditional systems of medicine have their own science behind them, in order to improve the outreach of these systems, serious attention is being paid to validate the traditional knowledge and bring that in conformity with the modern scientific paradigm. Efforts are being made to strengthen quality control and standardization by evolving pharmacopoeial standards and setting up State Drug Testing Laboratories. Indian Government has also made compliance of Good Manufacturing Practices (GMP) mandatory for Ayurveda, Siddha and Unani drug manufacturing units. Not only this, the GMP norms are being made more and more stringent to ensure compliance with the evolving world standards on GMP. In order to ensure quality of such AYUSH products which use minerals in their preparation, testing for heavy metals has been made mandatory for export purposes with effect from 1st January, 2006 (*Kurukshetra, July, 2007*, p. 27).

If herbal production in the State is known to the rest of the country, it can create an exhaustive job of collecting and collating in all researches and extension studies. It will create a new avenue in the job markets. Different types of medicinal plants grow in different climatic zones. The State may be divided into three zones on the basis of its different climatic conditions: tropical and subtropical zone and temperate and alpine zone. Some important medicinal plants with their botanical and trade names and local uses as medicine for the purposes are shown in Table 14.4.

Table 14.4: Tropical and Subtropical Zone.

Habit	*Botanical name*	*Trade name*	*Purpose*
Herb	*Amomum subulatum*	Sthul Ela	Digestion, tonic
	Andrographis paniculata	Kalmegha	Liver disorder
	Asparagus racemosus	Shatavari	Tonic
	Curcuma cassia	Kali Haldi	Joint pain/sprain
	Curcuma Longa	Haridra	Cough/ pain
	Mimosa pudicaa	Lajjalu	
	Rauvolfia serpentina	Sarpagandha	Hypertension
	Solanum Khasianum*	Kantakari	Swas cough
	Solanum nigrum	Kakamachi	Digestion
	Zingiber officinale	Ardraka	Cough, arthritis

(*Contd.*)

(Table 14.4 Contd...)

Climber	Cissampelos pareira	Ambastha/ Patha	Liver tonic
	Tinospora cordifolia	Guduchi	Tonic
Shrub	Abroma augusta	Pishach Karpasa	Gynaecological disorder
	Caesalpinia crista	Lata Karanj	Malaria
	Cassia alata	Dadmardan	Skin disorder
	Euphorbia royleana	Snuhi	Piles, fistula
	Jatroha curcus	Ratnajot	Tonic
	Justicea adhatoda	Vasaka	Cough, swas, pain
	J. gendrussa	Kala Vasak	Cough, swas, pain
	Rauvolfia tetraphylla	Sarpagandha	Hypertension
	Solanum torvum	Brahati	Cough, swas
	Woodfordia fruticosa	Dhataki	Dysentery, tonic
Scandant Shrubs	Cissampelos pareira	Patha	Tonic
	Embelia ribes *	Via bidang	Worm infestation, liver disorder
Tree	Tinospora cordifolia	Guduchi	Tonic
	Aquilaria agallocha *	Agaru	Aphrodisiac, eye, ear
	Bauhinia purpurea	Kovidar	Throat disorder
	B. Variegata	Kanchanar	Throat disorder
	Bombax ceiba	Semul	Aphrodisiac tonic
	Cassia fistula	Aragvadha	Laxative, purgative, tonic
	Cinnamomum tamala*	Tejpatra	Cough, tonic
	Cinnamomum zeylanica*	Tvak	Cough, tonic
	Gmelina arborea	Gambhari	Cardiac, nervine tonic
	Gynocardia odorata	Chaulmoogra	Skin diseases
	Oroxylum indicum*	Shyonaka	Tonic
	Salmilia malabarica	Salmili	Aphrodisiac tonic
	Saraca asoca	Ashoka	Uterine tonic
	Terminalia arjuna	Arjuna	Cardiac tonic
	T. belerica	Bahera	Digestive tonic
	T. chebula	Haritaki	Purgative
	Zizyphus jujubo	Badara	Digestive, diabetes

(Contd...)

(*Table 14.4 Contd...*)

Temperate and Alpine Zone

Habit	*Botanical name*	*Trade name*	*Purpose*
Herb	Aconitum heterophyllum*	Visha	Tonic
	Coptis teeta*	Maira	Liver disorder
	Picrorhiza kurroa*	Katuki	Liver tonic
	Swertia chirayita*	Chiraita	Liver disorder
	S. Ciliata*	Chiraita	Liver disorder
	Valeriana hardwickii*	Tagar	Cardiac, hepatic and nervine tonic
	Thalictrum foliolosum	Mamiri	Liver tonic
Shrub	Berberis aristata	Daru Haridra	Liver tonic
	Zanthoxylum alatum	Tumbru	Digestive tonic
Climber	Embelia ribes*	Vai bidang	Worm, liver
	Rubia cordifolia*	Manjishtha	Blood purifier
	Tinospora cordifolia	Guduchi	Tonic
Tree	Taxus baccata*	Talisa	Swas, tonic

Source: Regional Research Institute (Ayurveda), Itanagar, Arunachal Pradesh.

Note: *indicates that these medicinal plants are largely available in Arunachal Pradesh.

Reasons for Traditional using of Medicinal Plants

1. Lack of Globalization

Needless to say, India is moving into a new century and a new millennium. In this context, a State like Arunachal Pradesh with continental dimensions should not ignore the changes that are occurring in the rest of the country due to impact of globalization. India initiated the process of globalization and liberalization since 1991. Over the past decade globalization and liberalization in India has been discussed mainly in terms of foreign investment, industrial development, information technology and the tremendous growth of service sector, etc. and there has been substantial media coverage of all these aspects of the Indian economy. The advent of globalization brings with it a marked change in our outlook as far as management of national economy is concerned. Under economic globalization, country after country has opened up their economies to free flow of finance capital, technology and goods. The death of distance, the service revolution and the mobility of capital are the three pillars of globalization which are present tremendous opportunities for India. But the good fruits of globalization have not entered the State.

2. Lack of Transportation

After the independence of the country, the Government of India undertook the development of transport and communication with a view to open up this remote state of India and therefore to facilitate the rapid development of the State. The State is the poorest in having roads connecting the urban and semi-urban areas. The people living in the remote villages, which lie in hilly and difficult terrain, finds very difficult to bring their patients to health centre for treatment. That is why; many times they depend upon the village Priest and *Vaidya* (Ayurvedician) who are mostly illiterate.

3. Lack of Medical Facility

The health care institutions have been shaped in conformity with National pattern. The old health units and dispensaries have been restructured into Primary Health Centres and Health Sub-Centres to ensure comprehensive coverage of preventive as well as curative care. At present (2003-04), there are 3 General Hospitals, 12 District Hospitals, 31 Community Health Centres,78 Primary Health Centres, 386 Sub-Health Centres, 3 Health units, 17 Dispensaries, 37 Homeo Dispensaries, 3 Ayurvedic Dispensaries and 2 T.B. Hospitals and others functioning in the state (*Directorate of Economics and Statistics*, Government of Arunachal Pradesh, 2004). Their total number during 2003-04 is 581 covering the entire geographical area of the state i.e., 83,743 sq. kms. The geographical area per health centre is 144.13 sq. kms. The total number of doctors including all registered is 527 during 2003-04. If we consider the population as per 2001 census, we get the population per doctor is 2083. Again the doctors are living mostly in urban and semi-urban areas. The local doctor posted in health centre located in village areas are hardly living in government allotted quarter. As a result, the village people finding no way depend on locally available herbal medicine.

4. Believe

Most of the village people have good faith in village Priest and *Vaidya* (Ayurvedician). Many a times the priest is successful in healing and the *Vaidya* (Ayurvedician) in curing diseases.

5. Age-old Custom

There are many age-old customary practices which compel the people, especially village people to use medicinal plants in their suffering. Their ecological adaptation and understanding many a times have proved result oriented. There are many examples in context of this fact. The people of the state are conservative in mind. They want to maintain the age-old custom.

Now-a-days, Herb-drug interactions are a hot topic of debate and herbs are potentially dangerous to patients who are already taking prescription medications. The basic concept of interaction is that consumption of two substances (herbs, drugs) at the same time or within a short interval of each other, will result in physiological effect that are different from a simple summation of the effects (Barbara, 2000).

SECTION - III

This section tries to bring into notice of authority and policy maker about the sustainability of flora and fauna in the State. In recent years, the State's rich biodiversity has increasingly come under threat. The hastening paces of developmental activities in the last three decades, and the improvement in the communication network, have meant increased access. Road building has established communication but the blasting process involved has meant the loss of valuable habitat. The rapid monetization of the barter economies has meant increased trade in timber. A number of hydropower projects have been commissioned, and these projects are at various stages of progress. The urbanization process has meant the destruction of the forest cover adjacent to the new townships that have come up. Another significant threat to the fragile ecosystem and biodiversity of the State is the shifting cultivation and the shortening of the jhum cycle and introduction of commercial plantation.

Timber extraction in the State was taken up on a large scale till 1995-96. Hence, a large number of wood based industries cropped up. A timber trade in the State had also increased through the operation of tree permits. There was halt on this trade after a Supreme Court Judgement on 12th December, 1996 on a writ petition (civil) No. 202 filed by Shri T.N. Godavarman Thirumulkpad.

In addition, there is the illegal trade of forest projects such as timber, medicinal plants, orchids, animal hide, musk gland and birds, which are smuggled out of the State by poachers. Bio-piracy is a new challenge manifested in a number of ways. Sometimes, the operators enter the State, develop contracts, and smuggle out valuable species, mainly of flora, without the knowledge of the government. Given their highly sophisticated methods of operation, this type of biopiracy is very difficult to detect. The creation of public consciousness, apart from the enhanced vigilance of the government, can help to control this problem.

Impact of Shifting Cultivation

The extent of deforestation of tropical forest has caused worldwide alarm as tropical forests provide more than 50 per cent of modern medicine. Tropical forests are living museums and laboratories that have yielded only a tiny fraction of their treasures to scientific study. In course of shifting cultivation remarkable varieties of flora and fauna are disappearing, which need immediate attention for extensive and intensive studies.

The type of vegetations destroyed depends upon the length of jhum cycle. A dense forest of long cycle has more tree species than grasses, whereas a forest of short cycle has more number of grasses. All the forest resources are disappearing and become rare due to deforestation and illegal felling of trees. The ecological balance favouring the complete hydrological cycle has been seriously upset over vast areas due to ignorance or lack of appreciation of methods of conserving and managing natural vegetation (whether a forest, grassland or mixed type) and of clearing the vegetation for cultivation. This misuse and destruction of plants cover combined with great increase in human and livestock population has created intense competition for natural resources. In the continued absence of conservation and correctly integrated land use system, overall habitat deterioration has become very widespread.

Impact of Urbanizations

Till 1961 census the State of Arunachal Pradesh was entirely rural having no urban centre. There were 17 urban centres in the State as per 2001 census. All these towns are administrative centres in most cases. Before the establishment of administrative centres, these places were full of forest. According to 1991 census 12.80 per cent people live in ten urban areas while as per 2001 census 20.41 people live in seventeen urban areas. The decennial urban growth rate in the state has been recorded as 139.63 in 1971-81, 167.04 in 1981-91 and 101.24 in 1991-2001.

Impact of Population Growth

The human population census was conducted for the first time in Arunachal Pradesh in 1961. Population increases in 2001 by 326.23 per cent in comparison to the population of 1961. More population means more shelter, more food, etc. which directly accelerate the deforestation. The decennial population growth rate since 1961 in the State has been recorded as 38.91 per cent in 1961-71, 35.15 per cent in 1971-81, 36.83 per cent in 1981-91 and 26.21 per cent in 1991-2001. It is more than all-India average.

Impact of Transportation

Till 1947, there were only three jeepable roads between Pasighat and Kobo by 35 kms., Sadiya-Tezu-Denzing by 77 kms. and still well road 56 kms. (*Source:* N.C.A.E.R – *Techno-Economic Survey of NEFA*, 1967, p. 91). So, the total length of roads was only 168 kms., till 1947. Before independence the colonial government did not take any effort to initiate the development process and the British indifference towards the area was mainly due to the fact that the area did not possess any readily exploitable resources. After the independence of the country, the Government of India undertook the development of transport and communication with a view to open up this remote state of India and therefore to facilitate the rapid development of the State.

In the development plans, the government has been attaching high priority to the construction of roads and as a result the total length of roads constructed in the state stood at about 15021.80

kms. including 399.80 kms. under National Highway giving the road density of 17.9 kms. per 100 sq. kms. of area at the end of March, 2004. The impact of road transport is wide ranging which includes agriculture, industry, trade and commerce which cumulatively affect overall development of a region. But at the same time the State has to face deforestation and thereby to destroy the herbs.

Impact of Industrializations

Arunachal Pradesh, though endowed with abundant natural resources is still lagging behind in industrial development as compared to other States of the country. Lack of transport and communication, dearth of skilled/technical personnel, poor literacy among local people, and low capital formation for setting up industries in this hilly region are some of the major factors for industrial backwardness. At present the main thrust of the Industry Department is to promote traditional village and small scale industries and thereby provide employment opportunities and improve the economic conditions of the people of the State.

Due to the shifting cultivation, growth of urbanization, growth of population, growth of transportation, growth of industrialization and overall development programmes, the hitherto virgin vegetation has become a victim of sudden large-scale changes upsetting the balance of nature.

Medicinal Plants under Threat in the State

At conference in Guwahati, experts from the State Forest Research Institute, Itanagar, Botanical Survey of India and the G.B. Pant Institute of Himalayan Environment and Development, Itanagar made an assessment of 47 plant species lying under threat. Out of the 47, five are threatened at the global level and are red listed by the International Union for Conservation of Nature (IUCN). These endemic species include Amentotaxus assamica, *Coptis teeta, Gymnocladus assamicus, Piper pedicellatum, P.Peepuloides, Aquilaria malaecensis, Dienia muscifera, Rauvolfia serpentina* and *Smilax glabra* are reported to be critically endangered.

Steps Taken by the Government

Orchid Research cum Development Centre

Realizing the importance of orchids which are found in abundance in the State, an Orchid Research cum Development Centre has been set-up at Tipi in the year 1972. Over the last 20 years, the Centre has made considerable progress in conservation, research and development by establishing a good germ-plasm collection of 400 species housed in the Orchidaria at Tipi, Dirang, Roing, Jengging and Itanagar. An Orchid Sanctuary covering an area of 100 sq. kms. for *in-situ* conservation of 160 species naturally occurring in Sessa area of West Kameng District has been established (*Information Bulletin No. 27*, 2008).

Arunachal Pradesh State Medicinal Plants Board

On the directions of the Ministry of Health and Family Welfare in the Department of ISM and H, Government of India, a State Level Medicinal Plants Board has been constituted under the Department of Health and Family Welfare, Government of Arunachal Pradesh *vide* Government notification No. HOMOEO-98/3 dated Itanagar, the 5th February, 2002. Initially, the Board was constituted on 7th November, 2001 but it started functioning since 5th February, 2002. Now the Board has been fully shifted to the Department of Environment and Forests in July 2007. The Board has a full time Chairman and Principal Secretary (Environment and Forests) acts as Vice-Chairman. Director, State Forest Research Institute, functions as its Member-Secretary and Chief Executive Officer. The Board is required to be further strengthened. The Board has the following functions:

- Coordination with Departments/Government Organizations for development of medicinal plants.
- Assessment of demand/supply position relating to medicinal plants both within the state and outside.
- Advice concerned Departments/ Organizations on policy matter relating to schemes and programmes for development of medicinal plants.
- Provide guidance in the formulation of proposals, schemes, programmes etc. to be taken up by agencies.

- Survey, identification, inventorisation and quantification of medicinal plants.
- Promotion of *ex situ / in situ* cultivation and conservation of medicinal plants.
- Promotion of co-operative efforts among collectors and growers and assisting them to store, transport to market their produce effectively.
- Setting up of database system for inventorisation, dissemination of information and facilitate the prevention of patents being obtained for medicinal use of plants which is in the public domain.

Matters relating to import/export of raw materials, as well as value added products either medicine, food supplements or as herbal cosmetics including adoption for quality and reliability in the state of Arunachal Pradesh and outside (*Information Bulletin No. 27*, 2008).

Wildlife Conservation

Wildlife in Arunachal Pradesh is not confined to Protected Areas alone. Vast, remote and inaccessible high altitude tracts as well as reserve forests and other areas in the foothills are equally important wildlife habitat. Besides bringing more and more rich and representative wildlife areas under the protected area network, wildlife management has to take into account conservation of biological diversity outside national parks and wildlife sanctuaries. The damage to wildlife in recent years is attributable to habitat degradation, encroachment, fragmentation and poaching.

Hunting has been a part of local tribal culture. Till recent past when the area was virgin and hunting was for self-sustenance, the pressure felt on wildlife was not significant. The Wildlife Act of 1972 is applicable throughout the State and wild animals get legal protection outside protected areas also. Of late, it has been realized that wildlife conservation cannot succeed without involvement and support of the local people. To seek cooperation from the people living in the vicinity of protected areas, specially designed eco-developmental schemes are being contemplated. These schemes aim at development of the areas in the immediate surroundings of national parks and wildlife sanctuaries so that the biotic pressures on protected areas can be minimized.

Namdhapa National Park and Pakhui Wildlife Sanctuary also implement the Central Scheme on Project Tiger. Project Elephant launched by the Central Government in 1991 covers many protected areas, reserve forests and the migratory corridors. The project seeks to stabilize dwindling elephant populations by habitat improvement, corridor linking and control of poaching. Provisions for protection of life and property and compensation for loss of life have been incorporated in the project. The emphasis is on involvement and cooperation of the local people. This Elephant Reserve will be spread in East Kameng and Papum Pare Districts covering an area of 1892 sq. kms. This Elephant Reserve harbours Elephant, Tiger, Leopard, Clouded Leopard, Snow Leopard, Red panda etc. A total of 377 Elephants were counted during 2001 Elephant Census.

To impart education, promote awareness and also to keep captive stock of indigenous fauna, the State Zoo at ltanagar and Mini Zoo at Roing and Miao are being developed. At Miao captive breeding of White Winged Wood Duck has been undertaken. The State Zoo at ltanagar houses rare animals like slow loris, binturong, stumptailed macaque etc. It is a captive breeding centre for tiger, barking deer, sambhar, etc. Large enclosures and natural way of keeping the animals are noteworthy features of this zoo. The State Wildlife Advisory Board under Chief Minister is also functional in the State. This Board has many senior officials as members SFRI (*Information Bulletin No.27*, 2008).

SECTION - IV

In order to harness the vast and varied natural resource endowments of Arunachal Pradesh, the following steps may be suggested. The conservation and sustainable utilization of medicinal plants/ herbs and the conservation of wild lives through community participation can deserves attention. A sustainable management plan for this sector is essential. The plan must analyse the status of medicinal plants/ herbs in the State and identify the threats and opportunities, barriers to markets and investments, recognize indigenous knowledge and practices and help to preserve sacred groves, with the effective use of biotechnology. There is nothing beyond nature, behind nature and other than nature. The key to man's health lies largely in the environment. The purpose of environmental health is to create and maintain ecological conditions that will promote health and thus prevent diseases. The biological and physical environment mostly depends on forest, which needs its preservation and protection. In order to maintain and improve the human quality of life, the renewable natural resources should be conserved. In this regard the following suggestion may be considered.

1. The renewable natural resources are soil, water, air, plants and animals. These are functionally connected to each other and have the capacity to increase under suitable conditions. Women have a definite role to play in building a free, healthy, prosperous and moral society, because they are much closer to the nature due to their motherhood complex. So, women should be given proper training regarding the conservation of nature based resources.
2. "Nature can meet all the needs of men, not the greed", Mahatma Gandhi said, "Real education is possible only in the lap of the nature", said Rousseau. The greedy nature of the man disturbs the whole environment. There is a dire need to inculcate the feeling of environmental protection among all sections of the people. Environment is our heritage. Hence, it is the – you and I who can save our environment. So, we should adopt environment conscious life.
3. In order to improve the quality of life of the present and future generations we have to establish a system in which resources and human needs are matched and none is being destroyed.
4. For the management of renewable natural resources we should try to establish the best balance between human needs and the resources to satisfy them.
5. Programmes should be developed to raise consumer awareness and promote their active participation to achieve changes in consumption and production patterns.
6. Unauthorized cutting of trees should be strictly restricted.
7. Government should promote the use of solar energy for fuel, light and other purposes.

8. We should recreate the desolated areas by planting more fruit bearing and quality type of trees.
9. Seminar for conservation of animals and plants should be organized in almost every village to grow consciousness among the villagers. The illiterate and innocent hunter should be given allowances and imparted the good effects of conservation of biodiversity. To give punishment the hunter, the informer may be awarded secretly and community hunting is strictly prohibited.
10. A quick survey should be undertaken through a team of young and enthusiastic field experts borrowed from different organizations dealing with indigenous medicinal herbs and drugs to assess the nature and extent of availability of economic plants and above all to extraction herbs of economic value from the forest should be encouraged.
11. This should be followed by detailed survey for identification, classification and codification of economic medicinal herbs.
12. Considering the market demand both inside the country and the export market, projects should be drawn to cultivate herbs of medicinal value for their desired active ingredients.
13. Bankable projects should be drawn for cultivation and processing of known medicinal herbs.
14. Promotional programmes on the aspect of research and development should be undertaken of selected herbs of known use but unknown economic exploitation for their gainful utilization.
15. The authority should undertake the possibilities for establishment of pharmacological perfumery and other specialized industries.
16. The floral assemblage in the State can cause immediate concern to any investigator. The effects of growth of urbanization, population, transportation, industrialization and overall shifting cultivation on biological resources will have to be assessed on database and do accordingly for the preservation of natural resources.
17. The only one university, Rajiv Gandhi University in the State should establish a Herbal Science Department with the

following major areas of research as part of teaching and extension programmes.

(a) Development of natural products as drugs from living resources.
(b) Standardization of herbal drugs that are already developed.
(c) Validation of commercially available herbal drugs and formulation.
(d) Development of Agrotechnics for herbal plants.
(e) Development of human resources by commencing job oriented short-term teaching and training programmes on herbal sciences.

18. The existing Research Institute (Ayurvedic), Itanagar should be well equipped with enthusiastic field experts who have considerable expertise in dealing with herbal research so as to be awarded national and international patents on herbal products.
19. Government (Central/State) should sell cooking gas (LPG) at subsidized rate so that the people can use firewood as least as possible.
20. The women especially village women should be given training how to be preserve biodiversity in the State, because, in most cases, the women in the State are collecting the firewood from the forest. Deforestation for domestic fuel supply adds to the environmental crises.
21. Much of the forest wealth of the State is undocumented. A comprehensive Biodiversity Action Plan, beginning with an exhaustive listing of the important plant and animal species of economic value, as well as endangered and rare species, should be the first step towards the conservation and sustainable use of this priceless heritage.
22. For conserving and managing natural vegetation the jhum cultivation and illegal felling of trees, which are the root cause of deforestation, must be stopped immediately but not without rehabilitation of the *jhumias*. If the government is successful to protect the natural vegetation, the state will be the richest in having the herbs which can be sold in national and international markets. Hence, it is necessary first to develop

the market for herbs within the state where the local cultivators will be benefited economically. It will give an incentive to the local people to protect the valuable herbs from extinction.

23. For the betterment of lives, urbanization, transportation, industrialization are necessary but we can try to minimize the deforestation due to shifting cultivation and illegal felling of trees which are the main cause of disappearance of flora and fauna in Arunachal Pradesh. The Central Government as well as the State Government should give top priority to protect the herbs of economic value in the State which are endowed more than 50 per cent of herbs of the country. Days are not far when the Governments can generate employment as well as earn foreign currency from the export of the State's flora and fauna if they take keen interest to protect them from disappearance due to impact of the factors mentioned under Section II.

Conclusion

Roy Barman Committee's Report (1982) on Forests clearly stated that banning the practice is not likely to achieve the object in view and it might even provoke reaction. CSE (1985) reports that a number of features have led to the failure of schemes to settle shifting cultivators; low productivity, absence of tools and implements, failure to understand water management in settled cultivation, short-term government policies and above all change of socio-cultural ethos, have been listed as probable factors. Question arises if a change is brought looking at the entire terrain conditions of the region, will it be acceptable to the local people and fit into their pattern of life. In this regard it may be suggested that some scientific measures should be taken to put an end to the erosion of top soil and studies should be carried out to explore the possibility of introducing modern innovations on jhum land so as to obtain higher yield per unit area. Besides, replacements of crop cultivation by other types of alternative livelihood like plantations, economic and conservational forestry, horticulture, development of animal husbandry i.e., livestock rearing like poultry farming, sericulture, bee keeping and so on may also be encouraged. The problems arising out of jhuming in Arunachal Pradesh can be solved keeping in view the many facts of shifting cultivation, the socio-cultural life of the people, the feasibility of change over the expenditure involved and the maintenance of a changed pattern. Effects should be so made as to bring the change from within the society. The cultivators should be imparted proper training and education to adopt new innovations. They must also be educated about the danger of jhuming.

Our specific focus with regard to social concerns is community rights to resources – a concern that is central to many of the debates on natural resource management. Three arguments are put forth: (i) that while the environment has at one level assumed a non-negotiable presence in policy, social concerns are only highlighted to the extent that they are deemed not to be environmentally destructive, (ii) that the discursive are deemed harmful is overly simplistic and in need of re-examination, and (iii) that the changing nature of environmental discourse can only be understood within the wider shifts in development policy. Although there are many who could claim that the environment itself receives an inadequate attention in development policy, a contention that is at least partly true, we are concerned here with new emerging policies and legislations tackle social concerns given the socially constructed nature of the environment.

The recent debates and developments with regard to the draft of National Environment Policy (NEP), 2004 and the Scheduled Tribes (Recognition of Forest Rights) Bill (STB), 2005 are illustrative in different ways of the manner in which social concerns are dealt with in environmental policy and legislation in India. Yet, while the pros and cons of specific policies and legislations have been Central to the academic debates on the environment, very little attempt has been made to trace the changes in environmental policy making and the way of social concerns have been still problematized.

REFERENCES

Agarwala, Padma Guha (2006): "Role of North-Eastern Women in Conservation and Protection of Environment", *University News*, Vol. 44, No. 37.

Anderson, L.A. and J.D. Phillipson (1985): Herbal medicine, education and the pharmacist, *Pharm.* J. 236: 303-305.

Barbara, S. (2000), "Is US Health Really the Best in the World? *Journal of American Medical Association* 284(4):483.

Bhattacharjee, R.P. (2000): *Economic Development of Arunachal Pradesh*, Himalayan Publishers, Delhi, Itanagar, p. 17-18 and p. 45-49.

Eisenberg, D.M., R.C. Kessler, C. Foster, F.E. Norlock, D.R. Calkins and T. L. Delbanco (1993): Unconventional medicine in the United States. Prevalence, costs and patterns of use. *N. Engl. J. Med.* 328: 246-252.

Fahishi, A. (1996): Complementary medicine. Vol. 1. London: *Financial Times* and Health Care Publishing.

Ghosh, A.K. (1990): "Impact of Shifting Cultivation in Living Natural Resources", in Majumdar, D.N. (ed.): *Shifting cultivation in North-East India*, Omsons Publications, Guwahati and New Delhi, pp. 178-197.

Government of Arunachal Pradesh (2004): *Economic Review*, Directorate of Economic and Statistics, Itanagar.

Government of Arunachal Pradesh (2006): *Arunachal Pradesh: Human Development Report* 2005, Rajiv Gandhi University, pp. 171-72.

Harikumar, P.N. and *et al.* (2007) "Role of Ayurveda Centres in Promoting Backwater tourism in Kerala", *Southern Economist*, Vol. 46, No. 9, Sept. 1, Bangalore, p. 21.

Hegde, S.N. (1988), "Coptis Teeta Wall (Mishmi Teeta): A Rare Medicinal Plant from Arunachal Pradesh", *Arun for News* 6(I), pp. 27-29.

Jain, S.K. (1987): *A Manual of Ethnobotany*, Scientific Publishers, Jodhpur.

Johnston, G.A. (1997): Market Report. Herbalgram 40: 52.

Josh, M.C. (1997): "Role of Herbs and Drugs in Economic Development" in Pandey, B.B. (ed.), *Patterns of Change and Potential for Development in Arunachal Pradesh*, Himalayan Publishers, Itanagar, New Delhi, p. 174-184.

Kanjilal, U.N., Kanjilal, P.C. and Das, A. (1934): *Flora of Assam*, Vol. I, Government of Assam, Shillong.

Maclennan, A., D.H. Wilson and A.W. Taylor (1997): *Prevalence and cost of alternative medicine in Australia*, London: Mintel International Group.

Mandal, R.K. (2006): "Sustainability of Medicinal Plants and its Economic Viability in Arunachal Pradesh", *Resarun (Journal of the Directorate of Research)*, Government of Arunachal Pradesh, Itanagar, Vol. 31, p. 1-10.

Mandal, R.K. (2005): *Arunachal Economy: Socio-Economic Transformation*, Champion Publishing, Itanagar, pp. 116-117.

Mandal, R.K. (2006): "Sustainability and Economic Viability of Medicinal Plants in Arunachal Pradesh, India" *Plant Archives: An International Journal of Plant Research*, Vol. 6, No. 2.

Mandal, R.K. (2006): "Forest and its Sustainability in Arunachal Pradesh", in Joseph, T.M (ed.): *New Governance Paradigm: Issues in Development*, Kalpaz Publications, New Delhi.

Mandal, R.K. (2006): "Herbs and their Sustainability in Arunachal Pradesh", Kurukshetra: *A Journal on Rural Development*, Vol. 56 No. 5, March, Ministry of Rural Development, New Delhi.

Mandal, R.K. (2007): "Flora and Fauna in Arunachal Pradesh: Economic Viability and Sustainability", *Arunachal Review*, Vol. VIII, No. 23, Sept.-Nov., Directorate of Information, Public Relations and Printing, Government of Arunachal Pradesh, Naharlagun.

Mehta D.K., (1998): *British National Formulary. British Medical Association and the Royal Pharmaceutical Society of Great Britain*. London : The Pharmaceutical Press.

Menon, Ajit (2006): "Environmental Policy Legislation and Construction of Social Nature", *EPW*, January 21-27, Vol. XLI, No. 3, p. 188.

Pandey, H.C. (1988): "Some Healing Herbs of the Monk's Amongst the Minor Forest Produce", *Arun for News* 6(I), pp. 1-10.

Pantuck E.J. (1996): Stimulatory effect of vegetables on intestinal drug metabolism in the rat. *J. Pharmacol Exp. Therapy* 198 : 278-283.

Rao, V.M. (2003: *Tribal Women of Arunachal Pradesh*, Mittal Publications, New Delhi, p. 21.

Rimo, Y., Tamuk, A. Ranjan, S. and Mishra R. (2004): Some Prominent Medicinal Herbs of Arunachal Pradesh in Mishra, R. (ed.): *Recent Advances in Environment Biology and Ethnobotany*. Sunview Centre, Itanagar, p. 77.

Shrivastava, S.R. Barik, N. Mishra, S. Vengurlekar, G. Shrikarthi, S. Revathi, S. Jain (2006): "A Review of Herb-Drug Interactions", Plant Archives: *An International Journal of Plant Research*, Vol. 6, No. 2, October, pp. 423.

Sinha, G.N.(2008): Forest and Forestry in Arunachal Pradesh, *SFRI Information Bulletin* No. 27, Issued by Director, State Forest Research Institute and Mission Director, State Bamboo Mission, Itanagar, Arunachal Pradesh.

15

Floriculture Industry

Introduction

Demand of flowers is increasing day-by-day because change in human attitude towards social and religious values. Flowers are now used in almost all the functions in India due to which its domestic demand is rapidly increasing. International demand of cut-flowers soars up especially during X-mas and Valentine day. Flowers like roses, gerbera, carnation, gladiolus, chrysanthemum, orchids and lilies are in great demand. Actually, the demand for flowers has gone up with liberalization, due to changes in lifestyle, increase in income level, corporate culture, increase in standard of living, increase in purchasing power of individuals, increase in educational status, etc. Metropolitan cities like Bangalore, Delhi, Mumbai, Kolkata, Hyderabad and Chennai and other major cities have the major market places for flowers and plants.

Annual growth potential of floriculture industry is about 25-30 per cent. This rapid rate is based on its export potential. The market is vast and sky is the limit for export of Indian cut-flowers. Floriculture is now emerging as an important economic activity in India due to its vast domestic market. In the past, it is always considered as an object of joy and beauty, always firing up human emotions and imagination. It has become a potential money spinner for the third world countries. This industry was promoted for earning the valuable foreign exchange during Eighth Five Year Plan as extreme focused thrust area for Exports by allocating one thousand millions of rupees. The "Technical Experts Committee" identified Bangalore, Pune, Hyderabad and Delhi as ideal for establishment of Export Oriented Production Units. There are 122 projects with the production capacity of 245 million plants per year has been registered on tissue culture, out of which 90 projects have become operational with 192 million plants per year production capacity. Only few have successful records as per the estimation. With invent of this fashion driven technology and challenges in export of flowers to the distant foreign markets during the last two decades, it has led to the development of its domestic market. Now-a-days, floriculture is being viewed as a high growth industry both for domestic as well as export market (Rao, 2011).

The commercial Floriculture is being promoted under National Horticultural Mission (NHM), National Horticulture Board (NHB), National Bank for Agriculture and Rural Development (NABARD), Ministry of Agriculture, Agricultural Produce Export Development Authority (APEDA), Ministry of Commerce, Government of India, Horticulture/Agriculture Departments of State Governments, Private Sector Investments. The commercial banks are also providing financial assistance in the form of loans, processing the floriculture projects and analyzing the projects for economic viability (Thanur, 2008).

Ornamental Nursery Plants

The major production sites of the country are in East coast – Kadiyam, Rajahmundry in Andhra Pradesh, West Coast -Mannuty in Kerala, Bangalore in Karnataka and Kalimpong, Kolkata in West Bengal. The domestic market is highly fragmented and unorganized for these floricultural products, but it is expanding at a very high growth rate.

There is a great demand for good quality flower seed. Nursery stocks viz. bulbs, budded rose, corms and potted foliage plants have a good demand in the domestic market. The nursery stocks of important garden flowers are Roses, Carnation, Gladiolus, Chrysanthemum, Gerbera, Lilium, Alstroemeria, Freesia, Aster, Iris, Limonium, Liatris, Lisianthus, Protea, Bird-of-Paradise, Tulip, Nerine, Archilea, Gypsophilla and Statice can be grown successfully. Potted/Foliage plant viz. Ficus, Dracaena, Azalea, Kalanchoe, Begonia, Yucca, Saint paulia, Chrysanthemum, Poinsettia and Dieffenbachia have great demand for garden display.

Potentiality of Floriculture in North-East States

The North-East region is endowed with the rich natural resources, which needs to be transformed into wealth though entrepreneurship development. Floriculture is a labour intensive economic activity generates large employment opportunities. Hence, Floriculture will be one of the avenues for employment and empowerment for women, unemployed educated youth and development of weaker sections of the society and overall poverty alleviation programmes. Diversification of cut-flowers with high value flower crops, which have the export demand, is in urgent need of the hour for the Floriculture Industry. Anthurium, which is important exotic commercial cut-flower, which can be grown in North-Eastern Region of India (Mizoram, Meghalaya, Nagaland, Arunachal Pradesh). Other crops like Orchids, gerbera, lilium, bird of paradise, etc. can be cultivated successfully in this region. Government of India has also declared some of the hill states as Special Economic Zones (SEZ) for Floriculture due to certain strategic advantages in Sikkim and Jammu and Kashmir for Floriculture, Uttarakhand for growing Gladiolus flower crop (Rao, 2011).

The potentials of Commercial floriculture are increasingly recognized and the expectations are that the floriculture is an important growth engine for sustainable and widespread development, augmenting economic opportunity, income and employment in hilly states of the region viz., Arunachal Pradesh, Mizoram, Nagaland, Meghalaya and Sikkim. The economy of the north-east people can be strengthened through the Floriculture Village or cluster village model for rural development in areas with good accessibility. This involves the sustainable use of natural resources and introduction of the market driven non-farm enterprises business opportunities through post-harvest processing and value addition to primary products through cultivation of commercially important flower crops suitable to the region.

Due to the efforts of the centrally sponsored scheme on Technology mission for integrated development of horticulture in the north-eastern states including Sikkim in the form of 50 per cent subsidy in kind as planting material with production unit with buyback arrangement under contract farming developed large plantations of Anthuriums in Mizoram, Meghalaya, Nagaland and Arunachal Pradesh, other flower crops having the potential to commercialize in North-East region are orchids, Gerbera, Liliums, Asters, Gladiolus, Tuberose, Bird of paradise, Heliconia, carnations, Rose, etc.

North-Eastern Hills Region will emerge as a potential production centre for the high value flowers like Anthurium and Orchids and cut greens on commercial basis because of available rich natural resources, favourable climate, low operational cost, low cost of production and quality. The region is reported to have immense potential for floriculture development, since topographically and agro-climatically, there are wide ranges of variation. A total of 700 such anthurium production units in contract farming mode with production capacity of 100 millions cut stems per annum are come up in the north-east region. The first consignment of 100 kg of anthuriums grown in Mizoram and the Garo Hills of Meghalaya was exported to the UAE. Similar kind of projects has also been initiated in other flower crops such as Gerbera cultivation at Itanagar and orchids at Dirang Valley of Arunachal Pradesh (Rao, 2011).

Amongst floricultural crops, orchids like Cymbidiums. Paphiopedilums and Vandas are commercially important as foreign exchange earning items while anthuriums, amaryllis, begonias, carnations, dahlias, gladioli, hedychium, lilies, roses, rhododendrons, varieties of ferns and palms, conifers and other foliage plants offer excellent opportunities for commercial floriculture both in domestic and foreign markets (Hegde, 2008).

It is economically viable for flower production by taking the advantage of the most favourable climate of the North-East Region. Many people can easily take up flower cultivation with minimum investment. The operational costs and energy costs are very less due to congenial climate. This region has great potential to meet the demand for flowers on occasions like Valentine's Day, Christmas, Mother's Day, seminar/symposia, formation of bouquet, floral tribute etc.

Realizing the potentials of floriculture with an emphasis on orchids in the global trade and its abundance in the State, Arunachal Pradesh Government under the Department of Environment and

Forest has established an Orchid Research-cum-Development Centre at Tipi in the year 1972 in West Kameng District. Over the last three decades, the Centre has carried out pioneering works in the development of Orchids and promoted the floricultural activities not only in Arunachal Pradesh but also throughout the North-East India. It has made considerable progress in conservation, research and development by establishing a good germ-plasm collection of 400 species housed in the Orchidaria at Tipi, Dirang, Roing, Jengging and Itanagar. An Orchid Sanctuary covering an area of 100 sq. kms. for conservation of 160 species naturally occurring in Sessa area of West Kameng District has been established. Various other agencies like National Horticulture Board, APEDA, NEC, NEDFI, NABARD, etc. have also initiated promotional activities and assistance schemes for ventures in floriculture so as to achieve socio-economic upliftment of the people of this region.

Demand in International Trade

Flowers have good export trade and are a good source of earning foreign exchange. The Global Floriculture business based on consumption is estimated at US$60 billions of which cut-flowers contribute for 60 per cent share. India being a tropical moderate country is a treasure house of ornamental plants. The international floriculture market trade is estimated to be Rs. 125,000 crores of which cut-flowers accounts for about Rs. 80,000 crores. Out of this, India is having only 300 crores business. Hence, there is a good scope to increase its share in the international business. Netherlands is the world leader in trade and technology of floriculture products with contribution of US $13.2 billions (2005). The Netherlands exports ornamentals to 112 countries, while just 13 of these markets accounts for 90 per cent of the sales. Sales of cut-flowers and pot plants sourced from the Netherlands will increase by 36 per cent and 46 per cent respectively shown in Table 15.1. The sector will subsequently be responsible for sales worth ($ 4 billion 2006) $ 7.5 billion by 2016 of which 90 per cent will be realized by exports. Kenya, the important competitor for Indian cut-flower industry, caters to over 60 per cent of the global cut-flower demand and produces over 40 different types of cut-flowers (Rao, 2011).

Table 15.1 Top 10 cut flowers and pot plants auctioned in the Netherland

Top 10 cut flowers auction turnover in NLG Millions				*Top 10 pot plant auction turnover in NLG millions*			
S.No.	*Flower*	*Year 2000*	*Change 99/00%*	*S.No.*	*Crop*	*Year 2000*	*Change 99/00%*
1.	Rose	1,427	+ 10.6	1.	Ficus	97	– 0.8
2.	Dendranthema	709	+ 18.1	2.	Phalaenopsis	84	+ 22.9
3.	Tulip	390	+ 20.5	3.	Kalanchoe	74	+ 6.4
4.	Lily	330	+ 5.5	4.	Dracaena	68	+ 9.5
5.	Gerbera	221	+ 10.1	5.	Dendranthema	60	+ 4.3
6.	Dianthus	150	– 4.2	6.	Hedera	53	+ 5.8
7.	Cymbidium	143	+ 9.1	7.	Spathiphyllum	50	+ 15.4
8.	Freesia	137	+ 4.1	8.	Anthurium	49	+ 27.9
9.	Alstroemeria	97	+ 9.8	9.	Hydrangea	45	+ 14.7
10.	Gypsophila	94	– 2.6	10.	Rosa	42	+ 9.2

*Source:*This table has been taken from Rao C. Chandrasekhara (2011): "Opportunities and Challenges in Floriculture Industry for Entrepreneurship Development in North East Region of India" in Mandal, R.K. (ed.), Entrepreneurship and Rural Development in North-East India, DVS Publishers, Guwahati.

Cultivation of Flowers

Floriculture can be done in open fields or in poly-houses. However, culture in poly-houses is preferable as it provide artificially controlled environment in which threat from diseases, insects, high temperature, intense light, heavy rains, etc. are minimized. Hence, flowers are produced round the year without any seasonal constraint.

Potentiality in the Job Market

Floriculture industry requires persons of the followings categories:

(a) Skilled workers: Persons trained in manual work like cutting/harvesting of flowers, packaging, transport and storage in cold chambers.

(b) Junior Technicians: Class X pass with 6 months to one year training in techniques of floriculture, hydroponic /soil culture, packaging and storage, construction and maintenance of pipeline, sprinkler, drip, cold storage, etc.

(c) Senior Technicians/Floriculturists: Essential qualification for the post is B.Sc. in Agriculture/Floriculture/Botany with specialization in poly-house/greenhouse, drip irrigation and fertigation, hydroponic culture, transportation, sales, marketing and exports. Knowledge of computer is desirable.

(d) Scientist/Scientific Officer/ Manager: Persons having M.Sc./ Ph.D. in the field of agriculture/ floriculture/ microbiology/ virology with specialization in poly-house/ greenhouse, modern techniques of irrigation and fertigation, hydroponic culture, sales, marketing and exports.

Self-employment Opportunity

There is a good self-employment opportunity in this field. Small scale floriculture industry can be established with limited resources through which one can be gainfully employed. This industry has very high employment generation and foreign exchange earning potential.

List of some Floriculture Industries of India that can provide employment

- Pudumjee Plant Laboratories Ltd., Pune.
- Sharda Farms, Nasik.
- Sahil Agro and Farm Products, 24-Kapashera, Delhi.
- Al-Falah Blossoms Limited, A-22, Green Park, Aurobindo Marg, New Delhi.
- Shreyash Blooms, Raghu Ganj, Chawri Bazar, Delhi.
- Indus Floritech Ltd., Hyderabad.
- Jagdambi Agri Genetics Ltd., Hyderabad.
- Neha International Ltd., Pune.
- Praz Agro-Vision Ltd., Pune.
- Eden Park Agro Products (P.) Ltd., Pune.
- Agri-expo Biotech (I.). Ltd., Mumbai.
- Nagarjuna Agritech Ltd., Bangalore.
- Global Industries Ltd., Delhi.
- Sri Vasavi Florex Ltd., Bangalore.
- Nath Biotech Ltd., Aurangabad.
- Varlak Agrotech Pvt. Ltd., Bangalore.
- Eden Agro Flora (Aop), Bangalore.

- Turbo Industries Ltd., Punjab.
- Florence Flora, Krishna Apartment.
- Basappa Road, Bangalore.
- Horizon Flora (I.) Ltd., Induri, Pune.
- Century Flowers, Pune.
- Birla Floriculture, Shirgaon, Pune.
- Cooper Agro Products (P.) Ltd., Sahney Sujan Park, Pune.
- Kumar Biotech, Pune.
- Samarth Greentech, Bhawani Peth, Pune.
- Deccan Flora base, Pune.

List of some Institutions/Universities that offer courses in Floriculture

- IARI, New Delhi.
- National Centre for Mushroom Research and Training, Solan, H.P.
- Assam Agriculture University, Jorhat
- Birsa Agricultural University, Ranchi.
- Rajendra Agricultural University, Pusa, Samastipur.
- Haryana Agricultural University, Hissar.
- Shere-e-Kashmir University of Agriculture, Srinagar.
- University of Agriculture Sciences, Bangalore.
- Kerala Agriculture University, Trichur.
- Mahatma Phule Krishi Vidyapeeth, Rahuri, Ahmednagar.
- Dr. Punjabrao Deshmukh Krishi Vidyapeeth, Akola.
- Central Agricultural University, Imphal.
- G. B. Pant University of Agriculture and Tech., Pantnagar.
- Acharya N.G. Ranga Andhra Pradesh Agricultural University, Hyderabad.
- University of Agricultural Sciences, Dharbad.
- Himachal Pradesh Krishi Vishwavidyalaya, Palampur.
- Narendra Deva University of Agriculture and Tech., Faizabad.
- Punjab Agricultural University, Ludhiana.
- Rajasthan Agricultural University, Bikaner.
- Tamil Nadu Agricultural University, Coimbatore.
- Indian Agricultural Research Institute, New Delhi.
- C.S. Azad University of Agriculture and Technology, Kanpur.
- North Bengal University, Darjeeling, West Bengal.

Dry Flowers Production

Dry flowers have good demand both in Indian and international markets. From India it is being exported to countries like USA, Japan and Europe. India stands first in dry flower export owing to the availability of variety of plants. Dry flowers don't mean only flower parts, but also includes dried shoots, seeds, barks etc. Export of dried flowers and plants from India is about Rs. 100 crore per year. The industry exports 500 varieties of flowers to 20 countries. They are widely used to make handmade paper, lampshades, candle holders, jute bags, photo frames, boxes, books, wall quilts, topiary, cards and several gifts. The use of dry flowers in the making of these products enhances the appearance and beauty of these products.

Techniques in Dry Flower Making

Dry flower production involves two important steps.

1. Drying

Best time for cutting flowers for drying: Flowers should be cut in the morning hours after the dew has evaporated from the plants. Once cut, group stems into bunch using rubber bands and remove them from the sunlight as soon as possible.

Sun Drying: Sun drying is the easy and cheap method. But during rainy days we can't dry flowers in this method. The flower bunches are hanged upside down in ropes or in bamboo splits. No chemicals are used. Good aeration is must. Chances of fungal attack are very high in this method.

Freeze Drying: It is an improved method over sun drying. The freeze drying equipments are costlier. But the quality of the dried flower is very high and fetches good price.

Pressing: Either blotting paper or ordinary papers are used. The flowers will become flat and there is chance of higher amount of damage to the flowers.

Glycerin Method: Glycerin is filled after removing the moisture from the flowers. Very high quality products are obtained in this method.

Polyset Polymer: By spraying polyset polymer flowers get dried. Drying time is very less in this method. It improves the colour of the final product.

Silica Driers: Using Silica or Silica gel, we can improve the quality of flowers and it makes the flowers intact. Very delicate flowers and plants are dried in this method.

2. *Dyeing: Procion*

Type colour is best for dry flowers. Take 4 kg of dye-powder and mix with 20 litres of water. Dilute this solution in 800 litres of hot water and mix 2 litres of acetic acid. For very soft flowers add Magnesium Chloride to enhance the colour. Soak the dried flowers until they absorb the colour.

Commercial Dry Flower Products

Flowers and Parts of Plants: Cock's comb, jasmine, Amaranthus, Areca and Coconut leaves and cut-flowers come in this category. Also includes dry leaves and shoots used as fillers. Past 20 years India is exporting these types of materials.

Potpourri: It is a mixture of scented loose dry flowers kept in a polythene bag or normally kept in almirahs, drawers and bathrooms. More than 300 types of plants used in this method. Bachelor's button, Cock's comb, jasmine, rose petals, Bougainvillea flowers, neem leaves and nuts from the fruits are commonly used in India to make Potpourri. Our main customer is United Kingdom.

Dry Flower Pots: Dry stems and shoots are used. Though it has less market demand, it gives good price and mostly preferred by high income group. The commonly used materials are dried cotton skins, pine flowers, dry chillies, dry bottle-gourd, grass, tree jasmine, everlasting flower, asparagus leaves, fern leaves, tree barks and twigs.

Dry Flower Handicrafts: It is the latest development in dry flower market. Framed dry flower pictures, greeting cards, covers, bouquets, candle stands, and glass bowls are made using different coloured dry flower materials (Swarnapriya and Jayasekar, 2008).

Conclusion

North-Eastern Hills Region may emerge as a major production centre of floriculture in view of international market because of its strategic location provided good transportation. As floriculture is labour intensive, the employment and income per unit area from floriculture is much higher than any other crops. It takes not only less area in comparison to other crops but also needs less financial investment. The domestic market is not developed, again it is highly fragmented and unorganized but it is expanding at a very high growth rate. It may be hoped that in near future, the bottleneck for the development of floriculture will be removed and its market will be developed. Micro finance, micro credit through SHG can develop this small scale floriculture industry. There is steady growth in SHGs and many households are being helped through helped Micro Finance. To set up floriculture industry through SHG by micro credit will bring a healthy progress of the overall development of the rural people especially women in the north-east region in general and in Arunachal Pradesh in particular. No development can be achieved in rural north-east India especially in Arunachal Pradesh on sustainable basis until and unless its women are developed and empowered socially and economically. It is well understood today that without economic and social liberalization of women, no true liberation of women is possible and also without the provision of equal economic and social opportunities to women, no emancipation of women truly occurs.

REFERENCES

Chandrasekhar Rao, C. (2005): Radio talk on: *Floriculture as an Occupation*, for Intellects programme recorded on 1st August, 2005 at All India Radio, Pasighat.

Chandrasekhar Rao, C. (2011): "Opportunities and Challenges in Floriculture Industry for Entrepreneurship Development in North-East Region of India", in Mandal, R.K. (ed.), Entrepreneurship and Rural Development in North-East India, DVS Publishers, Guwahati, India, pp. 29-34.

Gudaganavar, N.V. and Gudaganavar, R.S. (2009): "Empowerment of Rural Women through SHG", *Southern Economist*, Vol. 47, No. 19, February 1, Bangalore.

Hegde, S.N. (2008): "Impact of Globalization on the Development of Floriculture *vis-a-vis* Socio-Economic Upliftment of Women of Northeast India" in Pandey, B.B. (ed.): *Impact of Globalization on the Himalayan tribes of India*, Himalayan Publishers, New Delhi, Itanagar.

Kumararaja, K. (2009): "Performance of Self-Help Group in Tamil Nadu", *Southern Economist*, Vol. 47, No. 19, February 1, Bangalore.

Thakur, P.C. (2008): "Employment Opportunities in Floriculture", *Employment News*, 4-10 October, Vol. XXXIII, No. 27, New Delhi.

Swarnapriya, R. and Jayasekar, M. (2008): "Agri-Business: Dry Flowers Production" Kurukshetra, *A Journal on Rural Development*, Ministry of Rural Development, Vol. 57, No. 2, December, New Delhi.

SECTION III
WOMEN EMPOWERMENT

16

Empowerment of Women Through Education and Some Selected Opinions

Introduction

Another debated topic in which Government of India as well as the Non-Governmental Organizations (NGOs) and inter-governmental organizations including UN is taking interest is "women empowerment". But it is true that the real development of society is neither possible nor desirable by leaving half of the population in dark and depression. Realizing this virtue Gandhi advocated for the "women empowerment". By supporting women empowerment he writes, of all the evils for which man has made himself responsible, none is so degrading, so shocking or so brutal as his abuse of the better half of humanity to me, the female sex, not the weaker sex. It is the nobler of the two, for it is even today the embodiment of sacrifice, silent suffering, humility, faith and knowledge. Therefore, he was in favour of educating women and giving them all freedom which men enjoy. He writes, man should learn to give place to woman in the country or community where women are not honoured. He even encouraged the women to join politics hand by hand with man but also warned them to be independent in their thinking without simply carry the wishes of their parents or husbands. When the country was still struggling to escape from the clutches of foreign ruler, Gandhiji was thinking about to rescue the womenfolk from the clutches of parochial caste ridden thinking of Indian male bastion. But this progressive thinking of Gandhiji is yet to be realized even after 60 years of independence of the country. Still women are fighting hard to get their political justice with limited success in Panchayati Raj Institution where the seats are reserved for 33 per cent of the women. The Women Reservation Bill is yet to be passed in our Parliament which seeks to equalize the advantage of women participation in politics at the national level. Therefore, this made Gandhiji's thinking more relevant as we are still struggling to match his wishes to place women on an equal footing in our male dominated society.

Women's empowerment and their full participating on the basis of equality in all spheres of society are fundamental for the achievement of equality, development and peace (Fourth World Conference on Women, Beijing, 1995). From time immemorial, women have faced the challenges of coping with a male chauvinistic milieu. Even after several years of planned development of India, the status of women in our country is low and their socio-economic conditions are much more depressed than that of men. Empowerment by means of education, literacy or modest income-generating projects is clearly insufficient to ameliorate the prospects for a higher quality of life for women. The process of empowerment is taking place at so many levels that it is quite difficult to gauge the actual nature and extent of empowerment in improving status of women. Certainly the process is entangled in the struggles of civil society against the state, and under the weight of historical practice and on going debates over the appropriate role of ideologies. Women constitute 48 per cent of the Indian population, but when we often sermonize human rights, we often forget that women as human beings are also entitled to fundamental human rights. We have denied and continue to deny them basic human rights. Even after 61 years of independence these women continue to live in a state of neglect and exploitation. The concept of women empowerment was introduced at the International Women's Conference at Nairobi in 1985. The term empowerment was defined as "a distribution of social power and control of resources in favour of women". Empowerment is not something which could be made available in the form of a capsule to those whom we think is in need of it. It is not just a concept that could be defined with the help of some universally accepted parameters. Empowerment is a process and includes the following components:

(i) Equal access to opportunities for using society's resources.
(ii) Prohibition of gender discrimination in thought and practice.
(iii) Freedom from violence.
(iv) Economic independence.
(v) Participation in all decision-making bodies.
(vi) Freedom of choice in matters relating to one's life.

The national policy of empowerment of women has set certain clear cut goals and objectives: The goal of this policy is to bring about the advancement, development and empowerment of women. The policy will be widely disseminated so as to encourage active participation of all stakeholders for achieving its goals. Specifically, the objectives of this policy include:

(i) Creating an environment through positive economic and social policies for full development of women to enable them to realize their full potential.
(ii) The enjoyment of all human rights and fundamental freedom by women on equal basis with men in all spheres-political, economic, social, cultural and civil.
(iii) Equal access to participation and decision-making of women in social, political and economic life of the nation.
(iv) Equal access to women to health care, quality education at all levels, career and vocational guidance, employment, equal remuneration, occupational, safety, social security and public office, etc.
(v) Strengthening legal systems aimed at elimination of all forms of discrimination against women.
(vi) Changing societal attitudes and community practices by active participation and involvement of both men and women.
(vii) Mainstreaming a gender perspective in the development process.
(viii) Elimination of discrimination and all forms of violence against women and the girl child.
(ix) Building and strengthening partnerships with civil society, particularly women's organizations.

Education is central to the process of sustainable development. The role of education in empowerment is not only learning of three 'R's (reading, writing and arithmetic) but includes:

- Raising awareness;
- Critical analysis of various structures, and
- Acquiring knowledge for empowerment at all levels.

Education should include not only formal education but also skill training and functional literacy. First and foremost of all is to demystify the myth that girls are not sent to school because they are girls and in view of their primary role as mothers and housewives. Girls and women are not only housewives and mothers but they are also 'workers' in the economic sense. They should be educated to perform an indispensable role in the home and in the household economy, as well as for bringing enlightenment and emancipation. Empowerment of women through education will develop:

- Self-esteem and self-confidence of women;
- A positive image of women by recognizing their contribution to the society, polity and economy;
- Ability to think critically;
- Decision-making abilities and action through collective process;
- Choices in areas like education, employment and health;
- Equal participation in development process;
- Knowledge and skill for economic independence, and
- Access to legal literacy and information relating to their rights.

Women of today certainly play a vital role in the development of the society. Man's natural tendency is to remain happy. For attaining peace, happiness and full-fledged satisfaction, we require certain basic steps. One such step is "Women Empowerment". Women Empowerment through education is considered as the only effective instrument of their capacity building. There is always a high degree of correlation between the attainment of education and the level of economic development. This notion is true both at the macro and micro level. If education plays a pivotal role in designing the course of development, it is the womenfolk that form the primary element of the development process. The pre-requisite in the development process is their empowerment and the initiatives for empowerment should, obviously, begin with education. The deprivations of women are significantly visible in various macro indicators like education, health, employment etc. In different spheres of life they are also subject to a lot of hurdles, which are necessarily gender specific. Sincere effort is urgently required for the emancipation of women from all distress. The significance of women empowerment has gathered momentum over the years. It is also reflected in the recent Union Budgets of the Government of India. The Seventh Five Year Plan had adopted the Women's Component Plan (WCP) to initiate a mechanism for identifying and monitoring the schemes, directly benefiting women. In the Ninth Plan, provision was made for allocating unconditional minimum quantum of funds for the women welfare related schemes run by the different Ministries/Departments. The WCP was the precursor of Gender Budgeting. The Tenth Plan went a step further when it decided to launch Gender Budgeting. In 2004-05, the Ministry of Women and Child Development, Government of India had adopted "Budgeting for Gender Equity" as a Mission Statement. Finally based on the recommendations of the Ashok Lahiri Committee on "Classification of Budgetary Transactions", the Government of India has introduced a statement on Gender Budgeting in Union Budget 2005-06. It included 10 demands for grants. The Gender Budgeting is, now, well institutionalized in India. The Draft Approach Paper to the Eleventh Five Year Plan aimed "Towards Faster and More Inclusive Growth" (Planning Commission, June 14, 2006). Its objective is to include the excluded and it gives stress on 'Gender Balancing'. All the steps echo the concern of the nation for women, for their overall development, and thus empowerment. The Government has recognized that education is the primary step towards women's empowerment. The policy of the Government gives stress on the removal of illiteracy among women and all the hurdles towards their access to education.

In India, at present, there are as many as 1578 women's colleges. Along with this, there are five universities exclusively for women. Today the importance of education in capacity building and empowerment is no longer any unfamiliar notion. If basic education forms the preliminary step of women's progress, the higher education is, perhaps, the best medium to ensure social, economic and political empowerment of women in India. When any one talks about women empowerment, the topic involves a large number of issues like economic opportunity, social equality, political representation, participation in governance, property right. The agenda is always to remove the gender-based asymmetry in all events. All the gender-asymmetrical issues in all events against the women can be removed through enlightening of education.

For centuries, under an artificial dispensation, women's intrinsic qualities had been suppressed, and they were forced to live a wretched life. Not being counted as human beings, women did not even have voting rights.

The statement recalled that it was on March 8, 1857, in New York City that the Suffragette Movement had brought a new awakening. Making it clear that women were no less capable then men, a sustained movement for women's rights had been launched.

Accordingly, the United Nations General Assembly had declared March 8 as International Women's Day, the statement noted, adding that this day is an occasion to examine how far the goals of equality among the sexes, peace and development have been achieved.

It is only when men and women work hand in hand that the economic and political problems facing Arunachal Pradesh can be successfully resolved (*The Assam Tribune*, 12th March, 2007).

A manual, developed after a year long intensive research by the Gender Training Institute (GTI) of the Delhi-based Centre for Social Research, deals with crimes related to dowry, illegal trafficking and domestic violence.

"The law is the same for both men and women. However, if those who implement it (policemen) lack of sensitivity towards women's problems, that gets reflected in their behaviour," say Sucharita of the Purogami Mahila Sangathan, a national women's organization that has been active for close to two decades.

However, Kiran Bedi, India's best known police woman feels that on its own, the manual will struggle to solve problems related to the way the police treat women. Welcoming it as a significant step, she says, "The manual is a very clear roadmap which tells the trainer exactly what path he should take. However, the problem may lie not with the trainer, or the training method, but with the trainee," she says (*The Telegraph* 12th July, 2006).

Human Resource Development Minister, Arjun Singh said, it is civil society to understand that a nation can only progress if the women are literate, since the child learns his words from her. The country can only be proud when the rate of literacy among all sections of society is high.

Women's empowerment and their full participating on the basis of equality in all spheres of society are fundamental for the achievement of equality, development and peace (Fourth World Conference on Women, Beijing, 1995).

From time immemorial, women have faced the challenges of coping with a male chauvinistic milieu. Even after several years of planned development in India, the status of women in our country is low and their socio-economic conditions are much more depressed than that of men.

Former M.P., Murlidhar Bhandare said it was necessary for the Government to take programmes of the female literacy on a war-footing and ensure that adequate funds are put at the disposal of the implementing agencies and Non-Governmental Organizations for the purpose (*The Arunachal Times*, 4th September, 2005).

The resolution on the National Policy on Education (1968) stressed the importance of women education in these words, "The education of girls should receive emphasis not only on grounds of social justice but also because it accelerates social transformation".

The United Nations Declaration on the Elimination of Discrimination Against Women (1967) took note of the great contribution made by women to social, political, economic and cultural life and the part they play in the family and particularly in the rearing of children and recommended the following in Article 9 of the Declaration: "All appropriate measures shall be taken to ensure to girls and women, married or unmarried, equal rights with men in education at all levels and in particular.

(a) Equal conditions of access to and study in educational institutions of all types, including universities and vocational, technical and professional schools;
(b) The same choice of curricula, the same examinations, teaching staff with qualifications of the same standards and school premises and equipment of the same quality, whether the institutions are co-educational or not;
(c) Equal opportunities to benefit from scholarships and other study grants;

(d) Equal opportunities for access to programmes of continuing education, including adult literacy programmes.
(e) Access to educational information to help in ensuring the health and well being of families.

Phenomenal Progress since Independence

Education is a vital channel to prepare people for the kind of effective role mentioned above, to achieve a sound democratic system, with full knowledge of the citizens' duties and rights. The benefits of education are many. Education is the best investment that a country could make, of lasting benefit.

Importance of education of women has been recognized since the achievement of independence. Accordingly strenuous efforts have been made in this area. The following figures in Table 16.1 reveal that literacy among women has increased proportionately as compared with men. Yet much more is needed to bring it at par with men.

Table 16.1: Sex-wise Literacy Rate 1951-2001 in India.

Year	*Per cent Literate*	*Male*	*Female*
1951	18.33	27.16	8.86
1961	28.31	40.46	15.34
1971	34.45	45.95	21.97
1981	43.56	56.37	29.75
	(41.42)	(53.45)	(28.46)
1991	52.11	63.86	39.42
2001	55.30	64.13	45.84

Source: Census of India, Various Issues.

Notes: (i) Literacy rate for 1951, 1961 and 1971 related to population aged five years and above. The rates for the years 1981 and 1991 relate to the population aged seven years and above. The literacy rates for the population aged five years and above in 1981 have been shown in brackets.

(ii) The 1981 rates exclude Assam where the 1981 census could not be conducted. The 1991 census rates exclude Jammu and Kashmir where the 1991 census was not conducted.

The number of women per hundred men since 1950 to 2000 is depicted in following Table 16.2 in India. From the very beginning the women were much lagging behind the men but in the later part they are getting much progress in the field of higher education.

Table 16.2: Number of Women per Men in Higher Education since 1950-51.

Year	*Number of women per hundred men*
1950-1951	14
1960-1961	17
1965-1966	24
1981-1982	38
1982-1983	39
1983-1984	40
1985-1986	42
1987-1988	46
1988-1989	46
1989-1990	47
1990-1991	47
1999-2000	55

Source: Ministry of Human Resource Development, Department of Education.

Causes of Slow Progress of Women Education

(a) Economic backwardness of the rural community.
(b) Lack of proper social attitudes in the rural areas for the education of girls.
(c) Lack of educational facilities in rural areas.
(d) Lack of women teachers.
(e) Lack of proper supervision an guidance due to inadequate women personnel in the Inspectorate.
(f) Lack of proper incentives to parents and children.
(g) Lack of adequate incentives.
(h) Lack of suitable curriculum.

Some Selected Opinions

President, Dr. A.P.J. Abdul Kalam, said, "Empowering women is a prerequisite for creating a good nation, when women are empowered, society with stability is assured. Empowerment of women is essential as their thoughts and their value systems lead the development of a good family, good society and ultimately a good nation".

Jawaharlal Nehru once said, "To awaken the people, it is women who is meant to be awakened, once she is on the move, the family moves, village moves and the nation moves".

Again, Jawaharlal Nehru stated once, "Truly no argument is required in defense of women's education. For my part, I have always been strongly of the opinion that while it may be possible to neglect men's education it is not possible to neglect women's education. The reasons are obvious. If you educate the women, probably men will be affected thereby, and in any event children will be affected."

M.K. Gandhi in his *True Education* said clearly, "As for women's education I am not sure whether it should be different from men's and when it should begin. But I am strongly of the opinion that women should have the same facilities as men and even special facilities where necessary. The question of the education of children cannot be solved unless efforts are made simultaneously to solve the women's education. And I have no hesitation in saying that as long as we do not have real mother teachers who can successfully impart true education to our children they will remain uneducated even though they may be going to schools. She must have special knowledge of the management of the home, care of children, their education, etc. –"

Again, Mohandas K. Gandhi stated, "There is no occasion for women to consider them subordinate or interior to men".

Dr. Radhakrishnan has very emphatically stated, "Women are human beings and have as much right to full development as men have. The position of women in any society is a true index of its cultural and spiritual level."

Netaji Subhash Chandra Bose said, "The best means of conquering lust are to visualize the mother image in all women, to invest women with the hello and to worship God in the mother form, such as Durga and Kali. When man contemplates God or Guru in the form of the Mother, we learn to see divinity in all women...."

Swami Vivekananda also once said, "There is no chance for the welfare of the world unless the condition of women is improved. It is not possible for a bird to fly on one wing". Likewise no nation can flourish keeping half of its population in negligence and ignorance, as women constitute half of its human capital. A modern society cannot bring all round development without utilizing the talent of its women.

If you do not raise the women who are living embodiment of the Divine Mother, don't think that you have any other way to rise. All nations have attained greatness, by paying proper respects to the women. That country and that nation which does not respect the women have never become great, not will ever be in future. You will find in the Vedic and Upanishadic age Maitreyi, Gargi and other ladies of revered memory have taken the place of Rishis. In an assembly of a thousand Brahmanas who were all erudite in the Vedas Gargi boldly challenged Yajnavalkya in a discussion about Brahman. —Swami Vivekananda (1863-1902) (The *Complete Works of Swami Vivekananda, Vol. VII*).

The union of man and women will represent a perfect co-operation in the building up of human history on equal terms in every department of life. (Rabindranath Tagore (1861-1941))

According to Vedas, women should have opportunity to attain knowledge of Vedas from all the four corners. —*Atharveda*: 14.1.64.

In Vedas, woman has been called updeshtri of knowledge and this indicates women as teachers.—*Rigveda*: 1.3.11.

From the point of view of reverence due, a teacher is ten-fold superior to mere lecturer, a father a hundred-fold to teacher and mother a thousand-fold to father.—*Manusmriti:* 2.145.

Where women are respected, there the gods delight, and where they are not there all work and efforts come to naught. There is no hope of rise for that family or country where they live in sadness.—*Manusmriti*.

Atreyi's reply was that 'In this region several savant sages like Agastya, etc., reside. I am coming from the ashram of Valmiki to study Vedas from them.' Clearly indicates women's educational pursuits in ancient India.—*Uttar Ramcharitmanas:* 2.3.

Indeed, if the education is to have its maximum result, it must begin even before birth. The part of education which the mother has to go through is to see that her thoughts are always beautiful and pure, her feelings always noble and fine, her material surroundings as harmonious as possible and full of a great simplicity.—Aurobindo (1987-1950).

> "Several forms of gender discrimination emerged from a contradiction in the Indian Constitution. It ensures equality for all before law and prohibits discrimination on grounds of religion, race, caste, sex, or place of birth but it also guarantees freedom of religion – the right freely to profess, practice, and propagate religion. This provision of religious freedom takes away much of the freedom and equality extended to women by the Constitution."
>
> —**Prof. S.C. Dube, Sociologist**
> (*Indian Society*, NBT, 1990)

> "If the Indian civilization has survived for the past several thousand years, while others there have vanished, it is because of our strong sense of culture and morality which is rooted in our families. Central to this is the role of women. Whether, the woman is a wife or mother, she has always played a crucial role. Can we afford to vulgarize her?"
>
> —**Promod Navalkar, Maharashtra Minister of Transport and Culture** (Replies to S. Balakrishnah's question),
> *The Sunday Times of India, August* 6, 1995.

> "Education must be illuminated and re-illuminated in the light of the soul.... The new community of girls and women in India must be a community of Light. And Light knows no distinction or creed or community."
>
> —**Sadhu T.L. Vasvani**

> "Despite my thirty years of research into the feminine soul, I have not been able to answer... the great question that has never been answered what does a woman want"?
>
> —**Sigmund Freud**

> "The history of woman is the history of the continued and universal oppression of one sex by the other. The emancipation

of woman is her restoration to equal rights and privileges with men".

—Tennesse Claflin

"The history of men's opposition to women's emancipation is more interesting perhaps than the story of that emancipation itself".

—Virginia Woolf

"Why are women ... so much more interesting to men than men are to women"?

—Virginia Woolf

(*The Times of India*, 8th March, 2007)

Conclusion

Education is a milestone for women empowerment because it enables them to respond to opportunities, to challenge their traditional roles and to change their lives. Similar ideas were supported in International Conference-1994. It was said that Education is one of the most important means of empowering women with the knowledge, skills and self-confidence necessary to participate fully in the development process. Educating woman benefits the whole society. It has a more significant impact on poverty and development than men's education. It is also one of the most influential factors in improving child health and reducing infant mortality. At least 60 million girls lack access to primary education and the gender gap in literacy persists till date. Although literacy and school enrolment among both girls and boys have increased dramatically, yet much remains to be done. More and more girls should be enrolled in school, and should complete their schooling. This will become true as the level of education increases. There are signs of progress, as enrolment of boys and girls in primary schools edges closer and closer to parity.

Every year, even at the university level, women are catching up and even surpassing male enrolment in some countries. In Kuwait, Bahrain, the Philippines and Cuba, more women are now enrolling in university than men. Although girls and women's access to education is improving, but they are often channelled into traditionally 'female' fields of study that reinforce their traditional roles in society.

The greater demands for more gender equality and women's empowerment that are being made both socially and politically are certainly not the result of public policy promoting gender equality, but rather emerge from past and present gender oppression and discrimination against women.

REFERENCES

Aggarwal, J.C. (2004): *"Development and Planning of Modern education"* Vikas Publishing House Pvt. Ltd., Ed'-8, pp. 273-79.

Ruhela, Sarya (1999): *"Understanding the Indian Women Today: Problems and Challenges"* Indian Publishers' Distributors, Delhi, pp. 164-66.

The Times of India, Thursday, March 8, 2007.

The Arunachal Times, September 4, 2005, Vol. 17, No. 89.

The Assam Tribune, Guwahati, Monday, March 12, 2007.

The Telegraph, Calcutta, Wednesday, July 12, 2006.

17

Tribal Women in the State

Introduction

Women show love, kindness, sympathy, patience, tolerance, perseverance and tenacity of purpose in the face of adversity. They do not try to run away from responsibilities. They possess immense talent and when used fully, the potential is really very high. Even if she holds high profile jobs which may demand time and energy, she never hesitates to discharge her role effectively. She fits into different roles at different places. Be it the role of wife, mother, and daughter, daughter-in-law or official roles — she accommodates herself to each situation quickly.

In Arunachal Pradesh, various tribal communities are at different stages of development; as such the status of women differs from community to community. However, in general the position of women in Arunachal Pradesh is respectable but not high. The prevalence of polygamy, victim of bride price, sex abuse and child marriage are quite in common. It has no doubt lowered their position. They are generally devoid of equal political and property rights. In Arunachal Pradesh, the sex ratios in the State were 1013 in 1961, 1007 in 1971, 1004 in1981, 998 in1991, and 1003 in 2001 (shown in Table 17.1).

The role and work participation of women has been everybody's focus of attention in every society and in every age. Naturally, it is vital with a view to bringing about the desirable changes for social mobility and granting them equality in the matters of rights and privileges. It was in this background that the need of praying into the hidden realms of the women of the tribes of Arunachal Pradesh was felt so vigorously that the research scholars decided to put their heads together to come out with veritable contributions based on observation and investigation, and the result is this present compilation of the research studies on the status of women of the tribes of Arunachal Pradesh.

The Principal inhabitants of the State of Arunachal Pradesh from East to West are the Wancho, Nocte, Tangsa, Singpho, Khamti, Mishmi (Digaru, Miju and Idu), Adi (Gallo, Padam, Minyong, Pailibo, Bokar, Bori etc.), Memba, Khamba, Apatani, Nyishi, Hill-Miri, Nah, Tagin, Aka, Khawa or Bugun, Miji, Sulung, Sherdukpen and Monpa, etc. scattering over an area of 83,743 sq. kms. with hilly terrain in the trans Himalayan region have occupied over 3482 villages under 16 districts of Arunachal Pradesh. The census-wise silent features of population in the State are shown in Table 17.1.

The census in Arunachal Pradesh has been being conducted regularly after every decade since 1961 (First census). It is a thinly populated state. Total population, males, females including ST total population, its males, females and also its percentage of total population, sex ratio (general), sex ratio (ST), Literacy rate in percentage including males and females and also the population density are shown in Table 17.1. As evident from Table 17.1, the comparative analysis of sex ratio in respect of general population and ST population in different census years reflects that it has been declining continuously with an exception in 2001 census.

The sparsely inhabited Arunachal Pradesh is a predominantly tribal inhabited State. Obviously in the past, the tribesmen purely inhabited it. During 1961, the tribal people formed 88.76 per cent of total population. The percentage of ST population was 79.02 per cent in 1971, 69.82 per cent in 1981, 63.65 per cent in 1991 and 64.22 per cent in 2001 census. Gradually, different census report has given different classification of total number of tribes, sub-tribes. While 1961 census mentioned 82 tribes and sub-tribes, 2001 census mentioned 26 major tribes and 110 sub-tribes.

It is interesting to find that the female population of Scheduled Tribes' (ST) has always been higher than that of males. While the generality in this case needs to be answered through systemic study of population genetics, this might be worthwhile to mention here

Table 17.1: Silent Feature of Population in Arunachal Pradesh (Census-wise).

Census	Population			Literacy Rate in Percentage			ST Population			Percentage of ST population to total population	Sex ratio		Population density
	Person	Male	Female	Person	Male	Female	Person	Male	Female		General	ST	
1961	336558	177680	158878	7.13	12.25	1.42	298439	148256	150183	88.76	894	1013	4
1971	467511	251231	216280	11.29	17.82	3.71	369408	184060	185348	79.02	861	1007	5.58
1981	628050	335941	292109	25.55	35.12	14.02	441167	220143	221024	69.82	862	1004	7.50
1991	864558	465004	399554	41.59	51.45	29.69	550351	275397	274954	63.65	859	998	10.32
2001	1097968	579941	518027	54.74	64.07	44.24	705158	352017	353141	64.22	893	1003	13.03

Source: Different issues of Census Report.

that female sex is generally stronger than that of males. Thus, there is all likelihood of the female to live longer than male. This could be supported by the evidence and the fact that in the advanced western countries, the proportion of women in total population is higher than that of males. Similarly, the female population number in the Scheduled Tribes (ST) population of Arunachal Pradesh has always been higher than that of the male population. While prenatal mortality could be a valid factor in general, but lack of maternity care, access to medical services in general and absence of the same in the interior areas, low awareness among females, hesitation to visit male gynecologist, superstitions during pregnancy, lack of care at home led to increasing chances of infant mortality in the instant case. Availability of data in this regard is the limitation of the study.

Arunachalee tribal women, being uneducated, indeed suffer most in their society and life. The literacy rate of Arunachal Pradesh since 1961 is shown in Table 17.1.

Table 17.1 shows that how much women are lagging behind their male counterpart regarding education. In view of education, the International Commission on Education (1996) states that a respect for equity demands requires a special effort to do away with all inequalities between sexes in the field of education. Gender inequality lies at the root of the lasting situation of inferiority that affects women at every stage at their lives. Education in general and higher education in particular are an insurance against economic need. Access to the higher education, both technical and professional, will guarantee economic independence leading to social status and hence empowerment to women. If education is to promote equality for women, it must make a deliberate, planned and sustained effort so that the new value of equality of sexes can replace the traditional system of inequality.

However, considering the fact of geographical isolation and inhospitable terrain, low levels of development in the State, as well as lack of modern facilities and technology in the health services sector, the general paucity of females in the State may be attributed to the following reasons.

Reasons for Paucity of Females

In sharp contrast to developed states of India, Arunachal Pradesh is characterized by backwardness, underdevelopment, and underutilization of its human resources. Very large segment of population in the State is residing in small and very small dispersed villages. The uneven distribution of population in the State follows a linear pattern mainly in the lesser and outer Himalayan zones of the central part of the State and uniform pattern in the gentle slope area of upper Brahmaputra river uplands. In the hills and mountain parts of the State, population is concentrated along the streams and on the banks of main rivers.

A considerable deficiency of females in its general population shows that there were 859 females for every thousand males in the State in 1991 (Table 17.1) and 893 females in 2001. Although more males are born than the females in every part of the world, yet that alone does not explain the general deficiency of females in Arunachal Pradesh. So far as the factors are responsible for the increase in number of females during 1991 as compared to 2001 census in the State are concerned, a good deal, like changed favourable attitude and consequently atmosphere for the female sex, improvement of medical facility, increased intra-state and inter-state movement of female, increase in the number of family stations in armed force, police force, other civil services, increased literacy and education and resultantly increased female representation in all services and so may be enumerated. The following discussions might help us to understand the general paucity of females in the State. The following discussions might help us to understand the general paucity of females in the State.

(i) This need to be emphasized here that the sex ratio in case of Arunachal Pradesh depicting a change may be attributed to first due to the reorganization of State during the administration of NEFA and subsequently to the Union Territory status to the Statehood in the late 1980's, when numbers of districts were delineated out of the then existing ones and new districts came into being. This while influencing the workforce structure of the State due to large scale immigration of workforce mainly from the other states of India, the head counts might also have bearing on the inflated population count in general and sex ratio in particular.

Further, the differences in sex ratio of most of the states in India are to be understood largely in the context of the differences in their mortality patterns of males and females. In addition, the factor of sex selective migration may have its own contribution to make. The sex selective migration of the male workforce leaving the family at the place of origin certainly inflates the sex composition in this instant case.

(ii) It is generally considered that the female foetus is biologically stronger than the male foetus. Since, the natural sex ratio in itself is governed by the differences in the prenatal mortality of the two sexes and since more males die before birth than females, it is often said that those countries with low prenatal losses show more masculinity in natural sex ratio and less masculine where the prenatal losses are great.

(iii) It is interesting to find that the female population of Scheduled Tribes has always been higher than that of males. While the generality in this case needs to be answered through systemic study of population genetics, this might be worthwhile to mention here that female sex is generally stronger than that of males. Thus, there is all likelihood of the female to live longer than male (as the gentler sex is biologically stronger) and hence more males die than the females not only at birth but also at all ages.

This could be supported by the evidence and the fact that in the advanced western countries, the proportion of women in total population is higher than that of males. Similarly, the female population number in the Scheduled Tribes population of Arunachal Pradesh has always been higher than that of the general population. While prenatal mortality could be a valid factor in general, but lack of maternity care, access to medical services in general and absence of the same in the interior areas, low awareness among females, hesitation to visit male gynaecologist, superstitions during pregnancy, lack of care at home lead to increasing chances of infant mortality in the instant case. Availability of data in this regard is the limitation of the study.

(iv) In India, 108 females are born per 100 males. There are genetic evidences to prove that during the gestation period more males are eliminated than the females because of recessive X-linked lethal genes eliminating males while having little or no effect on the viability of the heterogeneous females. This could be the valid reason for the state of Arunachal Pradesh also where female population composition is higher than that of male population for all the ethnic groups in general.

(v) The loss of more females in case of general population are due to insufficient attention and health care to them during the entire conception period as well as after birth. Women in general, suffer from a low status in the society which is an undisputed fact and generally considered with regard to all the states in India. Above all, the females are considered as social and economic liability while the males are credited as an asset to the family. All these together tell upon the health of the females and result in relatively high female mortality in all ages and all groups whether tribes or non-tribes population. In case of Arunachal Pradesh, there are hardly any separate maternity cares in the State's Health Service system. In addition to the above-mentioned points, the continued paucity of females may be attributed to recurrence of environmentally afflicted diseases which are endemic in nature such as malaria, diarrhoea, asthma, hepatitis, tuberculosis and other respiratory ailments.

(vi) Women in tribal society, lead a very busy life helping the menfolk in all walks of life. Tribal society enjoys an egalitarian status and women are considered as assets as the bride price is paid by the groom's family at the time of marriage. This is one of the valid reasons why females are better off in tribal society in contrast to the general population in the country as a whole.

(vii) A large number of women are living below poverty line; they suffer also from nutritional deficiency. Lack of alertness and access to balanced diet and right foods during pregnancy, insufficient intake of irons, proteins and micro nutrients such as iodine and vitamins is the principal cause of very high incidence of nutritional deficiency diseases like anemia, diarrhoea, night blindness, goiter, etc. Low body resistance due to malnutrition farther may complicate minor ailments and make it a health hazard. As a result, females' death rates in villages of the State are much more than males.

(viii) A high death rate at the time of puberty due to functional derangement and in the reproductive age bracket 11-19 on account of early marriage or child marriage among females could be one of the major reasons. Child marriage is very much prevalent in Arunachal Pradesh on account of socio-economic and cultural factors.

(ix) The practice of polygamy is in vogue. A man can take as many wives as he wants and can afford. More the number of wives, higher are the status of the husband in the society. This may also have adverse effect on favourable sex ratio.

(x) In Arunachal Pradesh where 80 per cent of the population lives in rural areas and 40 per cent below poverty line, poor medical facilities, extremely unhygienic living conditions, high infant mortality and absence of pre natal and postnatal care, high death rate among women, all give adverse effect on favourable sex ratio.

(xi) The son is considered to be the insurance against old age. This enforces preference in allotment of good diet and medical care in favour of males. That is why, infant mortality rates below 1 year of age is very high in the case of females as against of males in India.

(xii) High mortality rates among women in reproductive ages are also responsible for declining sex ratio. Death rate among women in the reproductive age group of 15-44 was about 30 per cent higher than that of the males as revealed by National Sample Survey.

(xiii) Sex determination tests are very rare in the State as a strategy to ensure desired family sex composition. Dowry system is also not prevalent in the system. Both have positive impact on a favourable sex ratio.

The unbalanced sex ratio bears many socio-economic implications like work structure of a populace, sex crimes, gender disparity and gender discrimination etc. Since, the two sexes play partly contrasting and partly complementary roles in an economy or in a society, in the absence of ideal sex ratio, the fabric of socio-cultural milieu of a society is bound to fall in danger and the growth of population is thus affected. Thus, in this paper an attempt has been taken to analyze the pattern of sex ratio in the State of Arunachal Pradesh.

The study of population characteristics is, therefore, extremely important in accelerating decision-making processes for decentralized development and planning of this backward State. As stated earlier, the transitional character and frequent reorganization of the State (the population statistics for a longer period of time is difficult to generate) poses several challenges to implementations and interventions in the name of development. It is with this focus in this background that study of pattern of sex ratio in Arunachal Pradesh bears an added significance.

The 20th century has witnessed many human achievements like technological breakthrough, unparallel economic prosperity, remarkable advances in human survival and transition of former colonial states to political independence. However, the fruits of progress have not been equitably shared. The major challenges include, eradication of mass poverty, protecting human rights, stabilizing the environment, empowerment of people especially women, rectifying economic inequalities and a sustainable economic development.

The lack of access of rural women to education, skill, health care facilities and resources limit their role in the emerging non-agriculture sectors, while their counterparts in the urban areas have better access to education, skills, basic amenities, resources and participate productively in the development activities. Central and State Governments have launched a number of schemes targeting the rural women, however, emphasis of most of these schemes is more on livelihood protection rather than on income and wealth generation on sustainable basis.

REFERENCES

Bhagabati, D. (April, 2001): "Education of the Tribal Women in Assam: Status, Problem and Hope", *Journal of North-East India Council for Social Science Research*, Shillong, p. 52.

Bora, M.M. and Bhattacharya, A. (1996): "Raising the status of Plain Tribes Women through Income Generating Training" in Medhi, K. (ed.), *Status of Women and Social Change*", Women's Studies Research Centre, Gauhati University, Guwahati, p. 102.

Dubey, S. (2000): "Tribal Women and their Political Empowerment: A case study of Arunachal Pradesh", Resarun: *Journal of the Directorate of Research,* Government of Arunachal Pradesh, Department of Cultural Affairs, Itanagar, Vol. XXVI, pp. 12-13.

Iqbal, A.B. (2007): "Social Face of India: Some Issues", *Kurukshetra,* A Journal of Rural Develooment, June, Vol. 55, No. 8, New Delhi.

Mandal, R.K. (2005): *"Arunachal Economy: Socio-Economic Transformation",* Champion Publisher and Distributor, Itanagar, p. 41.

Iqbal, R.K. (2005): "Literacy in Arunachal Pradesh: Trend, Features and Growth", *Rajiv Gandhi University Research Journal,* Vol. 8(2), December, Rajiv Gandhi University, Itanagar.

Iqbal, R.K. (2004): "Role and Work Participation of Galo Women in Socio-Economic Development of Arunachal Pradesh": *A UGC sponsored research project.*

Iqbal, R.K. (2006): "Trend and Growth of Population in Arunachal Pradesh", *Southern Economist,* January 15, Vol. 44, No. 18, p. 28.

Iqbal, R.K. (2006): "Position of Women in Tribal Society of Arunachal Pradesh With Special Reference to Galo Women", *Journal of Social Anthropology,* Vol. 3, No. 2, December, Serials Publications, New Delhi.

Iqbal, R.K.(2006), "Control of Jhum Cultivation in Arunachal Pradesh—Retrospect and Prospect", *Kurukshetra,* December, Vol. 55, No. 2, p. 18.

Iqbal, R.K. (2008): "Role of Tribal Women in Socio-Economic Development", *Southern Economist,* Vol. 47, No. 8, August, Southern Economist, No. 9, Bangalore.

Mandal, R.K. and Bhattacharjee, Madhuparna, "Pattern of Sex Ratio in Arunachal Pradesh: 1961-2001: Trend and Feature", a paper submitted to '*Indian Economic Journal*', New Delhi for publication.

Muralidharan, K. (2005): "The Globalized Women and Workforce: Issues Problems and Solutions", *University News,* December 12-18, Vol. 43, No. 50, p. 3.

Padmavathy, S. and Pandian, P.K. (2004): "Need of Education for Rural Women", *Southern Economist,* April 1 and 15, Vol. 42, Nos. 23 and 24, p. 15.

Pandey, B.B. (1997): "Status of Women in Tribal Society: Arunachal Pradesh" (ed.), Introductory Part.

Sharma, D.B and N. Romida (1996): "Violence against women: A case study of Meitei women in Manipur" in Medhi, K. (ed.), *Status of Women and Social Change",* Women's Studies Research Centre, Gauhati University, Guwahati, p. 142.

Sumathy, M. and Nagendran, K. (2007): " Women Empowerment—Ethics and Logics". *Southern Economist,* Vol. 46, No. 6, Bangalore, p. 6.

18

Gender Discrimination

A Holistic Approach Towards Intervention in Frontier State of Arunachal Pradesh in India

Introduction

The peculiar background against gender discrimination initially surfaced in the Indian context has led to many parallel thought processes and strands making it extremely difficult to come up with an overarching framework within which a cohesive interpretation of a number of fragmented and parallel discourses can be attempted. These discourses have been women centric emerging as a part of larger consciousness aimed at broad political or social change. Whatever may be the ideological underpinnings, a concerted effort has largely been made to create spaces for women within a larger socio-economic and political context. According to Sen, 'women issues' are multidimensional incorporating vast canvas covering multifarious role played by women specially in India in realizing the aspirations of the common people including themselves (Sen,1994). Women always depend upon others throughout her life: as daughter she depends upon father; as wife upon her husband and as a mother upon her son. Women had faced social and economic handicap for centuries. Despite the rights granted by the Constitution and special legislations, the reality is that there are widespread non-implementation of legislations, structural inequalities and power imbalances within the society.

Women's ability to influence decision-making at all levels is circumscribed because of their low socio-economic status and unequal rights as compared to men. They are not adequately represented at all levels of authority and administration, more so in less developed societies. Over the years, there has been a significant change in the overall status of women but the problem of violence and exploitation against women continues unabated. Women have been victims of ill treatment, humiliation, torture and exploitation since the dawn of civilization. But regretfully, female victims of violence have not been given much attention to, in nearly all the contemporary social and political structures nor has any attempt been made to explain why both the public and academicians have ignored them for so long. The hard fact remains, that the women have continuously and ruthlessly been exploited throughout the globe. The implementation of laws granting rights to women has been slow, lopsided and haphazard. Socially, economically and politically women are lagging behind men. Latest figure of crime record bureau reveal that South Asian Women continue to experience the grossest form of violence.

The report called Progress of the World's Women 2000 of the United Nations Development Fund for Women (UNIFEM), has found that apart from the four Scandanavian countries-Denmark, Finland, Norway and Sweden, four others Germany, Ireland, Netherland and South Africa follow close bridging the gender gap when it comes to women's participation in the fields of education, legislature and employment in services. Women who constitute half of the humanity have been subjected to the tyranny and oppression of a patriarchal order for centuries and in fact, most of them are suffering from the same even today. It is this aspect that needs to be closely examined because the future society in terms of its direction and pace is dependent on this question.

Gender and Good Governance

Men and women have different roles and hence their own different and unique needs. These differences must be considered in formulating the agenda of development particularly in deciding common priorities and allocation of national resources. Good governance means overall development and progress of country and fulfilling the needs of all citizens regardless of ethnicity, socio-economic status and gender. Gender responsive governance is good governance as it grants equal opportunity to both men and women to participate fully in governance and decision-making. The goals of good governance cannot be achieved without achieving gender equality. Giving due attention to the specific needs and interest of women could help in achieving good governance, this moreover, will improve the lives of the people. All programmes and projects of the country should be gender-responsive. Governance can be efficient and effective only if it articulates women issues and interests and can only be gender-fair if it is gender responsive at political, administrative and economic spheres as women have perspectives, which enhance the quality of governance. Practical experiences reveal that women are far better administrators and have much more organizational capabilities than their male counterparts and they tend to show much more respect for ethics and values of the society, they are generally more altruistic and community oriented.

The right to equality between men and women is a fundamental right in Indian Constitution. State is specifically permitted to make laws in favour of women as a deliberate affirmative action so as to enable them to overcome traditional handicaps. Further, respect for the dignity of women has been made a fundamental duty of Indian citizens and all actions derogatory to such dignity are liable to be stuck down. Conversely, the social institutions and customs are more resistant to change, because they are more rooted in history and more dependent on mind-sets. Gender equality is relatively recent concept and most patriarchal societies have ordained rampant injustices and discrimination against women in the family and outside in everyday life. It is indeed bad that women's status is undermined and subordinated but worst of all is that they have accepted their position as their destiny and in many cases they are found to be an instrument of exploitation.

This chapter is an attempt towards a progressive overview of concerns about gender issues as they emerged in post-independent India with special reference to the State of Arunachal Pradesh. An attempt has been made to deal with empirical analyses in some major sectors such as literacy/education, social, economic and political participation, etc.

In India, gender discrimination is stereotype, prevailing to a greater extent in every nook and corner. This is evidenced and found in every walk of life. Gender discrimination takes its root at the early stage of infancy. The starting point of this evil is the unit of family itself. This is a deep-rooted problem that continues and is carried on from generation to generation. Female members are most often regarded as "risks" and "liabilities". This gender discrimination leads to inequality, injustice, dissatisfaction and disputes. When gender discrimination is narrowed down through concerted efforts many problems would be solved and peace be established. The positive way to eliminate gender discrimination is to generate awareness level of the people about the causes and consequences of the phenomenon. Women constitute 48 per cent of the Indian population in our country and 47 per cent in Arunachal Pradesh but owing to the socio-economic situation, the women and girls are lagging behind in every sphere as compared to their male counterparts.

In almost every society, women/girls live in vulnerable conditions because the risk factor lies simply in being a female. Gender inequity works against girls throughout their lives. A wide range of discriminatory and violent practices are institutionalized in cultural traditions and thereby gets legitimated as 'social norms', so, routine discriminatory practices become invisible. Such practices are widespread not only in general mainstream societies but also in tribal societies in our country. The State of Arunachal Pradesh is no exception to this imbroglio. It needs immediate universal intervention in an equally systematic manner as Constitution guarantees equal rights for all. From time immemorial, women have faced the challenges of coping with a male chauvinistic milieu. Even after several years of planned development in India, the status of women in our country is low and their socio-economic conditions are much more down in the dumps than that of men.

The discrimination from one to another depends on their socio-cultural background. Phenomenon of gender discrimination is not caused by a single factor. It has multiple causes and therefore need a multiple strategy to tackle the problem. The problem of gender discrimination may be viewed from the various angles like the roles they assume (i) who does what, the responsibilities they share (ii) who is responsible for what, the resources they enjoy – who owns what, the constraints they face (iii) who has access to what, the regards they are entitled to (iv) who deserves what, the recognition they need (v) who gets recognized for what, the remuneration that is due (vi) who gets how much for the work, the representation they make (vii) who represents where, the regulations they make – who decides what, the restrictions imposed on them (viii) who submits to whom or what; Man or Woman! This is very much established in Indian society especially in rural communities in general and Tribal society in particular.

The tribal population of India constitutes about 67.6 million and women in the tribal community constitute half of the tribal population. In Arunachal Pradesh, major portion of population is tribal. They were 88.76 per cent in 1961, 79.02 per cent in 1971, 69.82 per cent in 1981, 63.65 per cent in 1991and 64.22 per cent in 2001. The sex ratios in the state were 1013 in 1961, 1007 in 1971, 1004 in1981, 998 in1991, and 1003 in 2001.The well-being of tribal community depends very much on the women. Status and condition of tribal women relating to their socio-cultural locale, their economic rights, their participation in management, their access to employment, food, health, and resources etc. have not been properly focused. Nutritional status of tribal girls is compromised and overlooked by unequal access to food, by heavy work demands, and by special nutritional needs (such as for iron), which makes females particularly susceptible to illness, such as anemia, trapped in a cycle of ill health exacerbated by childbearing and hard physical labour. There are many taboos and myths which are barriers to health practices and growing body of adolescence tribal girls.

Adolescence is a period of dynamic changes in physical, sexual growth and psychological development, influenced by both nutrition and ecological factors. If the nutrient intake is not adequate it will adversely affect their growth and will lead to poor performance in later part of their life. In Arunachal Pradesh with varying social customs and common beliefs against females there is a high prevalence of malnutrition amongst girls. The problems of tribal women differ from a particular area to another area owing to their geographical location, historical background and the process of social change in the phase of transition in development process.

The tribal women should be brought into mainstream, if they are to be benefited from the progress on the development front. Thus, like other women in different tribal societies, the tribal women are also not recognized by their social system regarding their freedom and rights. Women's empowerment and their full participation on the basis of equality in all spheres of society are fundamental for the achievement of equality, development and peace (Fourth World Conference on Women, Beijing, 1995).

Equality among Men and Women

There is a need to have equality for both men and women in Choices, in Opportunities and in Rights. Equality in the family can be ensured by participatory decision-making; sharing the responsibilities; trusting, loving and serving each other; respecting one another and economic independence for both men and women.

In a world where equality is often misunderstood, misinterpreted and exploited for political gains, it is imperative that "equality" should be redefined. Equality, irrespective of the sex of the individual should promise a life of freedom, choice, opportunities and dignity. The low value for female life is the biggest problem. The desire to have male issues has reduced the chance for girls to be born and thus female infanticide is on the rise. Economic conditions and cultural ethos of India have forged an invisible combination that threatens even the female embryo. Even if a female child is born against such heavy odds, she is not given a chance to survive. She suffers malnutrition, lack of medical attention, early marriage and frequent child births. The crude death rates fostered by abortions and child birth without proper medical care indicate the reduced life span of women. Another major problem is that of illiteracy. Despite a significant increase in the gross enrolment rate of girls in primary schools from 25 per cent in 1950 to 66 per cent in 1980 and 70 per cent in 1982, a large number of girls are still not receiving primary education, while 95 to 100 per cent boys are now enrolled in elementary schools.

Engels, the well-known economist, held that female subordination was the result of the emergence of private property, in particular the private ownership of the forces of production.

Karl Marx had opined that female employment would largely free women from economic dependence on their husbands and so from male dominance within the family.

Sociologists Blood and Hamlin's approach was that the employment of the wife outside the home did not appreciably alter power relations within the family: working wives had only marginally more power than whole-time wives.

Viola Klein believed that employment outside the home had some beneficial results; it helped to restore in women their sense of usefulness and renewed their self-confidence. Still the mother and housewife role remained primary. There was no evidence from her research data that paid employment produced demands for freedom from traditional female roles.

In our country, the status, role and the various characteristics and problems of women have been culturally much different from the women in the West. In the Post-Independence era, there has been a vast expansion of education and employment opportunities as well as provisions for the protection, welfare and development of our women and many of them are quite modern and advanced like their western counterpart. Women are the nucleus of our civilization. They have different roles to play in the ever changing social set-up. Women's development is directly related with the nation development. With the dawn of independence our Constitution guaranteed gender equality and a large number of schemes and programmes have been initiated for women's development. But the Indian women have to survive in a complex area of socio-cultural, historical, political economic realities.

The International recognition of the status and the problems of women all over the world have resulted in the United Nations declaring 1975 as the International Women's year and the period between 1975 and 1985 as Women's Decade. These are recommendations of the United Nations World Conference (Mexico, 1975) to initiate plans for raising the status of women and for ensuring their full involvement and integration in the process of development at all levels. In India, the appointment of the National Committee on the status of women in 1972 and the publication of its report in 1975 marked the first official attempt to study and recommended changes to improve women's position in society. Declaring 1975 as "Year of Women" by the United Nations, since then there is increased concern of women's sufferings and their empowerment in the society (Medel-Anonuevo, 1995). Very recently the UNDP has brought out its Human Development Report 2003, which speaks about the millennium development goals. It lists eight goals out of which the third goal to be achieved is gender equality and empowerment of women. In the budget presented before the Parliament for the year 2004-05, the Union Finance Minister has stressed on "gender budgeting".

Discrimination in Educational Opportunities in India

Only a few girls take up higher education in Arunachal Pradesh. Every year only about 10 per cent of the total girls who appear for plus two examinations take up higher studies. The remaining discontinues their academic pursuits due to myriad of reasons. The considerable reasons observed are; due to gender discrimination, such as traditional family decisions – not to invest in their daughter's future as there will be no financial returns, etc. In case of higher education the tendency is very much same with a greater decline. The proportion of the girl student which pursue higher education is too less when compared with the two plus level. When we look at the overall educational status there is a huge decline or variation in the proportion of education of girls from primary to higher education.

Phenomenal Progress since Independence

Importance of education of women has been recognized since the achievement of independence. Accordingly, strenuous efforts have been made in this area. The following figures reveal that literacy among women has increased proportionately as compared with men. Yet much more is needed to bring it at par with men. This is shown in Table 16.1 and Table 16.2.

Concerted efforts were made only after independence to advance the education of girls and women. The concept of women empowerment was introduced at the International Women's Conference at Nairobi in 1985. The term empowerment was defined as "a distribution of social power and central of resources in favour of women". Education is the milestone for women empowerment because it enables them to challenges, to confront their traditional roles and to change their lives. Similar ideas were supported in International Conference-1994. It claimed that education is one of the most important means of empowering women with the knowledge, skills and self-confidence necessary to participate fully in the development process. Educating women benefits the whole society. It has a more significant impact on poverty and development and even on men's education.

Position of Women in Arunachal Pradesh

In the tribal world of Arunachal Pradesh, various tribal communities are at different stages of development. Necessarily the status of women differs from community to community. Tribal women's right is customary in nature rooted in their tradition and mythology. Heritage status of women, it may be tribal or non-tribal, largely depends upon the kind of economic and political rights they enjoy. The position of women in Arunachal Pradesh is respectable but not very high. The prevalence of polygamy, bride price has no doubt lowered their position. Till recently child marriage was quite common. Victim of "bride-price", "sex-abuse" and "child marriage" in tribal society are generally devoid of equal political and property rights. Tribal women have a busy life, helping menfolk in almost every walk of life. From cooking to cultivation and from hard work to dance, they are always busy, in fact; they are the backbone of tribal pastoral economy. But economically they remain dependent on their male counterpart and thus they virtually hold a subordinate position. In Rousseau's modified language "Arunachalee woman is born free but everywhere she is in chains." Every society accords social status to women members as per its own perspective. The status and role of women in tribal society is also governed by their own norms and values. The tribal family is patriarchal. Kinship is recognized on the side of men. The tribal women's status in Arunachal Pradesh is lower than that of men. She faces many problems in all walks of her life simply because of being a female. In this male dominated society a women is considered inferior to a man. She is meant to depend on and under subjugation of man. The family in which she was born as a daughter does not consider her as a permanent abode. She is looked upon as a transient member to be handed over on marriage to her in-law's family. She cannot have a share in the immovable property at all. Decision making and exercise of authority go under power of men.

Educational Scenario

In Arunachal Pradesh, till independence literacy rate was only less than 1 per cent. In the succeeding Five Year Plans, an increasing percentage of expenditure on education has given good results despite of formidable constraints like inaccessibility of territory, people's unawareness of the need of education and traditional dependence on children for domestic and field work. Thus, with increasing emphasis through successive plans the State has achieved commendable progress in the field of education. The literacy rate census-wise from 1961 to 2001 in Arunachal Pradesh is shown in Table 18.1. Census started first in the state from 1961.

Table 18.1: Literacy Rate in Percentage in Arunachal Pradesh.

Year	*Person*	*Male*	*Female*
1961	7.13	12.5	1.42
1971	11.29	17.82	3.71
1981	25.55	35.12	14.02
1991	41.59	51.45	29.69
2001	54.74	64.07	44.24

Source: Census Report, Arunachal Pradesh, 1961, 1971, 1981, 1991 and 2001.

From Table 18.1, it is observed that the good fruit of education in the State is achieved though the females are lagging behind the males. Higher education in Arunachal Pradesh needs a far-reaching structural reconstruction. The enrolment of students in the colleges in Arunachal Pradesh during academic session 2004-05 and 2008-09 is shown in Table 18.2 and Table 18.4 and enrolment of lecturers in colleges during these academic sessions is shown in Table 18.3 and Table 18.5.

Table 18.2: Enrolment of Students in the colleges in Arunachal Pradesh during Academic Session 2004-05.

Sl.No	Name of college	Total Student			APST			Non-APST		
		Boys	Girls	Total	Boys	Girls	Total	Boys	Girls	Total
I.	**Govt. Colleges**									
1.	J.N.College, Pasighat	1147	686 (37.42)	1833	999	611	1610	148	75	233
2.	D.N. Govt. College, Itanagar	975	661 (40.40)	1636	845	569	1464	83	89	172
3.	I.G. Govt., Tezu	469	275 (36.96)	744	292	171	463	177	104	281
4.	Govt. College, Bomdila	329	189 (36.48)	518	289	160	449	40	29	69
5.	D.P. Govt. College, Kamki	284	169 (37.30)	453	279	162	441	05	07	12
6.	R.F. College, Changlang	77	48 (38.40)	125	71	43	114	06	05	11
7.	T.G. College, Deomali	121	85 (41.26)	206	98	60	158	23	25	48
	Total	**3402**	**2113 (38.31)**	**5515**	**2923**	**1776**	**4699**	**482**	**334**	**826**
II.	**Private College**									
1.	Don Bosco College, Jully	83	63 (43.15)	146	83	60	143	-	03	03

Contd...)

(*Table 18.2 Contd...*)

2.	St. Claret College, Ziro	46	41 (47.12)	87	43	37	80	03	04	07
3.	Doying Gumin College, Pasighat	12	04 (25)	16	11	04	15	01		01
	Total	**141**	**108 (43.37)**	**249**	**137**	**101**	**238**	**04**	**07**	**11**
III.	**Technical and Professional College**									
1.	NERIST, Nirjuli	822	157 (16.03)	979	75	06	81	882	16	898
2.	Rajiv Gandhi Polytechnic College, Itanagar	188	89 (32.12)	277						
3.	College of Horticulture and Forestry, Pasighat	27	36 (57.149)	63						
4.	NEHMC, Vivek Vihar, Itanagar	43	42 (49.41)	85	19	16	35	24	26	50
	Total	**1080**	**324 (23.07)**	**1404**	**94**	**22**	**116**	**906**	**42**	**948**
IV.	**Rajiv Gandhi University**	393	240 (37.91)	633	315	196	511	59	63	122
	Total I, II, III, IV	5016	2785 (35.70)	7801	3469	2095	5564	1451	446	1907

Source: Directorate of Higher and Technical Education, Govt. of Arunachal Pradesh, Itanagar.

Table 18.3: Total Number of Lecturers in Government Colleges of Arunachal Pradesh during Academic Session 2004-05 (Sex-wise).

Sl.No.	*Name of college*	*Male*	*Female*	*Total*	*Per cent of Female to Total*
1.	J.N. College, Pasighat	55	03	58	5.17
2.	D.N. Govt. College, Itanagar	43	17	60	28.33
3.	I.G. Govt., Tezu	27	nil	27	00
4.	Govt. College, Bomdila	14	01	15	6.66
5.	D.P. Govt. College, Kamki	15	01	16	6.25
6.	R.F. College, Changlang	12	02	14	14.28
7.	T.D.College, Deomali	11	01	12	8.33
	Total	**177**	**25**	**202**	**12.38**

Source: Directorate of Higher and Technical Education, Govt. of Arunachal Pradesh, Itanagar.

Table 18.4: Enrolment of Students in the Institutions of Higher Education in the State during Academic Session 2008-09.

Sl.No	*Name of Institutions*	*Total Student*			*APST*			*Non-APST*		
		Boys	*Girls*	*Total*	*Boys*	*Girls*	*Total*	*Boys*	*Girls*	*Total*
1.	Rajiv Gandhi University Rono Hills, Doimukh	969	484	485	393	408	801	91	77	168
2.	J.N. College, Pasighat	2221	1263	958	1111	846	1957	152	112	264
3.	D.N. Govt. College, Itanagar	2835	1598	1237	1457	1117	2574	144	117	261
4.	I.G.Govt. College, Tezu	1335	696	639	449	440	889	247	199	446
5.	Govt. College, Bomdila	635	310	325	263	270	533	47	55	102
6.	D.P.Govt. College, Kamki	961	568	393	538	406	944	13	4	17
7.	R.F. Govt. College, Changlang	240	116	124	110	117	227	6	7	13
8.	W. R. Govt. College, Deomal	393	203	190	197	147	344	24	25	49
9.	Govt. College, Yachuli	87	58	29	57	28	85	1	1	2
10.	Don Bosco College, Jully, Itanagar	486	234	252	228	239	467	6	13	19
11.	St. Claret College, Ziro	282	132	150	124	136	260	8	14	22
12.	Doying Gumin College, Pasighat	368	223	145	200	129	329	23	16	39
13.	St. Francis De Sales College, Aalo	85	44	41	37	33	70	6	9	15
14.	Arunachal Law Academy, Itanagar	95	84	11	84	10	94	0	1	1
15.	North-Eastern Regional Institute of									

(Contd...)

(*Table 18.4 Contd...*)

	Science and Technology, Nirjuli	1195	898	297	121	38	159	777	259	1036
16.	Rajiv Gandhi Govt. Polytechnic, Itanagar	379	223	156	129	109	238	94	47	141
17.	College of Horticulture and Forestry, Pasighat	133	77	56	13	12	25	64	44	108
18.	North East Homeopathic Medical College and Hospital, Itanagar Hospital, Itanagar	144	46	98	16	39	55	30	59	89
19.	Tomi Polytechnic, Basar	321	263	58	253	54	307	10	4	14
20.	Hills College of Teacher Education, Naharlagun	100	43	57	26	31	57	17	26	43
	Grand Total	**13264**	**7563**	**6701**	**5806**	**4609**	**10415**	**1760**	**1089**	**2849**
				(42,98)		**(44.25)**			**(38.22)**	

Source: Directorate of Higher and Technical Education, Itanagar.
Note: Figures in parenthesis show percentage.

Table 18.5: Number of Teaching Staff during Session 2008-09 (Sex-wise)

Sl. No.	Name of Institution	Total	Male	Female	APST Male	APST Female	NON-APST Male	NON-APST Female
1.	Rajiv Gandhi University, Rono Hills, Doimukh	85	66	19	17	10	51	07
2.	North-Eastern Regional Institute of Science and Technology, Nirjuli	140	122	18	06	01	116	17
3.	College of Horticulture and Forestry, Pasighat	34	31	03	01	01	30	02
4.	J.N. College, Pasighat	62	53	09	17	04	36	05
5.	D.N.Govt. College, Itanagar	62	44	18	17	10	27	08
6.	I.G. Govt. College, Tezu	24	23	01	06	01	17	00
7.	Govt. College, Bomdila	20	16	04	05	04	11	00
8.	D.P. Govt. College, Kamki	22	19	03	14	02	05	01
9.	R.F. Govt. College, Changlang	14	11	03	07	03	04	00
10.	W. R. Govt. College, Deomal	13	08	05	03	03	05	02
11.	Govt. College, Yachuli	09	07	02	06	02	01	00
12.	Rajiv Gandhi Govt. Polytechnic, Itanagar	19	13	06	02	05	11	01
13.	St. Claret College, Ziro	18	10	08	03	05	06	04
14.	Don Bosco College, Jully, Itanagar	23	11	12	07	08	04	04
15.	Doying Gumin College, Pasighat	15	09	06	06	02	03	04
16.	St. Francis De Sales College, Aalo	11	10	01	02	00	08	01
17.	Arunachal Law Academy, Itanagar	09	07	02	05	01	02	01
18.	North-East Homeopathic Medical College and Hospital, Itanagar	24	20	04	05	02	15	02
19.	Tomi Polytechnic, Basar	27	25	02	01	01	24	01
20.	Hills College of Teacher Education, Naharlagun	11	07	04	02	00	05	04
	Grand Total	642	512	130 (20.25)	132	65 (10.12)	381	64 (9.97)

Source: Directorate of Higher and Technical Education, Itanagar.
Note: Figures in parenthesis show percentage.

A comparative study of Enrolment of Students in the Institutions of Higher Education in Arunachal Pradesh during Academic Session: 2004-05 and 2008-09 is done in Table 18.6.

Table 18.6: Enrolment of Students in the Institutions of Higher Education in Arunachal Pradesh during Academic Sessions 2004-05 and 2008-09.

Session	*Total Student*			*APST*			*Non-APST*		
	Boys	*Girls*	*Total*	*Boys*	*Girls*	*Total*	*Boys*	*Girls*	*Total*
2004-05	5016	2785 (35.70)	7801	3469	2095	5564	1451	446	1907
2008 – 09	7563	6701 (42.98)	13264	5806	4609 (44.25)	10415	1760	1089 (38.22)	2849

Source: Directorate of Higher and Technical Education, Itanagar.
Note: Figures in parenthesis show percentage.

A comparative study of Enrolment of Teaching Staff in the Institutions of Higher Education in Arunachal Pradesh during Academic Sessions 2004-05 and 2008-09 is done in Table 18.7.

Table 18.7: Enrolment of Teaching Staff in Govt. Colleges of Arunachal Pradesh (Sex-wise) during Academic Session 2004-05 and 2008-09 (Sex-wise).

Session	*Male*	*Female*	*Total*	*Per cent of Female to Total*
2004-05	177	25	202	12.38
2008-09	181	45	226	19.91

Source: Directorate of Higher and Technical Education, Itanagar.

Causes of Slow Progress

(a) Economic and social backwardness of the rural community.
(b) Lack of proper social attitudes in the rural areas for the education of girls.
(c) Lack of educational facilities and infrastructure in rural areas.
(d) Lack of women teachers.
(e) Lack of proper supervision and guidance due to inadequate women personnel in the Inspectorate.

(f) Lack of proper incentives to parents and children.
(g) Lack of adequate incentives.
(h) Lack of suitable curriculum.
(i) Co-educational aspects.

Significance of Women Education

Dr. Radhakrishnan has very emphatically stated, "Women are human beings and have as much right to full development as men have. The position of women in any society is a true index of its cultural and spiritual level."

The resolution on the National Policy on Education (1968) stressed the importance of women education in these words, "The education of girls should receive emphasis not only on grounds of social justice but also because it accelerates social transformation".

The United Nations Declaration on the Elimination of Discrimination against Women (1967) took note of the great contribution made by women to social, political, economic and cultural life and the part they play in the family and particularly in the rearing of children and recommended the following in Article 9 of the Declaration: "All appropriate measures shall be taken to ensure to girls and women, married or unmarried, equal rights with men in education at all levels and in particular.

(a) Equal conditions of access to and study in educational institutions of all types, including universities and vocational, technical and professional schools;
(b) The same choice of curricula, the same examinations, teaching staff with qualifications of the same standards and school premises and equipment of the same quality, whether the institutions are co-educational or not;
(c) Equal opportunities to benefit from scholarships and other study grants;
(d) Equal opportunities for access to programmes of continuing education, including adult literacy programmes; and
(e) Access to educational information to help in ensuring the health and well-being of families.

Discrimination in Power

The concept of leadership has not been examined seriously from a feminine angle. Most of the researches have made an attempt to compare women's managerial capability with that of men, taking the latter as paragons of leadership. Such approaches are not loyal to the facts and there is a need to break new grounds to understand women's leadership potential. Being relatively more patient and considerate, women would be more sympathetic to public grievances, and beings dedicated to the task, they could take bold step to implement welfare programmes. If women constitute half of the population of the country, it is natural that their special aptitudes, talent and expertise are captured for doing well in different sectors (Goretti, 2002). Therefore, we need to deliberate on how to ensure adequate representation of women positions of leadership? What changes in policies and professional training may be required to attract and retain women in leadership positions should be the action agenda of today.

Amendment in Constitution in 1972 to strengthen the sharing of power by women at local level has opened a new chapter in the history of women's struggle for empowerment. The enactment of the 73rd Constitutional Amendment i.e., Panchayati Raj, in India is, no doubt a landmark event in this regard. It is important because of revolutionary measure by reserving 33 per cent seats for women at all levels in the local governance. Local governance interpreted as the active involvement of the local population within the territorial boundaries in local government is ensuring improved quality of service and leadership at the local government level. This is a significant shift in the approach towards the well-being of women from 'Welfare during Fifties' to 'Development during Seventies' and to "Empowerment during Nineties'.

Political empowerment at local level i.e., Panchayati Raj assumes particular importance as a means of producing democratic functioning and decision-making decentralized governmental power, thereby restructuring political institutions. This development i.e., amendment in the Constitution has brought the question of competitiveness of Indian women to the centre stage of controversy. In view of the majority of Indian rural women being illiterate and new in this role, this question has attracted the attention of the large number of commentators and researchers.

Women Empowerment in Political Arena

Political participation does not necessarily mean an active involvement into politics. There are two methods of political participation, one as a voter and the other one as an elected representative in the Legislature and Government. Despite persistent efforts, they are deprived of both the forms of political participation and continue to be marginalized. Owing to patriarchal set-up of society it is difficult to find a woman willing to contest elections and also finding a woman having a genuine interest in participating in election by registering her vote. A small fraction of women are, however, seen participating in this process with constant mobilization by feminist and female politicians. If women are to enter into politics there has to be a comprehensive understanding of gender issues by women to be successful in politics. They need a congenial environment and firm encouragement from family. Unfortunately, the traditionally assigned gender roles limit women's abilities in decision-making and thus compel them to assume the burden of household responsibilities. Specific measures have been taken to encourage the participation of women in decision-making in India by providing 1/3rd of seats in local councils. There are more than 800,000 women in local politics in both urban and rural areas in India. Unfortunately, they are not empowered to participate actively with the result there is no impact of women on policy and planning. It is true that women's representation should increase along with capacity building for new infrastructures. Efficient women in the governance are seen transforming their respective villages and towns. The decisions made at local level have a direct impact on the lives of the people. As women are the integral part of the society it becomes the fundamental duty of the local authorities to support the capacity building programmes to empower local decision-making structures. When the role of women is overlooked progress of the country is adversely affected and the quality of service deteriorates. Women can be empowered at all levels of society, solely through active participation.

In India only 8 per cent of Parliamentarians are women, and no South Asian country has reached the figure of 10 per cent. It is so because of lack of a healthy relationship between gender and governance and a good understanding for gender and development. A thorough grooming for young female leaders is required so that all anomalies in politics could be replaced by more people centred values. This, however, may not materialize, as the male counterparts will not easily provide enough space for these amateurs to spread their wings for their preliminary flights. In such circumstances, only those female who agree to adopt 'norms' of men can enter politics, which in turn generates unwillingness on the part of many women who automatically become reluctant to be like a man in order to compete on an equal footing. Bills for women empowerment are often tabled but remain undiscussed despite the willingness of high-level politicians. During the budget session of 2003 at New Delhi the proposed Women's Reservation Bill remained undiscussed because of severe criticism and strong opposition from majority of Parliamentarians of different political parties. They insisted that there should be a consensus among the different political parties for representing SC, ST and OBC minority women with separate reservation for them in the proposed Bill. A few maintained that a quota for women representation should be left for the individual party to decide. This demand, however, is kept alive by a number of women organizations involved in women upliftment by lobbying with female Parliamentarians and interested political parties; as they firmly support women empowerment and believe that without representation there can be no emancipation. Country's future development and good governance depends on politics and equal political representation at all levels helps social upliftment. Reservation for women does not mean creating a space for women into politics but it has much broader implication as women understand problems faced by them and thus can raise the issues, legislate rules and can formulate policies for their betterment. It is essential to bring women into the mainstream of politics because a society functioning with only males is an imbalanced society.

In spite of all this reservation for women's participation in the politics the desired goals up to a desirable limit have not been achieved because of lack of enthusiasm on the part of majority of women and reluctance because of a number of social dogmas. As women's reservation in politics is the need of the day, an adequate number of women representatives have got to be there. To some extent, a few desirable and efficient women politicians are seen engaged but the overall scene is not much inspiring despite the efforts put in by the government. For this, government is not alone to be blamed but a reluctant attitude of women to actively participate in politics at every stage is also responsible. Generally, those women who have a political background in a state that at least one of their family members is in active politics are seen enjoying the fruits of this reservation policy. People, who missed the opportunity to contest the election because of this reservation system, use their female family members viz., wives, sisters to fulfil their desires in politics. Most of the women candidates become a rubber stamp in the hands of the male relatives who became *de facto* rulers. Most of them become mere puppets in the hands of their male relatives and their relatives act on their behalf and they have no say in the process of decision-making. They remain totally ignorant about the facts. It is generally observed that their husbands work on their behalf and are designated as *Sarpanchpati*, *Parshadpati*, and *Memberpati* respectively, thus making a mockery of the entire process of empowerment. A number of Governmental and Non-Governmental Organizations raise programme to address issues related to social, economical and political problems of women, despite all these efforts, women still continue to be the vulnerable sector. The rhetoric of development and lip service has not improved the plight of women but has only proliferated her exploitation, subjugation and oppression. The lives of women are based on perceptual paradigms. The patriarchal values have placed women in extremely vulnerable positions and widened the male female gap.

The principle of gender equality is enshrined in the Indian Constitution, in its preamble, fundamental rights, fundamental duties and directive principles. The Indian Constitution guarantees equal rights to both women and men. But the representation of Indian women in politics at national level is lower than that of men. Although women constitute nearly half of the population, but politics has remained largely a monopoly of men because the condensation of power and authority mainly lies in the hands of this gender. (At present, there is a controversy about the 33 per cent reservation for women in Legislatures and in Parliament. The government has appointed a committee for the empowerment of women. But the failure of recent efforts to secure reservation for women in Parliament and Legislatives is well-known to all. Reservation and empowerment of women have a long way to go. However, the women's participation in politics has been very low in the past 62 years after gaining independence. It was found that year 1977 showed the lowest representation of women in Lok Sabha, it was 3.3 per cent only. The year 2004 shows that 9.5 per cent women participation in Lok Sabha. In recent Lok Sabha elections 2009, 61 women M.P. (11.23%) out of 543 have been elected and out of them 9 have become Ministers. This is a great achievement of women in the history of India.

Improvement in economic status is a more visible indicator of women empowerment. This naturally gets reflected in improved social, political and cultural status of women. Self-confidence and self-esteem of women proceed simultaneously with their empowerment. In brief, all indicators can be classified into two broad categories namely visible and invisible indicators. Amongst visible indicators a mention could be made of women's representation in Parliaments. Thirty per cent of total women Parliamentarians in the world come from just seven countries. Their share in national Parliaments of a few selected developed and developing countries is shown in Table 18.8.

Table 18.8: Seats in Parliaments held by Women (As % of total).

Developing Countries	*Per cent*	*Developed Countries*	*Per cent*
China	21.8	Sweden	45
Pakistan	21.6	Denmark	38
Morocco	10.8	Norway	36.4
India	8.8	Finland	36.1
Indonesia	8.0	Netherlands	36
Nepal	5.9	Iceland	34
Egypt	2.4	Austria	33
Bangladesh	2.0	New Zealand	29

Source: Human Development Report, 2003.

It can be seen from Table 18.8 that both in developed and developing countries women hold less seats than the men. However, in developed countries their representation is relatively higher than in developing countries. In this context, it can be said that increasing the number of women in Parliaments and also raising women's visibility in positions of authority and decision are quite necessary for their empowerment, politically and economically as well. Again, much of women's work never appears in the national statistics because it is seen as an extension of their carrying and nurturing functions rather than as materially rewarding activity. All of them are taken as unpaid family labour.

Women in tribal society in Arunachal Pradesh are generally not allowed to participate in the tribal Village Councils. Thus, the councils are male dominated institutions. Tribal people cannot easily think of women being a member in Village Council. Consequently, women are invariably discarded even today. But the introduction of Panchayati Raj (PR) at grass-root and Parliamentary Democracy at upper layer has armed the women with voting right and political rights on the equal footing of their male counterparts. Democratic creed and ethos have introduced the concepts of election through secret ballot boxes, adult suffrage and equality before law, rise of the sense of individualism, emphasis on social justice, social equity and social welfare. All cumulated together accelerate and speed up the process of social change. The statutory Panchayati Raj Institutions (PRIs) functioned from 1969 to 1997 in Arunachal Pradesh wherein there were some 24000 elected incumbents as Gram Panchayat Members (GPMs), Anchal Samiti Members (ASMs) and Zilla Parishad Members (ZPMs). Out of them, there had been only 4 women Anchal Samiti Members or Gram Panchayat Members. In 1987, at Anchal Samiti level, there was 1 and in 1992 there were 3 elected female representatives. The ratio of nominated female representatives has remained almost the same. Almost similar condition prevails in the traditional village council institutions. At present, there are total of 8077 Gaonburas, out of which 6731 are Gaonburas and 1346 are Head Gaonburas. In this traditional band of a huge number of so-called village authorities, a few women GBs have been appointed since 1998 onwards. The process of proliferation of Gaonburas since 1998 has facilitated to some 91 women to occupy the office of the GBs till date.

In the State of Arunachal Pradesh, tribal women are poorly represented in the ranks of power, policy and decision-making.

Women in Arunachal Pradesh are not just behind in the political and managerial spheres they are still far away from their actual sharing of power with their male counterparts. Total strength of women in State Legislature is altogether 9 in all the Legislative Assemblies put together within the span of 35 years from first Agency Council Election, 1969 to Seventh Legislative Assembly Election, 2004 where there are 60 seats in Legislative Assembly, at present. Women organization like APWWS (Arunachal Pradesh Women Welfare Society) along with the State Women Commission and Apex NGOs, Educationist and Social Workers of the State of Arunachal Pradesh, should engineer women Upliftment movement against the social catharsis like polygamy and child marriage, domestic violence and sexual harassment, sexual health of women etc., so that women do not become victims by themselves and also women do not become instrumental for the women exploitation. Women fold should be enlightened of their rights and their rightful position in the society.

The United Nations Development Programme (UNDP)'s Human Development Report (1995) opines "inverting in women's capabilities and empowering them to exercise their choices is not only valuable in itself but is also the surest way to contribute to economic growth and development". The report reaffirms that "Human development is impossible without gender equality". As long as women are excluded from the development process, development will remain lopsided. Sustainable human development implies engendering the development paradigm.

Reservation of Seats for Women in Panchayati Bodies

Under the framework of the 73rd Constitution Amendment Act, the one-third of the seats in Panchayat bodies is being reserved for the women for the first time in India. This was a new message for the rural population. Though the Galo society accords high status to the women in the society, the women never enjoyed such status in the corporate decision-making forum. Thus, the message of reservation was received with mixed response.

The tribal communities of Arunachal Pradesh had their own system of local self-governance. "Age old traditional system of self-governance in Arunachal Pradesh was replaced by Panchayati Raj

Institutions in 1968". With the coming into force of the Constitution (Seventy-Third Amendment) Act, 1992 with effect from 24th April, 1993, it was incumbent upon the state government to enact the Arunachal Pradesh Panchayati Raj Legislation. Reservation for women in the Panchayati institution have a stronger case because they can lead to empowerment at the level of local society. Through such empowerment social change is possible on broad scale.

The system ordained though the NEFA Panchayati Raj Regulation 1967 continued with regular elections till 1992. The Constitution (73rd Amendment Act) 1992 paved the way for restoring Panchayati Raj System in the State. It would suffice to mention here that several interactions across various levels were held to ensure to maintain the relevance and applicability of the act in the context of Arunachal Pradesh. The present strength of PRIs in the state is depicted below in Table 18.9.

Table 18.11: Present Strength of Elected Members of PRIs in Arunachal Pradesh.

(As on 29th August, 2003)

Sl.No.	*Level of PRIs*	*Nos.*	*Members*			*Chairpersons*	
			Male	*Female*	*Total*	*Male*	*Female*
1.	Gram Panchayats	1639	3924	2561	6485	1092	547
2.	Anchal Samities	136	1062	577	1639	86	50
3.	Zilla Parishad	14	91	45	136	8	6
	Total	**1789**	**5077**	**3183**	**8260**	**1186**	**603**

Source: Department of Panchayati Raj, Government of Arunachal Pradesh, Itanagar.

Note: Above figures do not include the allotted strength of Tirap District as PR elections were not held in that time.

In the above Table 18.9, it has been observed that the overall participation of women in PRIs is 38.5 per cent only. The Panchayati Raj Institutions also played a very important role in bringing about a major socio-political change in the traditional tribal society of Arunachal Pradesh with the increasing growth in education and political awareness at rural people and their increasing interface with the outside world due to greater mobility.

The Panchayati Raj Institutions serve as a training ground for rural people and equip them with both knowledge and experience about the democratic system of government in the country thereby enabling them to play more important and useful role in the state and as well as in the nation. The State Government is firmly committed to the reservation; development and strengthening of the Panchayati Raj Institutions throughout the state, democracy and women empowerment of the State have been the guiding policy for the state government. With the introduction of Panchayati Raj System in the State, a large number of elected Panchayat members would be involved in all development initiatives in rural areas in accordance with their levels (Srivastava, 2006).Change in the traditional concept of rural leadership based on the age factor. Thus, age is no longer a criterion for the emerging leadership.

Leadership of fair sex is altogether absent in Arunachal tribal world. Women, rarely contest elections. For this, some of the reasons may be: (i) mass illiteracy among women, (ii) low social statuses, in some cases where the more women a man has the greater social status he enjoys, (iii) lack of political training in leadership or political affairs. In most village councils, women are not allowed to participate or they do not participate whatever case may be, (iv) in many other aspects of life, women are subject to unequal treatment in a majority of the tribes. Devoid of property rights or rights over land or debarred from inheritance of father's property as the case may be, and also their economic dependence on men are a great issue for debate.

Jawaharlal Nehru once said, "To awaken the people, it is women who is meant to be awakened, once she is on the move, the family moves, village moves and the nation moves". Swami Vivekananda also once said, "There is no chance for the welfare of the world unless the condition of women is improved. It is not possible for a bird to fly on one wing". Likewise no nation can flourish keeping half of its population in negligence and ignorance, as women constitute half of its human capital. A modern society cannot bring all round development without utilizing the talent of its women.

Dr. Radhakrishnan has very emphatically stated, "Women are human beings and have as much right to full development as men have. The position of women in any society is a true index of its cultural and spiritual level."

Disparity in Sex Ratio

One of the important indicators of gender disparity is sex ratio. According to the Census of 1991 the sex ratio of our country was that for every 1000 males there were 972 female. It is decreased to 933 per 1000 in 2001. Male child is more favoured and celebrated for by the family. Mothers are more emotionally attached towards their sons and they want to marry their daughters at the early age (Thangamuthu and Rasi, 2003). Hospital records show that more male take admission to the hospitals for treatment than female. Several studies reveal that most of the boys are taken to more qualified doctors and more money is spent on their treatment. The girls receive less immunizing vaccines against childhood disease even though such facilities are available free of cost.

Pattern of Sex Ratio in Arunachal Pradesh: The findings of the study are elaborated below. The findings are deducted on the basis of sex ratio analysis based on secondary data from the census. Though all the aspects of the study do not provide a very clear picture about why female population in the State are lower than that of male population but certain inferences have opened a new vista to go for further studies on the lines of population genetics.

Table 18.10 below highlights the details about the sex ratio from 1961 to 2001 censuses concerning the population of Arunachal Pradesh and India. This may be significant to mention here that the first population census in Arunachal Pradesh took place in the year 1961.

Table 18.10: Sex Ratio—Arunachal Pradesh and India 1961-2001.

Census	*Sex Ratio-General in A.P.*	*Sex Ratio-ST in A.P.*	*Sex Ratio-General in India*
1961	894	1013	941
1971	861	1007	930
1981	862	1004	933
1991	859	998	927
2001	901	1003	933

Source: Census Report: 1961, 1971, 1981, 1991 and 2001.

The overall trend of general sex ratio in the State of Arunachal Pradesh as well as for the country as a whole shows a continuous decline, except for a marginal improvement in 1981. In 2001, there is an improvement in the proportion of females to 901 in Arunachal Pradesh and to 933 for India as compared to 1991 census. If we look at the change in sex ratio for India as a whole in the period flanked by 1991-2001, then it is observed that there is an addition of +6 for all India in contrast to the substantial addition in case of Arunachal Pradesh to + 42.

It is interesting to find that the female population of Scheduled Tribes has always been higher than that of males. While the generality in this case needs to be answered through systemic study of population genetics, this might be worthwhile to mention here that female sex is generally stronger than that of males. Thus, there is all likelihood of the female to live longer than male (as the gentler sex is biologically stronger) and hence more males die than the females not only at birth but also at all ages.

This could be supported by the evidence and the fact that in the advanced western countries, the proportion of women in total population is higher than that of males. Similarly, the female population number in the Scheduled Tribes population of Arunachal Pradesh has always been higher than that of the general population. While prenatal mortality could be a valid factor in general, but lack of maternity care, access to medical services in general and absence of the same in the interior areas, low awareness among females, hesitation to visit male gynecologist, superstitions during pregnancy, lack of care at home lead to increasing chances of infant mortality in the instant case. Availability of data in this regard is the limitation of the study.

In India, 108 females are born per 100 males. There are genetic evidences to prove that during the gestation period more males are eliminated than the females because of recessive X-linked lethal genes eliminating males while having little or no effect on the viability of the heterogeneous females. This could be the valid reason for the State of Arunachal Pradesh also where female population composition is higher than that of male population for all the ethnic groups in general.

The loss of more females in case of general population are due to insufficient attention and health care to them during the entire conception period as well as after birth. Women in general suffer from a low status in the society which is an undisputed fact and generally considered with regard to all the States in India. Above all, the females are considered as social and economic liability while the males are credited as an asset to the family. All these together tell upon the health of the females and result in relatively high female mortality in all ages and all groups whether tribes or non-tribes population. In case of Arunachal Pradesh, there are hardly any separate maternity cares in the State's Health Service system. In addition to the above-mentioned points, the continued paucity of females may be attributed to recurrence of environmentally afflicted diseases which are endemic in nature such as malaria, diarrhoea, asthma, hepatitis, tuberculosis and other respiratory ailments.

Women in tribal society, lead a very busy life helping the menfolk in all walks of life. Tribal society enjoys an egalitarian status and women are considered as assets as the bride price is paid by the groom's family at the time of marriage. This is one of the valid reasons why females are better off in tribal society in contrast to the general population in the country as a whole. A large number of women are living below poverty line; they suffer also from nutritional deficiency. Lack of alertness and access to balanced diet and right foods during pregnancy, insufficient intake of irons, proteins and micro nutrients such as iodine and vitamins is the principal cause of very high incidence of nutritional deficiency diseases like anemia, diarrhoea, night blindness, goiter, etc. Low body resistance due to malnutrition farther may complicate minor ailments and make it a health hazard. As a result, females death rates in villages of the State are much more than males.

Conclusion

A key policy intervention is the comprehensive promotion of the empowerment and rights of women and girls, including rights of descent ownership and inheritance as well as full social and legal status as human persons. The platform for action that has emerged from the series of conferences all over the world on Women must be taken seriously as a charter for action because the fate of today's women directly affects the fate of today's girls who may or may not become tomorrow's women. To do this in earnest, we need greater commitment, accountability and resources from government and society at large. The challenges are to implement the recommendations that have been agreed upon by the international community so that they will actually improve the life changes and realities of women and girls everywhere.

Women's empowerment is also children's empowerment. The promotion of women's reproductive health and reproductive rights would help ensure that every child is wanted and healthy; woman can exercise their reproductive rights only when they are empowered to do so. The control of women's fertility is also related to the control of their sexuality. Female genital mutilation continues to be inflicted on women and girl children as a customary means of controlling their sexuality and, therefore, their fertility. Women's rights over their own bodies thus constitute the foundation of their rights to economic and political resources (Dharagi, Malipatil and Basavaraj, 2007).

REFERENCES

Aggarwal, J.C. (2004): *Development and Planning of Modern Education*, Vikas Publishing House Pvt. Ltd., (Ed.)-8, pp. 273-79.

Iqbal A.B. (2007): "Social Face of India: Some Issues", Kurukshetra: *A Journal of Rural Development*, June, Vol. 55, No. 8, New Delhi.

Dharagi, J. and *et al.* (2007): "Gender Description in India—A need for Intervention", *Journal of Global Economy*, Feb. Vol. 3, No. 1, Mumbai, p. 37-39.

Ruhela, Sarya (1999): *Understanding the Indian Women Today: Problems and Challenges*, Indian Publishers, Distributors, Delhi, pp. 164-66.

The Times of India, Thursday, March 8, 2007.

Janaki, D. (2006): "Empowerment of Women through Education: 150 years of University Education in India", *University News*, Vol. 44. No. 48, Nov. 27 December, 3, p. 83.

Mandal, R.K. (2005): *Arunachal Economy: Socio-Economic Transformation*, Champion Publication, Itanagar.

Social Development Report, *Council for Social Development*, Oxford University Press, 2006, p. 78.

Participation of Women in Panchayati Raj: A Status Report, *Institute of Social Sciences*, New Delhi, 1995.

19

Socio-Economic Status of Tribal Women in Present Economic Environment

Introduction

Women are an integral part in every society. The status of women in society is directly linked with social and cultural traditions, stages of economic development achieved, educational levels and political attainments for women in society. Such factors affect the national and also regional characteristics of the status of women. The economic status of women is determined by the role played by them in carrying on economic and non-economic activities in society. The nature and type of economic and non-economic role played by women have undergone continued transformation in accordance with the changes in socio-economic factors, education levels and technological developments and with the changing concepts regarding the extent to which women's contribution is desirable and necessary. In the world over, it is now recognized that the status of women in society, both in the developed and underdeveloped countries, continues to be inferior to men. Although women's role is crucial in the family and household economy, women have not given equal rights in social, political as well as economic fields. The necessity of improvement of status of women has been recognized all over the world as an important aspect of national progress and development. It is also felt that the problem of poverty cannot be tackled without providing opportunities of productive employment to women. Productive employment to women would provide necessary economic base and improve their social status.

But it is still a fact that women in many countries of the world are facing discriminatory attitude if varying degrees on the ground of sex in employment and working conditions.

Women play a vital role in the society. Apart from the matriarchal society, women play a decisive role in most of the patriarchal societies also. The future of children depends, by and large, upon the mothers who generally stay at home and take care of their children's health and education. This is particularly so in countries like India where society and life of people are moulded by traditional and spiritual foundations. Though women are the key factor in the process of change and development, yet in many countries they are underestimated. For example, women in the traditional societies of Asia and Africa take equal part with men in producing foodstuffs, in addition to endless household works, yet their works are not given due weightage. In many parts of rural India women participate equally or even more in some societies with men in various agricultural operations.

Women are part of our socio-economic system. They uphold our rich cultural and traditional values as they have a strong bond with the society. Their progress is many often equated with the nation's progress and therefore, their participation in developmental activities of the societies is always a concern. The educational background of women has a direct bearing on her development. In general, women have lower literacy and education and hence less participation in social, political and scientific/technological fields. Hence, they are sometimes treated as the socio-economically weaker sections or vulnerable sections of our society. Quite often their contributions are unnoticed and un-reorganized and are less paid than that of their counterparts. But with the advent of technological and scientific development and public awareness, the overall developmental activities of women have changed nationally and globally. The women of seventies and eighties have lots of changes either socially or economically. Even their perceptions and participation in socio-political activities have drastically changed. With the passing of time the public has identified the role of women and their contribution to the society.

In most societies of the world, women have been defined largely in terms of their functions as wives and mothers. Many people including women themselves think that they cannot think of performing any role other than wife and mother. Feminists tried to shatter this long held notion about women's place and the accepted belief of their nature and function. Even then, most women faced the problem of dual role, whenever they took up employment outside home. Despite the seeming progress, women still occupied inferior jobs and faced discrimination in entry to jobs as well as opportunities for advancement.

Most Indian women do accept their traditional role of dependence on male relatives. But as possibility of economic independence through respectable employment becomes a reality for women, they do take advantage of the opportunity. The educated Indian women, when comes in contact with a broader culture than that of her home, learns about new role potentialities and would like to adopt certain changes in the traditional roles. Social change is possible only by empowering and educating women. Nehru once said, "to awaken the people, it is women who is meant to be awakened, once she is on the move, the family moves, village moves and the nation moves". Swami Vivekananda also once said, "There is no change for the welfare of the world unless the condition of women is improved. It is not possible for a bird to fly on one wing". Likewise no nation can flourish keeping half of its population in negligence and ignorance, as women constitute half of its human capital. A modern society cannot bring all round development without utilizing the talent of its women. President, A.P.J. Abdul Kalam, said, "When women are empowered, society with stability is assured. Empowerment of women is essential as their thoughts and their value systems lead the development of a good family, good society and ultimately a good nation".

Victimization of women is one of the serious problems resulting from the exploitation of women in different spheres of life in a male dominated society. The fact is that women do not enjoy equity with men in social, economic, political and cultural aspects of life. It is the root cause of large scale victimization of women. Economic helplessness, insufficient laws and prejudiced societal patterns have entrenched the philosophy of violence in the male Psyche.

In Arunachal Pradesh, various tribal communities are at different stages of development; as such the status of women differs from community to community. However, in general the position of women in Arunachal Pradesh is respectable but not very high. The prevalence of polygamy, victim of bride price, sex abuse and child marriage are quite in common. It has no doubt lowered their position. They are generally devoid of equal political and property rights.

The role and work participation of women has been everybody's focus of attention in every society and in every age. Naturally, it is vital with a view to bringing about the desirable changes for social mobility and granting them equality in the matters of rights and privileges. It was in this background that the need of prying into the hidden realms of the women of the tribes of Arunachal Pradesh was felt so vigorously that the research scholars decided to put their heads together to come out with veritable contributions based on observation and investigation, and the result is this present compilation of the research studies on the status of women of the tribes of Arunachal Pradesh.

The Principal inhabitants of the State of Arunachal Pradesh from East to West are the Wancho, Nocte, Tangsa, Singpho, Khamti, Mishmi (Digaru, Miju and Idu), Adi (Gallo, Padam, Minyong, Pailibo, Bokar, Bori etc.), Memba, Khamba, Apatani, Nyishi, Hill-Miri, Nah, Tagin, Aka, Khawa or Bugun, Miji, Sulung, Sherdukpen and Monpa scatterring over an area of 83,743 sq. kms. with hilly terrain in the trans Himalayan region. As per 2001 census the population is 10,97,968 with male 5,79,941 and female 5,18,027, number of village is 3649, number of major tribes is 22, density of population is 13 and literacy rate is 54.74 per cent. The sparsely inhabited Arunachal Pradesh is a predominantly tribal inhabited State. Obviously in the past, the tribesmen purely inhabited it. During 1961, the tribal people formed 88.76 per cent of total population. The percentage of Scheduled Tribes population was 79.02 in 1971, 69.82 in 1981, 63.65 in 1991 and 64.22 in 2001 census. Gradually, different census report has given different classification of total number of tribes, sub-tribes.

The State is inhabited by the world's largest variety of ethnic tribal groups and sub-groups, each tribe speaking their own-language and dialect has their own colourful festivals with different socio-political traditions. Their diverse and unique rich culture and traditional heritage constitute arts and crafts, fares and festivals, social structure, folklores in the form of songs and dances that still remain fresh and well preserved in this State.

An Arunachalee woman has no right to movable or immovable property, except her share of her mother's ornaments. In fact, in many tribes a woman she is a piece of property, first owned by her husband, and after his death by the eldest son. A widow's position is precarious if a son does not wish to support her. The widespread practice of marriage by "bride price" reinforces the concept of woman as useful property. In fact, the Taraon-Mishmi word for marriage is "buying a woman" (Baruah, 1975). But today, such type of social taboo is changing with the impact of globalization and education and every tribe tends to mix up with the mainstream of the country.

Women are very much lagging behind their male counterpart regarding education. Gender inequality lies at the root of the lasting situation of inferiority that affects women at every stage at their lives. Education in general and higher education in particular are an insurance against economic need. Access to the higher education, both technical and professional, will guarantee economic independence leading to social status and hence empowerment to women. If education is to promote equality for women, it must make a deliberate, planned and sustained effort so that the new value of equality of sexes can replace the traditional system of inequality.

Each of the indigenous inhabitants of Arunachal Pradesh has distinctive culture, customs, language and traditions of their own, which they have manifested through different socio-cultural, religious and political events. The women's role in different aspects of their traditional lifestyle of the people is immense.

Position of Women in Different Tribal Society

The *Wanchos* constitute one of the major tribes of the Tirap district who are scattered over the Patkoi range of Indo-Myanmar border in the foothills lying close to the plains of Assam. They are meek, mild and polite by nature. As agriculture is their main occupation, the women play important role in the family, fields and society. With the advent of education after the independence of India, employment opportunities increased and, as a natural consequence of this, women's interest was aroused and they joined certain categories of jobs in the offices, which in turn, provided them with ample opportunities to come into contacts with various cross currents in different fields of life. Though the *Wancho* family is patriarchal, patrilineal and patrilocal and, consequently, succession is counted through the male line, the women are allowed to take part in the social, religious and cultural functions, and enjoy certain privileges. The study of their status has brought in interesting facts opening further scope for more in-depth research.

The *Noctes* are another major tribe of the Tirap district. Educated Nocte women are seen actively participating in political, administrative and professional domains, as secretaries, doctors, teachers, lecturers, lawyers and stenographers. Though they have their own rights over their earnings they earn and do everything for the welfare of their whole family.

The *Tangas* inhabit the eastern hills of the central part of the Tirap district (now called, Changlang district). The women are dependent on man and considered transient members of the family. Men, being the bread-winners, control the family purse, and women's role is recognized in the domestic sphere and in a household affairs. But now-a-days, women are conscious of their rights and place in family, society and politics.

The *Singphos* are the second largest tribe inhabiting the Bordumsa circle of the Changlang district and living in joint families with father as the head. They have very interesting laws of inheritance according to which only the eldest and the youngest sons inherit the family property. Women take equal part with men in agricultural activities and enjoy freedom to choose the occupations they like with preference for office, jobs, business and contracts.

The *Khamtis* live in the lower part of Lohit District. They are exceptionally expert in rice cultivation. The women do not have purdah system and they enjoy the social and religious functions of family and society. With education and vocational training, they have taken up gainful jobs.

The *Digaru Mishmi* women play their important roles as daughters, sisters, wives, and mothers and shoulder various responsibilities of the home and the society.

The *Miju Mishmis* are no longer static. They come into contacts with several groups of people including outsiders and they do accept the changes in the society through education. Thus, Miju women are not far behind their male counterparts. Elections to the Panchayats, the Legislative Assembly and the Parliament are also arousing lots of interest for desirable changes in them.

The future of the *Idu Mishmi* women is bright because of their love for hard work and search for the place of honour in the society. They are no longer confined to the kitchen and the agricultural fields.

The *Galos* are numerically the largest tribe inhabiting the West Siang District. As per their customary laws only the male members of the family inherit the immovable property but with the proliferation of education, women also are inheriting the immovable property also. Thus, changes are taking place in the life of the Galo women.

The *Padams* and the *Minyongs* are the two major tribes of the East Siang district. Since they have patriarchal system, the Padam-Minyong women are subjected to men. However, they have now rights to choose their life-partners and divorce their husbands. Child-marriages are also on wane.

The *Bokars* and *Boris* are the major tribes in the Adi group. Women cannot inherit immovable property from their parents and husbands. They have usually rights over the property.

The *Pailibos* are the inhabitants of the Tato and Paym circles of the West Siang District. Men and women are engaged in agricultural occupations. Besides these, women are to perform the activities like food gathering, domesticating animals and weaving. But educated women are trying for the freedom and equality of position. Therefore, they have started taking part in political and socio-cultural activities.

The *Membas* are the inhabitants of the Mechuka Sub-division of the West Siang District. Men and women are busy with traditional cultivation for most of their time. The Memba women are, however, getting interest in education and politics. Movies and videos have also great impacts upon them.

The *Apatanis* are one of the major tribes of Ziro, the headquarter of the Lower Subansiri district. There is a sex-wise division of work between men and women according to which women are to look after all the domestic activities and other activities like sowing, weeding, harvesting and collecting firewood, green vegetables and fruits. Men are supposed to be bread-winners. Therefore, women are now trying for equal opportunities for education, training and employment.

The *Nyishis* constitute another major tribe of the Lower Subansiri, Papum Pare and East Kameng districts. Since, the Nyishis have patriarchal, patrilineal and patrilocal society, family descent is traced through male. Therefore, men exercise commanding authority over women. Women enjoy more freedom in the household chores. Now situation is changing and women are coming forward to take up higher responsibilities.

The *Hill Miris* inhabit certain parts of both the Lower and Upper Subansiri districts. Women in their society are subordinated to the male members. They shoulder most of the household chores. They do not have any rights to inherit the parental properties like land, cattle and valuable properties. However, the Government is now trying to remove the practice of discrimination against them by means of education.

The *Tagins* are one of the major tribes of the Upper Subansiri district. They have cultural affinity with the Galos, the Nyishis and the Hill Miris. Women have neglected and exploited in the past. With the opening of the political and social institutions, they have now begun to be conscious of their rights and privileges. Spread of education is also bringing about changes in their lives.

Women in the *Aka* tribe are simple, amiable and cheerful, by nature. However, agriculture being the main occupation, they take part in the activities related to agricultural and horticulture. Moreover, they take up activities like collection of firewood, jungle vegetables and fruits and water, cooling, serving the dishes, husking of paddy, cleaning of the house and washing clothes and utensils, weaving and looking after the babies.

The *Buguns* (*Khawas*) are one of the important tribes of the West Kameng district. They are basically agriculturists. Women's domain includes total responsibility of cooling after the light and comparatively soft work, including household management, child rearing work, and tending the domestic animals and poultry. However, education is making them gradually aware of the benefits of modernization.

The primary job of the women in the *Sulungs* tribe is looking after infants and household duties. They are also engaged in the activities like cooking, husking of paddy, cleaning the house and utensils, washing clothes. Preparing local beer and serving the members of the family. The Sulungs women do not enjoy freedom to choose occupations as per their choice simply because of lack of education. Thus, the Sulungs are the most backward tribe of the East Kameng district.

The *Mijis* are the inhabitants of the West Kameng district. The duties of women include kitchen-work, cooking and serving. Cultivation field work removing the dry leaves and weeds, sowing and harvesting. Now, various welfare schemes run by the Departments of Agriculture, Veterinary, Industry, Rural Development, etc. are bringing about changes in their society.

The *Monpas* are inhabitants of the West Kameng and Tawang Districts. They are Buddhist by religion. Cooking, cleaning, washing, housekeeping, looking after the infants, husking of paddy, grinding of cereals, brewing local wine, weaving and knitting are the activities normally taken up by women. Factors like cultural contacts, modern transportation system, and increase in opportunities for economic participation are now bringing about impact on the life of these tribes men and women and they are moving ahead in the matters of employment, commerce and training.

Overall Contributions of Tribal Women

No society can breathe without the rapturous existence of women as perceived by the sociologists. Their care and caresses cater to the needs of reading and preserving the cardinal virtues and values which provide human life with meaning and purpose. The constituent units of the life of women differ in the context of the various tribes of Arunachal Pradesh. With a forward march, development and changes in all spheres of life and culture of the people of Arunachal Pradesh have been observed. Notable developments have also taken place among the women. They have now enjoyed better way of livelihood and freedom of speech, etc. compared to those days in traditional society. Development is not uniform among all the tribes because of various factors. Impacts of developmental schemes are more on the urban inhabitants than on the semi-urban and rural settlers. Monogamy is the most common form of marriage and the love marriage and inter-tribal marriage is also in offing to a great extent. The boys and girls now have enjoyed greater freedom in selection of their mates. Most of the engagements made especially for the girls by their parents in childhood days are either rejected or avoided which has caused dissatisfaction among the older generation and also develop conflicts. The system of payment of bride-price in new form of marriage is not involved. In some cases marriage ceremony as per customs is also not performed. Gradually, such unions are accepted by the respective societies to cope up with cultural development. The women also demand now share in parental property. On economic point of view the women's movement for upliftment of their traditional economy is notable. There are number of women officials of different status as administrator, academicians, medical practitioners, engineers and other non-technical Ministerial staff in the Government and Non-Governmental Organizations. The women are also very much enthusiastic in establishment of small and medium scale industries. Of the small scale units in the state, more than 50 per cent are owned by women. These units are mostly carpet making, weaving, knitting and embroidery. Initially their counterpart menfolk, especially the older people were not in favour of active participation of women in commercial enterprises but gradually seeing economic benefits their attitudes have changed. A few of the energetic women have set-up educational institutions with missionary zeal. In religious activities, however, the women have to maintain their traditional status though women may become priest in some tribes to conduct smaller puzas but no significant development has been noticed. Direct participation in ritual performance is still restricted, but in other form of performance of the community festivals like Mopin and Sulung (Adi), Dree (Apatani), Nyokum Yalo (Nyishi), Si-Donyi (Tagin), Loku (Nocte), Mol (Tangsa), Oriah (Wancho), Tamlodu (Digaru and Miju Mishmi), Reh (Idu Mishmi), Changken (Khampti and Singpho), Losar (Monpa and Sherdukpen) women can participate freely and actively.

The tribal communities of Arunachal Pradesh had their own system of local self-governance in Arunachal Pradesh. "Age old traditional system of self-governance in Arunachal Pradesh was replaced by Panchayati Raj Institutions in 1968". On political front too, the women have developed a lot. Although active participation in the traditional village council is still restricted, yet they can contest Panchayat as well as Legislative Assembly elections. The Government has also reserved 33.33 per cent seats in the Panchayati Raj System for women. With the coming into force of the Constitution (Seventy-Third Amendment) Act, 1992 with effect from 24th April,1993, it was incumbent upon the state government to enact the Arunachal Pradesh Panchayati Raj Institution.

The Constitution (73rd Amendment Act) 1992 paved the way for restoring Panchayati Raj System in the State. It would suffice to mention here that several interactions across various levels were held to ensure to maintain the relevance and applicability of the Act in the context of Arunachal Pradesh.

It envisages establishing strong viable and responsible Panchayat at village, block and district levels and also to evolve adequate powers, responsibilities and finance upon these bodies so as to enable them to prepare plans and implement schemes for economic development and social justice. It is expected that active involvement of Panchayati Raj Institutions in the process of formulation and implementation of the plans will make possible maximum utilization of human and material resources in the rural areas. The election to the present Panchayati Raj was held in April, 2003 and Table 19.1 shows institutional-wise number of elected PRI members in Arunachal Pradesh.

Table 19.1: Present Strength of Elected Members of PRIs in Arunachal Pradesh.

Sl. No.	*Level of PRIs*	*Nos.*	*Members*			*Chairpersons*	
			Male	*Female*	*Total*	*Male*	*Female*
1.	Gram Panchayats	1639	3924	(39.5)2561	6485	1092	(33.37) 547
2.	Anchal Samities	136	1062	(35.2)577	1639	86	(36.76) 50
3.	Zilla Parishad	14	91	(33)45	136	8	(42.86) 6
	Total	**1789**	**3077**	**3183**	**8260**	**1186**	**603**

Source: Directorate of PR and RD, Itanagar.

Note: (i) Above figures do not include the allotted strength of Tirap District as PR elections were not held till date.

(ii) Figures in parenthesis show percentage of female members only of total elected members in PRI.

The Panchayati Raj Institutions (PRIs) also played a very important role in bringing about a major socio-political change in the traditional tribal society of Arunachal Pradesh with the increasing growth in education and political awareness at rural people and their increasing interface with the outside world due to greater mobility. The Panchayati Raj Institutions serve as a training ground for rural people and equip them with both knowledge and experience about the democratic system of government in the country thereby enabling them to play more important and useful role in the State and national level political bodies. The State Government is firmly committed to the preservation; development and strengthening of the Panchayati Raj Institutions throughout the state, democratic and empowerment of the state have been the guiding policy for the State Government.

With the instruction of Panchayati Raj System in the state, a large number of elected Panchayat women members would be involved in all development initiatives in rural areas in accordance with their levels.

The status and role of women especially in political parlance has changed at the grass root level after the implementation of Panchayati Raj Institutions Election on 1st April, 2003. In Zilla Parishad, the women members elected were 33 per cent, while in Anchal Samities, it was 35 per cent and in Gram Panchayat, it was 39.5 per cent. Again, the women chairpersons in Zilla Parishad were 42.86 per cent, in Anchal Samities were 36.76 per cent and in Gram Panchayats were 33.37 per cent. The status of women has changed immensely. Their role in developmental decisions has remarkably changed. Perhaps more and more impact of globalization changing are the present day mindset of the male dominated society and bring higher empowerment of women in the state.

Economical and Educational Position

The number of workers in this State during 2001 was 482,206, which is 43.97 per cent of total population. The female workers in the State were 188,657, which are 39.12 per cent of total working population

(*Source:* DES, Itanagar, 2003). Thus, about 4 out of 10 workers in the State are women and they deserved better empowerment as stakeholder for development of the State. The State Government has now constituted State Women Commission (SWC) and it will be a milestone towards empowerment in Arunachal Pradesh.

In higher education, the percentage of APST girls is 37.65 out of total enrolment of APST students in colleges and Rajiv Gandhi University in the State. Again, the strength of female lecturers of the seven government colleges is 12.37 per cent (*Source:* Directorate of Higher and Technical Education, Itanagar, 2004-05). In overall female literacy rate was 1.42 per cent in 1961, 3.71 per cent in 1971, 14.02 per cent in 1981, 29.69 per cent in 1991 and 44.24 per cent in 2001 shown in Table 19.1. The females are lagging behind the males. But the females have achieved much progress in education. Days are not far that the female literacy rate will be equal to their male counterpart.

For sound socio-economic development of the State and triple contributions of women i.e., participation in politics, workforce and education are must. Though they are lagging behind their male counterpart regarding of politics, workforce and education, their numbers are increasing very rapidly day to day. In addition to their triple contributions, they have to be empowered in decision-making in all respects of life. Especially, their decision-making in family planning can give more fruitful result in comparison to their male counterpart.

Reasons for their Empowerment

The National Perspective Plan for Women 1988-2000 AD (1988) which has made a free, frank and objective analysis of the impact of developmental plans and programmes of Indian women highlights the pathetic profile of women in India: There is continued inequality and vulnerability of women in all sectors – economic, social, political, education, health care, nutrition and legal. As women are oppressed in all spheres of life, they need to be empowered in all walks of life.

Further, the Constitution of India has guaranteed, 'Equal rights and equal opportunities to all its citizens, irrespective of sex, age, race or religion'. The rights are guaranteed by law, but yet to be legalized in custom.

Improvement of the status of women and their access to family planning services, again make a triple contribution of sustainable development such as: (i) they make their own contribution to the quality of life and eradication of absolute poverty, (ii) they contribute to economic growth, by raising the quality and skills of the workforce, and (iii) slowing down population growth thus reducing the burden on the environment which will improve sustainability. In brief, it can be said that women are to be empowered in the search for a safe environment, economic and social justice, adequate reallocation of resources, the survival of all species and the common goal of healthy planet in which the future generation can flourish.

Women development and nation building are the two immediate tasks before the State. In fact, there is a strong positive correlation between the two. Nation building is a collective task. Nation is to be built on the ground and in the hearts too. People come first. Governments must create conditions in which all citizens have opportunity to find reasonable secure, remunerative and productive employment to make the process of development more meaningful. It is, therefore, necessary that women do not lag behind in sharing this responsibility on equal footing with men. They are the ones who can provide a human touch to the entire exercises of economic development. But, first, what is women development? In my opinion, it is a process in which through their contribution in achieving broader goals of economic development.

In any society with inequalities of income distribution and wealth, there exists an underprivileged group. Arunachal Pradesh is in no way an exception to this general rule. Rural socio-economic structure of Arunachal Pradesh has been disfavouring this group. The underprivileged group is not able to get the benefits of reforms and economic development. Within the underprivileged group women are the worst affected as they are doubly disadvantaged, as underprivileged group and as underprivileged sex.

In terms of every set of indices of development and socio-economic status women have fared worse than men. In work, employment, earnings, education, health status, political activities, decision-making and exercising of authority, women are the underprivileged. On the one hand, in activities like agriculture, household, spinning and weaving, religious, social-cultural, women are privileged. But they are treated differently even in enjoying the benefits of growth including the chance for acquiring knowledge which is considered as an important index of development. The capability of poverty measure of human development considers lack of three basic capabilities. The economic benefits of education derive not just from increases in cognitive skills, but to a far greater extent from the increase in non-cognitive abilities as reflected by changes in a person's ideas, perceptions and attitudes. But women are deprived of all these benefits.

How to Uplift the Tribal Women

1. The policy maker and planner should think regarding the birth of a girl child, opportunities of education to women, preferential treatment to women, types of marriages prevalent in the contemporary society, conjugal relation between husband and wife, and the custom so that women have to assert themselves as equal partners in their relentless contribution to the growth of the society and human civilization.
2. But the role of the socio-cultural factors cannot be overlooked while considering women's economic activity. Despite social norms, taboos and conservative attitude, large number of women belonging to the lower strata of the society participate in economic activities for economic necessities which vary from region to region in the State.
3. Village-wise seminar, symposium, workshop etc., should be conducted to strengthen the attitude of women of Arunachal Pradesh so that they can play a major role in the economic reconstruction of the State. We can remember the United Nations Development Programme (UNDP)'s Human Development Report (1995) which opines "investing in women's capabilities and empowering them to exercise their choices is not only valuable in itself but is also the surest way to contribute to economic growth and development". The report reaffirms that "Human development is impossible without gender equality. As long as women are excluded from the development process, development will remain lopsided. Sustainable human development implies engendering the development paradigm".

4. Financial linkages required to be increased and for that more bank branches are required to be opened. This will raise the Credit Deposit (CD) ratio of all banks. Women should be given relaxation in getting loan from the financial institutions so as to empower the women economically that more and more women will come and take loan to open enterprises. Moreover, author thinks that Arunachal Pradesh possesses immense potential (God gifted) for the development of Tourism Industry where tribal women play a vital role more efficient.
5. Without educating girls, the State never brings all round development as women constitute a half of its total population. The State should enforce women's empowerment through higher education giving different favourable facilities such as bearing total educational expenses coupled with healthy environment in colleges like separate rest room for leisure period in co-education colleges and separate girls' college, etc. Female literacy, particularly in rural areas, in our country is extremely low, the drop-out rate among girls is very high. Girls are normally burdened with household chores. They are deprived of education and exposure to the outside world and therefore, they remain ignorant and superstitious. There is a need to convince the illiterate parents for girls' education *vis-à-vis* motivating these parents for adult education programmes. Female students can interact with such girls and persuade their mothers for their enrolment in colleges/schools. Cognitive empowerment of women carries her to self-confidence and self-reliance i.e., psychological empowerment which can lead to further social action or economic activity that stimulates political and economic empowerment. Different academic strategies and other plans are drawn out for this purpose. Training and education for empowerment of women in the State result in individual empowerment and social transformation whereby, women have more control over their lives and more of an effect in the changing society to eliminate of reduce gender bias and discrimination.

Conclusion

Women development and nation building are the two immediate tasks before the State. In fact, there is a strong positive correlation between the two. Nation building is a collective task. Nation is to be built on the ground and in the hearts too. People come first. Governments must create conditions in which all citizens have opportunity to find reasonable secure, remunerative and productive employment to make the process of development more meaningful. It is, therefore, necessary that women do not lag behind in sharing this responsibility on equal footing with men. They are the ones who can provide a human touch to the entire exercises of economic development. But, first, what is women development? In my opinion, it is a process in which through their contribution in achieving broader goals of economic development.

In any society with inequalities of income distribution and wealth, there exists an underprivileged group. Arunachal Pradesh is in no way an exception to this general rule. Rural socio-economic structure of Arunachal Pradesh has been disfavouring this group. The underprivileged group is not able to get the benefits of reforms and economic development. Within the underprivileged group women are the worst affected as they are doubly disadvantaged, as underprivileged group and as underprivileged sex.

In terms of every set of indices of development and socio-economic status women have fared worse than men. In work, employment, earnings, education, health status, political activities, decision-making and exercising of authority, women are the underprivileged. On the one hand, in activities like agriculture, household, spinning and weaving, religious, social-cultural, women are privileged. But they are treated differently even in enjoying the benefits of growth including the chance for acquiring knowledge which is considered as an important index of development. The capability of poverty measure of human development considers lack of three basic capabilities. The economic benefits of education derive not just from increases in cognitive skills, but to a far greater extent from the increase in non-cognitive abilities as reflected by changes in a person's ideas, perceptions and attitudes. But women are deprived of all these benefits.

REFERENCES

Bhagabati, D. (April, 2001): "Education of the Tribal Women in Assam: Status, Problem and Hope", *Journal of North-East India Council for Social Science Research*, Shillong, p. 52.

Bhattacharjee, R.P. (2006): "Globalization and Its Impact on Women Population of Arunachal Pradesh", *SIRD*-ARUN, Vol. I, p. 41.

Bora, M.M. and Bhattacharya, A. (1996): "Raising the status of Plain Tribes Women through Income Generating Training" in Medhi, K. (ed.), *"Status of Women and Social Change"*, Women's Studies Research Centre, Gauhati University, Guwahati, p. 102.

Buzarburah, R. (Oct. 1996): "Human Rights and Women" in Medhi, K. (ed.), *"Status of Women and Social Change"*, Women's Studies Research Center, Gauhati University, Guwahati, p. 27.

Das, G. (1995): *Tribes of Arunachal Pradesh in Transition*, Vikas Publishing House Pvt. Ltd., New Delhi, p. 31.

Dubey, S. (2000): "Tribal Women and their Political Empowerment: A case study of Arunachal Pradesh", Resarun: *Journal of the Directorate of Research*, Government of Arunachal Pradesh, Department of Cultural Affairs, Itanagar, Vol. XXVI, pp. 12-13.

Goswami, A.K. (Oct.1996): "Women in the vision of Kalidasa" in Medhi, K. (ed.), *"Status of Women and Social Change"*, Women's Studies Research Centre, Gauhati University, Guwahati, pp. 54-55.

Mandal, R.K. (2005): *Arunachal Economy: Socio-Economic Transformation*, Champion Publisher and Distributor, Itanagar, p. 41.

Mandal, R.K. (2005): "Literacy in Arunachal Pradesh: Trends, Features and Growth", an article accepted by Rajiv Gandhi University, Rono Hill, Itanagar.

Mandal, R.K. (2007): "Role and Status of Galo women in Socio-Economic Development of Arunachal Pradesh": *A UGC sponsored research project*.

Mandal, R.K. (2006): "Trend and Growth of Population in Arunachal Pradesh", *Southern Economist*, January 15, Vol. 44, No. 18, p. 28.

Mandal, R.K. (2006): "Control of Jhum Cultivation in Arunachal Pradesh—Retrospect and Prospect", *Kurukshetra*, December, Vol. 55, No. 2, p. 18.

Mandal, R.K. (2008): "Participation of Women in Agriculture in Arunachal Pradesh with Special Emphasis on West Siang District", in Singha, K.(ed.): *Village Development in North-East India*, Concept Publishing Co., New Delhi.

Mitra, Amitava (1996): "Female labour participation: A district level study in Arunachal Pradesh" in Medhi, K. (ed.), *"Status of Women and*

Social Change", Women's Studies Research Centre, Gauhati University, Guwahati, p. 91.

Muralidharan, K. (2005): "The Globalized Women and Workforce: Issues, Problems and Solutions", *University News*, December 12-18, Vol. 43, No. 50, p. 3.

Padmavathy, S. and Pandian, P.K. (2004): "Need of Education for Rural Women", *Southern Economist*, April 1 and 15, Vol. 42, No. 23 and 24, p. 15.

Sanajaoba, N. and Rashid, P. (Oct. 1996): "Women as Decision Maker" in Medhi, K. (ed.), *"Status of Women and Social Change"*, Women's Studies Research Centre, Gauhati University, Guwahati, p. 11.

Sarma, M. (Oct. 1996): "Status of Women: Need for Multi-dimensional Change" in Medhi, K. (ed.), *"Status of Women and Social Change"*, Women's Studies Research Centre, Gauhati University, Guwahati, p. 14.

Sharma, D.B and N. Romida (1996): "Violence against women: A case study of Meitei women in Manipur" in Medhi, K. (ed.), *"Status of Women and Social Change"*, Women's Studies Research Centre, Gauhati University, Guwahati, p. 142.

Srivastava, R. (2006): "Role and Importance of Training in Channelizing Demand for Participation in Development", *SIRD*-ARUN, Vol. I, p. 29.

Pandya, R. and Mathu, A. (2005): "Capacity Building for Effective Women Administrators of Tomorrow", *University News*, December 5-11, Vol. 43, No. 49, p. 1.

Pandey, B.B. (1997): *"Status of Women in Tribal Society: Arunachal Pradesh"*, (ed.), Directorate of Research, Government of Arunachal Pradesh, Itanagar, introductory part.

Vashistha, K.C. and Malik, S. (2002): "Some Strategic Efforts Towards the Empowerment of Women", *University News*, Vol. 40, No.5, February 4-10, p. 1.

20

Work Participation of Women in Agriculture

A Case Study in West Siang District

Concept of Participation

Participation is a tool to attain several distinct objectives. Once used and properly handled, the participatory approach can lead to changes in knowledge, attitudes, skills and distribution of power across individuals and community for their own development. "Differential degree" and "extent of participation" in development can be described as follows: (i) The mere use of a service; (ii) Participation through the contribution (or extraction) of resources, materials and labour; (iii) Participation through "attendance" often implying passive acceptance of decisions made by others; (iv) Participation through consultation on a particular issue; (v) Involvement in the delivery of service, often as partner; (vi) Involvement as implementers of delegated powers; and (vii) Most completely participation "in real decision-making at every stage: the study of feasibility, planning, implementation and evaluation" (UNICEF, 1986).

Women are an integral part in every society. The status of women in society is directly linked with social and cultural traditions, stages of economic development achieved, educational levels, attitude of the society towards women, social and religious taboos, women's own awareness and political attainments for women in society. Such factors affect the national and also regional characteristics of the status of women. The economic status of women is determined by the role played by them in carrying on economic and non-economic activities in society. The nature and type of economic and non-economic role played by women have undergone continued transformation in accordance with the changes in socio-economic factors, education levels and technological developments and with the changing concepts regarding the extent to which women's contribution is desirable and necessary.

It is almost universally accepted that the woman's primary role is performed specially as a home-maker and it is for the man to provide subsistence to his family. Under certain conditions, in addition to the role of a house-keeper, women also participate sometimes in the gainful activity of the community. Thus, we find that some women work and some do not. The question- "Why does a man work" — is not a significant one because he is regarded as the natural bread earner, therefore he is expected to provide subsistence to his family. However, the question — "Why does a women work" — assumes special significance when the whole range of her activities centres on household chores. Although a large number of women are engaged in the household activities, they are significantly contributing to the monetary and non-monetary inputs of our national income because their works, in the contest of Socio-economic setting, are generally either undervalued or not taken into account in the labour sector, inspite of fact that all the activities are productive. In this respect, the observation of Human Development Report, 1993 is worthmentioning "Women are often invisible in statistics. If women's unpaid housework were counted as productive output in national income accounts, global output would increase by 20 per cent to 30 per cent (Human Development Report, p. 25). In fact, the spatial variation in the level of female participation in work has started drawing greater attention since the seventies. Although the sociologists and economists (Boserup, 1970; Gulati, 1975; Sundaram, 1989; Nayyar, 1989) have analyzed the conditions and factors which influence the female participation in work, but their studies are based on analysis of data for a state, while others relate to the country as a whole. There cannot be two opinions that the majority of women apparently work out of economic necessities, at the same time the importance of socio-cultural factors cannot be overlooked, particularly while considering the female participation in economic activities. Another interesting aspect of female participation has been its wide variation from country to country and from region to region within a country.

The position of women and their status in any society is an index of its civilization. Women are to be considered as equal partners in the process of development. But, because of centuries of exploitation and subjugation, Indian women have remained at the receiving end. In this context, in order to provide a big push, Institutional support is necessary to empower Indian women in general and rural women in particular. Women empowerment demands a "Lifecycle" approach where empowerment is viewed as a process and not as an event, which challenges traditional power equations and relations. Empowerment in its simplest form means redistribution of power that challenges the male dominance. This does not, however, mean that the empowerment process adopts an antagonists approach. It is only to enable women to supplement and coordinate with men. Empowerment is an active process of enabling women to realize their identity, potentiality and power in all spheres of their lives (Sharma, 1992).

President, A.P.J. Abdul Kalam, said empowering women was a prerequisite for creating a good nation, "when women are empowered, society with stability is assured. Empowerment of women is essential as their thoughts and their value systems lead the development of a good family, good society and ultimately a good nation".

Education is a milestone for women empowerment because it enables them to respond to opportunities, to challenge their traditional roles and to change their lives. Similar ideas were supported in International Conference, 1994. It was said that Education is one of the most important means of empowering women with the knowledge, skills and self-confidence necessary to participate fully in the development process. Educating woman benefits the whole society. It has a more significant impact on poverty and development than men's education.

Social change is possible only by empowering and educating women. Jawaharlal Nehru once said, "To awaken the people, it is women who is meant to be awakened, once she is on the move, the family moves, village moves and the nation moves". Swami

Vivekananda also once said, "There is no chance for the welfare of the world unless the condition of women is improved. It is not possible for a bird to fly on one wing". Likewise no nation can flourish keeping half of its population in negligence and ignorance, as women constitute half of its human capital. A modern society cannot bring all round development without utilizing the talent of its women.

In case of India in its broad regional spectrum, we find that the Southern and North-Eastern States have a higher female participation than the Northern States. This has led Boserup to conclude that the influence from West Asian culture was strong in the Northern part of India-Pakistan sub-continent and only marginal in the Southern part (Boserup, 1971, page 71). In fact, the Southern and North-Eastern States have a pattern more like that of South-East Asian countries. For example, according to the 1991 census, the female participation is the highest in Mizoram (43.12%) followed by Manipur (38.96%) and Arunachal Pradesh (37.49%) and it is the lowest in Punjab (14.48%). Thus, the variations in the level and extent of female participation in economic activity are conspicuous at each level, starting from the regional level to the district level.

In Arunachal Pradesh, the female marginal workers in 1981 census were 14,995 and it has fallen to only 1117 in 1991. However, the female main workers have only marginally increased from 1,18,604 in 1981 to 1,42,100 in 1991. Let us discuss the sectoral classification of female workers of the state in Table 20.1.

Table 20.1: Sectoral classification of female main workers of Arunachal Pradesh,

1981-91 (percentage).

Year	*Primary*	*Secondary*	*Tertiary*
1981	95.12	1.99	2.89
1991	89.02	1.81	9.17

Sources: (i) Census of India, 1981 series –I, Primary Census Abstract, General Population Table part-II, (B) (i).

(ii) Census of India, 1991, Series-I paper-2 of 1992, Final Population Totals.

Table 20.1 reflects that during the 1981 census year more than 95 per cent of the female workers were engaged in the primary sector. However, during the last census i.e., 1991, there was a significant reduction in female workers in the primary sector. Thus, in Arunachal Pradesh we find that there is steady decline of Workforce Participation Rate (WPR) of females and at the same time there is significant decline of female workers in the primary sector. In this connection, the relationship between WPR of females and economic development through the "U" shaped curve (Anker, p. 27) can be referred to. According to this theory, in the initial stages of development, the female participation rate is higher and they mainly work as family workers in the primary sector. In the second stage of development the participation rate falls due to a lack of their geographical mobility from rural to urban areas. In the third stage, the female participation rate increases particularly in the secondary and tertiary sectors because of the spread of education and change in the attitude of the people.

As per the State Forest Report, 1999 (published by the Forest Survey of India), forest cover of Arunachal Pradesh is 68951 sq. kms. accounting for 82.21 per cent of its total geographical area. The recorded forest area of the state is 51,540 sq. kms. which is about 62 per cent of its total geographical area. Thus, the State is fortunate to have such high percentage of its area under valuable forests cover against the national percentage of 23.28. Again, out of its area, 70 per cent constitutes broad and narrow valleys, 10 per cent foothills and flat areas and 20 per cent constitutes snow clad peak areas. The agricultural operations are confined to only 5 per cent of the total geographical area, out of which 62 per cent to 65 per cent are under shifting cultivation *(jhum)*.

It is known through archaeological discoveries that in the Neolithic period around 1000 B.C., man's attitude to his environment underwent fundamental changes. It might be an accident when he took hoe from bow i.e., from hunter he became food producer. Man began to plant, cultivate and improve species of edible plants by selection. This is regarded as the first step in the transition from food gathering/hunting to food production. Among the food plants cultivated by the Neolithic people, rice, wheat, barley, millet, maize, yam, sweet potatoes provided staple food.

Almost all the tribes except Apatanis and Khamptis in Arunachal Pradesh are practising shifting cultivation. The Apatanis and Khamptis are engaged in settled cultivation. The *jhumias* (the man who practices *jhum* cultivation is called the *jhumia*) produce all the crops, which they need. These types of cultivation are widespread among the hill dwellers of Assam, Meghalaya, Nagaland, Mizoram and Arunachal Pradesh. It is known in different areas by a variety of local names. In North-East India, it is called *Jhum*. In these widespread areas, there is a remarkable uniformity of the method of cultivation. It is the most primitive form of agriculture which is still in vogue in most parts of North-East Hill Region of the country. According to 2001 census about 80 per cent of the State's populations are living in rural areas and all are directly and indirectly involved in *jhum* cultivation. It is also claimed that slash and burn agriculture leads to deterioration of the vegetative cover on the hills: forest lands degenerate into infertile grassland and barren land space. Therefore, it is contended that this system of agriculture is unsustainable and economically impoverishing of the tribal people depended on it.

The shifting cultivation is also called as slash and burn method of cultivation. It is labour-intensive process of farming with extensive use of land. It is also claimed that slash and burn agriculture leads to deterioration of the vegetative cover on the hills: forest lands degenerate into infertile grassland and barren land space. Therefore, it is contended that this system of agriculture is unsustainable and economically impoverishing of the tribal people depended on it. The technology being primitive, the level of production and income is very low. It occupies a distinct place in the socio-economic fabric of tribal economy of this State. The *jhumia* selects the field on the slope of the hill on rotation basis. Due to deterioration in fertility of soil the *jhumia* is compelled to shift his cultivation on another plot. He keeps the land fallow for a number of years for regeneration of forests. Again, he uses the same land. That is why, this process is also called shifting cultivation. Its chief characteristics are: (i) slash and burn operation of vegetal species, (ii) use of human labour as chief input, (iii) non-employment of animal, and (iv) use of simple implements such as dibble stick, scrapper, etc.

The cycle of agricultural operation in all these areas of North-East Region is marked by the following stages:

1. Selecting the forested hilly track.
2. Cleansing the forest track by cutting down the jungle during December-January.
3. Drying and burning of fallen shrubs/trees into ashes during February- March.
4. Fencing the cleared plots.
5. Worship and sacrifice.
6. Dibbling and sowing of seeds for mixed cropping.
7. Weeding operation.
8. Watching and protecting the crops against depredation by wild animals, pests, etc.
9. Harvesting.
10. Threshing and storing.

The area under shifting cultivation and number of families are engaged are shown in Table 20.2.

Table 20.2: Shifting cultivation in the North-East Region.

State	*Annual Area under shifting cultivation (sq. kms.)*	*Fallow Period (in years)*	*Minimum Area under shifting cultivation one time or other (sq. kms.)*	*No. of families practicing shifting cultivation*
Arunachal Pradesh	700	3 –10	2,100	54,000
Assam	696	2 – 10	1,392	58,000
Manipur	900	4 – 7	3,600	70,000
Meghalaya	530	5 – 7	2,650	52,290
Mizoram	630	3 – 4	1,890	50,000
Nagaland	190	5 – 8	1,913	1,16,046
Tripura	223	5 – 9	1,115	43,000
Total	**3869**		**14,660**	**4,43,336**

Source: The Task Force Report on Shifting Cultivation, Ministry of Agriculture, 1983.

The following Table 20.3 shows the position of different states of North-East India in respect of only shifting, shifting combined with permanent, permanent and not doing any cultivation.

Table 20.3: Shifting, Permanent and Combined Cultivation in the Tribal Society.

State	*Percentage of tribal households in respect of cultivation*			
	Shifting cultivation	*Shifting combined with permanent cultivation*	*Permanent cultivation*	*Not doing any cultivation*
Arunachal Pradesh	33.50	24.20	29.60	12.70
Assam	18.60	24.00	29.50	07.70
Manipur	46.10	24.50	15.40	04.10
Meghalaya	15.40	38.20	21.60	14.80
Tripura	12.10	11.60	53.20	23.10

Source: Patnaik, 1984.

Agriculture is still the single largest livelihood system and occupies an important place in the economy of Arunachal Pradesh and forms a major occupation of the people of the state. According to 2001 census about 79.66 per cent of the State's populations are living in rural areas and 58.44 per cent of the total workers are cultivators. It is not only the main source of employment, income and food, but it is also the main culture for rural families. It is seen that almost all rural women are involved in agriculture. Through women play a significant and crucial role in agriculture and allied fields, they are ignored. By and large they have remained 'invisible workers'. Because of low 'visibility' of their contributions, they are not regarded as equal partners in the developmental process. They work longer and harder than men. They also work on more tasks than men. Usually, the low income, low skilled and low productivity jobs are female specific. Almost always, labour intensive, back breaking and time consuming activities are the domain of the weaker sex (females).

Household and community roles among the Arunachalee tribes are also sharply gendered. Men and boys may hunt and fish, but good production and preparation is the women's responsibility. Men will perform certain specific tasks like slashing the trees for *jhuming* or using the plough for settled cultivation. Traditionally only men handled the spade to prepare the fields. But this seems to be changing as men withdraw from farming operations. The author saw many women in the fields using spades. Generally, tasks which require more physical strength are undertaken by men such as cleaning of jungle for *jhum* cultivation, setting fire to it before the seed is sown, collection of house building materials from jungle, etc. But the success of agricultural operation depends upon women as they are the ones who carry out most of the work like sowing, weeding, harvesting, etc. There is no division of labour as such between married and unmarried women. Thus, there is division of labour in the Galo society between men and women.

Geographical Area under Study

The West Siang District extends over an area of 12,006 sq. kms. approximately in central region of Arunachal Pradesh bounded by Tibet (China) in the north, Assam in the south, Upper Siang District and East Siang District in the East, and Upper Subansiri District and Lower Subansiri District in the West. Its topography is mainly mountainous interspread with gentle slopes and low-lying valleys kissing the plains of Assam. The altitude of this district varies from 200 m. to 1890 m. above the sea level. West Siang District comprises five sub-divisions and twenty circles with headquarters at Aalo.

Of all tribal groups of West Siang District, the Galo ranks first in population and are predominant at Aalo, Basar, Tirbin, Liromoba, Darak, Kaying and Likabali circles and sub-divisions-wise they are predominant in Aalo, Basar and Yomcha sub-divisions. Therefore, our study was confined only on Galo women. That is why, the study had been undertaken to investigate the work participation of women in agriculture of Galo society.

Agricultural Work of Galos

The main occupation of the Galos is agriculture both jhum and wet rice cultivation. In *jhum* cultivation, which are also called 'slash and burn' method of cultivation, several crops like paddy, maize, millet, chilli, bean, pumpkin, banana, sugarcane etc. are grown. Off late people find it more reliable and assured production, to adopt wet rice cultivation. Nevertheless, the *jhum* is still very popular. Because of its multiple cropping pattern, there is lesser chance of crop failure in *jhum* and always serve as support in the lean period. That is why; the people are still in the stage of *jhum* cultivation with a dibble. The whole area is a network of hills, on the slopes of which, the Galos have their agricultural fields. Some of the fields are even at a height of 4,000 to 5,000 feet. After the selection of sites for cultivation, the trees in the fields are felled, generally in the month of February and the whole area is cleared of grasses and creepers. These cut trees are left in the field for nearly a month to dry and by March, they are fired. Efforts are made to see that the whole field is burnt together. The Galo area has a heavy and continuous rainfall, March is generally a dry month having clear sun shine. After the fire is out, the products of this *jhum* fire are utilized in a number of ways. The ashes are left strewn all over the field, which serve as manure. The un-burnt or charred wood is utilized in three different ways: the big and massive logs are used for their indigenous methods of contour-logging, which, to some extent, checks the soil erosion; the thicker sticks are used for fencing the field; and finally, the smaller ones are used as fuel, which are carried everyday by women in their conical baskets, hung on the back, while returning from the field. At the time of felling the trees, cleaning the jungle, setting fire and fencing the fields, efforts are made to see that all the villagers do their respective work together, as these occupations are considered the responsibility of the whole village. Care, however, is taken to ensure that no *hilok* trees are cut, as these trees are believed to be the abodes of spirits. If, however, their cutting is essential, as it often becomes so, due to their abundance in the jungle, offerings of fowls and eggs are made to the spirits, so that they may not get annoyed and cause damage to the crops. *Pute Sidi*, another spirit, believed to reside on the trees in the jungle, is also propitiated with sacrifices (Mandal and etc, 2010).

A major portion of their time is devoted to agricultural activities, which demand a great deal of labour and hard work. Co-operation has its inherent social and psychological advantages. During the work, they feel that one is for all and all for one. Big plots, cleared in this way, contain a number of smaller plots, individually owned by different families. The individual families take care of their own plots. Only the fencing is jointly made, as it catered for the common interest of all the plot holders. But an individual has every right, guaranteed by social sanctions, to requisition the help of his co-villagers for sowing or harvesting his plot, in case he falls short of the required hands and in return, he has to entertain those, who participate in such activities, in a feast.

Crops

Together with paddy and maize is also sown broadcast in the same field. Maize is sown in separate holes and millet is strewn all over the field. Maize, however, is sown in three different ways; firstly, it is sown separately in the month of January and February; it is also sown in the same field with paddy or a little after the paddy has been sown; and finally, it is sown in an altogether separate field, depending upon the condition and the quality of the soil, in the months of June and July. Brinjal, Mustard, Chilli and Giyi (*Brassica species*) seeds are also sown at that time. The latter, however, is not utilized for extracting oil, but only the leaves are taken as vegetable. All these crops are sown together, and thrive almost at the same time. This mixed cultivation meets three major needs: food from paddy and maize; drink from millet; and vegetables from brinjal, mustard, chilli and giyi.

The corn is ripe by September-October, and then starts the harvesting. The time of harvesting may vary according to the time of felling the trees, burning them and sowing seeds. These are dependent on the rains and the time varies from area to area. Harvesting implements are conspicuous. In the harvesting of paddy, the long conical basket is suspended from the shoulders on the back. Ears of paddy are picked out by hand and put in it. When the basket is full of ears of paddy, then it is brought to the house made in the agricultural field and collected on the bamboo made mat. Some paddy ears are taken separately on the mat and pressured by feet frequently changing their position till the paddy is separated from the ears. After the harvest is over, the grains are brought to the village and stored in the granary.

Keeping in view the importance of this sector the State Government has always given priority to various agricultural programmes in development plans for attaining self-sufficiency in foodgrains. But the progress/ improvement in this sector has not been up to the expectation. The main reasons for this are its topography which is hilly one, predominance of shifting cultivation, lack of irrigation facilities, lack of technical know-how etc. However, efforts are being made to dissuade the people from shifting cultivation and induce them to take up permanent cultivation, where possible, and proper utilization of available cultivable land. In the beginning, the people showed a tenacious attachment to their indigenous methods of cultivation but, with the gradual propagation of the idea through the villages, some amount of success has been achieved. But the nature of land does not provide scope for bringing about permanent cultivation on a large scale, so that it can completely replace shifting cultivation. In the areas, where there is no scope for plough cultivation, terracing of the *jhum* fields with provision for irrigation by tapping the hill streams has been done. People, as a whole, still show a tendency to cling to their own traditional methods, having socio-religious sanctions (Mandal and etc, 2010).

Objective

The objective of the study was undertaken to investigate the work participation of Galo women in agriculture in West Siang District of Arunachal Pradesh.

Hypotheses

In the background of the above consideration and the objective, the research study proposes to examine the following hypotheses during the course of the study:-

(i) In subsistent tribal economies, the division of labour is more demographic in nature, i.e., based on age and sex parameters.

(ii) A large part of the work performed by the male in general and femalefolk in particular are confined to land resources particularly agriculture and forest. The extent of availability of these resources for livelihood as well as for commercial purposes likely to determine the variation in the nature and pattern of work.

Methodology and Data Source

It is defined that social science research is an enquiry or investigation, which has clearly defined parameters. It is a system of critical, controlled and empirical enquiry. There are three approaches of social science research, which the researchers are to follow in the field of research i.e., qualitative, quantitative and action research. The researcher has adopted the quantitative approach as well as qualitative approach in the present study. But the quantitative approach of research goes with the experimental research and survey studies. Moreover, the selection of method of research depends upon the nature of the problem in hand. The plan of works and the procedures of this study were formulated eventually through a format questionnaire-cum-interview schedule related to the predefined factors considered for observation. We selected five different villages in a circle in such a way that each village was chosen more or less equidistantly to each other. From each village of that circle 10 women were randomly sampled and interviewed for the collection of the requisite data in such a way that 3 were from the age group of (15-25) years, 4 from the age group of (25-35) years and 3 from the age group of (35-45) years. We were giving more weightage to respondents of age group of (25-35) years because our objectives were fulfilled more accurately. Respondents of age groups of (15-25) years are more advanced and those of age group of (35-45) years or above are traditional, that is why, both were given less weightage to some extent for our study. In this way 10 × 5 = 50 Galo women were selected from each circle. In the West Siang District, seven circles out of twenty circles where Galo are predominant were selected. In this way 50 × 7 = 350 Galo women were interviewed.

The inclusion of villages under study was subject to distance from the district headquarter, mode of communication and concentration of people. The women were randomly sampled and interviewed for the collection of the requisite data. This study was based on both primary and secondary data. While secondary data had been collected from different reports and journals, primary data had been collected through personal investigation with the help of structured questionnaire and participation method. Samples had been selected through random sampling technique without replacement.

Field Survey

The field survey was conducted in the month of January, 2007 only in some selected villages in the district of West Siang, where the Galo people are more in number. The report has been presented in Table 20.4 given below.

Table 20.4: Distribution of Work Participation in Ag.:culture among the Women at Different Age Groups.

Area under survey	*Age group*	*Respo-ndent*	*Agricultural Activities*			
			Regu-larly	*Frequ-ently*	*Occasi-onally*	*Never*
West Siang	15 – 25	105 (100)	20 (19)	35 (33.3)	39 (37)	11 (10.4)
	25 – 35	140 (100)	58 (41.4)	43 (30.7)	36 (25.7)	3 (2.1)
	35 – 45	105 (100)	57 (54.3)	25 (23.8)	22 (20.9)	1 (0.95)
	Total	**350**	**135 (38.57)**	**103 (29.42)**	**97 (27.71)**	**15 (4.28)**

Note: Figures in parenthesis indicate percentage.

The above Table 20.4 shows that there is difference in age composition among the little age (15-25), middle age (25-35) and old age (35-45) groups. None of the respondents was below 15 years or above 45 years. Because, the women between the age group of (15- 45) years remains very active in agricultural work. The highest number of the respondents (54.3%) of the old age group belonged to the age group of (35-45) years engaging in the agricultural activities regularly, however, the lowest number of the respondents (0.95%) of the old age group also belonged to the age group of (35-45) years in this respect in the district of West Siang. The respondents who worked regularly in agricultural field were 19 per cent in the age group of (15-25) years, 41.4 per cent in the age group of (25-35) years and 54.3 per cent in the age group of (35-45) years. The respondents who were engaged frequently in the agricultural activities were 33.3 per cent in the age group of (15-25) years, 30.7 per cent in the age group of (25-35) years and 23.8 per cent in the age group of (35-45) years while engagement in this respect occasionally were 37 per cent in the age group of (15-25) years, 25.7 per cent in the age group of (25-35) years and 20.9 per cent in the age group of (35-45) years.

If we want to see the respondents who worked never in the agricultural fields, we got the lowest percentage i.e., 0.95 per cent in the age group of (35-45) years, highest percentage i.e., 10.4 per cent in the age group of (15-25) years and 2.1 per cent in the age group of (25-35) years. As overall observations, we saw that 38.57 per cent women were engaged regularly, 29.42 per cent women were frequently, 27.71 per cent were occasionally of all the three age groups in agricultural activities. But 4.28 per cent of women were never engaged in the agricultural activities.

Findings

The percentages of women engaged regularly in the agricultural activities were increasing with the increase in the age groups in the district, while in this regard, those were decreasing in case of frequently, occasionally and never work with the decreasing the age groups in the district. As explanation we can say that less age group are diverting themselves from the agricultural activities and this diversion is seen more with less age group with the impact of globalization in the 21st century and the development of education in the state. It was also seen that the women who occasionally or never worked in agricultural field were mostly living in the urban and semi-urban areas engaged in highly prestigious government jobs or in highly sophisticated private business leading a very busy lives. This study, however, focused on the point that the Galo women of study area enjoyed lower status than man despite of their hard work in household and agricultural field.

In addition to the home work, the rural women played an important role particularly in the agricultural production which was the main occupation of the villagers. Most of them were directly and indirectly engaged in agricultural activities. A few of the village women were doing the salaried jobs like clerks, school teachers, etc.

Conclusion and Way for Development

Men dominate the women, but women also have ways of getting things done according to their desires and wishes. Indian women present a paradoxical picture for the interpreter of Indian society. The view is that the Indian women is disadvantaged and discriminated against behavioural reality, while her participation in the highest political and social spheres is another undeniable reality.

Efforts should be made so that cognitive empowerment of women can carry her to self-confidence and self-reliance i.e., psychological empowerment which can lead to further social action or economic activity that stimulates political and economic empowerment. Different academic strategies and other plans are drawn out for this purpose, training and education for empowerment of women in the state result in individual empowerment and social transformation whereby, women have more control over their lives and more of an effect in the changing society to eliminate or reduce gender bias and discrimination.

To maintain the proper quantitative balance between various economic activities was one of the principal functions of the economic system which should operate to give equal freedom of choice to men and women. Women are not playing only supplementary role but their role in economic development is vital, positive and essential.

Development will set momentum when it is part of all, when it is generated from all the segments, when all contribute in their potential best ways and when all share its benefits optimally. Development will be promoted with the integration of women, and will be constrained with the neglect of women. Development requires the effective participation of all, tribal, non-tribal, men and women. Effective participation will be possible only with increasing awareness, promotion of efficiency and skill, last-but not the least by the change in attitude and outlook.

The need for school going age girls to assist in economic activities such as agriculture and cattle grazing, household chores and child care prevent them from utilizing educational facilities. Incentives offered have been inadequate to meet the cost of education of girls of disadvantaged families. Families give priority to the education of boys as social norms tend to ascribe an exclusively domestic role for girls with their future circumscribed by early marriage and child-bearing and rearing.

Education is one of the most crucial factors that allow women to compete as equals in the professional world and to earn an income of their own. A certain amount of fund should be earmarked for women's education in every state budget and proper utilization of this fund should be done effectively.

In this regard, educated girls have an important role to play in terms of creating motivation for girls' education in the community by dispelling the fears that educated girls marry outside. To cope with the present situation boys also must go ahead in the line of education consequently the community's awareness about girls' education and attitude towards culture-specific role of girls will change. From the above study, it can be said that the participation of female labour in Arunachal economy is quite high and they are mainly employed in the primary sector of the economy. However, as the fast pace of economic development takes place and female literacy rate increases, the female workers withdraw themselves from the primary work due to the symbol of their newly earned status through literacy. As a result, there is a drastic fall in the work participation rate of female in all the districts of Arunachal Pradesh in 1991. Thus, the "U" shaped pattern as proposed by the various social scientists in relation to economic development and the work participation of females has been portrayed beautifully in Arunachal Pradesh. The overall effect of literacy in work participation of females is also found to be negative. As the literacy rate increases, the female workers withdraw themselves from the primary work. But they are not getting suitable employment opportunities in the secondary and the tertiary sectors, except for the government jobs, particularly in urban areas. However, the job absorption capacity in the Government services is also limited.

Suggestions

1. Women should play first a vital role to male decision with their male counterpart in their home.
2. Contemporary women should assert themselves as decision-

maker of all state bodies, Church, socio-cultural institutions, NGOs and organized bodies.

3. Education system has to play an important role in this direction, as it is the only medium through which the image of a girl-child as second class citizen can be removed. Mass media too has a very important role to play for bringing out a total revolution in social attitude and public opinion. The existing institutions should be de-institutionalized and they should be reconstituted on the basis of gender equality. Female editors should replace male editors on their own rights.
4. With development and change in the world on all front of life like economy, culture, political, trade, industry, education to the women movement have been noticed for the rights and welfare which indicate all round development and awakening. To cope up with the global change, tribal women require infrastructural facilities, mobility, new mechanized training, socio-economic open contact. For that it is required of support of the financial institutions, Government's full support, NGO's involvement, proper qualitative educational facilities and training etc.
5. The government should encourage entrepreneurs, specially the local people, and provides training facilities to produce more skilled men and women. Efforts should have been made by the government for improving the technique of production. Design is very important in handloom industry. A research design centre should be established in the territory for revival and revitalization of local arts and crafts and to conduct research on scientific line with an aim to preserve the local arts and crafts without losing their originality.

Acknowledgement

This paper is a part of UGC sponsored minor research project submitted in 2007. The author is grateful to the UGC.

REFERENCES

Alam. K. (1987): "The Changing Role of Women in the Rural Economy of Assam, Conference Volume of the Indian Economic Association". *Seventieth Annual Conference*, Jaipur.

Anker, Richard (1981): "Demographic change and the Role of Women" in Richard, Anker (ed.) : *Role of Women in Developing Countries*, I.L.O. Publications, Geneva, p. 27.

Behera, M.C. and Roy. N.C. (1997) (editor): "*Trends in Agrarian Structure in the Hills of North-East India*". Commonwealth Publications, New Delhi.

Bhorali. D. (1998) (editor): "*Economic Development of the North-Eastern Region*" Spectrum Publications , Guwahati.

Bhuyan, B.C. (ed.) (1993): "*The Tribal Women*", Omsons Publicatins, New Delhi.

Bora, M.M. and Bhattacharyya, A. (1996): "Raising the status of Plain Tribes Women through Income Generating Training" in Medhi, K. (ed.): *Status of Women and Social Change*, Women's Studies Research Centre, Gauhati University, Guwahati, pp. 102-03.

Bora. D.K., Duarah, D.K. and Paul. B. (1997): "*Impact of Urbanization in Arunachal Pradesh*", Director of Research, Government of Arunachal Pradesh, Itanagar.

Bose. M.L. (1997): "*History of Arunachal Pradesh*", Concept Publishing Company, New Delhi.

Boserup, Ester (1970): "*Women's Role in Economic Development*, George Allen and Unwin, p. 71.

Chetana, K. (1986): "*Social and Economic Dimensions of Women's Development*", Discovery Publishing House, New Delhi, pp. 6-9.

Chetana, K. (1986): "*Social and Economic Dimensions of Women's Development*", Discovery Publishing House, New Delhi, pp. 6-9.

Chowdhury, J.N. (1982): "*Arunachal Panorama*", Directorate of Research, Arunachal Pradesh, Shillong.

Das. G. (1995): "*History of Arunahcal Pradesh in Transition*", Vikas Publishing House Pvt. Ltd., New Delhi.

Das Lipi, Mishra, S.K. and Nath, N.C. (2006): "Decent Work and Empowerment of Women in Agriculture", *Kurukshetra*, Vol. 54, No. 7, May, pp. 21-22.

Duarah, D.K (1998): "*A Handbook of Arunachal Pradesh*", Frontier Publisher and Distributor, Itanagar, p. 28.

Directorate of Information and Public Relations (1968): NEFA, The Land and the People, NEFA Administration, Shillong, p. 14.

Dutta. S. (1997) (editor): *"Studies in the History, Economy and Culture of Arunachal Pradesh"*, (Ed.), Himalayan Publications, Delhi, Itanagar.

Dutta Choudhury, S. (1994): Arunachal Pradesh District Gazetteers, East Siang and West Siang Districts, Government of Arunachal Pradesh.

Gulati Leela (1975): "Female work participation, A study of inter-state differences," *Economic and Political Weekly*, January.

Jagdish. P. (1987): "Women in the Labour Force : A Case Study of Bihar", Conference Volume of the Indian Economic Association, Seventieth Annual Conference, Jaipur.

Goswami, A.K. (Oct. 1996): "Women in the vision of Kalidasa" in Medhi, K. (ed.), *"Status of Women and Social Change"*, Women's Studies Research Centre, Gauhati University, Guwahati, pp. 54-55.

Mandal, R.K. (2005): "Literacy in Arunachal Pradesh: Trends, Features and Growth", an article submitted to Rajiv Gandhi University, Rono Hill, Itanagar.

Mandal, R.K. and Etc, M. (2010): Women in North-East India, Mittal Publication, New Delhi.

Mibang, T. (1994): *"Social Change in Arunahcal Pradesh"* Omsons Publications, New Delhi.

Mishra, K. (1991): *"Women in a Tribal Community : A Case Study of Arunachal Pradesh"*, Vikas Publishing House, New Delhi.

Nanda, Santosh (2005): "Political Empowerment of Indian Women at Local Level—Key of Social and Economic Development", *Journal of Global Economy*, Vol. I, No. 4, Oct.-Dec., Mumbai, pp. 243-246.

Motiram (2006): "Scheduled Castes' Education in India; Issues and Challenges", *University News*, March 27-April 02, Vol. 44, No. 13, pp. 1-5.

Pandey, B.B. (1993): *"The Buguns : A Tribe in Transition"*, Himalayan Publications, Itanagar.

Srivastava, L.R.N. (1962): *The Gallongs*, Directorate of Research, Government of Arunachal Pradesh, Itanagar, p. 8.

Sundaram, I. Satya (2006): "Women Empowerment: Basic Issues," *Southern Economist*, April 1 and 15, Vol. 44, Nos. 23 and 24, p. 8.

Vashistha, K.C. and Malik, S. (2002): "Some Strategic Efforts Towards the Empowerment of Women", *University News*, February 4-10, Vol. 40, No. 5, p. 16.

Verma, B.M. (1981): *"Rural Leadership in a Welfare Society"*, Manthan Publication, New Delhi, p. 61.

Wahan, P. and Venatadasappa, T. (1998): "Female Labour Force Participation in Karnataka", *Indian Journal of Labour Economics.*

21

Panchayati Raj Institutions PRIs and Women Empowerment

Introduction

The necessity of improvement of status of women has been recognized all over the world as an important aspect of national progress and development. It is also felt that the problem of poverty cannot be tackled without providing opportunities of productive employment to women. Productive employment to women would provide necessary economic base and improve their social status. But it is still a fact that women in many countries of the world are facing discriminatory attitude in varying degrees on ground of sex in employment and working conditions. From time immemorial, women have faced the challenges of coping with a male chauvinistic milieu. Even after several years of planned development in India, the status of women in our country is low and their socio-economic conditions are much more depressed than that of men.

Every society accords social status to women members as per its own perspective. The status and role of women in tribal society is also governed by their own norms and values. The tribal family is patriarchal. Kinship is recognized on the side of men. The tribal women's status in Arunachal Pradesh is lower than that of men. She faces many problems in all walks of her life simply because of being a female. In this male dominated society a women is considered inferior to a man. She is meant to depend on and under subjugation of man. The family in which she was born as a daughter does not consider her as a permanent abode. She is looked upon as a transient member to be handed over on marriage to her in-law's family. She cannot have a share in the immovable property at all. Decision-making and exercise of authority go under power of men. Thus, like other women in different tribal societies, the tribal women are also not recognized by their social system regarding their freedom and rights. Women's empowerment and their full participating on the basis of equality in all spheres of society are fundamental for the achievement of equality, development and peace (Fourth World Conference on Women, Beijing, 1995).

According to the International Labour Organization (ILO), there is tendency to under value women's work in rural areas, where they are taken as unpaid family labour, but if it is quantified, the world's Gross National Product (GNP) would increase by 20-30 per cent (ILO, 1981-85). United Nation's Statistics envisaged that women perform 67 per cent of the world's working hours and earn only 10 per cent of the world's income. They have less than 1 per cent of the world's property. Women as human resource in India constitute about 50 per cent of the population and 77 per cent of them belong to rural areas. Majority of them comes from small, marginal and landless families. Their main occupation is agriculture and allied activities, involving them either as cultivator or, agricultural labourers. About 60-70 per cent of labour input is provided by women in production, processing and storage of grain.

In a world where equality is often misunderstood, misinterpreted and exploited for political gains, it is imperative that "equality" should be redefined. Equality, irrespective of the sex of the individual should promise a life of freedom, choice, opportunities and dignity. The low value for female life is the biggest problem. The desire to have male issues has reduced the chance for girls to be born and thus female infanticide is on the rise. Economic conditions and cultural ethos of India have forged an invisible combination that threatens even the female embryo. Even if a female child is born against such heavy odds, she is not given a chance to survive. She suffers malnutrition, lack of medical attention, early marriage and frequent child births. The crude death rates fostered by abortions and child birth without proper medical care indicate the reduced life span of women. Another major problem is that of illiteracy. Despite a significant increase in the gross enrolment rate of girls in primary schools from 25 per cent in 1950 to 66 per cent in 1980 and 70 per cent in 1982, a large number of girls are still not receiving primary education, while 95 to 100 per cent boys are now enrolled in elementary schools.

Engels, the well-known economist, held that female subordination was the result of the emergence of private property, in particular the private ownership of the forces of production.

Karl Marx had opined that female employment would largely free women from economic dependence on their husbands and so from male dominance within the family.

Sociologists *Blood* and *Hamlin*'s approach was that the employment of the wife outside the home did not appreciable alter power relations within the family: working wives had only marginally more power than whole-time wives.

Viola Klein believed that employment outside the home had some beneficial results; it helped to restore in women their sense of usefulness and renewed their self-confidence. Still the mother and housewife role remained primary. There was no evidence from her research data that paid employment produced demands for freedom from traditional female roles.

In our country, the status, role and the various characteristics and problems of women have been culturally much different from the women in the west. In the Post-Independence era, there has been a vast expansion of education and employment opportunities as well as provisions for the protection, welfare and development of our women and many of them are quite modern and advanced like their western counterpart.

Women are the nucleus of our civilization. They have different roles to play in the ever changing social set-up. Women's development is directly related with the nation development. With the dawn of independence our constitution guaranteed gender equality and a large number of schemes and programmes have been initiated for women's development. But the Indian women have to survive in a complex area of socio-cultural, historical, political economic realities.

The International recognition of the status and the problems of women all over the world have resulted in the United Nations declaring 1975 as the International Women's year and the period between 1975 and 1985 as Women's Decade. These are recommendations of the United Nations World Conference (Mexico, 1975) to initiate plans for raising the status of women and for ensuring their full involvement and integration in the process of development at all levels. In India, the appointment of the National Committee on the status of women in 1972 and the publication of its report in 1975 marked the first official attempt to study and recommended changes to improve women's position in society. Declaring 1975 as "Year of Women" by the United Nations, since then there is increased concern of women's sufferings and their empowerment in the society (Medel-Anonuevo, 1995). Very recently the UNDP has brought out its human Development Report 2003, which speaks about the millennium development goals. It lists eight goals out of which the third goal to be achieved is gender equality and empowerment of women. In the budget presented before the Parliament for the 2004-05, the Union Finance Minister has spoken about "gender budgeting".

Women as an independent target group, account for 495.74 million and represent 48.3 per cent of the country's population, as per the 2001 census. No country can achieve its potential without adequately investing in and developing the capabilities of women. In the interest of long-term development it is necessary to facilitate their empowerment. In many developing countries, including India, women have much less access to education, jobs, income and power than men. Even after five and a half decades of planned development Indian women, except a privileged minority, have not achieved expected success in the mainstream of life. If we cannot improve the status and role of women, then our country will be unable to compete over the world.

Women empowerment is a global issue, which has gained momentum in recent decades. In India, besides ratification of international conventions, there are provisions in the constitution and several Legislative Acts have been passed to ensure women empowerment. It however, appears that on this front the situation on ground is far from satisfactory. The position of women and their status in any society is an index of its civilization. Women are to be considered as equal partners in the process of development. But, because of centuries of exploitation and subjugation, Indian women have remained at the receiving end. In this context, in order to provide a big push, Institutional support is necessary to empower Indian women in general and rural women in particular. Women empowerment demands a "Lifecycle" approach where empowerment is viewed as a process and not as an event, which challenges traditional power equations and relations. Empowerment in its simplest form means redistribution of power that challenges the male dominance. This does not, however, mean that the empowerment process adopts an antagonists approach. It is only to enable women to supplement and coordinate with men. Empowerment is an active process of enabling women to realize their identity, potentiality and power in all spheres of their lives (Sharma: 1992). "I never define anything", said Swami Vivekananda smiling, "Still, it may be described as a development of faculty, not an accumulation of words, or as a training of individuals to will rightly and efficiently. So we shall bring to the need of India great fearless women-women worthy to continue the traditions of Sanghamitta, Lila, Ahilya Bai, and Mira Bai – women fit to be mothers of heroes, because they are pure and selfless, strong with the strength that comes of touching the fact of God".

There are several indicators of empowerment. At the individual level, participation in crucial decision-making process, ability to prevent violence, self-confidence and self-esteem, improved health and nutrition conditions and at the community level, existence of women's organizations, increased number of women leaders, involvement of women in designing development tools and application of appropriate technology, etc. are very crucial. At national level the indicators are, for example, awareness of her social and political rights, adequate representation in legislative bodies, and integration of women in particular in national development plans, etc.

There is scope for corruption in every step of the society when there is concentration of authority. There is a need that decentralization and dispersal of decision-making should be explored fully and effective provisions made in this behalf.

Improvement in economic status is a more visible indicator of women empowerment. This naturally gets reflected in improved social, political and cultural status of women. Self-confidence and self-esteem of women proceed simultaneously with their empowerment. In brief, all indicators can be classified into two broad categories namely, visible and invisible indicators. Amongst visible indicators a mention could be made of women's representation in Parliaments. Thirty per cent of total women Parliamentarians in the world come from just seven countries. Their share in national Parliaments of a few selected developed and developing countries is shown in Table 21.1.

Table 21.1: Seats in Parliaments held by Women (As % of total) in Developing Countries.

Developing Countries	*Per cent*	*Developed Countries*	*Per cent*
China	21.8	Sweden	45
Pakistan	21.6	Denmark	38
Morocco	10.8	Norway	36.4
India	8.8	Finland	36.1
Indonesia	8.0	Netherlands	36
Nepal	5.9	Iceland	34
Egypt	2.4	Austria	33
Bangladesh	2.0	New Zealand	29

Source: Human Development Report, 2003.

It can be seen from Table 21.1 that both in developed and developing countries women hold less seats than the men. However, in developed countries their representation is relatively higher than in developing countries. In this context, it can be said that increasing the number of women in Parliaments and also raising women's visibility in positions of authority and decision are quite necessary for their empowerment, politically and economically as well. Again, much of women's work never appears in the national statistics because it is seen as an extension of their carrying and nurturing functions rather than as materially rewarding activity. All of them are taken as unpaid family labour.

In India for the first time in 19th century women empowerment movement began under the auspices of Brahmo Samaj. Between 1910 and 1920 the number of social organizations for women increased rapidly. Mahila Samities, Women Clubs, Ladies Societies, etc., were formed in different parts of the country linking together women all over India. Activities of these organizations were centred on three fronts namely, health, education and employment. Swami Vivekananda summed up the national problems in India in two words: the women and the people. He traced the reason of continued downfall of India because of neglecting our women.

Empowerment is a multi-dimensional social process that helps people to gain control over their own lives and communities in their society. Empowerment occurs within sociological, psychological, economic spheres and at various levels, such as individual, group, and community and challenges our assumptions about the *status quo*, asymmetrical power relationships and social dynamics.

Empowerment of women involves many things—economic opportunity, property rights, political representation, social equality, personal rights and so on. The Indian society is a patriarchal system in which women's position within the structure and duties towards the family precede their rights as individuals. Many who argue for empowerment of women do so either with or without a full understanding of the conflicts between the historical and contemporary status of women in the patriarchy and the goals of empowerment. Certainly we may track a great many changes that have occurred in the direction of change in the status of women in India but women have yet to achieve or realize many of the ideal stages of social, psychological, economic and political empowerment. Hence, it is certainly more appropriate to define empowerment as a process rather than an end-point. Empowerment by means of education, literacy or modest income-generating projects is clearly insufficient to ameliorate the prospects for a higher quality of life for women. The process of empowerment is taking place at so many levels that it is quite difficult to gauge the actual nature and extent of empowerment in improving the status of women. Certainly, the process is entangled in the struggles of civil society against the state, and under the weight of historical practice and on going debates over the appropriate role of ideologies. Women constitute 48 per cent of the Indian population, but when we often sermonize human rights, we often forget that women as human beings are also entitled to fundamental human rights. We have denied and continue to deny them basic human rights. Even after 59 years of independence these women continue to live in a State of neglect and exploitation. The concept of women empowerment was introduced at the International Women's Conference at Nairobi in 1985. The term empowerment was defined as "a distribution of social power and control of resources in favour of women". Empowerment is not something which could be made available in the form of a capsule to those whom we think is in need of it. It is not just a concept that could be defined with the help of some universally accepted parameters. Empowerment is a process and includes the following components:

(i) Equal access to opportunities for using society's resources.
(ii) Prohibition of gender discrimination in thought and practice.
(iii) Freedom from violence.
(iv) Economic independence.
(v) Participation in all decision-making bodies.
(vi) Freedom of choice in matters relating to one's life.

Empowerment actually is a process that addresses all sources and structures of power. It is not enough to provide only education to women but they require access to the labour market and employment also. It will, however, not transform any gender and caste relations. The process has to work on an individual as well as on a collective level. Women have to be organized and acknowledged as a political force also. The process has to challenge both gender and social power relations. It is a process that is much about education, it does not come out of school books. It is a knowledge which has to be expanded. More importantly people should start thinking critically and question it. It generates new notions about power itself. Otherwise, when women enter the public structures, given the existing ideology, they operate with the so-called male notions of power which is presented as domination, patronage etc. The question that needs to be answered is that in a society where men control the destiny of women how is it possible to empower women? Before we discuss practical measures and associated difficulties in the process of empowerment of women, let us look at what does the national policy for empowerment of women in India do?

The national policy of empowerment of women has set certain clear cut goals and objectives: The goal of this policy is to bring about the advancement, development and empowerment of women. The policy will be widely disseminated so as to encourage active participation of all stakeholders for achieving its goals. Specifically, the objectives of this policy include:

(i) Creating an environment through positive economic and social policies for full development of women to enable them to realize their full potential.
(ii) The *de-jure* and *de-facto* enjoyment of all human rights and fundamental freedom by women on equal basis with men in all spheres—political, economic, social, cultural and civil.
(iii) Equal access to participation and decision-making of women in social, political and economic life of the nation.
(iv) Equal access to women to health care, quality education at all levels, career and vocational guidance, employment, equal remuneration, occupational, safety, social security and public office, etc.
(v) Strengthening legal systems aimed at elimination of all forms of discrimination against women.
(vi) Changing societal attitudes and community practices by active participation and involvement of both men and women.
(vii) Mainstreaming a gender perspective in the development process.
(viii) Elimination of discrimination and all forms of violence against women and the girl child.
(ix) Building and strengthening partnerships with civil society, particularly women's organizations.

The social welfare policies are built on the premise that women lack power, they are denied on basic rights as individuals, limited income and access to resources. It is clear that efforts to improve income and living conditions (the basis of the early social welfare approach) are insufficient in empowering women unless considerations of the basic patriarchal features of society are brought into the equation and the responsibility of states to address its negative effects. Policy-makers must also take note of the resistance that women have faced in their entry into public space, and coordinate vigorous efforts to continue legal reforms and enhance women's participation in social, economic and political spheres.

As we see the discrimination is deep rooted and perpetuated through patriarchy the task to empower women becomes even more challenging. While women in India have the legal right to own land, very few do. For those women who do own land, ownership rarely translates into control of the land or of the assets flowing from the land. The policy prescriptions and legislations assure the equality of right over land for women in India, such as, the Article 25 of the Indian Constitution permits freedom to all. Indian Constitution mandates gender equality. The theoretically non-discriminatory nature of law in practice cannot challenge the religious and customary law that guide issues and ideologies on status and treatment of women, property rights related to inheritance, marriage, divorce etc. The constitutional provisions and amendments to the inheritance laws are not sufficient in themselves to change the patterns of rural land ownership. Increasing women's property rights not just in theory but in practice can positively contribute towards the welfare of poor and would help in bringing about effective change in the nature of current status of poverty as women are more likely to spend income from land on education and meeting the basic needs of children and family. In fact, the right over property and land can be an important source of alleviating poverty from rural India.

Women empowerment came to be associated with social justice and equality. This was real barrier for the feminists and women's movement to grab and thrash the government, law makers, and implementers of laws and point out lacunae in social and political structure which were responsible for women being so powerless. The women groups started evolving strategies to achieve the two goals i.e., equality and social justice. Without further digressing into the issue of empowerment of women whether considered in absolute term or in comparison to men, it is concluded that women's fight is not against men but against the system of patriarchy and all its manifestations. Equality in social systems is a necessary condition for empowerment of women; however it is not sufficient for their development; as development and empowerment are not synonymous. Development refers to "progress of an individual/ group in economic, social, political and cultural context" whereas empowerment is defined as "distribution of social power and resources in favour of women".

Education is central to the process of sustainable development. The role of education in empowerment is not only learning of three 'R's (reading, writing and arithmetic) but includes:

- Raising awareness;
- Critical analysis of various structures, and
- Acquiring knowledge for empowerment at all levels.

Education should include not only formal education but also skill training and functional literacy. First, and foremost of all is to demystify the myth that girls are not sent to school because they are girls and in view of their primary role as mothers and housewives. Girls and women are not only housewives and mothers but they are also 'workers' in the economic sense. They should be educated to perform an indispensable role in the home and in the household economy, as well as for bringing enlightenment and emancipation. Empowerment of women through education will develop:

- Self-esteem and self-confidence of women;
- A positive image of women by recognizing their contribution to the society, polity and economy;
- Ability to think critically;
- Decision-making abilities and action through collective process;
- Choices in areas like education, employment and health;
- Equal participation in development process;
- Knowledge and skill for economic independence; and
- Access to legal literacy and information relating to their rights.

Participation of women in economic and non-economic activities has been universally recognized as an important element in the adoption of the small family norm, essential for the achievement of the twin goals of economic development and population planning. Such as recognition, however, presupposes not only that existence of a conflict between the economic employment of women and child rearing but also an association between employment of women and their socio-economic status. Social change is possible only by empowering and educating women. Jawaharlal Nehru once said, "To awaken the people, it is women who is meant to be awakened, once she is on the move, the family moves, village moves and the nation moves". Swami

Vivekananda also once said, "There is no chance for the welfare of the world unless the condition of women is improved. It is not possible for a bird to fly on one wing". Likewise no nation can flourish keeping half of its population in negligence and ignorance, as women constitute half of its human capital. A modern society cannot bring all round development without utilizing the talent of its women.

Until recently, in India as in many other developing countries, the roles of women in the economic activities of the nation were practically ignored. In fact, the preoccupations with specific patterns of economic development often resulted in the relative neglect of women's need and the process of development itself often had some serious negative repercussions on the status of women, thus worsening rather than improving their condition. Today women actively contribute the promotion of economic development in different 'capacities namely as officer, scientist, technician, executive, etc. Now-a-days their work is not confined to family and household chores but has also extended to research fields, factories, offices, administration, science and technology. With the spread of education and training, their mobility has increased and they have come out of their shells to undertake various types of duties and responsibilities. This is mainly to raise the living standard of their families.

Efforts should be made to move beyond land policy and law reform to reforming the laws of succession which continued to disadvantage women even when progressive land and property rights have been enacted. We must also improve land administration and management, secure tenure, and property rights by undertaking practical steps to bring about real benefits to women. In order for legislative amendments to change patterns of inheritance, the social and religious norms that impact inheritance (like bride price practices) must be considered, the public must be educated as to the purpose of the amendments, a plan must be developed for their enforcement, and an effort made to assure that inheritance practices change in accordance with the amendments.

There is a need for an examination of conceptual gaps in linking the formalization agenda more closely to the wider issues of enhancing the rule of law for the poor women; a review of existing policies aimed at securing the assets of the poor; a review of existing legal, institutional and financial mechanisms with a view to proposing for the legal empowerment of women; a review of potential risk factors to be managed proactively in formalization processes, including gender aspects of poverty and development, a programme that could enhance awareness in the media and general public about the benefits that could be gained by formalization approaches, including better legal protection of the assets of the women, and to propose steps that could bring such approaches higher up on the national agenda.

The Scheduled Tribes whose population is estimated in 2001 census at 89 million constitute about 8.5 per cent of the total population of the country. They are considered as a distinct ethnic group because of their peculiar socio-cultural traditions and economic practices. Another important feature of the Scheduled Tribes is that most of them live in remote, inaccessible hilly and forest areas. Hence, they are cut off from the national mainstream and lead a secluded life. Considering them as the most marginalized and deprived section of the society and in view of their special needs and problems, a special place was accorded to tribal development in the country's development agenda right from the beginning of the era of planned development.

Accordingly, different approaches and strategies were adopted and special programmes and schemes implemented for the development of tribal societies in different Five Year Plans. Even though, these approaches laid primary emphasis on the economic development of the tribal people, they are placed a special thrust on the development of education among the tribal. Under these approaches several programmes and schemes were implemented during different plan periods for the promotion of education among them.

Tribal societies of the State are generally characterized by the traditional types of work, often considered to be less 'productive' and more community-based. Such a society is considered as 'an aggregate of social relations' rather than 'set of individuals' and form its 'core-identify' in a specifically confined set of household environment that compels the people to alter the work-pattern. There are, therefore, no records of a significant change in the economic and social conditions of such society and, consequently, their pattern of work also shows the inclusion of basic attributes of work related to a greater emphasis on household activities and community work which are classified as 'unorganized' in strict economic terms, but 'well-organized' in terms of social norms. Such societies were in the past not very well exposed to other societies and were generally confined to the areas of their cultural cores which helped them retain their own cultural identities to a great extent. However, these 'semi-isolated' societies have undergone tremendous transformation in the recent decades under the impact of modernizing influences and market forces which have been responsible in breaking the core-identities of the social and cultural norms of these traditional societies. Urban areas which represent the nodes for infrastructure and productive activities and are the epicentre of the market forces considerably influence the work pattern and have not only altered the needs for work and employment, but also the pattern of work.

Arunachalee tribal women, being uneducated, indeed suffer most in their society and life. The literacy rate of Arunachal Pradesh since 1961 is shown. It shows that how many women are lagging behind their male counterpart regarding education. Gender discrimination is prevailing to a great extent. This is evidenced and found in every walk of life. Gender discrimination between men and women and boys and girls take root even at the early stage of life.

This paper tries to examine the political empowerment of tribal women through PRIs.

Political Arena in Arunachal Pradesh

The recommendations of the Ering Committee constituted in April 1964 by the Governor of Assam were accepted by the Government of India, and the President of India promulgated the North-East Frontier Agency Panchayati Raj Regulation, 1967, with effect from the 2nd October, 1968. The Regulation provided for the Constitution of Gram Panchayats at the village level, Anchal Samiti at the block level and Zilla Parishads at the district level. Panchayati Raj in NEFA generally followed the all-India pattern. Till the 14th September, 1997 i.e., before the constitutional impasse, only Arunachal Pradesh had retained the three tier system of Panchayati

Raj system among the North-Eastern States. In Assam, the three tiers Panchayati Raj system was reduced to two tier by jettisoning the middle tier. There, the district level body is not in existence, as the block level body is at Sub-Divisional level. In Manipur and Tripura, only Gram Panchayats are functioning, and in Meghalaya, Nagaland, and Mizoram, only tribal councils are working. The 1967 Panchayati Raj Regulation was subsequently amended in 1970, 1971, 1972, 1994 and 1997.

According to the 1967 Regulation, the term of all Panchayat bodies was to be three years. However, in Arunachal Pradesh, the Panchayati Raj Bill of 1994 has raised the term to five years, as per the 73rd Constitutional Amendmenti Act (1993). In Arunachal Pradesh (the then NEFA), the total number of Gram Panchayats in 1969, when Panchayati Raj was first introduced in the State, was 938 which came down to 837 in 1987 due to a change in the size of Gram Panchayats, but again increased to 2012 in 1992. Similarly, the total number of Anchal Samities in the beginning was only 38, which subsequently increased to 44 in 1972, 60 in 1987, and finally to 78 in 1992, when Panchayat elections were held last in the State. Likewise, the number of Zilla Parishads also rose from 5 in 1969 to 12 in 1992. Thus, after the 1992 elections on an average, each Gram Panchayat had 3 members, Anchal Samiti 16, and Zilla Parishad 13 members. (White Paper, 1998).

In the last three decades, since the introduction of the Panchayati Raj in Arunachal Pradesh, seven elections to Panchayat bodies were held in free and fair manner from 1969 to 1992. Though there was no provision for party system in Panchayati Raj elections in Arunachal Pradesh, the influence of party politics could not be stopped on Panchayati Raj elections. It has been observed that political parties played a big role in the elections though the names and symbols of parties might not have figured openly.

Although Panchayati Raj System, introduced in 1969, has proved to be a unique democratic institution and played a vital role in socio-political and economic development of the people in the last three decades, unfortunately this august institution was dissolved on the 14th September, 1997. The problem was that the 73rd Constitution Amendment Act, 1992, which provides for a uniform system of Panchayat throughout the country (except in a few scheduled areas) with provisions for reservation of seats for SC/ST and women within a stipulated time-frame, was itself the reason for it. In pursuance of the said Act, the State Government promulgated an ordinance in conformity with the provisions of the Constitution Amendment Act and later replaced it by a Bill called "The Arunachal Pradesh Panchayati Raj Bill, 1994", and passed in the Assembly on the 9th September, 1994.

The NEFA Panchayati Raj Regulation, 1967, which has been the basic and parent law on the subject governing the Panchayati Raj Institutions in this State for nearly three decades had not proved for any reservation to any others and it was purely an institution from the grass root level managed, controlled and administered by the tribals themselves for their betterment and development (Modi, 2001).

It shows that how many women are lagging behind their male counterpart regarding education. Illustrating the inequality of sexes in the field of education, the International Commission on Education (1996) stated that a special effort should be done with all inequalities between sexes in the field of education. Gender inequality lies at the root of the lasting situation of inferiority that affects women at every stage at their lives. Education in general and higher education in particular are an insurance against economic need. Access to the higher education, both technical and professional, will guarantee economic independence leading to social status and hence empowerment to women. If education is to promote equality for women, it must make a deliberate, planned and sustained effort so that the new value of equality of sexes can replace the traditional system of inequality.

Each of the indigenous inhabitants of Arunachal Pradesh has distinctive culture, customs, language and traditions of their own, which they have manifested through different socio-cultural, religious and political events. The women's role in different aspects of their traditional lifestyle of the people is immense.

In Arunachal Pradesh, various tribal communities are at different stages of development; as such the status of women differs from community to community. However, in general the position of women in Arunachal Pradesh is respectable but not very high. The prevalence of polygamy, victim of bride price, sex abuse and child marriage were quite in common. It had no doubt lowered their position. They were generally devoid of equal political and property rights. Today, the position of tribal women has changed. They have come to know that they are exploited by their male counterparts. The educated women are coming forward to shoulder the equal responsibility with the men for the socio-economic development of Arunachal Pradesh. But the realities of women in rural Arunachal Pradesh are difficult to comprehend. Women, most of the times, are even deprived of some of the fundamental human rights and this denial is justified often in the name of tradition. In rural areas, women are generally relegated mainly to household duties and cheap labour in agricultural activities.

The political empowerment can be defined as the degree of equality and freedom enjoyed by women in shaping and sharing of power and in the value given by society to this role of women. The recognition of women's political equality in the Constitution of India was a radical departure, not only from the inherited norms of traditional Indian Society, but also from the political norms of most advanced countries at that time. Thus, the women achieved the great political equality of franchise as well as right of being elected. In the Constitution equality on the basis of sex becomes one of the fundamental rights.

Empowerment has several other dimensions like social empowerment, economic empowerment, besides, of course, political empowerment. Social empowerment implies promotion of social capabilities such as education, health, cultural aspects and women's honour. Economic empowerment implies entitlement of employment, income, property, productive resources and benefit of development irrespective of gender difference. Political empowerment, of course, implies equal role in decision-making process in power structure from grass root level to national level. All these dimensions of empowerment are inferred related with each other.

The principle of gender equality is enshrined in the Indian Constitution, in its preamble, fundamental rights, fundamental duties and directive principles. The Indian Constitution guarantees equal rights to both women and men. But the representation of Indian women in politics at national level is lower than that of men. Although women constitute nearly half of the population, but politics has remained largely a monopoly of men because, its condensation of power and authority mainly lies in the hands of this gender. At present, there is a controversy about the 33 per cent reservation for women in Legislatures and in Parliament. However, the failure of recent efforts is to secure reservation for women in Parliament and Legislatives, the government has appointed a committee for the empowerment of women. Through reservation, empowerment of women has a long way to go. The women's participation in politics has been very low in the past 59 years after gaining independence. It was found that year 1977 showed the lower representation of women in Lok Sabha, it was 3.3 per cent only. The year 2004 shows that 9.5 per cent women participated in Lok Sabha which is higher in all the Lok Sabha.

Amendment in Constitution in 1992 to strengthen the sharing of power by women at local level has opened a new chapter in the history of women's struggle for empowerment. The enactment of the 73rd Constitutional Amendment i.e., Panchayati Raj, in India is, no doubt a landmark event in this regard. It is important because of revolutionary measure by reserving 33 per cent seats for women at all levels in the local governance. Local governance interpreted as the active involvement of the local population within the territorial boundaries in local government is ensuring improved quality of service and leadership at the local government level. This is a significant shift in the approach towards the well-being of women from 'Welfare during Fifties' to 'Development during Seventies' and to "Empowerment during Nineties'.

Political empowerment at local level i.e., Panchayati Raj assumes particular importance as a means of producing democratic functioning and decision-making decentralized governmental power, thereby restructuring political institutions. This development i.e., amendment in the Constitution has brought the question of competitiveness of Indian women to the centre stage of controversy. In view of the majority of Indian rural women being illiterate and new in this role, this question has attracted the attention of the large number of commentators and researchers. It also presents interventions promoted through local government to reduce poverty and promote socio-economic development targeted at women and seeking to bridge gender gaps.

Women in tribal society in Arunachal Pradesh are generally not allowed to participate in the tribal village councils. Thus, the councils are male dominated institutions. Tribal people cannot easily think of women being a member in village council. Consequently, women are invariably discarded even today. But the introduction of Panchayati Raj at grass root and Parliamentary Democracy at upper layer has armed the women with voting right and political rights on the equal footing of their male counterparts.

Democratic creed and ethos have introduced the concepts of election through secret ballot boxes, adult suffrage and equality before law, rise of the sense of individualism, emphasis on social justice, social equity and social welfare. All cumulated together accelerate and speed up the process of social change.

The statuary Panchayati Raj Institutions functioned from 1969 to 1997 in Arunachal Pradesh wherein there were some 24000 elected incumbents as Gram Panchayat Members, (GPMs), Anchal Samiti Members (ASMs) and Zilla Parishad Members, (ZPMs). Out of them there had been only 4 women Anchal Samiti Members or Gram Panchayat Members. In 1987, at Anchal Samiti level, there was 1 and in 1992 there were 3 elected female representatives. The ratio of nominated female representatives has remained almost the same. Almost similar condition prevails in the traditional village council institutions. At present there were total 8077 Gaonburas, but of which 6731 are Gaonburas and 1346 were Head Gaonburas. In this traditional band of a huge number of so-called village authorities, a few women GBs started being appointed since 1998 onwards. The process of prolification of Gaonburas since 1998 has facilitated to some 91 women to occupy this office of the GBs (Dubey, 2000).

Arunachal yet stands to be a male dominated society. The number of women legislators was altogether 9 only in all the Legislative Assemblies put together within the span of 25 years. The most educated among the women Legislators is Miss Komoli Mossang who has a post-graduate degree in Political Science. On the other hand, Mrs. Nyari Welly, another women legislator was the least educated having had no formal education. Ms. Komoli Mossang (1984-1990) became the first lady Minister of the State (Minister of Industries). Mekup Dolo was one of the four women candidates in the fray in the previous elections (Dubey, 2000).

Arunachalee tribal women are poorly represented in the ranks of power, policy and decision-making. Women in Arunachal Pradesh are not just behind in the political and managerial spheres they are still far away from their actual sharing of power with their male counterparts.

Women organizations like APWWS along with the NGOs, Educationist and Social Workers of the State of Arunachal Pradesh, should engineer women upliftment movement against the social catharsis like polygamy and child marriage so that women do not become victims by themselves and also women do not become instrumental for the women exploitation. Womenfolk should be enlightened of their rights and their rightful position in the society.

The United Nations Development Programmes (UNDPs) Human Development Report (1995) opines "inverting in women's capabilities and empowering them to exercise their choices is not only valuable in it but is also the surest way to contribute to economic growth and development". The report reaffirms that "Human development is impossible without gender equality. As long as women are excluded from the development process, development will remain lopsided. Sustainable human development implies engendering the development paradigm".

Reservation of Seats for Women in Panchayat Bodies

Under the framework of the 73rd Constitution Amendment Act, the one-third of the seats in Panchayat bodies is being reserved for the women for the first time in India. This was a new message for the rural population. Though the Galo society accords high status to the women in the society, the women never enjoyed such status in the corporate decision-making forum. Thus, the message of reservation was received with mixed response in the Galo society.

The tribal communities of Arunachal Pradesh had their own system of local self-governance. "Age old traditional system of self-governance in Arunachal Pradesh was replaced by Panchayati Raj Institutions in 1968". With the coming into force of the Constitution (Seventy-Third Amendment) Act, 1992 with effect from 24th April, 1993, it was incumbent upon the state government to enact the Arunachal Pradesh Panchayati Raj Legislation.

The system ordained though the NEFA Panchayati Raj Regulation, 1967 continued with regular elections till 1992. The Constitution (73rd Amendment Act), 1992 paved the way for restoring Panchayati Raj System in the State. It would suffice to mention here that several interactions across various levels were held to ensure to maintain the relevance and applicability of the Act in the context of Arunachal Pradesh. The present strength of PRIs in the state is depicted below in Table 21.2.

Table 21.2: Present Strength of Elected Members of PRIs in Arunachal Pradesh

(As on 29th August, 2003)

Sl.No.	*Level of PRIs*	*Nos.*	*Members*			*Chairpersons*	
			Male	*Female*	*Total*	*Male*	*Female*
1.	Gram Panchayats	1639	3924	2561	6485	1092	547
2.	Anchal Samities	136	1062	577	1639	86	50
3.	Zilla Parishad	14	91	45	136	8	6
	Total	**1789**	**5077**	**3183**	**8260**	**1186**	**603**

Source: Department of Panchayati Raj, Government of Arunachal Pradesh, Itanagar.

Note: Above figures do not include the allotted strength of Tirap District as PR elections were not held in that time.

These figures show that women's direct participation in PRIs is much below in comparison to their male counterpart. The overall female participation is only 38.54 per cent.

However, the Panchayati Raj Institutions (PRIs) also played a very important role in bringing about a major socio-political change in the traditional tribal society of Arunachal Pradesh with the increasing growth in education and political awareness at rural people and their increasing interface with the outside world due to greater mobility.

The Panchayati Raj Institutions serve as a training ground for rural people and equip them with both knowledge and experience about the democratic system of government in the country thereby enabling them to play more important and useful role in the state and as well as in the nation.

The State Government is firmly committed to the preservation; development and strengthening of the Panchayati Raj Institutions throughout the State, democratic and empowerment of the State have been the guiding policy for the State Government.

With the instruction of Panchayati Raj System in the State, a large number of elected panchayat members would be involved in all development initiatives in rural areas in accordance with their levels (Srivastava, 2006).

Age

Age is associated with experience and wisdom. "It has acquired a traditional importance in the society and considered to be an important factor in the Indian tradition of leadership. It symbolizes experience, maturity and equanimity of mind". "Age is a significant variable in the study of rural leadership because in the Indian Village Community, leadership has been the monopoly of the old persons who in the post dominated rural life in all its aspects". The same is the case with the leadership in various village councils in Arunachal Pradesh. But, the introduction of statutory panchayats and spread of party politics at the grass root level has given definite impetus to the entry of younger people in the leadership structure. The analysis of leadership in relation to its age composition simply explains the mobility of younger generation into the leadership position. There is difference in age composition between the traditional leaders and the modern leaders. There is a significant change in the traditional concept of rural leadership based on the age factor. Thus, age is no longer a criterion for the emerging leadership (Karlo, 2005).

Conclusion

President, A.P.J. Abdul Kalam, said empowering women was a prerequisite for creating a good nation, "when women are empowered, society with stability is assured. Empowerment of women is essential as their thoughts and their value systems lead the development of a good family, good society and ultimately a good nation".

Education is a milestone for women empowerment because it enables them to respond to opportunities, to challenge their traditional roles and to change their lives. Similar ideas were supported in International Conference, 1994. It was said that Education is one of the most important means of empowering women with the knowledge, skills and self-confidence necessary to participate fully in the development process. Educating woman benefits the whole society. It has a more significant impact on poverty and development than men's education. It is also one of the most influential factors in improving child health and reducing infant mortality. At least 60 million girls lack access to primary education and the gender gap in literacy persists till date. Although literacy and school enrolment among both girls and boys have increased dramatically, yet much remains to be done. More and more girls should be enrolled in school, and should complete their schooling. This will become true as the level of education increases. There are signs of progress, as enrolment of boys and girls in primary schools edges closer and closer to parity.

Every year, even at the university level, women are catching up and even surpassing male enrolment in some countries. In Kuwait, Bahrain, the Philippines and Cuba, more women are now enrolling in university than men. Although girls and women's access to education is improving, but they are often channelled into traditionally 'female' fields of study that reinforce their traditional roles in society.

As stated in the International Conference on Population Development (ICPD), 1994, countries must recognize:

(i) The value of ensuring that women begin and complete their education; (ii) To eliminate gender bias in all types of educational materials that enforce inequalities between men and women.

Educational programmes for both boys and girls must promote shared responsibilities. As soon as boys begin their education, they need to be taught to take care of their own domestic needs and to share responsibilities at home. Educating both boys and girls in non-stereotyped thinking about male and female roles is critical. Women need to be empowered to become equal to men and thus have equal access to developmental resources and benefits. In order to empower women we need not only to give them more economic power but also bring changes in the entire, social, political and legal systems of the countries because these are responsible for women's lower status in society and the main hindrance in their progress.

REFERENCES

Aggarwal, J.C. (2004): "*Development and Planning of Modern Education*", Vikas Publishing House Pvt. Ltd., New Delhi, pp. 273-279.

Alam, K. (1987): "The Changing Role of Women in the Rural Economy of Assam, Conference Volume of the Indian Economic Association". *Seventieth Annual Conference*, Jaipur.

Anker, Richard (1981): "Demographic change and the Role of Women" in Richard, Anker (ed.) : *Role of Women in Developing Countries*, I.L.O. Publications, Geneva, p. 27.

Azu, T. (1998): "Women in Nishi Society—A Case Study of Yachuli Circle in lower Subansiri District, Arunachal Pradesh 1998" (An Unpublished M. Phil. Dissertation. Deptt. of Tribal Studies, Arunachal University).

Baruah, S.L. (1992): "*Status of Women in Assam*" Omsons Publications, New Delhi.

Behera, M.C. and Roy. N.C. (1997) (editor): "*Trends in Agrarian Structure in the Hills of North-East India*". Commonwealth Publications, New Delhi.

Begum, Mustary (2006): "Women Entrepreneurship in India: Challenges and Strategies" *University News*, Arpil 10-16, Vol. 44, No. 15, pp. 13-15.

Bhorali, D. (1998) (editor): "*Economic Development of the North Eastern Region*" Spectrum Publications , Guwahati.

Bhuyan, B.C. (ed.) (1993): "*The Tribal Women*", Omsons Publications, New Delhi.

Bora, M.M. and Bhattacharyya, A. (1996): "Raising the Status of Plain Tribes Women through Income Generating Training" in Medhi, K. (ed.): *Status of Women and Social Change*, Women's Studies Research Centre, Gauhati University, Guwahati, pp. 102-03.

Bora, D.K., Buarah. D.K. and Paul. B. (1997): "*Impact of Urbanization in Arunachal Pradesh*", Director of Research, Government of Arunachal Pradesh, Itanagar.

Bose, M.L. (1997): "*History of Arunachal Pradesh*", Concept Publishing Company, New Delhi.

Boserup, Ester (1970): "*Women's Role in Economic Development*, George Allen and Unwin, p. 71.

Chetana, K. (1986), "*Social and Economic Dimensions of Women's Development*", Discovery Publishing House, New Delhi, pp. 6-9.

Choudhary, D.S. (1981):"*Emerging Rural Leadership in an Indian State*", Manthan Publication, New Delhi, p. 45.

Dubey, S. (2000): "Tribal Women and their Political Empowerment: A Case Study of Arunachal Pradesh", Resarun: *Journal of the Directorate of Research*, Government of Arunachal Pradesh, Department of Cultural Affairs, Itanagar, Vol. XXVI, pp. 12-13.

Karlo, R. (2005): "*Emerging Pattern of Tribal Leadership in Arunachal Pradesh*", Common Wealth Publishers, New Delhi, p. 51.

Modi, Milorai (2001):"Panchayati Raj System in Arunachal Pradesh," *Arunachal University Research Journal*, pp. 42-45.

22

Women's Micro Entrepreneurship and Economic Development in the State

Need of the Day

Introduction

The Agriculture sector has not been able to contribute adequately to the national economic development. Therefore, the industrial sector has assumed greater importance in economic development. Realizing this fact, our planners have aimed of speedy industrial development through utilizing the natural and physical resources that our country processed plenty. They also realized that the people and their potential ability have supreme role to play for economic development. The growing needs of the public on the one hand, and the inability of the government machinery to cuter to the ever-growing needs of people efficiently and effectively on the other hand, has accelerated the process of marketisation. This trend could be clearly seen in the field of industry and the business who's the potential entrepreneur comes forward to take up industrial ventures. It is worthwhile considering what role the women entrepreneurs can play in the context. Entrepreneurship is a vital input to industrial development as entrepreneurial talents and efficiency made the fortune of an enterprise.

The Government of India has accepted various challenges to fight against poverty on all fronts to improve the lot of the weaker sections of the society. By way of decentralizing the economic and the industrial concentration, in order to ensure the equitable distribution of the national wealth, particularly in rural areas, new strategies have been designed by our policy makers and planners.

The development of rural industries is one such strategy. Rural industrialization is not only crucial for accelerating industrial growth but also for achieving the social objective of dispersal of industry and equitable distribution of wealth. The rural industries will encourage the class of entrepreneurs, particularly technocrats and the educated unemployed to start their own industrial ventures.

The new Industrial Policy 1992 of the Government of India, envisaged that more stress has to be given to the Small Scale Industries (SSIs) in rural as well as in urban areas, which aims at providing all essential services, support and guidance to SSIs and tiny sector under one roof. Rural industrialization is important not as a means of generating employment opportunities in the rural areas with low capital cost and raising the real income of the people, but because it contributes to the development of agriculture and urban industries. Without rural industrialization, it would be considerably more difficult to solve the problem of agricultural unemployment and widespread underemployment. Rural industrialization promotes rural industry.

Since independence in 1947, the Indian economy has been on the whole, on a path of gradually self-acceleration development accompanied by reasonable stability. There has been a noticeable acceleration in the level of confidence and the performance of the Indian economy in the 21st century. The short-term prospects, despite recent global uncertainties, continued to be, by and large, benign for India. Over the medium-term, there are several challenges and opportunities. The public policy may therefore, have to specially focus on these aspects in order to meet not only the expectations of the global community, but also more importantly the aspirations of millions of people in India, particularly the poor and the underprivileged from diverse backgrounds.

Micro Enterprises

Micro enterprises are an important source of income and employment for a significant proportion of rural poor. In fact, this sector is perceived to be an essential part of survival strategy of poor households. The growing commercialization of rural economy, increasing dependence of agriculture on external inputs and growing educational opportunities have opened up new vistas for the micro enterprise sub-sector.

As per 2001 census, micro enterprises sub-sector accounts for 25 per cent of employment of all the main workers. The growth prospects of this sub-sector are highly promising. Certain product lines such as brick making, dairy products, retailing of electronic entertainment, soft toys making, chalk piece making, mushroom culture, candle making, agarbatti making, etc. are considered to have very encouraging market.

It is imperative to note the participation of women in economic activities as self-employed individuals. Many of the traditional occupations opened to women were mainly based on caste and creed and the nature of self-employment is based on the standard of living. Presently, women are not only generating employment for themselves in the unorganized sector, they are also providing employment to others. The country needs to mobilize and utilize fully all its resources including human resources. The participation of women in economic activities is necessary not only from a human resource point of view but also it is essential even for the objective of raising the status of women in society. The economic status of women is now accepted as an indicator of a society's stage of development.

Therefore, it becomes imperative for the Government to frame policies for the development of entrepreneurship among women. The long-term objectives of the development programmes for women should aim at raising their economic and social status in order to bring them into the mainstream of national life and development. For this, due recognition has to be accorded to the role and contribution of women in the various social, economic, political and cultural activities.

The economic development of region largely depends upon the success of industrial and agricultural sectors. The agriculture sector has not been able to contribute adequately to the sufficient economic development. Realising this fact, the policy makers and planners should aim of speedy industrial development through utilizing the locally available raw materials. The growing needs of the people of the region on the one hand, and the inability of the government machinery to cuter to the ever-growing needs of the people efficiently and effectively on the other hand, have accelerated the process of marketisation which depends on industrial ventures based on entrepreneurial skillness. Entrepreneurship is a vital input to industrial development as entrepreneurial talents can efficiently make the fortune of the region.

Entrepreneurship plays a vital role in Economic Development. Entrepreneurship involves taking risks and coordinating factors of production towards prosperity in an uncertain environment. Entrepreneurs and entrepreneurial qualities make the difference in the success or failure of an industrial organization. The development of right Entrepreneurship is one of the most urgent and acute problems faced by the developing country.

Women as Human Resources

The effective utilization of human resources is a necessary condition for the developments of any economy. Women occupy 50 per cent of the total Indian population and they constitute an important segment of human resources. Though women have undergone many kinds of exploitation and oppressions, after independence there is some notable change in their status, specially in terms of breaking the age old customs and traditional bondages. Women have been identified as potential contributions for fostering the pace of economic development. But the opportunities that exist in occupations are insecure and low paid. Agriculture is the major sector in which 70 per cent of the female working population is engaged. It is also low wage occupation and income potential from agriculture depends on favourable climatic conditions. Alternative employment opportunities are inaccessible to women due to their poverty and unskilled nature (Rani, 2006).

Women Entrepreneurs

Women entrepreneur may be defined as the women or a group of women, who initiate, organize and operate a business enterprise. Government of India has defined women entrepreneur to those who owned at least 51 per cent share in the capital of the enterprises, and at least 51 per cent employment generated by the enterprises should be for women only. With regard to ownership, an SSI or a SME managed by one or more women entrepreneurs in proprietary concerns, or in which she/they individually or jointly have a share capital of not less than 51 per cent as partners/shareholders/ Directors of Private Limited Company/Members of Co-operative Society is called a 'Woman enterprise'.

The girls today need to be exposed to the new value system that will enable them to emerge as 'new women'. The half of the total population is women in the north-east region in general and in Arunachal Pradesh in particular. That is why, all round economic development of the region never be possible neglecting its women. Women have predominant role to play in our country and there is a need to bring them into mainstream of economic development in general and industrial development in particular. Their talents should be canalized in to newer and fruitful activities of entrepreneurship. But they have not responded favourably as traditionally they are accustomed to be confined themselves into the four walls of home. But now times have been changing, they should be motivated and encouraged to force themselves to enlarge their field of activities. In view of their proverbial capacity for hard work, dedications, commitment and sense of duty and responsibility, they should have been properly motivated to show their talents into newer and fruitful activities and entrepreneurship. In the interest of the nation, all round development is necessary, that Indian women both urban and rural should be given importance without delay. There can be no doubt that they can make substantial contribution to the nations' development. The small scale sector provides many opportunities for their entrepreneurship.

The Indian women constitute 60 per cent of rural unemployed and 56 per cent of the total unemployed, though they have the ability to undertake various activity including industrial activities. It is, therefore, essential to develop women entrepreneurship in order to expose the various employment and profit generating avenues. In some part of our country women have proved and established their talents as successful entrepreneurs. But it has taken place only on cities. In rural areas, women have been suffering from the web of poverty, social traditions and restricting customs. It is necessary to emancipate them and bring them into the field of entrepreneurship. Women can be venture into business industry by providing proper training in entrepreneurship in the related area.

In entrepreneurship development it is necessary to give equal importance to prospective women entrepreneurs. The educated Indian women, when comes in contact with a broader culture than that of her home, learns about new role potentialities and would like to adopt certain changes in the traditional roles. Social change is possible only by empowering and educating women. *Nehru* once said, "to awaken the people, it is women who is meant to be awakened, once she is on the move, the family moves, village moves and the nation moves". Swami Vivekananda also once said, "There is no change for the welfare of the world unless the condition of women is improved. It is not possible for a bird to fly on one wing". Likewise no nation can flourish keeping half of its population in negligence and ignorance, as women constitute half of its human capital. A modern society cannot bring all round development without utilizing the talent of its women.

Areas of Women Entrepreneurship

Women entrepreneur in the earlier years after independence were confined to entrepreneurship in traditional areas like food, fruits, vegetables, pickles, papads, tailoring, etc. However, latter in 1980s and subsequently women entrepreneurs have branched out to several non-traditional areas like engineering, beauty-parlours, jewellery, handicraft, electrical, electronics, chemical and other manufacturing. Women have expanded from the traditional three Ps-Pickle, Powder and Papad to modern three Es such as Engineering, Electrical and Electronics.

The Indian SMEs sector is very gigantic. It consists of a large number of villages, tiny micro and medium industries. The sector consists a vast range of activities, where a women can perform better comparatively to its male counterpart. There are vast numbers of industries under SMEs sector where women are playing a major role, these can be listed in three categories:

1. *Agriculture and allied industries:* Sericulture, horticulture, dairying and animal husbandry etc.
2. *Home based industries:* Handicrafts, agarbatti and candle making industry, bidi industry, beauty parlour, printing work, doll making, textile and loom, jewellery, pottery etc.
3. *Out home Industries:* Electrical and electronics, computer, food processing, chemical etc.

Apart from these, there are women who have performed well in both organized and un-organized sector.

In Arunachal Pradesh, various tribal communities are at different stages of development; as such the status of women differs from community to community. However, in general the position of women in Arunachal Pradesh is respectable but not very high. The prevalence of polygamy, victim of bride price, sex abuse and child marriage are quite in common. It has no doubt lowered their position. They are generally devoid of equal political and property rights. To get rid of these tribulations, empowerment of women is very essential. Economic empowerment through entrepreneurship development is an easy way within a very short period. The emergence of women entrepreneurs and women-owned firms with their significant contributions to the economy are visible in India. These businesses are ready for continued growth in the future.

With the spread of education and awareness, women have shifted from the extended kitchen, handicrafts and traditional cottage industries to non-traditional higher levels of activities. During the 1970s, the decade of the International Women's Year, efforts to promote self-employment among women received greater attention from the government and private agencies. The new industrial policy of the Government of India has laid special emphasis on the need to conduct special entrepreneurial training programmes for women to enable them to start their own ventures. Financial institutions and banks have also set-up special cells to assist women entrepreneurs. The result has been the emergence of more women entrepreneurs on the economic scene in recent years, though the number is still quite low. Women entrepreneurship, on the whole, still remains a much-neglected field. While almost half the population of Arunachal Pradesh comprises women, the businesses owned and operated by them constitute less than 5 per cent. This is a reflection of social, cultural as well as economic distortions in the decades of development. However, women's contribution and participation in economic activity and production of goods and services are much greater than statistics reveal, since much of it takes place in the informal sector and also in households. In olden days, due to shyness and fear, they were not ready to come forward to undertake any work, job and business in the society. But now-a-days women have more awareness about the society, problems, circumstances and opportunities available before them.

They are ready to take any risk to come forward economically as they have more responsibility to take care of their children and more interest in the development of their family. As education has spread and compulsions for earning have grown, more and more women have started to go out of the homes and opt for employment for a wage or for an entrepreneurial career.

It is interesting to find that the female population of Scheduled Tribes has always been higher than that of males. While the generality in this case needs to be answered through systemic study of population genetics, this might be worthwhile to mention here that female sex is generally stronger than that of males. Thus, there is all likelihood of the female to live longer than male. This could be supported by the evidence and the fact that in the advanced western countries, the proportion of women in total population is higher than that of males. Similarly, the female population number in the Scheduled Tribes population of Arunachal Pradesh has always been higher than that of the male population. While prenatal mortality could be a valid factor in general, but lack of maternity care, access to medical services in general and absence of the same in the interior areas, low awareness among females, hesitation to visit male gynaecologist, superstitions during pregnancy, lack of care at home lead to increasing chances of infant mortality in the instant case. Availability of data in this regard is the limitation of the study. Arunachalee tribal women, being uneducated, indeed suffer most in their society and lives. Their literacy rate, number and sex ratio in the state since 1961 is shown in Table 22.1 shown below. Table 22.1 shows that how many women are lagging behind their male counterpart regarding education. Gender inequality lies at the root of the lasting situation of inferiority that affects women at every stage at their lives. Education in general and higher education in particular are an insurance against economic need. Access to the higher education, both technical and professional, will guarantee economic independence leading to social status and hence empowerment to women. If education is to promote equality for women, it must make a deliberate, planned and sustained effort so that the new value of equality between male and female can replace the traditional system of inequality.

Table 22.1: Salient Features of Population in Arunachal Pradesh (Census-wise).

Census	Population			Literacy Rate in Percentage			Sex ratio	
	Person	Male	Female	Person	Male	Female	General	ST
1961	336558	177680	158878	7.13	12.25	1.42	894	1013
1971	467511	251231	216280	11.29	17.82	3.71	861	1007
1981	628050	335941	292109	25.55	35.12	14.02	862	1004
1991	864558	465004	399554	41.59	51.45	29.69	859	998
2001	1097968	579941	518027	54.74	64.07	44.24	901	1003

Source: Different issues of Census Report.

The census in Arunachal Pradesh has been being conducted regularly after every decade since 1961 (First census). It is a thinly populated state. Total population, males, females, sex ratio (general), sex ratio (ST) and literacy rate in percentage including males and females are shown in this table. As evident from the Table 22.1, the comparative analysis of sex ratio in respect of general population and ST population in different census years reflects that it has been declining continuously with an exception in 2001 census. The sparsely inhabited Arunachal Pradesh is a predominantly tribal inhabited State. Gradually, different census report has given different classification of total number of tribes, sub-tribes. While 1961 census mentioned 82 tribes and sub-tribes, 2001 census mentioned 26 major tribes and 110 sub-tribes.

Each of the indigenous inhabitants of Arunachal Pradesh has distinctive culture, customs, language and traditions of their own, which they have manifested through different socio-cultural, religious and political events. The women's role in different aspects of their traditional lifestyle of the people is immense. The sex ratios in the State were 1013 in 1961, 1007 in 1971, 1004 in1981, 998 in 1991, and 1003 in 2001 (shown in Table 22.1). The well-being of tribal community depends very much on the women. Status of tribal women relating to their socio-cultural problems, their economic rights, their participation in management, their access to employment, food, health, etc. have not been properly focused.

Need for Women Entrepreneurs

The economy of the rural areas in the State remains stagnant. As per 2001 census 42 per cent of the rural population and 25 per cent of urban population live below poverty line because enterprises are concentrated in urban areas. Agriculture itself cannot provide full employment in rural area. As the growth rate of industrial sector is very slow and the number of industrial units is very small, the number of unemployment is growing very fast having no alternative way to be absorbed excepting the government sector which is already over saturated. Out of the above employment job seekers a major portion belongs to rural areas. Therefore, it is necessary to develop small scale industrial unit in rural areas, where there is chronic unemployment, dearth of capitals lack of appropriate technical know-how. To develop the underdeveloped state like Arunachal Pradesh, it is necessary to empower its women first. President, A.P.J. Abdul Kalam, said empowering women was a prerequisite for creating a good nation, "when women are empowered, society with stability is assured. Empowerment of women is essential as their thoughts and their value systems lead the development of a good family, good society and ultimately a good nation". Development of women entrepreneurship is one of the ways to empower the women.

Women Entrepreneur in Small-Sector and Rural Industries

Small-scale sector

The small-scale sector is a major area in which enthusiastic talented women can start a number of small units. It provides various assays where raw-materials and labours and other infrastructure facilitate are abundantly available. All entrepreneurs who are prepared to invest up to Rs. 75 lakhs in fixed assets can register a small-scale unit and those who can invest up to Rs. 10 lakhs in fixed assets can start a tiny unit in rural and backward areas.

Rural Industries

Any industry situated in rural area where the population does not exceed 10,000 which intends to manufacture goods and render services with or without using power and in which the fixed capital investment per head does not exceed Rs. 15,000 can be considered as rural industry. Rural industry requires limited capital and labour which is easily available and also limited technical know-how and limited market so that women can successfully start their units. Examples may be Agarbatti, Fire-works, weaving, doormats, bags manufacturing, candles, etc.

Recently, A "*Village Industry*" means – (i) "any industry located in a rural area which produces any goods or renders any service with or without the use of power and in which the fixed capital investment per head of an artisan or a worker does not exceed one lakh rupees or such other sum as may, by notification in the Official Gazette, be specified from time to time by the Central Government".

Provided that any industry specified in the Schedule and located in an area other than a rural area and recognised as a village industry at any time before the commencement of the Khadi and Village Industries Commission (Amendment) Act, 1987 shall, notwithstanding anything contained in the sub-clause, continue to be a village industry under this Act;

Provided further that in the case of any industry located in a hilly area, the provisions of this sub-clause shall have effect as if for the words "one lakh rupees", the words "one lakh and fifty thousand rupees" had been substituted.

(ii) ...any other non-manufacturing unit established for the sole purpose of promoting, maintaining, assisting, servicing (including mother units) or managing any village industry.

Challenges

The problems and constraints experienced by women entrepreneurs have resulted in restricting the expansion of women entrepreneurship in the state. The major barriers encountered by women entrepreneurs are as follows.

1. Entrepreneurial Lack

It is widely accepted that the availability of entrepreneurship is the most important determinant in the process of industrialization. The government in its efforts to create entrepreneurship in the underdeveloped regions provides for various monetary and non-monetary incentives like the development of an infrastructure, assistance in marketing and procuring raw materials, providing finance or granting subsidies on investment. With this thrust in view, the state governments have created various institutions to cater to the different needs of entrepreneurs. Specialized training to women in rural areas is absent.

It can be argued that lack of entrepreneurial skill of the local people and their deficient interest to invest and innovate has contributed in preventing the evolution of modern economic system in the State. One example of their lacking interest in manufacturing activities is that those tribal boys and girls who go for crafts training do not want to have their own business but like to join as craft teachers in government organizations (Krishna, 2000). The mindset of the tribal is not to establish their own enterprise or business but to venture either in politics, contract business, or government services to earn "easy money". This mindset can be termed as *psychological barrier* which has emerged very strongly in the context of present socio-political context of the State.

2. Financial Co-operation and Co-ordination

Nature of financial problem in this State is quite different from that prevailing elsewhere. Inadequate banking system, excessive dependence on agricultural economy, less inflow and more outflow of funds, low capital formation rate, lack of expert in knowledge in financial management, lack of co-ordination between financial institutions and the development agencies, lack of appropriate measures of expenditures, excessive procedural formalities, no-repaying tendency of borrowers are the obstacles for the financing of industrial sector.

3. Inner Line System

Main reforms of government institutions related to withdrawal of inner line permit and license policy are very urgent to ensure easy entry of investment and skill labour force into the territory for industrialization. In this way, employment of local people will increase and thereby insurgency problem will automatically disappear. Inner Line Permits system and government policy in issuing licenses only to local people most likely has worked against the opening up of market institution in this part of the country.

Inner Line System restricts the free flow of skilled and unskilled labours, information, raw materials and other equipments, etc.

4. Lack of Confidence

Women generally lack confidence in their own capabilities. Having accepted a subordinate status for long, even at home, members of their family do not appear to have total confidence in their abilities and on their decision-making. Society in general also lacks confidence in woman's strength, traits, and competence. The society in the state is male dominated and male person is the economical decision making authority. As she lacks of proper encouragement from the family, societies and government, she possesses low capacity to bear risks. In the absence of support, she may not have confidence to bear the risks.

5. Problems of Finance and Working Capital

Another problem faced by women entrepreneurs is lack of access to funds because they do not possess any tangible security and credit in the market. Since women do not enjoy right over property of any form, especially on the immovable property in the state, they have limited access over external sources of funds. Initially their counterpart menfolk, especially the older people were not in favour of active participation of women in commercial enterprises but gradually seeing economic benefits their attitudes have changed.

6. Socio-Cultural Barriers

A woman has to perform her family duties irrespective of her career as a working woman or an entrepreneur. In this society, more importance is given to educate the male child as compared to the female child. This results in lack of schooling and vocational training of women, their lack of attaining technical skills and thereby lack of awareness of opportunities available to them. The state is inhabited by the world's largest variety of ethnic tribal groups and sub-groups, each tribe speaking their own-language and dialect has their own colourful festivals with different socio-political traditions. Their diverse and unique rich culture and traditional heritage constitute arts and crafts, fares and festivals, social structure, folklores in the form of songs and dances that still remain fresh and well preserved in this state. The women's role in different aspects of their traditional lifestyle of the people is immense. Social attitudes, in male dominated society, denied of equal treatment for women especially in rural areas.

7. Production Problems

Production in a manufacturing enterprise involves coordination of a number of activities. While some of these activities are in the control of the entrepreneur, there are others over which she has little control. Improper coordination and delay in execution of any activity cause production problems in industry. The inability of women entrepreneurs to keep pace with the latest advances in technology and lack of technical know-how results in high cost of technology acquisition and machinery utilization. These problems result in increasing the cost of production and adversely affecting the profitability of the unit. Non-availability of raw materials and other necessary inputs in the hilly terrain remote state is the main problem for the development of entrepreneurship.

8. Inefficient Marketing Arrangements

Heavy competition in the market and their lack of mobility makes the women entrepreneurs dependent on middlemen. For marketing their products, women entrepreneurs are at the mercy of middleman who pockets a major chunk of profit. Further, women entrepreneurs also find it difficult to capture the market and make their products popular. They lack information on the changing market. In addition, women entrepreneurs face difficulty in collection of payments.

Unfortunately, the impact in transforming the primitive tribal economy into a market economy has been negligible conceivably because supply driven by government efforts is mismatched with the ground realities in regard to the existing institutional structure associated with the tribal mode of production prevailing in the State. Therefore, for the sake of economic progress it is extremely important to know the factors that have been impeding the emergence and development of market institutions which are deemed crucial for transformation of a primitive economy to a modern one. This new economic policy of the State Government, which is considered as a paradigm shift in the country's economic policy, is based on the capitalist mode of production where it is assumed that if markets are allowed to function freely it can efficiently achieve a marked improvement in economic life of the people in a country. Governments in the State have emphasized in building economic institutions through introduction of policies and programmes such as establishing different bank branches from zero in 1971 to 1999 at present for promotion of market-led development like in other parts of the country. The development of market depends on the institutional reforms where government can play a positive role in developing institutional arrangements for private investment.

9. *Production Cost*

So far the institution in production is concerned, for many products such as medicinal and herbal products and processed foods; marketing channel is almost missing in the State. But it is well known fact that more production and unrestricted exchange of goods and services will improve the well being of the community as a whole and an equitable distribution of income and assets may accelerate the tempo of development because all these activities are performed under such as institutional arrangement where economic agents find incentives to maximize benefits.

Suggestive Measures

1. Steps to be taken to change negative social attitudes towards women.
2. Raw materials may be supplied on priority basis.
3. Training schemes should be designed that women can take full advantage.
4. Financing cells public financial institutions and banks special cell may be opened for providing easy finance to women.
5. Marketing of products.
6. Supply of free electricity should be insured at least at preliminary stage.
7. For inexperienced women, special type of training and development programmes should be arranged to inculcate in them entrepreneurship abilities.
8. They should be suggested to use easily available (for example, locally available) human and physical resources.

9. Individual enterprise loans and advances should be provided to women entrepreneurs through public sector banks and private banks at concessional/less rate of interest.
10. Complicated legal and administrative procedures and formalities need to be made flexible and hassle free. Every time, government and its agencies should co-ordinate and co-operate to women entrepreneurs to make entrepreneurial environment friendly.
11. Steps should be taken to make women aware of financial and technical assistance available to them under government and non-government schemes and women should be encouraged to start small business enterprises by giving them concessions, subsidies and incentives.
12. Non-Governmental Organisations (NGOs) can play a significant role in empowering women entrepreneurs by providing gender awareness, basic education, motivating training, financial helps and so on. They can act as an agent of social change and development in view of changing technologies and transition in the society from traditional to modern. Many NGOs are successful in developing appropriate styles and strategies towards women's issues through raising their self-confidence and capacity building.
13. ***Women Welfare Programmes:*** Under the Scheme Directorate endeavours to create awareness amongst the women beneficiaries about various programmes of the State Government and Ministry of Social Justice and Empowerment, Ministry of Human Resource Development, Department of Women and Child Development aiming at the Welfare of the Women. The Women Groups are sent to different parts of the country to inculcate awareness amongst them about implementation of various women welfare and empowerment Scheme so that they are fully conversant with activities carried out by the Self-Help Group (SHGs) and Mahila Mandals to maintain their cultural heritage and economic upliftment, national integration, etc. They are taken to historical, cultural and economically developed places in the country for their awareness so that thereafter the women would implement the programmes of socio-economic development at their respective

places effectively and efficiently. In the year 2006-07, only 20 women were sent for study tour. The number of participants should be increased to at least 100 and sent to such places where the women have engaged in entrepreneurial works very successfully. The women who are very much active in entrepreneurial works should be selected.

Conclusions

Besides above remedies, society of the State needs to bring about an attitudinal change in regard to the role of women as an entrepreneur. This will lead to the development of an appropriate environment in which women will come forth and give vent to their entrepreneurial talents. Ultimately, women entrepreneurship must be recognized for what it is. Nationally, it has great importance for future economic prosperity. Individually, business ownership provides women with independence they crave for and with economic and social satisfaction.

Women entrepreneurship is an indispensable ingredient in the economic development of a country. It can reduce the problem of unemployment. It enables them to their best effort to attain higher standard of living for themselves without depending on others.

Women entrepreneurs have been facing, several social organizational and economic barriers in their growth and development. The effective implementation of all the above measures at rural as well as at urban will help in increasing entrepreneurship in economic development. It is true that if the women come out with a commitment and dedication into entrepreneurial activities, nothing can fail their efforts in their success. When women will shoulder their responsibility equally with their male counterparts with full efforts, days are not far from us when our noble country will be superpower developed country in the world.

There is a proverb i.e., "anything is possible with a help of woman. Similarly, anything can be demolished by a woman." But now-a-days most of the women concentrate in developing the family both in the case of nuclear and joint family. So both the government and men should encourage the women to become entrepreneurs in all fields. They must be motivated to establish business concerns which will help to develop their family income and the standard of income of the particular region and thereby a considerable contribution towards national income. Non-Governmental Organisations (NGOs) can play a significant role in empowering women entrepreneurs by providing basic education, motivating training, financial helps, etc.

Micro finance, micro credit through SHG can develop this small scale industry. There is steady growth in SHGs and many households are being helped through helped Micro Finance. To set-up small scale industry through SHG by micro credit will bring a healthy progress of the overall development of the rural people especially women in the north-east region in general and in Arunachal Pradesh in particular. No development can be achieved in rural north-east India especially in Arunachal Pradesh on sustainable basis until and unless its women are developed and empowered socially and economically. It is well understood today that without economic and social liberalization of women, no true liberation of women is possible and also without the provision of equal economic and social opportunities to women, no emancipation of women truly occurs.

Employment is the surest way to enable the vast numbers of people living below the poverty level to raise them above it. Village industries through development of entrepreneurship are capable of offering employment opportunities at the place of residence to a large section of population. This has the capacity to correct regional imbalances by initiating industrial activities on dispersed basis in the most neglected, backward inaccessible areas like most of the areas of North-East States in general and Arunachal Pradesh in particular where perhaps large scale sector is unable to penetrate. Village industry is a key to rural development and rural prosperity.

REFERENCES

Amin, M. (2008): "Entrepreneurship Development: An Approach To Economic Empowerment of Women", *Kurukshetra*, September, Vol. 56, No. 11, New Delhi.

Ganapathi, R. and Sannasi, S. (2008): "Women Entrepreneurship—The Road Ahead", *Southern Economist*, Vol. 46, No. 18, January, 15, Guttahalli, Bangalore.

Kamalakannan, K. (2008): "Rural Industrialistion and Poverty Alleviation", Kurukshetra, *A Journal of Rural Development*, Ministry of Rural Development, May, Vol. 54, No. 52, New Delhi.

Mandal Ram Krishna (2008): "Role of Tribal Women in Socio-Economic Development", *Southern Economist*, Vol. 47, No. 8, August 15, Guttahalli, Bangalore.

Mandal Ram Krishna (2005): "Literacy in Arunachal Pradesh: Trend, Features and Growth", *Rajiv Gandhi University Research Journal*, Vol. 8(2), December, Rajiv Gandhi University, Itanagar.

Mandal Deepali (2008): "Women Entrepreneurship and Economic Development in Arunachal Pradesh", *A Mimeographed Paper submitted in the Seminar* on "Development of Entrepreneurship in North-East States", D.N. Government College, Itanagar, August, 9.

Rani, G. Sandhya (2006): "Promoting Micro Entrepreneurship for Women Development", *Southern Economist*, Vol. 45, No. 1, May 1, Jamia Masjid Complex, Palace Guttahalli, Bangalore.

Rani, G. Sandhya (2008): "Role of NGOs in Women Development", *Southern Economist*, Vol. 47, No. 9, September 1, Jamia Masjid Complex, Palace Guttahalli, Bangalore.

❑❑❑

Index

Administrative centres, 44, 87, 90, 171, 292, 387, 456
Adult education programmes, 346, 551
Afforestation, 362, 410, 425
  compensatory, 414
Agrarian countries, 183, 205
Agricultural Produce Export Development Authority (APEDA), 469, 472
Agricultural sectors, 17, 117, 119, 196, 231, 272, 281, 602
Agriculture sector, 52, 118, 218, 600, 602
Agri-expo Biotech, 474
Agro-based industry, 203, 230
Agro-forestry, 408–10
All India Khadi and Village Industries Board (AIKVIB), 208–9
All India Spinners Association (AISA), 207, 209
All India Village Industries Association. (AIVIA), 207, 209
All-India Khadi Board (AIKB), 207
Alpine region, 432
Anchal Samiti Members (ASMs), 528, 593
APKVIB Act, 212
Aromatic industry, 262
Aromatic plants, 262, 408–9, 437
Arunachal Pradesh Bamboo Development Agency (APBDA), 194
Arunachal Pradesh Biodiversity Board, 413
Arunachal Pradesh Khadi and Village Industries Board (APKVIB), 209–10, 212–13, 215–16
Arunachal Pradesh Panchayati Raj Act, 85
Arunachal Pradesh State Pollution Control Board (APSPCB), 413
Arunachal Pradesh
  economy of, 118, 562
  forest revenue of, 365
  indigenous inhabitants of, 540, 590, 608
  local tribes of, 94, 438, 441
  patterns of urbanization of, 294, 299
  population structure of, 294, 300
  position of women in, 539, 590, 606
  rural, 591
  tourist destination, 98
  traditional tribal society of, 530, 595
  tribal soil of, 210
  tribes of, 60, 544
  western, 78
Arxian model, 53
Asian Development Bank (ADB), 114
Asian Highway, 259
Association of Southeast Asia Nations (ASEAN), 36, 250, 252, 259, 270–71
Auxiliary Labour Corps (ALC), 168
Ayurveda, 190, 448–50

Balance of Payments (BOP), 111, 299
Bamboo based biomass gasification system, 195
Bamboo based industry, 190
Bamboo sector, 191–192, 194, 426
Bharat Sanchar Nigam Limited (BSNL), 137, 150, 155, 159
Bilateral agreement, 257
Bilateral trade agreements, 251, 256
Bio-aesthetic impact, 372
Bio-diesel products, 245
Bio-diesel, 267
Bio-diversity, 29, 32, 34, 40, 262, 351, 362–63, 376, 378–80, 397–401, 404, 406–7, 417–18, 425, 454
  faunal, 32
  loss of, 381, 397–98, 401

marine, 397–98
mega, 420
unique, 446
values of, 397, 399
Bio-geo-chemical cycling, 400, 445
Bio-geochemical factor, 396
Bio-geographic region, 431
Biological Diversity Act, 32, 352, 414
Biological diversity, 32, 352, 398–99, 417, 431, 448, 459
Biological materials, 406
Biological resources, 363, 398, 414, 462
Biomass, 388, 407
Bio-piracy, 401, 455
Bio-resource centres, 419
Bio-resources, 390
Biosphere reserves, 418
Bio-technology, 118, 409, 460
Biotic elements, 431
Biotic interference, 376
Biotic pressure, 459
Bio-utilization, 414
Bird species, 95, 362, 432, 444
endangered, 444
Black money, 41, 125
Border Area Development Programme (BADP), 39
Border Trade agreement, 255
Border trade, 38, 120, 225, 244–45, 248, 258, 261, 268, 273
open, 255
Botanical Survey of India, 96, 359, 402, 433, 437, 457
Brahmaputra, 34, 62–63, 93, 95

Cane and Bamboo Technology Centre (CBTC), 193–94
Capital formation, 47–48, 51, 235
Capitalist mode of production, 116–17, 614
Capitalist sectors, 53
Capital-sparing sectors, 124
Cement plant, 248, 250
Central Agricultural University, 331
Central Government Industrial Policies, 239
Central Leather Research Institute (CLRI), 31, 211
Centrally Sponsored Scheme (CSS), 193, 239–40, 411, 470
Child marriage, 100, 495, 502, 513, 529, 539, 594, 606
Christian Missionaries, 318
CIS countries, 264, 403
Cluster village model, 36, 470
Co-education colleges, 346, 551
Coffee region, 266
Cognitive empowerment of women, 551
Communication, 4, 24–25, 38, 49–50, 58, 126–27, 135–36, 140–41, 143–44, 153–54, 163–70, 189–90, 244–45, 260, 456–57
electronic, 153
Community Forest Management, 415
Community land, 8–9, 372, 413
Community rights, 415–17, 465
Components
abiotic, 381
non-biotic, 449
Confederation of Indian Industries, 195
Consequences of Urbanization in Arunachal Pradesh, 277, 301
conservation of, 379–80, 404, 414, 417–18, 462
Constitution Amendment Act, 57, 85, 529, 546, 589–90, 594
Constitution of India, 6, 58, 548, 591
Convention on International Trade in Endangered Species, 370
Cooperation agreements, 257
Cooperative sectors, 188
Coptis teeta, 97, 402, 439–40, 457
Corporate sectors, 187
Cost-benefit analysis, 179, 271
Cottage industries, 25, 62, 208, 212, 228, 369
rural, 208
traditional, 606
Craft centres, 63, 218
Credit Deposit (CD), 551
Credit money, 24
Crude death rate, 198, 510, 576
Cultivation, 36, 119, 381, 383, 385, 437, 439–40, 455, 462, 470, 513, 560, 562, 564
Cultural moorings, 28
Cultural norms, 588

Deccan Flora base, 475
Decennial growth rate, 64, 69
Decennial Population Growth Rates, 64, 389, 456
Deforestation, 92, 369, 373, 380–82, 384–85, 388, 392–93, 396, 400–402, 409, 424, 446, 455–57, 463–64
Department of North-East Region (DONER), 39
Department of Science and Technology (DST), 190–91

Department of Telecommunications (DOT), 137, 150, 155
Department of Trade and Industry, 135
Developed industrial countries, 26
Development Centre, 458
Development policy, 42, 415–16, 465
District Industries Centre (DICs), 236, 239–40, 392
Domestic market, 191, 262, 469, 477
Dry flower making, 476
Ecological balance, 351, 354, 362–64, 367, 381, 385, 399–401, 407, 412, 425, 455
Economic activities, 40, 42, 64, 116, 122, 151, 166, 185, 346, 550–51, 556, 558, 570, 586, 602
Economic and Social Commission for Asia and Pacific (ESCAP), 251
Economic co-operation, 251–52, 259, 261
    regional, 256–57
Economic development, 16–19, 42, 45–48, 50–52, 61–62, 113–18, 122–24, 136, 165–66, 230–33, 243–45, 277–79, 281–82, 585–87, 602–4
Economic growth, 7, 17, 42–43, 48, 50, 113, 116, 136, 151, 164, 275, 280–81, 304, 311–12, 351
Economic independence, 483–84, 498, 510, 538, 540, 582, 585, 590, 607
Economic integration, 4, 166, 309
Economic liberalization, 108, 117, 138, 242, 270, 272
Economic power, 241
Economy
    agricultural, 122, 178, 611
    developing, 114, 165, 234–35
    dualistic, 52–53
    multinational, 109, 139
    regional, 39, 268
    rural, 30–31, 203, 211, 426, 601
    underdeveloped, 51–53
Ecosystem, 2, 34, 93, 376, 393, 396–98, 400–401, 407, 418–19, 423, 445–46
Eden Agro Flora, 474
Education
    benefits of, 308, 488
    economic benefits of, 550, 552
    formal, 318, 484, 585, 593
    higher, 333, 336, 521
    massification of, 317
    phenomenal growth of, 81, 320
    public, 339–40
    quality of, 309, 313, 340, 346–47
    role of, 483, 585
    vast expansion of, 511, 577
Educational opportunities, discrimination, 512
Employment exchanges, 186
Employment generation, 17, 62, 215–16, 281, 304, 411
Empowerment
    economic, 346, 570, 591, 606
    political, 485, 523, 588, 591–92
    social, 591
    women's, 346, 551
Endangered species, 370–71
Energy sector, 257
Entrepreneurial motivation, 49
Entrepreneurial talents, 232, 600, 603, 616
Entrepreneurship, 44, 124, 196, 222, 232–35, 237–38, 241, 373, 600, 602–5, 610, 613, 617
Entrepreneurship Development Programmes (EDPs), 238
Environmental policy, 373, 415, 465
Environmental problems, 393, 402, 407
Equitable development, 18, 282
Equitable distribution, 115, 124, 215–16, 600–601
    exotic, 263
Exploitable resources, 169, 391, 456
Exploitative development model, 423
Export market, 113, 192, 462, 469
Export promotion, 111, 236, 239, 244

Farm forestry, 372
Females
    general paucity of, 75, 498–99
    literacy rate, 548, 571
    participation rate, 559
    paucity of, 74, 501, 534
    population composition, 501, 533
    workers, 547, 558–59, 571
Five Year Plans, 47, 169, 179, 208, 266, 370, 513, 587
Flood prone zones, 34
Flora and fauna
    disappearance of, 369, 424, 464
    economic viability of, 436, 445–46
    elements, 398
    exotic, 30, 262
    florence, 475
    native, 361, 431, 438
    sustainability of, 436, 454
Floral assemblage, 462
Floral Diversity of Arunachal Pradesh, 442
Floral tribute, 471

Floriculture industry, 35, 468, 470, 473–74, 478
Foothill region, 433
Foreign countries, 177, 243
Foreign Direct Investment (FDI), 26, 109, 111, 113–14, 117, 120, 122, 126, 139, 263, 265
Forest Act, 393, 416–17
Forest Based Industries, 189
Forest biome, 381
Forest burning, 386
Forest conservation, 362, 395, 412, 418, 425
Forest degradation, 354, 364, 379–80, 385, 399–400, 406
Forest Development Agency (FDA), 194
Forest dwellers, 390, 399, 415
Forest economy, 365, 367, 373
Forest ecosystem, 390–91
Forest genetic resources, 418
Forest management, 370, 394, 407, 410, 412, 416, 420–21
Forest policy, 399, 421–23
Forest resources, 92, 195, 351–52, 354–55, 360, 364, 367, 369–70, 380, 382, 399–400, 407, 412–13, 418, 420–21
  banning exploitation of, 364, 400
  degradation of, 380, 407
  management of, 373, 423
  preservation of, 412, 418
Forest revenue, 364–65
Forest Rights, 373, 382, 415, 465
Forest urbanization, 386
Forest wealth, 29, 373, 435, 463
Forestry sector, 370
Forestry-logging sectors, 373
Forests
  alpine, 93, 443
  broad-leaved, 93
  clearing, 381
  conifer, 93
  deciduous, 95, 442
  degraded, 93, 353
  dense, 353, 355, 432–33, 442
  exploit, 388, 394
  extraction of, 69, 380, 407
  humid sub-temperate, 433
  light Alluvial Semi-Evergreen, 435
  luxuriant, 352
  man-made, 368
  minor, 368, 373, 416
  mixed deciduous, 442
  non-timer, 189
  pristine, 446
  regeneration, 383, 410, 412, 422–23, 560
  rich, 179
  scrub, 383
  sub-alpine, 394
  sub-tropical, 394, 433
  sustainable, 411
  swampy rain, 441
  temperate, 93, 97, 394, 434
  tropical moist, 32, 354
  tropical rain, 394
  village, 360, 369, 417
  virgin, 408, 423
Formal agreement, 258
Framework-Agreement, 260
Free movement, 4, 107, 110, 220
Free Trade Area (FTA), 257–61, 270
Free trade zones, 130, 199, 271

Galo society, 563, 594
Galo women, 542, 563, 567
Gandhi, M.K., 202–3, 206, 209, 376–77, 396, 481, 490
Garo women, 31
Gas Authority of India Limited, 109, 138
Gas sectors, 255
Gender discrimination, 100–101, 483, 502, 505, 507–8, 512, 582, 588
Gender equality, 494, 507, 511, 526, 529, 550, 572, 578, 584, 591, 594
Gender Training Institute (GTI), 486
General Agreement on Trade Services (GATS), 308–9
Geographical analysis, 294
Geographical proximity, 244, 256–57, 261
Global Environment Outlook (GEO), 397–98
Global market, 25
Global objectives, 417
Global Warming and Climate Change, 396
Globalization
  definition of, 110
  economic, 112, 452
  pillars of, 112, 453
  process of, 25–26, 28, 45, 109, 117, 135, 452
  impact of, 8
  trade, 333
Good governance, 45, 506–7, 525
Government sector, 40, 44, 609
Gram Panchayats, 85, 87, 547, 589
Gross Domestic Product (GDP), 5, 92, 112, 114, 310, 353

Gross National Product (GNP), 576

Handicraft sectors, 32
Handloom sectors, 224
Health sector, 252
High wage source nation, 114
Higher education, 80, 307–17, 319, 333, 335–41, 343–46, 485, 489, 498, 512, 521, 540, 548, 590, 607
  quality of, 307, 310, 333, 340
Hill Area Development Programme (HADP), 39
Hill-forest regions, 7
Hilly mountainous forest regions, 383
Hilly regions, 6, 239, 457
Home industries, 605
Household industry, 44
Human capital, 27, 32, 43, 47, 312, 405, 491, 531, 538, 558, 586, 605
Human Development Index (HDI), 83–84
Human development, 252, 303, 405, 529, 550, 594
Human Resource Development (HRD), 312–13
Human rights, 482–83, 581, 583
Human societies, 275, 279, 377
Hydroelectric Power Corporation, 265

Immigration, 15–16, 280, 296, 299, 302
Immovable property, 513, 540, 542, 576, 612
India and China Trade Relations, 252
India Spinner Association, 209
Indian Agricultural Research Institute, 475
Indian Airlines Limited, 109, 138
Indian Independence Act, 142
Indian International Trade Fare, 220
Indian Library Association, 136, 140
Indian National Congress, 207, 209
Indian Oil Corporation Limited, 109, 138
Indigenous Knowledge System (IKS), 446
Industrial centres, 18, 282
Industrial commitments, 421
Industrial entrepreneurship, 124
Industrial environment, 237
Industrial Infrastructure Development Centres (IIDC), 240
Industrial Policy Resolutions, 208, 216
Industrial production, 121, 185, 221
Industrial revolution, 127, 135, 163, 223
Industrial sickness, 123
Industrial structure, 236
Industrial timber, 425
Industrial undertaking, 123, 188
Industrialization, 44, 121, 124, 128, 130, 172, 182, 184–86, 188, 198–200, 221, 236, 281, 304, 313
  growth of, 17, 402, 436, 457
  high degree of, 121, 186
Industrialized countries, 26
Industries
  agriculture base, 25
  agro-based, 409
  allied, 605
  bidi, 605
  consumer, 409
  dispersal of, 115, 601
  domestic, 113
  forest-based, 352, 367–68, 373, 395
  fruits processing, 120
  handloom, 572
  heavy, 228
  intensive, 50
  knowledge-based, 307
  -lab-user linkages, 191
  medium scale, 121, 188, 218, 367, 392, 545
  non-Conventional, 203, 231
  pharmacological, 439
  rubber-based, 368
  sericulture, 123
  textile, 203, 231
  wood-based, 194
Informal sectors, 606
Information technology, 110, 134–36, 139, 141–42, 311, 330, 452
Inherited norms, 591
Inner Line Pass (ILP), 107, 220
Inner Line Regulation Act, 89, 284
Inner Line System, 106, 220–21, 611–12
Insurgency problem, 45, 130, 199, 611
International Conference on Population Development (ICPD), 597
International Labour Organization (ILO), 576
International Long Distance (ILD), 137
International markets, 35, 190, 192, 262, 369, 424, 436, 463, 476–77
International Union for Conservation of Nature (IUCN), 402, 457
International Women's Year, 511, 577, 606
Interstate movement, 499

Japan Development Institute (JDI), 248

Jatropha plants, 267
Jhum cultivation, 119, 369, 382–84, 386, 424, 463, 560, 563–64
Joint Economic Commission (JEC), 257
Joint Forest Management (JFM), 415–17, 422–23
Joint Forestry Management, 422–23
Joint trade agreement, 271

Kalam, Abdul, 490, 538, 557, 596, 609
Kalpavriksh, 416
Khadi and Village Industries (KVI), 31, 62, 208, 206–13, 215–21, 225–26, 228
  evolution of, 206
  growth and development of, 212
Klein, Viola, 511, 577

Labour
  agricultural, 44, 119, 576
  cheap, 591
  division of, 117, 234, 563, 566
  huge, 178, 269
  human, 177, 268, 560
  intellectual, 312
  local, 122
  manual, 100
  migration, 25
  rural, 303
  saving, 207
  skilled, 225, 310
  tea garden, 15
  unskilled, 298, 303, 612
Land Custom Stations (LCSs), 245–46
Land tenure system, 420
Least Squire Method, 389, 391
Less Developed Countries (LDCs), 51, 449
Liberalization, Privatization, and Globalization (LPG), 376, 463
Linton, Ralph, 3
Livestock, 354, 364, 399–400
Logging sectors, 366
Look East Policy, 36–37, 244, 255, 262

Malnutrition, 509–10, 576
  management, 391, 406
Manufacturing sector, 122, 367, 373
Margin money, 186, 212, 217
Marketisation, 231, 600, 602
Markets
  agricultural, 120, 165
  regional, 40, 121, 185
Marx, Karl, 50, 510, 577
Material resources, 124, 221–22, 313, 546
Maternity cares, 498, 500–501, 533–34, 607
Medicinal flora, 190, 361, 430, 436
Medicinal herbs, 436–37, 440
Medicinal plants, 94, 97, 189–90, 264, 360–61, 369, 390, 395, 401–3, 411, 431, 437–38, 441–42, 454–55, 457–60
Meditation, 337
Meghalaya, 1, 6, 8, 10, 15, 24–25, 29, 31, 33, 35–36, 40, 45, 96, 248, 470–71
Mekong-Ganga Cooperation (MGC), 260
Memba women, 542
Meso-regions, 140
Micro credit, 478, 617
Micro enterprises sub-sector accounts, 602
Microbiology, 474
Migrants, 18, 282, 294–99, 444
  early, 75
  international, 20, 288, 297
  temporary, 410
Migration, 15–16, 18, 23, 25, 75, 277, 282, 285, 294, 296–99, 301–4
  analysis, 298
  altitudinal, 444
  continuous, 296
  illegal, 252
  internal, 294, 297, 300
  international, 297
  rural-urban, 19, 296
  selective, 500
  urban, 18, 282, 289, 296
Migratory corridors, 460
Military personnel, 295, 300
Millennium development goals, 511, 578
Millet beer, 395
Mineral resources, 7, 164, 167, 266, 405
Mineral wastes, 393
Mineral wealth, 121, 186
Mini Zoo, 460
Ministry of Agriculture, 193, 469
Ministry of Commerce and Industry, 250
Ministry of Commerce, 469
Ministry of Environment and Forest (MoEF), 416
Ministry of External Affairs, 59
Ministry of Health and Family Welfare, 458
Ministry of Home Affairs, 59
Ministry of Human Resource Development, 339, 615

Ministry of Labour, 240
Ministry of Petroleum and Natural Gas, 267
Minor Forest Product, 32, 245, 352, 371
Missionary zeal, 545
Mobility
 geographical, 559
 increasing, 179
 skill, 24
 social, 495, 539
Modern civilization, 61, 98, 163, 278
Modern economic system, 125, 222, 611
Modernization phase, 140
Monasteries, 263, 361, 436
Money laundering, 256
Mongoloids, 7
Monogamy, 544
Monopoly access, 26
Moral character, 336, 338
Moral dilemmas, 335
Moral teachings, 337
Multilateral negotiations, 270
Multilateral trade agreement, 251
Multi-media technology, 161
Multi-National Corporation, 113, 261
Multinational diplomacy, 24
Multinational seed firms, 117
Municipal Act, 20
Municipal governance, 18, 281
Myanmar-India Friendship Centre, 256
Myers, Norman, 379

Nagarjuna Agritech Ltd., 474
Namdhapa National Park and Pakhui Wildlife Sanctuary, 460
Narendra Deva University of Agriculture and Tech, 475
Nath Biotech Ltd., 474
National afforestation programme, 413
National and Multinational seed firms, 119
National Bamboo Development Agencies, 195
National Bamboo Mission, 194, 413
National Bank for Agriculture and Rural Development (NABARD), 224, 469
National Biodiversity Act, 417
National Biodiversity Authority, 414
National Biodiversity Strategy and Action Plan (NBSAP), 416–17
National Centre for Mushroom Research and Training, 475
National Environment Policy (NEP), 113, 373, 415, 465
National Forest Policy, 399
National Horticultural Mission (NHM), 469
National Level Steering Committee, 195
National Long Distance Services, 137
National macro-economic policies, 302
National Mission for Bamboo Application (NMBA), 190, 194
National Parks and Wildlife Sanctuaries, 447
National Perspective Plan for Women, 548
National Policy on Education, 312, 487, 522
National Rural Health Mission (NRHM), 449
National Sample Survey, 502
National Telecom Policy, 137
Nationalized banks, 217
Natural calamities, 45, 360, 419
Natural drain areas, 301
Natural garden, 361, 431, 438
Natural Gas Commission, 34
Natural Gas Corporation Limited, 109, 138
Natural hazards, 301
Natural patches, 439
Natural regeneration, 396
Natural resource management, 415, 465
Natural vegetation, 369, 424, 463
NEC Reorganization Act, 2
Neha International Ltd, 474
Neofelis nebulosa, 443
Neohouzeoua, 30
New Internate policy, 137
New Telecom Policy, 147
Non-agricultural sectors, 183–84, 205–6
Non-aligned Movement, 25
Non-cognitive abilities, 550, 552
Non-cooperation movement, 207
Non-durables, 42, 125
Non-employment, 560
Non-functional effect, 38
Non-Governmental Organizations (NGOs), 226, 267, 372, 381, 400, 409, 411–12, 418, 481, 487, 526, 545, 572, 594, 615
Non-inclusion, 260
Non-Least Developed Contracting States (NLDCSs), 258
Non-migrants, 299
Non-monetary inputs, 556

Non-stereotyped thinking, 597
Non-substitutability character, 406
Non-teaching employees, 310
Non-tribal girls, 330
Non-viable economic sectors, 109, 139
North East Frontier Agency (NEFA), 58, 107, 220, 589
North Eastern Regional Institute of Science and Technology), 187, 330
North-East Council, 1–2, 39, 120, 170
North-East Frontier Areas Reorganization Act, 58
North-East Frontier Tract (NEFT), 58
North-East India (NEI), 1, 7–8, 30, 32, 45, 60, 127, 173, 197–98, 245–46, 254, 262–63, 270–73, 397–98, 402
North-Eastern Council, 2, 27, 39, 170
North-Eastern Region (NER), 2, 6–7, 9–11, 13, 27–30, 32–40, 44–46, 86, 172, 175–76, 243–46, 248, 261–62, 352–53, 398
Nurul Islam, 257
Nutrient cycle, 363, 397, 399, 407, 425
Nutrient recycling, 351
Nutritional deficiency, 363, 425, 501, 534
Nutritional status, 99
Nycticebus caucang, 443

Occupations
- agricultural, 542
- allied, 206
- based, 384
- forest-based, 360, 385
- low wage, 603
- major, 118, 383, 562
- preferred, 384
- traditional, 602

Oil industry, 34
Oil sector, 33
Optic network, 257
Orchid Research and Development Centre, 441

Paddy, 60, 563, 565
Palearctic region, 444
Panchayat Bodies, 529, 589, 594
Panchayat election, 86–87, 589
Panchayati Raj Institutions (PRIs), 57, 87, 89, 98, 482, 528, 530–31, 545–47, 588, 590, 594–96
Pasighat, 80, 90, 149, 168, 176, 187, 318–19, 331, 391, 456
Patriarchy, 581, 584
Per Capita Investment (PCI), 213–14
Pesticides, 119
Petroleum industry, 33
Petroleum manufacturing sector, 33
Phyto-geographical region, 445
Plan forest development, 421
Plan investments, 48–49
Plant species, 361, 370, 397–98, 402, 422, 431, 438, 445, 448, 457
Plants
- crop, 96–97
- economic, 462
- pot, 472–73
- seed, 436
- species diversity of, 355

Poaching, 459–60
Policy resolution, 188
Political economic realities, 511, 577
Political participation, 507, 524
Political problems, 486, 526
Politico-economic process, 182
Politics, 8, 125, 222, 335, 482, 524–27, 541–42, 548, 591–92, 611
Pollination, 397, 399
Polymer and Chemical based industry, 203, 231
Population
- concentration of, 18, 282
- decennial growth rate of, 64, 67, 69
- dense, 17, 281
- density of, 10, 13, 64, 71–72, 160, 277, 283, 286, 382, 388, 410, 496, 539
- female, 330, 500, 532
- growing, 388
- huge, 253, 314
- internal migrant, 294, 300
- local, 60, 188, 523, 592
- male, 283, 330, 498, 501, 532–33, 607
- mobile, 294, 300
- movement of, 18, 282
- natural wildlife, 363
- non-tribes, 501, 534
- tribal societal, 4
- variation of, 70

Power requirement, 126, 196, 364, 404
Power sector, 265
Powerloom sectors, 224
Prejudiced societal pattern, 538
Prenatal mortality, 498, 500, 533, 607
Preservation of forest, 370
Preservation plots, 418–19
Private sector, 45, 112, 124, 131, 137, 147, 199–200, 228, 331, 370, 411, 424
Private Sector Investments, 131, 200, 228, 410, 469

Processed foods, 120, 614
Product mix, 31, 233
Products
agricultural, 26, 176, 248
allied, 246, 248
common property resource forest, 41, 125, 222
handicraft, 218
herbal, 120, 430, 448, 463, 614
horticultural, 35, 246, 248
low-value manufacturing, 246, 248
major forest, 32, 352
Professionalism, 46
Property rights, 100, 382, 495, 513, 531, 539, 581, 584, 586, 591, 606
Protected area network, 459
Public sector, 124

Quality assurance, 310, 333
Quality of life, 33, 38, 99, 183, 198, 204, 232, 279, 303, 311, 461, 549
Quality seeds, 117

Rainy season, 159, 167, 175, 178, 269, 304, 394–95
Raw materials, 24, 123, 163, 179, 208, 218–19, 225, 234, 236, 240, 262, 354, 360, 390, 612–14
Reform package, 110–11
Regional development, 166, 168, 299
Regional disparity, 62, 151, 165, 238
Regional hierarchies, 166
Regional imbalances, 113, 236
Regional Research Centre, 403
Regional Research Institute, 264, 403
Regional Research Laboratory, 437
Religious norms, 586
Reservation of Seats for Women in Panchayat Bodies, 529, 594
Rice cultivation, wet, 563–64
rich, 245
Rural Employment Generation Programme (REGP), 186, 212–13
Rural industrial development centres, 240
Rural industrialization, 182–85, 203–5, 218, 230–31, 241, 601
importance of, 204
Rural sectors, 44, 233

Sanitation problems, 90, 285
Sectoral classification, 558
Sectoral outlays, 170
Sectoral planning, 416
Seed sector, 117–18
Self-employment, industrial, 62, 202
Self-Help Group (SHGs), 226, 478, 615, 617
Sex ratio analysis, 74, 496, 532, 608
Small Industries Development Organisation (SIDO), 236, 238
Small Industry Export Corporations, 239
Small Scale Industries (SSIs), 109, 139, 196, 205, 225, 228, 236, 238–40, 368, 457, 601, 603
Social analysis, 99
Social capital, 9, 43, 61
Social science research, 567
Socio-cultural problems, 99, 608
Socio-economic infrastructure, 17, 280–81
South Asia Free Trade Agreements (SAFTA), 258
South Asia Growth Quadrangle (SAGQ), 36, 260
South Asian Association for Regional Cooperation, 258
Special Economic Zones (SEZ), 35, 37, 470
State Bamboo Steering Committee (SBSC), 193–94
State Domestic Product (SDP), 118, 122, 167, 366
State Financial Corporations (SFCs), 239
State Forest Research Institute (SFRI), 96, 193–94, 402, 413–14, 458
State forestry department, 367
State Information and Data Base (SIDB), 419
State Khadi and Village Industries Boards, 209
State Peace and Development Council (SPDC), 256
State Women Commission (SWC), 529, 548
Sustainable Development (SD), 4, 45, 164, 188, 255, 276, 280, 304, 376–77, 379–80, 396–97, 399, 404–6, 411–12, 416
Systematic forestation, 370, 424
target, 397
Tea industry, 266
Teakwood Plantation Scheme, 371
Team building, 233
Technical Consultancy Organizations (TCOs), 237, 239
Technical know-how, 566, 609
Technological monopoly, 26

Telecom sector, 147–48
Tele-density, 148, 155
Telegraph facilities, 143–46
Telephone connections, 144, 149
Telephone density, 151
Telephone exchanges, 149
Temperate climate, 30, 63
Temperate Forest, 434–35
Terminalia chebula, 434
Terminalia myrocarpa, 435
Tertiary sectors, 112, 559, 571
Timber
  extraction, 400, 425–26, 455
  plants, 436
  treatment, 368
  trees, 95, 398, 419
Tourism industry, 117, 225, 448, 551
Trachypithecus pileatus, 443
Trade Liberalization Programme (TLP), 258
Transport and Communication sector, 169
Transport industries, 164
Transport network model, 178
Tree associations, 93
Tribal grass roots associations, 99
Tropical forest, deforestation of, 385, 455

Unclassified State Forest (USF), 426
UNESCO, 313
Uniform lending norms, 241
United Nations Conference on the Human Environment (UNCHE), 377

Village industries, 25, 202–3, 207–10, 212, 216, 228, 230, 610, 617
Village Industries Association, 209
Village Industries Boards, 209, 212
Village industries sector, 216

Wet rice cultivation, 563–64
Wet temperate Forest, 32, 354, 435
Wild Flora, 370
Wildlife Act, 459
Wildlife conservation, 459
Wildlife Preservation, 370–71
Wildlife Protection Act, 377
Wildlife sanctuaries, 447–48, 459
Wildlife species, 419
Women
  active participation of, 545, 612
  clubs, 580
  competitiveness of, 523, 592
  contemporary, 571
  cultural status of, 527, 579
  disadvantage, 586
  economic status of, 536, 555, 602
  educated, 538, 542, 591, 604
  emancipation of, 478, 485, 617
  equal participation of, 23, 27
  exploitation, 538, 594
  integration of, 570, 579
  legislators, 593
  participation, 482, 506, 524–25, 527, 530, 583, 592, 602
  positive image of, 484, 585
  realities of, 535, 591
  representation of, 525–526, 591–592
  reservation, 525
  role of, 513, 524, 537, 547, 575, 578, 591, 616
  rural, 503, 557, 562, 569, 579
  self-confidence of, 484, 585
  social liberalization of, 478, 617
  talented, 609
  trafficking, 272
  true liberation of, 478, 617
  underprivileged group, 549, 552
  welfare, 615
  work participation of, 495, 539
Women Reservation Bill, 482, 525
Women's Component Plan (WCP), 485
Workforce Participation Rate (WPR), 559
World Bank, 182, 204, 330
World Commission on Environment and Development, 376
World Conservation Strategy, 417
World Development Reports, 120
World Tourism Organization, 263
World Trade Organization (WTO), 26, 110, 112, 271, 308–9
World-Wide Web, 135, 338

Yagoon, 253, 256
Yajnavalkya, 491
Yandabo, 105
Yanmar border, 435
Yoga, 448–49
Yunan Academy of Social Sciences, 252

Zilla Parishad, 85–86, 547, 588–89
Ziro, 59, 90, 542
Ziziphus nummularia, 95
Zokhawthar, 255
Zoological Parks, 447